W9-CBX-536

"FOR HELL AND A BROWN MULE"

In 1939, during the emotional national debate over neutrality legislation, Millard Tydings was pressured hard by Maryland isolationists to vote the way they wanted him to vote or they would make things hot for him.

"I don't care for hell and a brown mule," Tydings shouted back at them. "I am going to do what I think is right."

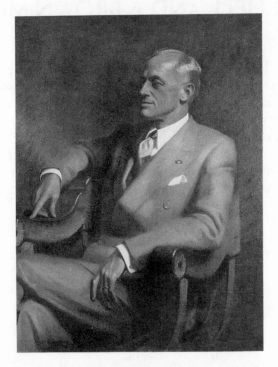

An oil painting of
MILLARD E. TYDINGS (*c.* 1946)
by Frank Salisbury, British portraitist.
Photograph courtesy of Mrs. Eleanor Ditzen.

"FOR HELL AND A BROWN MULE"

The Biography of
SENATOR MILLARD E. TYDINGS

Caroline H. Keith

Madison Books
Lanham • New York • London

Published by Madison Books
4720 Boston Way
Lanham, Maryland 20706

3 Henrietta Street
London WC2E 8LU England

Distributed by National Book Network

The paper used in this publication meets the minimum
requirements of American National Standard for
Information Sciences—Permanence of Paper for
Printed Library Materials, ANSI Z39.48–1984. ∞™
Manufactured in the United States of America.

Co-published by arrangement with the Maryland
Historical Society.

Quotations from James A. Farley's interviews with the
Columbia University Oral History Program are used
with the permission of the Columbia University Oral
History Research Office.

Library of Congress Cataloging-in-Publication Data

Keith, Caroline H.
For hell and a brown mule : the biography of senator
Millard E. Tydings / by Caroline H. Keith.
p.   cm.
Includes bibliographical references.
1. Tydings, Millard E. (Millard Evelyn), 1890-1961.
2. Legislators—United States—Biography.
3, United States.   Congress—Biography.
4. United States—Politics and government—1901-1953.
5. Maryland—Politics and government—1865-1950.
I. Title.
E748.T93K45   1991
328'.092—dc20   [B]   90-22850 CIP
ISBN 0–8191–8063–7 (cloth : alk. paper)

British Cataloging in Publication Information Available

TO MY PARENTS
John Johnston Keith
and
Caroline Masini Keith

Contents

Introduction and Acknowledgments

I undertook the research and writing of this biography through a grant from the University of Maryland. In December 1983 I received a call from a former professor at the university's department of history who knew of my work as one of the primary researchers for New York Senator Jacob K. Javits's autobiography and of my career as a writer and editor. The University of Maryland Foundation had asked her to recommend individuals qualified to research and write the biography of Senator Millard E. Tydings of Maryland, and she had given them my name.

Robert G. Smith, president of the University of Maryland Foundation, contacted me and explained that the Tydings family had approached the university for help in finding a historian willing to commit to such a work. A grant from the Millard E. Tydings Regents Scholarship would be awarded the individual selected to write the biography. Mr. Smith arranged a meeting with former Senator Joseph D. Tydings, and the two of us discussed my background and ideas about such a project as well as the family's thoughts on the matter. At subsequent meetings, Senator Tydings and I discussed in depth my concern that I be free to write a scholarly and objective work.

The Tydings family asked that they be allowed to review the manuscript upon its completion and to suggest changes, but agreed to grant me full authorial control over substance and interpretation. I am most grateful to them for their willingness to provide me with personal information, family correspondence, memorabilia, and photographs, and I am deeply grateful for their willingness to give me the freedom to write this book as I saw fit.

Many other individuals assisted me in completing this work. I owe an enormous debt of gratitude to the members of my writing workshop for their perceptive criticisms and suggestions for improving the manuscript, and for their encouragement: Julia Byrd, Marvin Caplan, John Coffman, Richard Lampl, Thomas Cleveland Lane, Peter Modley, Judith O'Neill, Elio Passaglia, Barbara Scheiber, Anne Womeldorf, and especially Shirley G. Cochrane, our once and continuing teacher; Roger O. Egeberg, biographer of General Douglas A. MacArthur, whose encouragement and support was sustaining; and Paul Herndon, whose knowledge of American history made his comments particularly valuable.

I want to thank Dr. George H. Callcott of the University of Maryland for reading my manuscript and for exploring with me Tydings's significance to the conservative tradition in American political history. It was he who suggested I write an epilogue (the Afterword) to satisfy the professional historian's need for seeing Tydings in the larger historical context. I also wish to thank Dr. Wayne S. Cole, my professor and adviser, and Dr. Marlene J. Mayo, professor and mentor, for their continuing support and interest in my work. I also am very grateful to Robert G. Smith for his assistance and guidance, and to his administrative aide, Doreen M. Bowser, for her cooperation and patience.

A number of people on the staffs of the different archives and libraries I used greatly facilitated my research: At the University of Maryland Archives, Lauren R. Brown and Leslie P. May were unfailingly helpful and extremely generous with their time, as were assistant curator Anne S. K. Turkos and student assistants Ann Andrews and Kathleen Copus. At the National Archives, Robert Coren, David Kepley, and John Taylor greatly aided my search for materials in the legislative and modern military records.

The manuscript went through many revisions. I want to thank my editors: Tim Wardell for ably helping me cut the manuscript to manageable length, and especially Vanessa Weeks Page for her superb and perceptive instruction on economy of expression.

Among colleagues, friends, and family, I thank Richard A.

Baker, Senate historian, for the single most helpful piece of advice I received (write as you research); James E. Miller, whose own career as historian and writer provided inspiration; Stephen Sniegosky, graduate school classmate, whose suggestions on sources proved invaluable; David Cutler, literary agent, whose advice on publishing and publishers was excellent; Jeffrey Hearn, whose efforts in tracking down the cartoons and photographs I wanted to use were exceedingly helpful; and Kenneth Otting, my high school history teacher, who made history come alive for me when he spoke in class of his experiences during the Korean War as they related to the conflict and its manifold political ramifications. And most of all I thank my family: my son, Abraham M. Ehlers, for his patience, support, and love; and my husband, E. Michael Ehlers, for being there.

Prologue

Physically and temperamentally he was built for war, and he fought one after another—both real wars and political wars. He knew the nightmare of gas and shells and the death-filled trenches in France, as well as the exhilaration of battle with Franklin Delano Roosevelt; and he knew the horror of the *walpurgisnacht*—night of the witches—of McCarthyism. His tall frame, lean, muscular, and agile, bristled with belligerent energy. He radiated confidence and ambition, spoke the language of the battlefield—of courage, strength, and the rewards of combat.

Esthetically and intellectually he was made for the Senate. With his military bearing and aristocratic profile—deep-set blue eyes, high patrician nose, chiseled prominent chin—and his quick intelligence, rapier tongue so suited to the cut and thrust of the Senate floor, he looked and sounded as if Hollywood had cast him for the part. He was a Democrat, as politically conservative as he was urbane. While his admirers believed he epitomized class and style, his detractors thought him arrogant and called him the greatest stuffed shirt in the Senate.

The range of his gifts and flaws was tremendous; the contradictions were outrageous and exasperating. He could be friendly and charming, then aloof and imperious, was described as whimsical and humorless, hot tempered and arctic—and he was all of those things. Millard Tydings was a man who aroused the strong emotions reserved for those who rise from nothing and reach the top but

appear to show insufficient humility, who are brilliant, effective, and
envied but also seem self-righteous and smug. He was either admired
or disliked. Few people felt neutral.

Those closest to him knew the warmth—recalled how he con-
soled others the night he went down to defeat and lost his place in
the Senate. When his wife Eleanor was unable to retrieve a treasured
necklace from the bank in time to wear it with her black evening
gown, he ordered a half-dozen gardenias and pinned them around
her neckline, creating a fragrant ivory frame. She was touched by his
thoughtfulness, but even she felt the chill. When he was angry he
grew cold, she said—"an iceberg would be hot in comparison." His
son, Joseph, remembered people suggesting Millard Tydings uri-
nated ice water.

Yet in private he wrote poetry, published under an assumed
name. He painted, wrote plays, and composed songs to play on the
piano to his daughter. When he turned on the charm, he was
irresistible. He was a superlative mimic and raconteur, holding
people spellbound as he regaled them with stories. A secretary to a
senator down the hall from Tydings's office remembered how he
sometimes strolled out into the corridor, wearing an immaculate
white linen suit and dapper Panama hat, smiling, waving, and
singing out, "Just wanted to see if anyone was alive!"

Reporters loved lobbing questions at him because his answers,
laced with irony, made good copy. When asked what a prospective
presidential candidate should do to attract voters in 1948, he replied
that he should "promise 120,000,000 jobs . . . drastic reductions in
rents, prices of food, clothing, and everything else people buy, and
the elimination of taxes altogether." "Anything else?" the newsman
laughed. "Well," Tydings deadpanned, "he should, naturally, appear
in a red bathing suit, providing his limbs will stand that kind of
public inspection. This will help to draw crowds and get him his fair
share of newspaper headlines no matter what he says. He must avoid
issues." He also could be testy with the press when they pricked his
well-known vanity. He once socked a photographer, shouting, "You
guys wait until I'm picking my nose before you shoot!" Either way
he made good copy.

He was a natural master of the public stage, a flamboyant
speaker whose long tapered fingers slashed the air to dramatize his

points. With a voice that alternately roared and whispered, needled and soothed, he unleashed a flood of facts and figures limned by a repertoire of parables, mimicry, and hyperbole, his sarcasm occasionally getting the better of him. His verbal brawls with Huey Long, Drew Pearson (whom he delighted in calling "Pew Smearson"), Harold Ickes ("Harold the Ick"), and Joseph McCarthy were legendary. The fireworks he provoked in debate drew crowds to the galleries and brought senators scurrying to the Senate floor.

He was incisive in committee, and privately he disdained colleagues who bumbled and mumbled along, politely coaxing agreement through stroking. With him it was, "Gentlemen, we're here to do this. I want a vote right away." Bing, bing, bing. "Good, gentlemen, we're adjourned." He could grasp, retain, and rattle off complex sets of facts with great rapidity, and he made mincemeat of those who came before him unprepared. Witnesses scheduled to appear often were warned by earlier victims: "Be careful what you say in the presence of Tydings—he'll put you in the hole if you don't say the right thing and he'll polish you off like nobody's business." He was considered the finest cross-examiner in the Senate.

His committed enemies were some of the biggest players on the national scene: Franklin Roosevelt, Thomas Corcoran, James A. Farley, Ickes, Pearson, McCarthy, Fulton Lewis, Jr.—men from opposite ends of the political spectrum. Many who felt the sting of his acid tongue preferred him as an ally, for he was a devastating adversary. He was not afraid of anyone, William Fulbright remembered, nor of taking an unpopular stand. Fulton Lewis called him "the viper-tongued Tydings."

But even his enemies conceded his ability and integrity. When he was given information that could have badly damaged Ickes and McCarthy but was of a highly scandalous nature, he refused to use it against them. When he told Ickes in public hearing that if anyone made an improper proposition to him he would say, "Get the hell out of my office," Ickes drily replied, "Your reputation is ample evidence that you would have said that, Senator."

He was called the goad and the conscience of the Senate, a realist and gadfly who could dissect and appraise with enviable clarity the substance—the pitfalls, advantages, implications—of measures pending before the Senate. He was a virtuoso debater, a man

with a will of iron who haughtily dispensed with the virtues of
consensus and compromise favored by those who subscribed to the
famous maxim "The way to get along is to go along."

He was one of the "Big Mules," his fellow Democrat, Lister
Hill, said of him, a veteran leader to whom newcomers looked for
guidance. He was a titan of the Senate, Richard Rovere wrote. He
was a powerhouse so firmly established that he dared to challenge
the president of the United States—and beat him at the great
American game of politics.

In his lifetime he was participant in and witness to every major
event of the first half of the twentieth century, from World War I to
the Cold War. He came from nowhere, fought his way up from
nothing, ascended through sheer strength of character, intelligence,
and boundless self-confidence to become one of the few privileged
to join the exclusive inner sanctum: the circle of men who ran the
U.S. Senate.

Neither Witch Hunt nor Whitewash

The Senate's famous marble-lined caucus room was standing room only on March 8, 1950, as members of a Foreign Relations subcommittee chaired by veteran Maryland Senator Millard E. Tydings waited for Joe McCarthy. The room, with its great crystal chandeliers, thick carpeting, and gleaming brass cuspidors, provided an appropriate setting for the drama that would be midwife to the birth of McCarthyism and deathblow to Tydings's career.

Tydings stood erect, confident, and trim in his three-piece suit with its starched linen triangle jutting crisply from the breast pocket. He remained immobile—immune to superfluous gestures such as straightening a tie, tugging at a sleeve, or smoothing the hair—eyes fixed on the doorway. Suddenly the klieg lights flashed on. As movie and television cameras whirred and a swarm of photographers set flashbulbs popping, McCarthy shambled into the room, red tie crooked, hair as rumpled as his suit. The crowd pressed forward. At a photographer's instruction, the two protagonists leaned across the mahogany table and glared. Several irreverent reporters growled like tigers in a pit. All that was missing was someone to declare, "Let the games begin."

Let the Games Begin

The spectacle had begun rather innocuously. An undistinguished freshman senator from Wisconsin, best known among colleagues for his careless attitude toward diligence and decorum, was scheduled to make a series of Lincoln Day speeches, starting in Wheeling, West Virginia, on February 9, 1950. There was nothing unusual in that. Half the Republican party was speaking during Lincoln's birthday week. But McCarthy, in describing a State Department riddled with communist infiltrators whose names he and the secretary of state knew, touched an emotional chord. He and his accusations made front-page news.

It did not seem to matter that McCarthy fiddled with the numbers (citing variously, in less than two weeks, 205, then 57, or 81, or simply "a lot" of Communists in the State Department), or that he was maddeningly evasive about the details of his evidence. The Senate, after hearing his revelations in a melodramatic six-hour speech on February 20, instructed the Foreign Relations Committee to appoint a subcommittee to investigate. Millard Tydings was selected as its chairman.

The choice appeared ideal. Tydings was a power in the Senate, a national figure known to be tough and shrewd. On previous subcommittees he had earned a reputation as a man of indisputable honesty who brooked no nonsense and cut straight to the marrow. His appointment reassured political observers and the White House, which hoped for a fair and thorough study—and efficient dispatch of the matter.

But the issue of Communists in government, so hastily dumped on the Foreign Relations Committee's doorstep, was an uncommonly uncomfortable one. Disputes arose over every aspect of setting up a subcommittee: bickering over the number of members (three versus five), and over who the minority (Republican) members would be. Bourke B. Hickenlooper of Iowa angrily accused the Democrats of partisanship for attempting to keep him off. Tydings only reluctantly accepted the chairmanship. He finally agreed because he believed the matter warranted scrutiny—and because no one else would touch it.

In early 1950 the subject of communism in government was a hot topic. Alger Hiss had been convicted on January 21. No one on Capitol Hill was eager to handle—or mishandle—such a politically hazardous issue. No one at the time thought of McCarthy as the most dangerous element involved. He was known as a maverick and rogue, but his skill at demagoguery remained unrecognized. No one then thought of it as a matter of who would bell the cat; it was the hearings that made McCarthy the dangerous creature who would have to be stopped.

Tydings's reluctance had not arisen from problems in the subcommittee's partisan makeup, nor from fear of McCarthy. It came, rather, from quick recognition of potential misunderstandings in the incendiary matter of communism in government. The directive Senate Resolution 231 had passed in a flurry of confusion on February 22, with conspicuous lack of caution following McCarthy's sensational speeches and headlines.

> Resolved, That the Senate Committee on Foreign Relations, or any duly authorized subcommittee thereof, is authorized and directed to conduct a full and complete study and investigation *as to whether persons who are disloyal to the United States are or have been employed by the Department of State.* . . . [T]he committee is directed to procure, by subpoena, and examine the complete loyalty and employment files and records of all the Government employees in the Department of State *and other such agencies against whom charges have been heard.* (Emphasis added.)

Tydings pinpointed ominous flaws in the resolution's language and balked at going ahead before the scope and procedure of the hearings were defined clearly. Skilled in unraveling legalistic tangles, he knew the risks of ill-defined objectives and vague terminology. He raised the matter at a February 25 meeting of the Foreign Relations Committee held to hash out procedure. He put it bluntly: "You can drive a horse and wagon through any place in this resolution," he complained. "Does it mean that we shall start with the Secretary of State and go all the way down through all the employees and take each one of them separately, or does it mean that we will investigate the charges that are laid before the committee of disloyalty in particular instances?" How broad was the mandate? "I don't want to be charged with not having done my duty," Tydings declared.

The wrangling had begun. "It does not mean that you are going on a grand witch hunt," the senior senator from Wisconsin, Alexander Wiley, retorted.

"But suppose," Tydings persisted, "there are 500 people against whom no charges or aspersions of any kind, shape, or form are filed. It is your thought that they should be investigated too?"

What worried him was the ambiguous language. The resolution could be misinterpreted a dozen different ways by fair men with the impartiality of Solomon. Imagine what others, with motives less pure, might do? All present and past employees? What of "such other agencies" and "against whom charges have been heard"? Heard by whom? McCarthy? Government officials? Or anyone who testified? It could go on indefinitely. Tydings pressed for a definite framework, concrete goals, and guidelines. He did not relish the prospect of sinking into a semantic and legalistic quagmire.

"If you want all the employees in the State Department investigated, I am willing to do that," he said. "If you want to limit it within some other range, which I think would be more sensible, I am willing to do that. But," he said, voice rising, "I am not going to allow myself to be maneuvered into the position where somebody is going to get up on the Senate floor and have the committee, of which I may be a member, charged with not having done a thorough and nonpartisan job."

Everyone jumped in with suggestions. Chairman Tom Connally: The Senate should reconsider the resolution and pass a sensible one. Theodore Green: The committee should draw up a set of clear questions and let the subcommittee act on them. Alexander Smith: The committee could make its own interpretation and present it. "I think that will be all right," Smith said.

"I think that is a very dangerous procedure," Tydings cut in. "With the intensity behind this resolution, and with an election year on, I'm not throwing any aspersions on anybody, this committee is liable to be put in the position where it can be charged with trying to cover up." He proposed his own remedy: "to get up a resolution by this committee and have the committee adopt it unanimously," with Connally then taking it to the floor to urge acceptance. "Reframe it," he said, "so the committee will not be open to criticism after the work is done."

Although his suggestion was adopted unanimously by the Foreign Relations Committee, it never got beyond the subcommittee's first executive session. They realized that resubmitting anything to the Senate would open up more acrimonious debate without changing a thing. The Foreign Relations Committee and its subcommittee (hereafter called the committee) were saddled with Resolution 231. It caused bitter disagreement from day one.

Tydings had seen the pitfalls of Resolution 231 and anticipated the consequences. "Darned if I'm going to be standing before the Senate committee and be accused of shielding Communists," he blurted at one point. Again and again during the two preliminary meetings he warned his colleagues that the hearings easily could lead to accusations of cover-up, of shielding Communists, or to the appearance of a partisan, mismanaged job. Tell the Senate "exactly what we are going to investigate," he cautioned, or they would have "somebody come in and say, 'You white-washed everybody.'" The symbolic vocabulary that so divisively characterized the proceedings was in place before Joe McCarthy ever set foot in the caucus room: witch hunt; cover-up; whitewash.

"We shall let the chips fall where they may," Tydings said to reporters after his appointment was announced. "This is neither a witch hunt on the one hand nor a whitewash on the other."

As he was promising "a full, fair, and complete investigation," McCarthy was expressing his satisfaction. "It looks like a good group of men," he told the press on learning that Democratic Senators James O'Brien McMahon of Connecticut and Theodore F. Green of Rhode Island and Republican Senators Bourke B. Hickenlooper of Iowa and Henry Cabot Lodge of Massachusetts were selected.

Indeed, because the five represented widely varying points of view and positions on the political spectrum and came from very different backgrounds, they were well received by all—the administration, the press, the Senate and House of Representatives, and the beleaguered Department of State. The handsome young Lodge, from upper-crust Boston, was an pugnacious as he was patrician, while Hickenlooper was a homespun product of the conservative plains. Green was highly respected for his eloquent evenhandedness, and James O'Brien McMahon, known to be as savvy as Tydings, was a feisty Irish Catholic who could go head-to-head with the Irish Catholic McCarthy. Everyone echoed McCarthy's praise and acclaimed them an outstanding group.

In its opening articles, the press explored a major element of the coming battle: the State Department employee loyalty files. Loyalty files contained all information gathered on department employees through routine and in-depth security clearance checks and summaries of FBI field investigations. The press speculated on what use McCarthy would make of them.

The files became McCarthy's weapon and refuge simultaneously. He made his famous (but ever-shifting) charges: There are 205 (or 57, or 81, or many) "card-carrying Communists" (or just "bad security risks") now in the State Department. When challenged—let us see the evidence, demanded Democratic Senator Scott Lucas of Illinois and others—McCarthy would reply nonchalantly that it was all in the loyalty files. They could get them for themselves. But he knew it was not so simple. President Harry S Truman in 1948 had issued an executive order discontinuing release of personnel data to congressional committees. McCarthy knew that and exactly how to play it. "The evidence is all in the files," he would chant to the public. "If the Senate wants to see it, all they have to do is ask."

Truman, he thought, would refuse their release on grounds of executive privilege, and then he could accuse the administration of having something to hide. When Tydings and the committee initially only delicately pressed Truman for the files (to avoid shutting doors later), McCarthy did indeed accuse all of them of concealing something. But when pressed himself to reveal his evidence, he hid behind the files. "Why aren't *they* getting the files?" he asked, insinuation permeating his words.

It was the perfect combination—bludgeon and retreat—and he played it cunningly for three months. When Tydings finally devised a strategy that let Truman release the material without jeopardizing executive privilege, McCarthy cried that it was too late. "The files have been rifled and raped," stripped of vital information, he claimed—depriving Tydings of an important victory while ensuring his frustration. The phrase "the loyalty files" came to represent the madness of the whole enterprise, and madness and anger set the tone for March 8, that circuslike day when the "games" began.

Tydings moved fast to pin down what McCarthy knew. He had heard that the 81 cases came from lists of individuals previously investigated on loyalty issues by congressional committees; he wanted to find out what substance there was to the charges. If McCarthy actually had something, he was prepared to shake the State Department top to bottom; but if it was all smoke, he wanted to clear the air fast. He abhorred misuse of facts and intended to demolish McCarthy if he was lying.[1]

"Now, Senator McCarthy," Tydings began after he swore in the scowling senator, "the information you presented to the Senate has been read by all of us, I am sure. You will want to supplement that, no doubt, and comment further on it."

"That is correct," came the reply.

"But, before you do," Tydings interjected, "there is one matter that, to make the record complete as of the congressional debate, I would like to ask you about for just a minute." And like a good prosecuting attorney, Tydings closed in on a curious matter. He quoted McCarthy's comments from the *Congressional Record* about case 14—a translator cited "as a bad security risk because he was flagrantly homosexual"—and then called McCarthy's attention to an unusual aspect of the case. According to McCarthy—and Tydings read McCarthy's own words—although "the State Department's own security agency recommended the discharge of this employee," the termination decision was rescinded because of "the attempt of a high State Department official to induce several individuals who had signed affidavits reflecting adversely upon the employee to repudiate their affidavits."

"Now, the purpose of reading that is this," Tydings said. "Is this . . . high State Department official whom you allege tried to doctor the records, one of the cases of the 81 that you brought before the Senate, or have you referred to him here only to substantiate the facts in case 14?" If such a person was still at the department, Tydings observed, the first thing they should do to eliminate subversive elements "is to find out who the man is."

McCarthy stalled. "I am afraid, Mr. Chairman, that you will have to let me go through those cases as I have them documented." He tried to muddle the numbers. "I will be unable to jump, say, from case 1 to case 72 back to case 58. . . . I can assure the Chairman that all the information he wants on case number 57 will be gotten to him, but I frankly cannot give him that information now, because I haven't arrived at that case this morning."

Tydings was waiting. "Just a minute. Just a minute. Just a minute! All I am asking you is this. This is a very serious charge—"

"Very serious," agreed McCarthy, interrupting.

"—that a high official in the State Department is tampering with the records to protect people who are charged with disloyal activities."

McCarthy repeated that he would bring the name before the committee. Henry Cabot Lodge broke in to protest that Tydings was not allowing McCarthy the courtesy of making his own statement in his own way. Tydings demurred. "We want to hear Senator McCarthy," he said. He looked straight across the table at him. "I have read over all of these cases three or four times, and I studied the possible ramifications of them. I would like to know whether we are to hear this as a collateral matter of proving case 14, or whether this man himself is to be charged with disloyal conduct as a separate case. You can certainly answer that. . . ."

"I will answer that. I will give the committee all of the information which I have," McCarthy promised. But he did not answer the question.

Tydings tried again. His face was flushed and his eyes glittered with anger. The frustrating dialogue had gone on for more than 20 minutes. "All I am asking you now is, do you know the name—I do not want you to tell it—but do you know the name of this particular high State Department official who is allegedly aiding disloyal persons in the State Department. Do you know the name?" He was nearly shouting.

"Mr. Chairman," McCarthy intoned, "when we get to case number 57 I will give you all of the names in that case. No names will be held back."

"You know whether you know the name or not, and you can answer 'Yes' or 'No' and we can end this right here."

"I tried to explain to you that I cannot give you information now on case number 57."

"I said case 14," Tydings snapped, his hand slapping the table.

The wrangling raged for more than 45 minutes, McCarthy evading, Tydings persisting, and Lodge—with Hickenlooper—protesting Tydings's treatment of McCarthy. "It seems to me this is a perfectly extraordinary procedure. I have never seen anything like it," Lodge had sputtered. "It is a perfectly amazing procedure to pick number 57 and then to pick number 14, and I suppose after you are through playing with that you will pick number 23. In the meantime the witness . . . has a prepared statement and he isn't given the common courtesy of telling his story in his own words." Lodge's indignation finally wore Tydings down. He agreed to let McCarthy bring the answers to the two questions at issue to the next committee meeting.

McCarthy was free to begin his statement uninterrupted— except for a brief but bitter dispute over naming names in public. It began when Senator McMahon sarcastically noted that innocent citizens could be hurt by untrue public accusations. When questioned about the wisdom of offering names in public hearing as opposed to executive session, McCarthy declared, "I personally do not favor presenting names, no matter how conclusive the evidence is." But he immediately equivocated. "The committee has called me this morning, and in order to intelligibly present this information I must give the names. I think this should be in executive session. I think it would be better. However I am here. The committee has voted to hold open sessions, so I shall proceed."

It was academic, anyway. McCarthy already had given the name of his first case to the press that morning before the hearing began. He had ignored Tydings's explicit instruction that he ask for executive session if he thought it appropriate. The issue of open versus closed hearings became another malignant misunderstanding that dogged the hearings throughout.

Lodge's description—that the procedure was "perfectly extraordinary"—was faultlessly apt. Tydings eventually was held to blame and excoriated for allowing open hearings, which gave McCarthy the chance to smear his victims publicly. And when, finally, hearings were held behind closed doors, Tydings was reviled for trying to hide secrets from the public.

Tydings knew all along the name of the "high State Department official" in question: Joseph Anthony Panuch. He was trying to show the flimsiness of McCarthy's evidence. Joseph Panuch was known as a rabid anti-communist who had forced a number of resignations from the department. In his February 20 speech, McCarthy had praised Panuch by name for "housecleaning Reds" and for trying to rid the State Department of case 41. It was due to slipshod home-work that McCarthy did not realize the "high official" he criticized in case 14 was the same man he applauded in case 41. Tydings, on the other hand, had taken time to study the material thoroughly. McCarthy unwittingly had left himself wide open for Tydings's attempt to expose the weakness of his evidence.

McCarthy's refusal to cooperate was not caused by fear of being trapped. He did not realize that Tydings was trying to reveal a contradiction. He was just protecting himself from looking foolish because he did not know Panuch's name—or those of most of his 81 cases. Sometime after his Wheeling speech, McCarthy had received a list of 108 names from Robert E. Lee, a man who once had served as head investigator for a 1947 House Appropriations committee probing into the Communists-in-government question. McCarthy had taken the list, along with case descriptions and old clippings stuffed in the dusty folders with it, and launched his February 20 speech. He barely glanced through the material and had done no real investigation. His exhaustive study consisted of lifting, almost verbatim, great chunks of the Lee files' descriptions—and embellish-ing them with a few sentences he added himself.

Tydings also was using the Panuch issue to test McCarthy's intention of cooperating, to see if he was going to turn over voluntarily the names of those he had charged, along with photocop-ies of evidence he claimed to have amassed. So far, the committee had not been able to get the names (or anything else) from McCar-thy, which meant it had not been able to begin investigating the 81 cases McCarthy said he intended to present. McCarthy had said a lot, but had shown nothing more than the "documents" he waved in the air as he would say, "I hold in my hand a list . . ."

Tydings realized that, if McCarthy had a genuine concern about Communists in the government—and solid evidence—he could have tried to save the nation in more subtle ways. He could have quietly approached President Truman, Secretary of State Dean Acheson, or the State Department's security section. If he did not trust Demo-crats or the department to clean house, he could have gone to the Justice Department or directly to J. Edgar Hoover and the Federal Bureau of Investigation. He could have asked advice privately of the Foreign Relations Committee; he could have sought guidance from the Republican Policy Committee; or, most obviously, he could have turned over his evidence to the House Un-American Activities Committee. But he did not. Instead he stood on the floor of the Senate, with its cloak of immunity, and stated that he had done enough investigation to come up with concrete evidence that 81 individuals employed by the State Department were known to be Communists. He took his case to the media. Of course, any Communists so openly forewarned would have had ample time to cover their tracks, resign, disappear, or defect.

It was small wonder that Tydings was skeptical of McCarthy's motives and chose to nail down the proof precisely. Tydings had no tolerance for devious or deceptive behavior. Once convinced of McCarthy's insincerity, Tydings sought to discredit him so no one would mistake his lies for truth.

Most of the press and the community of political observers saw things as Tydings did. McCarthy got the headlines, but Tydings got the praise. One columnist dubbed McCarthy "this 10-cent store Robespierre from Wisconsin." The headlines trumpeted comment on "MCCARTHY'S CREAKING LIMB," "MCCARTHY'S SMEARS," and "MCCARTHY'S ATTACK ON MCMAHON FLOUTS TRADITION AMONG SENATORS." Meanwhile, newspapers and magazines ran editorials extolling Tydings's conduct of the hearings: "His searching interrogations recall the great days of the wartime Truman Committee"; "Tydings appears determined to reclaim traditional canons of fair practice"; "The Tydings committee has so far gone about the business of investigating [McCarthy's charges] with diligence and a refreshing regard for decency and fair play."

But the general public did not see it that way. From day one, despite the persuasion of newspaper editorials, it was the unnerving McCarthy charges that stuck; they tended to strike home as fear was reinforced by disillusionment.

The wartime alliance with the Soviet Union bred hopes among many Americans for a postwar world of peace. The two nations had a mixed history of animosity and agreement—vast ideological, political, and economic differences measured against the shared heroics of the war. As the end of the war drew near, it became clear that the United States and the Soviet Union would dominate the world.

Should they divide into hostile camps, with Europe in ruins, America would bear the burden of defending the West from possible aggression. The need for accommodation was obvious; the search for methods to achieve it were many: mutual friendship societies, political think tanks, and, of course, the fledgling United Nations, an international organization devoted to cooperative peacekeeping arrangements. Wartime propaganda had nurtured images of a friendly, gallant Russia. Arthur Vandenberg, Republican senator from Michigan, led his party into active support of an internationalist foreign policy, quieting partisan divisions. There was genuine hope that a new and safer world could emerge from the wreckage of the war.

On August 6, 1945, a new force in the universe was unleashed that would disturb that rosy view. The true and terrible consequences of the atomic bomb came to be seen only gradually. By 1949, when it was learned that the Soviet Union also had the bomb, the horror was infinite. The earlier Berlin airlift and the partitioning of Eastern Europe behind the Iron Curtain had increased fears and confusion. Life could never be the same again.

When China entered the communist bloc after the shocking defeat of Chiang Kai-shek in 1949, Western nations were profoundly shaken. The State Department became the scapegoat in the American public's eyes. The erosion of Soviet–U.S. wartime cooperation and the cataclysmic loss of China put Soviet-American friendship societies under suspicion. Some, in fact, were dominated by communist influence. A number of social welfare organizations formed during the Great Depression to help the poor were fertile fields for communist exploitation. Many did become "communist fronts." Much of the membership quit when they saw what was going on, but the evolution among some groups created suspicion about growing communist influence.

In 1948 journalist Whittaker Chambers entered the news with his sensational story of secret papers hidden in pumpkins, implicating former State Department official Alger Hiss and others. Hiss was defended fervently by Truman, Acheson, some statesmen and senators, and many in the liberal press. "A red herring," said Truman. But some named by Chambers confessed; others, indicted for conspiracy, espionage, or subversion, were convicted. The revelations added fuel to an increasing national anxiety. When Hiss was convicted of perjury in January 1950—after such vigorous defense— the damage was irreparable. Distrust of the State Department grew. A belief that something was rotten among those pin-striped, arro- gant stuffed-shirts and fools who sold us down the river at Yalta became pervasive. Republican Representative Walter Judd declared, "Nobody has done as much to undermine the confidence in the Department of State as the Secretary of State."

Enter Joe McCarthy. People were ready to believe him. Joe, they thought, was trying to keep the country safe, keep it from being taken over right from under their noses. Maybe "fighting Joe" didn't go about it the best way, but he must be on to something, people were saying, or he wouldn't be saying those things. After all, he was a U.S. senator; and he was a regular guy—the kind most folks could identify with, plain spoken and persuasive.

Tydings was also a senator, but his arguments were based on logic, not emotion. He spoke urgently, but in complex terms. It was much easier to yell "Communists!" than to investigate and explain the perplexing reasons why some people were questioned more than once about security and/or loyalty.

Tydings was decidedly not a regular Joe. He was erudite, an intellectual. His immaculate suits were hand tailored. He had mar- ried a wealthy divorced socialite, Eleanor Davies Cheesborough, daughter of Joseph Davies, former ambassador to the Soviet Union and adviser to presidents who himself married one of the world's wealthiest women, Marjorie Merriweather Post Hutton. Tydings moved in elite circles, spoke with clipped precision, possessed the aloof bearing of a European dignitary, and would not stoop to good ol' boy backslapping with his constituents. He also would not tolerate sloppy homework or argument, was impatient when forced to suffer fools, and became belligerently combative when crossed. For those not close to him, he was not easy to know or like.

He was a member of the Senate's powerful inner club not because he was welcomed for compatibility, but because he was an effective senator who was highly respected, although slightly feared. Even the aggressive Huey Long was said to have been careful about tangling with Tydings.

The public often likes to see the high and mighty taken down a peg or two. Joe McCarthy did not look like much next to the elegant senator from Maryland, but there were those who got satisfaction out of seeing him give the patrician "MiLord" Tydings a good drubbing.

The second round of testimony saw greater crowds rush the caucus room. The lofty chamber bristled with an unlikely forest of tall television and movie cameras and hot klieg lights. There was a palpably festive atmosphere. All of Washington seemed more eager to witness another good fight than to hear an inquiry into serious issues. Another good fight was what they got: Tydings immediately asked McCarthy for the name that had caused so much controversy. By now he knew the name and knew that Tydings knew the name. McCarthy deliberately appeared to misunderstand Tydings in order to make a point he urgently wanted to exploit, a tactic he was to use brilliantly again and again.

And he said, "I understand the chairman wants me to answer two questions this morning. Number 1: 'Will you give the name of the individual in case number 14?' The answer is yes." He promptly handed Tydings a piece of paper that he said contained the name. "Number 2, can I give him the name of the State Department official mentioned in the secret files in that case, and am I making any charge against that official? The answer is no."

Before anyone could challenge him, McCarthy continued: If Tydings wanted the name, "I can tell him how to get it in a very simple and easy manner. That is by subpoenaing the files." Without yielding the floor, he stressed that to get the complete story the committee must get "not merely the State Department's—and this is important, Mr. Chairman—loose-leaf loyalty and personnel files, the State Department's two files, but also the files of the Civil Service Commission and the FBI." Because, he cautioned, "I and the American public will not be satisfied with a loose-leaf State Department file in which you can shove in and take out material."

McCarthy had cleverly impugned the files and identified himself with the public against the committee. But Tydings refused to be diverted from the subject—which was not to find out the name, but to determine publicly the accuracy of the evidence. He wanted McCarthy to come up with proof for every insinuation made and—

word by word, if necessary—account for purveying the damaging charges. "Senator, might I ask you whether the name of this individual is in your files," Tydings asked McCarthy.

McCarthy: "No."

Tydings: "It is not?"

McCarthy: "No."

Tydings: "It is not in the file in case number 14?"

McCarthy: "I have given the chairman all of the information in case number 14 on the Senate floor." If Tydings wanted the name, he could get it. "I can't," McCarthy said. "I do not have subpoena powers." But Tydings could "test the authority of the committee." McCarthy knew that subpoenaing the files was the last thing Tydings wanted to do. It would put him in a head-on collision with Truman over executive privilege.

Still, Tydings was unruffled. He had told McCarthy the day before that "you are going to get one of the most complete investigations ever given in the history of this Republic," and he knew the statement could be taken in two ways. If there was substance to McCarthy's charges, the inquiry would be exhaustively thorough. If not, McCarthy's evidence and methods would undergo such scrutiny that no one would doubt his charges were false. He, McMahon, and Green knew they had to pin McCarthy down at the outset or risk losing control, force him into cooperating if he would not do so voluntarily, make him realize he had to be straightforward with the committee.

The intensity escalated and bickering continued as the three-hour battle grew hotter and shriller. Tydings, McMahon, and Green were like bulldogs, trying to make McCarthy explain why, if the files were "replete" with evidence of malfeasance by a "high official," he did not know the culprit's name. And, of even greater importance, why wouldn't he show them his material so the investigation could proceed? McCarthy stolidly refused to discuss what was in his own files and repeated that all Tydings had to do was subpoena the government files.

Tempers went right off the edge. Tydings tried to gavel McCarthy into silence, his sharp blows seeming to shatter the room. McCarthy would not be stopped. He ground steadily on, interrupting constantly with his monotonous insistence that they could get the information if they wanted to—until Tydings, in a high-pitched voice breaking with anger, demanded, "Now you be quiet!" and protested, "That's not what I asked!" and finally roared, "I would like to say again and again and again and again and again and again that this committee will exhaust every avenue, investigate, request, and, I feel sure, obtain all the files that are in question."

"Except his," McMahon retorted sarcastically.

"That will do," said Tydings, trying to restore order with his gavel. But the fiery clashes continued unabated. Finally McMahon shouted, "Do I have to get a subpoena?" And McCarthy went on the attack. "You're not fooling me," he taunted. "I know what you want. I know what the State Department wants. They want to find out who is giving out information on these disloyal people so their heads will fall. You know you can get it." He twisted the knife. "You know the information is in the file. . . . I am very surprised and disappointed, Senator, that the committee would become the tool of the State Department." He went on to allude to rumors that the department was "rifling" its files, removing derogatory evidence. The inference was that Tydings, Green, and McMahon were conspirators in a plot to hide the files from the public until they could be stripped.

More insults flew as McMahon howled that he was "profoundly shocked" by McCarthy's "irresponsible speech," McCarthy insisted there was "nothing that the State Department would like better than to know what photostats I have," and Green, in the understatement of the afternoon, observed, "I cannot avoid the conclusion that you are trying to evade the question."

"You think so?" snapped McCarthy.

Tydings lamented, "You make so many speeches that we are getting along at a snail's pace." Moments later he complained, "That is not testimony. . . . It is nothing but an opinion. . . . Let's get on with the evidence." At last, exasperated, he changed his tactics to those of a neutral moderator. "Rather than argue," he said blandly, "proceed in your own way."

McCarthy then started to finish what he had barely begun the day before: testimony against Judge Dorothy Kenyon of New York, whom he accused of being a serious security risk because she belonged to as many as 28 communist-front organizations. The only effort Tydings made was to keep order. Before, each time McCarthy cited an organization Judge Kenyon and "other Communists" (Harry F. Ward, Louis Weinstock, Langston Hughes, Paul Robeson) belonged to or was associated with, Tydings had read into the record the entire membership list—coming across individuals such as Senators Arthur Capper of Kansas, Claude Pepper of Florida, and Elmer Thomas of Oklahoma, as well as Max Lerner, George Marshall, Upton Sinclair, his own father-in-law Joseph Davies, and a cast of hundreds. He would insist that dates of membership or association be compared with dates the organizations were cited as subversive. In every instance, Kenyon's affiliation long antedated any "communization" of the group.

Tydings's point came across loud and clear and—lest it be lost (he particularly sought the media's attention)—he carried an allusion to it over into the third day's testimony: "Senator McCarthy, you always read, as I recall, a few of the names. It would be very helpful, I am sure, to the press, if we could find the medium of letting the press have all the names." Again, a moment later, "I would like to tell the press that the date of the last exhibit, or the next to the last exhibit—what was that?"

McCarthy: "It was January 8, 1935. I read it."

Tydings: "And the date of the present exhibit is—*The New York Times* of October 9, 1944."

Tydings made his point, demonstrating how McCarthy was basing his case strictly on guilt by association, twisting facts to suit his needs without regard for truth. A later study by Tydings proved that a number of the groups McCarthy said were communist-front organizations never had been so declared. Judge Kenyon never had been a State Department employee. McCarthy's evidence looked so flimsy it was hard to believe even he could have confidence in it. The press concluded that his performance looked feeble. After the big talk about "57 card-carrying Communists" he had to fall back on the shabby device of guilt by association. Given the entire membership lists read by Tydings, it appeared easier to establish innocence by association.

Perhaps because the contrast between the two men was so clear cut, many descriptions of the proceedings focused as much on portrayals of personality as on discussion of what occurred: the quick, confident Tydings challenging the slow, determined McCarthy; the skilled duelist flashing a deadly sword as his antagonist ground steadily ahead, relentless as a great lumbering tank. That kind of dramatic coverage captured attention. And McCarthy loved playing to the crowds, nurturing the image of a heavy-bearded, glowering, unyielding defender of the anti-communist faith.

To Tydings it was not a game. From what he had learned of McCarthy, his charges and methods, the tone and direction of the first two days of hearings, he knew it was war—war over the most important aspects of American government and tradition: the prerogatives of the accuser versus the rights of the accused; rule of law versus vigilantism; structure versus anarchy; democratic tradition versus the Star Chamber. Tydings recoiled in horror as his rival bulldozed ahead, oblivious to rules of fair play, the constitutional or legal process, the Anglo-Saxon concept of equal justice under the law.

After another morning's stormy hearings, Tydings called his committee into executive session. He wanted unanimous agreement on procedures in order to avoid repeating the hostile confusion—without abandoning the right to challenge distortions of truth or disregard for the rights of the accused. Under his guidance the five men agreed to hear McCarthy out, reserving cross-examination until he completed his charges. Tydings invited Judge Kenyon and Ambassador Philip C. Jessup—a man McCarthy had named as having an "unusual affinity" for "Communist causes"—to address publicly the charges of communist affiliation that McCarthy had leveled at them.

When the hearings resumed on March 13, a wet and sullen Monday, the caucus room again was jammed to capacity, overflowing with the usual panoply of audiovisual paraphernalia. But the proceedings commenced in marked contrast to the earlier fire-and-brimstone. Tydings brought the committee to order and simply said, "The witness will proceed." McCarthy read testimony without interruption (save for Tydings sometimes reading into the record other sponsors and members of organizations with whom McCarthy said the four people he named had been associated).

Tydings also questioned McCarthy's refusal to testify that afternoon and thereby finish within four to five hours as promised. There was important housing legislation on the floor that he could not afford to miss, McCarthy said midway through his testimony. He would have to finish up the next morning at 10:30. That was precisely when Tydings had scheduled Judge Kenyon for rebuttal of the charges. He explained the conflict, appealed to the sense of urgency McCarthy had created: "If we could conclude with you today, I will sit here until 10 or 11 o'clock tonight. . . ."

But McCarthy was adamant. He "simply must be on the floor when we are discussing housing." Tydings suggested he could testify following Kenyon's appearance. Tydings knew McCarthy liked his morning words to make the afternoon papers. No, McCarthy protested, housing debates could go on all week, and, he added, "I do have other work to do, you see."

Tydings finally decided McCarthy should go on until recess and continue the following day, pending the situation on the floor. It was possible, he observed, that the housing bill might not come before the Senate that afternoon. He alerted a page to monitor the situation.

At Tydings's instruction, McCarthy resumed testimony (mostly lengthy quotes from old articles and books) until the noon recess when he demanded Tydings tell him as early as possible when to appear the next day. "I can't be called at the last minute . . . because it does take a tremendous amount of night and day work for me to get these cases in shape," he complained. Furthermore, he had changed his mind about the time he needed. He had to have more morning sessions. Tydings turned to converse with someone who had just entered the room, then announced that the housing matter had been deferred. The excuse for McCarthy's presence on the floor no longer existed. McCarthy brushed him off. "I have been working almost 24 hours a day getting these cases in shape," he said querulously.

Tydings was hardly the man to sympathize about how much time the hearings were taking. Few men in government bore so great a burden as Millard Tydings. He was chairman of the vitally important Armed Services Committee and served on the crucial Foreign Relations Committee. He was on the Joint Committee on Atomic

Energy, which dealt with the most critical matter in the history of the human race. His advice on military and foreign policy was sought by colleagues, the president, even by foreign leaders. He was regarded as one of the best informed figures in the U.S. government. His concurrence in committee was necessary and politically indispensable for the government to follow through on decisions.

Issues pending before the government in 1950 were of profound importance: adjusting shattered foreign policy objectives after the devastating shock of communist victory in China; decisions about defensive and strategic troop commitments to Europe; continued implementation of the Marshall Plan and North Atlantic Treaty obligations; promotion of disarmament talks (avidly supported by Tydings); the decision to go ahead with the first hydrogen bomb. And only one man sat on the three committees most crucial to these matters.

Tydings managed to contain what must have been certain contempt. "The committee is certainly not going to press you," he said to McCarthy. "You are carrying a heavy burden. We are all carrying a heavy burden, too," he grimly reminded him. "I haven't been in my office to do any work now for 4 or 5 or 6 days, and I have a bunch of people down there who are after me, almost beside themselves, to get some decisions."

But rather than raise another ugly ruckus, he scheduled McCarthy at 9:30 A.M. Kenyon would testify that afternoon. He knew McCarthy had managed to drag out his time on stage, but agreeing to one more morning of testimony, especially if it was an uninspiring as the tedious lists, flat biographical details, and passages cited from old periodicals and books presented so far, seemed wiser than getting into another fight with a man who played a game that sickened him. If the matter was of such grave importance to warrant investigation by the Senate without delay—and concerned the security of the nation—wasn't McCarthy's testimony important enough to outweigh housing legislation?

The committee eventually heard, over four mornings, charges against a total of ten people: Kenyon; Jessup; Haldore Hanson, a midlevel administrator in the State Department's office of Technical Cooperation and Development who had experience in Far East issues; Esther Caulkin Brunauer and her husband Stephen Brunauer (she, an American Association of University Women official for 17 years, now handled State Department liaison with UNESCO; and he, a decorated, retired Naval commander and chemist, worked for the Navy's Bureau of Ordnance); Owen Lattimore, director of the Walter Hines Page School of Diplomacy of Johns Hopkins University, who was a Far East expert and sometimes consulted for the State Department and the United Nations; Gustavo Duran, a veteran of the Spanish Loyalist Army and a naturalized American who once worked for the State Department and the United Nations; college professor Frederick Schuman of Williams College; astronomer Harlow Shapley of Harvard; and John Stewart Service, a State Department foreign service officer with years of experience in China. (Among them, only Esther Brunauer was on McCarthy's original list of 81, and only four were ever employees of the State Department.)

Of these, four tended to figure more prominently in the hearings, for one reason or another. Kenyon and Jessup were important because their responses were the first heard and because they convincingly shredded McCarthy's thin evidence. Tydings let them speak for themselves, which they did eloquently. He asked questions of clarification only, for their outrage and conclusive refutation of everything McCarthy had implied about them conveyed better than anything else the fraudulence of his "facts." It could not hurt to let others illustrate plainly just how much this production was McCarthy's doing.

Kenyon, visibly enraged, called McCarthy "an unmitigated liar." Her three hours of blistering testimony disproved, charge by charge, every McCarthy statement about her. Even Hickenlooper said that, although her affiliations were numerous, "I haven't the least evidence, nor do I have any belief, that you are subversive in any way." But those words could not change the fact that her name had appeared in major newspapers across the globe as a communist sympathizer and known collaborator.

Jessup was a State Department employee, a high-ranking, honored diplomat. He had been given but one reference by McCarthy on March 8—"Although I shall discuss the unusual affinity of Mr. Philip C. Jessup of the State Department for Communist causes later in the inquiry, I think it pertinent to note that the gentleman in question now formulating top-flight policy in the Far East affecting half the civilized world was also a sponsor of the American Russian Institute"—yet that single sentence earned him mention in papers everywhere. Jessup demolished the distorted picture made by the innuendo (and later he disproved other untrue accusations), but his career was damaged; his 1951 nomination for a top UN position was disapproved by a Foreign Relations subcommittee because of the fraudulent impression associated with him.

Lattimore and Service ultimately became more important because McCarthy was able to generate lasting public doubt about them. But his concentrated attacks on their past actions and writings did not gain credence among borderline believers until later. For now, Kenyon and Jessup made McCarthy look ridiculous. His performance nearly stalled. Tydings blocked McCarthy's attempt to make the caucus room his extended forum. Other news started to dominate the headlines. The press began to write his obituary.

Tydings appointed a staff—he had scrambled to assemble a first-rate group with proven ability and spotless reputations—presided over by a tall, experienced investigative attorney, Edward P. Morgan. Morgan, a highly respected former FBI special agent, was renowned for his consummate knowledge of the "isms." Communism, fascism, phalangism—if it was political and ended in "ism," he had studied and lectured about it. Tydings announced the appointments on March 14. The staff collated material already gathered to fashion leads—necessary because McCarthy, despite repeated requests for the 81 names and his evidence, still had produced nothing.

Meanwhile, Tydings, freed from the task of piecing together enough reliable data to consider McCarthy's testimony intelligently and to prepare thoughtful cross-examination, concentrated on the knotty problem of how to get McCarthy to hand over the names and evidence he said he had. At the end of his testimony on March 14, McCarthy gave Tydings 25 additional names to investigate. Tydings went after him, telling him tersely that the committee could not proceed until it had all 81 names. McCarthy retorted that there was "plenty to do on those 25" new ones.

"Don't you tell me how to run the committee," Tydings shouted. "I want today the 81 names." Although Tydings was unable to get any promise as to when they would be supplied, he had made an important point: McCarthy's unwillingness to cooperate was crippling the investigation.

Next, Tydings tried to corner him on discrepancies between his flamboyant, accusatory speech on the floor and the tamer morsels of insinuation he offered under oath. He suggested McCarthy's speeches from the *Congressional Record* be entered as sworn testimony. Tydings knew it might prove useful in trapping him into possible perjury charges sometime in the future. Since the 81 cases were already in the record, he said, "I see no reason why they should not be a part of the Senator's sworn testimony."

McCarthy tried to sidestep him. "I do not follow the Chair at all. . . . There is no way of making an oath retroactive."

"Certainly there is," replied Tydings, addressing the room: "All he needs to say is, 'All the things I gave in these cases on the Senate floor I would like considered part of my sworn testimony.' It is as simple as that." McCarthy repeatedly denied it could be done.

Tydings failed to force his hand, but he made McCarthy's evasiveness exquisitely obvious. Anyone who read the newspapers knew of McCarthy's brash boast: "I will not say anything on the Senate floor which I will not say off the Senate floor. On the day when I take advantage of the security we have on the Senate floor, on that day I will resign from the Senate." One could almost hear Tydings asking, "How soon?"

Tydings seemed firmly in charge. Even Republicans who had hoped McCarthy would give the Democrats fits admitted his performance was dismal. Some began distancing themselves. A full month after the famous Senate speech, McCarthy finally gave Tydings the names of the 81 cases. Tydings called a triumphant press conference, noting that—although he had, at long last, delivered the names—McCarthy had submitted "no substantiating evidence" to back up his charges. "Up to the present time," he commented acidly, "neither Senator McCarthy nor anyone else has given us the name of a single person who is accused of being a Communist or a card-carrying Communist."

The minute Tydings had the names he handed them over to Chief Counsel Ed Morgan, telling him to run a full check on who the persons were and their background data. When Morgan reported with confirmation that every individual was definitely from Robert

E. Lee's list—which meant all 81 had been subjected to loyalty investigations no less than four times by four different committees under a Republican Congress—Tydings went through the ceiling.[2]

All along his strong sense of propriety and morality had been deeply offended by McCarthy's uncooperativeness and disingenuousness. The misuse of information, procedure, and senatorial position was beyond anything he had confronted. As a man who had opposed issues and individuals he believed wrong in principle or unethical, he was scandalized by McCarthy's hypocrisy, baffled by his tactics, and enraged by the man's disregard for decency, truth, law, and principle—things Tydings held dear and had fought to preserve.

Tydings appealed to Democrats to speak out. Sam Rayburn, speaker of the House, Senator William Benton of Connecticut, and former Attorney General Francis Biddle attacked McCarthy for "irresponsible statements" and creating hysteria with his "witch hunting." Several McCarthy victims issued statements describing the humiliations they had suffered from "false accusations." The press continued to castigate him for the damage he was doing. Baltimore *Sun* political analyst Frank R. Kent wrote, "A storm of almost unprecedented violence has descended upon Mr. McCarthy's head. Not since 1917, when the late Senator Robert M. La Follette opposed our entry into World War I, has any member of Congress been as severely excoriated."

McCarthy was floundering badly. On the same day he relinquished the list of names, Tydings cut him off neatly when he demanded to interrogate Jessup, who was present for rebuttal. Tydings based his refusal on the tradition inherent in the Bill of Rights: Since the accused had been unable to confront the accuser when charges were made, it would be unfair to deny Jessup the chance to speak in his own defense. In fact, Tydings added, Jessup probably had more right to interrogate McCarthy than vice versa.

His statement drew loud applause in the caucus room. McCarthy, sitting just behind Tydings, leapt at the chance. He was quite ready to be questioned by Jessup, he said. Tydings, who knew exactly what he would do with the opportunity, snapped, "I haven't called on you yet." And he warned McCarthy that, when he did so, it was he, Tydings, who would be asking the questions. He would be asking about "discrepancies"—specifically in the original allegations of "57 card-carrying Communists in the State Department known to the Secretary of State. So far," he reminded McCarthy, "you have not named a single person as being a card-carrying Communist or a Communist Party member." Yet the unsubstantiated claims had been broadcast to the world as if they were fact.

McCarthy walked out. If he was not going to be extended the privilege of interrogating witnesses—he said, glowering for the cameras—attending future sessions would be "a waste of my time." He made this pronouncement and left Hickenlooper to take over. Hickenlooper presented no problem to Tydings. He was known as an habitual bungler whose ineptness had spawned the expression "to pull a Hickenlooper." He had little of McCarthy's aggressive tenacity. The first time he tried to interrupt Jessup, Tydings easily deflected him: "Would you like to let him finish, and then interrogate him so we won't be charged with heckling, or would you like to do it now?"

Hickenlooper immediately pulled back. "I shall bow to the suggestion of the Chair," he replied.

McCarthy had to regain the offensive. Surrounded by hustling news reporters on March 21, he unleashed another assault: He had the name—had given it to the committee—of the "top Russian espionage agent" in the United States. He was willing to press charges, he declared, and challenged the committee to get the man's FBI, State Department, and Civil Service Commission records because what they would find would "so shake the committee that they will quit playing petty politics and start investigating in earnest." Tydings called a closed-door session to grill McCarthy about the claim; but there was no new information, just embroidery of what had already been said about a man previously accused. The latest villain, among a total of 81 plus 9 plus 25—whatever happened to the 205 or the 57 was unknown (one senator grinned and said, "Maybe the 57 came off a catsup bottle")—was Owen J. Lattimore, mentioned twice before without designation as the "top Russian espionage agent."

As usual, McCarthy heaped on layers of rhetoric: Lattimore was "Alger Hiss' boss in the espionage ring in the State Department" and Hiss was "only one of the links. . . . If you crack this case it will be the biggest espionage case in the history of this country," he promised. But he would not reveal his evidence no matter how many times, and in how many different ways, Tydings asked. It was all in the files, he insisted.

"I am willing to stand or fall on this one," McCarthy boasted to the press after the executive session. Tydings was slyly noncommittal. So far, he told reporters, the committee only had opinion on names submitted, including Lattimore's—only McCarthy's opinion without substantiation, he reiterated in case anyone missed his point. Tydings persuaded Attorney General J. Howard McGrath to let the committee (minus Hickenlooper, who was campaigning in Iowa) make a special examination of Lattimore's file. In securing permission to review digests of FBI raw files, he scored a major coup. It was unprecedented. And it put J. Edgar Hoover in the awkward position of allowing information the FBI held to be evaluated by a congressional committee.

Lodge stated that "none of the charges has been proven," after he saw the FBI digests. Tydings followed with a strong summary: "It was the universal opinion of all of the members of the committee present" that nothing there showed Lattimore to be a Communist. When Hoover and McGrath testified several days later against releasing the loyalty files, Hoover hinted that the FBI had received nothing on Lattimore from McCarthy. Tydings took advantage of the opening. "The fact that [McCarthy] hasn't turned over any evidence has its own inference which I do not care to make," he said.

It seemed Tydings had him on the run, that things could be wrapped up in weeks. Three prominent Republicans—Henry Stimson, John Foster Dulles, and Arthur H. Vandenberg—had written open letters addressing the issues at stake. Vandenberg urged reestablishing bipartisan efforts regarding America's international responsibilities and invoked the need for law and order. Dulles pled for an end of "public dissemination of rumors and suspicions which create unnecessary confusion, division, and dismay." Stimson was more passionate: "This is most emphatically not the proper way to insure loyalty of Government employees," Stimson wrote to the New York *Times*. "The man who seeks to gain political advantage from personal attacks on a Secretary of State is a man who seeks political advantage from damage to his country."

It also looked as though Tydings would be getting the files from Truman—without having to go through the unpleasantness of subpoena. Tydings had known from the start that the loyalty files would be crucial to the hearings' outcome. If he could not get them, it would not matter whether he demolished McCarthy by exposing his phony evidence or turned up genuine Communists through his staff's investigations. Without the files, McCarthy would yell whitewash; enough people would believe him to further destroy State Department and administration credibility and effectiveness. Already the department and the White House had been forced to spend literally hundreds of hours a week dealing with the issue—time that took away from the other serious business of foreign policy and government.

Leaders all over the world, but especially in European nations that so desperately needed U.S. assistance, were horrified at the paralysis they were witnessing. To some it seemed as if what Hitler, Mussolini, and Tojo had failed to achieve over a period of years—to bring America to a grinding halt—a junior senator from Wisconsin had nearly accomplished in one month.

Tydings had chafed at McCarthy's manipulation of the public over the files. Early on, when speculation held that Truman probably would not release the documents, McCarthy voiced incredulity that Truman would withhold them from the three Democrats on the committee. "These men have demonstrated that they can be trusted with secret information," he solemnly had proclaimed. "I don't think anyone will believe the President if he says he can't trust them with information in the secret loyalty files."

Tydings was furious, knowing it had nothing to do with trust but rather executive privilege. McCarthy had taken a subtle swipe at his and the others' trustworthiness, and had cast suspicion on the "secret" files by trying to tie the whole thing to a sinister world of murky secrets. Determined to get the files, Tydings met with Truman on March 1, presenting persuasive arguments and drawing stringent ground rules to strengthen his chances: The files would be examined only at the White House; only the committee would have access; no notes would be taken. That would minimize leaks—and keep McCarthy from getting his hands on and doing what he wished with the information. The way he kept harping on the files seemed fishy to Tydings. McCarthy said it was all in the files, yet had not seen them. How did he know what was there?

The day after the meeting, Tydings wrote his first letter to Truman requesting permission for the committee to see the files. He conferred with the president again on March 11. Although no formal commitment was made, he was certain he had won agreement. He stated on two public occasions, without contradiction, that Truman had indicated the committee could see pertinent files at the White House. A "high authority" confirmed on March 18 that Truman was giving serious thought to opening the files. A confident Tydings contacted John Peurifoy, under secretary of state in charge of security and loyalty, to advise him to have them available by March 20.

Tydings knew Hoover and McGrath were adamant that the files not be opened. And unfortunately for Tydings, Truman was receiving conflicting advice. McGrath and Hoover were fearful lest Truman make a commitment. A nine-page March 20 internal Justice Department memorandum on the files detailed a wide range of options and problems from the Justice Department perspective. It broke things down by number: (1) If a promise to Tydings had *not* been made by Truman, then refusal to release would prevent leaks of unsubstantiated rumor, secret information, disclosure of procedures, and informant identity; release would set a dangerous precedent, would reveal cases where questionable State Department employees had perhaps been retained for several years, and would not satisfy McCarthy anyway, as he would charge tampering. (2) If a binding commitment *had* been made, then the question was whether the turnover of files should be voluntary or in response to subpoena; maybe Tydings could be persuaded that he would be criticized for failing to subpoena the files; Resolution 231 expressly ordered subpoena; neglecting to use it could allow McCarthy to claim that Tydings had hatched a behind-the-scenes cover-up with Truman. The main thrust of the memorandum was that, if there had been no commitment made, "it would be far better not to disclose the files."

To Hoover and McGrath, it was a territorial matter: protecting FBI procedure and prerogatives. The memo made clear they knew that disclosure without subpoena would mean "(a) no animosity will be created between the President and the members of the Subcommittee [and] (b) without such animosity the Subcommittee might perform a more objective job of evaluating the information [and also] (c) criticism that the administration has something to hide with respect to the loyalty of State Department employees will be reduced." Nonetheless, they lobbied Truman strongly to wait for a subpoena. On March 27 they appeared before the committee and repeated their arguments that opening the files would endanger FBI methods and operations.

On March 28, Truman sent a letter to Tydings denying release. He cited almost point by point the Hoover–McGrath arguments about unsubstantiated rumors, secret information, FBI procedures, and informant identity. The month-long process made Truman look indecisive, especially following Tydings's optimistic utterances—as if the president had waffled, rather than just kept his options open. It left the unfortunate impression that he was concealing something. And Truman had made Tydings look foolish.

Tydings was back to square one. Actually, Truman was not being totally rigid, for he arranged for a full review by the Loyalty Review Board—a bipartisan panel formed to handle loyalty questions—but Tydings could not accept the compromise. He had tried hard to avoid a collision with Truman that would put both in a tough spot; but he was also a defender of the system of checks and balances and would not surrender the Senate's right of subpoena. Further, Resolution 231 specifically ordered it; to disobey would put the entire venture at risk, inviting criticism. He served subpoenas on Acheson, McGrath, and the chairman of the Civil Service Commission.

Truman was testy. He ordered the subpoenas ignored. He wrote of Tydings in a March 29 note to Stephen Early, "His handling of the situation seems to me to have been rather discourteous, to say the least."

The lull was over. Just as Tydings's bid for the loyalty files fell through, McCarthy launched another offensive. He delivered a six-hour speech on the floor, a rambling rhetorical performance worthy of Scheherazade.

He began with a blast at Tydings (who was not present, having left to attend meetings at The Hague with North Atlantic Treaty defense ministers). It was all Tydings's fault, McCarthy claimed, that people had been identified in public. He had not wanted to do anything so unfair, but Tydings decided "that the first hearings would be open," and thus was to blame for the naming of names and the concomitant injury. "I think the Record should be made absolutely clear. [I] was very much disturbed by the very clever maneuvering of the Senator from Maryland in getting the names into public print." He made no mention of the unanimous committee vote for open hearings; no acknowledgment that on February 9, 10, and 20 he himself had volunteered the names of Gustavo Duran, Mary Jane Kenny, Harlow Shapley, and John Stewart Service; no reference to having told the press about Kenyon before the hearings began. He twisted the facts, successfully muddying the question of who was responsible, while casting doubt on the wisdom of holding open hearings—a subject that became controversial and for which Tydings ultimately was blamed.

Having disposed of Tydings, McCarthy moved on. Although he proposed to show Lattimore to be a Soviet agent and past, if not present, member of the Communist party, he eased up on the "top Russian espionage agent" aspect and instead emphasized another area: the Far East. (Lattimore was a respected scholar of Far East policy and political movements. At the moment McCarthy made his charges, he was, in fact, in Afghanistan for the United Nations, dealing with Asian political issues.) Lattimore was, McCarthy announced, the "principal architect of our far-eastern policy"—anything but a compliment, given the state of things vis-à-vis China.

As he often did, McCarthy repeated his charge a number of times that Lattimore was accountable for the "fantastic bill of goods" being sold to the American people about U.S. actions and goals in China. "I believe you can ask almost any school child who the architect of our far-eastern policy is, and he will say 'Owen Lattimore.'" Although the line brought outright laughter in the press gallery, with sufficient repetition the time actually came when many—even schoolchildren—if asked the question, would indeed answer, "Owen Lattimore." And McCarthy had a witness who was willing to testify under oath that Lattimore was a member of the Communist party. McCarthy did not identify his mystery witness, but emphasized his credibility. "This witness had been used by the Justice Department as a Government witness in another matter. The Department has trusted his veracity. . . ."

His other major sally that evening was the *Amerasia* case, a complicated, almost Byzantine episode of stupendous mismanagement. *Amerasia*, a bimonthly magazine, specialized in East Asian studies. The *Amerasia* case involved the investigation and arrest of six people (connected in one way or another with the magazine or its editors) for theft of classified government documents in early 1945, at a time when the nation was at war. It all began with the January 26, 1945, edition of *Amerasia*, which included an article entitled "The Case of Thailand." An Office of Strategic Services research analyst, who as part of his work read incessantly about Asia, noticed a stunning similarity between a secret OSS document he recently had seen and the Thailand article.

On checking, he found the article to be an almost word-for-word reprint. OSS security immediately investigated; and late at night on March 10, 1945, OSS agents entered *Amerasia*'s office in New York City without consent or search warrant. The office contained hundreds of classified documents, and one room held enough photocopy equipment to qualify as a laboratory. The agents combed through the documents and took 12 or 14 back to Washington, where the case was handed to the FBI. Unauthorized possession of classified government documents was a violation of the Espionage Act.

The FBI quickly realized that the documents obtained by the OSS agents were not admissible as evidence, since they had been seized without warrant. It launched an intense physical-surveillance investigation of everyone connected with *Amerasia*. Six people were considered culpable of theft or unauthorized possession of classified documents: Philip J. Jaffe and Kate Mitchell, coeditors of *Amerasia*; Lieutenant Andrew Roth of the Office of Naval Intelligence; Mark Gayn, a New York writer interested in Asian studies; Emmanuel S. Larsen; and Foreign Service Officer John Stewart Service.

For three months the FBI entered and searched—again without warrants—*Amerasia*'s offices and the individuals' apartments. They photographed what they found. Finally, on June 6, 1945, the FBI arrested the six and seized government documents found at the time of arrest. (In the cases of Roth and Service, none were found.) All six pleaded not guilty. A grand jury indicted Jaffe, Larsen, and Roth, while Mitchell, Gayn, and Service were released because of insufficient evidence.

The government's case immediately began to unravel. Larsen, on a hunch, plied his landlord with Southern Comfort and asked, "Say, Sager, how many times did you let those FBI men in here?" The landlord said, "Oh, do you know about that?"—and told him the number of times, what they asked, how they wired the telephone. The case collapsed. Larsen filed a motion to quash based on illegal search. The Justice Department, realizing Jaffe would waste no time in doing the same when he found out about Larsen's move (which he would, from the morning papers), arranged a hurry-up meeting at which Jaffe's attorney agreed to plead Jaffe guilty in exchange for the light sentence of a $2,500 fine. Larsen got off with pleading nolo contendere and received a $500 fine.

Had the issue involved less than a breach of the Espionage Act in wartime, that would have been it. But a howl went up that spawned numerous repeat investigations over the next ten years, including the one by Tydings. Each revealed the same: that the defendants insisted they were only practicing good journalism by trying to pry loose whatever government information they could (although they admitted they might have been overzealous). The material they collected dealt solely with East Asian matters, the magazine's legitimate sphere of interest. No one was proved to have tried to hide the documents or secretly pass them on. The State Department employees maintained that their possession and use of the documents was proper. Service, for example, had shared with Gayn and Jaffe only material he had permission to possess and declassify, as he had written and classified it himself. And why would a spy ring publish its hard-sought information if its business was espionage rather than publishing?

Nevertheless, it was easy to convince most people that espionage had been committed, that a prima facie case of espionage had been dropped, and that failure to prosecute represented a cover-up. The fact that the government's wound was self-inflicted due to illegal searches was not considered. The matter was regarded to be a whitewash of a conspiracy.

In his speech on March 30, 1950, McCarthy reopened the festering *Amerasia* case and linked it with Lattimore: Two of the

Amerasia defendants had been at the Lattimore home for dinner the night before their arrests. He underscored the cover-up question raised by the case's collapse with a vivid quote: "Months of painstaking work by scores, or perhaps hundreds of agents, developed what J. Edgar Hoover, the head of the Department, publicly referred to as a '100-percent airtight case' of espionage and treason." It did not matter to him that Hoover never made the statement and publicly denied saying anything of the sort. McCarthy repeated the "100-percent airtight" quote six times on March 30 and many times later, totally disregarding Hoover's denial. Through sheer repetition, his version eventually was believed. Tydings's committee had no choice but to reinvestigate.

Without realizing it, McCarthy had stumbled onto the two areas that would revive his credibility: the China/Asia nightmare and the *Amerasia* mess. It was easier to "prove" someone followed the Communist line than to prove someone was a spy; insinuations are more flexible than facts. But *Amerasia* appeared to be a certifiable case of espionage that had been dropped like a hot poker. Mere mention of China or Asia riled people as much as the idea of Communists or spies in government. China and *Amerasia* provided McCarthy an easy route for putting Tydings and the Democrats on the defensive. His real success with the public followed the March 30 speech.

Tydings heard with abhorrence McCarthy's misuse of the tangled elements encompassing the United States' China policy failure. The reason we lost in China—McCarthy said—was because the Lattimore, Service, and Jessup clique, led by Acheson, had promoted communist interests. Others also laid the blame on shortcomings of fallible men rather than on the corruption and arrogance of Chiang Kai-shek's government. The fallible men were called traitors. Senator William E. Jenner said, "There are some in our midst who are overjoyed at the prospect of a Communist victory in China. This is what they have been working for for years." (Tom Connally had a more down-to-earth interpretation: "Old Chiang's trouble was he didn't generalissimo enough.")

McCarthy never stopped crying "whitewash" when he spoke of traitors and spies allowed to go free. His message caught on among many who yearned for unambiguous answers where issues were increasingly complex and vague, and where clear answers did not exist. Tydings, Truman, Acheson, George Marshall, and other honest men were hard pressed to counter his oversimplifications and lies—as later Dwight D. Eisenhower, John Foster Dulles, Secretary of the Army Robert T. Stevens, and Republican Senator Ralph Flanders of Vermont were to discover to their great discomfort.

"Pure moonshine!" snorted Lattimore when informed of McCarthy's charges. "The Soviet Union ought to decorate McCarthy for telling the kind of lies about the United States that Russian propaganda couldn't invent. . . . No one likes being splattered with mud, even by a mad man." He flew back from Afghanistan and on April 6 appeared before Tydings's committee.

Sensational melodrama followed. Long queues of women and men stood at the doors of the caucus room waiting, and then the largest crowd yet—plus hordes of reporters, photographers, cameramen, and aides—scurried to find seats amid exploding flashbulbs. Alice Roosevelt Longworth, Mrs. Morris Cafritz, Mrs. Henry Cabot Lodge, Eleanor Tydings (she attended all sessions) and more than a dozen noncommittee senators came to listen. Abe Fortas and Paul Porter, Lattimore's attorneys, flanked him at the polished mahogany table. An unusually exotic element was created by the presence of a bronzed little man draped in embroidered purple satin robes: Dilowa Hutuktu, the "Living Buddha," whom Lattimore had rescued from the communists in Mongolia some years before. The white-hot klieg lights forced Henry Cabot Lodge to don green plastic-framed sunglasses to shield his eyes from the glare.

Tydings let Lattimore speak without interruption, and for more than five hours the bespectacled scholar drove home a number of points: that McCarthy himself was guilty of unauthorized use of secret documents obtained from official files; that he repeatedly had refused to submit evidence to a duly constituted Senate committee; that it was possible to hold views that disagreed with others' without being disloyal or pro-communist; that even officials of the U.S. government can oppose further aid to the Nationalist Chinese without being disloyal or pro-communist. "He seems to feel that everyone is disloyal whose opinions do not agree with those of himself," he said of McCarthy, who sat expressionless behind Tydings and watched.

When Lattimore finished refuting the charges, he mentioned the witness slated to testify that he was a member of the Communist party. "I make to you on my solemn oath the following statement: I am not and never have been a member of the Communist Party." He paused. "I have never been affiliated or associated with the Communist Party." He spoke deliberately. "I have never believed in the principles of communism nor subscribed to nor advocated the Communist or Soviet form of government either in the United States, in China, in the Far East, or anywhere in the world."

He then began a careful examination of U.S. policies in Asia—the historical context, the cultural aspects, the array of political realities. He was acerbic, sarcastic, and brilliant when lambasting McCarthy, deeply moving when making his solemn declaration, and dazzlingly lucid when delivering his succinct dissertation on Asian policy issues. He brought down the house. Or what was left of the house. The scholarly review had thinned out the crowd. McCarthy, too, had retired from the scene, without even leaving questions for the pliant Hickenlooper to ask.

At 4:45, Tydings leaned forward. Lodge's glasses slid into place as the lights came back on. "Dr. Lattimore," Tydings began, his face solemn and voice crisp, "your case has been designated the number 1 case, finally, in the charges made by Senator McCarthy. You have been called, substantially, I think, if not accurately quoting, the top Red spy agent in America. We have been told that if we had access to certain files that that would be shown." A tired Lattimore grasped the arms of his chair.

"I think as chairman of this committee that I owe it to you and to the country to tell you that four of the five members of this committee, in the presence of Mr. J. Edgar Hoover . . . had a complete summary of your file made available to them," Tydings went on. Hoover himself prepared the material, he noted. "And at the conclusion of the reading of this summary in great detail, it was the universal opinion of all of the members of the committee present, and all others in the room, of which there were two more"—it was obvious he was including Hoover—"that there was nothing in the file to show you were a Communist or had ever been a Communist, or that you were in any way connected with any espionage information or charges, so that the FBI file puts you completely, up to this moment, at least, in the clear."

Hickenlooper protested, "I have not been afforded an opportunity—"

Tydings abruptly cut him off. "I have arranged for Senator Hickenlooper . . . to see this file . . . some day next week."

Lattimore was beaming and visibly relaxed. He had knocked McCarthy right out of the ring. Tydings warmly shook his hand.

But McCarthy had not climbed back into the fight only to be declared down and out. He had not been stopped and began receiving some invaluable help.

The Beginning of the End

Republican Robert A. Taft of Ohio, Senate leader and an isolationist who had long been in contention with the internationalist wing of his party (which included Dulles, Stimson, and Vandenberg), had given McCarthy important—quiet—early support. Either Taft assumed the truth of the charges or saw McCarthy as an instrument for achieving political gain while reestablishing isolationism as the dominant Republican view. The divergent philosophies of Taft and Vandenberg had been vying since the end of the war to shape party foreign policy. Taft egged McCarthy on from the beginning, telling him to "keep on talking, keep them confused." When things looked good for Tydings and bad for McCarthy—and many other Republicans were unsure what to do—Taft ordered out the reserves. He encouraged Senator Styles Bridges of New Hampshire to join Kenneth S. Wherry of Nebraska in full support of McCarthy.

Taft's initial cheerleading behind the scenes grew bolder after March 30. He made a speech in Maine attacking Truman: "The only way to get rid of Communists in the State Department is to change the head of the government." He wrote an editorial for the Baltimore *News-Post* that accused Tydings of hounding McCarthy instead of finding Communists.

Republicans tended to gather around Taft. When it became

clear he had thrown his weight behind McCarthy, others began to close ranks. The political trend had worried Tydings, but Taft's actions shocked him. The two disagreed over some domestic and almost all international issues, but Tydings admired Taft and considered him a friend. He believed Taft's reputation for integrity and devotion to the law was well deserved. In 1948 he paid Taft tribute on the Senate floor. "He has an intellectual integrity—whether one agrees with his political philosophy or not—that is exceptional," he said.

Tydings was aware of Taft's strong partisan streak, but was stunned by his encouragement of McCarthy. Taft's attitude made it respectable for others to speak out for McCarthy or acquiesce in his methods. And his actions had frightening ethical implications. He was squandering his moral prestige to promote a strategy of expediency. The extremists—once basically harmless because they lacked respect—came out swinging.[3]

As the Taft faction grew more vocal, Hickenlooper made a public break that split the committee wide open. After seeing the Lattimore FBI digests, he challenged Tydings's deduction that Lattimore was cleared. The summaries were "completely inadequate," he said; the FBI and Justice Department "were not expressing any conclusions or evaluation" in their report.

Reporters dashed to question McGrath, who earlier had said that "as far as producing any spies" the McCarthy charges had "fizzled." Now McGrath said that Hickenlooper was correct: "Whatever conversation was had at the meeting and whatever files were shown, [both he (McGrath) and Hoover] were very careful not to draw any conclusions to influence the subcommittee members in their conclusions." This was all in accordance with Hoover's strict position that the FBI only gathered information and never passed judgment on it. Tydings's tart response to Hickenlooper's broadside—"I notice that Senator Hickenlooper doesn't say that the file portrays Mr. Lattimore as a Soviet agent or a Communist"—failed to undo the damage.

On the heels of that blow, Lodge defected. He disassociated himself from Tydings's Lattimore statement: "I have reached no final conclusions whatever on any phase of the investigation," he declared at a press conference on April 11. "When I do reach conclusions," he acidly added, "I shall announce them myself." He was taking a swing at Tydings, who apparently had spoken without authorization. The press reported that Green and McMahon, too, were surprised at Tydings's statement, for the Justice Department session was supposed to have been strictly confidential.

Tydings's error came back to haunt him. It undermined public faith in his judgment and made later statements suspect. And it brought the press down on him. Even sympathetic columnists wrote that he had damaged his cause. Noting that McCarthy's mystery witness had yet to testify, a Washington *Post* editorial stated, "Senator Lodge is quite justified in wanting to wait until all the evidence in the case has been presented before participating in a subcommittee 'clearance' of Dr. Lattimore."

The same day Lodge issued his statement of demurral, both he and Hickenlooper threatened to resign unless Tydings appointed a minority counsel. The press described a bitter showdown in which the two Republicans accused Tydings of partisan management of the investigation. A minority counsel, Robert Morris, was soon selected by the Republicans.

And as Hickenlooper and Lodge were dealing their blows, Hoover dropped a bombshell. He launched a sweeping investigation of Lattimore. The timing could not have been worse. Hickenlooper announced that McCarthy's charges prompted the probe, and newspapers lapped it up: "Senator Hickenlooper said after consulting with McGrath that the FBI is giving 'zealous' attention to McCarthy's charges that Lattimore is a Communist spy." Buried at the end of the article was a disclaimer: Investigation did not mean that "the FBI had uncovered any evidence to date substantiating McCarthy's charges or that the FBI suspects any will be found. Indications thus far are to the contrary." But the headlines and opening paragraphs were what most people read. That Hoover chose to open a full field investigation made it appear that McCarthy was onto something and that Tydings had made an egregious and premature judgment—or that Tydings was shielding someone.

Letters to the editor reflected the public's support of McCarthy and growing criticism of Tydings. "One would think that it were Senator McCarthy who is under suspicion or on trial," wrote an angry Washington, D.C., woman. "We know there are all shades of

Reds, pinks, and mauves in our Department of State." A Washington *Star* editorial noted that the masses of letters received "support Senator McCarthy and condemn his critics. . . . They are probably typical of thousands of such letters being received by . . . Senator Tydings and his colleagues."

They were. Tydings was bombarded with vicious mail. "How much do you charge to whitewash a barn?" asked an irate Texan who wrote in red ink.

The Baltimore *Sun* noted a peculiar contradiction. In judging the volume and character of its own mail as well as senators' constituent mail, it found that McCarthy had strong support. This was significant because "the great bulk of press and radio commentators, cartoonists and columnists have been vehemently critical, not to say denunciatory of Senator McCarthy from the start." Despite his earlier slump in public esteem, large numbers of people now seemed to be saying, "He must have *something* in all those charges." And McCarthy told reporters he was "snowed under" by 2,000 letters a day, 95 percent favoring his stand. The *Sun* was at a loss to explain it—beyond noting that most people were willing to believe the worst about the State Department.

A number of senators privately expressed apprehension over how Tydings and his committee were handling things—accepting witnesses' statements as truth without probing, functioning more as a front-line defense for the State Department rather than seeking facts. Off-the-record misgivings leaked into print, adding to Tydings's dilemmas. But he refused to buckle under the pummeling from Lodge, Hickenlooper, Hoover, McGrath, phantom whisperers, the press. The minute he returned from The Hague he reasserted control, launching an all-out effort to get the evidence. If McCarthy failed to produce, he would prove that the Wisconsin senator had no intention of cooperating.

Tydings wrote a letter on April 4 that he released to the press and sent by hand delivery to Bethesda Naval Hospital where McCarthy was being treated for sinus problems. Tydings reminded McCarthy of his still unfulfilled promises to give the committee his evidence. "You will recall that in the course of your speech on the Senate floor . . . which brought about this inquiry and the naming of our committee, you said that you would be 'willing, happy, and eager to go before any committee and give the names and *all the information available*,' " Tydings wrote, underscoring the operative words. "With this thought in mind," he continued, the committee requested "all information, documentary or otherwise, which you may have which has a bearing on the investigation."

Before noon Tydings received a refusal couched in cunning yes-but-no language. McCarthy offered to supply any material of value, but insinuated that Tydings was abetting the State Department in its efforts to uncover his sources. "Therefore, no information will be given the committee which would be of assistance to the State Department. . . . The committee is welcome to any other information, however, which I have or may be able to develop. I thought I had made this clear to the chairman and the committee on at least a dozen occasions," he wrote, adding insult to evasion.

Not so easily outmaneuvered, Tydings fired off a response, pouncing on the phrase "the committee is welcome to any other information." He wrote, "In line with this statement in your letter, will you please gather such information as you have together and turn it over to the Committee by noon tomorrow." He added for the record, "We do not desire to know any of your sources." Names of affiants and so forth could be deleted.

Tydings had publicly called McCarthy's bluff. Newspapers headlined the one-day, three-letter flurry, featuring McCarthy's refusal to cooperate. The high-handed response Tydings received the next morning—"It is rather difficult to understand the urgency of this request for further information before noon today, in view of the fact that you have done absolutely nothing with the great wealth of material turned over to you during the past five weeks"—was a desperate attempt to put Tydings back on the defensive.

Even in Wisconsin the air was turning chilly for McCarthy in early April. Major newspapers—the Eau Claire *Leader*, the Madison *Capital Times*, the Sheboygan *Press*, and the Milwaukee *Journal* (which had helped elect him)—attacked his inability to back up his charges. Only his hometown Appleton *Post–Crescent* and the Hearst chain's Milwaukee *Sentinel* defended him. The Milwaukee *Journal* summed up the feeling best: "His harum-scarum red hunt is rapidly turning out to be one of the great flops of our time."

Tydings called his committee into closed session on April 5 to discuss subpoenaing McCarthy's material. He had warned McCarthy to keep the files intact, indicating that, if they were not produced voluntarily, the committee might subpoena. Tydings had declined to do so originally in order to show "every consideration" to a colleague. He declined again later to preserve committee unanimity. At the April 5 meeting he pushed hard for subpoena as the one way to force McCarthy's hand. A bitter, polarizing partisan row resulted. The idea of subpoena was tabled permanently.

On April 24 Tydings again called the committee into executive session, this time with McCarthy present. He bluntly told McCarthy the committee wanted all the "information, evidence, or other data" relevant to the investigation. McCarthy indicated he "would be happy to comply." He never did.[4]

As a last resort, Tydings asked the FBI for copies of material McCarthy said he had handed over to them. The Justice Department's reply merely cited page numbers from the *Congressional Record*, where McCarthy had read documents into the *Record*, and quoted portions of his statements. The department did not acknowledge whether they had the material.

The long and the short of it was that no evidence ever was forthcoming from McCarthy. Tidbits thrown out at random on the Senate floor and during testimony exhausted his storehouse of "facts." In an angry progress update, Tydings expressed frustration: McCarthy, he said, despite repeated allusions to documentation, had yet to produce any "conclusive evidence that could prove or disprove disloyalty or sabotage or espionage or any other thing that might remotely be connected with this investigation." How on Earth, he asked, could he complete an investigation thorough enough to satisfy critics if denied this allegedly rich primary source?[5]

He composed a sharp reply to Taft's article (charging him with hounding McCarthy). Taft's premise was incorrect, Tydings asserted. "There is no one in America more anxious to get Reds and Communists out of all the Government departments than [I]. All we want is enough evidence to prove the case against any individual [and] expose the truth."

Confident that he had set the record straight about who was hampering the inquiry, and convinced that McCarthy would never cooperate, Tydings decided to take action. "I'm going to take it right now before the Senate and tell the story *now!*" he said bitterly to chief counsel Ed Morgan. Morgan managed to cool him down. Still urgently wanting the full Senate to know the extent of McCarthy's deceit, Tydings called in two top Washington newsmen. He reviewed the situation—stressing his certainty that the charges were nothing more than "a rehash" of earlier cases—and asked their advice.

"These men said," he later wrote, that ordinarily "it would be proper for me to go to the Senate and show that what McCarthy was charging was a rehash." But they cautioned that now, "in view of Hiss' recent conviction, Acheson's statement that he would not turn his back on Hiss and Truman's 'red herring' statement, if I did that it would look like an effort was being made to 'cover up'; that the public would not understand, even though the facts were presented to sustain such a position."

He put the idea into abeyance and embarked on a four-prong strategy to expose and thwart McCarthy. On April 11 he prepared a secret memo on procedures and precedents for the censure of a member of the Senate. In it he outlined what he considered ten relevant grounds for McCarthy's censure, including misleading the Senate about the actual language of his February 9 speech in Wheeling by altering "its most relevant passage"; failing to divulge his sources for the 81 cases; alleging his information was current; violating his promises to cooperate with the committee; damaging the State Department and executive branch "by unprincipled, irresponsible and unsubstantiated charges"; and injuring foreign relations programs and objectives. The last ground justifying censure dealt with ethics: "Senator McCarthy, in the sordid pursuit of political adventure has [injured the Senate] by subjecting matters of world import to partisan political attack, wholly divorced from semblance of truth, [and] has brought dishonor to the Senate by forcing formal action, and the waste of public funds, through reprehensible tactics."

He sent the memo to Morgan. "This is confidential, for your information," he wrote. "Please bring it to my attention at the proper time." Then he turned to the second item on his agenda: where to get support.

The White House, State Department, and Democrats in Congress and on the committee had let the investigation go on for more than a month with no coordinated plan. That error had to be rectified. He had to convince Truman that a plan of action was mandatory if McCarthy were to be countered, and that such a plan would require the loyalty files. He must renew his earlier efforts in this regard while appealing to Truman to take McCarthy seriously and move to checkmate him.

On April 12 he prepared a memorandum for Truman, detailing recommendations for action. The administration was "in the following position," he wrote: There was support for Truman's foreign policy (the Marshall Plan, North Atlantic Treaty pact, the Arms Implementation Plan), but the "domestic plan does not command the same support. I am not arguing its merits."[6] The opposition was exploiting public concern over deficit financing, agricultural problems, and the value of costly social programs. The Communist inquiry was being used as a wedge "to divide and weaken" U.S. foreign and domestic stability.

"How to recapture the lost ground?" he asked, and reeled off four suggestions, elaborating on the last: (1) Remove informant names from Lattimore's FBI file and have Hoover certify its accuracy and completeness; (2) give the file to the committee for examination at the White House; (3) give the committee and its investigators all files of the 81 McCarthy cases, with names of informants deleted; and (4) "then the President should go on the air and tell the American people what he proposes to do." The crucial part followed. In the broadcast, Truman must so convincingly make his case— telling the American people what he has done to combat communism—that he would co-opt McCarthy by assuming leadership in the fight himself.

"Tell them," Tydings urged, "that there was no [government] security program" until Truman set it up; "that you have appointed outstanding Republicans" as key figures in the Loyalty Review Board; "that your administration [prosecuted] Judith Coplon, Alger Hiss, [Valentine] Gubitchev, Harry Bridges and the 11 Communists in New York, all of whom were recently convicted. Tell them of the [Klaus] Fuches case [and] that all of these prosecutions were successfully completed through agencies of the Truman administration. . . . Tell the people you are the implacable foe of Communism."

He aggressively argued his case for getting the files. "Tell the people that you are breaking a long precedent because of the unusual nature of the times in making available" the 81 files. "Stick to your position that you will *not* make the FBI files public, using the statement of Mr. J. Edgar Hoover that he is opposed to this procedure."

Tydings warned the president in chillingly prescient prose what he risked by not moving fast. "[This] is the only way the Truman Administration can kill permanently the rumor and propaganda that 'there must be something bad in those files or Truman would not mind showing them'—'What is he trying to hide'—'There are Communists in the State Department. Truman is fighting Communism abroad and defending it at home.' " He warned that such quotes would be used by the Republicans in the upcoming elections "because it allows erroneous conclusions to be drawn from the old adage 'Where there is smoke, there must be fire.' "

Truman had been letting the investigation run its course. When he retaliated after some of McCarthy's more provocative charges, his comments were mere sarcastic jabs, as when he called McCarthy "the greatest asset the Kremlin has." In his memo, Tydings sounded the alarm. He hoped his hard partisan pitch would awaken the president to the dangers posed.

Truman indicated he would reconsider the files, and his administration began a counteroffensive. Vice President Alben W. Barkley spoke out to protest "rumors and suspicions" that threatened national freedoms. Secretary of State Acheson delivered a jolting speech before the American Society of Newspaper Editors, leaving his audience to ponder an awful dilemma: How could they as news reporters answer for abetting McCarthy? Truman himself laced into McCarthy in a speech before the American Bar Association, taking him to task for ignoring the real danger: communist imperialism abroad.

Another of Tydings's targets was his coterie of complaisant colleagues on the Hill. There had been sharp questioning of McCarthy by Democrats during both his February 20 and March 30 speeches, but they had not pressed the attack during the hearings. Lack of vocal support bothered Tydings. He called a meeting with McMahon and Morgan to thrash over how to rally Democratic support. Morgan suggested they get the House into the action to prove that the 81 cases had been cleared by four separate investigations. After all, Morgan noted, McCarthy's information originally came from the House committee that oversaw the State Department. Tydings and McMahon wrestled with the political overtones and finally agreed that the idea was worth a try. Tydings had Morgan prepare a pithy memo on the subject and together they went to see Sam Rayburn, speaker of the House.

The salty old Texan knew exactly what they wanted before they walked in the door. He needed little prompting to suggest that what they needed was "a little Roman Holiday on the House floor."

It was a bust, Morgan later recalled. "They muffed it. They didn't do it right because that was pretty dramatic stuff, if it had been laid out properly. [They] hadn't studied the situation. They had some member of their staff who didn't know a thing about it either prepare some little short speech for them to make on the House floor. And it, as we say, died aborning."

The fourth element of Tydings's effort to contain McCarthy centered on the investigation. Criticism stemmed from Tydings's skepticism over what McCarthy had charged; so, to satisfy the critics, Tydings announced that he was "broadening" the investigation. On April 17 he told the press that the committee had met behind closed doors and he had ordered his staff to begin inquiry through "new avenues." Reporters peppered him with questions. Yes, new areas would be covered, he explained; and yes, the *Amerasia* case would be part of it. They would "sift all clues, run down all leads, leave no loose ends," he promised, but refused to say what had prompted them to turn to *Amerasia*.

Tydings knew that McCarthy's mystery witness was set to testify in three days. Hinting at mysteries of his own, he stripped McCarthy of the limelight. The press pounced on his "sudden shift in policy" and its tantalizing secret aspects. His "mysterious and closed-mouth" performance commanded attention. His insistence on a wide-angle investigation reassured many. "Tydings was determined to see that justice and fair play were given to all those who were being pilloried by irresponsible accusations," said a *Sun* editorial. But it was not in the nature of things for one person to be able to control everything, no matter how skilled.

Tydings had scheduled Louis F. Budenz, McCarthy's finally named mystery witness, for testimony at 10:30 A.M. on April 20. Given the dramatic prelude, political adrenaline surged as the crowd began to line up before eight o'clock. Capitol police let in all who waited. The room, designed to accommodate perhaps 350 people, was crammed with almost double that number—hundreds of latecomers stood at the back and in the aisles while dozens of newsreel and television cameras commandeered half the space up front. Even senators had trouble finding seats. A hundred pencils were poised. Lodge's sunglasses waited at the ready in his suit pocket. Tydings's full water glass and empty ashtray were mirrored in the glossy tabletop. Microphone cords ran across the great expanse in parallel, emphasizing the division of the table into separate zones of combat.

Louis Budenz was a bitter former Communist party member who had renounced his political faith, rejoined the Catholic church, and participated in many investigations and trials of suspected communists. He was no starry-eyed youth when he entered the Communist party, having joined in 1935 at age 44 after years spent agitating with radical labor groups. He moved up in the party, hung on through the treacherous Soviet-Nazi wartime shifts of allegiance, and became managing editor of the *Daily Worker* from 1941 until he quit the party in 1945. As an informant for some of the most celebrated Communist prosecutions, he gave credibility to fears of communism in government. He had fingered Gerhart Eisler as the top American Communist in 1946 (Eisler was cited for contempt and fled to East Germany); he testified against Harold Christoffel (convicted of perjury); John Santo (fled under warrant of deportation); Alger Hiss (convicted of perjury); Alexander Stevens (fled); and the 11 New York American Communist politburo members (convicted of conspiring to teach the overthrow of the U.S. government by force).

What Budenz said gave credence to McCarthy's charges: The Institute of Pacific Relations harbored a Communist cell, and "in this Communist cell was Owen J. Lattimore," Budenz said. Furthermore, he had been told "to consider Owen Lattimore as a Communist" and was informed that, in the 1945 *Amerasia* case, Lattimore had "been of service" to the party. His story was far more injurious than anything anticipated. Reporters wanting to make the afternoon editions did not wait to hear the lengthy and sometimes incoherent testimony but, elbowing spectators aside, dashed to file dispatches that described the shocked silence followed by audible gasps from the audience.

Republicans leapt to confirm that Budenz validated McCarthy's charges. It "looks like another Alger Hiss case," crowed supporters. Moderates, too, believed the situation had been altered. Republican Ralph Flanders of Vermont convinced many with his observation from the floor that things had "taken a more serious turn."

Even prominent columnists were swayed by Budenz, if only temporarily—but long enough to give McCarthy credibility. Arthur Krock wrote of "many fair-minded persons" persuaded to change their minds, and William S. White reported in the New York *Times* that Budenz's story "was stronger and more explicit" than expected. Senate Democrats could find nothing to say.

Tydings and Morgan were stunned. Some very savvy legal and political minds had let themselves be convinced by hearsay—talk of "official reports" and "official information" uncorroborated by evidence. "Onionskin" messages that Budenz said identified Lattimore's code—"X" or "LX"—had been destroyed on "strict instructions." Budenz brushed off Lattimore's support of the Marshall Plan and 1940 aid to Finland—two clearly anti-communist programs. Lattimore had been granted "exemptions" to deviate from the official line, Budenz claimed. Every American Communist who had veered from Moscow's line had been expelled from the party but, if one were to believe Budenz, Owen Lattimore could think, say, and do as he pleased and remain a Communist in good standing.

After Budenz finished his statement, Tydings, Morgan, and Lattimore's attorneys—Paul Porter and Abe Fortas—probed inconsistencies in his story. Why had he specifically told a State Department security officer in 1947 that he had no information linking Lattimore to the party? Why had he written, in a 1949 draft of an article for *Colliers*, that Lattimore was not a Communist? Why in his forthcoming book had Budenz made no mention of Lattimore? His answers were evasive and weak. "In another book I am writing Mr. Lattimore is very prominent," he bleated.

It became clear under questioning that over the past five years Budenz had been in frequent touch with McCarthy backer Alfred

Kohlberg, the China Lobby's point and money man. More recently he had met with Robert Morris, the committee's right-wing minority counsel, and with a member of McCarthy's staff. His early denials of Lattimore's communism, the coincidence of recent contact with McCarthy backers, and his reputation as a professional anti-Communist (being an ex-Communist anti-Communist informer had proven quite lucrative) should have caused people to question his reliability.

Tydings grilled Budenz at a closed-door session on April 25 and hammered away at appearances before previous committees: In April and November 1946, March 1947, June 1948, and June 1949 he had testified about hundreds of Communists without once mentioning Lattimore. How could that be? Budenz lamely defended himself. There were so many names, so many hearings; he had focused on issues at hand. It did not escape Tydings's notice that of all the witnesses to appear—Kenyon, Jessup, Lattimore, et al.—only Budenz had not submitted character-witness letters. Lattimore, who in 1944 served as adviser to Chiang Kai-shek, had produced warm letters from Generalissimo and Mme Chiang Kai-shek—individuals unlikely to endorse communists.

The details revealed at this closed session, however, did not reach the public. Budenz's charges, the gasps, and all the public utterances were what captured attention, not the background information and discrepancies. What did emerge from the secret session was yet another sensational McCarthy charge accompanied by a savage attack on Tydings. The morning of April 25, before Budenz began answering questions, the confident chairman publicly humbled McCarthy by ejecting him from attendance at Budenz's second appearance. A rancorous 50-minute exchange had convinced Tydings that McCarthy's presence could only wreak chaos. (Lattimore and his attorneys had also been asked to leave.)

Such humiliation, witnessed by journalists positioned outside the door, enraged McCarthy. He sputtered his speechlessness, telling the press he could not think of a label strong enough to describe Tydings's high-handed behavior. And he took his revenge that afternoon on the floor. It was Senator William E. Jenner of Indiana who applied the lash, assailing Tydings for operating "the Interlocking Directorate of Whitewash Inc." He ensnared Tydings's father-in-law in the web. Wasn't it interesting, Jenner sneered, that Joseph Davies was a law partner of Seth Richardson, head of the Loyalty Review Board—the same Joseph Davies who had authored *Mission to Moscow*, a sympathetic portrait of the Soviet Union recalling his days as beguiled ambassador to that communist citadel? And wasn't it equally ominous that Edward Morgan had served with Richardson on the Pearl Harbor inquiry—another whitewash? "The men involved in the current investigation," Jenner snorted, "[are] well qualified in the art of swinging the whitewash brush."

In the midst of Jenner's onslaught, McCarthy gained the floor to trumpet a new charge: Budenz's secret testimony "had put [the] finger" on a high State Department official "as a member of the Communist Party." The impropriety of knowing in advance what Budenz was saying (Budenz remained closeted with the committee) did not concern McCarthy—nor did squeamishness over revealing secret testimony. And not one reporter questioned the propriety or accuracy of his charge, which later proved to be as empty as the others. He and Budenz dominated the news: "MCCARTHY SAYS BUDENZ BRANDS 'HIGH' AIDE RED."

It had been to prevent exactly such misuse of testimony and to protect the innocent from public accusation that Tydings had decided to finish the cross-examination in private. Because blameless people had been hurt, criticism of the public spectacle was growing, with blame often centered on Tydings. Yet the secret session pleased no one. McCarthy, with his strange genius for bending reason beyond recognition, made it appear sinister as he accused Tydings of treating him unfairly. Only witnesses against him testified in public, he complained, while witnesses supporting his charges were hustled off the stage as part of Tydings's cover-up technique.

Senator Herbert R. O'Conor of Maryland had hurried to the hearing room to warn Tydings of Jenner's and McCarthy's attacks. Tydings rushed to the floor. He parodied Jenner's windmill style as he shouted that he was sick and tired of "being stabbed in the back [by their] wild and reckless charges." But he held his tongue about Budenz. He remembered the backlash unleashed after speaking up prematurely in reference to Lattimore.

The parade of Communists and ex-Communists who followed told conflicting tales that titillated and further confused the issue.

Bella V. Dodd slashed up Budenz's story. She was a sharp New York left-wing radical who had joined the Communist party in 1943 and been expelled in 1949. She accused Budenz of making a career of denouncing former friends and colleagues, and she ridiculed his testimony, scoffing at the idea of "onionskin" communications. Not once, she swore, had she heard reference to Lattimore as a Communist.

Former Communist Party Chairman Earl Browder testified, as did Frederick Vanderbilt Field, a wealthy leftist who financed communist causes. They had to be coaxed by Tydings to say much, although Browder angrily refuted Budenz's version of party meetings and instructions on Lattimore. "It is hard to imagine," he said coldly, "how even a professional perjurer could think it up." Browder and Field denied that Lattimore was either a fellow traveler or a Communist. Their refusals to respond to other questions put them in a bad light; Budenz had warned that Communists are bound to lie under oath. Senator Jenner said that bringing Browder into hearings on communism was like "sending Baby Face Nelson to investigate John Dillinger." Tydings cited Browder and Field for contempt of Congress.

The last ex-Communist witness was Freda Utley, whose strident voice matched the occasional shriek from her microphone. In her 20-year career as a radical, she had run the political gamut from communism to China Lobby. Lattimore was not a spy, she said, but was a "Judas Cow," leading others to slaughter. She insisted on reading his works to prove her point, but interrupted with her own interpretations until Tydings cut her short. "It is not proper testimony for you to tell us what your opinion is. . . . We want facts, f–a–c–t–s. We are getting very few of them."

When Lattimore reappeared to refute Budenz's charges, the crowds were there again, but the atmosphere was less friendly. He ripped into McCarthy, Budenz, and Utley with savagery—calling them "a motley crew of crackpots, professional informers, hysterics, and ex-Communists"—until Ed Morgan asked for calm: "You and McCarthy are now even," he chided. Lattimore's rebuttal had little effect on public opinion. Budenz had said the country was crawling with Communists, and he had credentials as a government witness.

Republicans swarmed all over McCarthy's bandwagon. The

intense focus on the government's China/Asia policy failures put the State Department squarely to blame for everything. Communism became the central issue in several primaries. Senators Claude Pepper of Florida and Frank P. Graham of North Carolina, and Representative Helen Gahagan Douglas of California, went down to defeat because they were said to be soft on communism.

Tydings's confidence was shaken. The idea of such patently threadbare evidence carrying weight sickened him, and also frightened him. He met with Truman again—one of six meetings—to press for the files. He worked to reassure the public of the committee's integrity. "All the evidence we get in the matter will be turned over to the FBI," he announced in a radio address. "I think everybody in America, including myself, has a great deal of confidence in Mr. J. Edgar Hoover." Enlisting the FBI as committee ally could help its position. At a strategy meeting with Morgan and John Peurifoy of the State Department, he again struggled to find a way to contain McCarthy.

When Tydings broadened the investigation, he had ordered Morgan to track down every detail concerning the 81 cases. Morgan finally stumbled by chance on exactly where the names came from, confirming everything suspected. Now the rehash aspect of the 81 files could be proven—not just alleged—as could the depths of McCarthy's treachery and fraudulence. In retrospect it was stunning that the truth of the files' source had yet to hit the headlines. Morgan's contribution changed all that and crystallized Tydings's arguments for getting the data from Truman. It also persuaded Tydings that the subject could be aired and withstand the inevitable cries of whitewash.

On May 1, Democratic Representative Frank M. Karsten of Missouri launched the subject into print. The 81 cases were more than two years old and all previously investigated, Karsten wrote, and he could document it. "Inquiry should be made," he demanded, "as to whether or not a hoax, a deceit, or a fraud has been practiced . . . by someone, upon the American people." No one had trouble guessing whom he meant. The next day Peurifoy publicly denounced McCarthy's dog-eared list: "All Senator McCarthy had done was to shake two years of dust off of some old reports and produce them as his 'newly discovered evidence.' " He stopped just short of calling him a liar.

Washington *Evening Star* columnist Doris Fleeson detailed the history of McCarthy's "famous list" in a piece captioned "WARMED OVER BISCUITS." The list, Fleeson explained, was compiled by the Republican Congress of 1947–48, analyzed by four separate committees, and found to be so lacking in merit that it was dismissed without report. McCarthy, she bluntly observed, "stands in the grotesque position of accusing the only Republican-controlled Congress in 20 years of having failed to do its duty in rooting out communism."

With the stage thus set, on May 3 the Democrats launched a well-planned offensive on the Senate floor. Tydings made sure that word reached the press corps before it began. It was a tour de force, played by a troupe of nine with stunning precision. Scott W. Lucas, majority leader, led off, reading Peurifoy's speech into the *Record*; then, in an intricate exchange, the nine principals challenged McCarthy's credibility.[7]

Tossing questions back and forth, they explored arithmetic and semantics. How did McCarthy get from "a list of 205 that were known to the Secretary of State as being Members of the Communist Party" in his Wheeling, West Virginia, speech on February 9 to the "57 cases of individuals who would appear to be either card-carrying members or certainly loyal to the Communist Party" that he spoke of on the Senate floor on February 20? Why the shifts in numbers and wording? Why had McCarthy denied using the wording or figure contained in the "205" speech? McCarthy, they recalled, had said that what he read into the *Record* on February 20 was exactly what he said in Wheeling. Obviously not, the Tydings team asserted.

As proof, they brought in two affidavits from employees of the radio station that broadcast the February 9 speech, swearing that it was the "205" version. And the senators traced the origins of the numbers back over three years so there would be no mistaking McCarthy's intention of making obsolete material appear fresh.[8] The implication that he had lied under oath about most angles of the charges that occasioned the hearings was stark.

The prearranged procedural power play by the nine Democrats left observers in awe. For almost three hours, with flawless verbal choreography, they requested and yielded the floor, feeding Tydings questions.

> *Mr. Lucas*: I should like to ask the Senator from Maryland whether the Senator from Wisconsin produced any proof with respect to the 205 persons who, as the affidavits just read show, he said were card-carrying Communists employed in the State Department and helping to establish its policy?
>
> *Mr. Tydings*: Mr. President, will the Senator from West Virginia [Harley M. Kilgore] yield?
>
> *Mr. Kilgore*: I yield.
>
> *Mr. Tydings*: I should like to say . . . that all the testimony of the Senator from Wisconsin dealing with Communists or disloyal persons has been taken in open hearings and therefore the Senator from Illinois can draw the same conclusion from that testimony that I can draw. . . .
>
> *Mr. Lucas*: If I understand the Senator correctly, then, with respect to the 205 card-carrying Communists, so-called, anything that has been testified about them has been testified in the open?
>
> *Mr. Tydings*: By the Senator from Wisconsin.
>
> *Mr. Lucas*: Which has been nothing. . . .
>
> *Mr. Neely*: Has the Senator from Wisconsin given to the committee the names of 205 Communists who are employed in the State Department or who are shaping State Department policy?
>
> *Mr. Tydings*: The answer is "No."

When McCarthy was given the floor to ask a question but instead began reiterating his charges, the senators cut him short: "I yield for a question—not a speech." When he tried to evade yes-or-no questions, they would not let him get by with it: "If the Senator will not answer 'Yes' or 'No,' I must assume that he purposes to persist in evading my question," Neely shouted when McCarthy ducked a question for the fourth time. Tydings could not refrain from noting that "an honest man" could answer yes or no. Nor could he contain the pleasure McCarthy's discomfort gave him. "I am certainly very glad that the Senate has had the opportunity today to see . . . how difficult it is under some circumstances to extract information from witnesses."

The colloquy continued. At times Tydings refrained from responding. As chair of the committee, he said, he could not properly speak on matters still under investigation. His frustration emerged. "I have taken a good deal of vilification and abuse on the floor of the Senate," he noted, "but a long time ago I learned an old proverb that 'The spoken word is your master. The unspoken word is your slave.' " He meant no more premature disclosures, clearance of witnesses, or conclusions.

Newspapers characterized the debate as "a blistering exchange," but it was a cool, carefully orchestrated exhibition of muscle. Republicans had sat silent throughout. Wherry and Taft briefly challenged Lucas on grounds of procedure (insisting he be seated for calling McCarthy a liar through reading Peurifoy's speech), but Taft left at the oratorical climax. McCarthy was gone before the Democrats yielded the floor. No one besides Wherry had defended McCarthy from the splendid forensic fireworks.

Tydings was shocked yet again at learning how little defense McCarthy needed. Reporters who crowded around as McCarthy stalked out were promised an earful the next morning—and got it. At a press conference he announced that State Department employees "were part of the espionage ring" that handed atomic bomb secrets to the Soviet Union six months before the end of the war. The editors of *Amerasia* magazine were "collecting and transmitting to Russia the secrets of the atomic bomb" in 1945, and they got their information from the Department of State; a former Office of Secret Services agent, Frank Bielaski, was testifying before Tydings's committee behind closed doors about it that very moment, McCarthy declared.

The only part of his statement that held a grain of truth was that Frank Bielaski was testifying at a closed hearing. The former OSS officer, who led the illegal search of *Amerasia*'s office in 1945, recently had recalled seeing a document entitled something like "A Bomb Plan for Japan." When he testified before the Hobbs House Judiciary Committee investigation in 1946, Bielaski had made no reference to an "A bomb"; the expression was coined by newsmen long after the raid. No one else remembered such a document—and knowledge of the atomic bomb was so restricted that it is unlikely even Secretary of State Edward R. Stettinius, Jr., knew of its existence, much less lower officials. Bielaski's recent contact with McCarthy and Robert Morris undoubtedly stimulated his imagination into outstripping his memory.

Once again Tydings saw McCarthy distort an emotionally loaded subject. Coming on the heels of the Budenz debacle, his fear that *Amerasia* could become another minefield caused renewed anxiety. Only the day before, he had felt confident that this was one area where he was in control. He had said to the Senate, "I have accumulated a great deal of data [on *Amerasia*] about which even the committee knows nothing." He added somewhat arrogantly, "I believe I know a great deal more at this moment about the whole case and its ramifications than does any other man in America." Now he recoiled in horror as McCarthy's abuse of the facts damaged his hope of airing the case by orderly, judicious procedure. Order was McCarthy's enemy, and Tydings now recognized what that meant: The rule of law and justice would be subverted.

Just as Tydings was witnessing McCarthy's violation of the facts, another painstakingly managed part of the investigation met disaster at McCarthy's hands: the loyalty files. Tydings's meticulous work in piecing together the origins of the charges had given him the key to the files. He had convinced Truman that, since all the cases had been reviewed by four committees, his relinquishing them would not compromise executive privilege. Over Hoover's (and Seth Richardson's) continued vehement opposition—each threatened to resign if Truman gave Tydings the files—the president was persuaded by Tydings's arguments.[9] Release had been set for May 4, which, hardly coincidentally, was the day following the Democrats' show of force. Tydings and Truman wanted to dispatch McCarthy with a double knockout blow.

Like a cat with nine lives, McCarthy survived Tydings's every move. He had clawed *Amerasia* beyond recognition. Now he ripped to pieces Tydings's hope that the files might restore public confidence in him and his committee. They have been "raped and rifled," McCarthy crowed; it was a "phony offer of phony files." Though he was no longer dominating the headlines—newsmen were leery after finding his "sensational" charges to be so empty—he nevertheless continued to gain public support. The unraveling of Tydings's efforts accelerated.

Senate Democrats were meeting in the office of Leslie Biffle, Senate secretary, on May 8 when a distressed Tydings implored them to "go after McCarthy." He was far from the self-assured man who, after gathering facts, had marshaled forces to deter an unscrupulous man. The disarray now was overwhelming. And clearly he was exhausted. He routinely stayed up until 1:00 or 2:00 A.M. struggling over mountains of material, working on clues and procedures, or trying to catch up on other work. He looked drawn and anxious. The deep circles ringing his eyes almost resembled bruises. He was barely ever at home; and when he was, he was short tempered, impatient. His family grew concerned. Eleanor wrote her stepmother, "I am worried about Millard. He is so over-tired and I can do nothing with him."

Lucas had wound up the May 3 colloquy saying, "We have just started to fight." It was obvious to all in Biffle's office that Tydings needed all the help he could get. Senators William Benton of Connecticut and Dennis Chavez of New Mexico took up the cudgels. Benton characterized McCarthy as a "hit-and-run propagandist." Chavez exposed Louis Budenz as a violent opportunist who had committed (along with incest and bigamy) perjury and then hidden behind his Catholic conversion. In five years of talk with the FBI, Budenz failed to implicate Lattimore, Chavez noted in warning the nation about the caliber of men McCarthy used as witnesses.

Such attacks failed to tarnish Budenz and excited McCarthy to new heights of verbal abuse. Acheson, Jessup—the State Department—were "dilettante diplomats . . . pied pipers of the Politburo . . . prancing mimics of the Moscow party line . . . egg-sucking phony liberals," McCarthy jeered. The American people, gripped by the Cold War, psychologically vulnerable to fear of communism at home, were fearful, suspicious, vengeful. They were infected with McCarthyism and roused to a swelling wave of fury with which there was no quarreling. The anger Tydings expressed seemed feeble by comparison.

Tydings never had shied from battle. From the war and his political beginnings, he knew that the appearance of weakness draws big cats—and jackals—in for the kill. But, being committee chairman, he could not fight it out as he was aching to. For a powerful man accustomed to wielding enormous influence, the frustration was barely endurable. Unable to retaliate directly, he continued to press the investigation. He dug deeply into *Amerasia*. He also began searching for an alternative solution.

Early in April, Henry Cabot Lodge, unhappy about the growing partisan rancor, had suggested the creation of a bipartisan commission to take over. Tydings dismissed the idea. He had not assumed the chairmanship just to turn it over when the going got rough, he snapped. He also believed McCarthy's victims were owed the opportunity to respond and suspected that McCarthy would twist a nonpartisan proposal to his advantage, claiming cover-up.

By mid-May, however, Tydings was pleading for a nonpartisan commission. Knowing from painful experience McCarthy's skill at creating chaos inside a hearing room, he pressured Truman. No congressional committee could contain him. Only a nonpartisan group outside of Congress had a chance of restoring order. And on the expedient side, Tydings was up for reelection. His mail was so vindictive that he knew he was in serious trouble. He had to find a way to deflect accusations of whitewash. A commission composed of eminent jurists, generals, businessmen, and religious figures could ease him out of the hot spot.

Tydings had support. The New York *Times*, the Washington *Post*, and many of his colleagues (including Richard M. Nixon) promoted the idea. He appealed personally to Truman. To keep the effort low key, he eluded reporters by entering and leaving the side door at the White House; when confronted at his office, he declined comment. ("The spoken word is your master . . .")

Throughout May and June he lobbied his colleagues and Truman, explaining that he had no intention of stealing away—he could not, even if he wanted to—but that such a commission, authorized to review all charges and make its own report, could command public confidence. A study conducted by those who were "above politics"—with no constituents to answer to, no axes to grind—could provide an out for Senate and administration alike.

Tydings initially believed he had swayed Truman, but there were problems. Who would be willing to embroil themselves in the mess, and who would appoint them? Could Congress be convinced to transfer control? And, with elections not far off, Republicans were disinclined to cease pounding Democrats. Cries of cover-up and whitewash could be heard in advance by anyone.

Could a commission succeed in calming fears when the McCarthy/communist dilemma clearly played on a national state of mind? Popular emotional upheavals seldom are cured by rational dissection of facts. Some political analysts and practitioners might be sick of McCarthy, but the adulation he got wherever he went delivered a different message. He made people feel something was being done about the communist threat.

Tydings sat down with Truman and the Democratic leadership on June 22 at a secret night meeting at Blair House to debate the idea. Truman advisers Charles S. Murphy and Stephen J. Spingarn, who had opposed Tydings's original idea for a special group to relieve the committee, now vigorously promoted the establishment of a President's Commission on Internal Security and Individual Rights (PCISIR). Such a broad nonpartisan group could survey existing federal loyalty and security programs and the charges of the senator from Wisconsin.

Tydings, by then less worried about specific details than the need to stop McCarthy, argued passionately in favor of PCISIR. He wanted to wind up the hearings soon, he told Truman, but anticipated a firestorm of Republican criticism. Truman should appoint a commission—quickly. McMahon and presidential counsel Clark M. Clifford backed him up. But the majority of congressional leaders—House Speaker Rayburn, House Majority Leader John W. McCormack, and Senator Green argued against the idea, as did Vice President Alben W. Barkley. Attorney General McGrath feared a commission would hinder prosecution of Communists under the Smith Act. Although not present, Seth Richardson was violent in his objection.

Yet many other prominent Americans deluged the press with letters of endorsement. The Washington *Post* printed endless lists quoting those who added supporting voices to the debate—statesmen, academicians, bankers, industrialists, religious and military leaders. But there was little grass-roots demand. To Tydings's great distress, Truman tabled the idea.

No one can say if the appointment of a nonpartisan commission would have derailed McCarthy or rescued Tydings's committee, much less prevented what was later to befall Tydings. It hardly could have caused greater trauma than what did ensue. The whoops of "whitewash" with a second chorus, second verse, might have been louder, but could not have been worse.[10]

Even before it was clear there would be no commission, Tydings had forged ahead with the loyalty files. "We . . . are going through a complete examination of each," he announced when they arrived at the White House on May 10. "We've got everything—FBI, Q, X, Y . . . so there will be no excuses this time." He challenged his rival to prove they had been tampered with. "All McCarthy has to do is lay the evidence before us . . . and we will put whoever is responsible in jail. Otherwise it is just a lot of hocus-pocus."

His tart rejoinder did not end the complaints. When the State Department was unable to get the files to the White House for a week, McCarthy tauntingly said that the department had not "finished with their spring house cleaning." The minute Tydings claimed he had "everything—FBI, Q, X, Y," McCarthy set up a howl: Truman had not included the FBI raw data files, so crucial material was being hidden. Raw FBI data never were part of the deal, but his complaint hurt Tydings. Senator Green grimly remarked, "Nobody is going to satisfy McCarthy."

Tydings spent hundreds of hours examining all of the documents, working late into the night at the White House so he could tend to other business in the daytime. McCarthy's accusations grew extreme. Derogatory information had been weeded out as early as 1946, he charged. The State Department pointed out that there *were* no loyalty files in 1946—only personnel files—and any material removed was "solely from the standpoint of management and improvement and efficiency." But to the public a file was a file and weeding out was weeding out, so their virtue and value remained sullied.

Unfortunately no one thought to ask this important question until July: If the files had been stripped in 1946, why had McCarthy insisted they would prove his charges? But inconsistencies made no perceptible impression on the general public. Once McCarthy's version was planted, it became impossible to dislodge. Truth had trouble catching up with a lie as McCarthy's victims had agonizingly learned and poignantly stated before the committee.

Ultimately, Tydings found nothing to support McCarthy's charges, nor did McMahon or Green (each of whom examined all documents), and they said so in no uncertain terms. Hickenlooper and Lodge reviewed only 9 and 12 files, respectively. Although Lodge did not dispute Tydings's findings (Hickenlooper talked in circles), both Republicans claimed the files alone confirmed nothing. In the end, study of the files contributed nothing positive to the investigation, although not examining them would have been disastrous. And after thorough scrutiny, all Tydings could offer the public was his subjective evaluation. The information was strictly confidential. His opinion carried no weight with his opponents and very little with undecideds. As historian Robert Griffith noted, "The genesis of the controversy was not factual, and facts alone would not lead to its resolution."

In April, Tydings had promised a hard look at *Amerasia*. It was basically irrelevant to the communist issue, despite McCarthy's claim that it held the key to State Department espionage. Only two employees has been involved; one resigned (Emmanuel Larsen), and the other was cleared (John Stewart Service). The case was five years old and had been investigated in 1946. But McCarthy had focused on it, linked it to Lattimore, and attacked Service savagely; and the suspicions it raised about "something rotten" in the State Department had not abated. If nothing else was to be rendered unambiguous, Tydings wanted to see that *Amerasia* was.

So in May, as he studied daily at the White House, he set his staff to work on the evidence he had uncovered in preparation for the witnesses—the Justice Department prosecutors, the FBI and OSS officers, and, last, the six original *Amerasia* figures: Philip Jaffe, Kate Mitchell, Andrew Roth, Mark Gayn, Larsen, and Service. Service was of special importance because he was a bona-fide career foreign service officer, had served in China (and been excoriated for his views on the Chinese communists), and—although acquitted of wrongdoing—had been reprimanded for indiscretion.

After Frank Bielaski's "A bomb" revelations at the first *Amerasia* session May 4, there were no further appearances until the end of the month. In the interim, the country buzzed with speculation. One brief *Wall Street Journal* article on *Amerasia* used the words "mystery" and "mysterious" no less than five times. Then in late May the full parade of witnesses began, with all but Service testifying behind closed doors. (Lodge had insisted after Lattimore's last appearance that they "take this show off the road." Tydings concurred in the case of those not charged in public by McCarthy.) Besides preserving order by eliminating the tawdry circus atmosphere, closed hearings allowed for questions the committee hesitated to ask otherwise.

Tydings extracted the story with the care of an archaeologist sifting for artifacts. The sequence of appearance—Justice Department, FBI, and OSS figures preceding the six—made for careful groundwork. He retraced all events from the original article to the star-crossed prosecution, generating more than 500 pages of exhibits and testimony. He made public the 11 questions he asked the FBI and Justice Department to answer. He wanted no one to remain in doubt about what happened: how the documents got out of the State Department (in the hands of employees with gold badges authorizing them to take them); if any fell into foreign hands (no); if actual espionage was committed (no, questionable journalism was committed); if the FBI acquired any legally obtained evidence (no); why only three of the six were indicted (a grand jury cleared the others); why guilty pleas for Jaffe and Larsen were accepted the way they were (because motions to quash would have resulted in no indictments at all).

Tydings confirmed the Hobbs committee findings, and his lucid, meticulous disposition of every element the *Amerasia* case comprised should have strengthened his position—especially when, on June 12, a highly publicized New York federal grand jury conducting a simultaneous *Amerasia* investigation drew conclusions identical to Tydings's: no evidence of official misconduct. But it was his curse that organized political clamor outside the committee doors inevitably shaped public reaction. As with the Bielaski "A bomb" falsehood, other McCarthy tricks created rival attentions.

The first setback arose the day testimony resumed. Robert M. Hitchcock and James M. McInerney, Justice Department prosecutors in 1945, testified that "only one percent" of the 1,700 *Amerasia* documents seized were considered of "some importance." The rest they characterized as "casual and unimportant," "silly stuff," and "teacup gossip." Tydings, in trying to calm the public, passed that

information to newsmen. The words somehow were put into Tydings's mouth. The opposition pounced, denouncing him for brush-
ing off wartime acts of espionage as trivial "teacup gossip."

Then Robert Morris, committee minority counsel, got into the
act. Taking advantage of the opening Tydings gave him, Morris
revealed to Hickenlooper (but no one else on the committee)
information concerning the existence and contents of a small number
of *Amerasia* documents seen by the OSS but not seized during the
raid (to avoid tipping off the staff). That material did refer to vital
wartime intelligence: counterintelligence plans, U.S. fleet locations,
Chinese military operations. Hickenlooper leaked Morris's leak.
Tydings angrily denied the existence of the documents as he never
had been told of them. The cleverly staged effort to embarrass
Tydings worked. He appeared guilty of covering up important
information.

Morris and McCarthy met with former OSS officer Archbold
Van Beuren, the man in charge of the March 1945 black-bag
midnight raid on *Amerasia*. Together they cooked up a telegram for
Van Beuren to send them, accusing Tydings of wanting only to
discredit McCarthy's witnesses. Van Beuren later apologized, but the
damage was done. Another Morris deceit was the charge that
Peurifoy attempted to "pay off" Emmanuel Larsen with free legal
advice in exchange for testimony helpful to Tydings. It was bunk—
but good reading. Morris's actions represented such a breach of faith
that Morgan feared the Justice Department would refuse further
cooperation. He wanted Morris fired on the spot, but dismissal
would have ruptured the committee—and would have given the
opposition ammunition for "proving" the committee had been
fixed.[11]

None of those McCarthy–Morris charges held water, and eventually each was disproved; but with the leaks and tricks, the cumu-
lative effects discredited Tydings. Even among McCarthy skeptics, it
perpetuated a residue of uncertainty. Arthur Krock of the New York
Times—usually a perceptive analyst—wrote breathlessly about Bielaski and the "possibility that the transmission of atomic secrets to
Russia in 1945 is involved." Many people did not understand
Tydings's legal dialectics, but McCarthy's implications were absorbed easily—the right stuff to thicken a sinister plot.

And Tydings was subjected to scurrilous attack in the opposition press: "Rumors are flying thick and fast in the Capitol on the reward Senator Tydings (D) of Maryland will receive for his services in attempting to whitewash the Administration in general and the State Department in particular of splotches of communism." He had "sold out" for an ambassadorship ("possibly to Moscow where his father-in-law . . . once represented this country"), a Supreme Court appointment (he was "promised the post of chief justice"), or "the vice presidential nomination in 1952." Tydings had already been mentioned for the number-two spot on the Democratic ticket well before the investigation, so many found such rumors plausible.

Tydings was deeply wounded by such lies, by public reaction to McCarthy's falsehoods, and by the vitriolic mail pouring into his office. But instead of defending himself, he worked to draw attention away from McCarthy. He spoke about the dangers of Cold War tensions. He expressed hope that the Russians did not want war, but said he feared that "accidentally the powder keg may go off." Hurrying from an Armed Services Committee session he handed out a statement. Legislation "vital to national security" had been sidetracked. "At least three bills"—including extension of the draft, an urgent matter in view of the Cold War—"have run head on into the McCarthy investigation." Words of caution capped his message: "New plans and new problems are constantly springing up which must be dealt with."

His opponents scoffed and labeled his efforts to refocus the perspective of national needs as a trial balloon for escaping from the committee. That he was tragically prescient about "new problems" became clear little more than a month later. On June 25, North Korean troops swept across Korea's thirty-eighth parallel, and the nation was at war.

As chairman of Armed Services, Tydings immediately effected unanimous passage of an emergency draft extension. He appealed for approval of the long-pending billion dollar global arms aid bill: "Never, never, never, never again," he warned, will the country "have the time we had in World War I and World War II to get ready" for war. To the renewed Republican resistance against legislation he was pressing to a vote—on the part of Republicans who had built reputations as implacable foes of communism, but who opposed arms aid to North Atlantic Treaty programs and others—he replied, "Unless we act and act swiftly, Europe may be the next theater for such operations as we witness today in Korea."

His skilled efforts broke the partisan deadlock. Congress voted arms to North Atlantic Treaty nations and to Greece, Turkey, Iran— and Korea. Tydings acknowledged the entangling drawback of arms aid, but also understood the risks involved if the United States remained aloof. "I want to gamble on the side of having done all I can," he said. Economic and military assistance were "the physical sinews which bind the Atlantic pact nations together."

Tydings prescience may have gone unacknowledged, but his actions—and the war—swept McCarthy out of the news. James Reston spoke for many when he wrote that the "somber spectacle [of war] has finally overwhelmed the atmosphere of McCarthyism that has pervaded this city for months."

Tydings had been talking of ending the investigation before the war broke out; and the same day he effected passage of the military-draft extension, he brought up the matter of wrapping up. The meeting was acrid. Hickenlooper and Lodge were wild at the idea of terminating inquiry with areas of investigation left unfinished. Tydings had the ugly choice of continuing the probe interminably or ending amid charges of "whitewash."

The fourth estate—columnists, editors, radio commentators— in one voice prophesied that Tydings faced trouble if and when he tried to conclude. But no other option made sense to him. He knew military matters needed attention, and how much time, money, and effort had been wasted on one senator's fabrications; and he believed the country would rally behind Truman in the face of the North Korean attack. He also knew that in November he and other Democrats were up for reelection. Better to end it now, allow time for healing.

His concern was more than expedience. Not only was constituent mail negative and the opposition press vociferously pledging to defeat him, but the major news magazines *Newsweek*, *U.S. News and World Report*, and *Time* (which only in early April had listed him among the country's ten most effective senators[12]) openly speculated about his difficulties.

McCarthy immediately jumped in. "It's a good thing to bring

an end to the shoddiest and most disgraceful whitewashing ever seen in Congress," he said. But his splenetic reaction received only two short paragraphs buried at the bottom of a column headed, "TYD-INGS TAKES QUICK ACTION ON ARMS AID."

Tydings never blinked. Although it was obvious no consensus would be reached with Hickenlooper and Lodge, he voted for wrap-up. The committee voted three to two to close the investigation, and he instructed Morgan to draft a report. If there was half a chance, he planned to charge McCarthy with perjury and have him censured by the Senate.

McCarthy had plans of his own. He staged a visit home, his first since the crusade began. The Wisconsin press may have ridiculed him in April, but in June the people's welcome—he was mobbed, speeches interrupted with heavy applause—sent a message to Washington, stirring Republican National Chairman Guy Gabrielson's thinking. When Gabrielson later launched the party's vote-getting campaign, he declared that Americans "wholeheartedly agree with [McCarthy's] objectives." Telegrams from Republicans who could not condone his methods received no response.

McCarthy also drew Hoover into the fray. Earlier, when McCarthy had set off his clamor over the loyalty files' chastity, Tydings requested an FBI examination to ensure nothing was missing. Deputy Attorney General Peyton Ford of the Justice Department ordered two of his security officers to comb the files and advised Tydings that they were complete. But Tydings carelessly announced that the *FBI* had checked the files. McCarthy promptly wrote Hoover and received confirmation that "the FBI had made no such examination and therefore is not in a position to make any statement concerning the completeness or incompleteness of the State Department files." Tydings was caught in another blunder and was accused of trying to cover up the tracks.

A livid Tydings scurried to get Ford and McGrath to make a second check, this time by FBI agents. But the misunderstanding never was straightened out satisfactorily. McGrath's letter of July 17 affirming that the files contained everything (with a very minor exception) was challenged by McCarthy. Someone had sneaked the missing papers back in, he claimed. Right away Tydings asked the FBI to cross-check all material that Peyton Ford's officers saw in June with what FBI agents saw in July. But by the time Hoover got around to putting the charade to rest, Tydings's investigation had been over for a month and a half. Hoover's letter to Tydings on September 8 said, "This is to advise you that at the request of the Attorney General, we did make [the requested cross-check] on July 13, 1950 and found that the State Department files were intact, as indicated in the letter from the Attorney General to you dated July 17, 1950." But the false impression had already been created.

When Tydings read Ed Morgan's draft report he said, "I wouldn't change a single word." Senator Green concerned himself only with one sentence: "You make reference to 'human rights being immolated "before" this monster McCarthy.' . . . I think that word 'before' should be 'beneath.' " The draft became the Tydings *Report* and Tydings, Green, and McMahon signed it without hesitation. It was one of the most scathing reports filed by a committee in the history of the Senate, and no Senate document ever contained a more savage tongue-lashing of a colleague. More than 300 pages of lucid prose delineated charges, testimony, proof, issues, events, individuals, contradictions, and exhibits, all gleaned from 2,500 printed pages. Perhaps its sheer bulk—the madness of 3,000,000 words, the waste of five months, thousands of hours, thousands of dollars—inspired Tydings and Morgan to the potent mix of legal disquisition and ventilation of rage.

All aspects of McCarthy's nonexistent evidence and abusive conduct were laid out. There was no standard of decency he had not defiled, and Tydings made certain the report said so. "From the very outset the subcommittee was subjected by Senator McCarthy and certain segments of the press and radio to a campaign of vilification probably unparalleled in the history of congressional investigations," it stated, before proceeding to expose every lie—although that word never was used. "Untruth," "falsehood," "half-truth," "deception," "distortion," all of which were liberally used, made the unmistakable point.

"From the very outset of our inquiry, Senator McCarthy has sought to leave the impression that the subcommittee has been investigating him and not 'disloyalty in the State Department,' " they wrote. "The reason for [his] concern is now apparent. He had

no facts to support his wild and baseless charges, and lived in mortal
fear that this situation would be exposed."

> Starting with nothing, Senator McCarthy plunged headlong
> forward, desperately seeking to develop some information which,
> colored with distortion and fanned by a blaze of bias, would
> forestall a day of reckoning. . . . Any effort to expose the half-
> truths and distortions during our proceedings was countered by
> a charge that we were "seeking to protect the Communists." . . .
> We have the amazing spectacle of a United States Senator
> having made such charges with no facts or with discredited
> allegations of fact to support them. [McCarthy perpetrated]
> perhaps the most nefarious campaign of untruths in the history
> of our Republic . . . a fraud and a hoax perpetrated on the Senate
> of the United States and the American people. . . .
> We have seen the technique of the "Big Lie" elsewhere
> employed by the totalitarian dictator with devastating success,
> utilized here for the first time on a sustained basis in our history.
> We have seen how, through repetition and shifting untruths, it is
> possible to delude great numbers of people. . . .
> This has been done without the slightest vestige of respect
> for even the most elementary rules of evidence or fair play or,
> indeed, common decency. Indeed, we have seen an effort not
> merely to establish guilt by association but guilt by accusation
> alone. . . . Were this campaign founded in truth it would be
> questionable enough; where it is fraught with falsehood from
> beginning to end, its reprehensible and contemptible character
> defies adequate condemnation.

Tydings, McMahon, and Green had tested the evidence against
reality and judged McCarthy with a vengeance. The two Republicans
rejected the report, refusing to sign it. Lodge issued a report of his
own, and Hickenlooper said he would make a statement in lieu of a
separate report.

When the full Foreign Relations Committee met on July 18 to
consider the report, which had been released to the press the day
before, the two-hour brawl was one of the nastiest sessions on
record. Hickenlooper and Lodge in furious language disputed the
entire investigation, calling it a "perversion" of Resolution 231.
They argued everything—from who had wanted open hearings to

the right to file a minority report—shrilly interrupting, squabbling over whether the report should be "accepted," "received," or just "filed." Tydings fought ferociously to include "for transmittal to the Senate," a phrase he so unfailingly repeated that it took on the property of a refrain. As Lodge and Hickenlooper baited him, his impatience increased. "I am not asking them to pass on [the report], I am asking them to accept it and discharge our committee. I do not care what they do with it."

"Don't get sore," said Senator Alexander Smith of New Jersey.

"Well, I am trying to make it plain for the fifteenth time," an angry Tydings shouted. "I do not ask anybody to approve it or disapprove it."

Two hours and a dozen explosions later, voting was complete: unanimous on receiving the report and discharging the committee; nine to two for transmittal to the Senate. The full committee would not recommend, approve, accept, or comment. Tempers were too hot and the subject too inflammable. Tydings had done well to get it received "for transmittal to the Senate."

In the press conference following the session, Chairman Tom Connally staged a cagey duel with reporters that by its evasiveness illustrated the uneasiness over Tydings's report. When asked why Hickenlooper and Lodge voted no on transmittal, Connally replied, "I haven't got an hour to tell you."

"Will you have anything to recommend?"

"You haven't heard me say anything about it."

You mean, the reporters asked, looking for clarification, "the committee neither approved nor disapproved this report, it just received it?"

"That is all. We did not go into that, because we want to go home by Christmas."

"What do you think of the report, Senator?"

"Well, I think it is filed and I am going to send it to the Senate."

"Did you say 'vile'?"

Connally grinned. "When a fellow asks me a question like that," he said, "it reminds me of a man making a political speech, a man from Tammany over on the East Side, and there were some rough necks there, some tough ones, and he got up and asked if there were any questions." Connally paused. "Someone asked him some embarrassing question, and his bunch of thugs just went in and grabbed this fellow, gave him a good stiff kick in the pants, and took him to the stairway and pitched him down, and he bumped and bumped and bumped and finally out on the sidewalk, and then the orator said, 'Is there any other gentleman that wants to ask a question?' Are there any other questions?"

The press conference adjourned in laughter. But Tydings was not laughing. He knew the partisan bitterness within the committee promised more malicious reactions to come. McCarthy had called the report "a green light to the Red fifth column" in America. But now Tydings was free from the etiquette imposed by duties of the chair; five months of fury waited to be let loose by a master of mordant scorn as he presented his report to the Senate.

The tension on the Senate floor was palpable. Partisan lines, already drawn, visibly hardened. Three separate Republican efforts to block the receiving of Tydings's report were slapped down by straight party vote. A spiteful attempt to eject Ed Morgan was rejected by Senate President Alben Barkley. Then, with hostile parliamentary maneuvering over, the Maryland senator took the floor.

Tydings considered this speech to be the most crucial of his career. He had endured months of attack waiting for the day when he could speak openly about all that had transpired. Justice demanded that McCarthy be called to account before the very forum he had defiled, and Tydings urgently believed the Senate must be reminded of its best traditions and its sense of duty. McCarthy's conduct had mocked the Senate's standards and traditions, had injured the dignity and honor of the office. And this also provided a chance to dish out some of what he had taken.

His speech was a blend of passion and theater. Letting his voice rise and fall, wax self-righteous and then cold, sarcastic then angry, he left the audience, crowded into the chamber, cheering. Striding to and fro in the well of the Senate and gesturing, he spoke of the history, the responsibility, the meaning of the Senate; he spoke of "scars, wounds, misunderstandings, and misrepresentations by men of little character who preferred to serve their own ends rather than those of their country." McCarthy, he said, bristling with scorn, "has used every epithet and every term of approbrium and calumny to blackguard me." He reminded his colleagues that the accusations of whitewash as unleashed were tantamount to charges of complicity with treason. Did the Senate truly believe one of its committees guilty of treason?

When he turned to his props—charts, records, and a phonograph—he raised the pitch. "Come over and listen to me play my little Victrola," he urged, irony oiling his voice. He had McCarthy's own words in McCarthy's own voice to prove he had deceived the Senate. When Wherry objected, Tydings snapped, "I withdraw the request." But he suggested they listen to the record—"invitation by card only"—later, at a special playing. The caustic use of the word "card," as in "card-carrying," drew laughs.

Still he was not finished. Displaying his protean talents as a mimic, he delivered a devastating imitation of McCarthy. He rolled his eyes and hitched his trousers, and with glowering frowns perfectly captured the senator's monotonous cadence. His burlesque left the crowd howling as a stony-faced McCarthy sat silent, chin in hand. "There is the voice," Tydings exclaimed pointing to the phonograph, its coiled black cord trailing across the Senate's green rug. "And it is not the voice of truth. . . . If Senators are still in doubt . . . they will learn who has been whitewashing," he thundered, swelling to full ex-cathedra volume, "whitewashing with mud, whitewashing with slime, whitewashing with filth, whitewashing with the dregs of publicity at the expense of the love of people for their own country." With scathing contempt he ridiculed the Senator who "says there are 516, 205, 57, 108, or 25 or 1 spy in the State Department."

Tydings did more than tell colleagues and country they had been deceived by McCarthy. He appeared to be asking for censure. Whether shouting or speaking in near whispers, he repeatedly described acts of perjury without using the word. "[He] told us under oath that was not what he said, but the record stands there to challenge the statement. . . . That is why I said a hoax and a fraud was practiced on the people of the United States, and, by the eternal gods, that is true." All attention was riveted on him. "I am not going to ask the Senate what it is going to do about it. . . . I return the matter to the hands and the consciences of the members of the Senate."[13]

The press had no trouble interpreting his intent. William S. White of the New York *Times*, under the headline "TYDINGS CHARGES MCCARTHY PERJURED HIMSELF AT INQUIRY," opened his article, "Senator Millard E. Tydings accused Senator Joseph R. McCarthy today of perjury and left it up to the Senate's 'conscience' whether the chamber should take action toward censuring or expelling him."

Other newspapers' judgments were more colorful. "SENATOR JOE FAW DOWN AN' GO BOOM!" chortled a labor paper headline. "Joe McCarthy, the Senate's wild man, has had his ears pinned back by his colleagues," wrote the Washington *Evening Star*. The speech's elegant invective was proclaimed a spectacular display, and press support for Tydings was stunning. Despite the strong language, he was commended for his conscientious efforts to divine truth from McCarthy's chaos. "One cannot hope for a wholly judicial attitude from senators under attack by their opponents. By and large, however, Senator Tydings, who took most of the burden on his own shoulders, comes out very well," said an editorial in the *Sun*. As Doris Fleeson put it, Tydings's report "might have been less vehemently phrased had Senator McCarthy not so blithely indulged his penchant for character assassination." Labor considered itself no friend of the conservative Tydings, but the press nationwide praised his stance. It was salve for raw wounds.

Some media judges were not so convinced of Tydings's good faith. His hostility undermined the purpose of refuting McCarthy, the opposition press suggested. There were complaints that, out of the *Report's* 20 findings, the first nine focused on McCarthy, as if attacking him were more important than highlighting the State Department's clean bill of health. Some believed the *Report* was unfair to McCarthy; others feared Tydings had made him into a bigger figure—and still left the State Department vulnerable.

But most major papers, newsmagazines, and political analysts exonerated him for lashing back and defended him for concentrating on the truth. His performance was hailed as eloquent, justified, and even inspired. Marquis Childs wrote, "[Tydings's] answer [to McCarthy] was a masterpiece of analysis and denunciation."

It was not lost on observers that no Republicans rose to defend McCarthy. In fact, despite the straight party vote on Tydings's report, there were Republicans who let it be known they were repelled by McCarthy. Governors Alfred E. Driscol of New Jersey and James H. Duff of Pennsylvania had spoken out against him, as had Earl Warren of California and Thomas Dewey of New York to a lesser degree. Dwight D. Eisenhower, president of Columbia University, likened McCarthy's tactics to "behind-the-iron-curtain trick[s]."

Senator Margaret Chase Smith of Maine had epitomized political courage when she made her celebrated "Declaration of Conscience" speech in early June. McCarthy revolted her. Without saying his name, she railed against behavior that "debased [the Senate] to the level of a forum of hate and character assassination sheltered by the shield of Congressional immunity." The idea of the Republican party's capitalizing on "selfish exploitation of fear, bigotry, ignorance, and intolerance" sickened her. Victory would be worth nothing if principle were abandoned. What must be rejected, she declared, were smear tactics that bred "suspicions [which] spread like cancerous tentacles. . . . It is high time that we all stopped being tools and victims of totalitarian techniques—techniques that, if continued here unchecked, will surely end what we have come to cherish as the American way." Six of her fellow Republicans joined her in signing her anti-McCarthy manifesto.[14]

Tydings rejoiced at those sobering Republican words. McCarthy listened to Smith's rebuke in silence—his face halfway between grim and glum—and ducked out as Tydings and others crowded around her. Beaming, Tydings praised her "stateswomanship," calling her words "constructive, temperate, imaginative, and I believe fair," although he hastened to add that he did not agree with everything she said. Smith had not forgotten the Democrats: "I am not proud of the obviously staged undignified countercharges that have been attempted from the other side of the aisle," she had said.

Unfortunately, few other Republicans spoke up, and an incipient protest against McCarthy was flattened by the publicity he relentlessly generated. Irving Ives retreated from his position within days, cozying back up after McCarthy launched his next sensational assault. Respected Republican leaders such as Ralph Flanders, Leverett Saltonstall of Massachusetts, and H. Alexander Smith of New Jersey, also clearly uncomfortable with McCarthy's methods, by and large remained quiet—a silence that gave license to squalid partisan behavior sheltered under Robert Taft's umbrella of "respectability." When Smith appealed so poignantly for Republicans to come to their senses, Taft remained unmoved. No Republican organization ever repudiated McCarthy.

Democrats did little better. Throughout the hearings only 12 Democratic senators had raised their voices against McCarthy. Seven were first-term, little-known liberals. The rest remained silent— Harry F. Byrd of Virginia, Walter George and Richard Russell of Georgia. The great Senate leaders proved that timidity is indeed an occupational disease. Their silence contributed to McCarthy's increasing power.

The Republican response to Tydings's speech came the next day. Jenner led off, virtually calling Tydings a traitor for his "blasphemous perversion of the truth." Tydings listened impassively at his desk, arms folded, nibbling at an unlighted pint-size cigar. The entire attack was directed at him. Not a kind word was spoken on McCarthy's behalf—nor were his charges defended. (During Tydings's speech when Senator Warren Magnuson of Washington asked Lodge if he had found any evidence of communism, the Massachusetts senator had answered, "No, I did not.") As Jenner hurled his final words about "termites and vermin who . . . are gnawing away at the foundation of our freedom," the Republican abdication reverberated through the lofty chamber and the chance to vanquish McCarthy in his own arena slid by.

When Tydings stood up, senators and gallery spectators braced for another blast. Without so much as a glance at Jenner he quietly informed the chair that he wished to report two bills from the Armed Services Committee. The Senate settled down to work.

Tydings's forbearance had but a temporary sobering effect. When the printed report appeared, 45 typewritten pages of Lodge's dissent had been omitted inadvertently. Lodge went into orbit, believing it deliberate. A distraught Tydings denied it—an "unfortunate error," he lamented. The McCarthy claque roared into action, accusing Tydings of endless sins. The omission (and Lodge's outburst) hurt Tydings just as the American people were weighing the credibility of the whole investigation.

The hearings settled nothing. The report settled nothing, not in terms of guilt or innocence. Those who believed McCarthy in the first place continued to believe him. The proceedings only deepened doubts and increased public fears.

Despite his efforts to conduct the hearings fairly, Tydings had bad luck from the start. He held open hearings to prevent star-chamber tactics—and was accused of running a circus. He closed the hearings—and was accused of hiding the truth. He let the accused reply—and was charged with coddling subversives. He battled with Truman, Hoover, and Richardson to get the loyalty files—and McCarthy spoiled their value. He called McCarthy to book for withholding evidence—and was reviled for hounding the man who was going after the Commies. He agreed to Republican demands for a minority counsel—and Robert Morris wreaked havoc by collud-ing with McCarthy. He fully explained *Amerasia*—but McCarthy so abused the truth that few could parse the jumble of contradictions. He turned over to the FBI all the evidence he gathered—but the agency failed to assist him at crucial moments. He threw his support behind the bipartisan commission idea—and was accused of trying to weasel out of the mess. McCarthy could do anything and get away with it. Nothing stuck to McCarthy. Tydings seemed coated with glue.

But there was more at play here than bad luck. He made mistakes: his overconfident contempt for McCarthy; premature clearance of Lattimore; the loyalty files-Hoover snafu. And from the beginning, the language of Resolution 231 had spelled trouble. Those who hoped that the broad mandate would provide enough rope to let McCarthy hang himself were deluded. His followers transformed the resolution's language into loopholes, and McCarthy fashioned those loopholes into nooses. It was the Democrats who swung from the gallows.

Truman's unpopularity redounded on Tydings. Despite the fact that he and the president had major differences on many issues, Tydings inevitably was portrayed as Truman's "errand boy," a New Deal–Fair Dealer in Harry Truman's pocket just waiting for the 1952 Democratic National Convention when he could waltz away with the vice-presidential nomination. He nearly choked on his morning coffee when he read about Tydings the New Dealer.

J. Edgar Hoover's attitude also undermined Tydings. After the war, Hoover focused on the American Communist party. He was an unalloyed anti-Communist—but shrewd enough to know that keeping the FBI powerful and funded required targets that galvanized popular support. The public seemed to fear communism more than crime, so his pursuit of subversives met with almost universal approval. Frequent FBI warnings that 55,000 Communists and a half-million fellow travelers were subverting the U.S. government incited great public fear. Privately, Hoover probably had little regard for McCarthy, but the senator's facility for drawing attention to the communist threat gave Hoover and his FBI invaluable aid. Much as Taft found in McCarthy an apparent free ride to Republican power, Hoover saw a similar potential. His actions helped McCarthy's credibility.

Most of the press supported Tydings, yet it played a powerful role in his undoing. There was no rule that the media had to be consistent, and it wasn't. In March it generally praised Tydings's fairness in holding open hearings; by April it more often blamed him for creating an unruly atmosphere. His refusal to let McCarthy cross-examine drew condemnation. Tydings, in trying to keep the sessions from becoming a shambles, was labeled "arrogant." Most of the press disdained McCarthy, yet it kept his name before the public, increasing his power. The media fed the public's lust for sensational headlines, and a vicious cycle evolved as its coverage whetted an appetite for juicier stories. McCarthy used reporters to pass on what he wanted to sell. Sitting behind Tydings, facing the reporters, McCarthy would scribble away madly, scowling beneath his thick black brows, unworried about what Tydings said because his version got first coverage. And if what he said was shown to be patently false, the confusion already was created. Tydings could not dash willy-nilly out of the caucus room to hold press conferences every time a new idea struck home. The press, in its frenzy for exciting tidbits, let itself be used.

Partisan politics bedeviled Tydings every step of the way. The Washington *Post* once defined McCarthyism as "a reckless exploitation of popular anxiety about Communism." Tydings's committee got mauled by the war waged in the name of anti-communism. Out of power since 1932, a substantial number of Republicans appeared to believe that winning was what mattered—with any weapon and at any cost. When the issue of Communists in government surfaced, partisan bitterness already was sewn to its shirttail. Democrats, increasingly insulted by McCarthy, grew irate over moderate Republican failure to intercede with the extremists. But instead of trying to find common ground with Saltonstall, Smith, Flanders, Wayne Morse, and the like, the Democrats threw temper tantrums. Outside the Senate they saw a world in turmoil. The Korean War was going badly; a hoped-for surge of unity failed to emerge. On June 17, the same day Tydings released his report, federal agents arrested Ethel and Julius Rosenberg.

A frightened public cast about for scapegoats. Democrats stood out as a natural target. They were in power—and already blamed for the China debacle. The majority of Democrats closed their eyes and let partisanship dominate. Tydings bore the brunt of that warfare. China, Korea, and the communist issue had handed Republicans a deadly weapon. They inflicted deep wounds and shredded the facts before the committee. A committee as controversial as Tydings's never could have resolved an issue as touchy as communism.

Besides, the congressional committee procedure was the wrong method for discerning truth and for handling an emotionally loaded issue. Its inherent adversarial framework inevitably intruded; its open sessions drew sensational press coverage. Had Tydings opted right off for a closed investigation he might have robbed McCarthy of publicity. But in 1950 the subject of communism was hot, McCarthy's true nature as yet unknown, and Tydings's confidence too great. It was not in Tydings's nature to shrink from a head-on confrontation—as it was not in McCarthy's to allow quiet proceedings. It is doubtful whether *any* committee could have handled McCarthy's genius for subversion.

Could a bipartisan commission have succeeded where Tydings failed? As a body above politics, it would have denied McCarthy his all-important enemies, eliminated his open forum, and thus could have avoided his disruptive tactics. It could have conducted a dispassionate examination without public melodrama and might have restored confidence in government. But columnists, figures familiar with the hearings, and historians suggest that, had such a commission been appointed, it would probably still be sitting today if mandated to do what critics claimed Tydings failed to do: follow the myriad leads and scattershot charges; investigate every State Department employee; ferret out all disloyal persons from all departments.

Tydings himself was yet another element among the many contributing to the failure to stop McCarthy. Although gifted with a rare ability to speak his mind, he was too susceptible to unbridled anger. Razor-sharp words, intended to rebut, spilled political blood. His July 20 speech may have pleased those who saw through McCarthy and some among the press, but what the American people perceived was a caustic, haughty, power-entrenched bully backed by the Washington bureaucracy and its highly paid press staff, slicing up their hero. Poor old Joe, unpretentious public servant and indefatigable scourge of communists, was being mauled by a martinet named Millard.

Tydings's personality did not lend itself to easy camaraderie with press, colleagues, constituents, or the public. He was impatient, prickly, and inflexible, would rather fight it out than engage in devious games. He understood strategies of distraction and other diversionary tactics, and would coolly employ them to his advantage when pushing through legislation or coercing committees into action. He was also a master at using facts and logic to dazzle his opposition into submission. But unfortunately for him, nothing about McCarthy or the communist issue responded to those techniques. His frustration got the better of him and he lashed out. The public read it as abusive and partisan vengeance.

One of Tydings's great strengths as a Senate leader was his self-assurance. Because nothing about McCarthy or his evidence impressed him, his natural confidence made easy the step to overconfidence. He was so convinced that McCarthy was no match for him that he played right to his rival's strength by engaging in a slugfest. Instead of belling the cat, he punched the cat in the nose—an understandable reaction, but not a prudent one. McCarthy reveled in the stampede of men reduced to mice scurrying in his wake. He savored the uproar. The more confusion and anger, the less thoughtfully he was managed.

Tydings's own ethics made McCarthy a complete enigma to him. He could not comprehend that a senator of the United States was capable of behaving with utter disregard for all standards of fair play. He was the first to learn what Senator Stuart Symington of Missouri finally put into words: "If you are going to play with McCarthy, you have to forget about any of those Marquis of Queensberry rules."

Ultimately everything about him disturbed Tydings's sense of right and wrong. The contemptuous abuse of power and the hypocritical corruption of the democratic process sent Tydings into spasms of moral outrage. McCarthy's use of symbols, gestures, and well-staged appearances—briefcases overflowing with documents, a comfortably rumpled appearance, the folksy playing to the crowd— was in stark contrast to Tydings's self-righteous aloofness and creased sartorial splendor. McCarthy seemed to have a magic appeal; Tydings's refusal to work an audience the same way made him seem cold and unsympathetic. His strident moral posture engendered little sympathy.

People generally respond to personalities over issues, slogans over complexities. Americans sided with the personable McCarthy rather than trusting Tydings's insistence on intelligent analysis of fact. Tydings's twin flaws of arrogance and anger alienated the public and contributed to his ultimate downfall.

Notes

1. Several historians have written that before the hearings Tydings boasted, "Let me have him for three days in public hearings and he'll never show his face in the Senate again." Tydings denied any such statement. It was attributed to him by McCarthy in his book *McCarthyism: The Fight for America.*

2. The House Appropriations Committee, the House Committee on Expenditures in the Executive Departments, the Senate Committee on Expenditures in the Executive Departments, and a "committee of one" (Republican Representative Bartel J. Jonkman of Michigan) from the House Committee on Foreign Affairs, all investigated the 81 and cleared them completely.

3. Tydings's wife believed Taft nurtured a grudge against her husband because of an incident that occurred before Taft's speech: During a close game of golf, on the eighteenth hole, Tydings teased Taft to unnerve him. "You know, Bob, you're never going to be president," he remarked as they strolled up to Taft's ball. Taft stopped dead in his tracks. "What do you mean?" "Well, Bob, you're too partisan." Taft missed his shot, Tydings won

the match, but the friendship was never the same. Tydings related the story to his wife: "I'm afraid I really made the old man kind of mad this afternoon." She believed Taft held the remark against Tydings because the barb hit home.

4. At that same session, Tydings also cornered McCarthy on differences in wording between his February 9 Wheeling charges and what he said before the Senate on February 20. The point was important: If the Wheeling charges were not true, the whole investigation was based on fraudulent accusations. If he denied the language of his February 9 speech under oath before the committee, then he committed perjury because Tydings believed he had proof of exactly what he had said there. Tydings was gathering ammunition for charges of perjury and possible censure of McCarthy.

5. Most historians surmise that McCarthy possessed no authoritative evidence, that his files and bulging briefcases were stuffed with impressive-looking photostatic copies of heresay and secondhand gossip—phony "documents." Certainly Tydings believed he had established that the evidence was bogus. The Tydings Report concluded, "Our investigation establishes that the only logical reason for the Senator's non-cooperation and failure to supply information was the fact that he had no information to supply." Tydings later wrote, "Can anyone suppose for a moment that if McCarthy had proof of his charges that he would not run to a grand jury with it immediately? Can anyone suppose that if McCarthy, with his avidity for publicity, actually had proof he would deny himself the great acclaim that would come to him after proving his charges in a court of law?"

6. Conservative Tydings would not argue its merits as he opposed many aspects of Truman's Fair Deal domestic policy.

7. The nine Democrats were Lucas of Illinois, Harley M. Kilgore and Matthew M. Neely of West Virginia, Hubert H. Humphrey of Minnesota, Francis J. Myers of Pennsylvania, Herbert H. Lehman of New York, Burnet R. Maybank of South Carolina, Clinton P. Anderson of New Mexico, and Tydings.

8. He had not just plucked the "205" figure out of the air. What he held in his hand in West Virginia was a July 26, 1946, letter from Secretary of State James F. Byrnes to Representative Adolph J. Sabath of Illinois. Byrnes described a screening of about 3,000 State Department employees, transferred from other wartime agencies, that led to recommendation against the continued employment of 284. Out of the 284, 79 had been separated. Subtracting 79 from 284 left 205, whom McCarthy upgraded to communists. By 1950 all 205 had either been cleared or were no longer with the department. Equally specious was the origin of his 57. Investigators for a 1947 House Appropriations subcommittee composed a list of 108 case descriptions of State Department employees, past, present, and prospective, about whom security or loyalty questions had been asked. On

asking the department in March 1948 about the 108, they learned that only 57 still were employed there. McCarthy's 81 cases came from the list of 108. The numbers were important because they pinpointed the lie: Whether 205 or 57, McCarthy's case rested on fraudulent evidence.

9. Truman actually allowed the committee to see material added since the earlier congressional reviews—an action that, if known, could have set a new precedent vis-à-vis executive privilege.

10. The concept was resurrected occasionally during the summer, but no commission was established until 1951. Even then it never got off the ground as Senator Patrick McCarran, zealously protecting his new Internal Security Act, successfully sabotaged it.

Shortly after Tydings's election defeat in November 1950 he reflected on the meeting in a letter to William E. Boyle, Democratic National Chairman: "If . . . we had appointed a commission and turned this matter over, it not only would have made a difference to me in my campaign but would have helped others who suffered in some degree from the same tactics."

11. In fact, in a display of unparalleled gall, McCarthy threatened to stop "cooperating" unless Morris was allowed to "develop the facts." Even 35 years later Morgan recoiled at mention of the name. "Don't talk to me about that boy," he growled through clenched teeth during an interview.

12. *Pageant* magazine's formal poll of Washington correspondents earned McCarthy the "worst senator" title: He placed ninety-sixth out of 96.

13. The three committee Democrats considered censure and studied findings accusing McCarthy of perjury. A recommendation for censure and trial before the Senate for conduct unbecoming to a senator was voted down when Tydings noted that in such McCarthy would have the full opportunity to defend himself and present justifying evidence. That would prolong the agony. But if the full Senate would vote on censure without trial "to preserve the integrity of this body," he would go any distance to get it passed.

14. Her cosigners were Edward J. Thye of Minnesota, Irving Ives of New York, George Aiken of Vermont, Wayne Morse of Oregon, Robert C. Hendrickson of New Jersey, and Charles Tobey of New Hampshire.

2

A Despicable "Back Street" Campaign

If Tydings's situation was difficult in July 1950, McCarthy's appeared impossible. Humiliated by Tydings, left to fend for himself by Republicans, he worked desperately to redeem himself. Within a week he called attention to another State Department Communist he labeled "X." His sheer audacity got him attention: X was from the list of 81 so rigorously scrutinized. He promised photocopies of X's files and "a complete and air-tight case." Senator Wayne L. Morse of Oregon brushed him off. "I am still waiting for proof of the charges," he grunted; and the new case fizzled.

McCarthy tried another tack. Tydings was not the Armed Services Committee watchdog, he bellowed before a Milwaukee crowd, but Truman's "whimpering lap dog" who abetted "fellow travelers and their dupes." Where, McCarthy asked, was the $90 billion spent for military preparedness? Why was only $200 spent out of the $87 million appropriated for South Korea, he demanded to know.

But he spoke in vain. Reporters were tired of his hollow "sensations." Scratch a McCarthy charge and it disintegrated. Columnists considered him a boor; newspapers ignored what they now called his "daily fulminations." When he sent a letter of exhibit to the Associated Press in August, AP concluded that his "story lacked news value" and refused to use it. September's *CIO News* noted,

"Nobody is paying much attention to McCarthy these days." Tax troubles also silenced him. He had failed to pay Wisconsin state income taxes in four separate years. It looked as if truth, time, and Tydings had sidetracked him, made him back-page news.

McCarthy set out to exact revenge. Anyone who could read newspapers knew that Tydings's foreign policy positions linked him to President Harry S Truman and that, with an all-time low approval rating of 26 percent, Truman's unpopularity would hurt him. Anyone who could read maps knew Maryland wrapped around the borders of the District of Columbia and comprised a small area, in less than an hour, one might drive to the center of the state from Capitol Hill. Anyone who could read statistics could divine that the demographic face of Maryland's counties was changing. Baltimore— its sprawling new suburbs, large Catholic and labor populations, swelling numbers of registered Republicans, and growing black community—offered fertile ground for stirring disenchantment with the conservative Tydings. And anyone who could read a political pulse knew the whole electorate was jittery over communists. Mention of Tydings's name evoked instant association with the communist question.

Some people believed McCarthy was a moral illiterate; but he could read, and his political instincts and timing were uncanny. He did not waste a minute after Tydings's July 20 lambasting to begin campaigning against him in Maryland. Tydings unwittingly had given him an early boost. In March he had made speeches throughout Maryland to reassure people that there was no reason to get hysterical about Communist infiltration in government. "Not more than a handful, if that many, of the 20,000 State Department employees are a doubtful risk," he told his constituents. "The fact that two persons have been arrested, tried, and convicted should not make people think that the government in Washington is full of Communists," he insisted, referring to Alger Hiss and Judith Coplon.

Many Marylanders came away grumbling that he was treating a grave issue lightly. McCarthy grabbed that opening and exploited it, lamenting that Tydings was diluting the truth. By April, local Republicans were circulating petitions demanding Tydings withdraw as chairman of the committee. The Republican Activities

Committee denounced his "extremely unjudicious" clearance of Owen Lattimore and invited McCarthy to address them at Baltimore's Lyric Theater. Four other state Republican organizations joined in sponsorship. McCarthy eagerly accepted the invitation. Although he canceled at the last moment because of emergency sinus surgery at Bethesda Naval Hospital, the publicity focused negative attention on Tydings.

An entirely unexpected jolt came from Herbert R. O'Conor, Tydings's fellow Democratic senator from Maryland. In the middle of the hearings, not long after Lattimore testified, O'Conor took angry issue with some of Lattimore's views. If O'Conor (whose name was all but absent from the papers insofar as aiding Tydings) was in the mood to help at home, he might have kept still—or phrased his disagreement less harshly. When he attacked a figure already prejudicially linked to Tydings, O'Conor's actions—whether an intended slap or not—presaged trouble with state Democrats as well as Republicans.

In fact, Tydings had created problems for himself. Former Maryland congressman and mayor of Baltimore, Thomas J. D'Alessandro, later recalled that Tydings seldom bothered attending meetings of the Maryland congressional delegation. When D'Alessandro or other state congressmen asked him for favors, he made such a "big deal" out of it they regretted having asked.

Still worse was the way Tydings played political favorites. By virtue of seniority he was a major power—a "boss." When he threw his weight around, careers were boosted or set back. He favored conservatives over liberals; and as the number of liberals increased during the New Deal period, Tydings exerted his influence to promote fellow conservatives. But because Maryland's population traditionally had a basically conservative outlook, philosophical differences with liberals did not work to his disadvantage. What eventually did him serious harm were the continuous factional struggles that had less to do with ideology than with power.

And also he had drifted away from his constituents. Never the sweet-talking, chummy politico, he had gained a reputation early on for being distant—from constituents and local leaders. As he became busier and more powerful, and then married into the circle of Washington elite, the image of reserve he created deepened until, at some point, the public's perception of him shifted and crossed the fine line separating aloof from haughty.

By the early 1930s he was receiving letters warning him that Marylanders thought he had "gone Washington." "I find in many quarters an impression that you are 'high-hat,' unapproachable, that you won't fraternize at the cross roads, etc.," wrote John Marrinan, a newsman who frequently offered Tydings advice. Other loyalists echoed the complaint. Clarence Beach, who campaigned for him in 1938, wrote the campaign treasurer, "Personally, I believe the fight made on Senator Tydings [by Franklin Roosevelt] was the best thing that could have happened to him . . . as I believe the voters heretofore looked upon him as being a little 'high hat.' "

His insistence on having a small staff worked to his disadvantage. He wrote his own speeches, did his own homework, and thus retained few employees to field constituent requests and to handle visitors graciously. His secretary, Corinne Barger, served as administrative assistant; she had the help of two typists and perhaps six clerks. That was the whole of his Senate staff (although certain individuals in the state's legal, business, industrial, and banking communities served as unofficial advisers).

Maryland's proximity to the Capitol—if one may drive into the heart of Maryland within an hour, then the reverse is also true—meant that residents frequently showed up at his office, expecting an audience without appointment. Thousands lived within a trolley ride of his office, and more than a million could telephone for the price of a local call. Many a disgruntled constituent was observed leaving Tydings's office muttering about abrupt treatment. As an old-fashioned conservative, he abhorred fiscal waste and criticized the cost to American taxpayers of the federal bureaucracy. Keeping his staff small was a means of practicing what he preached, but it cost him dearly in political currency.

He was unconcerned about being seen as haughty. In 1933 he had written an article for the New York *Times*, "WHAT'S THE MATTER WITH CONGRESS?" which addressed "the chief impediments to reasonable legislative alacrity." Besides exploring national and international problems, he laced into constituent insensitivity. "The Member of Congress is too frequently forced to decide whether he is going to be a glorified office boy, attending with great punctiliousness to his mail, calling on departments for little favors for his constituents . . . or whether he is going to be a legislator," he wrote. Tydings intended to risk "the pique of a constituent" for the "more important field of legislation." Even though "the disappointed constituent berates him with having a 'swelled head' " and threatens to unseat him, a congressman must devote himself to problems of government, he argued.

Perhaps Tydings should have increased his staff to handle "office boy" business and placate favor seekers. His staff protected him from constituent interruptions, but failed to keep lines of communication open with local party leaders. For seven years Tydings had not answered the letters or talked with one of Baltimore's Democratic district leaders. When suddenly he needed help in 1950 and turned friendly, the man understandably was miffed. Sharper staff work could have kept his political bridges in better repair.

Labor, although traditionally Democratic, never had warmed to Tydings because of his pro-business proclivities. He believed the Great Depression not only brought massive poverty, but under-mined the secular values of hard work, social mobility, and material acquisition. Tydings was protective toward business because he believed its survival was essential to the survival of those values. And unionization threatened the workingman's freedom of choice: It attempted to force unions on workers and industry alike. It also interfered with self-sufficiency by promising higher wages, shorter hours, and advancement predicated on membership rather than merit.

The American climate was anti-business during the Depression; allies of business were easy targets. Tydings was warned by advisers that labor groups required management: "Certain angles" of his position should be highlighted, and from time to time he should make "at least one good wholly labor speech." Pro-labor Democrats should be handled gently. "Nicely phrased personal letter[s]" could keep the troops in line, wrote one confidante.

But given Tydings's voting record (he had refused to vote for Social Security; he voted against the Wagner Act, which created the National Labor Relations Board; he voted for the Taft–Hartley Bill), his anti-union and pro-business stances, and his opposition to New Deal social measures (predicated on the need for fiscal stability and a balanced budget), his relationship with labor was barely good enough to designate as an uneasy alliance. Only party loyalty had kept the labor vote by and large in his column.

The story was the same among black voters. His conservative views and Maryland's border-state status frequently caused columnists, constituents, and colleagues to classify him as a Southern Democrat. He was not a true Southern conservative. In 1924 he risked his career to speak out against the Ku Klux Klan. He verbally supported ideals of equality. Early campaign literature targeted for black voters read: "I am 100 per cent in my belief that everyone in our country is entitled to first class citizenship. Regardless of race, color or creed, every American is entitled to equality of treatment. This is so by moral law, by the Constitution of the United States and by the Supreme Court's decision, interpreting the Constitution"—hardly the language of a conservative Southern Democrat. And he refused to join the Dixiecrats in their walkout of Truman's civil rights plank in 1948.

Nevertheless his record on issues important to blacks was dismal. He had opposed the Fair Employment Practices Commission (FEPC), all anti-lynching and anti-poll tax legislation, and social programs involving housing, segregation, and educational discrimination. His negative votes were based on states' rights—the bedrock conservative principle underscoring all his opposition to New Deal and Fair Deal domestic programs. Blacks, however, did not see his arguments on lynching, poll tax, segregation, and the FEPC as principled. No matter how many times he espoused his "genuine regard for the colored man" and recognition that "they have had a bad deal," they saw him as a callous racist, not a conservative battling federal domination.

Tydings anticipated their attitude. In opposing the FEPC on the floor in 1946 because it forced federal regulation over the states and offered a false freedom—economic equality without social equality (which he believed would never happen)—he remarked, "I know that representatives of the colored people are in the gallery [and] I will be called an enemy of the colored race, a Fascist. . . . I do not care what they may say. . . . [M]y position is straightforward and honest," he declared. "People, whether they be black or white, will respond to truth and not succumb to misrepresentation."

His burst of interest in black housing and education at election time appeared cynical to blacks—a mouthing of platitudes. But it was not so much lip service as it was that other issues were more important to him during the 1930s and 1940s. The catastrophe of the Depression, and then wartime and postwar foreign policy threats, drew his attention. Remaining time and energy he devoted to protecting Maryland industries and businesses.

To place oneself too far in front of the average white citizen on an issue as volatile as race relations in a Southern border state meant political suicide. When he made another run for the Senate in 1956, his attitudes had changed, his outlook altered irrevocably by the McCarthy ordeal. He was more open to the influence of humanistic ideals. He listened to others about the rights and needs of blacks. To a great degree, his personal conscience reflected a changing national conscience. But in the 1930s and 1940s he was a product of time, place, and custom. Black Americans' problems were not high priority for the nation's white leaders. What black votes Tydings garnered came mostly from the growing black loyalty to the Democratic party.

Tydings had received early warnings about possible trouble in Maryland. A December 1949 analysis prepared for him spelled it out: "Too many people are mad at you for your own good." Yet despite Tydings's enemies and some voter indifference, the analysis predicted victory because Democrats and Republicans "who might give you trouble" would not run. McCarthy changed all that. The isolated but powerful constituent disenchantments and residual bad blood simmering beneath the surface in Maryland needed only a slight upturn of the heat to boil over. One lighted match might have sufficed to singe Tydings's reputation; McCarthy ignited a scorching election campaign.

Tydings did not announce his intention to run until July 8 and delayed campaigning until late in August. That was a mistake. Democratic opponents had the field to themselves. Former Democratic Congressman John A. Meyer entered the race with the backing of Maryland's AFL and CIO. The thrust of his campaign centered not on Tydings's conservatism or labor record, but rather on the "complete whitewash" of McCarthy's charges.

Another contender, Baltimore attorney Hugh M. Monaghan II, launched his campaign with rhetoric straight from the McCarthy lexicon: Tydings's report gave "the green light to Stalin's agents in this country to continue to gnaw at the foundation of our national security," Monaghan jeered. The incumbent, he charged, was largely to blame for American "unpreparedness" in Korea; just before the war broke out, Tydings had suggested talks with the Soviets. Neville Chamberlain looked "positively brilliant" compared to Tydings, Monaghan claimed. Catholics in particular listened. The Meyer and Monaghan offensives increased public uncertainty over Tydings's integrity.

Republican candidates were even more brutal in wielding the whitewash–communist–Korea–Russia weapon. Hagerstown Mayor Herman L. Mills, General D. John Markey, and Baltimore attorney John Marshall Butler all spouted the McCarthy rhetoric. Markey was the favorite; Mills pulled out. Butler, a prominent lawyer, was considered a lightweight. He had never run for office before. He concentrated almost exclusively on the whitewash–communist issue and focused on counties Markey ignored. Along with the McCarthy language, he adopted McCarthy techniques—because McCarthy adopted him.

Butler looked like good raw material to McCarthy. His enthusiasm in espousing the McCarthy line made him attractive; but more important, he was an amateur lacking a political organization, network, or manager. McCarthy and his staff sat down with Butler and his top aide in July. The meeting shaped Butler's strategy. He basically allowed himself to become the means to McCarthy's ends. Don Surine, Ray Kiermas, Mrs. Robert E. Lee (of the Lee-list Lees), Jean Kerr (McCarthy's research assistant and later wife), and others contributed time and talents to Butler's campaign. Butler may have been the nominal candidate—he gave the speeches and posed for the photographers—but McCarthy and his minions ran the show.

They sent Butler to Ruth McCormick ("Bazy") Miller, editor and publisher of the *Times–Herald*, the one Washington newspaper that applauded and abetted McCarthy as much as it berated Tydings. Miller, the niece of Colonel Robert R. McCormick, publisher of the pro-McCarthy Chicago *Tribune* and owner of the Washington *Times–Herald*, jumped at the chance to get Tydings. Through family contacts she set Butler up with Jon M. Jonkel, a Chicago public relations man who agreed to run the campaign. Miller supplied the airplane ticket, and Jonkel flew east. In theory, Jonkel could not assume the title of campaign manager under Maryland law, which prohibited importing outsiders; but in practice, his authority was absolute. He dictated strategy, handled money, and implemented propaganda techniques designed by McCarthy. Butler, who seldom showed up at campaign headquarters, did as he was told.

Tydings realized he was vulnerable. On June 5 he had met secretly with Democratic National Chairman William E. Boyle, along with other Democrats up for reelection. They discussed tactics for countering McCarthy. Clearly, what was on their minds was the heavy volume of mail that all the Democratic members of Congress were getting—letters dripping acid. Tydings especially seemed anxious.

He still believed his record would prevail. He banked heavily on his reputation as an international statesman. He would remind voters that he was the state's primary benefactor, having never failed to protect local industries, win defense contracts, and secure coveted military installations.

Maryland's defense industries regularly sought lucrative government contracts that provided employment and income. Tydings would not bend the rules or pressure Pentagon officials into accepting Maryland bids, but he always made sure that industry representatives received the opportunity to present their case.[1]

The port of Baltimore (which grew to be the nation's number-two port and Maryland's number-one industry during his tenure) faced possible ruin if the Saint Lawrence Seaway (first proposed by President Calvin Coolidge) were built. For more than 20 years Tydings fought legislation authorizing its construction. He fostered the port's prosperity by ensuring that Marshall Plan equipment worth billions of dollars was shipped through Baltimore. The Longshoreman's Union leadership solidly backed him in 1950 because his efforts protected the membership's jobs. He looked out for the Naval Academy, watched over white-collar firms and smokestack industries, and never forgot the smaller commercial interests—the oyster, crabbing, fishing, canning, and tobacco industries. Parkways, bridges, inland canals, and the international airport at Baltimore, all were funded and built under legislation sponsored by Tydings.

In early 1950 this particular one of the ten "most valuable" senators had seemed a cinch for reelection. Factional rivalries, liberal–conservative disagreements, labor disenchantment, black resentment—nothing new there. But signs of weakness caused by the McCarthy issue were becoming visible. In response to advisers' anxieties, he sent out questionnaires in June to party leaders to learn what concerned voters most. Only 30 of the 86 forms returned mentioned McCarthy or hearings-related subjects. Although 77 percent of the 30 said the hearings hurt him, they comprised only 23 percent of all respondents.

Perhaps the survey persuaded him that McCarthy's influence still could be deflected. In the cloakroom of the Senate he assured O'Conor, "Just you wait. Fifteen days after I start my campaign, all this opposition will disappear." A proud face went on record with the usual confidence—but it was a face that masked with effort steadily growing private fears.

Once the report was filed, Tydings looked less taut, less anxious. He relaxed for the first time in months, roared as he told Eleanor a joke making the rounds: "What is the shortest route from Baltimore to Washington? Go to Harvard and turn left." She wrote her stepmother Marjorie, "I can't tell you how happy I am to [see the] worry off Millard's shoulders." They left Washington for a much needed rest, joining Eleanor's father and Marjorie at Camp Topridge in the Adirondacks.

Before leaving he opened his campaign on August 1 with a press release. He decided, as his own campaign manager, that his best strategy lay in stressing his international experience. The release focused on six areas: his independent record; Korea's significance vis-à-vis a strong military defense; the vital task of achieving world harmony; the federal deficit; government spending on nonmilitary programs; the debilitating effects on individual self-reliance of compulsory, costly social welfare programs. McCarthy seemed to be relegated to a seventh catchall clause: "I shall from time to time discuss other issues of the campaign as occasion warrants."

It was an appeal intended to reach his traditional base of support. Longing to return to comfortable themes he ignored

McCarthy. In so doing, he overlooked changes that had occurred statewide. In the past he had run so strongly in the conservative suburbs and on the Eastern Shore—traditionally "Southern" areas— that he did not anticipate erosion in his position. His domestic social stance had become something of a liability, even in rock-ribbed conservative Western Maryland.

He returned from cool forests and lakes to brutal August humidity and disappointment. Chants of "whitewashing Commie-crat" echoed all over Maryland. He would have to confront the McCarthy-inspired issues head-on. Eleanor wrote her father, "The lies, half-truths and brick-bats from the Butler (Republican candidate) crowd are unbelievable! Many of Millard's old friends and supporters have been taken in." Joe Davies answered her quickly. Do not let anyone outside the family know how concerned she was, he counseled. "Some weak-kneed friends and supporters are apt to run for cover."

On August 31, before radio microphones and television cameras, Tydings went on the attack. The whitewash charges were so "utterly ridiculous . . . that it has been difficult for me to think that anyone in Maryland could believe them," he said, and urged listeners to consider what they were being sold: "propaganda to the effect that I have suddenly, almost overnight, surrendered my independence, thrown to the winds my patriotism and loyalty to my country and have even stooped so low as to connive to keep disloyal persons in the employ of our government." He set out to prove that his opponents' statements were "bare-faced and unmitigated" lies. Sixty minutes later he had covered every name, date, number, and falsehood of every McCarthy distortion.

The speech was an analytic masterpiece; as a piece of political oratory, it was dismal. The relentless pace and angry tone offered no humor to soften a mind-bending torrent of facts, no picturesque images or phrases to tug at emotions. He invoked the facts, but they were dry and numbing—and beside the point anyway. He continuously failed to grasp that the facts were not the issue. Just as he could not imagine anyone believing McCarthy, he could not fathom that logic and reality could fail to persuade. He assumed people would see the light, "do the right thing," if he explained it all. The righteousness implicit in his single-minded pursuit was annoying to many—and doomed to failure. The more he hammered away at truth, the worse he looked.

The loyalty hearings became the major issue. Tydings realized that being on the defensive was a poor campaign position and attempted to address other issues. He sent out another set of questionnaires, with demoralizing results: 57 Democratic leaders responded, and a full 81 percent concluded that the McCarthy matter hurt. Only two mentioned that the August 31 speech had helped. Prominent business and legal figures confirmed everything. "I was never so surprised and astonished to hear the comments about you all over the city," wrote Baltimore attorney Morris Schapiro who had been on vacation through August. "Hardly anyone I spoke to was going to vote for you. . . . [B]elieve me, Senator," he said, "you had better roll up your sleeves." Tydings went on the offensive to promote his record.

In the September 18 primary Tydings trounced his opposition: He received 172,572 votes, Monaghan 47,718, and Meyer 40,015. He was elated. But the numbers appeared less rosy on scrutiny. Meyer, and particularly Monaghan, were comparative unknowns. Their strong showing could be interpreted as voter unhappiness with Tydings. Also the gubernatorial ballot entry was marked by 120,000 more Democratic voters than was the Senate slot. (William Preston Lane got 173,769 to George P. Mahoney's 191,198.) The disparity suggested either a boycott of Tydings or greater interest in the gubernatorial race due to a sales tax issue. Lane had passed the first Maryland sales tax. It was so unpopular that it had split the party, adding to Tydings's woes.

In fact, the Lane-Mahoney campaign was so bloody and close that Mahoney demanded a recount. Despite Mahoney's 17,000 vote majority, Lane had won because of the Maryland unit vote system, which operated along the lines of the electoral college. (Until 1963 Maryland was broken into electoral districts; whoever took the most districts in a primary won, no matter what the individual vote tally.) Tydings tried to patch things up, and in October finally persuaded Mahoney to withdraw his suit. But he lost valuable time in the process, and a number of Mahoney's bitter-end supporters had defected to the Republican ticket, their mailing lists in hand.

John Marshall Butler squeaked out a miraculous victory on the

Republican side. Markey won the popular vote (34,791 for Markey compared to 32,899 for Butler), but Butler won the unit vote. He outspent Markey four to one. The ticket would be Butler for senator with Theodore R. McKeldin, a former Baltimore mayor and extremely popular figure, for governor. That boded ill for Tydings, given Lane's unpopularity and the postprimary bloodshed.

Once Tydings had reconciled the Lane-Mahoney groups he hit the hustings with a hard-stumping campaign in every Maryland county—towns, crossroads, and uncountable local headquarters. He left nothing to chance, touring alone as well as in caravan with other candidates, working the crowds, and once even hurdling a fence to escape a marauding bull.

He advertised widely. Postcards and press releases exhorted Democrats to attend his rallies. He drew good audiences. Pamphlets and posters bearing an unsmiling portrait extolled his virtues. His stern expression was that of the dedicated statesman; his pose was as stiff as his starched white collar and cuffs. Beneath the formidable visage ran the caption: "A man of international stature. . . . Millard Tydings is known and respected from Maine to California. He has put Maryland on the political map."

Meanwhile the senator from Wisconsin's mostly clandestine involvement in Butler's campaign escalated. McCarthy had spoken in Maryland only once before the primary, although he offered advice and assistance. Afterward he provided everything: speeches, fund-raisings, access to his wealth of Tydings material (no hesitation in opening his files this time, to ruin his archenemy), help in designing campaign propaganda, and generous use of his staff.

McCarthy-inspired pamphlets ridiculed Tydings's campaign literature. "THIS is the way YOU put us on the map Senator!" read a handout featuring cartoons of Tydings amid reeking garbage and dripping whitewash. McCarthy made three speeches in Maryland and a radio address broadcast over a number of local stations. He barely mentioned Butler in his eagerness to characterize Tydings, Brien McMahon of Connecticut, and Senate Majority Leader Scott Lucas of Illinois (all three were up for reelection) as members of the "Commiecrat Party" and "the whitewash committee." His words were heard or read by hundreds of thousands in Maryland and other parts of the nation.

Butler did not so directly accuse Tydings of near treasonable behavior. Under Jonkel's command he launched what came to be called the "big doubt" strategy. Since no one could prove conclusively that Tydings had deliberately concealed subversion, Jonkel decided the best course was to nurture uncertainty. His advice to Butler was this: "Let's not get into the business of proving whether or not it was a whitewash; let's stay in the business that a doubt does exist." Butler tried to tarnish Tydings's record by casting doubt on his integrity.

The ridicule was difficult enough, but the distortions of the record and vicious assaults were unbearable, especially for Eleanor. She wrote her father, "I think it is actually worse than 1938. Then we were only 'tools of Wall Street' and 'princes of privilege'! Now we are 'red Commies' and 'Truman's rubber stamp'!" She angrily scrawled, "Our Republican friends should be ashamed of themselves. Maybe it is the power of evil itself manifested in this man McCarthy and his henchmen."

This man and his henchmen kept the heat turned high—and knew where to find more fuel. Bazy Miller's network produced more than Jonkel. Colonel Roscoe C. Simmons, an elderly black family retainer, nephew of Booker T. Washington and Republican columnist for the Chicago *Tribune*, spoke in black Baltimore neighborhoods in an attempt to discredit Tydings. Given the senator's history on issues important to blacks, it was not difficult to do.

A brochure entitled "Back to Good Old Dixie" spotlighted detrimental aspects of Tydings's record, insinuating that he yearned to return "colored Americans [to] Dreamy Old Dixie." Three prominent black Baltimore leaders allegedly authorized publication of the pamphlet, but actually it sprang from McCarthy's fertile mind. None of the individuals named on the brochure had anything to do with its contents, publication, distribution, or financing. Only one of them saw it before it went out; one was unaware that his name was being used; and one would not have sponsored it if he had seen it because he believed it was "inflammatory." Yet it was passed off as independently published because it failed to bear the credit: "By authority Cornelius P. Mundy, treasurer, John Marshall Butler campaign."[2]

McCarthy's network produced more than speeches, speakers,

and unauthorized "literature." Right-wing supporters contributed big money. Millionaires and oil tycoons such as Alfred Kohlberg and Clint Murchison of Texas helped bankroll Butler, who outspent Tydings by three to one. And behind the scenes, McCarthy's staff "volunteered" long hours, the distinction between regular staff work and off-hours assistance blurring. Jean Kerr consulted almost daily with Jon Jonkel's crew while others assisted Bazy Miller's *Times–Herald* in preparing a special project—one among many of the under-the-table ventures McCarthy's staff planned in their crusade to unseat Tydings.

Miller had dropped substantial chunks of money into the Butler coffers and had made personal loans to Simmons and Jonkel. Her newspaper had attacked Tydings daily in editorials and one-sided articles. Now, in collaboration with McCarthy, she enlarged her paper's role by offering employee time and press facilities (at bargain prices) to Butler's campaign. The joint undertaking produced a vicious tabloid called "From the Record." Its four newsprint pages contained reprints culled from the *Times–Herald* morgue and Mc-Carthy's files. Eighteen items dragged Tydings's name through the whitewash–Korea mud while advancing McCarthy's version of events. The only piece that ostensibly promoted Butler—entitled "The Free State's Choice"—barely mentioned his name. "John Marshall Butler has devoted his life to his family and to his private law practice."

But the pièce de résistance of the production lay in the back cover's full-page photo section. Casually placed among individual news photos of the hearings' well-known cast—Lattimore, Philip Jessup, Dean Acheson, John Stewart Service, et al.—was a picture of Tydings in earnest conversation with Earl Browder, former head of the Communist party. The photograph (later characterized by the Senate subcommittee appointed to investigate McCarthy's and Butler's election practices as an "infamous" and "odious" part of the whole "despicable 'back street' campaign") was actually a slickly done composite. The *Times–Herald* photo morgue produced two separate photographs: one of Tydings listening to election returns (in 1938), and a recent shot of Browder talking intently while stroking his chin. Layout pros reversed the Browder image so that he faced Tydings and then rephotographed the cropped pictures together to make Tydings and Browder appear in intimate discussion. The caption, while noting it was a composite picture (a technique few people were familiar with in 1950), clearly implied a tête à tête: "Communist Leader Earl Browder, shown at left in this composite picture, was a star witness at the Tydings committee hearings, and was cajoled into saying Owen Lattimore and others accused of disloyalty were not Communists. Tydings (right) answered: 'Oh, thank you sir. . . .' " Half a million copies of the tabloid were stored in a Baltimore garage for distribution just before the election.

Unaware of the extent of McCarthy's activities on Butler's behalf, Tydings continued stumping the state. A memo instructing those speaking in his support warned against "being forced into a continued defensive position. There is enough in the Tydings' record to command public approval." It was a don't-explain-and-don't-defend prologue to suggestions on how to explain and defend the four big issues McCarthy (and Butler by proxy) constantly raised: Korea, Truman, the hearings, and Tydings's belief in peace through disarmament, which they portrayed as being soft on communism.

Tydings's supporters' speeches invariably stressed his war record, independence, and experience. Senatorial rank, respect, wisdom, courage, international reputation—the praise fit like a silk cummerbund. But noble sentiments grandly expressed often put people to sleep. If "war record," "independence," and "experience" had been translated more often into symbolic language—"patriotism," "rugged individualism," and "know-how"—accompanied by stories of his World War I battlefield exploits and his fight to keep Franklin D. Roosevelt from tampering with the Supreme Court, audiences might have been touched by the images evoked.

The one down-to-earth speech—delivered over the radio by Colonel William H. Triplett—portrayed a Tydings too many had forgotten. "He dug ditches; he washed pots and pans," Triplett said of Tydings's foot-soldier days on the Mexican border in 1916. During World War I, "His daily lot was the Hell we call war . . . the grime, the filth, the utter weariness, the hunger, the cold, the horror, the grief and the terrible responsibility of war." The American Veterans Committee (outraged over McCarthy's "Malmedy massacre" performance[3]) mustered stout support for Tydings among veterans groups, which enthusiastically joined his ranks.

A few liberals—ardent New Dealers who formerly never would have helped Tydings—swung his way. A local chapter of Americans for Democratic Action endorsed him. His old nemesis and sworn enemy Harold Ickes wrote, "I am sure that I am not the only citizen of Maryland who has been persuaded, to vote for you on November 7, by Senator McCarthy." Adam Clayton Powell, congressman from New York's Harlem district, dashed to Baltimore to speak for Tydings. Baltimore Mayor Thomas D'Alessandro, an important liberal Democrat who had fought him tooth and nail in 1938, endorsed him. A number of prominent Republicans wrote him that he had their votes.

Jewish leaders worked to rally Baltimore's Jewish community. Throughout his career Tydings had steadfastly combatted the ugly nativist anti-Semitism latent in American society. When he spoke against the Ku Klux Klan in the early 1920s, he protested their treatment of all minorities, including Jews and Catholics. In 1933 he was among the first senators to speak out against Adolph Hitler's treatment of Jews. He attended the New York rally at Madison Square Garden in 1934 to demonstrate against Germany's anti-Semitic policies.

But the Jewish community was liberal, pro–New Deal, and needed reminding of Tydings's efforts on its behalf. Herbert Levy, Tydings's former law partner, told for the first time of his behind-the-scenes work to secure recognition of Israel by the United Nations in 1948. When Israel's situation appeared desperate, Tydings was implored to use his influence to persuade Philippine authorities to abstain in the vote rather than tip the balance by voting no. Within a day he had gone one better, convincing the Philippine government to vote in favor of recognizing Israel.

Unfortunately the extent of liberal support failed to offset McCarthy's seemingly infinite resources. He dug up a 1947 Bryn Mawr College discussion series on the Soviet Union that listed Tydings and his wife among the patrons. Owen Lattimore had been a featured speaker and Alger Hiss a sponsor. The Tydings's involvement was nominal—they lent their names and paid their money without attending—but McCarthy inserted a damning news story about it on the front page of "From the Record" and fashioned a piece of campaign propaganda that reprinted the Bryn Mawr invitation with Tydings's, Lattimore's, and Hiss's names boldly circled and interlinked in crimson ink. The caption claimed, "Tydings Revealed as Patron of Lattimore at 1947 Lecture—Man He'd 'Never Seen' Before Probe Was Sponsored By Senator and Wife."

Tydings stuck to his plan. His refined literature and speeches promoted his achievements and set the hearings record straight. He put *Time* magazine's accolade to use in a pamphlet that combined its "one of the 10 leading members of the Senate" quote with lists detailing "what Millard E. Tydings did for the people of his home state." The harbors, bridges, airports, hospitals, military installations, and industry funding spoke volumes.

Another handout swept the reader through contemporary history: The "Man of International Stature" had authored the Philippine Independence Act and been awarded the Distinguished Service Star of the Philippine Republic. He had served as author, sponsor, or proponent of more bills to strengthen the national defense "than any other man in the Senate." He had been in Bikini to witness the first postwar atomic bomb tests, and had met with defense ministers and military leaders all over the world. "Besides being Chairman of the Senate Armed Services Committee," the brochure emphasized, "he is a member of the Senate Committee on Foreign Relations, and the Joint Committee on Atomic Energy. He is the only member of Congress serving on all three of these committees." Few American leaders could match Tydings's experience, and he appealed to Marylanders to value his skills and knowledge.

To counteract the McCarthy–communist thorn, he put out a pamphlet called "The Truth." Its stark black lettering on white gloss read: "When you hear the charge that the investigating committee 'whitewashed' or 'covered-up' disloyal employees in the State Department, tell them THE TRUTH!" It went on to spell out the facts of the four investigations of McCarthy's cases, Lodge's statement ("I did not find any Communists in the State Department"), and Hoover's acknowledgment that the files were intact. The unsmiling Tydings portrait, as usual, graced the back cover. His literature lacked the splashy visuals of the McCarthy–Butler efforts, and his speeches lacked the gossipy personal abuse that they had copy-righted.

The truth did not seem worth much in 1950. Then, in midau-tumn, several things happened that rendered truth more elusive. Fulton Lewis, Jr., a Mutual Network radio newscaster, began an all-out assault. He had attacked Tydings from the moment the hearings began, slyly offering opinion as fact on his broadcasts. Beginning on October 12, Lewis (who was fond of saying "McCarthyism is Americanism") devoted several 15-minute shows entirely to Tyd-ings—newscasts that were political speeches echoing the McCarthy line.[4]

Lewis was syndicated nationally on 535 radio stations—five in Maryland and another in Virginia that had a transmission range reaching into Southern Maryland. On October 12 he read Tydings's brochure "The Truth" and, after intoning sarcastically that it "sounds very impressive and very convincing," spent two shows twisting every item in it beyond recognition.

Tydings exploded. He denounced the broadcasts as "patently political" diatribes and demanded free time on Lewis's program to answer the smears. His telegram to station WCBM in Baltimore accused Lewis of blatant and unfair manipulation: "The clear politi-cal character of this broadcast was highlighted by a paid political advertisement . . . promoting the program in area newspapers. . . . No sponsor was indicated for this broadcast [so] it appears that free time was made available by your organization for this political and controversial speech."

When Lewis reported Tydings's demand for equal time, he shrewdly suggested Tydings send a reply that he would read on the air. "There was, as you know, nothing political in what I reported to you," he remarked in the broadcast. An apoplectic Tydings seethed at Lewis's "colossal gall": There was no more objectivity to these "pure and unadulterated tirades . . . than there are feathers on a whale!" The telegram he shot off to Lewis attacked his "offer" as "a smart trick." "It gives you a chance immediately to place such interpretation as you desire on my written statement without my having the right immediately to reply thereto. . . . Your cowardly reply indicates you are afraid." He challenged him to a debate. "I am ready to meet you on an equal footing of decency, honesty, justice and in the American tradition of a fair hearing for both sides. You wanted my statement and promised to read it over the air in full. I shall be listening."

Lewis refused to debate, but he did grant air time, which Tydings accepted with alacrity. On October 19 he showed up at the Baltimore radio station to deliver a slashing rebuttal—and did himself no little harm. He had expected to get minute-for-minute equal time, which would have meant at least two 15-minute slots. When he was informed by Hollis Seavy of Mutual News that he would have but one period for reply (11½ minutes after commercials), the setback put him in a froth. His voice was strident, and the speech sounded insolent.

He did himself further injury when he later learned that three minutes of his speech were not broadcast due to technical difficulties. Not for a moment believing the explanation, he lashed back with a 1,500-word telegram (which Lewis dubbed "The Thing") that accused Lewis of cowardice, cheating, and lying. Eight months of unremitting attack—accumulated grievances over the hearings, work interrupted, time away from family, and profound fatigue—had taken its toll. His telegram teetered between justified rage and rabid outrage. In his on-the-air comments, Lewis's honeyed baritone poured out snide commentaries that made Tydings's wrath appear ridiculous, even unbalanced.

Lewis condescendingly agreed to give him a second 15-minute spot, and Tydings repeated—with minor opening variations—his earlier speech. His shrill tone struck listeners as disproportionately belligerent. Critical letters flooded his office. "You make Benedict Arnold look like Little Lord Fauntleroy"; "Your terrible sarcasm was as sorry a batch of claptrap as I ever heard"; "That sneering, condescending accent and attitude used to carry weight." He was spared nothing. "You are a pansy." "You are a traitor." "Could it be your marriage to a cereal heiress and her fortune with its *Mission to Moscow* complex has turned your head and warped it?"

The truth did not matter. In fact, that was the point of McCarthyism. Any fiction could become fact. That the "cereal heiress" was Tydings's wife's stepmother—not his wife—was symbolic of everything that went wrong for Tydings and right for McCarthy. Bits of innuendo and false information became accepted as truth. When Tydings tried to straighten things out by separating insinuation from falsehood, he was perceived as evading the truth or splitting hairs. So what if Marjorie Merriweather Post Hutton Davies was his wife's stepmother? He was linked with her crowd, and *that* was what mattered. The propaganda succeeded because McCarthy worked his clever embroidery on existing Tydings flaws. His public image made certain things easy to believe; that made it easier to twist the rest into a confusion of half-truths and outright lies that came to be viewed as reality.

A few weeks before the election, he confided to Eleanor his fear that he might be defeated. She was incredulous. But he talked about retirement, enjoying quiet times together, traveling, perhaps buying a boat, doing the kinds of things they had never had time to do. After he left, she went for a long solitary walk along the Chesapeake Bay shore to take in what he had said. It wasn't like him to talk like that. He had told no one else his private thoughts. She, too, kept them unhappily to herself.

Stung by Lewis, the virulence of his mail, and unnerved by his own sense of doom, Tydings tried to regain his balance. Branding Lewis and McCormick's forces as meddling outsiders, he appealed to his constituents to remember how they had given Roosevelt a swift kick in the pants when he messed in Maryland politics in 1938. He had O'Conor, Senator Joseph O'Mahoney, and others speak in his defense; and in very early November he went on the offensive himself, attacking what he called a "carefully planned and executed campaign of propaganda, founded upon the technique of character assassination."

Then, just days before the November 7 election, the war in Korea took a disastrous turn. Chinese troops poured across the Yalu River and forced a humiliating American retreat. Butler, Lewis, McCarthy, and Bazy Miller's *Times–Herald* had a field day linking Tydings to the catastrophe. The tabloid "From the Record" circulated, coincidentally, at exactly that time. Several of its front-page articles ("TYDINGS GROUP HELD UP ARMS" and "KOREAN MONEY DISAPPEARED") resurrected McCarthy's stale charges that Tydings had prevented military supplies from reaching Korea and cited the canard that only $200 was spent in Korea out of more than $80 million appropriated.

The timing was diabolical and devastating. Over 350,000 copies of "From the Record" were mailed or delivered by hand to homes all over Maryland. Thousands more were distributed at the polls. Its effect was electric. Voters who had intended to cast their ballots for Tydings wrote him angry letters. "This is to advise you that on account of the attached picture appearing in the *Morning Sun* I am going to vote for the Republican candidate for Senator instead of you. Having fully made up my mind to vote for you, until I saw this picture in the paper this morning," wrote a Baltimore insurance agent after seeing a reprint of the composite photograph.

Appearance of the tabloid left Tydings on the defensive just as he was set to deliver a final campaign address. Only two days before the election, he was forced to respond to a contumelious attack instead of reinforcing his 24-year record. He issued a statement labeling it "a new all-time low," and exhorted voters not to be "hood-winked by this desperate last minute effort to obscure the truth and besmirch my character and the record I have made in the United States Senate."

Butler dismissed Tydings's complaints as "whining." Tydings was trying "to smear me by claiming he had been smeared," Butler asserted.

The next day—one day before the election—Tydings's final speech bitterly denounced Butler's campaign for both the tabloid and for a November 6 full-page advertisement in the Baltimore *American* that offered three new false charges against his handling of the committee: that Robert Morris was refused permission to cross-examine, that Morris was denied admission to executive sessions, and that Tydings had refused to call 35 witnesses the Republicans had wanted subpoenaed. "I have . . . kept the campaign, on my side, free from personal abuse, mudslinging, falsehoods, half-truths, fake pictures," Tydings cried as he launched another futile refutation of old and new lies.

He scorned Butler's disavowal of foreknowledge. "I was busy campaigning and I didn't see it until after it was issued," Butler said to newsmen as his headquarters refused to "confirm or deny that it had authorized the printing and distribution." When pressed, Butler reluctantly admitted "that he knew that some such thing was being published." Tydings scoffed, "Thus the cat is out of the bag. . . . It is a mystery to me that any man would aspire to such a high office as that of United States Senator, who is so devoid of common, everyday honesty," he said, his voice quaking with indignation. "I would rather go down to defeat a hundred times than to win [office] through such false and malicious propaganda and faked photographs as these."

He went down to defeat 283,180 to Butler's 326,291 in a campaign so dishonorable on the part of his opposition that the 1951 Senate investigation produced a searing bipartisan report that condemned every aspect: illegal use of finances; scurrilous literature; illegal outside influences; Butler's highly questionable and culpable comportment. This "was not just another campaign," the Senate report emphasized. "It brought into sharp focus certain campaign tactics and practices that can best be characterized as one destructive of fundamental American principles. The subcommittee unreservedly denounces, condemns, and censures these tactics." The Maryland campaign, "conducted by non-Maryland outsiders was of a form and pattern designed to undermine and destroy the public faith and confidence in the basic American loyalty of a well-known figure." The pain of losing to such tactics never would leave the "well-known figure" so viciously defeated in one of the dirtiest elections in American history.

The Senate and media were stunned. One of the titans of the Senate had fallen and Joe McCarthy was given credit. Tydings resisted that initial conclusion, blaming defeat on the national Republican trend; the vulnerability of Maryland's Democratic ticket headed by Lane; Korea; Truman; and "the smear campaign used against me and so on." McCarthy he dismissed as insignificant, although he did credit McCarthy-like propaganda and issues. But within a month, as the extent of McCarthy's involvement in the campaign was exposed—and as the story began to unfold through a private investigation he launched after hearing disturbing rumors—he came to believe that the Wisconsin senator's intrusion into Maryland politics was the crucial factor in his defeat. His incredulity gave way to a permanent righteous wrath.

Not all historians and political analysts agree that McCarthy was the decisive element. Historian Robert Griffith argued in *The Politics of Fear: Joseph R. McCarthy and the Senate* that his influence in the election has been overrated, as did David Oshinsky in *A Conspiracy So Immense*. In analyzing the subject, Griffith, Oshinsky, Richard Fried (*Men against McCarthy*), and Louis H. Bean (*Influences in the 1954 Mid-term Elections*) cited the demographics and political dissension, and especially the labor, black, and Catholic votes, as comprehensive factors. Bean statistically demonstrated that by 1954 McCarthy's influence in midterm elections actually had become a plus 5 percent factor in Democrats' favor: That is, where he was involved, Democratic candidates did 5 percent better than in contests he ignored. Bean posited that McCarthy's influence on elections in the early 1950s had been misconstrued; the perception of McCarthy as invincible was incorrect.

In referring specifically to Tydings's 1950 defeat, however, Bean noted that it was quite different from subsequent elections. The communist issue was then at its peak. In weighing the important Catholic factor, the factional disputes, and the national trend from Democratic to Republican, Bean ultimately concluded, "The more realistic view, supported by the findings of the Congressional investigation of this most unusual election campaign, is that the McCarthy operation was more effective in Tydings's defeat than the underlying trends and intra-party conflict."

There can be no disputing that Tydings was unpopular with labor, liberal Democrats, and blacks; that Catholics were affected strongly by the communist issue and exploited by McCarthy; that Maryland grass-roots leaders and his constituents resented his arrogance; and that the Lane situation hurt him badly (Lane lost to McKeldin 275,824 to 369,807 votes—a 93,983 vote loss compared to Tydings's 43,111). The national trend indeed was Republican. Korea was a handicap; Truman an albatross. But without the McCarthy factor in Tydings's 1950 campaign, the unifying issue of Communists in government would have been absent. Without McCarthy, the extreme emotionalism that gripped the campaign would not have existed. If Tydings had not chaired the committee, brutally called McCarthy's bluff by exposing his lies, and endangered McCarthy's newfound attention and power, McCarthy would have had no interest in Tydings one way or another.[5]

Only in hindsight is history a tidy chain of events. As history is being made, it is random options, unknowns, surprises. It is not a linear sequence that can be predicted with the same assurance with which it is later interpreted. In retrospect the reasons for events seem clear because the path backward is traceable. In retrospect it becomes simpler to distill the separate ingredients of an upset such as Tydings's. Historic events in retrospect appear inevitable. It was unthinkable before the election that Butler actually could unseat Tydings. Before McCarthy entered the picture, Tydings appeared a shoo-in. On March 26 a Baltimore *Sun* editorial had commented on Tydings's unshakable hold on his job. Nineteen days before the election, the New York *Times* predicted he would "weather the rough going." Even on the election's eve, Baltimore bookmakers had Tydings a five-to-one favorite.

Maurice Rosenblatt, head of the National Committee for an Effective Congress (NCEC)—an organization dedicated to stopping McCarthy (among other things)—believed "it was inconceivable that Millard Tydings . . . would be defeated. [He] had been here and had acquired such a hold on the public and on the general institutional concept in the Senate that [he was] a part of the marble." Speaking of the NCEC, Rosenblatt said, "We just didn't think of a man like Tydings as being defeatable. . . . If you didn't find the NCEC supporting [him] in 1950, it probably was because we would never have thought of him as vulnerable." "This is pure hypothesis," he added, "but let us suppose Tydings had refused or some way side-stepped that chairmanship, had not got into a slugging match with Joe—then . . . I think he would have won."

Without McCarthy's presence in the campaign—both symbolic and actual—Tydings's opposition would have been hard pressed to find a focus for its efforts. Who would have run against such a powerhouse? What Republican could have raised the funds necessary and gained access to unlimited amounts of research materials and an established professional staff? What foolhardy Democrat would have ventured into the primary without a lethal weapon? Factional elements poised to exploit a chance to take him on if he looked politically wobbly would have had to tread carefully; if they challenged him and lost, it could be dangerous. Tydings held many IOUs; patronage jobs lived in his pocket. He could call the shots in Maryland—at least until McCarthy salted every wound and fostered unity among unlikely allies.

Even with the communist–McCarthy–Korea issues, the Democratic primary had drawn only two relatively unknown challengers. Former Baltimore Mayor Howard W. Jackson, a formidable campaigner and powerful figure, decided not to run because of the incumbent's strength. Tydings was vulnerable but still had power and powerful friends who rallied to block Jackson. So strong were his allies that Jonkel found that even Theodore McKeldin, Republican candidate for governor, was not enthusiastic about being associated with Butler. Jonkel later observed, "Very few people in the State, especially people of stature, wanted to get out and campaign against Senator Tydings."

Of course, if Senator William Fulbright was correct in saying that any candidate who becomes too closely linked with foreign relations issues inevitably loses, perhaps Tydings could not have won in 1950. He was linked inextricably to the administration's international programs. But it is hard to see who, besides McCarthy, could have galvanized opposition in Maryland among potential rivals, disaffected Democrats, and diverse interest groups. Fulbright lost his Senate seat in 1974 and believed it was because he was chairman of the Senate Foreign Relations Committee during the war in Vietnam. But he lost in the primary. Tydings won his primary by almost 90,000 votes despite the communist issue, Korea, Truman, and all-out assaults from his competition.

In the 1938 purge election, he had won his primary by a mere 65,000 votes but went on to trounce his Republican opponent by more than two to one. In 1944 he carried Maryland by 131,000 votes while Roosevelt barely defeated Thomas Dewey with a 20,000 margin. That year Tydings even won Baltimore's seventeenth ward (the black district) by 51 percent; in 1950 he got only 15 percent there. The 1950 election showed extraordinary voter interest because of the highly charged issues. Turnout was 75 percent—27,000 more votes cast than in the 1944 presidential election and twice that of the 1946 midterm Senate contest.

Without McCarthy, Tydings could have avoided the position of constantly refuting charges. He could have harkened back to his roots. He was not as out of step in Maryland as most contemporary observers reported. The state's history of fiscal stringency and conservatism continued into the postwar era; it did not come to a halt in 1950. Those who argue that his defeat represented a consolidation of New Deal liberal, social, and political changes neglect evidence of Maryland's continuing, deep conservative orientation. O'Conor, an economic and political conservative, was reelected in 1952. Butler, who was reelected in 1956, could in no way be considered a liberal. When he lost in 1962, it was another Republican conservative, J. Glenn Beall, who unseated him in the primary and went on to win the general election. Democrat J. Millard Tawes, a Tydings protégé, was elected governor in 1958. The repudiation of Tydings was less the ousting of an old-fashioned conservative than the defeat of a badly wounded candidate who campaigned as an indispensable commodity rather than courting the voters with the humility and intensity of a freshman running for his political life.

Maryland's population had grown by almost 60 percent since Tydings entered the Senate in 1927. The age of his constituents had undergone a great change. Younger voters knew nothing of his achievements—knew only the name. McCarthy came along and, through Butler, painted the picture he wanted portrayed. Too many voters knew Tydings only through what his nemesis said about him.

Tydings was a particular individual caught in the crucible of McCarthyism. And eventually he did come to believe that McCarthy had made the difference between victory and defeat. In December 1950 he filed a complaint with the Senate and requested the election be investigated. He wrote articles and letters insisting that he "would not have been defeated if it had not been for the 'whitewash' charge which started two weeks after Hiss was convicted, and which in the middle of my investigation was accentuated by the outbreak of the Korean War."

Time described "the defeat of elegant, sarcastic Millard Tydings" as "spectacular" and "unexpected." Its postmortem said, "The thing that chiefly beat him was the charge that he had whitewashed the McCarthy investigation of Communism in the State Department." *Newsweek*'s account began, "[Senator Tydings] seemed the hands-down favorite against political newcomer [Butler]." And it went on to say, "Whenever Communism and Asiatic policy were heavily emphasized, Administration senators and congressmen lost." The New York *Times* wrote, "[McCarthy] contributed a heavy part, if not the decisive part," to Tydings's loss. Columnist Drew Pearson—no friend of Tydings—credited McCarthy with being the campaign's pivotal figure.

The *New Republic* analyzed the aftershocks in an April 2, 1951, article that described a "sinister . . . new gang of assassins." It left no question about who was responsible: " 'Political Murder, Inc.' is led by Col. Robert R. McCormick of Chicago, Senator Joe McCarthy of Wisconsin, and Fulton Lewis, Jr. . . . Together, as their first job, they killed off a four-time U.S. Senator from the state of Maryland last November." Tydings's reelection had seemed a sure thing, wrote *New Republic* analyst Helen Fuller, until he was selected to investigate McCarthy's charges.

McCormick himself had no doubt about who beat Tydings. He expansively declared his organization responsible. Jonkel was sufficiently convinced of his importance to take credit for the deed. He bragged about how he discerned and played on Tydings's weaknesses. The fact that Tydings "had not given the kind of answers to the charges against his conduct of the hearings that would let people feel confident [was] the thing that stood out like a sore nose. . . . Any propagandist would pick that up right away," he told the Washington *Post* in a postelection interview.

Historians may continue to disagree, but the people, the media, and the Senate believed that McCarthy defeated Millard Tydings. That perception became the reality. It remained the reality because nothing else could fully explain the incredible upset. McCarthy achieved what Roosevelt had not in 1938. He knocked a major power out of the Senate.

It is impossible to know the might-have-beens of history, but it is tantalizing to speculate. Had Tydings won, McCarthy surely would not have been so feared. He was credited with slaying a giant, and the results increased his power. Equally important, it increased his appetite for more power and more victims. It put his show back on the road for four more years. McCarthy became a man to be cultivated, or at least tolerated, by those looking to 1952. He was a person to be avoided by those who valued political survival.

Tydings's former colleagues looked around, wondering who was safe if such a master at intimidating and confusing his opposition had been unable to shake the stubborn McCarthy. A sobered

Senate went weak at the knees, and shrank into silence at the specter of the proud Tydings felled by the rabble-rousing hack from Wisconsin. William S. White, covering Congress for the New York *Times*, wrote of a "general expression of fear that what had happened to Mr. Tydings, with all his standing in the Senate, could happen to any other man in the Senate." Tydings's defeat gave rise to the legend of McCarthy: the "myth of political invincibility." The rest, as they say, is history.

For Tydings it suddenly was all over: 34 years of service to state and country, 24 in the Senate. A career vanished overnight. A few in Maryland wept, but many appeared gleeful at the humbling of the proud. Letters to newspapers gloated over putting an end to his "strutting and grinning," and terminating his "holiday jaunt" in the Senate. Tydings's devotion to truth and fair play, his reverence for the Constitution and traditional democratic values, and his many accomplishments were obscured by an arrogant demeanor.

There's an old and very American legend that has as its theme the comeuppance of the supercilious snob—the dandy who gets bested by a guy from the wrong side of the tracks. A certain distrust and dislike for the wealthy runs deep in American tradition. Tydings seemed to epitomize those who get their due because they appear to look down long aquiline noses. The way he held high that great chin made people want to see him taken down a peg or two. Retribution is all the sweeter if the high and mighty are humbled at the hands of the humble—for another well-known American theme is the triumph of the little guy who doesn't seem to stand a chance.

Joe McCarthy was the antithesis of a "strutting and grinning" aristocrat. He looked plain, dressed plain, shambled along like a good-natured puppy, and talked plain talk that was easy to understand. He appeared to be the quintessential underdog, America's favorite hound. Many Americans thought justice had been served when Tydings was rudely unseated.

There was great irony in the fall of Millard Tydings at Joe McCarthy's hands. McCarthy liked to portray himself as a war hero. He was "Tail-gunner Joe" and boasted of carrying ten pounds of Japanese shrapnel in his leg. In fact, he had no shrapnel in his leg or anywhere else. During a hazing stunt he had broken his leg when he fell down a ship's stairwell with an iron bucket tied to his foot.

That was his only war wound; he parlayed it into ten pounds of shrapnel complete with a limp that developed years later. He also parlayed it into a letter of citation. In February 1944 he forged his commanding officer's name to a letter he wrote, and then sent it through channels for Admiral Chester Nimitz's signature. He used the resulting citation in his campaign literature as evidence of his heroism.

Actually, McCarthy's career in the rear gunner's seat entailed little to brag about. In his overseas service (as an intelligence officer) he went along on missions. Grabbing the rear gunner's seat, he mowed down everything in sight; any coconut tree could harbor Japanese snipers was apparently his theory. When he signed on, the crew seldom returned with ammunition. McCarthy once shot his own plane's tail section when he lost his grip on the "twin 30" guns. Marines hung a sign on his tent: "Protect the coconut trees—Send McCarthy back to Wisconsin." He applied for and received a Distinguished Flying Cross in 1952 for flying 32 combat missions. (The DFC could be granted those with 25 missions or more.) McCarthy had flown only 11 combat missions, but had altered the record. Along with the Nimitz citation, his DFC (as well as an Air Medal and four stars) were obtained fraudulently. Tydings, a genuine war hero, had been pictured as a traitor by Tail-gunner Joe, scourge of the coconut palm.

McCarthy presented himself as the defender of the common man, referring constantly to his years as a judge devoted to the canons of judicial ethics. In truth he had violated his oath as a judge so flagrantly that the bar association brought a disbarment suit against him in 1949. He had destroyed court records in a case he dismissed that was coming up before the Wisconsin supreme court; he ran for political office while serving as a judge, which was a violation of state law; he operated a "quickie" divorce mill for prominent McCarthy contributors, even in cases outside his circuit— all blatant abuses of his position. Although the State Board of Bar Commissions stated that he "willfully placed the gratification of his personal ambition above the interests of the public . . . and chose to defy the rules of ethical conduct prescribed by the constitution, the laws of the state of Wisconsin, and the members of the profession," the state supreme court ruled that, although he was guilty, they would not disbar him because he probably would not repeat his offenses. His career was riddled with examples of corruption (including the income tax evasion). Yet McCarthy painted Tydings as unfit for office—a man no one should trust. In an awful irony, McCarthy had fashioned a sow's ear out of a linen handkerchief.

Tydings's background and origins represented perhaps the greatest irony of his defeat at the hands of McCarthy. Another typically American legend is Horatio Alger's poor young nobody who works hard and makes something of himself. McCarthy, who liked to wallow in his humble origins, made something of himself Alger never had in mind. Tydings was in fact the quintessential American success story. He was not, as so many thought, patrician born and bred. He came from a small town, from a family of ordinary circumstances, and attended the proverbial one-room school. Over the years he drifted away from his constituents, away from his roots. But when he began his career, he personified the expression "local boy makes good."

Notes

1. Former Senator Stuart Symington of Missouri recalled when, as secretary of the air force, he was authorized to handle business aspects of the air force without being responsible for deciding military matters such as what planes to buy. "I had one experience with Millard Tydings that impressed me a great deal," he said in an interview. "There was a manufacturer of airplanes, the Glenn L. Martin Company. . . . In 1948 or 1949, Glenn Martin himself came over to see me and said, 'I want you to buy such and such a plane,' and I replied, 'But the military don't want that plane; in fact, yours was third in the competition.' Martin became very upset. . . . One day Senator Tydings called and said, 'I'd like you to come over and have lunch with me.' I had a hunch he was wanting to talk about this matter, so [I] asked General [Hoyt S.] Vandenberg, Chief of Staff, to go with me. Vandenberg and I went over to Senator Tydings' private office in the Capitol. There also was Mr. Martin. In due course, Senator Tydings said, 'Glenn here has a plane he thinks you should buy, and he's upset you aren't buying it.' I answered, 'That's not my part of the shop. You had better ask General Vandenberg about it.' Vandenberg, former Head of Tactical Air for [Dwight D.] Eisenhower in Europe, looked Martin in the eye and said, 'The

reason we didn't buy your plane is because we believe two other planes are better.' Martin: 'But that's not right; my plane is the better.' Vandenberg replied, 'That's your opinion, but not ours.' At that point, if Tydings hadn't been the kind of man he was, he could have made it rough on us. [But he] said, 'Glenn, there it is. The military head of the Air Force doesn't want the plane. Stuart can't help get the plane if they don't want it.' As a result of this experience, I had great admiration for [Tydings]."

2. Two campaign-financed pieces of Butler literature failed to bear the Mundy credit: "Back to Good Old Dixie," and "From the Record." Because it was illegal to finance material passed off as independently sponsored, these became important exhibits in a 1951 Senate investigation of this election, as discussed in Chapter 11.

3. In December 1944, during a final assault on Allied lines in Belgium, Germany's First SS Panzer Division captured 150 Americans near a small Belgian village, Malmedy. The unarmed GIs, led into a wheat field, were slaughtered by machine-gun fire. After the war an American war crimes court convicted 73 SS troopers and sentenced them to death for the 'Malmedy massacre." In 1948 the German defendants charged that prosecutors had employed torture in extracting confessions and asked the U.S. Supreme Court to overrule the convictions. The Court refused to hear the case, but there was further investigation. By 1949 McCarthy had become involved. Perhaps the large number of Germans in Wisconsin accounted for his interest; possibly it was media attention. For undetermined reasons, he defended the SS before an Armed Services subcommittee investigating the controversy. He was not on the Armed Services Committee, but was allowed to sit in as a matter of senatorial courtesy. He took over and soon was bullying the subcommittee and witnesses with his manipulative techniques. His accusations made headlines: "MCCARTHY CHALLENGES TESTI-MONY!"; "MCCARTHY CHARGES WHITEWASH!" Eventually the subcommittee determined that the trials had been fair, despite a few instances of improper management, that the defendants had received abundant review and redress. McCarthy charged the subcommittee with white-wash. Armed Services Committee members—Republicans, Democrats, and chairman Millard Tydings—were furious and chastised McCarthy for irresponsible behavior by signing a bipartisan Resolution of Confidence in Senator Raymond Baldwin, Republican chairman of the subcommittee, whom McCarthy had attacked brutally. War veterans were scandalized by the outrageous claims on behalf of the SS. They never forgot or forgave McCarthy's conduct.

4. Lewis had strong ties to Colonel McCormick, Bazy Miller, and McCarthy. McCormick owned 19 percent of the Mutual Broadcasting Network. Lewis assisted with the "From the Record" layout.

5. A friend of McCarthy's remembered the Wisconsin senator's rage at Tydings for the disdainful July 20 speech, for trying to wreck his career. "Joe was so preoccupied with Tydings that he'd sit by the hour figuring ways to get revenge."

3

Chesapeake Childhood

In 1890, Havre de Grace, Maryland, was a sleepy Chesapeake village, its streets still paved with oyster shells. Nestled into the western shore of the Susquehanna River where it flowed into the world's largest estuary, the community inhabited a wooden shoreline of exceptional natural beauty. Millard Evelyn Tydings was born there on Easter Sunday, April 6.

His father's family had come to Maryland in 1645 from England, although originally the Tydings were Highland Dutch named Tideeman. The O'Neills, on his mother's side, emigrated from Ulster, Ireland, by way of Virginia in 1788.

From the Chesapeake area two Tydings brothers migrated west; one remained in Maryland where his descendants established farms throughout the colony. Millard Tydings's grandfather farmed in Calvert County near Prince Frederick. He also operated boats on the Chesapeake. He had a large number of children and named one of his sons Millard Fillmore Tydings after the thirteenth president, a custom of the times. But he died before his children were grown. His widow, forced to sell the farm, moved the family to Baltimore. By the age of 12, Millard Fillmore Tydings was working along with his mother and older siblings to keep food on the table. It was a hard and dreary life, cutting short his childhood and education.

Perhaps recalling memories of his father's boats, young Millard Fillmore joined the navy, became an engineer, and (after a stint as a tax collector) was drawn back to the Chesapeake. By his mid twenties he had been on his own for years, having struggled to achieve a degree of financial security.

John O'Neill, 18 years old, ambitious and penniless when he landed in America in 1788, entered the military under General Henry Lee. After serving in Harper's Ferry as superintendent of the U.S. Arsenal, he married a widow, Mary Hartshorn, and they established a small business. Believing opportunities would be greater elsewhere, the O'Neills moved to Havre de Grace where they operated a successful nail factory and reared a family. Mary Bond O'Neill was a fourth-generation daughter of the O'Neills of Havre de Grace.

Millard Fillmore Tydings met Mary O'Neill by chance. He managed a fish hatchery on the Battery, a small Chesapeake island, where the 17-year-old Mary had gone for a summer's excursion. Her mischievous blue eyes and pretty face, framed in golden-red hair, caught the attention of the serious-looking young man. He was tall and intense, with a handsome, masculine face. They married the next year, in 1889, and settled in Havre de Grace.

Millard Evelyn, first born of three children, was their only son. The boy was spirited, with a cheerful disposition and a propensity for clowning. His coloring and temperament favored the clear white skin, gingery red hair, and genial spunk of the O'Neills.

Havre de Grace boasted a sturdy economy, a stirring patriotic tradition, and a historic setting. Its history, among the oldest in Maryland, dated back to 1638 when the first settlement was established. The Old Post Road, opened in 1666, passed through the Susquehanna hamlet where ferries linked the South with New York and New England. The village, called the Susquehanna Lower Ferry until after the Revolution, experienced little military action during the Revolutionary War; but its citizens, including Colonel John Rodgers whose heroics won him acclaim, marched in the quest for freedom.

With victory, Lower Ferry resumed life as a small settlement in a new country and gained a new name—credited to the Marquis de LaFayette. The young Frenchman, come to North America to aid the colonists in their fight for independence, traveled the Old Post Road. Crossing the Susquehanna, he is said to have been transfixed by the beauty of the hamlet hugging the shoreline at the confluence of two pristine bodies of water. Its resemblance to Le Havre de Grace in France allegedly caused him to exclaim, "C'est Le Havre de Grace." Once the community was large enough to require formal government, the Maryland General Assembly incorporated it as Havre de Grace.[1]

The village grew. Fishing was the major industry; Susquehanna herring was in constant demand throughout the fledgling nation. Great fish floats stretched across the river's mouth, yielding incredible harvests. Canneries processed locally grown corn and tomatoes. The town became a center with its feed, hardware, and general stores; its blacksmiths; its wagon, gun, and nail factories. Arrival of the railroad in 1836, and the Tidewater and Susquehanna Canal in 1840, meant more trade and businesses. With construction of the railroad bridge in 1866, rail traffic became reliable.[2] Townspeople had visions of a booming future.

The railroad was important, but the Tidewater Canal—extending 45 miles from Wrightsville, Pennsylvania, to Havre de Grace—was a trade route of tremendous magnitude. Lumber, coal, and grain arrived in Havre de Grace for distribution by rail or steamship. Operation was profitable and picturesque with towlines, mule teams, and the high clear bugle calls that alerted lock-keepers of arriving barges. But terrible floods in 1889 proved catastrophic. Although the canal continued operating until 1900, subsequent flooding further eroded the canal banks, and competition from the growing rail systems siphoned off business. By the time Tydings was ten, operation was shut down. But the community's chance to become a major trading center had dimmed well before the canal's demise. Baltimore, with its great natural harbor and central location, had developed more rapidly. Still, from a hamlet of "fifty good dwelling houses" in 1695, Havre de Grace had become a thriving mercantile center—and then by 1890 drifted into small-town lassitude, boasting a proud history, a charming ambience, and a population of approximately 3,000.

Like all children in Havre de Grace, Tydings absorbed its rich heritage merely from growing up there. The names of the streets told the history of the nation and the town's intimate role in it—Revolution Street; LaFayette, Washington, Adams, and Franklin

Streets; Congress Avenue; Union Avenue; and Freedom Alley—and the stories told by his family brought that history alive.

The Revolutionary War had not directly touched the town, but the War of 1812 and the Civil War permanently marked it with glory and destruction, with bitter divisions and heroes. Accounts in schoolbooks confirmed legends the old-timers told. Stories of the Rodgers family's deeds sent Tydings's imagination soaring. Commodores John and George Washington Rodgers (sons of Colonel John Rodgers of Revolutionary War renown, proprietor of Havre de Grace's Rodgers Tavern) founded one of America's greatest naval families. Nine sons and grandsons achieved the rank of admiral. The War of 1812 witnessed the brothers' gallantry as John Rodgers's defense of Fort McHenry in September 1814 squelched the British attack on Baltimore, forcing the British fleet to retreat down the Chesapeake Bay. The battle's spectacular shellfire inspired Francis Scott Key to write "The Star Spangled Banner."[3]

Provocative narratives, especially those concerning hometown heroes whose celebrated tavern was just around the corner, were heady brew—even for boys nurtured on firsthand accounts of bloody Antietam. The citizens of Havre de Grace felt linked to the past in a profoundly personal sense. And Tydings's fascination with the Rodgerses' exploits was especially keen. His own family had been involved in an earlier battle of the War of 1812. When King George III's fleet blockaded the Chesapeake in 1813, it burned towns and factories as it went, with cannon foundries near Havre de Grace targeted. The town had only three pieces of artillery and a 50-man state militia for defense—mostly undisciplined and nonuniformed older and disabled men.

Forty-four-year-old Lieutenant John O'Neill, in command of the ragtag gang the morning the British fleet appeared, was summoned at sunrise by a lone sentry. O'Neill raced to the cannons adjacent the town at Potato Battery and with a small group opened fire. The roar of British rockets returning fire so frightened his men that they fled. Alone, he continued firing until the big gun, in recoiling, ran over his leg. He made it back to town and with a hand musket commenced shooting at the British landing force of 400—a number equal to the entire population of Havre de Grace (which had taken refuge in the woods). The British burned the village and took O'Neill prisoner aboard the *Maidstone,* Rear Admiral George Cockburn's ship. O'Neill's account of the ordeal was published on May 15, 1813, in the Baltimore *Weekly Register:*

> On the third instant [May 3], we were attacked by fifteen English barges at break of day. . . .
>
> When the alarm was given, I ran to the battery and found but one man there, and two or three came afterwards. After firing a few shots, they retreated. . . . I loaded the gun myself without anyone to serve the vent, which you know is very dangerous, and fired her. When she recoiled and ran over my thigh, I retreated down to town and joined Mr. Barnes of the nail manufactury, with a musket, and fired on the barges while we had ammunition, and then retreated to the common where I kept waving my hat to the militia who had run away, to come to our assistance, but they proved cowardly. . . .
>
> At the same time an English officer on horseback, followed by Marines, rode up and took me with two muskets in my hand. I was carried on board the *Maidstone* frigate where I remained until released three days since.

That was only the beginning. O'Neill descendants and townfolk tell a further story of courage. Cockburn had sentenced O'Neill to hang. As dazed citizens emerged from the woods to save their smoldering town, his 15-year-old daughter Matilda heard of her father's capture and the threat to his life. She rushed to the shore where the British were leaving and pleaded to see him. On learning where he was, she set out alone in the first undamaged skiff she could find to where the *Maidstone* rode at anchor.

Cockburn wasted no time informing her that civilians who fired on soldiers pay with their lives. Matilda stood her ground. Her father was a soldier of the militia, not a civilian, she argued. She implored the admiral to spare his life. Cockburn was unconvinced: Her father wore no uniform nor insignia. The girl refused to give up. He was commissioned by the state of Maryland, she insisted, and therefore must have papers proving his commission. She begged for time to produce them.

The admiral must have been impressed by Matilda's determination and concern for her father. He promised to wait. She found the papers in their partially burned home. The admiral released O'Neill. Before they left the *Maidstone,* Cockburn handed Matilda a small, glittering object and reportedly said, "Keep this for remembrance of Admiral George Cockburn, who admires loyalty and bravery in his enemies as he rewards the same virtues in his men." His token was his personal snuffbox—a gold-mounted tortoiseshell case. Matilda's mother, enraged over the torching of the town and imprisonment of her husband, flung the snuffbox to the floor, cracking it. But the family preserved Cockburn's gift as a symbol of two acts of heroism.

It did not hurt that President James Madison had threatened to hang two British officers if Cockburn hanged O'Neill. Still, whether it was Matilda O'Neill or President Madison that made the difference, nothing could detract from the courage displayed.[4] And Tydings relived those tales of audacity with each telling. The show of courage made a lifelong impression and the words "courageous" and "cowardly" took on intensely personal meanings.

Those were not the only stories that shaped a passion for courage and principle. His great-great-grandfather had freed his slaves before the Civil War. And he listened rapt to his grandfather's stories about Antietam, Bull Run, the Wilderness, learned about family who sided with the South, the pain such division caused. He mourned with his grandfather relatives and friends who had not returned. His great uncle, Captain Charles O'Neill, was killed at the Wilderness. The conspicuous bravery of his kin made him feel intimately tied to the central events of the nation's history.

All of this wove into the fiber of Tydings's character. Throughout his career he referred to those markers. "My own immediate ancestors fought and died—and I mean died—in the Civil War, shot down in battle wearing the uniform of the Blue," he told the Senate when challenged over the sincerity of his commitment to black Americans. "My own great-great grandfather freed slaves in his will, in 1820. He did not have many; he had only three. But he provided as best he could for their maintenance."[5] Tydings was proud of his heritage and as a boy became determined to measure up.

Lieutenant Henry O'Neill (wounded five times during the Civil War) adored his grandson, and he took the boy on walks through Havre de Grace from the time the child could toddle. Hand in hand the two would stand on the pier jutting out into the bay where the great river mouth yawned beneath the magnificent wooden-latticed trellises of the Susquehanna railroad bridge. O'Neill had a wry sense of humor and an affectionate nature. When together they visited members of his regiment, he teased his wartime comrades and let the boy in on the jokes so he could laugh with them comfortably. He valued education; O'Neill himself had some schooling and a cousin, William O'Neill, had gone to Maryland Agricultural College. Henry wanted the best for Millard and encouraged him to follow the family's example.

Havre de Grace was an idyllic place for children. Tydings loved the bay, that shimmering wonderland that attracted dozens of different waterfowl—Canada geese, mallards, swans, canvasbacks—and offered fresh- and saltwater fishing in the swift river currents and placid brackish inlets. One of his childhood escapades, so vivid in his memory that he recalled the words exchanged 40 years later in recounting it to his wife, reveals an early sense of pluck, a cool intelligence, and an affinity for mischief.

One broiling July morning when he was eight, he was target-practicing with a bow and arrow set that his grandfather had given him. As the sun simmered and sultry air clung to his sweaty clothing, all he could think about was the cool water lapping the shore behind Market Street—and the new town ordinance forbidding swimming except in proper bathing attire. Neither he nor any of his friends owned such a garment. A whistle came from across the fence. "Hey Chief! What say we go swimming? It's hotter'n Billy-be-damned!"

Tydings went over to the fence. "I don't have a swim suit. My father said anybody caught without one will be put in jail."

"Come on, Chief," his friends implored.

The boys would not go without him. Among the children of Havre de Grace, Tydings was known as a daredevil who usually got away with anything because of quick wits and impish charm. And he had even organized the boys into regiments so they could reenact the battles of Antietam and the War of 1812. Tydings pondered the pros and cons. His father wielded a hard hand. He felt rivers of summer sweat plaster his shirt to his back. "Let's go," he said.

In the foliage along the banks the boys stripped off their clothes. His friends hid theirs behind a large bush, but Tydings spied a board on the beach where he concealed his. They scrambled into the cool water and swam out—but not quickly enough to evade the eagle eye of Julius Jenkins, the fat old constable who, guessing some youngsters might be tempted to test the new law, was lurking nearby. Roaring mightily he waddled to the water's edge: "You boys come back here! I know you haven't any swim suits on."

Tydings had ducked beneath the water at first bellow. When he bobbed up for a breath he saw his friends charge out of the water and head for home, naked as jaybirds up Market Street, with Jenkins panting and shouting, "Come back here you young scalpies and put your clothes on!" Sliding back under the water, he stayed beneath the surface, popping up now and then like a seal to breathe and survey the shoreline.

Old Julius did not give chase for long, but returned to take custody of the clothing. Finding three sets of clothes, which matched the number of boys he had witnessed catapult out of the water, he was satisfied that he had nabbed his culprits. But back in the river one cool, clever boy floated and played. Once the law and startled ladies left the coast clear, he glided ashore and dressed rapidly, confident no one had seen him. A hand grabbed his damp collar. "How was the water, Millard?" an amused voice asked.

The boy grinned up at Henry O'Neill. "It was great, Grandpap." As they walked home the old man listened to the boy's recognition of luck and wile—and concern for his friends. Once convinced that he would not try it again, O'Neill slipped him a silver dollar to buy a bathing garment.

At school "Chief" was precocious, excelling at mathematics and debate. As acknowledged class cutup, he once played hooky for two weeks without getting caught, and could charm his way out of anything. He won the coveted job of wood boy for his one-room school, arriving early to lug in logs and kindling to keep the potbellied stove stoked red hot all day. By 1901 the town had a new school where the various grades had their own rooms and teachers. Tydings and his 11 classmates became "The Class of 1908." A 1904 yearbook included prophesies, with class prophet Milton Hopkins writing of "the future of 'Old Chief,'" Class Treasurer Tydings: "Looking again upon [the] stage . . . I saw the most comical clown it has ever been my pleasure to look upon. I knew it was Millard Tydings."

In winter Tydings and his friends raced horses on the frozen bay. When automobiles arrived—before age restrictions and licenses—they raced cars on the ice. One time they skated seven miles across the bay and back. He saved the life of a friend who had fallen through the ice into water six or eight feet deep. Tydings did not run for help, but lying flat on the ice reached for the boy's hands, pulled him to the surface, then to shore.

But Tom Sawyer adventures were only a part of Tydings's childhood. At ten he went to work to bring home needed money. He rose at half-past four to meet the train from Baltimore with the big-city papers and deliver them before school. At 14 he worked summers at the American Can Company, 11 hours a day, six days a week—eight hours on Saturday—for 5¢ an hour. Looking back he remembered, "Six of us kids packed all the tin cans that 150 men could make. It was hard work but it was great fun and I have yet to taste anything as good as the ice cream sodas we used to buy on Saturday afternoons." In college he worked summers, lugging 100-pound blocks of ice or helping to build a new Baltimore & Ohio railroad bridge across the Susquehanna at Havre de Grace. It was back-breaking labor, but provided funds for school.

Hard work was not the only hard part of his life. His parents' marriage was strained. His father was away for long periods of time, as chief engineer on the Chesapeake tugs *Pacific, Champlin,* and *Murray Vandiver* that towed larger boats through the draw of the railroad bridge, and later as superintendent of water transportation at the U. S. Proving Grounds at Aberdeen.[6] His mother was left to manage the children alone. Tydings's younger sisters, Naomi and Kathryn, were six and one, respectively, when he was 16. Mary Tydings loved her children fiercely, but like any mother was exhausted by their antics. And like other wives with an energetic brood, she turned to her husband for comfort and encouragement when he was home. But although he provided a steady living for his family, the solemn young man had grown moody and irritable. He was a stern, fair disciplinarian with his children, and never was playful. It was not in his nature to offer the kind of succor his wife sought.

The daughter of jovial Henry O'Neill—and great-grandniece of the impassioned Matilda—was a fun-loving, intelligent woman of striking appearance. It was precisely those qualities that had attracted her husband's attention, just as she had found his serious nature and rugged good looks appealing. Mary loved to sing and dance, write poetry, play the piano. As a young woman she enjoyed home theatricals, her ability at impersonations considered "professional." Affectionate by nature, she wrote verse to slip among her husband's linens. But he was little interested in what he considered frivolous. She grew hurt when he took no pleasure in her loving gestures.

Puzzled and deeply wounded, Mary Tydings became increasingly unhappy. As time went on, the dancing Irish eyes dulled perceptibly. Smiles failed to mask a melancholy cast to her face; her mouth took on traces of hardness. Nothing in her background prepared her to understand a dour and sour nature. She had made a desolating error—confusing character with temperament, believing that a person of good character would possess a good disposition. Little seemed to please her husband. Confronted with his relentless moodiness, she turned increasingly to her children and became ambitious for her son.

Tydings adored his mother, believing her to be the epitome of everything brave and beautiful in the world. He was very much like her—charming, quick-witted, fun-loving. He too loved to dance, write poetry, play the piano. His proficiency as mimic surpassed even his mother's. At some point he realized she often was unhappy. Drawing on his comic skills he would clown to make her laugh; he became a source of strength. But as he matured and sought to decipher the puzzle of her sadness, he came to resent his father bitterly for making her life grim and loveless. Painful observation taught him that life was not fair; his warm and beautiful and intelligent mother often was engulfed in tears. Perhaps his lifelong quest for fair play was an attempt to compensate for the unfairness of his mother's lot.

Childhood hardships endowed him with strength of character, but with a toughness rather than compassion. He developed a will of steel and a resolve that he would never tolerate being a victim of injustice. His belief in the fundamental importance of ethical behavior was spawned from emerging insight. An anger was planted deep inside him, lying in wait for events that would bring it to life—a profound anger over life's injustice and its unfathomable, capricious nature. He was born with a talent for making people laugh and a gift for speaking his mind; adversity taught him that humor and words could also be used as tools, as shields, and as weapons.

As resentment at his father grew, Tydings reached out to Grandpap. The old man kept a loving eye on his grandson and at some point replaced Tydings's father in the boy's affections. Grandpap, with his optimism and encouragement, served as mentor and—with his daughter's support—encouraged the boy to go to college. When Tydings's father scoffed that *he* had not gone to college and had done well enough and then refused to pay for it, Grandpap came up with the money. Later, when his sisters were of college age, Tydings remembered his grandfather's generosity and paid Naomi's way through the Girls Latin School in Baltimore and Kathryn's through Hood College in Frederick.[7]

Although Tydings was in the class of 1908, he breezed through his courses and graduated in 1906 at the age of 16. Impressed by stories of the Rodgers family, he yearned to go to the Naval Academy in Annapolis. Perhaps he was also reaching out to his father—coupling his father's seafaring vocation with the O'Neill military past. Whatever the motive, from his youngest years he wanted to be an admiral. But there were no competitive examinations then to qualify for admission; lacking any political clout outside of Havre de Grace, he failed to receive an appointment.[8] He enrolled instead at the Maryland Agricultural College (MAC) in College Park, which offered military training along with degrees in engineering. He would design bridges such as the one he had helped to build across the Susquehanna. Tydings became an army cadet, dressed in the same uniform worn at West Point, and was trained in military arts as he pursued a degree in mechanical engineering.

At MAC he was recognized as having a first-rate intellect. He had loved debate in high school, and at College Park became the prize pupil of Professor Charles S. Richardson, head of the Public Speaking Department, acquiring a remarkable vocabulary, excellent grasp of theory, and keen analytical skills. By the end of his sophomore year he had won the prestigious Schley prize and William Pinckney Whyte medal for debate and oratory. Senior year he was selected captain of Company A, won the Whyte medal again, and was president of the Morrill Literary Society, athletic editor of the yearbook *Reveille,* editor of the college newspaper *Triangle,* a champion track star and pole-vaulter, and valedictorian of his class.

But young Tydings was far from all business and grind. He had the lanky build of an athlete, an attractive appearance, and a ready lighthearted repartee. His sense of humor and personal charm made him popular. When mumps broke out during his senior year and threatened to quarantine all students for the entire Christmas vacation, he called a meeting of Company A. "We are not going to stay here in quarantine for Christmas," he announced. "As your captain I dismiss you all. Go home." They did. So did the rest of the school. The college's military headmaster (whom Tydings had informed of his plans in advance—thus demonstrating an early political acumen) acknowledged that he could hardly fire the whole school. Tydings became something of a hero.

He also became famous for his bantering, which inspired imitation. The Tydings profile in the 1910 *Reveille* showed an affectionate ribbing:

> It is as an orator, however, that "Chief" shines. . . . [H]e became endowed with his infantile erudition in the schools of his native town. . . . In the chapel he has orated on practically every subject from "Women Suffrage" to "Buttermilk" and he is usually showered with applause and other things. The school . . . can stand almost thirty minutes of him at a time . . . [a rare] claim to distinction in the line of enduring torture.

In his senior year he took the gold medal in the Oratorical Association of Maryland Colleges' statewide contest. *Reveille* lauded his "splendid oration." His subject, prophetic of a future interest, was "A Plea for Universal Peace." He soundly defeated a rival from Washington College who expounded on "The Degeneracy of the Senate."

On graduation in 1910 Tydings joined the Baltimore & Ohio Railroad in West Virginia to work on tunnels and bridges—dangerous and poorly paid work. During a rainstorm he fell from the top of a bridge. A workman on a lower span miraculously caught him. The fall—and the revelation of how little the head engineer was making after years with the railroad—convinced him that engineering was not for him. He was ambitious; and he missed the give-and-take of debate, the stirring sensation of an audience roused by his words. He returned home to consult his grandfather. It did not take long to decide: He entered the University of Maryland's School of Law in 1911, completing the three-year course in two while teaching mechanical drawing in Baltimore County's public schools to pay his tuition.

Henry O'Neill was aware of his grandson's strained financial situation. In 1912 he helped him buy a four-acre farm on the Gunpowder River well outside of Havre de Grace. Tydings paid $110 outright, and Grandpap lent him the $1,200 needed to gain title. The farm was Tydings's grubstake. From 1912 through 1919 he made payments with interest to reimburse his grandfather.

In 1913 he passed the bar and entered the practice of law in Havre de Grace. His work was largely routine—settling small estates and the like. But his practice was not the only thing on his mind. The Tydingses had been staunch Democrats from the days Thomas Jefferson organized the Democratic-Republican party. In 1912, as Tydings was in the midst of his legal studies, a historic event in American politics was taking shape. Since before the Civil War, just one Democrat—Grover Cleveland—had occupied the White House. In 1912, a promising candidate—one very different from the provincial William Jennings Bryan (who had determined the party's direction for several tortured decades)—strode onto the scene. Woodrow Wilson, idealist and intellectual, with his program of the New Freedom, captured the attention of many Democrats, Tydings among them. "I was the original Wilson man in my county," he remembered later. "I first became interested in politics at the time of his contest for the presidency."

That was the beginning of his political career. Initially he had no intention of seeking office. He was finishing law school, preparing to pass the bar, and contributing extra time to Harford County political figures. But a chance insult propelled him into the fray. Michael Fahey—a sage, old-time Havre de Gracian—ran town politics as his own personal club. He was amiable, a delight to shoot the breeze with, but had no use for the political neophytes beginning to cluster around James J. Archer, a Harford County activist allied with Senator Blair Lee's progressive movement. In particular, young

Tydings's high-profile efforts irritated Fahey and the old guard. They moved quickly to slap the upstarts down. "A lot of us first voters organized a Democratic Club up at Havre de Grace," Tydings observed in 1926 when asked how he began his career. "Some of the older men didn't like it."

In fact, they disliked it very much and made clear they did not think Tydings had the right equipment to be a legislator. "I had no idea at all of running for office," Tydings observed. He just did not like the way he was treated. "When it was announced that, anyhow, young Millard Tydings couldn't go to the Legislature, I just naturally had to go and get myself elected," he said. He challenged Fahey in 1915, found himself in the midst of a free-for-all, and loved it. He exulted in the verbal brawls and had a genius for turning attacks on himself to his advantage. Out of all elected delegates, he won the highest vote total in Harford County. Tydings, Archer, and Blair Lee's forces wrested control from the fading Fahey clique.

Tydings immediately made a name as a powerful debater. The press wrote about the "affable," "ebullient," and "spunky" new Annapolis figure. A Baltimore *American* editor thought so highly of his abilities that he framed an article about new House of Delegates members around him. In the sole photograph accompanying the text, all Tydings's trademark characteristics—the perfectly creased three-piece suit, the gleaming watch chain and tie clip, the white collar starched to within an inch of its life—made their debut.

He set to work in a blaze of energy. In a crusade for economy, he introduced and secured passage of measures abolishing useless state offices. And he managed to free Havre de Gracians from an unfair burden. When the Susquehanna railroad trestle was replaced, a wealthy group of businessmen bought it for $700. They wangled a charter from the state legislature exempting it from taxation and allowing them to charge tolls: 3¢ per foot passenger; 5¢ per sheep, swine, bicycle; 10¢ per horse, mule, cattle (driver 5¢ extra); 20¢ for loaded wagons; automobiles 50¢; and trucks $1.50. The bridge was the major link between New York and the South. Havre de Gracians became a captive group as the value of the bridge rose from $700 to over $500,000 in less than ten years.

Tydings believed tolls were a cruel distortion of the old practice of carrying locals for free. He was outraged by the excessive profits made at the expense of ordinary people. He proposed and achieved passage of a bill reducing all tolls by 50 percent until 1921, when they would cease and the state would purchase the bridge through issuing a bond. Harford County cheered. A bronze plaque later attached to a slab of granite beside the bridge read: "To Millard E. Tydings, United States Senator From Maryland, Through Whose Efforts This Has Been Made A Free Bridge. Erected By His Fellow Citizens In Token Of Their Esteemed Appreciation. 1928."

Tydings was mentioned prominently as a compromise candidate for speaker of the House of Delegates, with the backing of the powerful Lee forces—nearly unheard of for a freshman who was the youngest in the legislature at 26. But he barely had started up the political ladder when trouble on the border with Mexico called. Mexican revolutionary Pancho Villa's raids into U.S. territory had finally provoked President Wilson into ordering the army to pursue Villa back into Mexico. Delegate Tydings immediately joined Company D, the Maryland militia regiment he had formed, and found himself aboard a troop train bound for the Southwest. Instead of rising to make speeches on the House of Delegates floor, he found himself rising at dawn at Eagle Pass, Texas, to the sounds of reveille.

Notes

1. Legend has it that the town verged on permanent greatness when it came within one vote of becoming the new nation's capital city. A vote between it and a location on the Potomac River allegedly was tied at 27 to 27, with Southern members of the Continental Congress pushing for Havre de Grace; Elias Boudinot, speaker of the Congress, was said to have cast the deciding vote. But research by Havre de Grace historian J. Alexis Shriver reveals that this vote was one of several taken on Susquehanna locations proposed for reasons of regional pride by Maryland and Pennsylvania delegates in 1789. The present Potomac River location was not selected until July 9, 1790.

2. Before construction of the bridge, trains were ferried across. With the invention of steamboats, railroad operations speeded up greatly. During severe winters, tracks were laid across the ice to provide year-round service.

3. In 1931, legislation sponsored by Tydings established "The Star Spangled Banner" as the national anthem.

4. The city of Philadelphia, in gratitude for John O'Neill's actions

(which some credited with distracting the fleet from completing its Chesa-peake Bay sweep and pressing on to attack the city), presented him with a handsome sword. Both the snuffbox and sword are in the Maryland Histor-ical Society's collection in Baltimore. The O'Neill family was given the office of Keeper of the Lighthouse at Concord Point off Havre de Grace in perpetuity, in recognition of O'Neill's deeds. As a sinecure the position held prestige. A member of the family attended the duties of the lighthouse until the 1920s when an automatic electric signal was installed. Harry O'Neill, Millard E. Tydings's uncle, was the last to serve as Keeper. Havre de Grace also honored John O'Neill's courage with a monument in the town's park.

5. Tydings's great-great-grandfather, John O'Neill, actually had eight slaves. His will ordered all set free by age 35.

6. Tydings's father was nicknamed "Chief" because he was chief engineer on the tugs. As a boy Tydings was called "Little Chief"; as he grew older he earned the nickname "Chief" through force of his personality.

7. Liberal columnist Joseph Alsop wrote in a 1938 article deriding the conservative Tydings that Murray Vandiver, a prominent Havre de Gracian and chairman of the powerful Democratic State Committee, helped Tydings get a scholarship to Maryland Agricultural College and helped him through law school. No information available confirms Alsop's claims.

8. If Murray Vandiver had indeed taken an interest in Tydings, his political clout surely would have secured Tydings a place at Annapolis.

His dream of being like Commodore Rodgers lingered. On the Senate Naval Affairs Committee he fought to build up the navy. In 1939 he wrote a whimsical letter to Princess Abigail Kawananakoa of Hawaii, Republican party chairwoman, whom he had met as chairman of the Territories and Insular Possessions Committee. "Dear Princess," he wrote, "When I was a boy of 16, i.e. ten years ago, I tried very hard to get an appointment to the Naval Academy but was not successful that year, and so became a Senator instead, thereby robbing our Navy of, perhaps, the best Admiral in all its history. . . ."

4

This Is the End, God Take Care of Me

Back in August 1914, war had exploded in Europe. President Woodrow Wilson pledged to keep the nation out of the hostilities, but newspaper stories and photographs delivered images of death and destruction into American homes. Tydings followed the war's progress attentively.

Recognizing the likelihood that the United States would be drawn into the conflict, he felt compelled to renew the military training he had begun in college. He went to see the captain of Harford County's National Guard, Milton A. Reckord, a friend of his. "If you organize a platoon for Aberdeen and Havre de Grace," Reckord told him, "we'll swear them in and make you a second lieutenant and platoon commander" in the Maryland National Guard.

Tydings recruited two dozen young men. They were sworn in on a Saturday morning in June 1916; that same afternoon the unexpected happened. Responding to Pancho Villa's border forays, Wilson federalized the National Guard. Tydings's platoon was headed for Texas.

Eagle Pass, Texas, had little to recommend it. The thermometer hovered around the 100 degree mark, and little clouds of dust rippled at the drop of a cigarette butt. Eyes and teeth never were free of the grit of sand that salted every meal and filtered its way into every bedroll.

Sixteen men from Havre de Grace were at Eagle Pass, including Percy Fyle, Bob Frederick, and Joe Davis—close friends of Tydings, especially Fyle. As boys they had gone camping together. They had become Democrats and cast their first votes together at 21. In Texas, to make the long nights less boring, they borrowed two suits of "circular clothing" and crossed into Mexico to explore. That, and sweating through maneuvers, was the only action they saw. Instead of grumbling, Tydings joked about the weather and the absurdity of defending nothing from no one, calling the experience "that bloodless and comic war." Yet the discipline required to survive the heat and tedium prepared him well for what was coming.

Tydings barely had returned home when Wilson declared war on Germany. Without breaking stride he reenlisted. He and 15 others from the Havre de Grace contingent found themselves aboard another troop train, this time bound for Anniston, Alabama. They arrived in August and marched through miles of mud to reach Camp McClellan, 19,000 acres of rolling terrain in the rugged Blue Ridge Mountain foothills. Mosquitoes, flies, and the steamy Alabama heat tortured the men of the newly formed 29th Division.

Training went beyond maneuvers in the mud to encompass the beginnings of regimentation in order to curb individualism in favor of divisional command and inculcate regimental camaraderie—essential to performance as a unified entity. Many gathered there hailed from National Guard units of Maryland, Delaware, Virginia, and the District of Columbia, home from duty on the Mexican border. A strong bond sprang up among them. And many other Marylanders were billeted at the camp, among them a group who had left behind young careers in public life, as had Tydings. E. Brooke Lee, William Preston Lane, Hall Hammond, and William C. Walsh would become Tydings's lifelong friends. After the war those veterans, who had shared the seminal experience of their lives, formed the nucleus of a new and powerful political force that eventually came to dominate state politics.[1]

To encourage spirit, the 29th Division chose a name. In the Civil War, units with distinctive designations had performed unusually well and developed a special esprit de corps. The men of Camp

McClellan were from both North and South—Union and Confederacy—and were in a Southern camp named for a Northern general. The name "Blue and Gray Division" was adopted unanimously. The Blue and Gray attracted war correspondents, some of whom stayed with them from Anniston until the Armistice. The Baltimore *Sun*'s Raymond S. Tompkins showed such an interest in the Blue and Gray, and displayed it with such humor and loyalty, that he won the affection of the division. His stories did much to publicize Tydings's war record.

Regional ties, the divisional name, stories reaching hometown papers, and an inherent patriotism bound the men together. Like his comrades, Tydings felt such deep devotion to the division that throughout his Senate career his staff had standing instructions that any Blue and Gray member who came to call should be shown into his office immediately, no matter what he was doing.

Tydings enlisted as a private, but because of his experience was promoted to second lieutenant and then to first lieutenant by August. After basic training, the army made good use of his mathematics and engineering skills, sending him to the School of Fire at Fort Sill, Oklahoma, for four weeks of special training as a machine-gun officer. He graduated top of his class, and in January 1918 was promoted to captain in command of a company of the 110th Machine Gun Battalion, then was appointed second in command to Major D. John Markey, 112th Machine Gun Battalion.

The Blue and Gray, eager to get "Over There," felt keen disappointment at all the endless delays. Liberty Bond drives took advantage of boredom, patriotism, esprit de corps—and their small salaries. Many griped over the double jeopardy of pledging their lives and then pledging their money, but the 29th raised more than $1.2 million—a fact that became tangible in the number of finely engraved bonds appearing in the great army crap games.

Spring, with its fragrant beauty, reinvigorated the men; the Blue and Gray sailed for France. Crossing the Atlantic provided a first taste of fear. At night every porthole was covered so no glimmer of light could betray the ship's location to the Kaiser's "Hell Divers," the deadly U-boats. Interior passages were illuminated by ghostly blue lights. The convoy of 13 troop transports zigzagged to confuse lurking submarines. Yet the steady throb of the engines, the sight of spouting whales, porpoises skimming beside the bow, soothed the men. Residual fear was lessened by the ubiquitous army therapy: the floating crap game. When the commanding officer learned how much money was involved, he announced, "If I catch one of you with a pair of dice I'm going to send you right back to America!" Tydings would later laugh in recounting how that part of the ocean must be paved with dice.

One day airplanes appeared in the sky. A faint blue outline emerged on the horizon. In a book written about his war experiences, *The Machine Gunners of the Blue and Gray Division,* Tydings described a scene that entranced them as a tidal wave of men disembarked, struggling to regain their land legs:

> The harbor at Brest, France, is beautiful. A long, tapering finger of water points inland from the Atlantic and from it on either side verdant hills roll their picturesque undulations over the horizon. Old castles and forts, many of which have lost their usefulness long since, reach from water level to hill top; and, by design, which savors of the middle ages, offer mute evidence of the importance of this sea center in times of yore.

French children crowded the docks, begging for pennies and selling *vin rouge*. It was new and exotic—the language, their countryside billets in fourteenth-century monasteries, the abundance of wine, the shrugs and expressive hands of the French. There were chateaux and towns that had existed for centuries, medieval streets bathed in moonlight. Tydings was not the only American to fall in love with France in the springtime of 1918.

The Blue and Gray entered the Allied lines in Alsace, near the historic city of Belfort at the front called "Center Sector Haute-Alsace"—the far southeastern end of the war's long western front, stretching from Switzerland to the North Sea. Tydings, with other machine-gun captains, was sent to a special school at Châtillon-sur-Seine and spent four intense weeks learning all he could about barrages, angles, indirect fire, and the guns themselves. "Blindfolded we took down each piece and part and blindfolded reassembled them. Mules we groomed, groomed, groomed," he wrote. "At night everyone wrote letters home narrating his experience and impressions and describing in detail his scrumptious apartments in Monsieur's hayloft."

Tydings graduated first in his class at Châtillon-sur-Seine and was elated. His performance would reflect well on the Blue and Gray. At the railroad station he and others waiting to return to their divisions joked and chattered "like children just out of school," he wrote in a highly personal, reflective, and harrowing handwritten chronicle of his war experiences, which he never published. "The front! The front!—with roaring cannon, raids, dugouts, attacks, counterattacks, comrades—a roulette wheel on which I would be a number, with death acting as croupier."

Another young officer sauntered up to him, hands gesturing and shoulders shrugging, spouting what sounded like *"Bon jour, pomme de terre ral le bongor sol attis magli vasso,"* all the time raising and lowering his eyebrows as if inviting Tydings to join him in French conversation. Waving hands rising to the challenge, Tydings replied, *"Quell heure, oui, bong com satti ama cam de fricalle?"* They spoke perhaps 60 words of mangled French—had invented the others "found in no language on earth"—yet their "comrades were amazed. . . . It went about the group that we could speak French as well as English."

While changing trains, the group decided to secure a hotel room to continue the inevitable crap game. Obviously fluent in French, Tydings was asked to bargain for the room. Seizing a moment when the others were distracted, he said to the concierge, *"Chambre"*—gesturing to show it must be big. *"Oui, oui,"* replied the concierge who gave them a large front room. Reputation secure, Tydings won $100 after the dice began to roll.

At the end of the line, aboard a divisional truck, Tydings was swallowed up by the eerie paraphernalia of war. The road was camouflaged heavily with huge continuous sheets of burlap painted green with yellow daubs to blend with the countryside, strung along both sides on 12-foot-high wire frames. Strips of burlap were draped apron-fashion across the top every 50 feet or so. The "burlap alleys," as he styled them, made it hard for airplanes and observation balloons to see troop movement below. Through rips in the aprons he saw piles of artillery shells, corrugated iron, wagons—as well as farmers tranquilly tilling the soil, cattle grazing on the green hillsides, as if the bizarre-looking road were the only war zone. He pointed up to a balloon. "Boche," the driver said. He heard rumbling, a shriek followed by an explosion. "Twilight song," remarked the driver. His nerves tightened.

The division's commanding general sent word for him to report on arrival. "The reports came today," the general said, looking up at him. He referred to his excellent work at Châtillon-sur-Seine. "That reflects credit on the division. Join your company."

Trench warfare had stopped the forward and rearward movement of armies, so civilians had returned to Alsace to renew their daily lives. The Germans were reluctant to fire on Alsace's ethnic Germans, and an odd implied understanding between Germans and Allies in Haute-Alsace had developed: "You be nice and I'll be nice." Haute-Alsace had thus evolved into a "quiet sector." But the silence was deceptive. Alsace had changed hands between France and Germany a number of times over the generations. Many in the area were German sympathizers who spied on French and American positions. Tydings was warned to keep papers and maps secured. The command of the Blue and Gray, having replaced a nonchalant "I'll be nice" French division, began to liven things up. The morning after he arrived, Tydings was summoned to headquarters.

"Can you put down a short barrage on a particular section of a German trench?" General Bandholtz demanded to know.

"Yes, sir."

"Then do it tonight." He was to select time and place; Colonel R. H. Kelley, the division's machine-gun officer, would show him the ropes.

Tydings heart raced. "It was on my tongue to say, 'But sir, I've never been to the front line,' but to say that seemed cowardly. . . . Outwardly I presented a calm far different from the feeling within." He pored over Kelley's maps and aerial photographs. Newly dug German emplacements stood out clearly. Kelley suggested that he take four machine guns with 750 rounds of ammunition for each, and that he should shoot and run for cover. Still, Tydings felt anxious. "Didn't they know I had never been all the way up [to the front]?" His inexperience might be the end of him—and his men. But he chose ten men and set out on foot. The heavy guns and bulky equipment went by truck. He studied the map and pictures again. A wooded knoll, with its commanding altitude and leafy cover, offered excellent strategic position. His target was Ammerzviller Trench, a section of the zigzagging German front.

Setting up a machine-gun barrage required intricate preparation—all to be done under the Germans' noses. Vickers machine guns were too large and heavy to be carried by one soldier. A supply team was needed to haul the many accessories and ammunition—not to mention the maps, photographs, and careful mathematical calculations.

In *Machine Gunners,* Tydings described the steps that went into laying a machine-gun barrage. Officers calculated firing data and from it placed aiming stakes in the ground. Gun crews positioned the heavy weapons over gun stakes and pointed them at the aiming stakes so that the guns, if fired that way, would shoot in a line with due magnetic north. Next, wooden bases—planking two inches thick and six inches wide—were nailed together in the shape of a cross and put under the gun's tripod legs. Without the T-bar, a firing gun's weight and vibration would bury the legs in the ground, changing its true aim and elevation and endangering friendly troops. Sandbags were used to barricade each leg for further stability. Then each gun was bolted to the tripod.

Gunners had to aim and elevate each gun carefully, to carry the bullets to target. An officer's mathematical calculations then came into play. The gun's position was located on the map and a pencil line drawn through each gun position running parallel to north and south lines. Another was drawn from gun position to target. Those two penciled lines crossed at the gun location and formed an angle at that point. The angle showed how much the gun had to be swung from due north in order to align with the target. A circular dial on the tripod, marked in degrees and minutes, measured the angle so the gunner could aim accurately. Guns then were locked into true aim with "foolproofs"—stout sticks driven into the ground on each side of the gun jackets, with two horizontal sticks nailed so that the gun projected through a square wooden frame. The setup prevented the gun barrel from moving and thus rendered its aim, indeed, foolproof.

Flash hiders were the final touch. Six square feet of burlap on vertical wooden frames were erected so the flash of the gun could not be seen by the enemy. Water was needed to keep the burlap from igniting—and to keep the gun jackets cool so they did not give off telltale steam. Ammunition sometimes was carried up by the soldiers. But for raids requiring thousands of rounds, trained burros were used. Ammunition boxes would be thrown over the back of a burro; it would be led to the gun emplacements, unloaded, and led back. Again the ammunition would be loaded. This time the animal would be pointed in the path, given a slap, and unattended would return to the men. Another slap would start the unloaded burro back. The work had to be done in silence and with minimal movement to conceal their presence from the vigilant Germans.

"Nine-thirty came. Dark clouds were flying over the sky. Thunder and an occasional exploding shell broke the quiet. We started for the guns." Rain made the path slippery. "Hearts began to pound. Breath came faster." At the top of the knoll Tydings made certain that the guns had not been disturbed. Everything was okay. "When I say, Fire! cut loose like hell. . . . Every man stays at the guns until I blow the whistle. . . . Now wet your flash hiders and load!" There was a clicking of bolts and bullets and the slosh of water. "Fire!" The air rang with the din of four guns.

> All our guns had fired one belt and were now on the second 250 bullets. It seemed like hours had passed. . . . When would the shells come after us? Maybe in the next second. They were shooting the third belt. Hurry! Hurry! One gun had finished its 750 rounds. The other three were tack, tack, tacking away. Hurry! Hurry! All through but one. God, Man! Hurry!

When he blew the whistle, bolts clicked, feet scuffled, men cursed and laughed as they scrambled in all directions. Tydings ran down the path, lost his footing, and slid for yards on the seat of his pants. Somewhere German shells were exploding, but not near them. In ten minutes the panting men assembled in the communications trench, baptism by fire behind them. The raid's success raised the morale of Tydings's company and greatly increased his confidence. But the reality of what it meant stayed with him.

I wondered if we had caught the Germans working. How many of the poor devils had we killed or wounded? Maybe, now some of them were being carried to the rear. . . . I thought of my own Mother. I imagined her getting a telegram—"We regret to inform you your son was killed . . . !" Our house would be made dark. She would sit in it and stare and think and think. I felt wretched. Perhaps our aim had been bad. . . . I doubted this, we had used such care. . . . Maybe the Germans had quit working in the rain. . . . War in a day had lost all its romance. This was legalized murder. Two days ago, I had been shooting crap. Today, I had been killing men. . . . Who had started [this war] anyway?

The next morning brought devastating news. Joe Davis had been killed—a lifelong friend. His death, coming on the heels of the sobering raid, shook Tydings profoundly. Joe was the first of the Havre de Grace boys to die in France. "Who would be next?" he asked himself.

Germans raided American trenches the following dawn, using liquid fire—*flammenwerfer*. Hand grenades dispatched those who escaped the flames. The Americans opened up as the Germans faded back through the lifting mists of no-man's-land. Tydings was impressed by the courage of German soldiers who returned to retrieve their dead. "Such men were brave fellows. They had paid back our machine guns' attacks on their trench. The score was even."

The quiet sector heated up. The Americans began harassing the Germans with raiding parties covered by artillery shelling and machine-gun barrages. Tydings wrote, "Fritz's attitude was at first one of tolerant surprise." But when the raids continued, "Fritz came down off his aloof, dignified perch, got real mad . . . and came after us with artillery."

Tydings and Captain E. Brooke Lee of the 115th Infantry were summoned to headquarters to plan a raid. Lee's infantry were to enter German lines while Tydings's gunners covered with a box barrage—15 Vickers firing a stream of bullets for a half hour, boxing in the trench. They had two days. Hammers, saws, nails, shovels, and burlap were carried to the front by various routes. Security was tight; the men must know nothing until the last minute, to keep Alsatian spies uninformed. At the front, as Tydings studied the terrain, the men sprawled on the ground playing craps. "Good," he observed. "This would keep the men together and keep their minds employed."

> Shooting crap is the soldier's golf. It is his books; automobile; moving pictures. Warfare offers little chance for any other pleasure or diversion. To keep one's thoughts continually on the killing of men leads to madness. Crap is the soldier's counterbalance. While he is playing it he softens; forgets; becomes a human being again.

Dice did not pave the forest at Alsace; they were too important to be ordered tossed away.

After he determined the angle and details of attack, he set to work with the men. They dug pits for protective emplacements. Dirt was sandbagged to make three-foot-wide walls. Steel rails formed rafters, and more layers of sandbags on more rails on more sandbags completed the four-foot-thick roof. Adrenaline kept them from feeling the fatigue of digging, lifting, carrying, and placing aiming stakes, tripod T-bars, flash hiders, and the rest.

They were ready. Firing was to commence when the artillery opened up at 4:40—eight dark hours to wait. Tydings told the company what was in the works. "If anyone wants to write letters let him do it at once." He later wrote, "I doubt if there were six letters written. Thoughts were not susceptible to paper expression."

He remembered the night vividly. "No smoking. Talking in low tones only. Sleep if you wanted to; but who could?" In no-man's-land, flares and star shells lit up the sky, hung opalescent before falling silently. Behind them a red rocket shot up in the air. Tydings thought it unnerving.

They smelled gas. "Gas! Gas!" someone shouted. Frantic, everyone grabbed for his gas mask. In his haste, Tydings bobbled his, dropped it, put it on upside down, then righted it. Klaxon horns sounded a warning for those in the trenches. The thud of helmets resounded on trench duckboards as men knocked them off to put on their masks. Minutes seemed like hours.

"God!" he suddenly thought, was this another *flammenwerfer* raid? "I remembered our machine guns all were aimed not to protect us in front but to hit the enemy trenches to our left. . . . We could not fire a shot to stop them. We couldn't change the aim of these guns." His men were sitting ducks. "Every man out of his emplacement," he called, "and draw your revolvers. Look for a raid." Every nerve in his body tightened. "Test for gas!" There seemed to be little. He took off his mask and walked into the wind to look. A nightly sanitary patrol had spread chloride of lime. The breeze had blown the fumes straight to their positions. "Damn dumb fools," he raged at the stupidity of throwing chlorine upwind of guns the night of a raid.

The men giggled over the joke, but Tydings suddenly remembered the others in the trenches. He had to let them know it was a false alarm. He crept over and called quietly, "Hey fellows." In an instant there was a bayonet at his breast, another at his belly. "Hands up! Give us the pass," a voice snarled.

"Wait a minute. You scared it out of me," Tydings said weakly. "I'm from the machine gun company right over there." He was sickened by the thought that he might be killed by his own men. With hesitation they let him go. Tydings fell limply.

There were still two and a half hours to go. The wait grew unbearable. Finally a faint light appeared in the east. The raid had been called off. The rocket, fired by an Alsatian spy, possibly had tipped off the enemy. Tydings believed the general acted wisely. "Raids must succeed, not fail," he wrote. "Failure kills the dash and fighting spirit of the troops. . . . But what a night!"

Immediately after that, Tydings was promoted to major and transferred from Company A of the 112th Machine Gun Battalion to take command of the 111th. He was thrilled, but felt anguish at leaving. "I was greatly attached to the men," he wrote. In the six months of his captaincy there had not been a single AWOL, no man confined to the guardhouse, not one case of venereal disease. "There had, no doubt, been women," he acknowledged. "That was the business of the individual. Our company was no Sunday School." Above all, he was proud of their courage. "As I shook hands with each of them I was almost sorry for my promotion."

Now Tydings commanded four machine-gun companies and two regimental machine-gun companies of the 57th Brigade, a combined strength of 72 guns. He and Kelley surveyed all gun sites in his new sector. They decided to alter the positions to handle at least two indirect fire missions and one or more direct missions, so they could defend themselves in case of attack. The aiming devices' foolproofs were redesigned so gunners could swing from one target to another in the dark. And a new phase of warfare began. They were ordered to harass the Germans at least six times each 24 hours. "The main idea," Tydings wrote in *Machine Gunners,* "was to keep Fritz worried and guessing as to just where and when he could expect to receive these steel invitations to quit the gun for the plow." Two platoons handled the hit-and-run barrages—firing on enemy lines twice a night and once in daylight, 1,000 bullets per sortie. It was exciting work. The problem lay in getting to safe cover fast.

The infantry detested having the machine gunners set up nearby, because inevitably the Germans tried to destroy the guns. "Don't you put those goddamn guns here!" they would yell.

"Where would you have us put them?" Tydings would ask.

"I don't care a damn where you put them. . . . You want to get the hell shot out of us? . . . Why don't you go some place else with them?"

"That's a good suggestion. Shall we carry them over to the German trenches and shoot them from there?"

Such exchanges occurred dozens of times. A sense of humor helped.

Air battles grew nasty. Daily, four German observation balloons floated high in the air, while behind Tydings's position French balloons sailed. French and German planes swooped about trying to shoot down the balloons and each other. Machine-gun squadrons on airplane duty sent up streams of bullets, but the Germans sometimes got through. Balloons would burst into flames, and men would watch the French observer bail out in his silk parachute.

The front came noisily, vividly alive. Shells exploded, night patrol rifles rang out, and machine guns rattled staccato bursts. Dainty white smoke plumes blossomed in the sky as anti-aircraft shells sought to destroy inquisitive aircraft. Silent flares and star shells produced a surrealistic Fourth of July display. Tydings's chronicle pulsed with sounds and images: a shell's concussion extinguishing a candle flame, the high whine of bullets, a thud followed by trembling earth, geysers of soil raining to the ground, the cannon's booming rumble, a soft "pop" of a signal flare, red streaking flames, thick black smoke—the dreaded nightsong; the "hymn of hate."

At this time, mid-September, Tydings's billet was five kilometers from the front, in the home of a French farmwoman. He commuted to the front by motorcycle sidecar. When there was activity, he slept in the trenches; when quiet, he stretched out between clean sheets. One night a plane droned low overhead, barely 100 yards from the ground, illuminated by moonlight. "Is it ours or German?" he wondered. Two rockets fired by the pilot brought an instantaneous answer. The entire structure shuddered. Screaming women raced into his room, then dashed down into the cellar. He started to go with them, but changed his mind and leapt into bed. The shells were coming from far off—eight or ten miles—and were of large caliber.

> Z Z Z Z Z Z Z Z Z Z Z Whitz Z Z Z Z Whitz Ger-Boom, Ger-B o o o mmm. God! One would come through the roof next. I tried to take my mind off of it but couldn't. . . .
>
> Cries outside. A woman and children burst in the front door and into my room in the darkness. The children were screaming and crying. I turned on a flash light and ushered them down in the cellar with the others. Then back into my bed. . . . Oh, for a hole in the ground!

After 20 terrible minutes it was over. The women and children crept out of the cellar, the children whimpering softly. It was hours before he could sleep. In the morning his hostess led him to the back door. "*Voilà!*" she exclaimed, pointing to a huge shell hole not 50 feet from the house. There was another in front, and Tydings saw dozens of large earthen clods scattered about the slanted roof. He felt lucky to be alive.

Local Alsatians had revealed headquarters location to the Germans. Tydings decided to write home about the incident, but changed his mind. "They were already imagining enough. 'I'm in excellent health. We are still in a quiet section,' I wrote to Mother." But he dwelled on his narrow escape: "A feeling that if I was to go, I would be killed and if I wasn't to go, I wouldn't be killed came into my thoughts. . . . I had become a fatalist," he wrote in his memoirs. "I felt that I would come out of the war unhurt."

Tydings's group was chosen for another major raid. They needed telephone communication to coordinate the action. Signalmen ran wires from each machine-gun company to where Tydings would direct the barrages. All conversation was heard by induction, which meant the Germans could listen in. So codes were devised: "Wilson" meant "all right," "Belfort" meant "commence firing," and "hot dogs" meant "cease firing."

At the appointed hour Tydings, who had taken up position in a tree, yelled, "Belfort!" In an instant his three companies opened fire, as did the artillery. Bullets crackled over his head. "The air was sick with noise," he wrote. Suddenly a Very-pistol light fired from no-man's-land: The raiding party was headed back. Tydings seized the phone and shouted, "Hot dogs!" Two of his captains answered, "Wilson!" No word from the third. The line had been severed. He could hear the guns. They might hit the returning men—and the Germans would see the men when the mist lifted.

Tydings dropped out of the tree. He had to reach them before daylight. He found his driver, Allen, with the sidecar in the woods. When they reached a narrow road Tydings yelled, "Give her hell!" Allen hit the gas so hard that Tydings nearly flew out of his seat. By the time they got there, the company had ceased firing. Many of the men were shell shocked. "Great work, boys," Tydings said in praise. "You fellows were the real thing."

The raid demolished the trenches; the enemy counterraided. Tydings began staying at the front at night: It was safer there. Like everyone else, he had a perpetual case of the nerves, imaging he heard Germans sneaking across no-man's-land. He detested the game, and meditated on it at night in the trenches.

> Over there are Germans standing in their trenches just as we are here. They have had four years of this. Poor devils. They must be sick of it. They [too] have wives, mothers, families. . . . Strange how much asininity is engendered by national boundary lines. Those boundary lines were made by man, not God. God gave man the whole earth. . . . Is national pride a curse or a virtue? . . .
>
> Suppose on a certain spot all the Germans and French, English and Americans would be assembled. We could settle the thing in an hour. . . . If I could meet with the Germans over in

that trench we could fraternize over a bottle of beer and turn the whole thing over for arbitration. . . . There have been wars and wars and wars. . . . Why can't we settle the thing? It seems so easy, yet it is so difficult. It's like having a key in your hand in the dark and feeling for the keyhole. . . . After the war is over, they will go on just the same until the next one. The people will forget, and besides, there is more universal greed in peacetime than in wartime. When war comes, people think, but during peacetimes they don't bother to think. . . .

I think of [home and] visualize large crowds at the seashore. They are bathing, laughing, dancing, . . . beach strollers move up and down and there will be chaps splashing water on flirtatious women. . . . There will be complaints about the flies and mosquitoes. All life is comparative. Little luxuries to some are big luxuries to others. Here I don't mind too much the lice or rat tails running over my face at night. . . .[P]eople back home will never understand, or correctly imagine this war as it is over here.

Tydings received a rare reward; eight hours' leave with permission to go to Belfort, a lovely town of 10,000 with restaurants, white tablecloths, civilization, and women. "I long to feel the touch of a woman's hands, hear a woman's talk and laughter. I would like to hold one in my arms. . . . Allen drives me in the side car. We separate to meet again at eleven. I think I know what's in Allen's mind. Does he guess what's in mine?"

In early September "latrine gossip" had it that they were to move to another sector. When it was confirmed, the news did not make them happy. They knew the Haute-Alsace and felt relatively secure. They also knew they undoubtedly would join bigger battles, perhaps in worse places. On September 23 a new division arrived to replace them.

The next morning the Blue and Gray machine gunners assembled in heavy rain to head north. There was scant space in the boxcars, so the soaking men crammed themselves on top of guns, equipment, and carts. The downpour continued as they marched ten muddy miles to Rembercourt, where they were herded alongside army trucks driven by Indochinese drivers imported by the French, and were told to wait. Three miserable days and nights were spent in drenching rains. Forbidden to board the vehicles or to pitch tents, they slept on the ground. Flu and pneumonia took their toll. Tydings was incredulous over the stupidity of the orders. "I pass the word that orders forbid this [sheltering or sleeping in the trucks] but all officers are assembling at the rear of the column. That is enough. They understand . . . and climb into the trucks." Other officers were not so solicitous; most units awaiting orders at Rembercourt suffered many casualties from illness.

Yet Tydings savored a sweet respite while stranded there. His close friend Jack McGuire, an infantry surgeon, came searching for him. He had stumbled onto a two-inch-thick beefsteak and two young French women who he swore were raving beauties. Tydings needed no further inducement.

"One is a handsome brunette, brown, black-lashed eyes, fine strong features. The other, brown haired and blue eyes. . . . I'm more than content with the brunette. The mother of these two sisters came in. She is a widow, whitehaired, in dark dress," he wrote of the pleasant interlude.

"*Tres belle, n'est-ce pas?*" one of the daughters said, referring to the steak. "You wish him now?" A long-handled pan over hot coals, with a lump of real butter, held the steak, which produced a tantalizing aroma and sizzle. McGuire brought out two bottles of genuine champagne.

"We fall on the beefsteak [and learn] that the French family has had [none] for weeks," he wrote. One brother has been killed in the war; another is at the front. "[But] they do not allow us to dwell long on the unpleasantness of the war," he noted. "At the door I cling to her hand and press it tightly. . . . Doctor Jeckyl and Mr. Hyde—I am transformed from a dinner guest to a soldier on leaving."

The Allied armies were on the move, poised to cross the Meuse River to begin what would be the war's last major offensive. The battle had commenced while Tydings's men were at Rembercourt, covered by what was the greatest artillery barrage in history. The army's advance along the river's west bank had gained perhaps ten kilometers; the Blue and Gray's 58th Brigade had crossed at Charny and driven the Germans back. Tydings's men finally received orders (the empty trucks one morning abruptly drove off), and they marched for four rain-soaked days to Moulin Brule, south of Verdun, slogging 15 kilometers at night, sleeping days to avoid observation by enemy airmen.

The route to the front was snarled with two-way traffic; men, mules, horses, trucks, carts, wagons, ambulances, supplies, food, and ammunition trekked up one side and straggled back the other on a narrow road pock-marked with shell craters. All unnecessary noise was avoided; no talking. Only the roar and flash of artillery accompanied them. There were no good places to sleep. Tydings despaired over the suffering of his troops. "I hunted up a French farmer and bargained for enough straw for eleven hundred beds for my battalion. Without any authority whatsoever I signed an order directing payment which I gave to the farmer." His men slept well.[2]

On October 7, as the battle raged, the 57th Brigade prepared to cross the Meuse. General LeRoy Upton ordered Tydings to take his men upriver to a new bridge and report to him at the Côte de Roches. They marched about four kilometers and left the road, but the bridge had been destroyed. Tydings deliberated whether to retrace their steps through the valley or take a direct route over a high hill to the bridge Upton's infantry had crossed. He and the men opted for the latter. A downpour began. Mules and horses strained, but their hooves sank deep into the soil and they refused to pull the equipment. Tydings and others tried to shove the carts themselves, and then rehitched several of the animals to a single cart to draw each of the 200 carts. "I have been up and down that hill a hundred times," Tydings wrote of the ordeal. "We are dead tired and covered with mud. So are the animals."

Artillery blazed away nearby. Someone told Tydings 3,000 pieces of artillery were firing. "They light the sky with streaks of flame. The big guns roll and thunder," he wrote. "All we know is that it is a tremendous attack and that soon we will be hurled into it."

The exhausted men and beasts pushed on. At each road leading toward the river Tydings searched for a bridge. An officer they met told them the bridge they sought had been blown up. They must go back. They struggled back to the base of the infamous hill. Tydings ordered rest while he reconnoitered. In seconds, the men, mules, and horses were asleep. He found a dugout in the hillside. A sleepy voice told him that the closest bridge was at Charny, six kilometers in the opposite direction. All others had been destroyed. Close to panic, Tydings urgently described to the lieutenant of engineers how they had searched all night for a bridge, his men were totally worn out from marching 12 hours in the cold rain and mud, and that, if he could not cross the river, his division would have to attack without machine-gun cover. "I've got every machine gun company in our brigade out here on the road!" he gasped.

"Well you can't help it," the lieutenant in the dugout said. "It's not your fault. . . . You can't possibly make Charny by day light."

One of Tydings's officers entered the dugout. "Major, if you say 'push on' we'll do it. But the men are exhausted. Besides, I don't believe the damn animals will pull." It was 3:00 A.M. "Let the men sleep til daylight," Tydings said. He collapsed onto a wooden table nailed to the dugout wall and fell dead asleep in jam spilled all over it. At dawn they moved out to Charny where a pontoon bridge lay intact. The attack—as it turns out —was planned for the *following* day, so Tydings's story only made General Upton laugh.

When finally the attack began, Tydings went on horseback with Colonel William Pope as artillery and gas shells sprayed the advancing columns. Pope and Tydings rode forward to rally the men. "The two horses are flying past the troops toward the head of the column. Pope is a good soldier. His galloping past them this way cannot but put heart into his men."

They surveyed the front. Tydings dismounted. He cautiously crept forward, past the front line, sneaking up quietly on a pit six feet deep with a German Minniewerfer within and several machine guns nearby. Three German soldiers lay dead, one hit square in the face, head mashed in; and three others, crouching and slowly raising their hands, cried, "*Kamerade!* " He took them prisoner and rejoined Pope.

Ormont Wood, on the crest of a slope, became the Germans' main line of resistance. Assault would be difficult, given its open valley in full enemy view. But orders came from the French high command to attack—and for the two regimental machine-gun companies to join the infantry to get their weapons to the front. The heavy guns could not be fired when carried, though, and borne on shoulders, they slowed the men down. For artillery cover, there would be only four three-inch cannons. Tydings was furious. But reluctant to complain to officers of a foreign army, he detailed the two machine-gun companies, led by Captains William Keating and George Butcher, to accompany the assault. "I felt that I was issuing sure death warrants," he wrote.

He could not sleep and raced to headquarters to find the American in charge. "The air was so hot and stuffy I could hardly breathe. . . . I found [Colonel] Brown in a little room at one end. He had his coat off and was dripping perspiration. . . . This had to be his first battle"—an unnerving realization. Tydings brought up the lack of support: Something had to be done. "Going up that hill without any artillery cover to keep the Germans down in their trenches will be murder," he said. If the colonel would let him, he could provide cover. Brown was elated. Tydings pressed to get Keating and Butcher's companies withdrawn from the assault to help furnish the barrage. No, the colonel said, they had been ordered to go.

At least they would have cover, Tydings grimly said to himself, and sent for Captain Dennis Doyle. They devised a plan for Doyle's 12 guns to take a position overlooking the German trenches and commence firing as the assault began. He knew Doyle's group would suffer casualties, but without them the infantry and his machine gunners would incur terrible losses.

For 15 minutes prior to the attack, the four French guns lobbed shells about Ormont Wood; heavy German artillery shelled the American area. Doyle's guns opened up. His men were so well hidden that Tydings could not see a soul, but the hail of bullets loosed on enemy trenches called down on them the hottest barrage Tydings had witnessed. "It literally rained shells . . . the ground there was a series of earthen fountains. Through the din I could still hear Doyle's machine guns tack, tack, tacking away. But it was sickening to see the shelling they were taking." Tydings turned to Colonel Pope. "They can't possibly live through it."

Still the guns fired steadily. But the advance was in trouble. German machine guns extracted a heavy toll; shells blew some of the men up into the air. Tydings looked back at Doyle's emplacement. Daggers of flame from shell fire flashed about it. "I was sick," he wrote. The two machine-gun companies with the assault battalions were helpless. "All they could do was lug their pieces over the open ground from shell hole to shell hole." And Doyle's men were being massacred. When Doyle's guns grew silent, Tydings raced through the woods to summon stretchers. A few men came over the hill. That was all that was left, he agonized. Then Doyle appeared, helping carry some wounded. "I embraced him in my delight at seeing him still alive."

One of the wounded was a youth of eighteen or nineteen, hit with parts of a shell in the abdomen. "I know he is dying and take one of his hands in the two of mine. His eyes move over to me with a fixed look. I want to tell him something but words are difficult to utter. 'The barrage you boys fired saved many a life, soldier. . . . God bless you.' " A faint smile answered him, and Tydings turned away to hide tears.

They had taken the west end of Ormont Wood—now called "Death Valley." General Upton returned to command. He was furious over the assault's inadequate artillery support. "It was murder," he said.

The front on the east bank of the Meuse River was nearly a straight line. Other attacks had given the Americans the hills to the left of Death Valley, overlooking the deep Molleville Ravine; but one section of Ormont Wood was yet to be taken, an area of wooden heights. From there the Germans threatened Pope's flank and rear. Upton decided on a morning attack. He ordered the kitchens to the front before the men moved out. Horses drew up under cover of dark, and the kitchen corps carried coffee, hash, and water all night to the front. At dawn the Germans, seeing movement or smoke from the kitchen, let loose a withering barrage. Tydings raced over to help.

It is a ghostly sight. Dead horses are strewn about . . . [others] have broken loose. Some are walking about dragging their intestines. There are wicked cuts and gashes on the bodies of others. These poor animals stand about trembling. The cooks and men of the kitchen force had jumped into the cover of fox holes. There was not time to look after the horses. . . . Strangely I feel almost more pity for these dead and wounded animals than I would feel if they were human beings. . . . They rely on us to protect them, and we have broken this trusting faith.

They took Ormont Wood. Now that they had crossed Molleville Ridge, only Etraye's Ridge remained in German hands. From there the Kaiser's army looked down the ravine, streaked red and yellow by cold October nights, and threatened the entire front. The Blue and Gray at Meuse-Argonne now formed the center of a front hundreds of miles long—a giant arc. They were the pivot of an invisible steel bar prying the enemy back, and the area of wooded hills above the Meuse was the fulcrum. Pressure must first be applied on the heights of Etraye's Ridge to break that last German hold inside the Allied line.

It was Tydings's turn to lead the reserve company's cover of the impending attack. He refused to use those who had survived the previous assault. He consulted with Keating, just off the front line. "Keating takes his strenuous days in front of Ormont Wood very philosophically," Tydings wrote. "I feel he is damn loyal. He showed me a picture of the girl whom he is going to marry after the war. Will I stay for supper he asked."

Six of them squatted down with beefsteak and potatoes in their mess pans and ate until their hunger was alleviated. Then they talked about all manner of things: how good the steak was, how women fought in the Russian Army. Someone asked if Tydings thought the diplomats were trying to settle the war. "Yes," he responded, "and quarreling over the phraseology of documents while we hold the front."

Would they ever get relief? "When we get relief I want a woman first of all," said one, voicing the thoughts of every man there, Tydings wrote.

They dispersed. The stars were out—as were high explosive shells and phosgene gas. A captured German possessed papers that translated: "Hold the line! Remember the Fatherland!" Tydings reflected on the evening's events: "How alike is the tone of [the orders we read]—ours and the Germans. Even in the forthrightness of war one finds a wealth of hypocrisy. Necessary? Yes, because the sophistries of peace fit us for the sophistries of war." A new divisional order that praised their conduct at Ormont Wood and ordered the taking of Etraye's Ridge ended on this note: "Fortunately what is ahead is not so serious or trying as what is already behind." Tydings contemplated the phrase.

Is my death ahead? That's damn serious to me and mine! Nevertheless, like all the rest I'm glad to get this indirect word of communication. It makes killing other men worthwhile because, if we *can* kill them all, the praise will be the more lavish. That's it! I'm to live for just two things now. First to kill! Second to be rewarded for killing! But what of the dead? Where is their praise?[3]

And there were so many. One company of six officers and 266 men had come out of the Ormont with a remnant of 36. Among the dead were Percy Fyle and Bob Frederick. With Joe Davis's death, that meant three of the 16 who started together were gone. Tydings sat quietly remembering when he and Fyle crossed into Mexico in the blistering heat of Eagle Pass. Fyle, he recalled, had played the piano. "The last time I heard him, he played Chaminade's Scarf Dance. . . . I'll miss him!—miss him! Why did he have to go?"[3]

Keating and Butcher's machine-gun companies had been weakened badly. Word of new casualties kept coming in. The sense of loss and waste at Fyle's and Frederick's deaths hit him hard. "A feeling of vengeance possessed me. By the gods, they shall pay for this. Just wait! No. There is nothing in that view. It's the game. It's the war. Haven't the Germans had friends killed too—and what about their families?"

General Upton sent for Tydings on October 20. He had ordered the signal corps to lay telephone wires. For security, everyone was addressed in code. Tydings's code was "Mustard." "Hello, Mustard," Upton said as he opened a large map marking their positions in red crayon. "We're going to take Etraye's Ridge . . . on October 23, commencing at dawn." Pointing to illustrate, Upton told him they needed plenty of machine-gun cover. "Look the area over, then give me a plan."

In the morning Tydings glided through the woods, passing several new cemeteries with fresh graves and wooden crosses hung with metal identification tags—Americans, Austro-Hungarians, and Germans side by side. In a beautiful meadow he saw at least 30 American dead laid out, coats over their faces.

He arrived at the front line on the south side of Molleville Ravine. The woods were thick, the underbrush nearly impassable.

Across the ravine the Germans were entrenched at Etraye's Ridge. The bottom of the ravine was 50 yards wide and bare. At Etraye's Ridge it was some 300 feet deep so that Etraye's towered 100 feet over Molleville Ridge. Without the thick woods and underbrush, the Germans—from their fortified observation nests and towers—could have seen the Americans dug into the front of a mere quarter of a mile away. From the famous Pylone Observatory on Etraye's Ridge they had an unobstructed view of Allied lines as far away as Verdun.

Tydings knew the slope on the ravine's south side would afford excellent cover. He marked the ten best locations and headed back. The strategy he devised to execute Upton's plan was brilliant and unorthodox.

Upton intended an attack from the east. All previous attacks in the Meuse-Argonne offensive had been to the north. Now, instead of advancing north, Upton's infantry would go along the east–west ridge, hitting the Germans in the flank. Heavy artillery would precede and accompany the attack. The 110th and 112th Machine Gun Battalions, positioned behind the troops, would fire over their heads.

Tydings planned to divide his 111th into four groups 200 yards apart along Molleville Ridge, all ahead of the infantry advance. Each would have five or six guns. Only one group would fire at a time. As the infantry advanced, Tydings told Upton, his gunners would shoot directly across their front line, so that the bullets would fall 150 yards in front of them, keeping the Germans on Etraye's Ridge under "an endless band of steel bullets."

Since Upton called for the men to move 100 meters every 10 minutes, the 111th's fire would move at the same rate. When the troops arrived opposite the first group of machine guns, the second would take over and gradually move their fire eastward until the infantry picked up the third, and then fourth, group of guns. The line of fire—continuous and withering—would stay ahead of the men until the objective was reached, instead of having to cease abruptly—as with an overhead barrage—when the troops approached. His strategy, an interlocking barrage paralleling the line of advance, was approved without hesitation by Upton.

The next day Upton called him in. "I'm sorry, Mustard, but

Division Headquarters has sent word that we cannot use your machine guns." Shooting across the front of assault troops was too dangerous. Tydings argued and explained the series of five aiming stakes for each gun: Every ten minutes the gunners would swing the guns gradually from west to east, from one aiming stake to the next, each stake calculated to represent a 100-meter advance. There was no other way, Tydings insisted, to penetrate the thick German cover. Given the terrain, it was safer to shoot ahead of them than over their heads in the usual manner.

"Let's see what can be done," Upton said. He got on the phone. "About this plan of Mustard's. You understand? I think it's a mistake to abandon it." A long conversation ensued. Tydings could hear only Upton's occasional, "I would like to use them. . . . I don't agree. . . . Wait a minute." With his hand over the transmitter, Upton asked, "Are you ready to assume full responsibility for the safe use of those guns?"

"Yes, sir."

Upton said into the phone, "Yes, I'll assume full responsibility." After he hung up he told Tydings, "I want you to make sure everything goes right."

Headquarters' refusal of his plan planted doubts in Tydings's mind. He refigured all the firing data and found no errors. He told his captains—Doyle and Norman White—about Upton's call. "For God's sakes, fellows, watch those gunners. Make sure they keep swinging their guns. . . ."

"What the hell does an operations officer know about machine guns?" Doyle snorted. "Those swivel chair artists at headquarters!"

At dawn on October 23, a deafening artillery barrage commenced. At 6:15 A.M. the men moved due east, and White's guns opened up due north to begin the interlocking barrage. As the troops moved, the guns swung. German machine guns, pointing down the barren pathway in the ravine, were ineffective. The advance cleared White's first group, and his second opened fire; then Doyle's companies put down their curtain of fire. Enemy shells fell on the ravine below, on the ridge, and up and down the roads. As Doyle's second group withdrew, Etraye's Ridge was in American hands. They held the highest ground east of the Meuse River. Infantry losses were light. More than 60 abandoned German guns were found as they overran Etraye's Ridge.

Spirit and morale among the officers and men was sky high. Everyone was talking about Tydings's barrage. No one in the advance was hit by the 111th's fire. White, Doyle, and Tydings were jubilant. Upton gloated. "I guess G-3 will let us alone now." Headquarters, too, credited Tydings's gunners with the success. "Damn good day's work!" Pope congratulated Tydings.

"Thank God it's over," Tydings replied.

But it wasn't. Airplanes went up to determine exactly where the front line was. This was essential information as the artillery had to maintain a barrage while the troops consolidated, but must not mistakenly shell their own. But Pope had not been able to pin down precisely the location of the front. Artillery was pressuring him. Intelligence had not come up with anything. Pope's phone rang. It was Upton, wanting Tydings. "Mustard, there's not a damn word yet as to our positions on Etraye's. . . . I sent two dumb fools up there to locate it and I've no answer yet." Find the front, he ordered, "and don't come back until you do. Better take an orderly with you."

Tydings was in a fury. "These goddam infantry men, you've got to shoot them to an objective and then go find them," he raged. "Can't the damned infantry find the position on a map? . . . Intelligence officers!—a lot of damn ignorant damn fools—intelligence officers!—who named them that anyhow."

He finally cooled down. As he passed a nearby company, he ordered a first sergeant to accompany him. He stripped off his oak leaves. The front line would be thinly held, and he could walk right into the arms of the Germans. He and the sergeant walked briskly up a hill, the sergeant about 50 feet behind so they could not be felled by the same shell. It was nearly dusk, twilight serenade in full crescendo, shells falling in the woods beside the path.

Tydings's mind was fixed on the sergeant. Dragging him along was nothing but cowardice, he chided himself. "Suppose he gets hit; his blood will be on your hands." He argued with his conscience. "But suppose I'm hit there may be no one to see it and I may die. Yes, but . . . having him with you won't stop you from being hit." He stepped behind a large tree and signaled the sergeant. " 'I don't see any use of your going along,' I said, half regretting my words as I uttered them."

The sergeant refused to leave. But Tydings knew the young man had to be as torn as he was. It took some persuasion, but soon the sergeant was loping back down the path. Tydings watched him go. A beautiful mackerel sky was spread out over the horizon. The sun's low rays transformed tufts of clouds into "rubies and fiery opals." Trees were silhouettes. He looked at the sight, determined to remember.

"Suddenly an aeroplane flying low came over Etraye's Ridge straight toward me." He leapt into the brush. The sky showed no glint of metal. He resumed his descent. In a moment a trail of dirt churned behind him and he ran through the bush, tearing his face and hands in the briers, ripping his uniform as he threw himself on his stomach. He lay there until the plane had gone. He stood up. In seconds the plane swooped over the ridge and Tydings ran like a wild man through the brush, slashing his hands and face until blood trickled. Near panic he sat immobile in the darkening woods until the plane had not returned for five minutes. The injustice of his mission came back into his mind: "I thought I could shoot down those intelligence officers who had failed to do their work . . . if I could find them," he wrote.

German shelling was formidable. At the bottom of Molleville Ravine he found a dugout with 20 men and an officer inside. The officer had broken from the pressure. "For God's sake get me out of here," he began shrieking at Tydings. "I'm not fit to command." Tydings immediately noticed the men watching him. The effect of a hysterical officer was devastating to morale. "I fell back on the sophistries of our divisional order hardly without thinking. 'It's all right now, old fellow. We licked them,'" he said. "'Lie down and get a rest and you'll be all right.'" He backed out of the dugout. "This damn fellow had unnerved me."

Shelling grew heavier. He suddenly saw Captain Butcher with an infantry major named Stone. They dashed into an old German dugout. It was packed with men. They decided it would be safer to run for other cover. Butcher and Stone dashed into a sandbagged hut with Tydings close behind. They found a candle and examined the shelter. Built in the side of a hill, it was 12 feet long, eight wide, and seven high with a wooden floor, stout planking door, no windows. A sound like pebbles on tin drew their gazes up. The roof was thin, corrugated iron. A shell could rip it like paper. The fear returned.

Helplessly listening to the explosions was maddening. The ravine's steep sides caught the noise and hurled echoes back and forth. They considered abandoning the hut but decided it would be worse outside. Shrapnel battered the door and pounded on the iron roof. Tydings was certain he was going to die in that hut. Sitting on the edge of a cot he began to pray. "This is the end, God take care of me," ran endlessly through his mind. Each explosion sounded as if the next would burst through the metal overhead.

"This is the end, God take care of me." Thirty minutes had gone by. "Yes, you ask God to take care of you when you're going to die," Tydings railed at himself in silent communication. "Why didn't you think more of Him when you were back in civil life? God take care of me. I promise I'll be a better man if you do."

The men finally tried talking to each other to bolster their spirits and control their fear. Suddenly the shelter shuddered as if it would fly to pieces. "We each jumped up instinctively and for a moment blinked before we knew that it had not killed us." Butcher cracked. "I can't stand it, I can't stand it," he screamed, both hands to his head, "I'm going mad!"

"Stone and I put our arms around him. He had but expressed our own thoughts which we were fighting to keep within us," Tydings wrote. Butcher dropped to the cot, weeping. More pebbles hit the roof.

"Finally a quiet came upon me and I resolved to die," Tydings wrote. " 'God forgive me my sins and bless my mother, father, sisters and everybody.' I was still afraid but not nearly so much. The shelling had killed my spirit of resistance." Then a strange thought struck him. " 'The Germans are your brothers—pray for them. God bless the Germans,' I said inwardly. And so we sat in silence. Butcher became quiet, too, and after two hours the shells stopped falling next to us."

They went out into the ravine where darkness had settled like a blanket. The moonless sky was brilliant with stars. They breathed in the fresh, chilly air. There was nothing Tydings could do to locate the front line in the pitch black night. As Stone and Butcher left to find their units, Tydings pulled some blankets around him and fell exhausted onto the cot.

At 4:00 A.M., light shelling jarred him instantly awake. At daybreak he set out, walking and crawling to the top of Etraye's Ridge. Climbing a tree, he gained an unobstructed view of the German lines and sketched a careful map of their positions.

Once back safe behind the lines, he searched for the head commanding general's dugout. The deep underground passages were unfamiliar, running endlessly in many directions. In a state of agitation he finally cornered someone to direct him. The man looked him over with undisguised curiosity; covered with mud, Tydings wore a two-day stubble of beard and no insignia on his tattered uniform. He staggered on, knocked on the designated door; no answer. He knocked again.

> Same result. I turned the door handle and walked in. The General, clad in an abbreviated night shirt, was about to get into bed. "Mustard reporting, Sir."
>
> "What the hell do you mean, walking into the quarters of your Commanding General!" he roared, red-faced with anger.
>
> "I'm sorry, Sir, but I thought it important—"
>
> "Butcha didn't knock! Who the hell are you?"
>
> "Sir, you wanted me—" I began but his bellow interrupted me. "Butcha didn't knock. Now get out!"

Tydings slumped out the door trembling with rage. He reported to one of the aides, and John Koch found him to give him his bedroll and food.[4]

Just before the 29th was relieved from duty at the Meuse-Argonne, heavy artillery and machine-gun barrages were launched by the enemy to prevent the arrival of fresh troops and supplies. Orders came to strengthen positions in case of counterattack. A machine-gun squad of the 114th Company was assigned to fire a barrage. The enemy shelled them severely; the gunners took refuge in a dugout contaminated by poison gas. Captain Keating found the men in terrible shape and called Captain Butcher for assistance; together they volunteered to fire the barrage themselves. The Germans spotted them. A blizzard of shells killed both. Tydings went numb. They had been through so much together and survived, only to have an heroic gesture kill them.

On the nights of October 29 and 30, the Blue and Gray marched to Bar le Duc, 30 miles behind the front and began to overhaul their equipment for the next operation. Tydings was promoted to lieutenant colonel on November 7 and made divisional machine-gun officer for the Blue and Gray, replacing Colonel Kelley. On November 11, 1918, he and his men were marching to Metz to participate in the planned capture of that great fortress city, the last stronghold of the German Army. While moving wearily along they received word that the Armistice had been signed. A friend of Tydings's, who also was marching that day, had seen the lieutenant colonel leading his machine gunners down the road. "I will never forget him or the fellows coming alone the road to Metz," he told the senator's wife long after the war. "They were the most exhausted, discouraged looking bunch I ever saw, slogging along toward what they all must have figured would be certain death."

Tydings had used those exact words himself in describing his fears at the time. It would surely be his turn, he had thought as he grimly trudged through frozen mud. The following day, after 11:11 A.M., church bells in the villages began to peal. Throngs of people appeared, some dazed, some shouting, and others weeping in joy and relief. Finally it was truly over.

In the years following the war, after he grew powerful, Tydings often was criticized by rivals and the press for being arrogant and so confident that he appeared untroubled by doubts. Those who so labeled him knew little of what lay beneath the proud facade. The young man who served in the war had lived with self-doubt, fear, and fallibility as daily companions. His personal writings candidly reveal a frightened soldier, sometimes angry at exposure to mortal danger. They also depict a brave and intelligent leader, compassionate and psychologically astute with those under his command.

His chronicles delineate an abhorrence of war, a reverence for life. His reflections resonate with acute discomfort over the "sophistries of war" that sanctioned legal slaughter. He had witnessed the madness and absurdity of war and knew it for what it was. His later crusade for disarmament was born in the trenches of World War I.

He demonstrated an ability to function and lead even while overwhelmed by near-debilitating fear. He was fully cognizant that signs of distress serve no purpose—and can be destructive. That knowledge demanded he separate personal feeling from outward attitude. He willed himself to live a double life, one private, one public. He felt a deep sense of responsibility for his actions—the consequences in terms of flesh and blood and death. Internal dialogues focused on values and philosophy, cowardice and courage. He understood that the closer men were to combat, the less they should dwell on it. He spent hours chatting with them about food, women, faraway places, helping put the war at a distance. Incompetence infuriated him, but fear he understood and tried to soothe. He would go to almost any lengths to satisfy orders yet protect his men.

His experiences reinforced and refined two innate qualities: optimism and tenacity—attributes the army considers essential to leadership. *Infantry in Battle,* a basic army source book (George C. Marshall, director), defines "optimism" as the conscious ability to resist discouragement, and shore up determination; and "tenacity" as the relentless pursuit of the specific goal, without being so stubborn as to be unable to change one's method. Tydings became the consummate practitioner of optimism and tenacity. Then there was courage: to be vulnerable and still take a stand. Soldiers and officers of the Blue and Gray recognized Tydings as one of the few graced with those qualities. What was innate in the boy became etched into the character of the man. The major who convinced the colonel to use a machine-gun barrage at Ormont Wood, who fought for his plan at Etraye's Ridge, was a far cry from the hesitant captain frightened by the prospect of laying a two-minute barrage on Ammertzviller Trench in Alsace.

He was loved by his men and loved them in return. He inspired loyalty, motivated those in his command by example and obvious concern. Exhausted, bloody, emaciated, lice-infested, muddy, nerves strained to the breaking point, he and his men came out of their experience radiating pride in achievement. "The thing that made us love him was because he *led* his men," said one of his wartime comrades.

Tydings's handwritten record becomes more revealing when contrasted with his book, *The Machine Gunners of the Blue and Gray Division*. The impersonal voice of the latter—stunningly different from the emotional, often harrowing manuscript—tells none of his own story, it makes no mention of his acts of courage, strategic innovations, or misgivings. He refused to glorify war the way some do after surviving its hardships. The separation he maintained between public and private writings mirrored the separation he effected to keep from showing fear. Yet compassion slips out between the lines in *Machine Gunners* as he singled out not only Doyle, Keating, and Butcher, but those who seldom rate mention in accounts of war: the cooks, chaplains, burial details, the mule skinners, the horses. He understood the integral connection among all segments of an army, no matter how unglamorous the roles, and understood the pain engendered by the brutal, random finality of death.

In the book, the Ormont Wood assault—where the handwritten account says he despaired bitterly over Keating and Butcher's companies' unnecessary exposure, and volunteered a defensive barrage— is described in a removed tone:

> The attacking troops had very little support in the way of artillery and it soon became evident that their mission would be an exceedingly trying one. . . . The commanding officer of the 111th Machine Gun Battalion, on his own initiative, ordered Company A, 111th Machine Gun Battalion, Captain Doyle commanding, to take up a position on the hill about one-half mile southwest of the Bois d'Ormont, for the purpose of delivering an overhead barrage.

Only by sifting through the appendix can a reader discover that the commanding officer was Tydings himself.

As to Etraye's Ridge and his interlocking parallel barrage, the book contains no mention of the brilliance of his plan or the exhilarating vindication. "Both the artillery and machine gun fire was co-ordinated and moved forward in pursuance to a schedule, or time-table, which had been carefully prepared," he wrote. "This attack was a complete success from every angle. The machine guns were effectively and sensibly used and for four hours and thirty minutes kept a continuous barrage in front of our advancing men."

No reader would know he was a hero, yet his strategy at Etraye's was important enough to be incorporated in *Infantry in Battle* as an example of superb use of terrain in defensive cover for an assault. Prepared under the direction of Colonel George C. Marshall, and first published in January 1934, the book is used today as collateral reading at West Point and the other major U.S. Army artillery, infantry, and command staff training schools.

Following an explanatory description of Tydings's strategy at Etraye's Ridge, the text states that the results achieved "were due, almost entirely, to an appreciation of the possibilities proffered by the terrain. . . . It was the ground and its relation to the front line that made this unusual and highly effective machine-gun support possible. As told, it all appears simple and obvious. The terrain was there and the relative positions of the opposing forces offered the opportunity. [But] in this case it was recognized."

Tydings emerged from the war a hero, deserving of the honors bestowed on him: the Divisional Citation, the Distinguished Service Medal, and the Distinguished Service Cross.

The war's experiences critically shaped his life. Everyone has some natural guard and the potential to exercise it to greater or lesser degrees. In childhood he had developed a cautiousness to manage the strain of divided loyalty due to his parents' unhappy marriage—yet had retained an openness with his grandfather. During the war, for reasons of morale and sanity, he learned not to allow others to penetrate his carefully erected wall. He kept outward display of feelings controlled, developing a will of iron to do so. Ed Morgan, committee counsel for the State Department loyalty investigation, said of Tydings many years later, "This man had more total command of himself than anyone I've ever known." He learned that control in the machine-gun emplacements and trenches. The handful of men who had served with him were the only ones he allowed to be close to him after returning to civilian life.

Mayor of Baltimore Thomas D'Alessandro visited Tydings after he became ill late in life. He never forgot the sound of Tydings's voice calling out as if he were back on the battlefield. For when

Tydings lay dying, his mind would sometimes drift free from its moorings and roam unfettered through time and space—not to the wars with Joseph McCarthy or Franklin Roosevelt, but rather to the terrifying and exhilarating days near Verdun, the wretched and noble trenches of the Meuse-Argonne.

Another experience from his days in France taught him to build protective walls and pushed him farther into himself.

At war's end Tydings was ill with the flu; his lungs had been burned by mustard gas. His feet were severely scorched: One night in the November cold, feet nearly frozen, he had placed his leather boots too close to the fire to dry them. When he forced his still tingling feet inside, impurities in the leather seared the soles of his feet. He limped badly from the pain and required medical attention. Once the Armistice was signed, he and his friend "Doc" McGuire were furloughed together to Nice on the French Riviera for rest and recuperation. The warm sun, superb cuisine, and pristine beauty of Southern France worked their magic. Tydings recovered quickly from the flu and the immediate discomfort from the gas—although his lungs suffered a light, permanent scarring. His limp diminished and would eventually disappear, though his feet forever retained deep discolorations.

One afternoon, strolling the promenade beside the sparkling turquoise Mediterranean, Tydings and McGuire noticed two strikingly attractive young women approaching. Tydings's eyes blazed. When the women drew near, he remarked in intentionally loud but conversational tones, "What beautiful girls, Doc. Do you suppose they speak English?"

"Yes, and a lot better than you do," the prettier of the two retorted. The four of them laughed and lingered to chat. The one who had spoken was the daughter of a distinguished French general and had lived in Vienna and London. They all became friends. The spirited young woman and Tydings became inseparable companions. He fell head over heels in love, wrote long romantic poems to her, sang love songs, pursued her tenaciously, gracefully, and ardently. She was a communist by political leaning—most likely a starry-eyed one, a rebellious youth, he thought, given her father's position.

With no promise that she would marry him, he had to return with the army to the United States. He promised to return as soon as he could, and he kept his word. Every summer he sailed to France, waging his transatlantic romance. The last trip was in 1923. He had asked her father for her hand; but time, distance, and a rival apparently as persistent as he had wooed her away. He was a French politician, a member of the Socialist party's left wing, which was engaged in serious flirtation with the Communist Internationale. Tydings was staunchly conservative and just beginning his first term in the U.S. House of Representatives. She married the Frenchman. He turned his formidable energy to politics.

Those deeply wounded by love sometimes do not allow evidence of hurt to show. The positive side of such behavior is the avoidance of self-pity; the negative is a hardening, a retreat to conceal pain. Such personal toughness became characteristic of Tydings. In recalling the wounds Tydings suffered in his 1950 election defeat, Ed Morgan said, "He would not reveal that sense of hurt even to me." His wife was keenly aware of it, too. "He was a man who bottled up his emotions," she remembered.

He did not marry for more than a dozen years although widely considered Washington's most attractive and eligible bachelor. The private man was kept in check; the proud, self-confident public face masked his true feelings. When asked in a 1926 interview, during his first run for the Senate, how a man as attractive, successful, and as avidly pursued by beautiful women as he was, had managed to slip the marriage noose, he was reported to have laughed and said, "Not my fault. All I can do is ask them."

Notes

1. Colonel D. John Markey also served in Tydings's division—the same man who lost the 1950 Maryland Republican primary to John Marshall Butler while excoriating Tydings for whitewashing the loyalty investigation. Tydings's and Markey's careers continuously crossed paths as they continuously crossed swords. Wartime ties were severed by political disagreement and rivalry.

2. A year after he left the service, the War Department sent Tydings a memo asking about the purchase. He explained. They paid the French farmer.

3. A chaplain buried Percy Fyle in a shallow trench with an overcoat over his face. In 1926 Tydings returned to Ormont Wood to try to locate

his grave. He spent three days searching for the mound where Fyle was buried but could not find it in the dense brush that had overgrown the area.

4. When Tydings was in the Senate in the 1930s, this same general—not General Upton—came to see him about a military matter. "We have met before, General," Tydings said evenly as the general made himself comfortable on the other side of the desk. The senator's mind's eye was filled with the picture of that muddy, exhausted young major and the angry general in his nightshirt. The general believed he was mistaken. "No," Tydings said. "In the battle of Etraye's Ridge. When I came to report where the German lines were, and you said, 'But you didn't knock.'" The general had no recollection. Tydings never forgot or forgave.

5

The Accidental Senator

Wars create opportunities for the underdog in America. Old occupations are flung open to greater numbers; new occupations spring up; expansion of industry generates wealth and opportunity. Youths who have risked death and returned as heroes are willing to take risks to succeed, and the infinitely smaller risks of peacetime seem easy compared to what they have endured. They are hungry for challenge and full of confidence which, channeled intelligently into civilian fields, can offer a fair shot at the brass ring.

Coming in on cloud nine, Tydings's first act as a civilian in June 1919 was to buy a fire-engine red Stutz Bearcat. By Christmas he had set up a law partnership with Major Robert H. Archer of the Blue and Gray and purchased a 212-acre farm for development with what was left of his war savings and a bank loan. And he buried his beloved grandfather. Henry O'Neill was ill when Tydings returned, but had welcomed him home joyfully. Just before the old man died, Tydings brought him his faded Civil War flag from the cemetery. He took care of Grandpap's small estate; after paying off debts, he gave his share of the inheritance to his mother. Henry O'Neill's legacy of advice and loans did not make Tydings wealthy, but ensured him a comfortable life.

He considered settling down in Havre de Grace. His law practice was growing and several of his properties sold quickly for a fair profit. (He gave one parcel of land to the town for a park.) Still, he was restless and ambitious, found the life of a country lawyer in a small town too tame and predictable. He missed the exhilaration of debate and action at the Maryland Assembly in Annapolis. Then, too, the politically sophisticated daughter of a French general who knew the capitals of Europe might be bored in rural America—but might find its politics intriguing. By year's end he had won back his old seat in the House of Delegates.

What providence had not done for Tydings, the war did. He had started up the political ladder with no organizational backing, no family wealth or name, just his own confidence and intelligence. Now with his war record and wartime friendships—E. Brooke Lee, William C. Walsh, and William Preston Lane were politically well-connected men from prominent families—Tydings became the fair-haired boy of Harford County. New social and business connections enlarged his network, and college and law school acquaintances remembered his debating genius and analytical skills. He gained support and publicity easily. (During the war his photograph, set above captions such as "Swatting the Hun," had appeared in local papers and in the *Sun*'s photogravure section; articles noted his "unusual precocity" in rising to command a machine-gun battalion nicknamed the "Suicide Squad.") In both the primary and general elections in 1919 he won the largest number of votes cast in the county.

Immediately his name was proposed for speaker of the House, a position of power as well as prestige. He wanted it badly and this time would not let the Baltimore bosses use him as in 1916 when they backed him solely to make the sitting speaker compliant—and forced Tydings to step down when that goal was achieved. The experience taught him how to work with the leaders—and how important independence was. To control his own destiny, without alienating the power brokers, he would build his own personal network. Lee, Walsh, and Lane were rising members of Democratic Governor Albert C. Ritchie's circle. Lee's father, former U.S. Senator Blair Lee, was a Ritchie ally. He was impressed with Tydings, who became a Ritchie leader in Harford County; Ritchie backed him for speaker. The Baltimore machine gave him no trouble.

As speaker he racked up an extraordinary record for economy. The political philosophy that guided him throughout his career began to take shape: his unswerving belief in a classic, conservative, small-"d" democracy; faith in the Jeffersonian ideal, which says the government that governs least, governs best. From the beginning he fought those who opposed his fiscal conservatism, who did not share his mistrust of a federal government steadily encroaching on individual and states' rights. Tydings believed that individuals and states had the right to choose their destinies, and that those rights were fundamental to the American political tradition.

Such ideals and values were more than politics to him. They represented a way of life he fought to preserve. Whether the issue was Prohibition, taxation, creation of new state or federal departments, or alteration of the size of the Supreme Court, he judged it by the effects on individuals' and states' rights—and the power, size, and cost of government. Anything that threatened the American tripartite system—the balance of power among the executive, legislative, and judicial branches—he fought. A centralized government too large and powerful threatened the economic stability of a state or nation, he believed, because bureaucracy inevitably perpetuated itself through the expenditure of money.

In later years Tydings was accused often of being so rigid in his fiscal orthodoxy, so intransigent in his defense of individual and states' rights, that he was insensitive to the poor. The charge was easy to make against those who opposed social programs that enlarged the government's role in people's lives. It was not always a fair assessment. In the Maryland Assembly, he secured a settlement for farmers displaced by the Aberdeen Proving Grounds, as well as fighting for benefits through extending the Workmen's Compensation Law. Veterans' issues always received his special attention.[1]

Of all that he championed as speaker of the House of Delegates, Maryland leaders past and present believed that introducing and effecting passage of the 1920 bill creating the University of Maryland was his most important act. Getting the bill through the Assembly was no small feat. Four attempts from the 1670s to 1907 had been made to found a state university system, but the first three had been foiled. Nevertheless, the idea of consolidating proprietary, religious, and professional colleges and universities in Maryland into a unified system continued to tantalize educators.[2]

In 1912 Maryland Agricultural College suffered a devastating fire, an event that revived the idea of a university system by bringing change: MAC went coed, trimmed its military emphasis, and was renamed Maryland State College of Agriculture. After the war, the American Medical Association decided to eliminate proprietary education; University of Maryland medical faculty frantically sought an undergraduate college to act as base for the formation of a state university. After rejection by St. John's College and others, they approached Maryland State. Their reluctance to merge with a mere agricultural and technical school was mirrored by Maryland State's reluctance to be saddled with the university's enormous debts. Negotiations took months, but by March 1920 the law school had drafted a bill making Maryland State College's trustees the sole directors and owners of all university property—and debts. The combined institutions would take the name University of Maryland.

On March 12 the trustees named a committee "to take the necessary steps to have the bill introduced in the House of Delegates." The committee asked Tydings, an honors graduate of Maryland State College and the University of Maryland Law School, and one of the most influential State House leaders, to introduce the bill. Tydings was happy to help his alma maters. Despite opposition from Governor Ritchie (who thought a merger would prove too costly), Tydings lobbied hard for swift enactment. "The skids were greased," he told his son Joe years later, and the bill slid through the judiciary and education committees within a week. On March 30 it passed the House in an 86–0 vote. The state senate likewise passed it unanimously, and Ritchie signed it into law on April 9, 1920. "Speaker Tydings's Bill" laid the groundwork for what would become one of the world's largest universities.

Tydings did not appear to realize immediately the full import of his achievement; for when he was invited to speak at College Park in June 1920, he dwelled mainly on farm issues, speaking only as a prominent alumnus and not as legislative father of a great university. But Speaker Tydings's Bill was an act of historic importance for higher education in Maryland. In later years he took great pride in having helped to found a new university.

The word on his tenure as speaker was "fairness." Journalists, apparently happy to have a lively young fellow to match wits with, described him as "mischievous," "honest," "unflinching," "affable," and "fair." An editorial summing up his potential commented: "The

Old Democratic war horses recognized him as one of the most promising colts in the pasture."

Tydings was no sooner inaugurated as a state senator (after trouncing a primary rival and burying his Republican opponent) than he set his sights on Congress. He was determined to run without a political machine; but, while not seeking the Baltimore machine's active support, he could not afford to ignore it. Maryland's second district comprised not just Harford, Carroll, and Baltimore counties, but several heavily populated wards in the city. The two main Democratic factions there had locked horns over power for years, with top bosses John J. "Sonny" Mahon and John S. (Frank) Kelly usually at war. Neither was a particularly savory type. Mahon's philosophy—"Politics is my business and I make it pay; I would be a fool not to"—spoke volumes about his character, as did Kelly's nicknames: "Slot-machine Kelly" and "King of the Underworld." Their legendary feuds (they once went four years without speaking) were punctuated by grim truces. In 1922 the Mahon and Kelly factions were quarreling, but the two men were on uneasy speaking terms.

To nail down the congressional nomination and prevent their opposition, Tydings needed their consent. He went to Mahon first. Mahon told him to see Kelly. Kelly referred him back to Mahon, who sidestepped him again. One noon, a frustrated Tydings spied the two lunching together at Baltimore's Rennert Hotel and plunked himself down uninvited. "I want to go to Congress," he said. "I've asked each of you for help several times. Each has sent me to the other. Time is getting short and I want an answer."

The older men glared at each other. Each feared endorsement might force the other into a rival camp in the race. Finally Kelly broke the tension. "Well, you're running, aren't you?" he growled.

"Yes," answered Tydings, grateful for the opening because until that moment he had not been sure he would get to.

"Then get out of here and get going," said Mahon. He did. As neither expressly approved his candidacy, he gained the support of the two factions with no obligations. He ran hard, campaigning on issues that mattered most to Marylanders: economy in government, and modification of the Volstead Act—the law that enforced America's "noble experiment," Prohibition.

The Prohibition issue attracted most attention and gave Tydings his first taste of dirty politics. The Maryland Anti-saloon League, headed by George W. Crabbe, was zealously committed to stamping out alcohol and stomping out "wets," moderates, and anyone else not a lock-stock-and-barrel "dry." Tydings, a moderate, favored local option on drinking and earned the wrath of Crabbe and the League. Dry fanatics everywhere sniffed the air for any scent of alcohol-related scandal. A late-night episode in Annapolis gave them the chance to pounce on Tydings.

After a few drinks at a wild party (he left at midnight just after the girls from Baltimore arrived), Tydings returned to Carvel Hall in a pleasantly mellow condition. A few colleagues were gathered in the smoking room, among them Delegate Horace Davis, driest of the drys. Tydings succumbed to impulse. Squashing Davis's hat down over his ears, he dragged him from his chair, urging cheerfully that they bend an elbow together. Davis, a man without a trace of mirth, rejected the invitation and turned escapade into scandal: Tydings, he announced the next day, had been shockingly intoxicated, had disgraced himself in a drunken brawl, and, furthermore, was bought off by the liquor interests.

Tydings's sense of humor had made him popular in Annapolis. Friendly publicity, his war record, and his skill at demolishing those who would spend frivolously had made him a tough opponent. The Anti-saloon League was desperate for ammunition with which to shoot him down. Tydings had handed Crabbe and the league a loaded gun—and they promptly shot themselves in the foot by accusing him of selling out to the liquor interests. He sued Davis and Crabbe (who had publicized Davis's story) for libel. Four of his colleagues who were present that night backed up his statement that he was only indulging in a little "intentional horse-play" by imitating a drunken person.

He wrote a blistering letter to the Baltimore *Sun:* "I want to ask Mr. Davis in the columns of your paper, . . . did you not have a fist fight with the keeper of a hotel in Snow Hill? And what was your condition of sobriety at the time?" The voters should know, he wrote, what some former mayors and a hotel proprietor knew about the holier-than-thou Mr. Davis. As for Crabbe, who was furious at being sued, "I cannot repress a smile at the acrobatics of Crabbe. It is all right for him to defame me . . . but if I attempt to defend myself by suing . . . I become a foul person." Crabbe was buried in a shower of stars and stripes. "I wish to say to Crabbe that, while he was sitting upon a swivel chair with his feet upon his desk, . . . I had the low position of standing in the muddy trenches of France by the side of real men . . . upholding the Constitution of my country."

Sun readers had gotten their first look at the Tydings modus operandi. Not once did he say that he had not been intoxicated nor that he did not drink.[3] Instead he counterattacked, wrapping his argument in sweet patriotism. In the primary he swamped his dry opponent and won in a landslide in November.

In Washington, Tydings became a careful student of government, quietly learning the fundamentals of parliamentary procedure. The few times he spoke on the House floor he focused on spending and states' rights, arguing against new federal departments. The bigger the bureaucracy, he said, the greater the cost, duplication, and waste—and the more it encroached on areas belonging to the states. He went on record against raising income taxes and proposed that states manage estate and inheritance taxes. Additional federal taxes would extend federal power at the expense of the states, he warned.

He spoke out against the Ku Klux Klan, an action considered risky. When the Klan tried to discredit him for his anti-Prohibition stance, he denounced it and chided its anonymous spokesman. "He hides behind the pen and ink of a false name just like the Klan hides behind its nightgown in the dark. He demands courage of me and shows cowardice himself," he wrote in a letter to the press. Maryland voters showed their appreciation of his aggressive style and conservative stand by reelecting him by an overwhelming majority in 1924.[4]

By 1926 Tydings had grown comfortable in Congress, earning the sobriquet "Glad" Tydings for his outgoing manner. His confidence increased. So did anti-Prohibition sentiment across the nation. Prohibition made his name known outside of Maryland and earned him his spurs on Capitol Hill.

Tydings did not believe in legislating morality. And he regarded the Eighteenth Amendment as encroachment on states' rights and on individual liberties. Local areas should be free to choose, he said on the House floor. It was wrong and unconstitutional for Iowa or

Texas to dictate to Maryland (which had local option regarding liquor before Prohibition). Tydings was no longer merely a moderate, but a whole-hog wet; and, as tempers flared in Congress, he emerged as the new wet leader in the House. Questions designed to bait him drew stinging rebuttals that exposed fundamental flaws of Prohibition—and revealed his skill as a verbal tactician. He believed it unfair that those who wanted to modify Prohibition were accused of being un-American. "So long as I am temperate in habits, what right have you to lay down a code of morals for my personal conduct?" he asked angrily. He denounced its proponents as "superkings" who would deny individuals free choice.

Did not Tydings know, asked Representative William D. Upshaw of Georgia, that the Eighteenth Amendment, "which closed every saloon in America," was passed by due governmental process?

"Oh," crowed Tydings, "Nobody but a blind man would say that prohibition has closed every saloon." The vital point, he argued, was outsider meddling. What harm was there in making a mint julep and sitting around under a tree with friends on a hot summer afternoon? "If that is sin and hades is peopled with those who do no worse, then send me to hell immediately!" he said to a roar of appreciation. Upshaw admitted he was "the smartest wet I have ever locked horns with." Philadelphia's *Public Ledger* called him "a new light" among wets, who reduced his opponents to silence.

The publicity helped at a crucial time. Up for reelection in 1926, he had set his sights on the Senate seat held by Republican Ovington E. Weller, a taciturn, elderly first-termer. Tydings thought he had a good shot at the nomination. He had been lucky in politics so far; and although a number of analysts called him too young and inexperienced, he had learned from playing craps in the army to go with the luck while the streak held. He also knew he had made intelligent use of his two terms in Congress, having spent time learning and growing—studying new issues such as international economics and foreign policy. He knew not to spread himself too thin, not to get out in front on too many issues; and he worked on matters important to constituents: veterans rights, a bridge across Chesapeake Bay, the burgeoning federal budget, and Prohibition. He believed he had earned the right to make a run at the nomination, so he spread word that he wanted it.

Solid backing came instantly. Robert Archer (once his law partner and now the powerful state commissioner of roads), E. Brooke Lee (speaker of the House of Delegates), and others in his personal network pumped hard for him on the inside. Second-district constituents, who liked their accessible young congressman, rallied behind him. The business community formed a powerful block of support. Tydings was a Bourbon Democrat—pro states' rights, balanced budget, and business; a Grover Cleveland Democrat who believed businesses large and small must be protected from government interference. He had cultivated business leaders; they saw in him a philosophical ally, a rising political star to whom they could hitch their wagon.

Reporters, attracted by his flamboyant style, aided the Tydings boom. Articles about the "dashing" young representative from Havre de Grace recounted his "brilliant" war record and "meteoric rise" in politics. High visibility and solid support made him a viable candidate.

He faced tough competition. Older, richer, and more powerful Democrats also were interested—Ritchie intimate Howard Bruce (nephew of Senator William Cabell Bruce); well-known Baltimore businessman Howell Griswold, Jr.; and prominent attorney Omer F. Hershey—as were rural county Representatives T. Alan Goldsborough and Steven Gambrill. The Baltimore *Sun* was not enthusiastic: Tydings was hardly "the best material [available] for duty in the Senate." Perhaps he was "industrious and shrewd, courageous and attractive," but his experience was "wholly parochial," sniffed the *Sun*—while conceding that "quite possibly a seat in the Senate will one day be his [for] he seems to be destined to go very far in politics."

Weller, a Republican senator basking in the Coolidge era's prosperity, was considered unbeatable. Dozens of Democratic leaders warned Tydings not to run because Weller would win. Ultimately it was the Baltimore bosses who decided. Sonny Mahon and Frank Kelly, the aging machine leaders, had been eclipsed by Frank A. Furst; but both still had to be reckoned with. Mahon, along with Baltimore Mayor Howard W. Jackson, opposed Tydings; Ritchie's first choice was Hershey, who had the support of factions preferring a candidate from the city over a county man. Other elements, while friendly to Tydings, believed only an older, more conservative candidate of means could defeat the patrician Weller. With the party on the brink of hostilities, Ritchie called a conference to consider the nomination—an idea applauded by the *Sun,* Furst, Mahon, and others who thought it would end the confusion without openly forcing anyone's hand or risking a divisive primary.

A half-dozen meetings were required to reach consensus. County leaders preferred Hershey if a city man were to run and Tydings if a county man were to run. Furst, the Baltimore boss, wanted a man from the counties and liked Tydings: "A man who went to the Texas border as a private, came back from the World War as a lieutenant-colonel, became Speaker of the House of Delegates and afterward State Senator and has been elected twice to Congress and has done all this by his own efforts and without any wealth to help him hasn't done it all by accident," he reminded the conferees.

Tydings's greatest asset, it seemed, was that he was poor. There was no suspicion that what Furst so indelicately referred to as "boodle" had played any part in his past. Ritchie was persuaded. He liked being governor, but it was prudent to keep one's options open. Rumors suggested Ritchie had swung behind Tydings so the kid could "keep a seat warm for him in the Senate." Mahon capitulated too, saying, "What's the use of having advisers if we don't heed their advice? I'm going along with the boys."

Tydings surprised almost everyone when he came out of the mess with the nomination. He was nearly apologetic about his luck. "In a sense," wrote liberal editor Oswald Garrison Villard, "he is an accidental United States Senator"—chosen by Boss Furst as a compromise candidate because he was poor but honest and smart and charismatic.

Once he had the nomination, Democratic harmony prevailed. The Republicans were not so fortunate. Their primary split the party, leaving it vengeful and floundering. Tydings found the campaign less strenuous than the nominating process. The contest pitted the demonstrative Tydings against a man once described as the "Greatest Living Rival of the Sphinx." Tydings did not have to try to steal the headlines. Stories saturated the state about his go-get-'em attitude and pungent speech, his infectious smile and colorful style. He was colorful in a literal sense as well, with his red hair, piercing blue eyes, and white skin that reddened splendorously when he got excited.

In fact, he was too colorful for some. The opposition tried to discredit him for his anti-Prohibition stance and propensity for strong language. Rumors from the past surfaced in print: "Some of us remember that in the Rennert Hotel, shortly after Mr. Tydings was elected to Congress, he used his memorable statement: 'What the wets of Maryland need to do is summon up all their courage and tell the drys to go to hell,' " a letter to the Baltimore *Sun* reported. "Some Democrats hold the idea that men who use that kind of language do not deserve a place in the United States Senate. Then some Democrats remember that a year or two ago Mr. Tydings was charged with being drunk and playing the full part one night in Annapolis." Tydings was baffled over how to combat such charges. Taking on Weller was easy, but being on the defensive made him uncomfortable, and fighting rumors made him feel helpless and angry. He told the *Sun*, "On the other side it is going to be a whispering campaign. Already anonymous letters and clippings have been sent broadcast over the State which are intended to mislead and deceive the voters," and lamented, "I don't know how to fight that way."

Tydings clobbered Weller in November. Yet no one, including Tydings himself, expected him to be more than a one-term senator. Ritchie was waiting in the wings, and 1932 was a presidential election year. Maryland usually went Republican in presidential years with Senate-seat coattails in full operation.

Tydings set about finding a place in the national Democratic party. Ritchie, who recognized a strong rival when he saw one, and who would have shed few tears had Tydings lost, thought he was acting "too smart and fresh in trying to set up political shop for himself." But Tydings knew what he was doing. In 1916 he had been denied the speakership; now he was damned if he would suffer nomination by conference, bossism, or outside fickle power. He would establish his credentials and develop party ties on the national level to increase his strength and make him more visible and important in his state.

Havre de Grace went crazy. "OUR BOY, OUR HERO, OUR WARRIOR" and "CONGRATULATIONS, CHIEF" raved editorials and banners. The town fathers put on a "monster parade," the biggest in local history, with four bands, blazing torches, colored lights, and a dance at the Bayou Hotel.

Havre de Grace may have been thrilled, but the Washington *Daily Mirror* moaned that the likes of Hugo L. Black, Alben W. Barkley, Robert F. Wagner, and Millard Tydings would not raise the level of the Senate. Others expected strong careers for Black and Barkley and predicted great things for Wagner and Tydings; a New York congressman said that, with his force in debate, infinite wealth of facts, and brilliant cross-examination, Tydings would become "one of the great men of the United States Senate."

Tydings discerned that Weller's hallmark was obscurity. His name never appeared in newspapers outside of Maryland; he was a nonentity behind the scenes, and quiet as a tomb on the floor. Obscurity was not on the Tydings agenda. From his seat in back, far from the aisle, he ignored the notion that new members should observe in silence. His filibuster against Muscle Shoals (a controversial plan that, if approved, would find the government producing electrical power and fertilizer in competition with private corporations) won him attention despite its failure, because he discussed the issue at hand instead of droning on reciting from the Bible, the almanac, the *Congressional Record*, the Declaration of Independence—the usual filibuster fare.

Attired in evening dress (he was summoned from a dinner party) and speaking without notes, he argued the bill's inequities for three hours—its violations of local sovereignty, its distortion of government's traditional role. "This government was designed to govern, not to go into business," he exclaimed. Exercise of eminent domain to sell fertilizer was legalized larceny. He brought the few senators in the cavernous midnight chamber to laughter with self-deprecatory wit: "I am very much flattered that the entire Senate is at attention now, with every seat occupied. . . . I trust Senators will not keep up their applause because I am afraid I will be called to order." The *Sun*, his reluctant supporter, gave him a rave headline: "TYDINGS GIVEN LEADING RANK AMONG NEW MEM-

BERS OF SENATE." Coverage in the New York *Times*—a step into the national limelight—brought respect.

By the end of the 1928 session he was unanimously elected chairman of the Democratic Senate Campaign Committee, charged with gaining control of the Senate in the upcoming elections. The post was considered a plum—contact with top party leaders—although Frank R. Kent, the *Sun's* veteran political analyst and writer of the acclaimed column "The Great Game of Politics," belittled its importance. The position had no substance, he wrote, and disparaged those who equated it with power: "The truth is, the job is a joke."

That may have been the reality, but the perception remained that the job was important; and Tydings worked to make reality match perception. He already had experience speaking on the hustings. In 1927 and early 1928 he appeared in Narragansett, Rhode Island; Sedalia, Missouri; Kansas City; Omaha; Chicago; New York—sometimes accompanying Governor Ritchie, a presidential contender. Tydings impressed party leaders as an interesting political figure in his own right, on occasion upstaging Ritchie. "If named for vice president, Colonel Tydings would add great strength to the Democratic ticket," said a Colorado Springs newspaper about "the brilliant young Maryland statesman."

In speeches he cited chilling statistics on farm foreclosures, commercial bankruptcies, and bank failures (1927 saw four times more bank failures than 1917 through 1920 combined). Republican prosperity was for the few, he said; and his facts debunked the Republican "myth of prosperity." He had the ability to hold audiences, from his opening quips ("prohibition is better than no liquor at all") through attacks on "the dragon head of bigotry"—a reference to attempts to discredit Democratic presidential hopeful Alfred E. Smith of New York because of his Catholicism. His mix of humor and straight talk brought him more attention.

In June he was appointed to the Democratic Platform Committee at the national convention in Houston. When Ritchie withdrew from the race in favor of Al Smith, Tydings went all out for Smith. He was made (in addition to chairing the Senate Democratic Campaign Committee) chairman of the Speaker's Bureau, responsible for lining up speakers for the candidate. Frank Kent remarked that some in Smith's inner circle seemed worried about the attention Tydings got from Washington newsreporters. So they annexed Tydings, Kent wrote, and brought him to New York where they could keep an eye on him.

The 1928 election excited the prejudices of bigots and snobs. With the KKK and some Protestant elitists using the pulpit to spread intolerance, the ideals of democracy and liberty took a trashing. Rum, Romanism, Racism, and Bossism (the latter referring to Smith's Tammany Hall connections) were catchwords echoing an earlier ugly election. On Maryland's Eastern Shore, Tydings witnessed the Republican tactic of hiring blacks to ride around in cars with Smith banners. Besides its intended result, the strategy reinforced in black voters' minds the growing image of the GOP as a white party, and they continued their drift away from Abraham Lincoln's party (although it was 1948 before blacks would become staunch Democrats). A few Republicans refused to pander to religious bigotry. Senator William E. Borah of Idaho canceled a number of scheduled addresses when the Reverend J. E. Skillington of the Methodist Board of Temperance, Prohibition, and Public Morals asked that Smith be denounced "from every pulpit of the Methodist Church in America." Tydings respected Borah for showing such character. They became good friends.

Tydings himself made frequent speeches for Smith. The campaign evoked a troubling sense of déjà vu for him, with all the rumors of drunkenness that dogged Smith. It was another "whispering campaign." The religious bigotry enraged him. He asked listeners to reject prejudice and to endorse "the principles of equal opportunity for all citizens to hold public office and to aspire to the pinnacles of fame, the right of religious freedom and the right of local self government in all matters not essentially national."

Objection to Smith because of his humble origins stirred his indignation. "The real aristocrat is not the person who inherits wealth, nor the person who had a famous grandfather, nor the person whose manners are perfect," he said, "but the real aristocrat has brains, courage, perseverance and energy, he is the person who has won his way through opposition." In speaking about Smith he used words that could be applied to himself as well.

He ridiculed Republican candidate Herbert Hoover's speeches

for lack of substance. All he could glean, he said, was that Hoover favored "the Ten Commandments, better homes, sweet womanhood and sweet childhood."

In 1928 radio was used for the first time, through nationwide hookups, to educate an entire nation. Irving Berlin made his radio debut for Smith. Tydings, who had opposed the Susan B. Anthony Amendment granting suffrage to women, reformed his ways and organized leading women to make radio addresses. Times Square crowds witnessed an amazing display: huge Movietone News films screened outdoors at night with amplification—a spectacular new way of featuring speakers. New York candidate for governor Franklin D. Roosevelt, New York Mayor Jimmie Walker, and Tydings were among the first illuminated on the big screen. Television made its first campaign appearance: "HOOVER'S NEWARK SPEECH LIKELY TO BE TELEVISIONED" ran a New Jersey headline.

The Senate saw only nine Democrats elected and Smith lost, but Tydings came out of the campaign a respected player in the big leagues. He had worked with the movers and shakers: Democratic National Chairman John J. Raskob and Al Smith's "Cabinet," which included the retiring Democratic Chairman Jouett Shouse and Mrs. Franklin D. Roosevelt. His dual role, the press said, provided connections impossible to achieve through ordinary personal contact.

Once back in Congress, Tydings continued his war against Prohibition, assuming the role of leading wet with humor ("Let him who is without gin among you throw the first stone") and hardball politics. To embarrass opponents, he proposed an enforcement appropriation totaling $83.75 million—a sum large enough to ruin the economy—to call attention to the fact that Prohibition was unenforceable. In an April 1, 1930, speech he refuted every claim made for Prohibition: that it would end drunkenness, decrease crime, abolish saloons, make roads safer, cause savings to grow and taxes to lower. He touched a torch to a powder keg, the press gleefully wrote, by exposing what had actually happened during ten years of Prohibition: drinking. For example, after a 1927 Army–Navy game, with President Coolidge, the Cabinet, and many members of Congress in attendance, police cleaning up the stadium disposed of more than 1,000 empty glass flasks—one for every 80 people—with the silver, nickel, and gold flasks carried home by the revelers unaccounted for.

Tydings had announced his speech in advance and, as he anticipated, the galleries were packed. He was cheered (despite Vice President Charles Curtis's threats to clear everyone out) as he mixed statistics with irony to prove that production of the crops necessary to make beer, wine, and hard liquor—which had dropped when Prohibition began—had made an astonishing rebound. Thirty-two million gallons of bootleg liquor were seized in 1928 alone, he said—nearly one-third the amount consumed per year before Prohibition. "Do you think, Mr. President, that they seized all of it? Did they get one-half of it or a third of it or a fourth of it?" he queried. Tydings demonstrated that, in gallons of beer, liquor, and wine, Americans had spent $1.3 billion on alcoholic beverages in 1927 alone. Bootleg liquor represented a staggering tax-revenue loss and incurred enormous costs for enforcement. The effect on the economy was overwhelming: a loss of nearly $400 million.

He raised other, ugly, aspects: crime and corruption. Prohibition was supposed to end crime, he argued, but so many agents were on the take that the Prohibition force had a 330-percent turnover rate, and 1,365 citizens had been shot to death by agents—many of them innocent victims. Senator Frank Greene of Vermont had been shot critically during an afternoon stroll because an agent, aiming at a moonshiner fleeing up an alley off Pennsylvania Avenue, had missed his intended victim. And there was gangland lawlessness. Al Capone and organized crime flouted the law, encouraging hypocrisy and disrespect for authority. Senator Thaddeus Caraway tried to discredit Tydings's biblical quotations: Tydings had said, "If Christ himself were on earth today, even He would be put in jail for turning water into wine." The Arkansas senator told Tydings to leave God out of the discussion since "every man has a right to express his own opinion." "We have not that right," Tydings snapped, pouncing as Caraway fell into his trap by voicing what Tydings was leading up to: Prohibition was more than a fight against disdain for the law. It was also a battle for states' rights. Instead of legislating idealism, Prohibition encouraged lawlessness and denied people the right to self-government.

Tydings published his mindboggling collection of facts in *Before and After Prohibition,* published by Macmillan. The book was reviewed as a dissertation that "proved conclusively" the folly of it all. The reality of Prohibition was a failure, wrote Tydings; and the failure, he underscored, lay in trying to enforce a local responsibility.

Other problems of a national nature—defense, war debts, armaments—began to command Tydings's attention. In 1922 at the Washington Naval Conference, the United States had agreed to scrap 15 old battleships and cancel construction of as many new warships—two-thirds of the entire battle fleet. Some conferees believed the country was committing suicide, but the United States, Britain, and Japan signed a pact fixing the famous 5:5:3 ratio governing naval power. Tydings believed that, with the rest of the world becoming an armed camp on land and sea, it was time to rectify naval deficiencies by building 15 new cruisers to keep the United States from falling behind the 5:5:3 agreement. The strength of the army, minuscule compared to others in the world, meant that a stronger navy was a necessary first-line shield of defense in case of war—to protect trade, the Panama Canal, and the island possessions of Hawaii and the Philippines.

But more than the cruiser bill was on his mind. The size of armies was not covered by the Washington Naval Agreement, or any agreement. As a member of the Naval Affairs and the Banking and Currency committees, he had educated himself on military and economic matters. By 1929, he believed he was witness to a world heading for disaster. He hoped that explaining the complex relationship of war debts to loans to armaments might awaken people to the danger.

Armed with an arsenal of facts, he strode onto the floor in January 1929—days after the Senate approved the Kellogg Pact outlawing war—and painted a ghastly picture. Japan and all of Europe were maintaining enormous standing armies. France had one in 55 citizens in its army (the U.S. ratio was one in 800), and—counting reserves—one in eight under arms. At the same time, European nations owed the United States $12 billion in war debts, $8 billion in other government loans, and $3 billion in loans from private corporations, yet they continued to borrow—most of the money going for national defense. In 1927 they borrowed $2.6 billion and spent $4 billion on defense—meaning, Tydings said, the

United States was subsidizing two-thirds of their arms expenditures. The Senate must vote for the cruiser bill to defend America's shores, he argued—for, with the whole world arming, it would be foolhardy to ignore America's vulnerability—but more, the Senate must try to stop what was happening. "How amusing and paradoxical the whole thing is, . . . the entire world joining in a peace pact to outlaw war, with the standing armies of the sizes I have stated," he said angrily. "What a lovely peace-time picture to behold!"

He introduced two resolutions opposing all government loans to nations maintaining peacetime armies or navies in excess of peacetime requirements. (Private lenders could lend at their own risk.) In effect, he told the world: You signed the Kellogg Pact, now put your money where your mouth is.

The cruiser bill passed, Tydings having persuaded many to change their votes; but his resolutions were rejected and attacked. It was arrogant for an American to dictate to other nations, essentially exercising a veto over how they spend their money, his critics said. The *Wall Street Journal* accused him of trying to put Europe "on a bread and water diet."

He answered them sharply. He was not dictating how foreign governments spent their own money. They could do as they chose. The resolutions in no way curtailed loans from private corporations or nongovernment sources. But if they asked to borrow U.S. taxpayers' money, the government should be interested in how it was spent. No legitimate banker would let 75 percent of his loans go toward nonproductive purposes, offering little chance of repayment. And Tydings stated that he was trying to help Europe off its starvation diet. "My way to get them off a bread and water diet is to insist that the money derived from our loans should go into productive enterprise—something to create wealth . . . instead of more debt, and hence, more poverty through the use of much of our money for military establishments."

Tydings was unperturbed by the criticism. His speech dissecting the problem precipitated a national debate, and that was his goal. His forte was defining and exploring issues through discussion. When later criticized for having authored little legislation of importance, he replied, "I do not care to be known as the introducer of bills and resolutions. I think I can do more good by studying the bills that originate in the executive departments and in the committees of Congress."

Tydings had become one of the Senate's workhorses, but still made time for matters of lesser significance and for himself. He proposed establishing a national board of painting and sculpture to sponsor an annual competition, the five winners to be awarded compensation for the surrender of their creations to a national gallery of art. The art collected would tell the story of the United States. Had such a program been instituted 80 years ago, he said, the gold rush, the Civil War, slave life, western roundups, pioneer aviation, and other episodes in American life would have been preserved in a gallery in the nation's capital. "The softening and civilizing influence resulting from an appreciation of art is of great worth," he said. His plan would cost only $50,000. Artists supported it enthusiastically, but it never was voted into existence.

His interest was both cultural and personal. He had long been known for his interest in writing—he was an amateur playwright and poet—but what was less known was that he was an aspiring artist. He had bought a home in Georgetown; it was a "commodious mansion with double drawing rooms," and was quite "suitable for entertaining," burbled the press. But what really tickled high society's fancy was the discovery that he had fixed up an artist's studio in the attic. The news, as gossip columns put it, provided society "with the choicest gossipy tidbit. . . . The new picture of the talented painter seeking relaxation and amusement over the easel and palette thrills Washington tea parties." According to the stories, "Senator Tydings wears a purple frock frightfully smeared with daubs of pink, green, red and white paint."

Uncomfortable with questions about his work, he would rapidly change the subject, but the news hounds would not let him alone and described in lurid language the few works seen: "His latest picture presents a gorgeous slinky blonde holding in leash a brace of eager English setters"; the blonde, of course, had "swimming voluptuous eyes." One portrait aroused particular curiosity because no matter how often he was asked, he refused to reveal its subject. It was a bust of a young, black-haired woman. He would only say that it was painted from a sketch made years ago on a trip to Europe.

The main reasons for Tydings's popularity with the regular press were his friendliness and intelligence. He always had time for reporters, stopping to have a cigarette with them, helping them get tickets to plays; and he was quotable. Gossip columnists loved him because he was handsome and single. He was mobbed for interviews; his parties were "smart" and "interesting." When he failed to show up at some social gathering, news squibs running under tags such as "Millard Is Missing" gushed, "Ladies sighed in vain for the guiding arm of Senator Millard Tydings, the Maryland Beau Brummel." Society matrons threw their daughters, nieces, and unmarried sisters in his path.

When leap year in 1932 inspired a new spate of inquiries into his private life, he finally said he was going to accept the first woman who asked him. Tydings became known as a ladies' man despite his protests that he might remain a bachelor for the rest of his life. "It's all written on the scroll of fate," he told newswoman Ruth Ayer of the Baltimore *Post*. "I don't get time to fall in love. . . . Perhaps I shouldn't take my job as seriously as I do. Yet I like it so much better than anything else."

Stories about his personal life—embarrassing as they were—increased his popularity in Maryland and in the Democratic hierarchy. He started to move in prominent circles. He led some senators, businessmen, and other professionals in establishing a private fishing and hunting club on three private islands purchased in the Chesapeake, the Jefferson Rod and Gun Club. The sine qua non of membership was being a Democrat. It was to rival the Republican's Camp Rapidan, mixing politics, pleasure, and power—and providing jobs and money in an area hit hard by the Depression. Charter members included Bernard Baruch, John Raskob, and Jouett Shouse.

When the stock market crashed in October 1929, the country blamed Hoover and the GOP. Tydings stated through the Democratic National Committee that leaders who were "yelling prosperity" last year were trying to "find a scapegoat in the face of a $15,000,000,000 loss in one week. . . . If things have gone awry, they must take the responsibility."

Until spring 1930 the stock market rallied on and off, but in

May and June it broke again. Grim realities of the Great Depression began to sink in despite Hoover's repeated bromides to the effect that recovery was just around the corner. Tydings came out of the 1930 midterm elections (this time the party realized a net gain) acutely aware of the Depression's all-pervasive effects. He struggled to understand the causes and persistence of the economic castastrophe. He had long considered Republican prosperity to be rotten to its domestic core and had voiced concern over Europe's precarious war debts and arms situation. Now he began an intensive study of the world's prevailing economic policies.

President Warren G. Harding had met the postwar agricultural crisis with an emergency tariff setting high duties on agricultural products, the Fordney–McCumber Tariff Act of 1922. Its scope soon was extended to raise duties on industrial goods. Angered Europeans fought back with protectionist policies of their own. Following the market crash, Congress—pushed hard by Hoover's administration and Republicans—enacted the infamous Smoot–Hawley Tariff. The GOP predicted prosperity would return within a month of its passage. Instead, it delivered the coup de grâce to any chance of recovery. Within two years, all European countries had hiked their tariffs in retaliation. World trade dried up, commodity prices collapsed, production dropped, unemployment increased, and a profound global Depression deepened so drastically that the world would not recover until the beginning of World War II.

During the Smoot–Hawley debate, Tydings's major concerns were war debts, peace, and Prohibition. While playing no major role in fighting the tariff, he voted against final passage. He often failed to show up for votes on the endless amendments offered to protect special items—from tinsel to tomatoes. But he was counted among the Progressive–Democratic coalition opposed to higher tariffs, along with Borah, Wagner, Robert La Follette, Gerald Nye, and George Norris. During the seven-month battle, tempers ran so hot that the Senate floor was likened to the New York Stock Exchange during a panic. Each of the 29 in the coalition, with the exception of Norris, broke at times, changing their votes on goods important to their states.

Tydings switched only three times—on tomatoes, cement, and straw hats—but even that inconsistency engendered criticism. Columnist Frank Kent accused him of betraying party and national interests. H. L. Mencken, the famed Sage of Baltimore (who earlier had been sent to Washington to appraise Tydings for the still skeptical *Sun* and returned an admirer of his "breadth of intellect" and "independence and courage"), lashed out at him for caving in to special interests like a common political hack. "No one man can intellectually justify every vote he casts," a frustrated Tydings lamented. He was stunned by the fury of the attacks.

Smoot–Hawley passed in June 1930, raising tariffs to their highest levels in history. In July, Tydings attended the London Disarmament Conference and witnessed the European delegates frothing at the mouth over the tariffs. He also witnessed the widespread unemployment in Britain and learned of the extent of unemployment and trade depression in the rest of Europe. Things were worse than he imagined. The events of that summer—the personal abuse he took and the world's reaction to Smoot–Hawley—constituted a painful learning experience from which he absorbed two lessons: what happens when a politician bows to pressure; and the significance of tariffs. They had the potential to destroy world trade. Smoot–Hawley, he said, "walks like a shadow in our factories, now still and shrouded in gloom."

His concern emerged in written form. *Counter-Attack,* published by Bobbs Merrill, was a 141-page dissertation outlining the causes and cure for the Depression. Tydings knew that books on international economics, currency, and tariff are usually deadly dull—"dry-as-dust." He wanted his book read by the man in the street, the taxpayers, not just by economists and politicians. So he decided to write—as he phrased it in his preface—"with sufficient imagery and allegory" to enliven his factual recital.

The enemy was the "Army of Depression." Its four metaphorical leaders were "The Four Horsemen of the Depression: Captain Tariff & Embargo, Captain Depreciated Currency, Captain War Debt, and Captain Armament." His use of sustained military imagery compensated enough for the dreariness of his subject that the book was widely read, went into paperback, and was reviewed by newspapers—the New York *Times,* the Cleveland *Plain Dealer*—as a minor miracle: "distinctly readable" and understandable, a "literary campaign" that put manifold problems into perspective. He got high marks for his sound philosophy, clarity of vision and analysis—and colorful style. A few found his figurative language silly, but "the author deserves to be forgiven," wrote one reviewer, for getting people to read about economics.

As delineated by Tydings, the fundamental causes of the Depression were crippling tariffs, unstable currencies, outstanding war debts, and the costs and perils of world rearmament. Shortsighted, nationalistic philosophies had the whole world committing "commercial hari-kari." "Riders of devastation wear the camouflaged trappings of friendship," but their tunics and helmet inscriptions differed ("Buy American"; "Protect American Labor"; "Buy British"; "Protect British Labor"). His solutions (revival of world trade, settlement of war debts, stabilization of currencies, and disarmament to a peacetime basis) were presented with workable strategies.

His studies prepared him for leading the debate on the 1932 revenue bill. Hoover's primary effort to combat the Depression—the Reconstruction Finance Corporation (RFC), legislated in January 1932—had made few inroads on the problems of unemployment, hunger, and industrial and financial collapse. Tydings initially supported the RFC as a necessary remedy to a desperate domestic situation; but when Hoover requested another $1.5 billion to enlarge the program—government money to be channeled through private concerns for public works programs—Tydings balked at spending nonexistent money and railed at the idea of government going into business with business. He was one of a handful who voted against expanding the RFC.

He realized the country was "practically in a state of war" due to the suffering brought about by the Depression. But he saw another peril: The federal deficit, already at the $2 billion mark, was threatening to soar into the stratosphere. In spring 1932, when Hoover submitted his budget message, Tydings was ready to do battle to spare future generations of Americans from an inconceivable burden of debt.

The $2 billion RFC appropriation, the $2 billion deficit, Hoover's $4.5 billion budget request (plus farm and veterans relief) added up to a $9 billion obligation; taxes were projected to raise only $2.5 billion. Tydings believed that appropriating huge sums of money

without careful thought about where it would go and who ultimately would pay was wrong and unproductive. Communities and
states should exhaust their own resources before invoking federal
aid. He was arguing the flip side of states' rights: states' responsibility. And he was arguing the traditional conservative's position: that
a government must not prematurely spend what it does not have,
leaving itself without reserves. "We must keep some semblance of
financial order," he pleaded. "If the depression is to go on indefinitely . . . eventually the Federal Government itself may have to enter
the field . . . but I for one do not believe that we should do that as
an initial step."

Those who looked to government had not fully considered the
ramifications of raising taxes. There were some 17 million unemployed, 34 million without incomes, and millions more with greatly
diminished incomes. If manufacturers' taxes were slapped on con-
sumer items—soap, small appliances, automobiles—those items
would be farther out of the reach of people who could barely afford
them now. If income taxes were increased, they would be levied on
people already reeling from reduced incomes; and the unemployed
had no incomes to tax. Thomas Jefferson had believed that each
generation should clear the books, leave no deficit to saddle its
descendants. Tydings, too, believed that a durable political and fiscal
philosophy was essential to a society's existence and survival. When
Royal S. Copeland of New York protested, "No sort of political
philosophy can stand up in the face of human distress. . . . I am
content to go forward and let the future take care of itself so far as
political philosophies are concerned," Tydings despaired. It was
especially in times of crisis, he believed, that such philosophies must
be respected as stabilizers, guidelines, safeguards.

There were ways, he said, for the government to help without
ravaging its credit, increasing taxes, and adding to the deficit. He
proposed an amendment providing federal funds directly to states—
not advanced as loans to private corporations—with the states
"morally bound to repay." His amendment was defeated, but he had
injected a note of caution into the debate and scored points with La
Follette, Wagner, and a few others who understood he was not being
coldhearted in opposing relief measures, but hardheaded in warning
of the risks involved. He had become the fiscal conscience of the
Senate.

His failure to sway his colleagues sent him digging deeper into his storehouse of ideas. Throughout his battles over war debts, disarmament, tariff, and the revenue bill, he had not given up his fight to repeal Prohibition, but had been both stung and struck by criticism from Hugo Black for wasting the Senate's time on Prohibition, a minor matter compared to the horrors of the Depression: "We hear from all over the Nation that the people are starving and cold. Does not the Senator think that the people of this country are more interested to-day in whether or not they are going to get some bread than they are in whether or not they will get a glass of beer?" Tydings had reexamined Prohibition in light of the country's ills, and saw in repeal or modification a workable way to raise revenue, provide relief money, create employment, stimulate industry and agriculture, and make inroads on the growing federal deficit.

Eschewing anti-Prohibition rhetoric, he proposed the Tydings Constructive Amendment to the pending revenue bill. He would float a $1.5 billion bond issue for public works, which would bring into the Treasury $500 million a year. The bond would be self-liquidating because it would be repaid entirely by a tax levied on 2.75-percent beer at the rate of 24¢ a gallon. Using 1914 consumption figures, Tydings projected minimum revenues of $2 billion in four years, plus desperately needed bonuses: Beer production would mean new jobs in coal mines, breweries, glass factories, construction, transportation, on farms, in cities. Everyone would benefit (although staunch drys declared that they would rather vote billions for bread and see the country go broke than vote one cent for booze).

It could be accomplished by "simply taxing an article that anybody can now buy," Tydings said. "Al Capone and his henchmen are getting the money. Why not let the government get it and put the unemployed to work?" The Senate galleries burst into applause. Labor embraced the idea. A group of ten senators worked hard for his amendment—especially Wagner of New York. None came to the defense of Texas Senator Morris Sheppard, author of the Eighteenth Amendment. But Tydings's pleas to Hoover ("Bootleggers grow rich [while the Finance Committee plans] to tax automobiles, radios, theater admissions") went ignored as the president remained mute. Tydings was furious. "I don't want to hear after this session is over the Chief Executive has come out and said he favors modification

. . . after we have sandbagged industry for $1,200,000,000 instead of getting half of that from beer," he shouted. "It is my belief that if the Anti Saloon League [were] sent to the North Pole . . . Congress would repeal the Eighteenth Amendment within twenty-four hours." But his proposal was defeated 61 to 24.

With his amendment out of the way, the tariff emerged as the focus of attention. Tydings and Senator Cordell Hull of Tennessee led the fight to take all tariff items out of the revenue bill. They had no place in a tax bill and were delaying its passage; a "locust swarm of lobbyists" for oil and copper, lumber and coal, had stalled the bill. The media and national leaders were shocked that the White House had taken no steps to prevent injection of tariff items into a tax measure as the deficit strained the nation. Tydings grew so incensed that finally he cried out, "Have we gone mad? . . . We sit here [taking] care of some little interest in this State or that State instead of rising above the petty sectional interests of the moment. . . . Over and over I have listened here to the whine about My State! My State! . . . Is there no man here to put my country first?"

When Senator Huey Long, a diehard supporter of high oil tariffs—whose constant interruptions made a shambles of debate—cried, "A point of order," Tydings turned on him. "An interruption of that kind is a point of disorder," he shouted. "Will the gentleman yield?" asked Long. "I decline to yield to a Senator who has yet to learn the meaning of courtesy," Tydings said savagely as Long sat down.

He and Hull lost their battle but won praise. Calling the tariff debacle a "sickening spectacle," Frank Kent and the *Sun* chastised as "looters and vultures" the 18 senators guilty of taking advantage of a national emergency by holding the deficit hostage to special interests. The "one ray of consolation is the fact that a Maryland Senator did his best to prevent disgrace. Millard Tydings justified his election," wrote the *Sun*. Frederick William Wile, veteran political analyst for CBS, singled him out, as did Mencken, who ridiculed the Senate's fourth-rate caliber but noted that on occasion "a really competent man slips through. . . . I point to Senator Tydings."

In 1927 Tydings had become a U.S. senator by the grace of God, good luck, and Frank Furst. By 1929 local newspapers were promoting him for governor. He knocked the idea down hard—he liked the Senate—but it revealed the power he wielded. Wile, returning from a 30-state tour, was quoted as saying, "Senator Tydings is one of the truly useful members of Congress. . . .The Democratic Party might go far and do worse in 1932 than to consider Tydings for the presidential nomination. He is one of the half dozen presidential possibilities who have the serious consideration of the Democratic Party nationally." When 1932 rolled around, there was no question who the nominee for the Maryland Senate seat would be. Governor Ritchie's seatwarmer had secured the seat for himself.

He also had learned a trick or two. Ritchie had never given up his presidential aspirations, and in 1931 Tydings had helped establish Ritchie for President Clubs in Maryland and other states. At the Democratic Convention in 1932 he was selected to make Ritchie's nominating speech. The delegates sat up and took notice; his impact outweighed Ritchie's. Tydings now called the shots in Maryland.

Some in the state still spoke of him as a "political accident," but his colleagues characterized him as the kind of senator who set the Potomac on fire. He learned that it was political death not to be in the news. (He later facetiously advised Senator George Radcliffe of Maryland to do something—anything, rob a bank, stand on his head—to get his name in the papers, or join the ranks of the unemployed.) Tydings's vision had expanded as he matured. His interests evolved and his perspective broadened. He listened to others, but made up his mind based on his own judgment. Constituents could yelp all they liked if they disagreed, he said, but he would be guided by his own sense of what was right.

He came into the Senate an accident, a political daredevil who loved a brawl and who was known for tempering his forensic blows with an infectious smile. He returned for a second term as a statesman, a national figure attuned to national problems, determined to articulate the conservative philosophy he believed should be the backbone of public policy—a course that must resist the counsels of expediency. His first term was, in effect, a metamorphosis. Tydings's discipline, confidence, intelligence, and hard work won him membership in the inner circle of the U.S. Senate.

Notes

1. In addition to supporting veterans' benefits, Tydings was among those who established the American Legion. He was first commander of the Joseph L. Davis Post No. 47 in Havre de Grace.

2. The 1907 effort to merge the University of Maryland professional schools with St. John's College of Annapolis and Maryland Agricultural College in College Park failed when MAC officials decided to continue its focus on agriculture. Attempts to attract other colleges foundered because of the university's debts. Another obstacle was the fact that the Assembly had established a curious precedent by financing public, private, religious, and proprietary schools. Not only did MAC and the University of Maryland schools receive state appropriations, but St. John's, Loyola, Morgan, Goucher, Johns Hopkins, and others looked to Annapolis for money—to the tune of nearly $1 million annually by 1920. Hence, each had a strong interest in maintaining the status quo. Joining a state system meant loss of independence; not joining surely meant loss of subsidy. The idea was lambasted as socialistic.

3. In fact, according to Mary Risteau, Tydings's House of Delegates colleague, he could not claim sobriety. When he failed to support her for state senate in 1925, she wrote him on January 11, 1926, voicing disappointment and saying that she had made enemies on his behalf: "When Crabbe attacked you, I stood by you even though those on [sic] the party had told me the whole *true* story." And Davis had written Crabbe in August 1922 and described the exchange between him and Risteau: " 'Mr. Davis, you had quite an exciting scene at Carvel Hall last night, I understand.' I said, 'What have you reference to, Miss Risteau?' and she answered, 'I understand my friend, Mr. Tydings, was—well—lit up.' " Tydings's January 13, 1926 reply defended his story. (Correspondence from Risteau Papers, Maryland Historical Society)

4. The presidential election year of 1924 saw Republican Calvin Coolidge win by a large margin; Democrat Tydings had swept his district in an otherwise Republican year. When Tydings met Coolidge shortly after the election, the president—in his usual loquacious manner—asked him, "What district, Congressman?" "The second of Maryland, Sir," said Tydings. "How did it go?" Coolidge queried. "You carried it by about 5,500 votes," Tydings responded. "What was your majority?" the president wanted to know. "I carried it by about 5,500, too," Tydings said smiling. "Must be an extraordinarily intelligent district," Coolidge remarked.

6

The Squire of Havre de Grace Takes Aim at the Squire of Hyde Park

In early 1933 it was not obvious that Millard Tydings would become one of President Franklin D. Roosevelt's most tenacious and hated adversaries. True, Tydings had supported Maryland's Governor Albert Ritchie over Roosevelt for the 1932 nomination, believing the New Yorker too liberal, too glib, and too vague in his positions. Also true, the two men had little in common beyond their bedrock self-confidence and pugnaciously thrust-out chins. Roosevelt was born to wealth, the scion of a patrician family. In the eyes of political observers he was a frivolous and vacillating man, the antithesis of the self-made, decisive Tydings. Walter Lippmann's famous remark—that Roosevelt was "a pleasant man who, without any important qualifications for the office, would very much like to be President"—epitomized the opinion of his opposition, including Tydings.

During his campaign Roosevelt committed himself to a platform favoring, among other things, sound currency, lower tariffs, reciprocal trade treaties, a balanced budget, and repeal of Prohibition. Although his speeches revealed contradictions—he would slash federal spending yet increase assistance to the unemployed—and his elusiveness on specifics was maddening, he remained firmly committed to cutting costs. "I regard reduction in Federal spending as one of the most important issues of this campaign," Roosevelt declared in an October speech in Pittsburgh. "It is the most direct and effective contribution that Government can make to business."

Those words reassured Tydings, who kept any residual reservations to himself and worked hard for Roosevelt, the Democratic ticket, and his own reelection. He sought to calm those who questioned Roosevelt's sincerity. "I'm getting a little sick of hearing this talk that Roosevelt is not safe," he chided audiences. At campaign's end, Roosevelt won Maryland by a whopping 130,130 votes. Tydings won even bigger, garnering an unprecedented 154,853 majority.

The two men seemed in agreement on economic philosophy and were in total accord on Prohibition. During the campaign Tydings ridiculed the Republicans' Prohibition plank (drawn to appeal to wets and drys) as "not a plank at all but a collection of splinters"—so hypocritical that their slogan, he scoffed, should be "Nobody knows how dry I am." When the lame duck session of Congress convened in January 1933, Tydings—usually quietly dressed—appeared sporting a necktie emblazoned with the words "Repeal! Repeal! Repeal!" He wore it once a week to the delight of the press corps covering his fight for "straight, unadulterated, and unembellished repeal." On February 17, Congress voted to end the ignoble experiment. Prohibition officially ended in December, when Utah became the thirty-sixth state to ratify the Twenty-first Amendment. Repeal, joked observers, had been the first card in the New Deal.[1]

Before the famous "100 Days" of 1933, during the lame duck period, Tydings set himself up as a force to be reckoned with through a bold opening gambit. He proposed that a Treasury/Post Office bill be recommitted to the Appropriations Committee (on which he served) and be adjusted in connection with all other appropriations so the federal spending total could not exceed the $2,949,100,000 estimated revenue for the next fiscal year. "I simply ask by this resolution that the government bring its expenditures within its income," he said. His challenge to Democrats to honor their platform hit like a bombshell. Party leaders leaned hard on him to relent. He did eliminate specific figures from his resolution, but was determined to dramatize the issue. "If we don't make these cuts [in expenditures] it will be because of political fear," he exclaimed in frustration. "If I can't vote my sentiments here, to hell with this job."

Humorist Will Rogers, writing in a column, ridiculed the Senate for opposing Tydings's stance: "That is, if you didn't have any money you could not dole out any. Well the Senate like to mobbed him, they called the idea treason, sacrilegious, inhuman, and taking the last vestige of power from a politician—that is, the right to appropriate your money, which you don't have." The incoming administration, put on notice that Tydings would hold them to their promises, did not find his attitude endearing.

Roosevelt's plans for dealing with the national crisis had not taken shape even as he assumed office. Historians may argue forever whether, in fact, his ideas ever crystallized into a coherent program or remained trial-and-error improvisations. What was clear in March 1933 was a desperate need for action. Bernard Baruch and other Wilsonian figures whom Tydings respected had Roosevelt's ear and urged him to "cut government spending—cut it as rations are cut in a siege. Tax—tax everybody for everything." Congressional progressives—Fiorello La Guardia, Robert La Follette, Robert Wagner—all counseled against deficit spending. Roosevelt's first two emergency measures—the Emergency Banking Act and the Economy Act, designed to relieve the banking crisis and slash federal spending—had support across the political spectrum. Tydings worked for both; he voted for raising taxes through legalizing beer and for the formation of the Civilian Conservation Corps (CCC).

Tydings's concern over the New Deal's direction was first aroused by the Agricultural Adjustment Act (AAA) and the related Thomas Amendment, an inflation bill giving Roosevelt authority to devalue currency. The banking and emergency bills already had given the president wide discretionary powers. The AAA contemplated creating a great bureaucratic authority, a new federal control Tydings distrusted; the Thomas Amendment threatened uncontrolled expansion of credit and imprudently cheapened money. The prospect of a sea of paper money flooding the country—just as the world was seeking monetary stabilization at the London Economic Conference—seemed madness. Inflation was like a fire, Tydings warned, "easy to start, but hell to exterminate." Remedy lay not with "stupid nationalism," but in treaties with other nations. "You can't cure a sick man by mending his broken thumb. And you can't mend a sick world by inflating America. This depression is world-wide," he argued. Republicans chortled as he publicly broke ranks with the administration.

Still, Tydings voted with the administration on the Federal Emergency Relief Administration (FERA), the Truth in Securities Act, the Emergency Farm Mortgage Act, the Home Owner's Loan Act, and the Farm Credit Act. But he violently opposed the National Industrial Recovery Act (NRA) and the Tennessee Valley Authority (TVA). Debate was all but curtailed by the avalanche of major legislation that descended on Congress in a matter of weeks, and by the images of crisis across the country: Iowa farmers nearly lynching a foreclosure lawyer, and breadlines, poverty, despair everywhere.

Tydings believed the AAA, NRA, and TVA were bad legislation—panaceas. He distrusted panaceas and mistrusted intrusion in business, increases in the size and power of government. Roosevelt's direction, and the alacrity with which New Deal programs were introduced and enacted, worried Tydings. Indeed there was a national emergency; but action for the sake of action, speed for the sake of speed, seemed reckless. And he was totally unsympathetic to an apparent philosophy of national autarchy, inimical to the tradition of Jeffersonian democracy so much a part of Tydings's personal and political makeup. He, perhaps more than Roosevelt's other opponents, embodied the wish and effort to reclaim the America of sturdy farmers, small businesses, corner groceries. To those who said that such an America never existed, except in the dim past or in myth, Tydings had a sure reply: Come to Havre de Grace and let me show you.

Whether one agrees with Henry Steele Commager that Roosevelt's New Deal was not a revolution but an extension of the progressive democratic tradition as deeply rooted in America as Jeffersonian democracy, or accepts Samuel Lubell's interpretation that it did indeed represent a break with the past, Tydings himself unquestionably viewed the New Deal as a distinct, deliberate change in social and political philosophy. He believed the president was moving beyond recovery to reform using means dangerous to democracy, the rights of the individual, the rights of the states, and the Constitution.

He became a leader in the fight against what he believed was a radical destabilizing shift, a swing into economic irresponsibility. Roosevelt's experimentation was not prudent or safe—it was flying by the seat of the pants—and was unlikely to have redeeming results. Even if Roosevelt achieved temporary success, Tydings feared the long-term effects would include runaway debt, bankruptcy, potential economic collapse, and perhaps even the end of U.S. democracy. Roosevelt might buy time with expensive improvising, but the piper would be waiting to be paid down the road and the American way of life would risk sliding into autarchy.

Roosevelt's displeasure over the senator's independence and growing antagonism was obvious. When Treasury Secretary William H. Woodin selected a Marylander, Dean Acheson, as undersecretary in May 1933, the president neither consulted nor informed Tydings in advance, even though Tydings would manage Acheson's confirmation in the Senate.[2]

Tydings (who had voted against four out of ten key New Deal policies) still refrained from an open break with the president. With loss of faith in business and financial leaders, and the near-paralyzing pessimism gripping the country, Americans needed reassurance. In a May 17, 1934, interview with the Washington *Post,* he praised Roosevelt's courage. "The President is at present not only the political but the moral and spiritual leader of the country. . . . [I]n the dark days immediately following his inauguration [he] saved the United States from serious disaster." He knew Roosevelt's popularity was one of America's greatest assets.

Roosevelt—or his administration—was in another way one of Tydings's important assets. For the first time since Woodrow Wilson, Democrats enjoyed access to federal patronage. The abundance at Tydings's command gave him formidable power in Maryland. After victory, James A. Farley, Roosevelt's campaign manager, had decided that Democratic senators would get the first say when it came to spoils. Tydings was "sitting pretty," the Baltimore *Sun* remarked. Whenever someone wanted something, he was the man to see. And see him they did. Every day more than 100 people requested interviews. The phone never stopped ringing. Job seekers overflowing into the hallway outside his office had to be lined up by Capitol police. He received 15,000 applications for 100 jobs. More than 40,000 letters went out by June in response to inquiries. Desks were piled shoulder high. An incredulous Senate postmaster, on running a check, revealed that Tydings received more mail than any other senator, including those from New York and California.

He had to hire extra clerks after two typists suffered breakdowns. His secretary, Harold Scarborough, resigned due to overwork. Tydings hired Corinne Barger to head his new staff. He issued a public appeal asking constituents to refrain from requesting personal meetings unless the matter was of "grave importance." "This may be misunderstood," he acknowledged, "but with the volume of mail, calls, and interviews, in addition to committee hearings, congressional sessions, and legislative study, "I find that, even working far into the night, it cannot be done. I like the job. This is no complaint. All I ask is helpfulness."

The *Sun* made his plight the subject of an editorial, saying, "Ordinarily the woes of politicians don't excite us over-much, but we confess to a feeling of sympathy on reading Senator Tydings' pathetic plea for relief from the importunings of jobseekers." He took to locking his office door every day at 1:00 so his staff could catch up. News reporters joked that it was easier to get out of jail than to get into Senator Tydings's office.

His patronage experience made him cynical, and he gave a press conference on the subject. "In the making of recommendations I have been moved at times between amusement, pity and disgust. One leader endorsed 13 men for the same job. Only one could be named for the position, yet the other 12 believed they would have gotten it if I had followed this leader's recommendation." Such people had lost his respect. "I pretty well know by now whose word is good and whose is worthless. In times of great distress it has been a matter of regret that people who really are out of work and need assistance should be toyed with like that."

Patronage did more than consume Tydings's time and open his eyes to ugly realities. It put him in hot water in Maryland. Baltimore Mayor Howard Jackson was convinced that Tydings was in collusion with Governor Ritchie and his crowd; Ritchie suspected that Tydings was in league with Jackson. Tydings was accused of setting himself up as "king bee," of aspiring to "bossdom," the governorship. He was furious at the insinuations. He had invited the different factions to gather a handful of men to help decide the fairest way to fill patronage jobs; but after six weeks, when they failed to agree among themselves on anything, he made the appointments as even-handedly as possible. He was proud of his success. "I don't want to boast," he boasted to the news people, "but I'll venture the assertion that more people from Maryland have found employment with the Federal Government since March 4, with the possible exception of New York, than from any other State in the Union."

When midterm elections rolled around in 1934, Tydings rallied voters to support Roosevelt and the party. There was distinct ambivalence toward the New Deal in Maryland. Ritchie, who was running for reelection, minimized New Deal issues so as not to be forced to support or oppose them. Even Democrats who favored New Deal measures—such as George L. Radcliffe, candidate for senator and friend of Roosevelt—specified that, once the crisis abated, extraordinary powers must be given up, and government returned to its usual role.

In Maryland and some dozen other states, Tydings stumped for the three Rs—Roosevelt, Radcliffe, and Ritchie—telling voters that, if they believed the government had helped resolve the banking crisis, saved homes and farms from foreclosure, and created jobs, they should vote Democratic. He campaigned "as the Democrat who voted against more of the recovery legislation than any of my colleagues." Crowds roared when he repeated the refrain, that he was not "sent to Washington to be a rubber stamp for anybody!"

Tydings's outspokenness—insisting that expensive relief programs were not meant to be permanent—set teeth on edge at the White House and inspired the Republican Senatorial Congressional Committee to decorate him (along with Al Smith, John Davis, and Senators Carter Glass and Harry Byrd of Virginia) for "warning against the piling up of appropriations by the Federal Government under the present Administration." He took the GOP's attempt to make political capital at his expense with good humor, grinning as he said, "I have heard that there is an election coming on."

Its results were stunning. The Democrats gained nine seats in the House (making it 322 Democrats to 103 Republicans and 10 Farmer-Laborites or Progressives). They also gained nine Senate seats, with no incumbents lost: Democrats now outnumbered Republicans by a two-thirds majority, the largest margin held by either party since Reconstruction. Roosevelt's popularity was vindicated, with little need to placate conservatives. The greater chore would be restraining the big spenders. Harry Hopkins knew his agenda. "Boys—this is our hour," he announced. "We've got to get everything we want—a works program, social security, wages and hours, everything—now or never."

Tydings, too, knew his agenda. He was ready when Roosevelt presented his legislative priority in January 1935, an enormous emergency public employment program—$4.8 billion for work relief, the largest single appropriation in history. The money was to be used by Roosevelt as he saw fit, signifying a transfer of power from Congress to the president. Congressional radicals opposed the Federal Emergency Relief Appropriation (FERA) as insufficient. Conservatives were appalled at the size of the figure and the political implications. The bill ignited a three-month battle and marked the beginning of Tydings's complete disaffection from Roosevelt and the New Deal.

Pure "stop-gap legislation," he cried, protesting what Roosevelt claimed would "prime the pump." Don't prime it, he shouted, "repair the valve on the pump so we can get some more water out of it." Such spending would not put the country back on its feet; it would keep government in the business of providing jobs. Who was prepared, he asked, to vote for another $3 billion or $4 billion appropriation every year? It would bring back the 1920s' "mad dance of the millions" when "high priests of finance" threw money around with no regard for sane economics or worldwide problems with trade, tariffs, or disarmament. "Men here complain about costs in one breath and then in the next breath vote to drive the public debt sky high," he roared. "You are not going to get that money from the rich alone. The poor also are going to have their pockets pretty well picked."

Tydings's tirade against FERA (a "whirlwind of conservative opposition," said the Washington *Post*) was merely his opening blast. Days after its easy passage he took to the Senate floor with a vengeance. The chamber was nearly empty as he began speaking on April 2, but word circulated that Tydings was on the warpath. It was not long before most senators were seated, the galleries filled, and many members of the House gathered.

They got an earful. He attacked, preached, and pleaded, berating the administration for "running the Government on hot air, on money pulled down from the heavens. . . . A billion dollars is treated just the same as if it were a hundred thousand." The AAA and NRA drastically raised prices of manufactured and agricultural commodities when people had scarcely any money to spend. "Take cotton," he said, stabbing the air with a long bony finger, "we are plowing under our cotton, and while we are plowing it under Brazil and Egypt and India are raising more and more." "Think of it!" he shouted and asked sarcastically whether farmers were supposed to raise automobiles. "God knows, I do not believe there ever was a man in the White House who wanted to do more for the underprivileged people," he said, but Congress had to "reassert itself or let us quit calling this a democracy." The New Deal's palliative measures, the NRA, the AAA—"alphabetical institutions" and "monstrosities," he called them—must be repealed.

"I have voted for all of the unpopular measures of the administration and for practically none of its popular ones," he reminded colleagues. When the time came to turn off the faucet, it would require a lot more courage than he had yet witnessed. And the administration had failed to confront the fundamental problem: "There will not be any return to prosperity until there shall be a return to healthy world trade." It was time to end the temporary policies, he said, to revive world trade, stabilize international currency, settle the war-debt question, and work toward international cooperation and disarmament. If that was not done, he thundered, they would only continue "to pursue mad policies which already have brought Europe to the brink of war and may, before we know it, plunge all of Christendom into a holocaust. . . . The time will come when we will rue the day that there was no speaking out."

Tydings had given the press a new expression to play with: alphabetical monstrosities. Every major paper in the country gave his speech coverage. Some called his denouncement vitriolic, Cassandra-like calamity howling, and then hurled the ultimate insult, branding him a "Tory Democrat." But most gave his stinging rebuke strong editorial support. The administration would do well—the national press by and large agreed—to swallow the bitter spoonful from Tydings's bottle, whether or not the dose was palatable.

The speech launched a spate of articles attacking Roosevelt while Tydings graduated from being "the watchdog of the Treasury," as the *Sun* had labeled him, to being considered one of government's most articulate men. He could bring any discussion "down from the realm of cloudy speculation to the solid ground of specific application," said an editorial in the *Evening Sun*. He was the target of "bouquets from congressional colleagues and other quarters," for his "sledge-hammer attack," said the Washington *Star*. "It's many a moon since any member of the administration party has taken his courage in both hands and spoken right out in meeting as Tydings did. . . ."

Such responses inspired pundits, gossips, and colleagues to speculate on the side effects and publicity of such a dramatic speech. Might he be seeking to serve as rallying point for Democrats opposed to Roosevelt and the New Deal in 1936? The *Star* suggested he was just the right age "to aspire to national honors at no too distant day. . . ."

He was a hot news item, but was not about to sit back and preen among the thousands of congratulatory letters, telegrams, and phone calls. He followed up with a resolution to balance the budget, provoking another round of debate on New Deal direction and costs. He became a sought-after speaker, and was invited to address the National Economy League at New York's Biltmore Hotel (along with Lewis Douglas, the former budget director who resigned in the summer of 1934 in anguish over Roosevelt's fiscal policies). It was an excellent forum for elaborating his theme. "Unthrifty governments can never translate prosperity to the masses," he argued. The country must wake up and realize there was no panacea. The longer the day of reckoning was postponed, the more painful the aftermath.

Tydings's balanced-budget proposal was doomed—raising taxes in an election year is not for the fainthearted—but his salient jabs at the New Deal provided a focus for Roosevelt's opposition and invaluable fuel for the conservative cause. The coverage he got was a publicist's dream; editorials, cartoons, and newsreels gave favorable exposure to his philosophy and gave the nation a good look at his incisive intelligence and sardonic wit.

The president was not amused. In public he breezily dismissed Tydings, Lewis Douglas, and other conservatives, calling them members of the "Liar's Club." Supporters laughed along with him at the small group of self-appointed alarmists. But many in Washington believed the president only revealed his inability to tolerate criticism. And Roosevelt's private reaction bordered on censorship. Metrotone News had interviewed Tydings and released a newsreel containing the story "Our Own Mounting Debt Brings Warning of Disaster from Senator Tydings of Maryland." White House Secretary Marvin McIntyre had Sol Rosenblatt of the NRA complain to the Motion Picture Producers and Distributors of America that the film, lacking an opposing view, was unbalanced. Metro-Goldwyn-Mayer subsequently ordered a number of theaters to cut the subject and return the release; the president of Motion Picture Producers, Will Hays, nervously wrote Rosenblatt that the problem of balance was tricky. "Since the newsreel must be entertaining as well as news," he wrote, including a second "balancing" interview would jeopardize achieving an amusing variety. "In the near future," he added, "we are going to have a meeting of the newsreel editors where this may be further discussed. They are very anxious to do the right thing."[3]

Tydings probably never knew of the White House effort to suppress the Metrotone piece, but come summer of 1935 he knew he was in a serious battle with the most powerful man in the country. He relished the prospect.

While the president was not amused, some of his staff and Cabinet were made rabid by Tydings—especially Secretary of Interior Harold L. Ickes. Ickes, with his elfin ears, bristly eyebrows arched over thick-lensed rimless glasses, fleshy jowls, and stocky build, looked like a mischievous owlet; but he was a formidable fighter, a dictatorial type so sure of himself that nothing—facts, logic, persuasion—could change his mind once he had formed an opinion. He was a notorious hothead renowned for shouting matches, an imaginative retaliatory style, and grudges. He became famous for loathing Tydings.

Their first public clash erupted during hearings investigating accusations of maladministration in the Virgin Islands. Both men had strong proprietary interests in the West Indies, for the islands were administered by the Department of Interior but came under the jursidiction of the Territories and Insular Possessions Committee chaired by Tydings. Neither wanted to give an inch when they disagreed over the validity of a tangle of charges leveled at the islands' governor, Paul M. Pearson.

The Virgin Islands, which were purchased from Denmark during World War I, had muddled along with scant attention paid to the near-feudal conditions there. The population was 10-percent white (wealthy gentry) and 90-percent black (poor illiterate peasantry). In 1931 President Hoover appointed Pearson (father of columnist Drew Pearson) to be governor. It was not long before many island residents—government attorneys as well as frustrated native leaders—became disillusioned and began working for Pearson's recall by Hoover, and then by Roosevelt. By 1934 serious trouble was brewing. Eli Baer, a man Tydings recommended for U.S. district attorney, and Paul Yates, whom Robert S. Allen (Drew Pearson's by-line partner) had recommended as Pearson's executive assistant (Ickes appointed them both), each came to realize that the islands' problems were being compounded by inept management.

Paul Pearson was a decent soul but an ineffective governor. Careless and inefficient, he was a promoter more than an administrator. He trusted wealthy distillers, businessmen, and landowners—men who put their own interests above those of the territory. Yates had Baer investigate Pearson's record, which the attorney was delighted to do: Baer was a Democrat, Pearson a Republican; and for Baer, everything was political. He compiled perhaps 100 charges, and Yates—going over Ickes's head after he tried to derail the investigation—wrote a confidential letter to Roosevelt outlining the unsavory situation: Pearson was poorly organized, his cronies corrupt, his expensive programs failures; he was passive to the point of complicity in certain public works scandals that he had tried to "whitewash"; an Ickes minion had tried to force Federal Judge Webber T. Wilson to return records the judge had legally impounded. It was a sordid account, and Yates urged remedial action.

Ickes was enraged by Baer's politically motivated investigation and Yates's perfidious behavior. He angrily fired them both. But in firing Baer without consulting Tydings, he had disregarded all courtesy and protocol. Ickes was no maven of protocol, but he knew his actions would incite Tydings. Ickes was spoiling for a fight with the most vocal of Roosevelt's antagonists, and he got it. Tydings launched a study of island conditions and found that Yates's charges had merit. He announced that the Territories Committee would investigate. The furor began as the players jockeyed for position. Ickes immediately tried to maneuver himself into control. He wrote Tydings asking to appear first, and he announced to the press, "I asked the privilege of producing witnesses and of cross-examining witnesses."

Tydings wasn't buying. He did not trust Ickes, with good reason. The secretary publicly maligned Yates to discredit his testimony. Tydings suspected Ickes's opening remarks would be a carefully calculated attack and wisely refused him the chance to run away with the show.[4]

The opening session, on a sizzling July 2 morning, was tense. Robert Allen arrived early and pounced—fists flying—on his erstwhile protégé, calling Yates a "double-crosser." Before Capitol police could break it up, Yates sustained cuts and bruises and was taken to the Senate infirmary. Allen was hauled off to jail. Ickes arrived with an entourage—six high assistants, three departmental press agents, and his wife—only to find Tydings sticking to his guns and to learn that, with Yates out of commission, the lead witness was a minor player. The secretary folded up his papers and left.

Ickes never stopped trying to manipulate the hearings, though. He held daily press conferences. He impugned unfriendly witnesses, calling them drug addicts, "not quite normal mentally," or guilty of "judicial misconduct." He had an assistant ostentatiously hand Tydings an envelope of affidavits refuting testimony. Face reddening, Tydings slammed the table and snapped, "I wonder why the Secretary of the Interior does not present his case [instead of giving] interviews to the papers." Ickes's next move was more provocative. He wrote a vitriolic letter accusing Tydings of whitewash and demanding anew the right to cross-examine.

A livid Tydings counterattacked. Claiming that anti-Pearson witnesses were being intimidated and clearly implying the intimidation's source, he threatened to shift the investigation's focus from the Virgin Islands to the Department of Interior. When Ickes then released his scorching letter to the press, Tydings really had his fill. His reply, which he too gave to the press, exuded contempt. If Ickes wanted "to tell the United States Senate how to conduct its business," he should "first get elected to that body." The committee would survive without his "gratuitous advice."

Ickes dismissed Tydings's letter as "a perfect tirade." The senator, he smirked, had gone completely berserk. Ickes had deliberately used the media to fight Tydings and thought he was winning. He discussed his strategy in his diary, how he had his staff arrange for reporters to ask questions that allowed him to publicize his viewpoint. "My theory is that since we are denied the right of cross-examination and since Tydings seems bent on smearing us all he can we ought to fight back day by day through the newspapers."

With the two men on the verge of a brawl, Roosevelt was compelled to step in. He summoned Ickes to his office for what the press called a "presidential spanking," and met at length with Tydings and Senators Joe Robinson and Pat Harrison (who had appointed Judge Wilson) to discuss a settlement. Leaving the White House by the side door, a tight-lipped Tydings would only say, "We have discussed various phases of the Virgin Island situation."

Tydings had the support of his entire subcommittee. The Senate closed ranks, seeing Ickes's challenge to Senate prerogatives as out of line. Rumors abounded that Pearson would be forced to resign. Consensus held that Tydings cleanly bested Ickes—who had left Roosevelt's office looking like a fellow returning from a trip to the woodshed but when asked by reporters if he would be smoking the peace pipe with Tydings had replied, "I haven't smoked a pipe in years."

The president met with Ickes and Pearson on July 22. Paul Pearson was offered the job of assistant director of housing in charge of the Public Works Administration (PWA) social welfare agency. To placate Ickes, Judge Wilson was transferred to the Federal Board of Parole. Lawrence W. Cramer, the lieutenant governor of Saint Croix, was appointed governor of the territory. Tydings suspended the hearings indefinitely.

Tydings performed a valuable service to the Virgin Islands, whether Ickes and Roosevelt liked his manner or not. The Yates–

Pearson feud had paralyzed its government for two years—until Tydings threatened to air the whole sorry story. The hearings were a catalyst that brought to a close an untenable status quo. And Tydings wasted little time plotting against Ickes. He worked out on a "constructive basis" universal suffrage for island natives, 90 percent of whom were disenfranchised. He tried to simplify administration systems and costs, effected tax reform, delegated powers of eminent domain to the government-owned Virgin Islands Company to break up plantations, and pressed for administrative justice and economic stability. He developed legislation that became the Virgin Islands Organic Act, signed by Roosevelt on June 22, 1936. That act ensured territorial self-government and provided that the president appoint its governor with the advice and consent of the Senate.

Harold Ickes knew how to hold a grudge. He never forgave Tydings, never overlooked an opportunity to needle him. He licked his wounds in furious diary entries and awaited the chance to wreck Tydings's career.

And Tydings gained another powerful enemy. Columnist Drew Pearson was beyond livid. He barged into Tydings's office saying, "All right Millard, up to now I've been your friend but I know a lot of things I could write about you which would make juicy reading in Maryland." Tydings rang for Corinne Barger, told her to give Pearson any files he might want, then took Pearson by the collar and bodily threw him out. When Paul Pearson died two years later, Drew Pearson held Tydings responsible for his father's early death. He never missed a chance to take a vicious swipe at Tydings and his family.

As Tydings was embroiled in the acrimonious hearings and power struggle with Ickes, his war against Roosevelt's so-called Second New Deal heated up. Roosevelt, in January 1935, had not limited his agenda to the FERA. He had introduced other legislation that, for reasons known only to himself, he had allowed to languish: social security, a banking measure, and a public-utility holding company bill. Suddenly in June, as Congress anticipated adjourning for vacation, the president leaped into action. Those bills became "must" legislation, as did a radical new "soak the rich" tax scheme.

He also threw his support behind Senator Robert Wagner's labor relations proposal.

Two years of struggle against federal power, growing bureaucracy, deficit spending, and encroachments on individual rights had created a hardcore band of conservative Democrats committed to safeguarding values they believed Roosevelt's recovery and reform endangered. The five leaders were Carter Glass and Harry Byrd of Virginia, Thomas P. Gore of Oklahoma, Josiah W. Bailey of North Carolina, and Tydings—easily the most articulate and uncompromising, and unquestionably the one detested most by New Dealers. Until that summer the group had not drawn consistent support from some Democrats uncomfortable with the New Deal but wary of denouncing it. The "Second 100 Days" of 1935, with its unfolding opposition to the "Second New Deal," brought Tydings's group increased power. To a man the five debated, fought, and voted against each of Roosevelt's measures throughout the long, steamy summer.[5]

Wagner's labor bill proposed establishing a National Labor Relations Board as an independent and permanent agency empowered, first, to hold elections to determine suitable bargaining agents and, second, to prevent business from engaging in "unfair labor practices"—i.e., firing workers for belonging to a union or fostering company unions controlled by employers. Wagner believed company unions were subterfuge efforts to sidestep the right to collective bargaining. Tydings was convinced that enactment of the plan would allow unions to tyrannize workers and breed crippling strikes just as industries and businesses were beginning their recovery from the worst of the Depression.

To ensure a fair chance for company unions to survive, Tydings introduced an amendment guaranteeing employees the right to self-organization free from coercion "*from any source*. . . . It shall be unfair labor practice for any person to coerce employees in the exercise of their rights . . . or to coerce employees in their right to work or *to join or not to join any* labor organization" (emphasis added). It was just as important, he argued, to forbid interference by labor unions in employee elections as to forbid employer interference. But Wagner furiously opposed the amendment. It would restore the terrible conditions existing before the Norris–LaGuardia

Anti-injunction Law (when business and industry busted unions with impunity). It would hamstring labor by protecting company-dominated unions, which were altogether different from employee-organized unions.

"Well, if my amendment weakens this bill," Tydings retorted, "then words don't mean what they say." His amendment (drafted by the National Association of Manufacturers and offered at the request of Maryland Steel Company employees who preferred affiliation with a company union) was defeated 50 to 12; the Wagner Act passed, creating the landmark National Labor Relations Board (NLRB), a radical legislative innovation giving government the power to compel employers to accept unionization.

On the heels of that defeat came two far greater legislative challenges to the conservative philosophy: the utilities holding company bill, and a "tax the wealth" plan. Through use of federal authority, these would diminish the power of large-scale corporations. They became the showdown issues that split the Senate Democrats.

The holding company bill sought to break up the great utilities that controlled the nation's electrical power. They grew ever richer, while avoiding state regulation through complex arrangements. A "death sentence" provision sought to eliminate holding companies; any utility holding company that failed to justify its existence would be forcibly dissolved by the Securities and Exchange Commission (SEC) as of January 1, 1940. Roosevelt chose to make the "death sentence" a party loyalty test and, for the first time, moderate Democrats in significant numbers were drawn into agreement with Tydings. In the Senate the conflict was over the [William H.] Dieterich Amendment, which substituted regulation for dissolution, killing the "death sentence." New Deal forces won by one vote, 45 to 44, but 24 Democrats had joined with Tydings's group. Although they lost the vote, a break had been made. It would be easier to break another time.

And just such an opportunity presented itself with Roosevelt's "soak the rich" tax bill, which he sprang without warning on June 19. The idea of heavily taxing corporations and large concentrations of capital had been kicking around the Treasury Department for more than six months, yet Roosevelt had little interest in making great changes in the tax structure. But as Huey Long began drawing millions of converts to his "Share the Wealth" plan to "make every man a King," Roosevelt had second thoughts. He considered Long one of the two most dangerous men in the country (Douglas MacArthur was the other); and although the Louisiana senator appeared to be a vulgar buffoon, Roosevelt recognized that in reality he was a brilliant demagogue. In the words of historian Charles A. Beard, Long's "thunder on the left" spurred Roosevelt to action. His tax proposal was a sweeping measure calling for major revisions: stiff inheritance and corporate taxes, a gift tax on large fortunes, and an increased surtax on high personal incomes. The move to "steal Huey's thunder" actually reflected Roosevelt's own mistrust of tremendous wealth.

Tydings and his four fellow "irreconcilable" Democrats were outraged at the president's plan and at his launching it as a surprise; they were joined by many equally appalled moderate Democrats. They considered it vindictive class legislation, targeting a specific group for "punishment" without greatly enlarging revenue or balancing the budget. Tydings seethed over Roosevelt's tactics, distrusted his intentions. Punitive taxation was counterproductive. Corporations were employers and producers; inflicting damage on productive companies that paid wages to millions was sheer insanity.

He and his conservative and moderate allies waged a two-month fight as hot as the Washington summer. They could not defeat the plan. But the final bill was softened. It eliminated inheritance taxes and reduced the incremental corporate income tax, but increased gift, estate, and capital stock taxes and raised the personal surtax to its highest rate. Roosevelt's Wealth Tax Act of 1935 engendered the deepest resentment among business of all New Deal measures and inspired even greater hostility in Congress. The small coalition had been joined by 19 moderates. The rift in the Democratic party was widened. Those moved to action would not easily be silenced in the future.

The only defeat Roosevelt suffered that summer was at Tydings's hands. He staged a devastating filibuster against the $465 million rivers-and-harbors bill, brilliantly picking the costly bill to shreds item by item. Dressed in crisp white linen suitable for the tropics, he wound up the last late-night session before Congress adjourned with two and a half hours of sarcasm that reduced the crowded galleries to laughter as the chair gave up trying to gavel them to silence. Word that Tydings was on had drawn a large audience that, before the advent of television, enjoyed watching one of the greatest shows on Earth: the U.S. Senate. That night they hoped Huey Long would rise to bait and be baited, and hoped, as the *Christian Science Monitor* wrote, "this would be one of the times [Tydings] would slice Long into pieces like so much baloney." Tydings loathed the "kingfish" and was delighted to oblige.

Ignoring the sultry heat and ill-humor of his colleagues (Congress was enraged at being labeled a "rubber stamp"), he mimicked Long's filibuster style, pumping and thumping his fist as he mourned, "Poor old Louisiana. The way they leave Louisiana out of these large Federal appropriations breaks my heart and fills my soul with well-nigh unbearable grief." As the galleries roared, Huey rose to interrupt the burlesque, demanding to know why Tydings had not protested big appropriations for Baltimore in the works relief bill. Tydings stopped him dead, haughtily announcing that not only had he spoken against it, he voted against it. "I am not bribed easily with a good chunk of pork," he shouted as Huey slunk back into his seat.

"Of course I lived in a State with no water in it," he continued, his usually acid voice oily with irony. The Chesapeake Bay, the Susquehanna (the largest river east of the Mississippi), the Potomac, Patapsco, Patuxent "would make most of these so-called 'rivers' look like rain trickling across the pavement from a broken rainspout in a five minute April shower," he snorted.

Even mountainous landlocked Vermont was not spared his crocodile tears. Wiping mock droplets from his eyes he demolished decorum completely.

> You know, Vermont very much resembles Holland. It is low, flat country. [Laughter]
> They have to have a lot of dikes up there or the sea will come in and absolutely wipe Vermont off the face of the earth.
> Have you ever been to Vermont in tulip time? [Laughter] You see those great plains . . . , canals weaving through them like beautiful silver threads on a green carpet . . . and the Vermonters,

with their pink cheeks and their wooden shoes clattering. . . .
[Laughter] But always there is the sea [laughter] threatening any
minute to come in and dash this beautiful picture, this actual
madrigal into smithereens.

Alabama fared no better. Modestly denying he was much of a mimic
he oozed into the Southern drawl of an Alabama mayor trying, over
mint and bourbon, to persuade a U.S. senator to appropriate
$500,000.

"Suh, I want to thank you powahful much for giving me this
opportunity. . . . Now I know that a good many of you Yankees
ain't been down since you took your carpet bags in 1870 when
Wade Hampton ran you out with the red shirts and you flew
north to more peaceful and more lucrative puhsuits."

Well, the mayor's honey-coated words were sorely tempting to
Tydings's poor beleaguered senator, who recalled wrestling with his
conscience.

"Gentleman, although the temptation of that mint julep—even
now in my mind's eye I can see its amber beads; I hear the
tinkling of the ice against the brim, and in it I see the green
emerald flag waver o'ver its top. When I think of all those velvet
drops floating down my throat like a dewdrop burying itself in
the heart of the rose, it is all I can do—I must save this money
for the people. I must see that it is spent wisely, I wish the
witness would pardon me while I wipe a tear of regret from my
right eye."

And Tydings paused as the galleries dried tears of laughter.

The gathering had gotten its money's worth, and Tydings was
credited with stabbing the bill to death with the sharp sword of
satire. The New York *Times* wrote that he "attained the top most
heights of Congressional humor . . . and gained a reputation that is
nation-wide for doing his own thinking, and when he has reached
convictions, for refusing to swerve from them."

Except for that single victory Roosevelt had steamrollered Congress to get his way and riled Congress to near revolt. Faced with

reelection in 1936, he had seen each issue as vital. But columnist Drew Pearson summarized the verdict on the president's willfulness: His poor leadership made him "a poor general." He had won, but at great cost.

Prominent conservative Democrats smoldered, and anti-Roosevelt sentiment bubbled to the surface. Bainbridge Colby, a former secretary of state under Woodrow Wilson, promoted the idea of a national convention of anti-Roosevelt Democrats to be held before the regular 1936 convention so they could adopt the identical platform Roosevelt accepted in 1932 and violated ever after. Former Governor Ritchie declared the New Deal "on the rocks." Ray Tucker's "National Whirligig: News Behind the News" column gossiped about William Randolph Hearst's "dramatic gesture": urging conservatives to form a Jeffersonian Democratic party using Al Smith's name as lightning rod. "Once the public warms to the Jeffersonian idea the real candidate can be sprung. Informed sources believe he will be Senator Millard Tydings of Maryland."

Smith took an initial step on his own. With John Davis, Jouett Shouse, Irenee DuPont, and other prominent citizens, he formed the nonpartisan American Liberty League. Its avowed purpose was "to uphold the Constitution" and to "protect property and personal rights." Ickes, the New Deal's bluntest instrument, cheered them on, hoping they would take Tydings, Glass, Byrd, Gore, and Bailey to their bosom and keep them there—thus effectively achieving political realignment. "I'd like to see all the progressives together and all the conservatives together," he announced. "Then you'd always be facing your enemy and not worrying about what is happening behind your back."

But the five senators denied any intention of joining an organization containing Republicans. They issued separate statements through the Democratic National Committee. Tydings expressed confidence in the president. "I did not subscribe any more than many Americans did to the wisdom of each and every proposal" promulgated by Roosevelt, he said, and the president himself had "frankly confessed that some of them were experiments and after trial might be found wanting and if so would then be abandoned."

What Tydings would not abandon was his crusade to force moderation of the New Deal—or replace Roosevelt in 1936. The president's apparent shift from recovery to reform—its greater spending and burgeoning of federal power—had privately alienated a larger percentage of Congress than votes revealed. Columnist Frank Kent had written as early as April 1935 that 90 percent of Tydings's colleagues sided with him in spirit even if they lacked the courage to do so outloud. "It is difficult to name six Senators— particularly Democratic Senators—who at heart believe in the Roosevelt policies," he wrote.

And there was growing evidence of party disaffection. Tucker's "National Whirligig" of August 5, reporting a confidential get-together of Democratic veterans, wrote that former Massachusetts Governor Joseph B. Ely, Senators Royal S. Copeland of New York, Matthew M. Neely of West Virginia, and Tydings, and New Jersey Governor Arthur H. Moore all feared their states would end up Republican in the next election (as would Delaware and Pennsylvania) unless the New Deal was modified. Editorials continually addressed the New Deal's uncertain popularity, especially in the South. Negative predictions were not necessarily "authentic gospel," concluded Tucker, "but nobody at Democratic headquarters laughs off this bad news."

Tydings grew bolder, speaking throughout the East to promote ideas to cure the Depression in language resembling a political platform: "I would not run the government on borrowed money. I would tax and pay as I went. If I had to levy high-income taxes I would do it. I would not waste money," he said. At the Fiftieth Annual Dinner of the Southern Society at New York's Waldorf Astoria he again urged an international congress to restore world trade. "Nations, no more than individuals, can spend themselves into prosperity, or out of debt, or away from difficulty, any more than a drunkard can drink himself sober," he declared. His words were quoted favorably—and his motives scrutinized. The press insisted that he was making a bid to challenge Roosevelt. He issued no denials or comment.

Editorials and articles about political power struggles counted him among the party warhorses who were wheeling away from the president. In the Washington *Herald* Tydings headed a list of 18 senators who "already have one or more feet off the New Deal reservation." He became a rallying point for opposition to a Roosevelt second term. For a time he was linked with the American Liberty League after Jouett Shouse, with Tydings permission, published a pamphlet titled "Straws Which Tell." It included excerpts from letters that Tydings had received praising his April 2 denunciation of the alphabetical monstrosities. The Baltimore *News–Post* posed the proposition that he was angling for highest office: "BETCHA Senator Millard Tydings is playing with the idea that Presidential lightning might strike him when nomination time comes around." Just after his December speech at the Waldorf, the *Herald* revealed, "He has been urged by friends to seek the Democratic presidential nomination, but has refused to make any move in that direction."

When the Supreme Court declared the AAA unconstitutional in January 1936, after having ruled the same of the NRA in May 1935, the setbacks jeopardized Roosevelt's chances for renomination. In Maryland there was revived interest in Tydings as a favorite son, for the Court's actions vindicated his views. And when Roosevelt requested $2 billion more in 1936 for the Public Works Administration—as Tydings had prophesied—his arguments against the FERA were borne out. Ralph J. Sybert of the *News–Post* wrote that Tydings had his "eye on the White House"; there had been talk that he had approached state leaders about what support he could expect and that Howard Bruce had hosted a private conference with Jackson and Ritchie to discuss the subject. Tydings's famous painting smock started to be referred to as "Millard's imperial purple toga" by those who thought he was being groomed for the presidency in 1940.

In February, however, something occurred that gave Tydings pause. Al Smith publicly bolted the Democratic party, saying, "There is only one of two things we can do; we can either take on the mantle of hypocrisy or we can take a walk, and we will probably do the latter." The headline-making departure forced Tydings to clarify his thinking. Just as he believed silence was not useful, neither was walking away. His options were either to continue opposition to the incumbent's renomination, or to make peace with the intricacies of conscience and expediency and then make his views heard at convention platform time. Senators Byrd and Bailey already had set the anti-Roosevelt movement back severely when they formally announced that they would support Roosevelt in 1936. Unlike

Tydings, the two were up for reelection and, unable to remain independent, had swallowed hard and submitted.

Roosevelt, being vitally interested in all things political, was far from indifferent to the speculation centered on Tydings. He moved to cut him off whenever he got the chance. At a festive dedication of the Choptank River Bridge on Maryland's Eastern Shore, he gave Tydings the cold shoulder, inviting freshman Senator George Radcliffe aboard his yacht the *Sequoia,* and leaving heretic Tydings far from the glory of presidential pomp. High atop the shore ramparts overlooking the scene, Tydings was heard shouting to the swelling crowds to stop them from surging forward and being pushed off the ledge. One reporter immediately saw the symbolism and quipped, "There's Millard again, warning against going off the deep end."

Liberal columnist Raymond Clapper warned Roosevelt in an editorial that he would need Tydings in 1936; giving him the "large royal snub" would make it hard for Tydings to help. It was better, Clapper believed, to "allow some tolerance within the party than to risk having the whole New Deal overthrown because of too strict a purity test. . . . Petty vengeance is poor politics." Criticism within a party was a legitimate, time-honored duty.

A February 18, 1936, newspaper blurb offered testimony that both men had come to terms with political reality: "Senator Millard E. Tydings of Maryland, who often has disagreed with Administration policies, called on President Roosevelt at the White House today. He described the visit as 'purely social.' " His attempt to sidestep inquiries fooled no one. Louis Azrael's *News–Post* column quoted his "Spy who wallows in politics" as saying that Tydings would not qualify for the "Al Smith Walking and Social Club." Frank Kent was livid. Tydings had let himself be charmed by the sweet-talking Roosevelt. New Dealers laugh, Kent wrote, as they tell how simple the "taking of this Senator into camp" was. "It isn't easy to respect Senators like this who 'rise above their principles' but it is easy to understand them."

Kent's harshness was an isolated reaction. Still, many wondered if the man who had refused to jump through New Deal hoops whenever Roosevelt, Ickes, or Farley cracked the whip finally had been tamed. Maryland Democrats raced to join Roosevelt's bandwagon, apparently stampeded by the White House meeting and by a much publicized upcoming speech that was to display Tydings's party solidarity. The journalists kicked up a storm of speculation over what he would say to the Young Democrats of Maryland on March 5 in Baltimore.

Tydings proved to be master of the keep-them-listening technique, sustaining suspense through 45 minutes of Republican-bashing before finally—grudgingly, to some—stating his position: The New Deal was not popular in Maryland, but "let this fact stand out in letters of fire, that whatever may be said either pro or con about the present Administration or some of its policies, it cannot be truthfully said about it that either it or its policies brought on the depression." No one could argue with such praise—if praise it was. "There are only three courses open," he continued. "We can support the Democratic ticket; we can support the Republican ticket; or we can 'take a walk.' . . . I do not propose to 'take a walk.' "

He unveiled his strategy—undoubtedly his quid pro quo for having agreed to support Roosevelt. Democrats must "urge upon the convention a platform" ensuring modification of emergency measures; they must nudge the party back to its traditional role; they must press to separate "the Federal Government from local problems." Unspoken—but obvious to all astute listeners—was the fact that Roosevelt was sure to be renominated and, since Tydings liked his job, he could exert more influence by not opposing Roosevelt.

The day of Tydings's speech, Roosevelt announced his candidacy. He would enter primaries in Maryland, Ohio, and Massachusetts, and make his campaign debut in Baltimore. Tydings was credited (except by Kent) with maintaining his integrity as he met the dilemma. "He may still say he wears no man's collar," wrote Franklyn Waltman in the Washington *Post*. Mencken judged Tydings's arguments as sensible, unlike Al Smith who was "barking up the wrong solution." Tydings had resolved the dissenter's quandary by fighting from within.

Roosevelt's campaign opener—a splashy foray into Maryland replete with a star-spangled entourage including the vice-president, the secretaries of war, interior, agriculture, and commerce, and 39 senators including Tydings—was a tremendous success. With easy primary victories, the next stop was the Democratic National Convention in Philadelphia in June.

The convention was as boring as a rigged wrestling match. Some delegates were unhappy. Not only was the nomination sewn up, as anticipated, but Roosevelt had a New Deal platform all but in hand. Unable to wage a fair fight for their beliefs, six senators flatly refused to serve on the Resolutions Committee: Tydings, Glass, Byrd, Tom Connally of Texas, William Dieterich of Illinois, and Alva B. Adams of Colorado. They would not contest the platform, but neither would they support one that would embarrass them. The *Sun* noted, "The one thing that the Democratic conservatives are making sure of is that, whatever finally emerges from the Platform Committee, will be branded as Mr. Roosevelt's and not their creation."

Tydings went so far as to refuse to deliver Maryland's seconding speech for Roosevelt. This was more than Roosevelt or Jim Farley, his campaign manager, could stand. In a high dudgeon, Farley exerted "pressure of the strongest sort"—badgering and threatening, enlisting others to work him over—until finally Tydings succumbed and spoke a meager 169 words that addressed the need for sound economic policies and only in its last phrase could no longer avoid the task: "The Democratic Party of the Free State of Maryland, united, determined and in fighting mood, pledges its enthusiastic and loyal support to the great fighter who stood upon the frontiers of chaos and despair and who has battled for the rights of mankind—Franklin D. Roosevelt."

That time he barely escaped with dignity intact. Mencken fled the room, hiding in the convention hall basement until the debacle was over. Franklyn Waltman wrote that Tydings had "damned the President—not with faint praise—but without praise at all." Those without sympathy for Tydings laughed at seeing him left hanging pitifully from a limb. "If he now finds himself minus his dickey, pin feathers and pants, he has no one to blame but himself," huffed the Harford County Bel Air *Times*.

Republicans chose Alfred M. Landon, governor of Kansas, to run against Roosevelt. Tydings privately believed the two men's economic philosophies were nearly indistinguishable—"it was Tweedle Dee and Tweedle Dum," he later remarked—but because personal attacks on Roosevelt "would serve no useful purpose to the country or to myself," and because he was committed to party if not administration, he campaigned for Roosevelt.

Sitting next to Farley at an August meeting of the Democratic hierarchy in New York, Tydings had the campaign manager nodding in approval as he declared he intended to do "all I can, actively, to insure the election of Roosevelt." Farley kept smiling as Tydings, grinning broadly, added, "After Mr. Roosevelt is elected I shall continue to oppose any policies he may propose which I think unwise." Reporters appeared more interested in Tydings's views than those of other congressional figures present. Tydings dominated the event, to Farley's discomfort. "Senator Tydings today climbed right up to the driver's seat of the Roosevelt bandwagon beside Jim Farley," reported the *Sun*.

Being an astute politician, Tydings knew he would get national exposure by moving out front in the campaign. Throughout the autumn he spoke all over Maryland and in New York, New Hampshire, Ohio, Illinois, and Indiana. He and his new bride, the former Eleanor Davies Cheesborough, held a huge Roosevelt rally on September 5 in the garden of his new estate, Oakington Farms. Eleanor had convinced her husband that mobilizing Maryland's Democratic women to register and vote would significantly contribute to the campaign and would be good politics too. More than 2,000 women (and a sprinkling of men) attended. It was the largest gathering of Democratic women ever held in the state and a great success, with perfect weather shining on those gathered beneath the tall fir trees clustered in a grove beside the stone manor house.

Despite the fact that most newspapers endorsed Landon (hoping to "Save the American Way of Life" as the anti-Roosevelt slogan put it), and despite opposition from most business and industrial leaders (some of whom foamed at the mouth from mere mention of his name[6]), Roosevelt won 60.7 percent of the vote. Tydings's generous prediction—"I would be surprised if Landon gets as many electoral votes as Hoover received four years ago"—was not generous enough. In 1932 Hoover carried six states; in 1936 all but Maine and Vermont lined up in the Democratic column. Jim Farley took the old saying "As Maine goes, so goes the nation" and quipped, "As Maine goes, so goes Vermont."

Tydings was comfortable with the outcome. Despite the size of Roosevelt's majority—perhaps *because* of the size of his victory—the nation's press cautioned the president not to misinterpret the mandate. He had gained the freedom to do whatever he wanted in his second term, the Washington *Post* explained, but should not underestimate "the intelligence, self reliance and probity" of the average citizen by believing remedies could come only from the central government. The New York *Times,* even before the election, had warned Roosevelt to make his second term "more conservative than his first." The tide of public opinion was running "against hasty experimentation," and the *Times* concluded, "There is urgent need for the restraining influence of the party's conservative wing." The *Sun* (which had endorsed every Democratic nominee except William Jennings Bryan in 1896 and 1908) refused to endorse Roosevelt because the New Deal's economic foundation undermined "long range hope for prosperity."

Newspapers justified Tydings's position with their consensus that the administration must consolidate programs and abandon experimentation. Byrd, Glass, Tydings, and other conservatives could speak up in good conscience. They had been loyal Democrats and could not be accused of being Hooverites, turncoats, or Liberty Leaguers. They stood on firm ground, having delivered their judgments as conservatives, not obstructionists.

Tydings had emerged as one of the Senate's—and the nation's—leading spokesmen for the conservative cause. He moved up in the Senate ranks. He became, in addition to chairman of the Territories and Insular Possessions Committee, a ranking member of the Naval Affairs Committee and seventh on the powerful Appropriations Committee. Franklin Roosevelt had only experienced the first round with Tydings, who had gained new power and stature.

Notes

1. Although Tydings again introduced legislation to legalize 3.2-percent beer and raise revenue, the law Roosevelt signed was his own. Tydings was not invited to the White House signing. But Walter Winchell gave him a verbal "orchid" for leading the drive, and local florist Z. D.

Blackistone presented Tydings with a real one. (After beer became legal, Coca Cola sales plummeted. Budweiser's first team of Clydesdale horses made its appearance.)

2. Confirmation was no easy matter. Acheson had represented the communist government of the Soviet Union for the Washington law firm of Covington & Burling and so was accused of being a communist sympathizer. Tydings defended his character and integrity, spelling out that "an attorney does not have to sleep with the man who hires him." In 1950 this came back to haunt him when Joseph McCarthy said Tydings long supported the "Red Dean," knowing his communist connections.

3. Not all theater owners ordered by MGM to cut the reel were oblivious to what was going on. The owner of the Capitol Theater in Charleston, West Virginia, wrote to the Charleston *Daily Mail* complaining that "if anything is not favorable to the administration it has to come out." The unfairness disgusted him. "The Capitol isn't going to be restricted from showing whatever it sees fit to show," he concluded.

4. Tydings was right. In his diary Ickes referred to his planned remarks as "the attack that the statement I prepared . . . would have constituted."

5. In Tydings's case there was an exception. Although he disliked abandoning fundamental ideals of self-sufficiency, in the most inscrutable and confusing move of his career he voted "present" on the Social Security Act, thus taking no stand. He was criticized for the action, which he never satisfactorily explained.

6. Although Roosevelt inspired real devotion among throngs of supporters, he also aroused hatred within business, industrial, and professional communities. Calling him "That Man" or "That Madman" rather than using his name, they believed he had undermined the American system of individualism by injecting socialism into the economy. High taxes crippled industry; millions remained unemployed; the TVA and Home Owner's Loan Corporation competed unfairly with private enterprise; Wagner's NLRB encouraged strikes. Unforgivably, Roosevelt had abandoned his 1932 promises of sound money and a balanced budget and instead created a bureaucracy that threw billions away on relief while the national debt spiraled beyond $35 billion. States' rights had been trampled, the Constitution violated, the Bill of Rights betrayed, and the checks and balances of America's government threatened by Congress's reduction to a rubber stamp by a man they feared was moving toward dictatorship. The fate that had befallen Germany and Italy, they believed, could happen to the United States.

7

A New and Independent Nation

During Tydings's second term the New Deal was not his only focus. Serving on the Territories and Insular Possessions Committee, he educated himself about the Virgin Islands, Puerto Rico, Hawaii, and the Philippine Islands. Among those possessions, the Philippines grew increasingly important as Filipino leaders stepped up pressure for independence. The idea of granting the Philippines independence dated back to acquisition in 1898 and surfaced periodically. U.S. presidents since William McKinley had acknowledged it to be the ultimate goal; and each, in his own way, had furthered that policy through expansion of self-government.

Questions surrounding the issue—determining when the Filipinos would be ready, formulating terms of agreement, assuring protection of both U.S. and Filipino interests—posed difficult dilemmas. Several congressional bills sponsoring independence had failed for various reasons, including a curious ambivalence on the part of Filipino leaders. In 1930 a few men on the House and Senate territories committees believed the time had arrived to prepare a bill so carefully drawn that it would resolve the many problems. Democratic Representative Butler Hare of South Carolina and Democratic Senator Harry B. Hawes of Missouri and Republican Senator Bronson M. Cutting of New Mexico were the main forces behind the move, backed by Key Pittman of Nevada and also Tydings.

Before joining Hawes in heading the fight for independence, Tydings immersed himself in the islands' unsettling history. As a

225

schoolboy he had read about the exotic land acquired in the United States' "splendid little war" with Spain; Admiral George Dewey was one of his heroes. Later, keenly interested due to his Senate assignments, he grew intrigued by the Philippines' past and incensed over the U.S. role—the dark side of the story, ugly details glossed over in favor of positive aspects of U.S. rule. Those studies shaped his attitude and reinforced his resolve to produce fair legislation.

Three centuries of Spanish rule over the Philippines had been severe, but "Hispanicization" of the Malay–Chinese–Indonesian population by and large was achieved peacefully through Catholic missionary efforts. By late nineteenth century, the rise of a Westernized elite aware of democratic ideals led to demands for greater political equality. From 1807 to 1872, 11 separate native revolts kept the islands in turmoil. When the leading Filipino patriot, José Rizal, was executed in 1896, a nationwide rebellion began. The Spanish agreed to reforms provided that rebel leader Emilio Aguinaldo and his chiefs expatriate themselves, which they did. When Spain failed to honor its agreements, the struggle resumed. By April 1898 when the United States declared war on Spain over Cuba, the Philippines were in open rebellion.

The U.S. role in the Philippines started well. Dewey urged Aguinaldo's return; and in May 1898, Aguinaldo took command of Filipino forces and linked up with guerrillas throughout the archipelago. Outnumbered Filipinos kept the Spanish confined in Manila while providing their new American partners with valuable intelligence about enemy numbers, positions, and the absence of mines in Manila Bay. Dewey destroyed the Spanish fleet.

But Aguinaldo grew uneasy. His American allies refused to put in writing support for Philippine independence. Dewey was ordered to distance himself from Filipino leaders, lest he compromise U.S. freedom of action. British, French, Japanese, and German warships steamed into Manila, hoping to succeed Spain as master of the Philippines. The city itself was yet to be captured. The Navy Department decided that would be done best without Aguinaldo. Negotiations with the Spanish produced a secret agreement: The Americans would stage a mock assault on Manila without bombardment (Aguinaldo was told his army would be fired on if he tried to enter), as the Spanish put up mock resistance before a prearranged surrender. Spain saved face; the Americans were saved casualties; and on August 13 the American flag was raised over the old walled city, Intramuros.

Aguinaldo was enranged. Fighting erupted between Filipino and U.S. forces—allies the day before—as the Americans forced the Filipinos from their strategic positions. Bad relations grew worse. Aguinaldo, who had established a government and declared independence on June 12 (in a declaration patterned after the American one), convened a revolutionary congress that approved a constitution in November. Meanwhile, U.S. forces were consolidating their hold throughout the islands to prepare for transfer of rule between the world powers, without regard for the constitutional proceedings.

The Treaty of Paris, signed December 19, 1898, ceded the Philippines, Guam, and Puerto Rico to the United States (Cuba was granted independence); in return the United States agreed to pay Spain $20 million. The nature of the payment—not intended as indemnity nor purchase price—never was adequately clarified. Historian Leon Wolff described it as "a gift. Spain accepted it. Quite irrelevantly she handed us the Philippines. No question of honor or conquest was involved. The Filipino people had nothing to say about it. . . ."

Outraged Filipinos saw it as uncategorically immoral. "People are not to be bought and sold like horses and houses," wrote General Antonio Luna in his *La Independencia* newspaper. To President McKinley's December 21 proclamation of policy—"benevolent assimilation" with "justice and right" rather than "arbitrary rule"— Aguinaldo replied with a threat of war. The constitution was promulgated two days before Aguinaldo's inauguration as president of the Philippines on January 23, 1899.

Fighting broke out on February 4, after three Filipino soldiers were slain by two American privates on patrol duty. A two-year war commenced. Aguinaldo decentralized his army into guerrilla bands, forcing the Americans to fight an enemy that melted into the countryside. Atrocities on both sides matched anything recorded in the terrible annals of colonial war. Aguinaldo, captured in May 1901 by Philippine Scouts fighting for the Americans, called for the rebellion to end. He saw its futility and swore allegiance to the United States, which already had set up governmental institutions with the goal of eventual independence. More than 4,000 American and 16,000 Filipino soldiers died; some 200,000 civilians perished, mostly from disease and starvation. McKinley declared, "The Philippines are ours not to exploit but to develop, to civilize, to educate, to train in the science of self-government."

Spain's legacy—built on an indigenous heritage rich in arts, a written language, distinctive culture and industries, and commerce with Asia—left the Filipinos largely Christianized, partly Westernized, unified through a central authority, and with a European culture and system of jurisprudence. That foundation offered fertile ground for sowing the seeds of democracy.

McKinley's First Philippine Commission (1899), in its recommendations, stressed the need for civilian government and noted the native passion for independence. The Second Philippine Commission (1900) set up a judicial system, a legal code, and civil service, and provided for popular election of tax collectors and provincial governors. A police force—the Philippine Constabulary—was formed to control bandits and handle unpacified insurgents. Civilian rule replaced U.S. military rule on July 4, 1901.

The elite classes' aptitude for sophisticated political strategy (given their former exclusion from self-government) impressed American colonial figures. The Philippine Organic Act of 1902 provided for a two-house legislature, the lower to be popularly elected and the upper to be appointed by the U.S. president; two Filipino commissioners to represent the islands in the U.S. Congress; and extension of the Bill of Rights to Filipinos. The first archipelago-wide elections were held in July 1907. Filipino hopes and policies were expressed through formation of political parties that vied aggressively at the polls yet shared the goal of independence. The Jones Act of 1916 (the second Philippine Organic Act) explicitly stated the United States' intention to grant independence as soon as a stable government was established. It replaced the appointive Senate with an elected body, effectively granting legislative control of the islands to the Filipinos.

Augmenting political and judicial efforts to restructure the Philippines, land reform saw the Catholic church's property sold in small parcels to the peasantry. Cholera and small pox were all but eradicated. Hospitals, roads, and schools were built—the hunger for education filling the 7,000 free public schools built, enrollments rising from 5,000 to some 1 million students by 1920.

The Americanization of government and education occurred under Republican administrations from 1901 to 1913. The Filipinization of the island's civil service, and actual encouragement of nationalism, occurred under Woodrow Wilson's administration. During those years a new generation of leaders entered provincial politics. Manuel Quezon, Sergio Osmeña, and later Manuel Roxas rose to prominence and practiced lessons learned from Aguinaldo's failed revolution: Pragmatism, patience, and conciliatory policies offered the best hope for independence.

Until the end of the 1920s, the islands achieved a balance between native ambition and imperial rule. It was a vital period of development, allowing Filipino leaders time to reflect and test; for as much as they committed themselves publicly to "immediate, absolute, and complete independence" (the phrase that served as slogan), privately they were frightened by the reality. American historian Theodore Friend wrote that, when a 1916 bill—the Clarke Amendment, providing independence within four years—was defeated narrowly by Republicans in the House of Representatives after having passed the Senate, Quezon and Osmeña, who had lobbied forcefully for it, had been sick with worry lest it actually pass. The 1924 Fairfield Bill languished due to the pair's quiescence—although in the Philippines they supported the measure with rousing declarations, Quezon insisting he would "prefer a government run like hell by Filipinos to one run like heaven by Americans." He seemed to prefer the adulation and political support to be gained by damning U.S. rule over the work of replacing it. Years later, Carlos Romulo recalled Quezon lamenting, "Damn the Americans! Why don't they tyrannize us more?"

In truth, there were good reasons to delay independence. U.S. political policies had aided the Filipino aptitude for self-rule; but economic policies were contradictory, some fostering self-reliance and others dependence. The Payne–Aldrich Tariff of 1909 and Underwood Tariff of 1913 forced reciprocal free trade on the Philippines, resulting in a tremendous growth in Philippine–American trade at the expense of Philippine trade with others. In 1930, 79 percent of exports went to the United States, while the islands received 63 percent of its imports from the United States. This severely limited the Filipino capacity to develop industries—and undermined the desire for independence. Without free trade, independence would be disastrous to Filipino investment, agriculture, and business.

Besides promoting dependence, the United States failed to provide a basis for Philippine self-defense. No island taxes were used for military outlays, thus the territory had no navy, air force, army (besides the Philippine Scouts, a well-trained force of 7,000 whose full costs were borne by American taxpayers), or military–industrial base. In the absence of an American program, the islands would become an independent nation with no defensive capability.

Despite U.S. economic and strategic inconsistencies, and despite the Filipino leaders' private fears, the popular appetite for independence grew and converged with a series of powerful external influences: the Depression; the rise of Japanese militarism; Democratic victories in 1930 and 1932; and racial hostility in the United States to Filipino immigration.

The Depression hit American labor and agriculture hard. Their lobbyists mounted campaigns in support of Philippine independence to eliminate competition from its exports (especially sugar) and cheap labor. Many came to think that, given the strains imposed by the Depression, the country would be better off without its colony.

Japan's 1931 invasion of Manchuria forced U.S. leaders to consider the nation's role in the Pacific. Although Secretary of State Henry Stimson, President Hoover, and the Departments of War and Navy believed that Japanese aggression made retention of the Philippines more important, the general public and many in Congress favored noninvolvement in foreign disputes. For them, Japan's belligerence confirmed that the United States should withdraw its inadequate Asiatic Fleet to Hawaii. No less a figure than Theodore Roosevelt had called the Philippines an American Achilles heel.

The Democratic party was troubled from the beginning by the acquisition of the Philippines. The collective American conscience, with its strong anti-imperialist ideals, suffered. When Democrats took control of the House in 1931 and the presidency in 1933, the pro-independence movement gained momentum.

America's West Coast had attracted large numbers of Filipino laborers. Because the islands were a U.S. colony, there were no immigration restrictions as there were against other Orientals. With the Depression, labor groups and bigots alike saw a chance to end the influx of cheap, nonwhite workers under the honorable umbrella of anti-imperialism. Patriotic and nativist organizations joined the independence bandwagon. Raising the flag of a new and independent nation as the Stars and Stripes were lowered would bring satisfaction and honor to both nations—even if some motives were mixed.

Economic interests did play a major role in the movement for independence, as did social and strategic considerations; but without the anti-imperialist principles that occupied a central place in the American conscience, the drive for independence could not have been consummated.

Tydings entered politics during Wilson's anti-imperialist administration and believed in the Philippines' right to independence. But one aspect troubled him: the military effects in the Pacific. Even before the Japanese invasion of Manchuria, he foresaw dilemmas. Would independence "lay them open to attack?" he asked in a speech on the floor in February 1929. Would the United States be obligated if asked to repel an invader? He was concerned lest the Philippines "become the vassals, so to speak, of some other nation that might not deal with them as kindly." Except for his close friend Hawes, and for Pittman, a few other Democrats, and Cutting (the majority wanted to get rid of the colony to protect American cooking oil, sugar, and cordage interests), few senators cared enough to sustain a debate.

By 1932 the question took on greater urgency. Debate centered on a bill drafted by Hawes and Cutting. Hawes, like Tydings, was not easily influenced by special interests. Each was committed to independence—on terms favorable to Filipinos, yet acceptable to Congress and the American people. Both fervently believed any new government would need time to prepare for economic independence—as separate from political independence. They wanted a definite length of time—a commonwealth period—between acceptance of independence and actual formal separation from the United States. Tariffs must be applied gradually. Quotas should be fair to

Filipinos, yet fair to American farmers. As Hawes and Tydings repeatedly pointed out, the immediate high tariffs and ruinously small quotas sought by American farm groups would leave the Philippine economy in chaos, wrecking all chance for a secure future—one safe from Japan.

Hawes was harassed by powerful lobbies and individuals representing the gamut of opinion pro and con—from the nakedly racist ("God gave the nonassimilable Asiatics a place in the sun and that place is the Orient") to the militantly imperialistic (William Randolph Hearst insisted that "only decadent nations contract while the vigorous expand"). In between a cacophony of voices vied for attention, with the "Manila Americans" (U.S. citizens residing in the islands), American overseas investors, exporters and importers, and manufacturers staunchly opposing independence while the American Federation of Labor, the American Legion, the National Grange, and agricultural associations hurled themselves into action in support of independence.[1]

There was little agreement on anything within the pro-independence lobby. Labor and agriculture (joined by bigots) pressed for immediate independence, full tariffs, and complete cessation of immigration. Among internationalists, most preferred delayed independence and insisted that the United States retain military and naval bases there. Isolationists, citing the danger posed by Japan, wanted total and immediate withdrawal. Even among Filipino leaders and citizens there was disagreement. Business people and those with land and capital defended the status quo. The propertied classes wanted a long transition period or even permanent ties. Emilio Aguinaldo and Judge Juan Sumulong stood fast for immediate and complete freedom and argued against U.S. naval and military bases as a danger (they might draw enemy attack while ill equipped with men and matériel sufficient for self-defense).[2] Planters and millers fought any tariff limits, which Osmeña came to consider the price of independence. All groups detested the insult of immigration exclusion or quotas.

Quezon and Osmeña still privately vacillated—sometimes belligerently demanding immediate and total independence, and other times leaning toward some sort of permanent relationship. In a wide-ranging discussion with Secretary of State Stimson in 1928

Quezon said, "Give us certainty and we will take dominion status." To protect his standing back home, however, he added, "like your President T. R.—if you quote me on this, I will say you lie."

Hawes, as he prepared to take the issue before the Senate, feared that the Filipino leaders' inconsistencies made them appear insincere. When Senate hearings opened in January 1930, he invited the Philippine delegation (then headed by Manuel Roxas, Osmeña's stalwart ally) to a private meeting. "Do you and your people honestly and truly want independence?" he asked them. Roxas recalled he and the others "almost stumbled over each other" in their eagerness to answer yes. Hawes vowed to help.

The Hawes–Cutting bill was presented on the floor in April 1932. (Butler Hare's House bill had quickly passed, thanks to procedural maneuvering by Speaker John Nance Garner.) But it ran out of steam in the face of a filibuster by Arthur Vandenberg and the Senate's absorption with emergency legislation relating to the Depression. Tydings, one of the bill's floor managers, agreed in July to postpone action until the December lame duck session.

The six-month hiatus could have given Filipino leaders time to prepare a unified campaign. Hawes once advised them to court journalists, lobbyists, and legislators to further their cause. Unfortunately that was not to be. Quezon and Osmeña—alternately colleagues, allies, and rivals—had jockeyed for power for nearly two decades as Roxas rose to become Osmeña's main supporter. Quezon accused Osmeña of using the independence issue to project himself as the foremost Filipino leader. Quezon divided the Nationalista party, heightened Filipino–American animosities, and gathered other political leaders into a united front. Osmeña was relegated to second place by Quezon's powerful appeals to nationalism. Quezon's faction assumed the right to articulate the dream of independence as he attempted to make himself the personification of the Philippine nation.

In 1932, with independence a near reality, Filipino leaders fell all over each other in unseemly rivalry. Quezon, in the Philippines, feared Roxas and Osmeña—in Washington as leaders of the Philippine mission—could take control at home if they achieved their goal in the United States. He tried to force their return. But they refused. In staying they perhaps could usurp Quezon's position; in leaving they risked failure of the bill, for Hawes and Hare planned to retire. The new Congress might drop the whole thing to concentrate on the economic disaster.

Osmeña, Roxas, and the mission stayed. Quezon fumed and plotted. Hawes warned them that the impressions they made affected their cause and told them that a "high official" had remarked, "They are a 'soft' people, given to exciting and impressionable conduct, but lacking in earnestness and perseverance." Filipino power struggles at the top threatened the cause.

The Senate resumed debate as Franklin D. Roosevelt's administration prepared to succeed Hoover. Because of the economic crisis, independence was hardly a burning issue for the public or Congress. Tydings often spoke out alone in favor of the bill. "Aside from a speech by Tydings, scant attention to that matter was paid today," commented a newspaper article on December 14.

The Hawes–Cutting bill, as it stood then, proposed a 17–19-year commonwealth transition period, an immediate constitutional convention in the islands, a plebiscite on independence at the conclusion of the transition, gradual implementation of tariffs (so the burden would not fall all at once), U.S. retention of military and naval bases, an immigration limit of 50 Filipinos per year, and an American high commissioner with less power than the present governor-general. Hawes, Cutting, Pittman, and Tydings faced stubborn efforts to weaken the bill on the part of sugar and farm state senators determined to slash quotas and on the part of Arthur Vandenberg, who offered a replacement bill.

Vandenberg, a Hoover supporter, wanted a longer commonwealth period, with the constitutional convention to follow the years of trade adjustment. By then the Filipinos could better judge the situation (and perhaps decide against independence, having tasted the bitter tariff provisions). Vandenberg insisted that the United States retain control over Philippine domestic security and foreign relations by increasing the power of the high commissioner. Invoking old warnings from Theodore Roosevelt, he argued that, under Hawes–Cutting, the United States, would be left holding the bag in "a twilight zone of authority," charged with responsibility but stripped of authority. As example he cited rebellions by the Moros— Muslims from Mindanao and Sulu—who warred for independence from Manila. Retaining a commissioner with only casual power "[invites] trouble makers to make trouble for the purpose of getting us to intervene."

Tydings knew the Filipino position regarding a too-powerful high commissioner. "[That] could happen under either bill," he argued. "There are about 400,000 Moros and 11 or 12 million Christians [who have] a trained army with ammunition, field guns, machine guns . . . whereas the Moro has only his knife and his bolo." There was no difference between Vandenberg's bill and Hawes–Cutting. And, he asked, what about America's responsibility if the islands "had some controversy with another power?" Then what difference was there? Vandenberg was forced to concede, because under both bills the United States was responsible for Philippine foreign relations.

After Vandenberg, Iowa Republican L. J. Dickinson leapt in with an amendment to cut the transition period to five years. It was defeated by one vote; but Huey Long and Edwin Broussard of cane sugar–rich Louisiana won their campaign for pared-down, duty-free quotas on sugar. An angry Tydings reminded them what it was they were shredding.

"We are dealing not only with the question of independence, but we have written into the bill limitations upon Filipino trade with this country without giving them any counterright to limit importations from the United States," he said in summing up years of bickering over what Americans might sacrifice to honor the long-standing promise of independence. The bill already was rigged in favor of the United States, he noted. "As a matter of simple justice" it was "outrageous" that anyone should demand privileges he refused to give. He refused to yield the floor to Broussard. "They have no agent upon this floor . . . who can speak," he said impatiently. "Is it too much to ask that they at least be given a decent opportunity . . . to set up an independent government which will function and not bring economic chaos upon the new nation no sooner than it has started to work?"

Broussard demanded to hear Tydings's reasons for not imposing taxes after three years and raising them quickly. Tydings let him have it. "In the Philippines to-day they have no insular service, they have no diplomatic service, they have no army, they have no navy.

. . . Does anyone think that in a period of three years this nation can take over all their own affairs, have their trade representatives. . . , develop an army [and navy]?" he asked incredulously. He spun around to address the chair. "It is asinine to say that in seven or eight years [they] can assume all of the functions of an independent nation." Turning back to his colleagues he queried, "What is the use of granting them independence if that independence is not strong enough to permit them to be the success which we say we want them to be?"

Tydings proposed his own amendment, a 12-year transition: seven years to set up an economic system before tariffs, followed by five years of gradually increased restrictions. When debate resumed, it became clear that the sugar and farm blocs never would support a plebiscite but would allow a longer interim. The compromise hammered out allowed ten years for transition with popular ratification of a constitution. Filipinos could express their reaction to the new government's framework, but were refused a plebiscite for approving or rejecting its form.

The bill went through further modification to reconcile differences between House and Senate versions. What emerged gave Filipino leaders most of what they had asked for. The political terms provided for a ten-year transition, no plebiscite (Quezon, Osmeña, and Roxas opposed one, fearing it was too hot an issue for the first national vote), and an American high commissioner symbolically subordinate to the commonwealth president (who would occupy Malacañan Palace and thus appear preeminent to Filipinos, although the commissioner retained the right to intervene in crucial matters). The economic provisions spared American goods from Philippine tariffs until independence, while Filipino exports had five years without duties followed by five years of gradually increasing taxes; quotas on sugar, oils, and cordage were set at the higher figures of the House bill (850,000 tons of sugar and 200,000 tons of coconut oil, substantially higher than the farm lobbies had wanted); and Filipino immigration was not summarily halted until independence, with a token quota of 50 being allowed entrance annually until then.

On military and diplomatic matters, the Filipinos had not pressed for U.S. withdrawal. Despite a clear congressional preference for the abandonment of bases after independence, Democrats inserted a provision to retain them to appease anticipated Republican condemnation on strategic and balance-of-power grounds. Quezon and Osmeña indicated they would accept retention of bases as they had not opposed it earlier; Quezon at one time actually had spoken in favor of bases. The point, at that time, appeared insignificant to them compared to economic matters.

The Hare–Hawes–Cutting (H–H–C) bill went to Hoover in late December. He vetoed it on January 13, 1933, on grounds that it endangered peace in the Pacific. His veto was swiftly overruled by both the House and Senate.

Independence now lay in the hands of the Filipinos. Henry Stimson, who believed H–H–C was an evil bill, wrote in his diary, "Poor little Quezon now has the entire burden thrown on him of stopping it." During the year's negotiations, the diminutive Filipino leader was in a frenzy of apprehension. Opinion in the islands was split: Those for acceptance viewed H–H–C, for all its faults, as progress "not to be gambled away"; while those for rejection were convinced that it would cripple commerce and that the United States, with control of the military bases, "would be in a position to exercise practical suzerainty." Egypt provided them with an unnerving example of what kind of independence was enjoyed in the "presence of English navy and army reservations."

Quezon, although he had been in the Philippines throughout the Osmeña–Roxas mission, had lived in the United States as resident commissioner for more than eight years. He knew how the system worked and the nature of the American stance—the need to diminish the islands' special trading position to ensure harmony among competing interest groups. With Roosevelt's victory—before passage of H–H–C—Quezon had seen the chance to wring a more favorable bill from the Democrats. He sent a delegate, Benigno Aquino, as his personal envoy, with instructions to work for Senator William H. King's bill. King—from Utah, a beet-sugar state—had sponsored a bill for immediate independence.

Osmeña and Roxas had told Quezon that King's bill would never pass; and Aquino realized, on arrival in December, that the Hawes–Cutting measure offered their best bet. In reply to Quezon's cable declaring "let there be no bill" if immediate independence proved impossible, the strong-willed Aquino urged him to accept:

Nothing better "could be expected in the future." Thwarted in his attempts to improve H–H–C, Quezon grew determined to defeat it. He cabled the mission that the bill was "a joke." His stance contributed to Hoover's veto. Osmeña, Roxas, and Aquino—painfully aware of the bill's shortcomings—realized it was all they could get. But Quezon, knowing the American system, still argued for better terms. It was more likely, given that he knew who dictated the terms, that the chance to sink his rivals outweighed other considerations. He sailed for Washington in March 1933 to continue his battle.

A preoccupied Roosevelt was busy; Quezon was forced to negotiate with Osmeña and Roxas. On April 25 he signed an agreement at the Willard Hotel recommending that the Philippine Legislature accept H–H–C with two clarifying caveats: that the military and naval reservations exclude bases adjacent to Manila and other major ports; and that the Philippine Legislature be allowed to modify the trade provisions during the transition period or that the transition be reduced to five years. At a Capitol Hill meeting with Tydings and other senators, an emotional Quezon described the irony of some future Filipino president trying to run his nation in the midst of fluttering American flags. Senate majority leader Joe Robinson blurted out, "Why don't you come clean and be frank? We believe you don't want independence." Robinson's explosive remark revealed the deep uncertainty about Filipino leadership, and Tydings's skepticism over their sincerity deepened on witnessing Quezon's performance.

Quezon, on leaving, told Osmeña and Roxas that the Willard Hotel agreement was finished. But after wangling a meeting with Roosevelt and hearing him insist that the Filipinos must act before the United States would consider anything further, he once more decided to go along with Osmeña and Roxas. The men sailed together for Manila, Quezon assuring them he would comply. But less than a week after landing they split again. Quezon drew on his power base as Roxas and Osmeña challenged him to let the populace settle the matter by plebiscite.

As Osmeña and Roxas had worked in Washington for an acceptable measure, Quezon had been busy consolidating support. The president of the University of the Philippines, Rafael Palma, had been outspoken in favor of H–H–C. Quezon slashed the institution's budget by a third. Palma resigned to prevent further retribution. One of the Philippines' two biggest newspaper chains, the *T–V–T* (*Tribune–Vanguardia–Tabila*), openly opposed Quezon; the other, the *D–M–H–M* (*El Debate–Mabuhay–Herald–Monday Mail*), was not in either camp. Quezon persuaded wealthy backers to purchase *D–M–H–M;* and he snared *T–V–T* 's Carlos Romulo, a brilliant young journalist, to promote his positions.[3]

Money was next on the list. Quezon launched a fund-raising drive against H–H–C in the early summer of 1933, drawing huge contributions from wealthy Filipino businessmen and from longtime supporters Joaquin (Mike) Elizalde and Andres Soriano. Sugar interests contributed generously.[4]

But Quezon also needed to have the people behind him. He courted Juan Sumulong and General Aguinaldo, men with strong popular support who militantly opposed H–H–C because of their commitment to immediate independence. With his odd coalition, Quezon had Osmeña and Roxas against the wall. They were forced to attack the popular leader in public by casting doubt on his patriotism—an effort that backfired, for Quezon reveled in the role of aggrieved innocent whose love of country was being impugned.

Quezon settled on three grounds on which to fight H–H–C: (1) the naval and military bases, (2) the economic aspects, and (3) the indignity of the immigration clause. Osmeña, in frustration, defended his mission's compromise; he read the Willard Hotel agreement before the Philippine Legislature and described the Byzantine maneuvering Quezon had engaged in. But Quezon won. On October 7, 1933, after a marathon all-night session, the Philippine Senate rejected the terms of independence offered by the United States. At a time when Mohandas Gandhi and Jawaharlal Nehru were in and out of jail in India, and Vietnam's Ho Chi Minh and Indonesia's Sukarno were living in exile, Manuel Quezon was demanding a better deal.

Immediately after the legislature rejected H–H–C, Quezon again sailed for Washington. Osmeña and Roxas refused his request to accompany him. Roxas was sick of what he called the "two Quezons, [the] astute and slippery politician who babbles immediate, absolute, and complete independence" and the "high-brow, superbly conservative statesman . . . who speaks of a political partnership with America and is a devotee of free trade with the United States." Osmeña hoped Quezon would be left holding the H–H–C bag. Quezon asked a friend, just returned from a decade of promoting the Philippines in Washington, what his chances for success were. "None, virtually none," was the reply. The reception awaiting him was no better than his send-off. Key Pittman remarked, "Mr. Quezon may be political dictator at home but [the U.S.] Congress refuses to be dictated to."

With Hawes retired, Tydings, new chairman of the Territories Committee, took over management of Philippine independence. The blatant political overtones of the H–H–C rejection had angered Tydings. Quezon especially appeared insincere, selfish, and shockingly ambitious. Tydings, impatient with devious ploys, had little tolerance for Filipino maneuvering. When Hawes–Cutting had passed a year earlier, he had openly spoken his piece. "I was one of those who tried to keep out of the bill every discrimination against the people of the islands"—and in so doing, he said, "demonstrated my friendship for their cause." But, he admonished, "let me say it is not only doubtful that another bill as acceptable to them as this one can be passed if they reject it, but . . . rejection of this bill by the Filipinos will be construed by the people of the United States as indicating they do not want independence."

That should have served as a warning. Now, in the face of the Philippine Legislature's action, Tydings was blunter than ever as he issued what Filipino writers called his "famous *pronunciamento*" and what Americans called an ultimatum: There would be "no [new] Philippine legislation . . . at this session of Congress." But, he said, because the Filipino people had had no voice in the legislature's rejection of H–H–C, Congress would consider an extension of time; if the new legislature (there would be elections in June) failed to act or voted adversely, that would serve notice that the Philippine people "do not desire independence and desire to continue their present status. . . . [I]f the Filipino people do not want it, no better bill can be written and passed." Roosevelt, he noted, favored H–H–C, so Congress had expressed his wishes. In short, take it or leave it.

On hearing of Tydings's statement, Quezon said to Henry

Stimson, "I see nothing but to go home and teach my son to rebel."
Nevertheless he stayed.

Quezon had arranged meetings with Stimson—retired from
government but still influential—and with Secretary of War George
H. Dern. He warned them that under H–H–C economic ruin or
Japanese attack would lead to bloodshed, revolution, or both, but
said that special trade relations could prevent catastrophe. Quezon
met with Roosevelt, but the president was immersed in the American
economic crisis. He warned Quezon that—considering the mood of
labor, sugar, and dairy groups—"if you insist upon better economic
considerations, you may get your independence in 24 hours." When
Quezon replied, "if it is the intent of the United States to no longer
have interest in the Philippines in the Far East, now or in the future,
we may as well have independence as soon as possible," Roosevelt
suggested he prepare a written proposal and later urged him to take
stock of congressional opinion.

Tydings and Quezon had one brief meeting in January 1934
that proved neither productive nor destructive. After Roosevelt
called the congressional leadership to the White House to discuss
the stalemate, Tydings and Quezon had several more meetings.
Perhaps the president persuaded Tydings to reconsider new legislation. Filipino newspapers credited him (and Quezon, which was
unlikely) with softening Tydings's stance. Whatever the reason for
the shift, following separate White House conferences with congressional leaders and Quezon, Tydings arranged a series of negotiating
sessions with Quezon.

During those meetings Tydings had no intention of letting the
wily Quezon draw him into the ambiguities, sophistries, and complexities that he played with the genius of a virtuoso. "You want to
play draw poker," he said point-blank to Quezon, "but I'm playing
showdown."

Roosevelt was right, Tydings went on, in saying that any
changes Congress would make would be for the worse. The
H–H–C sugar quotas—low as they seemed to Quezon—had required hard-fought battles; reopening debate might produce lower
quotas. The "present temper of Congress" was not favorable for
economic concessions. But it might be possible to improve the
military terms, he said, given the growing isolationist sentiment and

army officers' concerns over the vast exposed defense perimeter in the Pacific. Eliminating the Philippines would shrink the defensive sphere to the army's liking. The navy, however, wanted to expand its fleet to maintain a balance in the region. Tydings put his cards on the table. He would commit himself to eliminating army bases and making naval bases negotiable at the time of independence. In exchange, he insisted that Quezon promise to support those changes. He drew up his proposals in memorandum form, signed it, and waited for Quezon to pick up the pen.

Quezon appeared to stall. He would be willing, he said, to accept H–H–C with Tydings's amendments if Tydings would publicly state that a committee would travel to the Philippines "with a view of finding out whether further amendments should be made after acceptance by the legislature." Tydings agreed, if Quezon would advocate acceptance of the modified legislation. Finally, after perhaps 15 minutes of hesitation, Quezon hastily scrawled his name on Tydings's memorandum.

Tydings had no evidence then that Quezon had been "playing draw poker" all over town; but Quezon previously had given Senator King the impression that he backed King's bill for immediate independence, and he had journeyed to New York to persuade Teddy Roosevelt, Jr., that he still hoped for dominion status. He had played the alternatives the way some do horses—betting win, place, and show on the assumption that three chances are better than one. Tydings had sized up Quezon accurately and was leaving nothing to chance.

He described the scene to his wife. "I will write the bill giving you your independence," he said he told Quezon, "but you've got to give me your word that you'll stick with it if I fight for it on the Senate floor." Quezon had agreed he would. Tydings insisted he put it in writing.

After securing Quezon's signature, Tydings cabled his allies, opponents, and prominent Filipino independents to gain their consent. Osmeña and Roxas were hesitant. They requested the military changes be offered as confirmation of their interpretation of H–H–C, but Tydings refused any conditions. He had Hawes help persuade them to comply. By February 24 he had the endorsements of Aguinaldo, Sumulong, Osmeña, Roxas, and every Filipino leader of consequence. He also obtained agreement of Secretary of the Navy Claude A. Swanson, his assistant secretary Colonel Roosevelt, and Secretary of War Dern.

With all loose threads carefully gathered and modified legislation ready, Tydings met again with the president and told the press that "important developments" were in the works. He assured Roosevelt that Congress would consider new legislation, leaving the president satisfied that the next moves were up to Congress. "It looks like we are getting somewhere now," Roosevelt told newsreporters. Tydings would head the effort to modify H–H–C into a bill acceptable to all Filipino and American interest groups.

In February, after working with Democratic Representative John McDuffie of Alabama, chairman of the House Territories Committee, Tydings wrote Roosevelt a letter and memorandum outlining the essentials of his negotiations and requesting a presidential message to Congress for swift passage of the Tydings–McDuffie Bill. "Senator Quezon and his associates have stated they will accept the bill as amended and advocate its acceptance by the Philippine legislature and people," he wrote, adding that, to "avoid future misunderstanding," he had cabled the substance of the enclosed memorandum to Filipino leaders and all favored acceptance. The memorandum, drafted jointly by Tydings and Quezon, proposed: "Where imperfections or inequalities exist in it they can be worked out later upon proper hearing and, I hope, in fairness to both peoples." On March 2, 1934, Roosevelt requested that Congress enact new independence legislation.

Its reintroduction before the Senate reopened debate on all the old issues with all the old players. Vandenberg, calling the idea of independence a "counterfeit luxury," introduced a bill for independence in two years. King sponsored one for immediate independence. Iowa's Dickinson reintroduced his five-year bill, with Huey Long's vigorous, colorful support.

Quezon reappraised his chances and decided to back Dickinson. Knowing that Tydings would not want to rewrite the bill on the floor, but apparently believing he could bluff his way to force changes, he wrote Tydings that he wanted independence in five years, not ten. "I do not want you, my dear Senator, to feel that . . . I am turning my back against our agreement. . . . You have no reason to believe that I am moved by any purpose other than to get the best out of a bad situation." But before he could have the letter delivered, Tydings was tipped off that something was afoot. He sent word to Quezon, saying, as he later told his wife, "You just open your mouth and I will read this note [the statement he had forced Quezon to sign] to the Senate and I will destroy you." He called the delegation to his office and warned them against supporting Dickinson's bill. Undoubtedly fearful of what the chairman of the key committee might do, they quickly backed down.[5]

Senate Bill 3055, the Tydings–McDuffie Independence Act, was introduced on March 14. Tydings quickly moved to undercut competing bills by reading a message from Quezon recommending Congress enact the measure. (The letter read in part: "Senator King . . . expressed surprise that I, together with other Filipino leaders . . . should endorse the McDuffie Tydings bill . . . when we all have disapproved of the Hare–Hawes–Cutting bill. . . . Our main objection [has] been eliminated.")

After the Vandenberg, King, and Dickinson bills were defeated, Tydings blocked attempts to water down his measure. His bill should be considered the reintroduction of something already fully worked and debated, he said. "We spent 18 months in attempting to get this legislation in a condition in which the majority of Congress would support it—and I say 'this legislation' because the parliamentary situation indicated it was advisable to reintroduce the whole bill." The Filipinos did not ratify the act, he said, but now "have come back to us unanimously and asked us to pass the bill again. . . . [T]he Filipino leaders of all factions in the islands have agreed to accept it, and Philippine independence will be on its way."

To those who would slash the commodity quotas, he reminded them he had fought cuts before and would again. "We should write no limitation" on their exports to the United States until independence was "an accomplished fact," he argued. It would be "an outrage [for] greedy sugar interests . . . to usurp the entire market while 14,000,000 people in the Philippine Islands are thrown into economic chaos." He impatiently suggested his colleagues use their heads. "Some think only about what the Filipino people sell to us. Did it ever occur to us that we are selling them practically an equal amount of goods?" If they cannot sell, how can they buy? American workers "will be thrown out of work" if Filipinos can no longer sell and thus no longer buy.

Nothing about the issue was simple, he said. "It is frequently stated that . . . all that is necessary is simply to pass a bill, and the Filipinos will have independence overnight." If it were as simple as that, "I should be the last one in the world to want to delay the transition," he declared. "[But] independence is not going to depend upon the will for liberty. . . . The ultimate success of Philippine independence is going to depend upon the ability of the Filipino people to evolve an economic existence in the new state of affairs in which they will find themselves."

He reminded them how the United States acquired its colony— how Filipinos helped Dewey defeat Spain and how the United States repaid its ally with a double cross. "[If] circumstances were reversed, how we would rave about the injustice . . . ! In Heaven's name, give the Filipino people this opportunity!"

Tydings's measure passed 68 to 8 on March 23, 1934, and was signed into law by Roosevelt the next day. The Philippine Islands would become a sovereign nation in 1945. "Well, you are on your way now," Tydings said to Elpidio Quirino, a member of the Philippine delegation, who had stopped him to thank him. Hawes, who had dreamed of having his name on the independence act, sent compliments to his friend. "Dear 'Glad,' " he wrote. "You are going to write big history . . . , international history."

Tydings was more humble in his self-assessment. "It is not the bill I would have written, [but] a bill not wholly good was, if they wished it, better for the Filipinos than no bill at all," he wrote to the Baltimore *Sun*. He knew the dilemma facing Filipinos and stated it often: "I do not doubt for a moment that [Philippine leaders] would prefer a different bill . . . , but I think these men have all found, from contact with Members of Congress, that this is about the best they can get . . . and their acquiescence does not mean that this is the bill which they themselves would like to have."

He was correct. But as unsatisfied as Quezon, Osmeña, Roxas, and the others were with the Tydings–McDuffie Philippine Independence Act, they worked for unanimous ratification by the Philippine Legislature. On May 1, 1934—the anniversary of the date on which

Dewey steamed into Manila Harbor and destroyed the Spanish fleet—the legislature ratified it.

Whatever Quezon thought of Tydings privately (and it undoubtedly was not flattering), publicly he gave him credit. He wrote the *Sun* to complain that the senator's name had been omitted from a newspaper discussion of the bill's passage. "Senator Tydings, more than anybody else in the present Congress, is due the credit of the enactment of this law," he wrote. "It was through his efforts that the advocates and opponents of the rejected Hare–Hawes–Cutting law in the Philippine Islands have been brought to agree upon the acceptance of the new legislation."

The Philippine *Free Press* wrote that the change in Tydings's attitude since his "famous *pronunciamento*" had taken him from malediction to benediction, had converted bad news into good tidings. The Tydings name, which had become known in the Philippines—not always fondly—would be associated forever with independence.

Roosevelt barely had signed Tydings–McDuffie when Congress moved to raise tariffs on coconut-oil imports—a step that would damage the Philippine economy and, in Tydings's opinion, alter the bill's hard-won provisions. He was furious. "In the bill we said if they would do certain things we would give them independence. . . . Now, when the ink is hardly dry upon that document we come here shooting them in the back," he complained in disgust during debate on the tariff. "What we are about to do to the Philippine Islands is exactly what England tried to do to the Thirteen Colonies prior to the Declaration of Independence."

During the years of debate on independence, Tydings had been indignant at times over American treatment of the islands; but the prospect of his country going back on its word appalled him. "I do not think it was fair for the United States to take the Philippine Islands in the first place," he raged. "We took them at the point of the bayonet and finally bought them from Spain. We then promised them independence." Justice demanded that they help the Filipinos retrieve their lost independence "under favorable conditions, after we have forced our will on them for a period of 36 years."

It was morally wrong—a thousand times wrong—he told the

Senate. "It is nothing more than an attempt to tax a helpless and unrepresented people to satisfy a few people in the United States. . . . It is cowardly for a great Nation like this to have passed an independence bill only a month ago and now shoot the people in the back as they are going home with the document."

His effort to amend the tariff bill to exclude the Philippines failed. Despite the provisions of Tydings–McDuffie governing trade, the Senate wrote into a new law conditions that Tydings believed violated the covenant. All the good will the act might have brought the United States in the Orient—"because every Senator knows that the United States, in its foreign relations in the Far East, is judged primarily by its treatment of the Philippines"—would be lost. "Those people know that we are breaking our word." The Senate disagreed. Connally of Texas wrote off Tydings's lecture as "het up" breast-beating. "We gave the Filipinos independence last spring and they would not have it. If a little processing tax on a few of their coconuts is going to keep them from accepting independence, they have not got any business with independence."

Tydings's strong objections did force some change, for the Senate agreed to Nebraska Senator George W. Norris's proposal to refund the taxes collected to the Philippine government. This move prompted Huey Long to remark, "We have done a whole lot of fighting here for nothing. I do not blame my friend from Maryland for smiling. He has maneuvered us right into his camp. I compliment the Senator." It was a small victory, but it did mitigate the tariff bill's impact on the Philippine economy.[6]

After the Tydings–McDuffie Philippines Independence Act was passed and accepted (it did not take effect until May 1935 when Roosevelt approved the constitution), Filipino leaders became frantic over the prospect of losing their special trade advantages. Quezon returned to Washington in October 1934 to persuade the U.S. government to continue free-trade privileges after independence and to adjust the unilateral restrictions imposed during the commonwealth period by Tydings–McDuffie. But Cordell Hull, Roosevelt, and Secretary of War Dern believed that reopening the act to modification could scuttle the entire bill or end up to the Philippines' disadvantage.

An unhappy Quezon hurried home to meet with the U.S.

congressional mission already in Manila to study conditions there. Tydings had promised Quezon such a delegation. In his memorandum to Roosevelt, and in Roosevelt's message to Congress (with the president using Tydings's language almost verbatim), they had promised, "Where imperfections or inequalities exist . . . , they can be corrected after proper hearing, and in fairness to both peoples." Hence in autumn 1934, four men (Tydings, Democratic Senators Kenneth D. McKellar of Tennessee and William G. McAdoo of California, and Republican Senator Ernest W. Gibson of Vermont) made the trip to Manila to consider possible changes in the independence act depending on what they learned.[7]

Tydings's party boarded the SS *Monterey* at Los Angeles on November 14, 1934. After a few leisurely days in Honolulu, where he met the beautiful, intelligent Princess David Kawananakoa with whom he corresponded for many years,[8] the delegation sailed on November 22 on the SS *Empress of Canada*. With them on the *Empress* were Babe Ruth and Connie Mack, who were leading a group of big-league baseball greats on an exhibition tour as athletic ambassadors scheduled to play games in Japan, Shanghai, and the Philippines. News accounts noted that the exuberant ballplayers stole the show from the closed-mouthed senators, who smilingly declined to comment on their mission.

Tydings's liner cruised toward shore amid a flotilla of small craft on December 9; the Philippines *Herald* had anticipated the biggest waterfront reception in the history of Manila. There would be a 17-gun salute as the first line from the ship was fastened; and then a 12-car motorcade—Tydings in the lead—accompanied by outriding motorcycle police, their lights flashing and sirens wailing, would escort the senators to Malacañan Palace. Thousands were expected to line the docks and roads in welcome—although the paper admitted it was difficult to say whether the Washington VIPs or the baseball stars created the greater excitement.

While in Manila they were entertained lavishly—champagne, gala balls, glittering Filipino society. At a reception in their honor, the palace was decorated inside and out with brilliantly colored electric lights shimmering from hedges and trees. Elegantly attired Filipinos, the women wearing stunning European gowns or Filipino costumes, danced in a blaze of color and light. Newspapers, along with a number of people, criticized the extravagance, fearing the exquisite parties and luxurious surroundings would show a superficial prosperity and mislead the mission, causing its members to miss the terrible poverty underlying that sparkling veneer. They need not have worried. Tydings was not interested in being entertained and was not beguiled by charm and glitter. The mission set to work, meeting with national leaders and heads of business and agriculture, touring the islands from Bataan and Corregidor to Iloilo and Mindanao, holding hearings wherever they went, and gathering a mass of data, suggestions, and impressions.

There was no question in Tydings's mind that free trade after independence was impossible. Other nations would clamor for equal treatment. Once the Philippines were sovereign, they must be sovereign like all others, must deal with the world as a peer—not as a demipower, politically independent while economically dependent. His chief goal was to determine how best to stabilize mutual commerce during the transition period. The mission would study the results of the recent tariff on copra, look into shortening or prolonging the commonwealth period, and weigh the wisdom of cutting loose the islands considering the political climate in the Pacific.

Filipinos, desperate for a preferred market, were torn over the paradox of security versus autonomy. Organizations such as the Philippine–American Trade Association and their lobbies went to great lengths to protest that they were not asking for free trade, but for reciprocal relations to prevent a shattered economy. But clearly, most Filipino leaders desperately wanted continued free trade, no matter the euphemisms used. Only Aguinaldo believed the economic issue was secondary to the political. But realizing that Tydings–McDuffie's provisions could block economic progress, Aguinaldo noted, "America gave Cuba a preferential tariff when the latter was granted freedom. . . . [W]hy should not the Philippines enjoy free trade which was imposed upon her if the United States really desires to help our country?"

Tydings was hounded by reporters asking what his mission would decide. He stubbornly maintained silence. "We want to look around," he told them. "We'll play ball with you fellows after we find out what we have come to learn." "Curt" was a word often used in accounts describing Tydings's reaction to being asked the same questions over and again. When General Pablo Araneta remarked he could see no justifiable explanation for the sugar quotas granted Cuba compared to those granted the Philippines, the papers wrote that "Tydings replied curtly, 'Many things in this world cannot be explained.' " He was impatient when Filipinos discussed the issues solely from their own viewpoint, without taking into account U.S. constraints. Such narrow vision annoyed him and, as at home, he let his annoyance show.

To a people unaccustomed to a direct or blunt confrontational manner, Tydings was hard to understand and deal with. Filipinos admired and sought to practice a sensitive diplomacy and delicacy— *delicadeza*—in their personal relations. They employed evasion and euphemism to avoid tactlessness. They deemed American brusqueness unpleasant, but endurable because it was a foreign trait. Tydings, in turn, saw their indirection and tactful white lies as devious and hypocritical.

The mission spent two weeks touring, listening, and learning. They often dodged photographers and the press to avoid making public comment. But rumors derived from off-the-record remarks by mission members unsettled the Filipinos, for the clear sense was that chances of amending the law were zero.

December 22 was the date of a much anticipated event. Tydings was scheduled to address the Constitutional Convention to explore how his studies would affect chances for remedying the "imperfections and inequalities" of Tydings–McDuffie. He refused to release advance comment on his speech (which would be broadcast by radio hookup throughout the islands) and had requested that Quezon be on the rostrum, raising the question among the Manila elite, "Why did Tydings request Quezon to be present?" "Maybe he has a big surprise for Mr. Quezon," was the customary answer.

Any Filipinos expecting a pleasant surprise were disappointed. Tydings had not been misled by wealthy Manila's display of prosperity. He always had understood intellectually that independence would bring hardship, but his theoretical understanding of the adversities was nothing compared to his firsthand scrutiny of the reality: poverty, economic fragility, the disparity between Filipino hopes and the facts.

Tydings and the mission members, convinced that prospects for an easy independence were nonexistent, now believed that altering Tydings–McDuffie to extend free trade from the stipulated five years to the entire ten years would be fatal. The burden of tariffs would crush the economy and would not provide sufficent revenue in the meantime to liquidate outstanding debt. (Under the act, export taxes would accrue to the Philippine government and would be used as a sinking fund to pay off the territory's bonded indebtedness, allowing it to start its life as a new nation with a clean slate.) As far as the mission was concerned, Filipinos were living in a fantasy world if they thought immediate independence was possible and if they thought it would be anything but a terrible shock even in ten years. Tydings's speech laid it on the line.

"It is fitting and wise that we counsel together and, in an atmosphere of an unalloyed truth and complete frankness, search for the means and measures most likely to achieve our avowed purpose," he said moments after expressing gratitude for the invitation to address them. He spoke without platitudes or flights of rhetoric designed to evoke sentimental images, gave no voice to soaring (but empty) optimism. Half of his address analyzed and defended the hated export tax on Philippine products, and the rest graphically described the bleak economic future after taxes were in force and U.S. markets were virtually closed to their products.

It was a long, gloomy recital, with excruciating detail of tonnage, dates, and pesos, of what those taxes would mean (beyond settling accounts between the two nations through liquidation of debt). In 1931, 1932, 1933, he told them, the Philippines sold P522 million worth of commodities to the United States—cane sugar and coconut oils, cheroots and shells—items sold without payment of any tax because they were part of the United States. Had they been independent, taxes would have totaled P440 million, he said, and payments received would have been only P82 million—a loss of P440 million in income. That illustration proved not only the coming hardships, he said, but justified imposition of export taxes commencing in five years to prepare them gradually for the loss.

If their ability to adapt was not demonstrated, business interests would fail to receive loans; natural resources could not be developed.

National defense would be costly. It would be "illogical" for the United States "to bear responsibility for the acts of a nation over which it has no control. . . . Sovereignty and responsibility walk hand in hand," he said. Health, construction, education, sanitation, and transportation still would require revenue. "It is my belief that persons in both countries who are conversant with economic factors, whatever their emotional, political, and spiritual impulses may be, will not, after a full examination of the facts, contend that immediate independence is the best solution of this problem," he said pointedly. "It is doubtful whether such a contention would be made by informed persons if they had the real welfare of the Filipino people at heart or if they did not wish to destroy all the accomplishments of the Philippines" since 1898.

His concluding passage sought to cleanse the American conscience. "I have ventured," he said, "to comment briefly upon your future problems, to explain why certain measures have been adopted and to point out the obstacles which yet lie ahead so that hereafter it may be said that nothing was concealed from the people of the Philippine Islands."

Nothing was concealed. Intellectually, Filipinos knew the United States was not about to subsidize an independent nation. They knew a people could not be independent and dependent at the same time. But the harsh reality—hearing it said with terrible candor by the spokesman for the one force that could grant respite—was depressing and demoralizing.

Reaction to the speech was careful. A few—especially businessmen—were glad he had spoken honestly, although some were alarmed, fearing his graphic presentation was an attempt to frighten them away from independence. Many were disappointed: He had engaged in scare tactics but offered no suggestions. One unidentified American listener remarked, "He did not talk like a Democrat, suave, accommodating, full of promises, but like a Republican, combining common sense, frankness and a measure of hard-boiledness."

Filipino leaders were circumspect in choosing words for public attribution. Quezon called it "a great speech showing the speaker's analytical study of the Philippine independence problem." Osmeña said, "The Tydings speech reveals that the independence question is definitely settled. Only its attendant problems have to be faced and solved." Roxas said, "The speech is very good. It has portrayed vividly and in true colors the situation. . . . I hope the people will . . . devote all their energies and intelligence to the wise solution of those problems." Aguinaldo refused comment.

Speaker Quintin Paredes called it a realistic "exposition of facts by a lawyer," and added, "It might be disagreeable to some but it is true." Elpidio Quirino, who had thanked Tydings in Washington, said, "In spite of the gloomy future he has pictured . . . , I am not afraid of independence." Carlos Romulo never forgot how "frank" the speech was. "There was nothing jovial about Senator Tydings' address," he recalled. "It was a somber picture."

Press reaction was stronger. Some papers applauded. The Manila *Advertiser* commented, "The country owes an enormous debt of gratitude [for Tydings's] austere truth." The Manila *Daily Bulletin* was "impressed" that he relieved mind and conscience "by presenting the facts fully without regard for the question of whether these facts are welcome or unwelcome." He was no "dreamer living in a world of make-believe."

Others saw his clarity as discouraging—and his tone condescending—and threw *delicadeza* to the winds. The Philippines *Herald* wrote, "Senator Tydings took occasion to paint a gloomy picture . . . but he was not offering any remedy. . . . To make us see an abyss of darkness ahead and not point the light to us, is to make us misunderstand America's motives." His attitude, the editorial said, was "you asked for independence, and therefore you must suffer the consequences. . . . It is but another way of saying: Take it or leave it."

A *Herald* columnist used stronger language (his wrath perhaps responsible for the mixed metaphor): "Senator Tydings reminds me of the hangman who tells his victim at the moment of death: 'God have mercy on your soul!' and then cuts off his head." But, he admitted, Tydings's logic was unassailable. "You cannot refute him for his facts are indisputable, and you cannot accuse him of hardness for that would imply your own cowardice," he wrote. "You can only say he is a hard logician . . . that he has a head clear as crystal and a heart hard as stone [and] the head must rule the heart. . . . Perhaps," he concluded, "the harshest thing we could say of the Maryland senator is that he has a deadly sense of rectitude."

Aguinaldo's rebuttal, spoken in Tagalog and translated, was made when the mission members were his guests in Kawit, Cavit. He challenged Tydings's thesis that no thinking person still could believe in immediate independence: "Grant us independence first and develop later, side by side with it, the Philippine economic stability." Tydings's curt reply was widely regarded as condescending: "God gave us heads for thought. A wise man uses God's gift wisely. The best thought would be none too good for the best interests of the people of the Philippines." Yet few agreed with Aguinaldo in the wake of Tydings's warnings, and a number of Filipinos began to rethink independence with some renewed interest in partnership or dominion.

Mission members, noncommittal through their weeks of study on the main areas of disagreement (sugar quotas, export taxes, and transition time), remained silent even after Tydings's speech. At a closed-door meeting between mission members and Filipino leaders at Malacañan the day after Christmas, another flood of petitions was presented. But no agreements were reached. The Americans would not comment on changes to Tydings–McDuffie. Everything would depend on what Congress instructed them to do, they insisted, as well as on the petitions. "The Filipinos cannot expect to get all they asked for, but one thing is certain, that any of their petitions will receive careful consideration" by Congress, Tydings assured them.

He understood the complexity of the problems tormenting Filipinos, but was impatient with their indecisiveness. In one of the rare interviews he granted, an intrepid Filipino newsman managed to persuade him to open up a bit just before his December 22 speech. Tydings discussed the leadership's need for "moral courage to tell the truth," and his disappointment over what he thought was cowardice. His anger was scarcely concealed.

> Then I ask if they [the Filipino leaders] have the real moral courage to tell the truth, to go out to their people and tell them that all this agitation has been a political bluff. . . . And they reply, "But Senator, you don't understand, that would be political suicide for us." Well, what the hell, I tell them that they are supposed to be so patriotic that they would die for their country, but they are not patriotic enough to commit political suicide for it.

As the American delegation prepared to depart on December 28, 1934, Tydings talked with reporters, fielding their questions brusquely.

> When will the Philippine question come up again in Washington, Senator, in connection with your survey here?
>
> I imagine that the Philippine question will remain as it is at its present status unless a delegation of Filipinos should come to Washington and ask for future consideration of some phases of the Philippine question.
>
> What are the prospects of another legislation on the Philippines in congress?
>
> That is answered by my answer to the first question.
>
> Do you believe, senator, congress in its coming session will have time to discuss any legislation tending to improve the imperfect provisions of the Tydings–McDuffie law?
>
> I believe that is also answered by my answer to the first question.

Asked to outline the problems that would come with independence, he replied, "I have already mentioned them in my speech before the constitutional convention." When queried about the differences between Hare–Hawes–Cutting and Tydings–McDuffie, he said only, "The philosophy of the two laws is the same. They are the same except in some changes." A foolhardy journalist who persisted, asking, "Are those changes substantial?" received the ungracious admonition: "You can read the two laws and compare their provisions. You need not ask that question."

Changes in the law would come only if Filipinos could make the case for them. On that note the mission departed, sailing for New York by way of Bali, Suez, and Europe. Tydings arrived back in Washington on February 7, having sailed around the world in the first of many such trips.

During the course of the Philippine visit, the mission members had swung away from independence because of their unanimous pessimism over the economic situation. McKellar hoped Filipino leaders would request modification of Tydings–McDuffie, allowing the United States to retain full sovereignty and continue controlling tariffs, immigration, and defense. The Philippines could enjoy full and complete self-government politically, but would be spared economic ruin and domination by Japan, he said. Republican Senator Gibson reported to the Senate that he regretted ever voting for Tydings–McDuffie. He openly advocated a permanent commonwealth.

Tydings, who withheld his support until after the Filipino mission left Washington (as did McAdoo), also had grave misgivings. "It is my personal opinion that congress made a mistake in passing the Tydings–McDuffie Act in its present form," he said on January 31 as he was leaving Paris. He believed the Filipinos were making a fatal error in forcing independence—both from fiscal and defensive points of view. Back in New York he described the act as of "dubious wisdom." But he was opposed to withdrawing the law that bore his name. Independence was "inescapable. . . . We gave our word. [The Philippine Islands] must accept the disadvantages that come with being a nation. . . . As a matter of conscience I explained the hardships . . . so it could not be said that the Filipino leaders took their steps in ignorance."

The Filipinos, headed by Quezon, arrived in Washington in March acutely aware that independence no longer could be mistaken for Utopia. Quezon, in Manila, had appeared to propose again an "economic and cultural partnership" with the United States, but it was grimly apparent that going backward was impossible. The Filipino people wanted autonomy. Undoubtedly goaded by the negative McKellar, Gibson, and Tydings statements, Quezon, Quirino, and others made firm declarations in support of Tydings–McDuffie. It was possible that Tydings deliberately had denigrated the act, believing he could force the Filipinos to defend it and put an end to their vacillation. In fact, there was no room left for coy games. Congress, disillusioned by its mission's discouraging findings and beset by the Depression, grew more anti-imperialistic. The tables were turned. It was Americans, now, who wanted absolute and total independence from their colony by a designated date.

Tydings was not so rigid as his initial utterances made him appear. Before the Senate he urged revision of trade policies because failure to safeguard the islands' economy would "cause economic dislocation [and] engender discord . . . and may encourage nations with grasping tendencies to intervene." But America must keep its

Millard E. Tydings during tenure as Speaker of the House of Delegates, Annapolis, c. 1920. (Susquehanna Museum of Havre de Grace, Inc.)

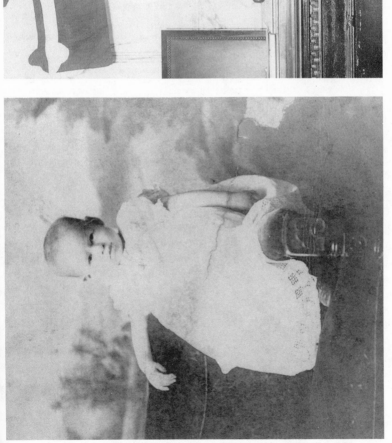

Millard E. Tydings c. 1891. (Susquehanna Museum of Havre de Grace, Inc.)

"On the carpet."
Malone cartoon
inspired by Tydings's
April 2, 1935 speech
castigating the New
Deal. (Special Collec-
tions, University of
Maryland at College
Park Libraries)

ON THE CARPET

SENATOR MILLARD TYDINGS CERTAINLY GAVE THE OLD DONKEY A HEART-TO-HEART TALK IN THE SENATE THE OTHER DAY, AND DEMOCRACY JUST SAT THERE AND BLINKED ITS EYES WHILE THE SENATOR FROM MARYLAND CAUSTICALLY REFERRED TO THE INCREASING NATIONAL DEBT AND THE UNBALANCED BUDGET. MR. TYDINGS DIDN'T APPEAR TO ENJOY HIS ROLE AS THE DENOUNCER, WHILE THE DENOUNCEE DIDN'T ENJOY IT AT ALL, BUT THE REPUBLICANS, SITTING IN RINGSIDE SEATS, VOTED IT A SWELL SHOW. —malone

"Look What Came
Out of Your Purge."
Berryman cartoon of
FDR and Jim Farley
lamenting the 1938
purge election results.
(Special Collections,
University of
Maryland at College
Park Libraries)

CHIEF, LOOK WHAT CAME OUT OF YOUR PURGE!

TYDINGS FOR PRESIDENT CLUB

JOIN NOW!

Tydings with Vice President John Nance Garner.
(Susquehanna Museum of Havre de Grace, Inc.)

Joseph Davies, Joseph D. Tydings, and Eleanor and Millard Tydings at the Democratic Convention in Chicago, 1940. (UPI/Bettmann)

After a successful morning of duck hunting Millard and Eleanor relax with their Chesapeake Bay retriever. (Photograph courtesy of Mrs. Eleanor Ditzen)

Senator George L. Radcliffe, FDR, Maryland Governor Herbert R. O'Conor, and Tydings on an inspection tour of Maryland defense facilities in October 1940. (Special Collections, University of Maryland at College Park Libraries)

Tydings and Maryland Senator Herbert R. O'Conor (to Tydings's left) celebrate with Alben W. Barkley (right) as he wins the Democratic Party's nomination for the vice presidency in Philadelphia in 1948. (Susquehanna Museum of Havre de Grace, Inc.)

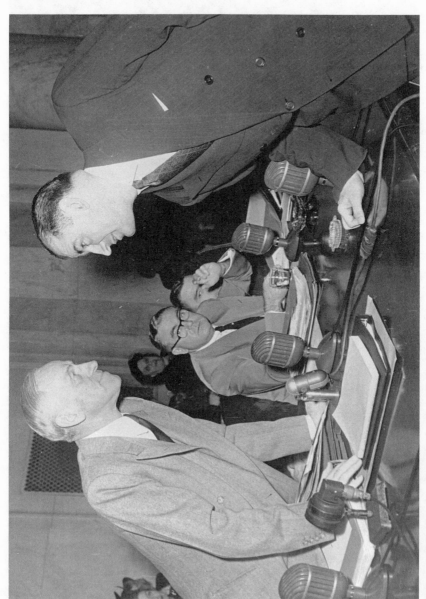

Tydings and Joe McCarthy square off at the Foreign Relations Committee's State Department Loyalty Hearings on March 8, 1950. (Globe Photos)

Henry Cabot Lodge, Bourke B. Hickenlooper, and Tydings during Owen Lattimore's testimony. (AP/Wide World Photos)

The infamous composite photograph published in "From the Record" purporting to show Earl Browder and Tydings in intimate conversation. (UPI/Bettmann)

Following his defeat, Eleanor and Millard Tydings sailed from New York on January 19, 1951 on a fifteen-day luxury cruise to the West Indies. (Special Collections, University of Maryland at College Park Libraries)

word: No changes could be undertaken by the United States "except upon the request" of Filipinos, and the terms must "realistically" deal with the matter so independence would be "real rather than an illusion." There was no reason, "idealistic or selfish," he said, to grant the "promised independence under circumstances which are harsh, cruel and inhuman on the one hand while laying us open to the charge of insincerity and materialism on the other. Too much has been done, too much has been spent, too much life has been lost, too many promises have been made and reiterated by the United States for our country not to see this venture through fully, humanely, even generously, if you please."

> Our course, our standards, our methods, our sincerity in the last analysis will be judged largely by the Filipinos, by the Orient and indeed by the World, by the final chapter we shall write in this all together novel world adventure.
>
> The story up to now has been too noble and inspiring for its final chapters to be written in a different spirit.

Despite Tydings's conciliatory attitude, Quezon's hopes went unmet in 1935. But President Roosevelt accepted the Philippine Constitution. At a White House ceremony on March 23, Roosevelt, in the presence of Tydings, McDuffie, Key Pittman, the new Governor General Frank Murphy, Quezon, Roxas, and other dignitaries from both nations, signed his approval—an action representing the last step necessary in establishing the Philippines Commonwealth. On July 4, 1946, the Philippine Republic would be brought into existence to join the world's family of nations.

Quezon hastened back to the Philippines to urge popular approval of the Constitution in a scheduled plebiscite and to campaign for president of the new government to be inaugurated that November. He was in a hurry because he feared Aguinaldo, who was running against him, would successfully parlay his stance—for immediate independence and against Tydings–McDuffie—into votes.[9]

The Filipino people overwhelmingly approved their constitution on May 14, 1935. It was 25 to 1 in favor of ratification.[10] Tydings made a speech on the Senate floor timed to coincide with the plebiscite. His speech, said the Baltimore *Sun,* was "viewed in the Philippines as exceedingly significant, serving to write into the Official record a declaration of policy from the one person in the Senate most qualified to make such a statement."

He reminded Filipinos that the United States had made good on its promise. If they wanted changes, it was up to them to move "now, and not 6, or 8, or 10 years from now." It warned Americans that they were pledged irrevocably to honoring their promise of 35 years. "Many arguments against complete independence have been made in both countries," he acknowledged. "But now that we have offered it and they have accepted, our hands are tied against making such arguments any more. . . . Whether independence is good or bad, we would be without honor or logic to attempt to reverse the situation now." U.S. policy was clear. Tydings's speech to the Filipinos in December, broadcast on radio, had reached "every nook and corner of the islands." They had been "apprised of what independence will mean. . . . There has been no deception," he said. Then he thanked the Senate for yielding him time "so that I might set the people of that country straight as to the attitude of the United States toward any change in their future status as I see it."

In April 1937 Roosevelt created the Joint Preparatory Committee on Philippine Affairs to study trade problems and recommend solutions. When Quezon returned to Washington that spring to pursue a remedy to economic "injustices and inequalities" (which was how he rephrased the Tydings–Roosevelt reference to "imperfections and inequalities"), he met with the president. Together they selected a group of experts from both countries to serve on the committee.

Its report, issued in May 1938, was the most penetrating analysis ever made of the Philippine economy. Its recommendations sought to ease the economic adjustment and extend its time-frame. In place of sudden imposition of full tariff in 1946, the committee urged a 15-year period during which regressive duty-free quotas would replace progressive export taxes on most goods and commodities. Products already controlled by quotas would be subject to progressive increases: Twenty-five percent in 1946 and 5 percent more each year until 1961 when tariffs would reach 100 percent.

That would dispose of Tydings–McDuffie's "shocking inequality." Subject to congressional approval, Roosevelt agreed to back the committee's recommendations. He knew it would be difficult, for Americans would oppose it and Congress was unpredictable. The committee's suggestions, written into draft legislative form, were sent to Capitol Hill for action in January 1939.

When the new special mission, headed by Osmeña, asked Tydings to take up revision of trade in January, he introduced legislation incorporating the committee's recommendations, but went no further. The State Department and Osmeña's mission were forced to trim their goals. Yet without Tydings's support, even the drastically curtailed proposal had little chance for success. Osmeña wrote Quezon in May, "We don't know whether he is inspired by his animus against Roosevelt, or if it is against you and all of us." The senator was, Osmeña said, "an indecipherable enigma."[11]

Roosevelt swallowed his pride and in May 1939 personally called Tydings to the White House for a conference. The second bill flew through both houses with few amendments. But the Tydings–Koscialkowski Act of 1939 left untouched recommendations for the post–1946 period; trade matters remained unresolved. With the outbreak of war in Europe in September 1939, Americans' attention shifted away from the Philippines—until the Japanese launched surprise attacks on Pearl Harbor, Guam, Wake Island, the Philippines.

Tydings's injured pride had not been the only stumbling block to long-range trade arrangements. The isolationists' noisy anti-imperialism had eviscerated the Joint Preparatory Committee's recommendations. And the Filipinos themselves were not blameless. The commonwealth government—rather than altering marketing and production methods, and diversifying the economy—looked instead to a trade preference arrangement as a panacea. Quezon found it easier to blame imperial policy for the islands' poverty than to deal with his government's inefficiency and corruption in the agricultural industries.

In drawing independence legislation, Tydings had worked hard to protect both American and Filipino interests as he labored to establish and defend solid economic foundations for the future

Philippine Republic. Concessions—no matter how little Americans liked them—were essential to prevent the islands' collapse, for independence with all hope of success destroyed would have made a mockery of the bold experiment underway. And Tydings understood the significance of what the United States was doing: writing the "final chapter . . . in this all together novel world adventure."

He realized that Tydings–McDuffie had its flaws—"imperfections and inequalities"—and he knew that political observers had criticized the more materialistic aspects of the law. But later in life, his wife remembered, among his many accomplishments Tydings was proudest of his authorship of the Tydings–McDuffie Independence Act.

Philippine independence was an odd concoction: a blend of materialism, isolationism, and idealism—with a dash of undiluted altruism thrown in. Given prevailing American attitudes, perhaps that was the only workable recipe. In the long view, those mixed motives did not subtract from the historic significance of Tydings–McDuffie. For the first time in the bloody history of East–West relations—or world relations, for that matter—a conquering power voluntarily relinquished its hold over a possession and offered an orderly, scheduled progression to national liberation. Perhaps liberal columnist Oswald Garrison Villard phrased it best when he wrote, "It is to Senator Tydings' lasting honor that his name is associated with this final act of justice to the Philippines."

Notes

1. The agricultural lobby attacks were illogical. The Philippine market was one of America's top customers for dairy and wheat products. Philippine exports—sugar, coconut oil, and cordage—had minimal impact on U.S. markets; 90 percent of its sugar competed with Cuban sugar. But dairy, milk, and sugar associations used scare tactics to convince farmers that tariffs would improve their positions. In fact, the main beneficiaries would be banks anxious to protect Cuban investments from revolutionary turmoil and the worldwide Depression.

2. Historian Theodore Friend notes that most Filipinos, reflecting their culture's strong familial ties, believed the world itself was a family of nations committed to peace as evidenced by the League of Nations, the

Washington Naval treaties, and the Kellogg–Briand Pact. And since their defense had remained in imperial hands for centuries, they remained untroubled by foreign policy and defense considerations. The words of a prominent Filipino, "Almighty God will take care of us," illustrated their political naiveté.

3. Theodore Friend noted that Romulo "switched sides in the middle of the fight" in opting to go with Quezon.

4. Many years later Filipino Senator Claro Recto disclosed that Quezon managed to raise a million pesos "to get a new independence bill."

5. Small wonder that Quezon later told Carlos Romulo that Tydings had effective ways of persuasion. He always knew exactly where the senator stood, Quezon said; and he added that when Tydings thought someone was wrong he never minced words, never dealt in half-tones, sometimes spoke bluntly, but always spoke knowing that he was an American senator. And when he gave his support, his word could be trusted.

6. Unfortunately the long term proved negative, for the Philippine government increased its spending rather than adjust to the income reductions that inevitably would accompany independence.

7. A much larger delegation originally was slated to go, but Tydings—always concerned about costs—insisted the appropriation for the trip be kept to $15,000, which enabled only four to go.

8. The half-Scottish, half-Hawaiian Princess Abigail (David) Kawananakoa, who had married the heir to the Hawaiian throne, was Republican National Committee chairwoman for the territory. She opposed statehood, was fearful of Japan, and was deeply concerned over the dwindling number of pure Hawaiians left—somewhere between 20,000 and 40,000 at the time. She worked on issues important to the native population, such as homes on the big island of Hawaii where they could live in the traditional manner. Tydings, as a supporter of local responsibility and rights, helped the princess.

9. Quezon patched things up with Osmeña. They ran together for president and vice-president, respectively, and won—stirring fears of oligarchy.

10. The Philippine Constitution, patterned on that of the United States, vested sovereignty in the people, extended them a bill of rights, renounced war as an instrument of national policy, and pledged itself to foster education and social justice. It provided for a unicameral legislature of 120 members, an 11-justice Supreme Court, a president and vice-president. Women's suffrage would be possible if 300,000 women voted for such at an election held within two years. The president, elected for one six-year term, could not succeed himself.

The legislature, "in times of war or other national emergency," could declare a dictatorship and thus give almost unlimited power to the president—a provision that reflected the residual Spanish *caudillo* heritage. J. R. Hayden, in government service in the Philippines during 1934–1935, took a dim view of that provision, fearing the dangerous possibilities inherent in "an irresponsible autocracy, with power concentrated in the President, the Speaker, and to a much lesser degree, in a few of their intimate political associates."

11. Tydings, the Hill's key player regarding the Philippines, had been embroiled in a power struggle with Roosevelt for years. In 1938 the president had attempted to purge Tydings from office when he was up for reelection, but failed. Tydings found vindication and increased power only slowly soothed his wounded pride. If Roosevelt wanted cooperation, he would have to eat humble pie. Quintin Paredes, newly elected Filipino National Assemblyman, interpreted Tydings's election victory as a set-back for Filipinos. They would have "rougher seas to sail" because of the "personal differences between President Roosevelt and Senator Tydings," he told Filipino newsmen in 1939.

8

At Home in Maryland

By the mid-1930s Tydings dominated Maryland politics and wielded sufficient clout in Congress to protect local industries. When France put high tariff restrictions on tobacco (it usually bought almost the entire Maryland crop), Tydings got Secretary of State Cordell Hull to include tobacco in a pending trade agreement. When the Chesapeake Bay crabbing industry was endangered by indiscriminate overfishing of blue, sponge, buchran, and peeler or soft-shell crabs, he introduced legislation mandating federal regulation—an unusual strategy for a states' rights advocate. Alarmed Maryland and Virginia officials, who until then had consistently failed to agree on a coordinated conservative program, quickly coordinated state laws covering fishing and crabbing, thus avoiding federal control.

When Midwestern interests renewed the push for a Saint Lawrence–Great Lakes waterway to the Atlantic, Tydings again successfully deflected them. He framed his arguments in economic terms: Given the huge federal loans made to financially troubled railroads, it would be "kissing good-bye to many millions of dollars" to build a competing mode of transportation while also putting more East Coast workers on the dole. But his goal was to protect a major Maryland industry: the port of Baltimore. He may have said, "I do not want to be provincial and think only of Baltimore and Maryland." But when all was said and done, it was Baltimore and Maryland he was fighting for. His constituents were grateful.

He promoted federal projects benefiting the state and had tremendous influence when it came to channeling New Deal money to Maryland. Although he voted against the Public Works Administration (PWA), once its programs were in effect and federal funds available, he supported applications for construction projects of permanent value—highways, bridges, hospitals, airports—that would provide jobs for the unemployed as they built structures essential to future growth. He introduced legislation to build parkways from Gettysburg to Washington and Baltimore to Washington, an international airport, a Baltimore Harbor tunnel, and a bridge to span the Chesapeake Bay.[1]

Maryland politics—fratricidal, rough-and-tumble as anything New York's Tammany Hall could boast—was something Tydings sought to avoid. As a senator he was not in the mainstream of local politics as were state and city leaders: Governor Albert Ritchie, Baltimore Mayor Howard Jackson; old-time bosses like Frank Furst; would-be power brokers and candidates such as William Curran and Herbert R. O'Conor. Tydings was neither machine politician nor independent pragmatist. He was an independent ideologue fitting no conventional mold save, perhaps, that of conservative Jeffersonian Democrat committed to a small federal government, blended with conservative Bourbon Democrat concerned with safeguarding business. His power base rested primarily on a personal organization built through patronage; he never was part of any faction.

Not everyone liked his method. The Bel Air (Maryland) *Times* remarked that he was "the recognized distributor of many gallons of political largess dished out of the very honorable James A. Farley's political swill trough. In other words, no one gets a job or favor unless he genuflects to Millard." But by staying clear of Ritchie's state machine, he had saved himself from being beholden to it. Many young aspiring county politicians had been chewed up and spit out by Ritchie's organization, never to surface again. By building his own group around himself, Tydings protected himself from such a fate.

After his 1932 reelection victory he came to appear invulnerable and was crowned by some as kingmaker, boss of the Maryland machine. But he had little inclination in that direction. Uneasy with machine types, he valued his independence, linked up with or sidestepped the machine when advantageous—a delicate tightrope act. No matter how often he voiced disinterest in the role of kingmaker and reiterated a preference for his maverick ways, he was too powerful to escape the pressures of machine politics. The 1934 battle for the Maryland governorship forced him to the center of the ring and tested his political balancing skills whether he liked it or not.

Governor Ritchie had overcome Frank Furst's opposition to a fourth term in 1930 only by promising no fifth term. But with Furst's death in January 1934, Ritchie went back on his word—against the advice of friends, advisers, and Tydings. Baltimore's Mayor Jackson, who had waited 15 years for the chance to succeed Ritchie, already had filed to run when Ritchie announced for a fifth term. Without Furst—the consummate mediator—the war was on.

Rumors reported impending battles between Ritchie and Jackson, Ritchie and Tydings, and Jackson and Tydings. Then Frederick, Maryland's Dr. Charles H. Conley joined the field, forcing state leaders to rethink their situation. E. Brooke Lee, a Ritchie top lieutenant, believed that, if feelers to the voters indicated a Ritchie nomination bode poorly for victory, a conference should be called; otherwise, Democrats could only hope for a party-wrecking Republican primary to offset their free-for-all. Lee learned that Maryland Democrats in general did not want Ritchie. There had been too much discord during his last term: bank failures; his unpopular handling of lynchings on the Eastern Shore (he had sent troops to arrest lynching suspects). And he had just plain been around too long. But having broken with tradition to succeed himself (only one other governor had done so since the Civil War), Ritchie now dared to challenge the fifth-term bugaboo.

Tydings from the start opposed a Ritchie fifth term. Publicly he refused to take sides between Ritchie and Jackson (never considering Conley a viable contender), while privately he worked to convince Ritchie not to do what he believed would be disastrous. A series of meetings attended by all factions failed to break the stalemate. Maryland Democrats, faced with what was called the "gubernatorial primary fight of the century," looked to Tydings—titular head of the party—to lead them out of the mess.

Tydings saw several possible escapes. Maryland's other Senate seat, held by retiring Republican Phillips Lee Goldsborough, was open. If Ritchie could be persuaded to run for the Senate, with Jackson for governor, that would give each man something, save face, and avoid the dreaded bloody primary. But Ritchie made it clear he was uninterested. Tydings did not give up. Clearly, for Ritchie to go from powerful governor and presidential contender in 1932 to low man in the Senate was hardly appealing. He privately offered to resign his own seat to give Ritchie senior rank—if Ritchie would reappoint him to the junior senator's seat. Ritchie refused.

Having failed twice, Tydings decided to force him to run for the Senate by supporting a compromise candidate for governor. He had been told by William Curran (Ritchie's Baltimore backer, Jackson's die-hard rival, and a would-be boss) that Curran and others would back Ritchie for the Senate if a man whom they could support was persuaded to run for governor. Convinced that Ritchie's nomination would elect a Republican governor, Tydings privately urged his friend George L. Radcliffe to enter the race as a third candidate. Radcliffe was widely respected for his work as PWA regional director and was a good friend of President Franklin D. Roosevelt, whose blessing would help.[2]

Meanwhile, groups antagonistic to Ritchie tried to mix things up further. They suggested that Tydings secretly conveted the governorship. He moved fast to spike such rumors, issuing a flat denial when asked. "No, I'm going to run for Senator," he insisted. Since that election was four years off, he meant he definitely was not in the current race. But he failed to quell all doubts. He could serve as governor and still run for the Senate in 1938. Those who so insisted neglected the point that doing so would entail two hard campaigns within four years and, if successful, return him to junior status. Nevertheless, gossip persisted—because others, in fact, were trying to force him into the race as the compromise candidate. He better than anyone else could stave off party disaster by sidetracking a suicidal primary.

During that time Jackson's people desperately sought his support. Only with the senator's "federal group" allied with the mayor's "municipal group" against Ritchie's "state machine" could Jackson force Ritchie out of the race or defeat him in a primary. Tydings, faced with allegations that he and Jackson were conspiring against Ritchie, kept a strict neutrality, which irritated supporters in both camps (except E. Brooke Lee and William Walsh, close Tydings associates who understood his stance). Ritchie was aggravated by Tydings saying, in effect, that Ritchie could not be reelected. It was the "height of effrontery." Rumors that Ritchie wanted Tydings's Senate seat in 1938 began to circulate, passed on by newsreporters: Ritchie "wants to take the measure of the Honorable Millard Tydings, who has let it be known that he proposes to seek reelection as Senator in that year, *Deo volente.*"

Newspapers viewed Tydings as the "probable balance of power" in Maryland. The *Sun* commented that he was "beginning to talk and act more and more as if he were boss." When reporters pressed him for enlightenment he would repeat, "I have nothing to say." He was seen increasingly as Machiavellian, vengeful, and power mad. The Baltimore pundit who signed himself "OSWALD" wrote, "Dear Millard, It begins to look as if the boys are going to call you BOSS whether you like it or not." Tydings disclaimed any wish to wield that kind of power. "My desire," he said, "is not to hurt or hinder anybody but to help Maryland and the Democratic Party." His statements satisfied no one. Stories persisted that he was intent on showing who ran the show.

He said he was willing to "sit down around a table" with state leaders to discuss the situation. But Jackson and Ritchie remained unmovable, vowing to stay in the race to the end. Tydings's position grew more uncomfortable. Many lamented the absence of Frank Furst, whose conciliatory ways, restraining influence—and dictatorial power—always had kept politicians in line, thus avoiding damaging antagonism. A good old boy to take the heat was a thing of beauty; uninterested in holding office himself, he could be trusted and could wield power from above without arousing paranoid reaction.

Tydings finally called for a peace parley. His statement, issued from his Washington office, began, "I have been reluctant to inject myself into the coming election. . . . Not even now would I venture to make a statement . . . were it not for the fact that the Democratic party, which has honored me so much, seems headed into a bitter factional primary." The battle would be suicidal, he warned, and therefore, "Governor Ritchie and Mayor Jackson and such others as they care to summon should be called into a conference with the aim and hope that unity and harmony will result." To avoid charges he was acting as boss he added, "I have no desire to sit in this conference if it is called unless the two leading aspirants want me to be present. . . . I have no desire to be State leader, as has been charged in some quarters." He far preferred to devote his "time and abilities to the national emergency rather than to factional party matters."

His appeal won the applause of Baltimore business leaders, who supported his efforts to avoid a difficult primary, and a few state figures. But the main players ridiculed his suggestion. Curran—who earlier had said, "Our party is in the temper for a good old-fashioned primary fight"—indirectly called Tydings a crackpot by remarking that those who believed conferences settled anything were "crackpots." "Perhaps," Curran added, "the Senator is so engrossed in national and international emergencies that he has lost touch with things in this little State." Ritchie was furious at the implication that he was less responsible to party and state than Tydings. Jackson parried the whole idea, saying he had no objections to a conference but believed it unnecessary.

Some interpreted Tydings's move as support for Jackson. Some believed he was trying to bury Ritchie. Others chastised him for being unduly cautious. His "excessive timidity has permitted him to see 'goblins,'" said a columnist. He was called autocratic, out of touch, and power hungry. Tydings was bemused by the reactions, especially the interpretation that he was trying to end-run a possible Ritchie challenge in 1938. When pressed on his plans for 1938, he replied with a deliberately stern expression that shifted to mock sinister. "I have as yet no political plans for 1938. But I am working on political plans for 1948 and 1968 and my political plans for 1998 are simply wonderful. They are very Machiavellian."

Tydings now worked actively to encourage George Radcliffe to file for governor and finally, after numerous meetings (including one with Radcliffe's friend Franklin Roosevelt), convinced him to consider it. On May 28, Radcliffe announced he would run if Jackson and Ritchie would withdraw. When he received no reply, he and Tydings closeted themselves for four hours. At the end of the session, Radcliffe reannounced that he would run, period. He left his ticket open in hopes that Ritchie would join it.

Ritchie was furious at Tydings. His camp had to regroup. Then another player joined the fray. Herbert O'Conor—an attractive, young, rising politician—eyed both the Senate seat and governorship. He was courted immediately by both Ritchie and Radcliffe for attorney general. O'Conor had little love for Tydings. He believed that, if things were arranged so Radcliffe ran for the Senate, with Ritchie for governor, Tydings would either be isolated or forced to join Jackson. Such an outcome would please O'Conor—who wanted to see the field cleared for his own future aims.

Nothing Tydings tried changed the situation. Ritchie would not budge. Jackson would not budge. Tydings arranged a meeting with Lee and Walsh and admitted defeat. In capitulating, he urged Radcliffe to run for the Senate on a Ritchie ticket; and on July 7, Radcliffe announced he would run.[3]

Ritchie was delighted. He immediately backed Radcliffe and brought O'Conor aboard as candidate for attorney general. When Curran's forces succumbed and backed Radcliffe for senator, the effect was devastating to Jackson. Tydings, Curran, O'Conor—all lined up behind Ritchie. Jackson was forced to withdraw (and threw his support to Ritchie). Ritchie believed victory was his. But Frederick's Dr. Conley refused to throw in the towel. Calling Ritchie "Prince Albert the Fourth," he forced the Democrats to endure a primary anyway.

Tydings was seen as humiliated. Newspapers called his foray into kingmaking a monumental flop and painted a ludicrous image of Tydings charging up the hill and sneaking back down. He was self-bloodied instead of "sitting pretty," which he would have been had he let well enough alone. Franklyn Waltman of the *Washington Post* wrote, "Mr. Tydings at this time appears to be the most unpopular Democrat in Maryland." James A. Newell of the Baltimore *News–Post* described the animosity between Baltimore Democrats and Tydings: "Some of those leaders regard Senator Tydings as a political Boy Scout, a child of destiny, who has mounted to political eminence by a series of lucky breaks. They would not be sorry, it is said, to see the Senator less eminent, not to say in eclipse."

He had squandered a great deal of political currency. Jackson was livid. His spokesmen growled that Tydings's "mysterious and inexplicable wanderings from one candidate to another have damaged the Democratic party." Curran was also in a fury. He called Tydings's supporters "malevolent." The man who had implied that Tydings was a crackpot—hardly a gracious loser or paragon of savoir faire—added, "They come around to play, lick the molasses off my bread and then call me 'nigger.' " Ritchie accused Tydings of seeking power and complained that he had tried to prevent the populace from selecting their own candidate by angling to handpick a slate in closed-door meetings in smoke-filled rooms. Tydings brushed that off as tommyrot: Had party leaders encouraged a fifth term, Ritchie would not have opposed hashing things out to avoid a primary; and stepping aside for party harmony was hardly unheard of.

There were few winners in the mess, which, as one paper remarked, had more switches than a Chicago railyard. Ritchie defeated Conley three to one in the primary—Conley's strong showing surprising everyone. The Republicans suffered a divisive primary too, with retiring Senator Phillips Lee Goldsborough, Baltimore Chairman of the Public Improvement Commission H. Webster Jackson, and Baltimore attorney Harry C. Nice engaged in a three-way race. Nice won.

In November, Ritchie ran with Tydings's support, Jackson's forces behind him, and with Roosevelt and Jim Farley speaking on his behalf. But the unthinkable happened. Maryland voters, who only twice since the Civil War had elected a Republican governor, handed Ritchie the only defeat suffered that day by a Democrat on the state or national ticket in Maryland. The Ritchie upset was so stunning that the New York *Times*—not given to reporting other states' elections—called Baltimore a "slaughterhouse. . . . To an outsider the result looks like a game of cutthroat politics, the revenge and opportunity of disappointed rivals."

Tydings was vindicated. The *Sun* wrote that, if his strategy had been followed, the party would not have lost the governorship. The paper observed that the outcome also made Tydings the state's "undisputed party leader." Had Ritchie run for the Senate as Tydings had urged, his domination "would have remained fully intact" because the state organization would have continued to center around him. Smaller and larger newspapers agreed, and the New

York *Times* noted the "natural progression of the title of State leader to United States Senator Millard E. Tydings."

Tydings had retained his composure in the face of blows aimed at him. He remarked, "There were just too many barnacles on the good ship Ritchie for it to have survived the hazards of another battle for the governorship." Jackson took the *Times* "cutthroat politics" statement personally, calling it "unfair and untrue." Tydings never believed it was aimed at him, a point he reiterated to journalist Holmes Alexander in a lengthy explanation of his role in the campaign. "I honestly tried to save Governor Ritchie from himself," he wrote Alexander, adding that he never was allied with Jackson in the contest, "never felt that the New York *Times* article was directed at me," and pointing out that Ritchie later "was fair enough to say after the election that my advice had been sound and genuine." He emphasized that he had "no desire to be leader or 'boss' and wished fervently that Ritchie had carried the mantle of that difficult role. . . . The only motive I ever had was to keep the Democratic party in such shape, as far as I was able, that it could produce a winner. I was only partially successful."

Although he never aspired to bossdom, it was thrust upon him. He clearly wanted his influence to count, but he had no desire to run the state. State politics degenerated too often into plotting and power brokering. He knew how the game worked but found it abhorrent. When forced to play, his hardball game won few admirers. He was not interested in backslapping, cajoling, patient persuading. Smoothing the ruffled feathers of those with inflated egos was an activity for which he was temperamentally unsuited. He loved a good romping, stomping fight; but petty squabbles offered no glory or pleasure. That part of politics was a dirty job, and he preferred to let someone else do it. He might have done better ruling with an iron hand or ignoring the matter completely—the former unappealing and the latter seemingly impossible. He resented making time for things he considered unimportant in comparison to the national crisis, Philippine independence, and the growing threat of German and Japanese militarism. Still, once regarded as head of Maryland's Democratic party, he had to be active enough to hold his people together and maintain friendly relations with traditional factions.

It was clear to all that Tydings had mishandled the 1934 gubernatorial election (despite being right about Ritchie's electability). On the national level he mishandled another issue and again found himself ridiculed and humbled: In the summer of 1935, the Navy and War Departments asked him to introduce legislation designed to thwart attempts to incite insurrection through urging sailors and soldiers to disobey regulations. The bill, as drafted, applied solely to the military and provided for punishment of "whoever publishes or distributes any book, pamphlet, paper, print, article, letter or other writing which advises, counsels, urges or solicits any member of such military or naval forces of the United States to disobey the laws or regulations governing such military or naval establishments." The military had in mind communist agitators whom they feared might try to subvert the nation's service personnel.

A howl of indignation went up among journalists, editors, and civil libertarians as they pointed out the potential for abuse. They believed such a measure could lead to fascism. Tydings was accused of abetting "a most formidable attack on the freedom of the press and free opinion," and of endangering the First Amendment of the Constitution. He was surprised at the vehement reaction. "Its real and only purpose as far as I am concerned is to promote the discipline of our army and navy and nothing more," he declared in response to a *Sun* editorial entitled "Attacks on Liberty."

The *Sun*—aware that Tydings had neither drafted nor enthusiastically sponsored the bill, having only introduced it on the Senate floor as a favor to the military—said in his defense, "Anyone who knows Senator Tydings and his public record [knows he] is the kind of man who would be quick to seek and apply remedies for any talk against the discipline of the armed forces and is equally the kind of man who would be impatient and contemptuous of any open suggestion to suppress the civilian's freedom of speech or of press." But, the editorial continued, "it remains a pity that Senator Tydings does not meet with the foes of the legislation and seek to understand their point of view." He and Democratic Representative John W. McCormack of Massachusetts, the bill's House sponsor, apparently were taken in by "people who cannot go to sleep without looking under their beds for the revolution. . . ."

H. L Mencken was incredulous at Tydings's involvement. "It is hard to understand Senator Millard Tydings' support of the McCormack bill. He is one of the most intelligent men that Maryland has ever sent to Washington, and his career in the Senate has been marked by extraordinary independence and courage, yet here we find him arguing for a measure that is not only idiotic, but . . . palpably dishonest . . . vicious and preposterous. . . ."

The "Disaffection Bill"—as the infamous piece of legislation came to be known—died a quick death in February 1936 when Secretary of War George Dern, who also had suffered massive criticism, publicly disavowed his creation. Tydings immediately wrote Dern a letter, which he made public, saying that if "the Secretary of War is not especially in favor of the bill then there is no reason why I should have been asked, even as a matter of courtesy, to introduce it." He reminded Dern he had played no part in drafting it. "I have never been an advocate of bills restricting freedom of speech. . . . It was represented to me that a campaign had been carried on to [incite members of the army or navy to disobey the laws] by agitators." But if Dern had no interest in the bill, then he, too, was "justified in dropping it."

He hoped that was the end; but, as usual, the press had the last word. The *Evening Sun* scored him for the undignified way he wiggled off the hook: He should have found a "better excuse" for abandoning "this ridiculous measure. . . . He could well have argued that his bill flies directly contrary to everything he has hitherto pretended to admire." But no, in haste to take the easy way out of his "unpleasant plight," he gave reasons that were "shallow, even fatuous. . . ."

Tydings never admitted that the bill went beyond legitimate necessity. He believed it analogous to Britain's "Defense of the Realm Act," which made it illegal to incite the British Army and Navy to revolt against the Crown, disobey officers, or mutiny. And as such, he believed it would not be misused in practice nor misinterpreted by American courts. In defending his actions for political writer Holmes Alexander, Tydings confessed he had introduced the bill "without thought or study." But he also emphasized, "Lest I seem equivocal I said then and I believe now, the bill was not a bad bill, that it would not have been abused." When the War and

Navy Departments ducked "in a cowardly way, of course, I withdrew my sponsorship of the measure."

It was Tydings's attitude—his refusal to concede he might have made a mistake—that most annoyed liberals. Oswald Garrison Villard, in one of the "Pillars of Government" articles featuring Tydings in the *Forum* magazine, spoke for them all when he wrote that newspaper editors believed Tydings "should have had the courage to admit in a manly way that he had erred and then apologize."

Despite the setbacks, Tydings's career flourished. His reputation as a man about town never ceased to be the subject of Washington gossip columns. Maybelle Jennings of the Washington *Herald* was one of the few who wangled an appointment to interview the "debonair bachelor Senator" at his apartment. He had moved from his Georgetown home (he rented it out) to an apartment in the Anchorage that he shared with Sam Rayburn, another bachelor. Jennings was fascinated by the "nautical atmosphere" of Tydings's decor—from a ship's model door-knocker to maritime pictures on the walls. He was "charming, charming," she wrote, "a good conversationalist, and altogether likeable."

Other columns twittered about how he was "far and away the most soignée member of the Senate," and had "human appeal." When 82 of the 470 members of the Capitol Hill Press Galleries of Congress took an informal poll among themselves, Huey Long was voted the best dressed and least helpful; William Borah of Idaho the best orator; Henry Keyes of New Hampshire the quietest; Elmer Thomas of Oklahoma the handsomest; and Robert Wagner of New York the most popular. But Tydings was voted the senator "with the most sex appeal."

When he stopped in Hollywood on his way to the Philippines in 1934, gossip columns there reported his comings and goings. A regular piece called "Snapshots of Hollywood collected at random" noted that "Lady Edwina Mountbatten arrived in town by plane Wednesday morning to visit Marion Davies; Marlene Dietrich and Senator Tydings from Maryland met at a luncheon given by Mrs. Lionel Atwill in the Paramount commissary today; the Senator greatly admires the Dietrich."

In 1935 he was voted among the best-dressed men in the

nation's capital along with Rexford Tugwell, "Tony" Biddle, Jr., and other notables. The article's text read, "To see him on a springlike day on the floor of the Senate, tall, lean, clad in perfectly pressed gray flannels, a blue or mauve tinged shirt, with a darker tie of the same color, is indeed a joy to females sensitive to and appreciative of the artistic things in life." In 1937 the Merchants Tailors Designers Association selected 16 best-dressed American men. Tydings, President Roosevelt, and Senator Henry Cabot Lodge, representing Washington, shared their billing with Fred Astaire, William Paley of CBS, and Edwin Goodman of Bergdorf-Goodman.

Drew Pearson long had called him Maryland's Beau Brummel senator. Even a dignified columnist such as Raymond Clapper could not resist tweeking that patrician nose when criticizing his conservatism, calling him "Maryland's dapper bachelor, darling of Washington's cocktail hour, at which time he is known as 'Glad Tydings,'" the "five o'clock hero."

His social prominence nearly compromised his name when a lobbyist under investigation for improper conduct cited Tydings in his testimony. Bernard R. Robinson, called the "suave cocktail lobbyist," was summoned to testify before Congress about how he entertained senators and representatives. He dated their secretaries and devised ways to sponsor parties at clubs, homes, hotels—parties paid for by his client, the Associated Gas and Electric Company. Those methods of meeting government officials were called "indirect salesmanship" and "insidious social lobbying." In August 1935 Robinson testified under oath that Tydings was one of the prominent men he had entertained in the course of lobbying against a bill that would have affected Associated Gas.

It had been just one of those things. Joan Diehl, a glamorous San Francisco socialite visiting Washington, was engaged to marry John Heinz II, heir to the Heinz pickle fortune. Robinson took advantage of the opportunity to throw a pre-engagement party in her honor. At the time, May 1935, Robinson knew relatively few of the Washington elite, so he asked the daughter of an old friend to give the party jointly with him. Young Evelyn Walker, eager to play hostess for such a glittering social event, had no inkling it would be paid for by corporate funds as a pretext for lobbying. Tydings was one of the unsuspecting Washingtonians she invited. Robinson's testimony made no mention of the Heinz–Diehl engagement or Evie Walker's innocent participation.

Tydings was furious at Robinson's insinuation that he had been entertained by the utilities lobby. He burst into the hearing room and, bristling with indignation, raked Robinson over the coals. "Mr. Robinson," he shouted, "Did you invite me to a party at the F Street Club?"

"You attended a joint party—you were there," a shaken Robinson replied.

"Who invited me?" Tydings barked.

"I think you were invited by a young lady."

"Who is she?" he persisted.

"Miss Evelyn Walker."

"Well, if I did accept her invitation to a club to which I belong, why did you say I was at a party you gave?" Tydings demanded to know. "Did she have any connection with a public utility lobby?"

"I never said she had."

"Then what do you mean by saying that I was a guest at a cocktail party given by you, and paid for with utility company money?"

"It was a joint party, Senator, given by Miss Walker and myself. I saw in the society columns that you were present."

"That's where you get your information, is it?" Tydings scoffed. When a chastened Robinson mumbled something about not knowing if Tydings was there or not, Tydings exploded. "I have never been invited by you to a party or have never gone to one given by you," he yelled, shaking his fist. "After this, when you use my name in your testimony, be damned sure you are right," he said. Turning sharply, he strode out of the hearing room.

The Washington *Herald* said the episode had "nothing more sinister about it than an olive at the bottom of a Martini," but a frustrated Tydings was shocked at the casual misuse of public officials' names. He also was becoming shocked by another Washington ritual: how some women, especially married ones—wives of friends, colleagues, powerful men—attracted by his growing status, his looks or personality, tried to seduce him. Women for years had pursued him. When they were single, it could be flattering. But he never ceased to be surprised and unsettled when someone's wife made it abundantly clear that she was willing—in fact, trying—to be lured to bed.

A story he liked to tell expressed perfectly his attitude toward such behavior. One afternoon at the Maryland Club in Baltimore he ran into General Edwin Warfield, the uncle of Wallis Warfield Simpson, who was in the midst of her sensational affair with the Prince of Wales, Edward Windsor. As they lunched together, the general asked Tydings, "Millard, what do you think of my niece, Wallis?" Without waiting for a reply he went on, "I received a letter from her asking me to send her a copy of our family tree. I wrote back and told her to start acting like a lady and she wouldn't need it."

Tydings was lonely. At 45 he was reaching his stride as a powerful man in a city full of powerful men. Yet he was close to no one special woman. The papers may have been rife with accounts of a glamorous social life; but alone in his off-hours, he put his thoughts into the form of poetry, producing a long manuscript of poems titled "Thoughts of a Madman." He wrote of war, of tears, of love, of dreams. Few who knew him would have believed the poems were his—so full of yearning, passion, and understanding of life's joys and bittersweet pain. "All who drink the wine of life must drink both heaven and hell," he wrote. His artist's eye recalled colors and scenes from his past, and his poet's soul remembered thoughts and feelings.

> At Châtillon-sur-Seine when June's a maiden
> Horse-chestnut rows are candle-coned in white
> And most profuse of leaf;
> The sun sifts through the boughs
> Etching with spendthrift hand infinite shadows
> On the white, dusty streets beneath, freckling them.

"The greatest tragedy in this flicker for all of us / Is naught but this: There is only one first time / For everything," he wrote.

> I could tell you of a case when I was young.
> She loved me. She really did. And I was not unfond myself
> Of much of her. . . .

If you want to moor your soul
Then tie it with a lock of woman's hair.

"There is one sense and only one—not more— / We see, hear, taste, smell and touch with / The fibres of the heart," he wrote in his solitude. He was sad, but he hid his sadness behind what the press called "his famous grin."

I'm sad. Sad? No! I'm happy
With sweet pain. Like a little boy whose tiny hand
Crushed has touched his mother's lips. That's it.
I'm sad with happiness, Ha! Ha! That's it. Let's laugh.
Ha! Ha! I'm happy with sadness.
I'm sane with madness
I'm suffocated with emptiness.
Isn't it fun to watch a train come out
Of a hill and slip along on the backs of steel snakes
With one eye stabbing into the night, and coughing?

He longed for someone to love him and sensed the need for a mate, not only for his soul but for his daily life.

In 1935, in the midst of the Depression, life in the United States was not all breadlines and New Deal. The beer can, Alcoholics Anonymous, Bugs Bunny, the Folger Shakespeare Library, Social Security, and George and Ira Gershwin's *Porgy and Bess* were born. Bruno Richard Hauptmann was convicted of kidnapping and murdering the Lindbergh baby. Joe Louis demolished Max Baer. The eccentric, the good, and the notorious died: Lawrence of Arabia and Will Rogers killed in accidents; "Ma" Barker, Dutch Schulz, and Huey Long gunned down like dogs. Mussolini invaded Ethiopia. Persia became Iran. The Moscow subway opened. The graceful *China Clipper,* flying from Alameda, California, to Manila in seven days, made the first commercial flight across the Pacific. Manuel Quezon was inaugurated president of the Philippine Commonwealth. Mary Pickford divorced Douglas Fairbanks. Barbara Hutton married Count Von Haugwitz-Reventlow; Marjorie Merriweather Post Close Hutton married Joseph E. Davies. And Millard Tydings met and married Eleanor Davies Cheesborough.

As a Washington bigwig, Tydings was invited even to New Deal soirées. Joseph Davies, liberal Democrat, friend of Roosevelt, and prominent attorney (he had come to Washington from Wisconsin to join the Wilson administration), often invited Tydings to dinners at his Massachusetts Avenue mansion. He liked the intelligent young senator and enjoyed their verbal sparring. Once Tydings noticed an oil portrait of a young woman and asked Davies who she was. Davies replied, "That's my daughter. She's married"—and abruptly changed the subject. But Tydings remembered the vision of pastel and blonde loveliness and one day in February 1935, just back from the Philippines, saw her sitting in the Senate Ladies Gallery and bowed to her from the floor.

Eleanor Davies Cheesborough was a natural beauty—tall and slim, with large, soft eyes and flawless creamy complexion set off by a mass of golden curls. She was intelligent, poised, and well bred, yet vivacious and witty, possessing an innate self-confidence strengthened from having been happily indulged with love and the safety of wealth. She was first born, and had two sisters, Rahel and Emlen, but no brothers. Her father adored her and called her his "son-daughter." She was adventurous by nature; her radiant smile and passion for life attracted people to her—especially men—without trying.

She was raised to be genteel—at home in a world of privilege during the 1910s and 1920s, when wealthy young women were expected only to be well mannered, well traveled, and concerned with the proper arrangement of love lives, social calendars, and clothes. They filled leisurely days planning extravagant evenings with young men whose main activities were playing passable to excellent golf, tennis, and perhaps bridge, who danced superbly, held their liquor well, and behaved like gentlemen while their family and college connections helped them achieve professional aspirations. A social conscience was a prerequisite for nothing in that luxurious world of material ambition. Good and charitable deeds were performed as a matter of noblesse oblige.

Eleanor was Vassar educated, concentrating in English, journalism, and French; and although offered two highly desirable jobs after graduation—one on the staff of *Vogue* magazine, and the other at the American University in Beijing—she never seriously considered either. Her career, taken for granted by her parents and herself, was to be marriage. In 1926, as Millard Tydings was celebrating the victory that secured him a seat in the Senate, she was walking down the aisle at the age of 22.

Her nine-year marriage to Thomas Patton Cheesborough, Jr., produced two beautiful children but very little happiness. Finally overwhelmed by the painful realities of living with an alcoholic, she left her husband at their Connecticut house and went home to seek her parents' advice. The thought of divorce—the disgrace—terrified her. She dreaded facing her family, especially her father, and admitting that her life was unbearable and that she could not change it alone. Her father's reaction stunned her. If she still loved Cheesborough, he said, he would help her; if she could no longer endure her situation, she should divorce "now, while you are still young enough to have a happy and rewarding life. . . . [Y]ou and the children can live with us here." Eleanor was speechless. There never had been a divorce in the family. There was the matter of custody of the children. "They are Tom's as well as mine," she reminded Davies. She stayed until she reached a decision.

Before Eleanor had arrived in Washington, an old family friend—"Aunt" Loretta Hines from Chicago—had come to visit. Senator Joe Robinson hosted a luncheon for her at the Capitol. Eleanor was invited. Her mother, believing her daughter needed a respite, encouraged her to attend. Eleanor later remembered saying, "All those fat old senators bore me to death." But her mother replied that she had entertained one at dinner parties who was neither old nor fat, but exceedingly attractive, and was the senior senator from Maryland. Eleanor had heard of him and had heard, she wrote in an unpublished autobiography, "how he had escaped the wiles of my brother-in-law's sister, the beautiful Evie Walker, and all the other Washington lovelies!" She ultimately decided to go out of sheer curiosity.[4]

Mrs. Robinson escorted her guests to the private Senate Ladies' Gallery before the luncheon and identified various senatorial lions prowling the floor below. Eleanor noticed a tall, slender man stride from the Democratic cloakroom to a desk on the aisle. "I had never seen a man with such a magnificent carriage," she remembered. "His shoulders were broad, hips narrow, and his thin face was handsome in an aquiline strong-chinned way." She asked Mrs. Robinson who he was. "Senator Millard Tydings from Maryland," came the reply; and as she spoke Tydings glanced up, smiled, and bowed to the young woman whose face he remembered from the portrait. She smiled back and returned the bow. "I thought you didn't know the Senator," Mrs. Robinson said in surprise. She didn't, Eleanor answered.

He came to the party and immediately engaged her in conversation, telling her he had admired her portrait but, on inquiring, had received a short reply from her father. He said he had just returned from the Philippines and had visited the South Sea island of Bali. "For two cents," he told her, "I would walk out of here and just spend the rest of my life on that lovely island, painting pictures of it." She replied that for two cents she just might go with him. But it was a while before she saw him again. At a lunch at the Mayflower Hotel, an acquaintance from Vassar was at a nearby table with Evie Walker. The two convinced Eleanor to stay on in Washington for a dinner they were hosting in March at the F Street Club. In recounting the names of the guests, they uttered the magic words: Millard Tydings. She accepted.

With trepidation—she was still married and uncomfortable with her situation—Eleanor wrote a formal note inviting him to her parents' home for cocktails before the dinner. He accepted.

Later she learned from Tydings's secretary, Corinne Barger, that on reading her note he leaped up and danced around his office—a sight Barger never had witnessed before.

She decided to proceed with a divorce. With men like Millard Tydings in the world, she wanted more than ever to be free. She reported her decision to her father. He suggested she return to Connecticut and in June accompany him to Europe where he intended to join his wife Emlen and Eleanor's youngest sister Emlen; the two women would leave for London in April and await them there. Eleanor perhaps could get a divorce in Paris.

She delayed telling her husband her plans but proceeded to reorganize her life. Tydings telephoned and wrote. His calls and letters were welcome. He invited her to New York the evening he addressed the Southern Society dinner. When she told Cheesborough she was having dinner with a senator, he laughed in disbelief.

As she danced with Tydings at Central Park's Casino to the music of Eddie Duchin, she told him her divorce decision was definite, and he replied, "When you are free, I will come to court you properly."

In love and eager to be free of the burdens of the past nine years, Eleanor summoned the courage to confront her husband. Shaken, he begged her to delay action until she returned from Europe. She consented, but felt it better to return to her parents' home rather than stay on with him.[5]

In Washington, Tydings introduced her to Maryland, land of her ancestors. Her maternal forebears had arrived in 1634 among those privileged to trace their roots to the *Arc* and the *Dove*. Zooming about the springtime countryside in his sleek black Packard roadster, Eleanor saw the shimmering Chesapeake and visited Antietam, where they learned that each had grandfathers who had worn Union blue and fought in the bloody battle there.

He had not asked her to marry him, but she was sure he would the moment she was free. She confided in her parents who were pleased but skeptical. "Millard Tydings is the most eligible and attractive bachelor in Washington. Every woman in town is after him," her father cautioned. Then he added, "I would rather have him for a son-in-law than any man in the world."

When the time came for her to sail to Europe, her father said that, if the senator came to New York to see her off, he would believe his intentions were serious; if not, then she was no more than a "passing fancy." She was unnerved by the thought—all the more so when, on the evening before he was to arrive, he telephoned to say that the Senate had failed to come to a vote on an important bill and, if debate carried over into the next afternoon, he would be unable to come. At the Plaza Hotel the next afternoon she rushed to the clerk to find a waiting telegram that read, "When you receive this, I will be on my way rejoicing." He arrived bearing orchids and roses and books.

The two months in Europe became a nightmare. A client of her father, Marjorie Post Hutton, was aboard ship with a retinue of maids, secretaries, and friends. She was rumored to be divorcing her husband, Edward F. Hutton. Only in London did Eleanor learn from her mother that her father had asked for a divorce himself. He was going to marry Marjorie. The only happy moments she knew were those spent writing Tydings and reading his letters.

In August she, her mother, and sister sailed for home. Her mother was miserable. Eleanor was anxious to see Tydings, and her children, and proceed with her divorce. In midocean an urgent telegram arrived from Tydings. "Imperative you come to Washington by Monday next." When she cabled back to protest that it would be nearly impossible to move in four days, a barrage of cables ensued insisting she must be in Washington by Monday.

While Eleanor was gone and after Joe Davies returned, Tydings spoke to him about marriage. One of the questions Davies asked his prospective son-in-law was where they would live. With Tydings's mother gravely ill with heart trouble—he had nurses staying with her around the clock—living in the family home in Havre de Grace was out of the question. "I have a house here in Georgetown," he said to Davies. "I'm renting it." Then he told Davies about an estate on the Chesapeake called Oakington Farms.

He had learned sometime before he met Eleanor that the estate south of Havre de Grace—a place he had admired as a boy and longed to own—was for sale. He was lunching with friends from Harford County when one of them said, "Millard, Oakington is for sale." He had replied, "Yes, I know. It's been for sale for some time." When his companion asked, "Why don't you buy it?" Tydings said in astonishment, "Are you crazy? I couldn't any more afford to buy Oakington—" He was interrupted. "It's for sale for practically nothing. It's a darn good investment." Tydings exclaimed, "Why that's no place for a single man! I'll never need a place like that."

But the conversation had put the bee in his bonnet. When he talked with Davies and described the place, Eleanor's father generously offered to help. But Tydings wanted Eleanor to see the house before signing anything. He had gotten an option to buy that would expire on Wednesday—hence the urgency. On Monday she arrived, exhausted but curious.

To get there from the Old Post Road they had to ford a stream in the woods. She murmured, "My, this is country, isn't it?"—a phrase that became a family joke. Stopping his roadster under great white pines bordering a lane that entered brick gates, he said, "This is it." As he showed her around the grounds he was "in a rosy dream," she remembered, seeing it in his mind the way it had been when he was a boy and walked the Chesapeake shore in front of the great graystone house. In August 1935, however, it was a wreck—shutters falling off, hinges rusted, plaster cracked, and a basement flooded with water. The grounds were a jungle—flower beds choked with uncut grass, weeds chin high, huge banks of azaleas and rhododendron running wild.

The house would come fully furnished, including some Oriental rugs, and possessed a graceful entry hall with a handsome chandelier. Seven fireplaces, all with marble mantels, graced the foyer, drawing room, the arched-entry dining room, library, parlor, solarium, and master bedroom. There were ten other bedrooms, nine baths, servants quarters, and a gigantic picture window from which she could see a breathtaking view of the Chesapeake.

Oakington also boasted an illustrious history. Surveyed in 1659 for Colonel Nathaniel Utie, the property—550 acres of rich farmland—commanded a magnificent site at the confluence of the Susquehanna River and the Chesapeake Bay. The original building—a square stone colonial built in 1812 by John Stump—was now a wing of the 29-room mansion designed by architect Stanford White for James L. Breese, a Wall Street millionaire who had acquired the property in 1905. The next proprietor, Commodore Leonard Richards of the Atlas Gunpowder fortune, spent $100,000 remodeling it, allegedly with more money than taste. Nearby was Sion Hill, homestead for generations of the Rodgerses, the naval family so revered in Havre de Grace.

The English boxwood enclosing the formal gardens were more than 200 years old and alone were valued at $75,000. A six-car garage was housed in a building composed of three ten-room houses. There were wisteria arbors, a greenhouse, a tennis court, tenant cottages and, a galaxy of farm buildings. All was in sad disrepair. But Eleanor fell in love with Oakington. Tydings and Davies closed the deal, buying it from the Richards estate.[6]

No matter how discreet Tydings tried to be, there were no secrets in Washington. In September, when Eleanor and her mother traveled together to Reno to seek divorces after he bought Oakington, the gossip columnists had a field day, especially because the Post Hutton–Davies connection provided a titillating double bill:

"DAVIES DIVORCE STIRS REPORT OF HUTTON MATCH: WIFE WINS DECREE, LAWYER MAY REWED: DAUGHTER AND TYDINGS LINKED" ran one headline. "Mrs. Thomas Patton Cheeseborough [*sic*—rare as concern for privacy was the copywriter who spelled Cheesborough correctly], who is now seeking a divorce in Nevada, will marry Senator Millard E. Tydings of Maryland, most wary of all Capitol Hill bachelors." Inevitably, Oakington was mentioned: Tydings "recently purchased a 600 acre estate. . . . Why, the social gossips wanted to know, should the bachelor and World War hero want a place this large unless he were going to settle down?"

When asked point-blank about rumors that he would marry, Tydings flashed his famous grin and said, "That's very flattering, but I don't know whether President Roosevelt will carry the Ohio and Mississippi Rivers or not."

"Do you know the lady?" reporters asked.

"Our families have been friends for years but really the only way that America can get prosperity is by buying from foreign countries as well as selling to them."

Reporters laughed, and one was heard to remark, "It's quite flattering that it ain't as cold today as it is yesterday, was it?"

Mother and daughter were granted uncontested divorces a day apart and, once the decrees were final, public curiosity increased geometrically. One column noted Tydings had seemed "so established in bachelorhood that even Lloyds, which insures anybody against everything, would have considered him a bad matrimonial risk." A Marylander posed an intriguing question in a letter to the editor: "What about Senator Tydings' new country estate? Does he expect to use it as a summer White House?" Eleanor became the object of curiosity, criticism, lavish compliments, and even jealousy.

Formal announcement of their engagement on December 5, 1935, introduced less flattering coverage. Along with the traditional wording—"Announcement was made today of the forthcoming marriage of Maryland's forty-five year old bachelor senator, Millard E. Tydings of Havre de Grace, to Mrs. Eleanor Davies Cheeseborough [sic], prominent New York and Washington socialite"—came embellishments that caused the couple anguish and embarrassment:

Mrs. Emlen Knight Davies, the bride's mother, divorced her husband, Joseph E. Davies, former chairman of the Federal Trade Commission, in Carson City [*sic*], Nevada just one day before the daughter obtained her decree. Mr. Davies and Mrs. Edward F. Hutton, aunt by marriage of Countess Barbara Hutton Von Haugwitz-Reventlow, will be married December 16. Mr. Davies was Mrs. Hutton's counsel during her divorce suit recently. Mrs. Hutton's palatial yacht, the four-masted bark *Sea Cloud*, which has been lying off Annapolis, will be brought to dry-dock for overhauling. Mrs. Hutton will not return to the vessel until after her honeymoon.

Not every announcement carried that array of detail, but seldom did Eleanor and Tydings escape being linked to Marjorie's divorce and remarriage to Eleanor's father—sometimes cruelly so. Drew Pearson wrote, "Eleanor Davies is now expected to marry Millard Tydings, dapper bachelor Senator from Maryland whose presidential ambitions are to be furthered financially by his prospective mother-in-law Mrs. Marjorie Post Hutton"—a claim as untrue as it was in bad taste. Even the venerable New York *Times* touched briefly on the dual divorces and Davies–Hutton rumors.[7]

But people in general seemed excited over the romance. At a Carroll County meeting of Democratic leaders from all over Maryland, the usual references to President Roosevelt and the party were applauded, but mention of Tydings's engagement inspired wild ovation. A bewildered senator said to the cheering crowd, "I don't understand why there is so much fuss about my engagement. People are getting married all the time."

The fuss arose partly from spontaneous reaction proving the truism that all the world loves a lover. But it was more than that. The romance was a political story. The "Senate's most eligible bachelor and the infinitely lovely Eleanor Davies Cheesborough" were written about nationwide. Many articles echoed the Martinsburg (West Virginia) *Journal*'s headlined analysis: "SENATOR MAY BE ACQUIRING A WIFE WHO WILL BECOME FIRST LADY OF LAND IN FUTURE YEARS—SHOULD SERVE TO OPEN EYES OF READERS TO UNDERSTAND WHY WEDDING STIRS FRIENDLY INTEREST." As one paper remarked, "Not since the Bachelor President Grover Cleveland, 49, was making arrangements to receive pretty Frances Folsom in the East Room of the White House has Washington been so thrilled and so keenly interested in impending nuptials."

The lavishness of the Post Hutton–Davies nuptials on December 16 drove the press into a frenzy that embarrassed the Davies women. The five-foot-high, three-foot-wide, 150-pound wedding cake, the roomfuls of white chrysanthemums dyed pink (costing almost $7,000), and the floor-length pink gowns so generously trimmed with costly white fox worn by Marjorie and her two attendants—daughter Nedenia ("Deenie") and granddaughter Marjorie ("Mahwee") Durant—riveted media attention, much to Eleanor's consternation.

Although Tydings, who had become very close to Davies, attended the wedding—riding to New York with a trainload of Davies's friends—Eleanor refused to go, out of loyalty to her mother. Emlen Knight Davies, unwilling to hide as if in disgrace, informed Eleanor that they were going to a concert at Constitution Hall where she had a box, and that Mrs. Woodrow Wilson and Mrs. William Borah would accompany them. It seemed to Eleanor that every pair of eyes in the auditorium was fixed on them.

Perhaps the sensationalism surrounding his engagement unnerved Tydings. Perhaps an attack of cold feet, brought on by the whirlwind nature of the romance and its rankling linkage to too many highly publicized divorces and remarriages, stung his Protestant conscience and engendered a sudden surge of distrust. What if Eleanor were just another predatory Washington woman, the kind who had caused him to doubt the morals of certain members of the female sex? He suddenly questioned his actions, wondered if he had made the right choice. Uneasy with Eleanor's youth and attractiveness, he found himself jealous of men who flirted openly with her during their courtship. He became angry with her for not trying harder to discourage such advances.

Such male behavior in her world was so commonplace that she had not considered it disrespectful. Nor had she anticipated Tydings's reaction. Her experience—including with husband and friends—had led her to believe men were more amused than angry when others expressed admiration for their wives. She never took seriously the passes made and believed, perhaps naively, that those who flirted with her were as innocent in their intentions as she. For her it was fun to be admired. For Tydings it was a serious matter of what was proper and what was not. He came from a different background, had lived a very different kind of life. His small-town and impoverished upbringing, and his lifetime of ceaseless hard work, seemed far removed from her life of ease. Perhaps their roots and values were too disparate. His stern conscience and sense of rectitude made his judgment of her unthinking but guiltless behavior all the more harsh.

He also had another worry, of heart-wrenching intensity, on his mind. His mother, sick and frail for a long time, was dying. Just before he first met Eleanor, he received word while returning from the Philippines that his mother had been hospitalized with a severe heart attack. He had rushed to Havre de Grace from the pier in New York. Gravely ill, her condition worsened and in June she suffered a paralyzing stroke. Mary O'Neill Tydings's health, and her son's obvious devotion, was covered in Harford County papers and in Baltimore and Washington too, the *Sun* reporting that the senator's 70-year-old mother, "great-granddaughter of John O'Neill who defended Havre de Grace single-handed during the War of 1812," was ill and that "her son hurried from Washington to her bedside and has spent much time with her since."

Throughout earlier illnesses he ensured that she was cared for properly and spent many weekends with her. Knowing the doctors insisted she avoid all excitement, he went to great lengths not to upset her. Acting carefree to raise her spirits, just as he had as a boy, he made no mention of political vexations. With his mother's condition so precarious, possibly terminal, he feared her reaction to hearing he had found the woman he wanted to marry. Eleanor met her just once before the wedding. It was traumatic for him, to be ardently in love with a beautiful and vibrant young woman, while in torment watching another—a woman always deeply loved, once also beautiful and vibrant, now grown old and wretched—dying.

That terrible conflict coincided with his misgivings. For one of the only times in his life, he lost his composure. Influenced by a mixture of grief and uncertainty, and under the influence of champagne that had flowed freely at the New York extravaganza, he arrived at Washington's Union Station barely able to pour himself out of the midnight train onto the platform where Eleanor awaited him. The usually ramrod straight senator swayed up to her and icily informed her he never wanted to see her again. She was shocked. Not so much at what he said. The wily Evie Walker had phoned from New York with "a mysterious warning": Eleanor must talk with her before seeing Tydings—an offer the mistrustful Eleanor declined. She was shocked at the shape he was in. Never before (and never again) had she seen him intoxicated.

Experienced in handling such a condition, she calmly said that he never need see her again but would be better off at her mother's home than trying to find a hotel at such a late hour. After downing sandwiches and milk, they had it out in the sun parlor. He raved and ranted: She was a frivolous woman, she would not be a fit wife, and so on. When he ran out of steam she replied that, if that was what he thought, she wouldn't marry him if he were the last man on Earth, goodnight. She stormed out and wept until dawn. The next morning, partly hung over, partly contrite, surely ashamed, he asked to see her. In the clear light of day they set the wedding date for December 27.

The service, held at 5:00 P.M. in the drawing room of her mother's home, was limited to family. Eleanor's mother gave the bride away as their sisters looked on. Tydings's mother was unable to attend. Attempts to keep the date and time secret failed despite Corinne Barger's efforts to throw the press pack off the trail. She delayed getting the marriage license until 3:00, but newsmen and newswomen staking out the palatial Davies home spotted a telltale sign that something was afoot when violinist Anton Kaspar and his daughter Krispa, carrying violin case and sheet music, were spied entering the house. A small army of shivering reporters converged on Massachusetts Avenue.

The 40-plus reception guests (including Senators Radcliffe, Borah, Tom Connally, and their wives, and Roosevelt press secretary Marvin McIntyre, Secretary of State Cordell Hull, close friend E. Brooke Lee) snarled traffic as their limousines slid in slushy ice. A police cordon relaxed its vigil when the bride and groom stepped outside for pictures, Eleanor wearing a long gray velvet gown with matching fox trim. A family member admonished, "Just one shot."

The photographs were ghastly, and the Washington *Herald*'s write-up captured the groom's nervousness and the strain of the past month. "Usually very much at ease the Senator was stiff and straight as a robot. His bride joined him, in gray from slippers to her broad brimmed hat. She too was unsmiling," the article began. "A photographer called out, 'Just one smile, Senator.' The Senator stared straight ahead, across the snowy yard and street. Mrs. Tydings looked up at him, nudged his arm, smiled. He relaxed, their smiles became shouted laughter, and they rushed back into the house as shutters snapped."

Word was leaked to the press that they were honeymooning in New Orleans. They then sneaked out to drive through the snow to Oakington—unaware that Tydings's office staff, led by Miss Barger, had attached a "Just Married" sign to the back of his roadster.

Throughout the fall, workmen had repaired, replastered, re-painted, and redecorated the old mansion—the decorating a gift from Davies.[8] Marjorie generously provided handsome rugs; there was Eleanor's furniture from her ten-room Connecticut home and Tydings's from his Georgetown residence.

By the time of the wedding, the house was beautifully finished and staffed by Robert Livingstone and his wife Nadene.[9] The Livingstones welcomed them warmly. Tydings swept Eleanor into his arms, across the threshold and up the wide staircase to the enormous master bedroom where hot chocolate, sandwiches, and cake were set on a table in front of the marble fireplace. She suggested a romantic fire, but the damper was closed and clouds of smoke billowed forth. Tydings pushed Eleanor out the door and slammed it shut. While he doused the fire, she sat on the top stair alone. She teased him unmercifully ever after for throwing her out of their bedroom on their bridal night.

Eleanor's father and Marjorie—unable to be with Eleanor on her wedding day—invited the couple to join them on the *Sea Cloud* in the Caribbean. In Nassau the British Governor General Sir Bede Clifford and his wife insisted the honeymooners spend the night at their beach cabana. The bed—a pullout arrangement—accommodated two, but on separate mattresses, one higher than the other and each sloping toward the floor. Worse, the cottage was infested with sand fleas. As they slipped and scratched through the night they engaged in a vigorous argument about women's suffrage, which, Eleanor had learned to her horror during dinner, he had opposed and voted against.

Back in Washington she opened her mother's home—during the week when the Senate was in session they stayed at Massachusetts Avenue—to guests, giving "at home" teas to meet the wives of other senators. Friendly and at ease with the groups of mostly older women, she became well liked for "her unaffected and natural manner." They received more invitations than ever to parties and receptions; and when they attended, they would dash home early to have time alone. Washington took notice of Tydings's contentment. "Millard's smile these days seems even more expansive than Mr. Roosevelt's," remarked a friend quoted in the Washington *Post*. Walter Winchell's "On Broadway" column said in March, "The Senator Tydings are infanticipating."

It was premature speculation. They very much wanted to have children, but to their great disappointment they as yet were unable to conceive. After they had been married awhile, when Tydings learned that Eleanor had discussed with her father her children's situation—Joe was ten and Eleanor six, and if something happened to her they would be remanded by the courts to the care of their father, who continued to drink and who, she feared, would be irresponsible—Tydings told her he wanted to adopt them.

He had everything. Fame, fortune, a family, power, the world on a string. When they went to the Democratic convention in Philadelphia in 1936 (where he swallowed his pride to give the Maryland seconding speech for Roosevelt's renomination), he and Eleanor were photographed, written up, and talked about as the next president and first lady. The only fly in the ointment—if it could be called such—was the unending publicity linking them to Eleanor's stepmother, Marjorie Davies. When Davies was appointed ambassador to the Soviet Union by Roosevelt, the farewell parties made society pages everywhere, with Tydings inevitably mentioned. The irony of proletarian Russia receiving one of America's richest, bejeweled capitalists was too good to miss; the Davies "wealth and luxury" would be "a Bolshevist eye popper." The last of the dinners was the epitome of opulence: "Social elegance has returned to Washington this season. The farewell dinner given by Joseph Davies and his wife, reached Lucullan proportions. Senator and Mrs. Tydings were guests at the dinner which . . . marked the return of predepression spending in the Capital."

The luxury of the *Sea Cloud* disturbed Tydings. Marjorie had studied marine architecture and planned every detail. Constructed in Kiel, Germany, in 1931 at a cost of $3 million, the vessel was 354 feet long with a 50-foot beam and weighed 3,600 tons—a sail and diesel square-rigged clipper in a class by itself. The graceful golden bowsprit, teak decks, immaculate silver-painted engines, and four towering masts were the least impressive attributes. It was the dramatic circular staircase, wood-burning fireplace, grand piano, eighteenth-century furniture, ten master cabins, pink marble bath with gold fittings, and exquisite paintings that left guests breathless.

Their first summer at Oakington, the Tydingses had full use of the *Sea Cloud*. With the ship's crew of 70 they boarded at Oyster Bay, New York. The second day aboard, Tydings told Eleanor he had received a wire and had to go back to Washington. Later he admitted that he just could not stand the thought of the ship's operating costs. Even some of Davies's wealthy colleagues found it hard to take. The president of American Express was aboard one afternoon, pacing furiously up and down the deck, face red as if angry. Eleanor asked his wife, "What is the matter with Bobby?" "Oh," she replied, "he's just figured out how much it costs to run this ship every time he draws a breath." Tydings said he knew exactly how he felt.

Marjorie also lent them the use of her enormous place in the Adirondacks, Camp Topridge, and invited them to her Long Island estate, her Fifth Avenue apartment, and the Xanadu of the East Coast: her Palm Beach estate, Marilago. At Christmas she showered them with gifts like a fairy-tale godmother, giving away furs and gowns she had worn only a few times, a diamond bracelet, silver serving plates that had belonged to the czar. After parties she loved to "hash the party," whereby she would "take the guests apart and not bother to put them all together again." Tydings was uncomfortable and troubled by such largess and wealth.

It was not long before he was partied out. He had been wined and dined half to death before he met Eleanor; as a bachelor senator he would not have had an evening free if he so chose. Now he yearned for quiet. They spent weekends at Oakington. She grew interested in politics, spearheaded the founding of the Harford County Women's Club, a member of United Democratic Women's Clubs of Maryland, and in 1937 made her first public address, to a women's group at the University of Maryland on peace through international trade.

He flung himself into his work. There was more than enough to command his attention, for, with the president's landslide reelection in November, the New Dealers' agenda came to include an item that would provoke one of the most bitter and significant political battles in the history of the Republic: Franklin Roosevelt's Supreme Court packing plan.

Notes

1. Once funding struggles were resolved, Tydings's efforts saw completion of the Washington–Gettysburg Memorial Parkway, the Baltimore–Washington Parkway, Baltimore's international airport, bridges spanning the Susquehanna at Havre de Grace and the Potomac at Morganstown, deepening and widening of the Chesapeake and Delaware Canals, and construction of the Chesapeake Bay Bridge. A few other bills, unsuccessful during his tenure, laid the groundwork for projects finished later, such as the Baltimore Harbor Tunnel. Certain ventures forced him into bitter confrontation with Roosevelt and Interior Secretary Harold Ickes, who headed the Public Works Administration (PWA), the major source of federal money for public works construction.

2. Radcliffe had been Roosevelt's superior when both were vice-presidents of a New York surety company in the 1920s. The two had remained close.

3. Radcliffe, in a memo written long after retiring from the Senate (the document is among his papers at the Maryland Historical Society), maintained that he had not wanted to run for any office: "Senator Tydings on various occasions in the early spring of 1934 urged me to run for governorship stating that Ritchie could not be re-elected. I told him again and again that I did not want to run for governorship or any other position as I had never been a candidate for office." But, Radcliffe went on, Tydings continued to pressure him and secured an appointment to meet with Roosevelt to discuss the matter: "Senator Tydings told President Roosevelt that Ritchie could not be reelected but that I could, he believed. President Roosevelt asked me why I was not willing to fit in with the wishes of himself and of the political leaders in Baltimore. He stated that he had no intention of interfering in Maryland politics

or doing anything detrimental to Ritchie but that he thought I should give careful consideration to any attempt to clear up the muddle." Radcliffe bowed to the wishes of Roosevelt and Tydings, acquiesced again when Roosevelt and Mayor Jackson "repeatedly urged me to run for the Senate insisting that I would have little opposition and that my candidacy would be of assistance to them and to other people who had gone out on the limb for me for governor."

Radcliffe's later resentment at Tydings's dominance as senior senator surfaced in the memo when he noted that he had refrained from building his own political faction because to do so might damage his relationship with Tydings and cause discord within the Maryland Democratic party. "Also I realized that such a restraint on my part would possibly make it a bit less troublesome for Senator Tydings to carry out his ambitious personal political policies," he wrote. He also resented the way the press favored Tydings for voting against the New Deal: "He was often lauded as bold and courageous and I was a 'rubber stamp,' " Radcliffe lamented.

4. Eleanor's sister Rahel had married Aldace Walker in 1933. His sister Evie was, in Eleanor's words, "a wild, harum-scarum girl who loved men and horses in that order. She was also possessed of a lethal wit." It was Evie Walker who had invited Tydings to the Diehl–Heinz engagement party in May.

5. Eleanor Cheesborough's two children, Joe and Eleanor, stayed on in the family home with their nanny and father until August when they spent time at their maternal grandmother's summer home on the Brule River in Northern Wisconsin. They rejoined her after the divorce was final and in time for Joe, who was then seven, to enroll in school.

6. Davies preferred to keep his wedding gift secret, even from Eleanor. He wanted it known that Tydings bought the property. He formed a corporation, the Oakington Company, to handle it. For several years the property title would be in the corporate name, then would transfer to the couple jointly. The purchase price was $52,500. In 1948 it was valued at $100,000.

7. So inextricably linked were their names that some well-known and otherwise careful historians have mistakenly written that Tydings married the heiress to the Post cereal fortune.

8. During renovation the house was wide open. Everyone in the area knew Tydings had bought the old Breese place; local lore had it that there was not a house in Harford County that did not display some souvenir from Oakington.

9. Livingstone was head busboy at Pierre's Restaurant at the Washington Anchorage. When he learned Tydings had bought a country estate, he asked if he and his wife—a cordon bleu cook—could work for him. They had a baby and the idea of leaving the city appealed to them greatly. Tydings was delighted to hire the young Scotsman. He gave them a large apartment on the third floor of the house. They stayed for 25 years, until the year before the senator's death.

9

The Squire of Oakington at War with the Squire of Hyde Park

When Congress reconvened in 1937 following Franklin Roosevelt's stunning election victory, Tydings immediately challenged the reinvigorated president. Believing Roosevelt would interpret his 46-state sweep as a mandate for the New Deal, Tydings intended to put him on notice that conservatives in Congress had no intention of playing dead. He reintroduced his resolution for an automatically balanced budget just four days after Roosevelt submitted his "balanced from the layman's point of view" 1937 budget.

Tydings's resolution, like his 1936 one, would impose strict controls on spending: Congress could appropriate no more money than it expected in revenue without raising additional funds through taxes or Treasury borrowing amortized over 15 years; and Congress could not increase funds allocated to individual bureaus and departments unless an equal amount was deducted from another bureau or department. Tydings's point was that Congress had to consider each appropriation in relation to the needs of other departments, and in relation to funds available for all government operations. Otherwise the country would suffer unbalanced budgets and growing federal deficits year after year.

Although the *Wall Street Journal* hailed his plan as "fiscal sanity," his colleagues assailed him: Such a step would breed fierce conflict between the House and Senate—and the proposal would interfere with congressional power. "I should be very reluctant to vote for any sort of a measure which would limit the absolute power of the Congress to appropriate money for any purpose at any time it wants to," Tom Connally announced. "It is one of the glories of democracy that it has the right and power, if it wants to do so, to act as a damned fool, and if Congress spends more money than it should, the people back home, if they are wise, will retire us." Tydings's resolution was sent back to the Appropriations Committee.

Of Justices and Justice

If Roosevelt felt any gratitude toward Tydings for promoting the ticket in 1936 it was short lived. Conservative–liberal animosities among Democrats had not been soothed by the campaign's expedient reconciliations. Although the victory was stupendous—there were only 16 Republicans in the Senate and 89 in the House—Tydings and his fellow conservatives remained alienated from New Dealers and would require careful handling. But Roosevelt, intoxicated by his success at the polls, became imbued with a sublime confidence that he could call the shots and did not need the conservatives. Any chance of the rift being healed was shattered when, on February 5, 1937, he introduced his bombshell judicial reform measure: the Supreme Court packing plan.

The Congress, the press, the nation, even Roosevelt's Cabinet and close advisers—all were stunned. In theory the idea of judicial reform was nothing new; discussions exploring curbs on the Supreme Court's powers dated back to Thomas Jefferson and had resurfaced periodically. When the Court threw out Roosevelt's National Industrial Recovery Act (NRA) in May 1935, declared his Agricultural Adjustment Act (AAA) unconstitutional in January 1936, and struck down other New Deal measures such as the Guffey Coal Bill and a New York State minimum wage law, proposals designed to rein in the conservative Court were reexamined. Editorials on the subject frequently were published nationally. Those predicting action proved accurate.

Roosevelt was infuriated over the High Court's rulings. It had stymied his good intentions—and had frustrated his pleasure in wielding power. For two years he and his advisers had discussed strategies for making the Court more amenable to New Deal goals. Now, given what Roosevelt saw as the Court's willful reactionary obstructionism, its "horse-and-buggy" attitude, its arbitrary unfairness, all New Deal reform legislation seemed endangered. The most controversial decisions were five to four; a few reactionaries—all Republican appointees—had shut down the New Deal and thwarted the two other branches of the American government. Roosevelt came to believe reform of the High Court was necessary to achieve his NRA and AAA objectives.[1]

The president was not alone in desiring court reform. Many Democrats in Congress—Speaker of the House William B. Bankhead of Alabama, Chairman of the House Judiciary Committee Hatton W. Sumners of Texas, Senate Majority Leader Joseph T. Robinson of Arkansas, Chairman of the Senate Judiciary Committee Henry F. Ashurst of Arizona, and Senators George W. Norris of Nebraska and Burton K. Wheeler of Montana—were sympathetic to the idea, as were White House advisers Benjamin V. Cohen and Thomas G. Corcoran and labor leader John L. Lewis. They all believed the Court was out of step, was usurping power in ways not intended by the Founding Fathers. Some had proposed plans of their own, most based on constitutional amendment. The president himself had briefly considered reform through amendment, but decided that would take too long. Expanding the Court became his solution of choice.

Working in almost total secrecy, Roosevelt broke his usual pattern of brainstorming the idea with Felix Frankfurter, Cohen, Corcoran, and others; he consulted with and confided in no one from his inner circle, Congress, labor, agriculture, or the liberal community. From his Cabinet only Attorney General Homer S. Cummings, Solicitor General Stanley F. Reed, and a Cummings assistant knew of the plan and worked on drafting the legislation and the president's accompanying message to Congress. He did call on two unofficial advisers—Judge Samuel I. Rosenman and attorney Donald R. Richberg—to review the documents. At the last minute he could not resist showing them to Corcoran and several others, but they—horrified at what they read, as they had advised against such a plan—suppressed their reactions. They knew the die was cast.

Later critics blamed Roosevelt's obsession with secrecy for his failure to see warning signs. Had he let himself listen to any among the Democratic leadership, he would have been told that his packaging would fool no one, that disguising his real aims with arguments about judicial delays and old age was a transparent deception and—worse—could be considered downright dishonest. Tampering with the Court would stir an outcry from those already fearful that Roosevelt wielded too much power. But Roosevelt went ahead with his plan. (A late-morning meeting at the White House on February 5 was convened to inform Cabinet and Capitol Hill leaders—Bankhead, Sumners, Robinson, Ashurst, and Representative Sam Rayburn of Texas—but not to seek their advice.) Under the guise of judicial reform, the president proposed—among other things—that, for every judge of any federal court who had not retired by age 70, another could be appointed, with Supreme Court membership limited to an additional six. Not coincidentally six judges then sitting were septuagenarians. Passage of the bill would enable Roosevelt to pack the Court with six more justices.

At noon on February 5, a White House messenger walked down the Senate aisle and read a message from the president. Eleanor Tydings, seated in the visitors gallery, listened intently. When she realized what she was hearing—a plan to retire aged judges who "cease to explore into the present or inquire into the future," to replace them with "younger blood to vitalize the courts"—she turned to some "roaring New Dealers" behind her and angrily exclaimed, "So that's the way he's going to get to the Supreme Court!"

The Senate's reaction, initially confined to the privacy of the cloakrooms, ranged from abhorrence to elation. Vice President John Nance Garner held his nose while making the Roman thumbs-down gesture (although publicly he paid obedient lip service). Robinson, who had turned red and stared at the table during the White House meeting, expressed approval and predicted passage. (Robinson's loyal but not impassioned support—privately he called the scheme "pretty raw"—was complicated by Roosevelt's promise to him of the first Court vacancy). Ashurst, also noncommittal at the meeting, where he had studied the ceiling, took a day to think it over before issuing a terse statement in support. As expected, Republicans gnashed their teeth and raged.

Only a few of the staunch Democratic conservatives announced opposition immediately: Edward R. Burke of Nebraska, Harry F. Byrd of Virginia, and old Carter Glass of Virginia, who was ill and was reached by telephone. "Of course I shall oppose it," Glass fumed in response to a reporter's question. "I shall oppose it with all the strength which remains to me, but I don't imagine for a minute that it'll do any good. Why, if the President asked Congress to commit suicide tomorrow they'd do it." Tydings and others held their fire for the moment. It was a time for careful thought.

Tydings, before Roosevelt's thunderbolt, had invited a few colleagues to dinner that night at the Massachusetts Avenue residence—a conservative gathering assembled to plot strategy for cutting the federal debt and opposing Roosevelt's spending measures. In the wake of the Court message, Tydings's dinner became the first council of war against the scheme. The first step was to count noses—who had gone on record for or against the bill, and the number left agonizing. Once they could determine the strength of the opposition, they could plan their attack and organize recruitment of undecideds. To a man they were against it, but Tydings counseled patience until they could assess the overall situation.[2]

The next morning's editorials heartened them. Only three of the nations's major presses—the New York *Daily News,* the New York *Post,* and the Philadelphia *Record*—failed to join the assault on Roosevelt's plan. Prophecies of dictatorship were not limited to the predictably conservative press. Editors nationwide roared their disapproval, columnists denounced the idea in shrill and unequivocal language, and the people themselves spoke up in telegrams and letters that were nine to one opposed. Prominent citizens issued statements condemning it; bar associations protested; state senates and assemblies passed resolutions against the bill. Church officials nervously wondered if a politically altered Court could protect religious freedoms. Tydings's mail ran 50–1 against the plan.[3]

Within days Tydings's hardcore bloc included—in addition to Byrd, Frederick C. Van Nuys, Peter Goelet Gerry, and Guy M. Gillette—Glass, Burke, Josiah W. Bailey of North Carolina, Ellison

("Cotton Ed") Smith of South Carolina, Walter F. George of Georgia, and Royal S. Copeland of New York. Some committed publicly; some, like Tydings, operated behind the scenes to work on those they believed they could recruit. The grapevine burned with rumors of liberal defections. Representative Hatton Sumners had declared his opposition on the way back to the Hill from the White House saying, "Boys, here's where I cash in my chips." The great progressive leader Wheeler, who had been in New York on February 5, was clearly outraged by Roosevelt's methods. The president's supporters squirmed unhappily. For both sides, recruiting the undecided took on aspects of a crusade.

Within ten days of Tydings's first dinner, a dozen or so men committed to fighting the Court plan met again at his home. Their strategy began to take shape. Instinctively they knew their best chance for defeating Roosevelt lay in finding a liberal Democrat to assume the lead—someone who could better convince liberals to join them. Wheeler's name came up immediately, and Tydings called him on the telephone.[4]

Wheeler at that point was the crucial Democrat, for the Senate's other great progressive leader, George Norris, had let himself be persuaded to go along with Roosevelt's plan although he openly detested it and refused to lead the fight. A powerful orator, Wheeler was tenacious, honest, skilled, and suspicious enough by nature to anticipate the opposition's next moves. For both sides his stance was almost a matter of life or death. The White House sent Tom Corcoran to woo him. They met for lunch at the old Grace Dodge Hotel a week after Roosevelt's message. In the dim dining room, safe from scrutiny, Corcoran obliquely led Wheeler to believe that, if he acquiesced, he could nominate several of the new Court members. Wheeler would not consent. They debated the merits of the bill. When Corcoran pounded the table and insisted, "It's going to pass!" Wheeler responded, "Well, Tommy, he *isn't* going to get it." He, too, slammed his fist angrily: "What's more, I'm going to fight it with everything I've got." (There is no evidence that the Roosevelt people tried to get Tydings's support; they undoubtedly wrote him off from the start.)

At Tydings's home, Wheeler stood and surveyed the faces of those seated at the elegantly appointed banquet table. There sat almost every conservative Democrat he had fought on almost every

New Deal measure. Aside from Tom Connally of Texas and perhaps Bennett "Champ" Clark of Missouri, he saw what he considered the Senate's bloc of standpat reactionaries and remarked that he knew he was in strange company. He would lead them in the fight, Wheeler said, but on one condition only: If they could muster the votes to beat the plan, he would fight to the bitter end; if not, they would have to agree to some compromise. They accepted his terms.

Sitting around Tydings's dinner table they discussed tactics. They would meet daily—always in a different Senate office or Capitol hideaway—to assess their strength, check progress in recruiting votes, alter strategy according to shifting events. They selected a nine-man steering committee. Wheeler would be the front man, Gerry their whip. Tydings would direct from behind the scenes; when the timing was right, then he would make public his stand. They all must work ceaselessly to convert waverers—at parties, dinners, in the Senate chamber, cloakroom, corridors, lobbies, offices, in private conversations. They would beg, cajole, call in their IOUs. Each must keep his antenna tuned for the slightest hint of a change of mind, and all intelligence collected was to be passed to Gerry for his weekly progress and status lists.

They knew the opposition would use the power of patronage—the threat of withholding PWA projects and funds, the carrot of diplomatic and judicial appointments—as leverage. They knew they must take pains to ensure that time and place of the secret meetings were never planned too far in advance so the opposition could not spy and draw accurate conclusions as to their strength. They even suspected that their phones would be tapped.[5]

Roosevelt was surprised by the national reaction. Respected liberals—Oswald Garrison Villard, Arthur Krock, Raymond Clapper—spoke out against the plan. William Allen White wrote, "Assuming, which is not at all impossible, a reactionary president, as charming, as eloquent and as irresistible as Roosevelt, with power to change the court, and we should be in the devil's own fix if he decided to abridge the bill of rights by legislation which he could easily call emergency legislation." Even Felix Frankfurter, a very close Roosevelt adviser, allowed his disgust to leak. He was especially offended by the suggestion that age could disqualify someone as vigorous and astute as Louis D. Brandeis, the 80-year-old justice—

and New Deal supporter. But the president maintained his take-it-or-leave-it attitude, refusing advice that he compromise by settling for two new justices or some other method of reform. He believed in the long run the country would support him. Again and again he repeated, "The people are with me. I know it."

Originally Roosevelt had intended to push his bill through the House, which had been so pliable in the past. But Sumners, chairman of the House Judiciary Committee—outspoken in opposition—had convinced a majority of five to oppose the bill in committee. House leaders persuaded Roosevelt that ramming it down their throats would prove too blatant a show of strong-arm tactics and could hurt if the House, embarrassed by its own spinelessness, should rebel. On February 19 the White House decided to make its stand in the Senate. It would be Wheeler, Gerry, Tydings, and their band of 18 against Majority Leader Joe Robinson, the only Senate leader willing to lead the administration's battle.[6]

On the day the White House decided to fight it out in the Senate, the president's supporters numbered 30, the opposition claimed the equivalent, and those remaining—perhaps 33—became the center of attention as the two sides strove to draw them into alliance. All but two of those uncommitted were Democrats. (Henrik Shipstead and Ernest Lundeen, both from Minnesota, were members of the Farmer-Laborite party.)

The undecideds were torn. Loyalty to such a popular president was a strong political instinct. That was reinforced by a belief that something must be done about the Court's intransigence. But side by side with such considerations arose feelings that Roosevelt's methods were wrong, that his action resembled an unconstitutional grab for power and smacked of dictatorship. Success might destroy a venerable institution. They could sense swelling public indignation. Across the Atlantic and Pacific, totalitarian governments were whittling away freedoms. It was imperative that the United States send the message that fascism could not threaten a healthy constitutional system. The lessons of fascism inspired a new appreciation for the institutions of liberty—and a new fear of how easily democratic freedoms could be lost.

The White House pulled out all stops. Patronage threats and enticements were wielded. Uncommitted senators were invited one or two at a time for private visits with the president. The Roosevelt charm failed to work its magic. The issue was too emotional and too controversial back home where the great masses of the middle class were uneasily pondering the wisdom of such a step. Instead of commitments, Roosevelt received warnings of trouble.

The initial appearance that the White House could keep its troops in line had been misleading. Defections by Connally and then Joseph C. O'Mahoney of Wyoming had hurt. And many of the committed were distinctly unenthusiastic: Norris's early statement, "I am not in sympathy with the plan to enlarge the Supreme Court," had converted no one. The Senate's formidable masters of debate stood solidly arrayed against the president's position. Wheeler proved to be an invaluable asset. He beat Bob La Follette to the draw in converting left-wing Republican Senators Gerald Nye and Lynn Joseph Frazier of North Dakota, and later rounded up Shipstead, bringing home crucial liberal votes.

Within two frantic weeks, lines had been drawn and strategies set. Tydings sent his father-in-law Joe Davies, the new ambassador to the Soviet Union, a long letter analyzing the fight and possible results. "The country rocks over the Supreme Court issue," he wrote. "Most of the republicans, 'Jeffersonian democrats,' and a few of the Rooseveltians are against the '6 more judges' proposal. Mail pours into the capital in a veritable avalanche. Score 50 against to 1 for." Although Roosevelt still held the bulk of the people, Tydings admitted, "I feel the P will have his hands full to jam it through the Senate, for all—or nearly all—the debating ability is lined up against him. . . . My surmise is that the '6 new judges' cannot get by the filibuster which seems in the offing. Result—Roosevelt suffers a reduction in popularity."

> If the fight goes on it is likely wounds will be opened and the party may split in 1940. . . . Talk of R for a third term comes more often.
>
> My concern is less about the placing of the six new judges, per se, than in the results flowing from such a course. For, it is my guess that once the court is friendly to F.D.R. a string of legislation both costly and regimenting will be passed and upheld which will lead to a mild form of socialism or perhaps farther left than that. We will then have a quasi-totalitarianism here. . . .

Here the court proposal is looked upon as the most far-reaching change in our set-up since the adoption of the constitution. Maybe the boss is asking for much to get a little. . . .

Personally I'm trying to keep a cool head—no stampedes—and hoping he may come around to something less far-reaching. If not . . . I shall fight it to the death if there is nothing else to do in the end, for we will be headed for the dictatorship about which up to now I've pooh-poohed. There comes a time in the lives of men when movements they start, hoping to check at a point further along, cannot longer be controlled—and, if the president wins his six judges—labor and others are going to say, "All right, now F.D.R., go ahead," and he will be a disillusioned man. . . . The day will come when F.D.R. will want the court more than anybody else in the U.S.A.

In late February, Joe Robinson told Joe Keenan, the Justice Department attorney assigned to the White House for the duration of the fight, that he could count 54 or 55 votes (only 30 were on record). On February 23, Tydings became the thirty-third senator to go on record against the bill. His timing was intentional and symbolic: Thirty-three votes were necessary to prevent imposition of cloture during a filibuster. His move received nationwide publicity—partly because the swing vote on cloture was so important; and partly because, as a veteran senator, his decision had tremendous impact. His announcement (some news reporters who knew little about him called it a "defection") gave the president's opposition greater credibility, which some analysts suggested could help in countering the accelerated effort to pressure labor and farm leaders to line up behind the administration.

As a part of Roosevelt's secrecy, he had deliberately neglected to consult labor and agricultural leaders. But with the opposition gaining strength to a degree he never anticipated, and with observers predicting the contest would last through the summer, Roosevelt went on the offensive. He summoned the three top agriculture leaders to the White House (Edward A. O'Neal, president of the Farm Bureau Federation; Louis J. Taber, president of the Grange; and E. E. Everson, president of the Farmer's Union). A disappointed president coaxed but one endorsement—that of O'Neal. And even O'Neal would not commit his organization, saying emotions ran exceedingly high. Pleading was to no avail as nothing Roosevelt or Secretary of Agriculture Henry A. Wallace promised or said changed the opinions of the three. That was Roosevelt's first personal taste of the profound popular antipathy stirred by the Court plan.

He fared no better with labor. During the election, the AFL and CIO—rival unions often at war—had joined in support of his reelection, and Roosevelt expected them to do so in favor of his bill. AFL President William Green did support the bill, but his view was not unanimous among AFL leaders; the union, a loose collection of independent organizations, could not exert sufficient influence to sway undecideds.

Roosevelt turned with hope to John L. Lewis and his CIO. The CIO owed its existence to Roosevelt—or so he believed—but Lewis, a national power due to the union's clout, was an independent and ambitious man who believed in politics (not ideals) as a means to his own ends. He trusted his destiny to no one. He distrusted the president's too-charming manner, knew Roosevelt himself was suspicious of potential rivals who grew powerful. Lewis also was miffed at not having been consulted in advance. He endorsed the bill but made no effort to influence waverers.

Roosevelt was on his own. Corcoran and Cohen persuaded him to use his strongest weapon: his resonating aristocratic voice. He alone could sell the plan to the people. Until then he had remained silent, letting his staff and Robinson lead the campaign. With 1,100 Democratic victory dinners scheduled nationwide on March 4 to celebrate his election, he agreed to deliver a Court bill speech at the Mayflower Hotel gathering for 1,300 of the party's most loyal jobholders. His speech would be broadcast live to the other dinners. On March 9 he would follow up with a "fireside chat" to the people. The speech was a resounding success, with it famous cadence:

> Here is one third of a nation ill nourished, ill clad, ill housed— now! Here are thousands upon thousands of farmers wondering whether next year's prices will meet their mortgage interest— now! Here are thousands upon thousands of men and women laboring for long hours in factories for inadequate pay—now! Here are thousands upon thousands of children, who should be at school, working in mines and mills—now! . . . If we would

keep faith with those who had faith in us, if we would make Democracy succeed, I say we must act—now!"

Wheeler thought it the most demagogic speech he had ever heard, but the audience roared support. Still, his later nationwide radio appeal to the people—a combined attack on the Court and defense of his plan—left the country cold. Columnist Joseph Alsop wrote that there were "no signs that [Roosevelt's] speech had changed the situation in any important fashion."

The anti–Court expansion bloc's counterattack was devastating. Carter Glass, the feisty octogenarian from Virginia, delivered an emotional speech bursting with indignation over "a proposition which appears to me utterly destitute of moral sensibility." His references to "parading . . . political janizaries paid by the federal treasury," his sculpted phrases ("judicial marionettes to speak the ventriloquisms of the White House") and his appeals to Americans "who value liberties" were so full of conviction that few remained unmoved.

Tydings, too, now entered the fray. On March 2 on the Senate floor he ridiculed Roosevelt's statement that justices over 70 tended to "see through the dim spectacles of a bygone age." The late Chief Justice Oliver Wendell Holmes had served until he was 90; Brandeis was 80. Who was the president trying to fool, he asked, implying age had a bearing on the quality of Court opinions? The NRA decision, he pointed out, had been unanimous. Brandeis and Benjamin Cardozo at times voted with the conservatives. Roosevelt's premises were full of inconsistencies so glaring as to be outrageous.

His most pointed attack was reserved for the March 4 victory dinner that he attended as featured speaker in North Carolina at the invitation of Senator Bailey. He refrained from explicit mention of the Supreme Court but made his point by discussing principles of democracy. The nation needs "a government of justice, a government of law and not of man, a government of three branches," he said, and urged his listeners against yielding "to the temptation to take short cuts" at the expense of the democratic process and philosophy.

And as he avoided mentioning the Court, he also avoided—at that dinner celebrating his party's president's reelection—mentioning even once the name "Roosevelt." He spoke of "dictators," and "regimentation," and "subversive trends of government," and said "the Chief Executive of our nation is a Democrat" (the closest he got to saying Roosevelt's name). His speech, which had been anticipated eagerly in light of his Court stance, drew no applause from the astonished Raleigh crowd. At the reception, almost no one came near Tydings. Paul Mallon wrote in the Washington *Evening Star*, "Mr. Tydings shook hands only with himself." Governor J. C. B. Ehringhaus said, "It was like the play of Hamlet with Hamlet left out." The columnist OSWALD wrote, "Dear Millard—You might tell the Governor of North Carolina you thought he already knew the name of the President."

Tydings, notorious for raising New Dealers' blood pressure, succeeded again with his barbed, wickedly timed, and widely publicized speech. In answering critics he said, "I had rather be right than pleasant." Had Warren Harding, Calvin Coolidge, or Herbert Hoover tried to pack the Court he would have fought them, too. "If that be treason," he said, "make the most of it."

The drama continued when Harold Ickes decided to retaliate. Ickes, taken by surprise along with the rest of the Cabinet, had remained a bystander. But the Tydings speech went too far. On March 10 he delivered a speech of his own at a hastily arranged second dinner in Raleigh. Slyly titled "Tidings of Victory," his talk invoked the Roosevelt name no fewer than 18 times. To make sure his listeners knew exactly what he was up to, he spoke of "Sad Tidings," and laughingly remarked that the previous dinner speaker should have said, "I came not to praise the Democratic Party but to bury it."

The acid-tongued duo provided national entertainment. But Tydings's speech had involved more than clever swipes at Roosevelt, for he had examined the dangers inherent in concentrations of power and had warned against passive acceptance of basic change in the American system of government, cautioning that those who surrender power buy tragedy.

The mutual pummeling continued. The opposition had a field day when the Judiciary Committee hearings began on March 10. Photographers, reporters, spectators, and senators, Tydings among them, jostled for seats. A number of Senate wives, including Eleanor, ensconced themselves in the front row of the gallery. Wheeler, Tydings, and the steering committee had decided the best strategy lay in having pro–Court expansion witnesses appear first. Committee members Connally, Van Nuys, and Burke were to pounce on them and expose the fraudulence of Roosevelt's arguments about crowded dockets and too many "aged and infirm judges." Their questioning was meant to force witnesses to admit that what Roosevelt really wanted was a Court that thought as he did; their arguing would deliberately prolong the hearings, educate the country by keeping them going. Headlines and publicity would help promote the idea that the bill was inherently bad and deceitfully presented, would help shape national opinion.

Corcoran and Keenan, in a frantic attempt to speed things up, tried to convince Connally to limit each side's presentation of witnesses to two weeks. With the firm backing of the Wheeler–Tydings steering committee, he refused. Corcoran and Keenan turned to committee chairman Henry Ashurst. Ashurst was on record as a supporter, but many in the opposition believed that, in his leisurely, colorful way, he was doing what he could to stall. He had come out forcefully against invoking cloture if there were a filibuster against the bill. (In their autobiographies, both Connally and Wheeler explicitly stated that they believed Ashurst privately was opposed to the plan.)

Tydings, too, saw that Ashurst was doing nothing to expedite the hearings and believed he deliberately was letting the bill sink slowly into the quagmire of senatorial procedure—a subtle delaying tactic as deadly as controlled doses of arsenic administered over a period of time. When Corcoran and Keenan approached him, Ashurst parried: "Gentlemen, gentlemen, you know how hard it is to get senators to agree to anything. . . . No haste, no hurry, no waste, no worry—that is the motto of this committee." The hearings went on for more than two months, until May 18.

Roosevelt's position also was damaged by the fact that the committee as a whole was against the bill, with Republicans Borah of Idaho, Warren R. Austin of Vermont, and Frederick Steiwer of Oregon on record against it and Democrat Joe O'Mahoney known to be opposed privately. Carl A. Hatch of New Mexico and Patrick A. McCarran of Nevada remained uncommitted. Norris's support was tepid at best. Only Matthew M. Neely of West Virginia, George McGill of Kansas, and William H. Dieterich of Illinois—none of them considered quick witted—were willing to do battle for Roosevelt. And Dieterich's backing was not wholehearted. Initially opposed, he felt the screws put to him by Chicago's Kelly–Nash machine. As he explained to one of the opposition, he could not "kick the President in the pants and get renominated."

Under Ashurst's cheerful management, Connally, Van Nuys, and Burke demolished Attorney General Cummings, Assistant Attorney General Robert H. Jackson, and several outside legal experts and labor leaders with sarcasm—and with the help of a battery of lawyers the American Bar Association and major law firms had provided. They pointed out endless inconsistencies, exposing Roosevelt's true purpose: It was not new blood in terms of age he wanted, but in terms of point of view. They proved inefficiency another phony issue.

When the Connally–Van Nuys–Burke onslaughts had consumed well over a week on less than half of the scheduled administration witnesses, Corcoran made a tactical error. He decided to close the administration's case rather than let the ruinous filibuster continue. It was a grave mistake because immediately the opposition brought its many distinguished witnesses to the stand: former administration official Raymond Moley; columnists Dorothy Thompson and Oswald Garrison Villard; prominent scholars from Columbia, Princeton, and New York University's schools of law. They dominated the headlines for more than a month with brilliant speeches and devastating testimony against the bill. It was hardball politics and hardsell instruction. The nation got a high-caliber course in constitutional government.

But it was the leadoff witness who found a way to stop the presses. Wheeler had been scheduled as the first opposition witness on Monday, March 22. He, Tydings, and the steering committee knew that if they could persuade Chief Justice Charles Evans Hughes to testify on the question of judicial inefficiency (Cummings had argued that the Supreme Court did not have the capacity to do its work effectively or efficiently) it would have tremendous impact. Wheeler and two of the Judiciary Committee's members called on Hughes, but failed to persuade him to appear.

Then on March 20, Mrs. Brandeis paid a call on Wheeler's daughter, who had just given birth. As she left Mrs. Brandeis said, "Tell your father I think he's right about the Court bill." Wheeler took that as an opening for action. He telephoned Brandeis, who immediately invited him over. Although Brandeis would not agree to appear, nor would he suggest to the chief justice that he appear, he told Wheeler to telephone Hughes and let him know where he was calling from. Wheeler presented his arguments to Hughes and pleaded, "You can't just lie down and let them do this to you." Hughes asked him to come over at once. On hearing that Brandeis had said Hughes would give Wheeler a letter—"Did Brandeis tell you that?" he asked—he agreed he would. That Sunday, Wheeler got a call from Hughes. As he walked into the Hughes home to pick up the letter, the chief justice said soberly, "The baby is born."

On Monday, Wheeler took the stand. Tydings and other insiders seated in the crowded Senate caucus room tried not to look too smug. Wheeler heard Ashurst whisper to the fellow next to him, "I don't know what he's going to spring but it'll blow us out of the water." It did. Wheeler drew the letter slowly from his inside coat pocket, saying, "I have a letter by the Chief Justice of the Supreme Court, Mr. Charles Evans Hughes, dated March 21, 1937, written by him and approved by Mr. Justice Brandeis and Mr. Justice Van Devanter." He recalled in his autobiography, "You could have heard a comma drop in the caucus room while I read the letter aloud. It struck down, one by one, every point raised by Roosevelt and Cummings."

Alsop called it a "masterpiece of exposition" that refuted every procedural argument advanced; Wheeler was elated at the letter's "sensational" result. "The newsreels photographed it, newspaper reporters clamored for copies, and it was all I could do to keep it from being snatched from my hands when the session was recessed," he wrote. Tydings was jubilant. Their strategy was proving more successful than they could have dreamed.

Roosevelt's men were reeling, furious at Hughes for playing unfair politics; but the president seemed confident that he would ultimately win. Perhaps he assumed the truth of the old saying that party members never stray far from a popular president who is head of their party. He was seen as complacent to the point of arrogance.

When Vice President Garner and two of Roosevelt's staunchest supporters in the Senate—Bryon "Pat" Harrison of Mississippi and James F. Byrnes of South Carolina—had talked to him about fiscal and labor policies, he treated their advice too cavalierly. Roosevelt wanted $1.5 billion for Works Progress Administration (WPA) relief and had taken little action over a series of sit-down strikes—views the three men found irresponsible. More spending and continued labor conflict would further damage the economy. Then Roosevelt reneged on a promise to set a $1 billion cap on his relief appropriations request and failed to act on the strikes. By late March, Garner, Harrison, and Byrnes were so outraged at Roosevelt's behavior that any inclination they might have had to help him on the Court bill was diminished drastically. The president lost a galvanizing force.

Then the Court itself—in what Alsop called "A Switch in Time Saves Nine"—altered the situation dramatically. On March 29 it upheld a Washington State minimum wage law. Two weeks later, on April 12, it upheld the Wagner Act. On May 24 it upheld the Social Security Act. The Court's reversals stunned the White House, surprised the nation, and brought Tydings, Wheeler, and their group to ecstasy. Surely, they thought, Roosevelt now would withdraw the plan, would agree to a compromise—for, as James Byrnes phrased it, "Why run for a train after you've caught it?" Moderates would be more recruitable, given the shift. Robinson met with Keenan and suggested compromise. "I can get [the president] a couple of extra justices tomorrow," Robinson said. "What he ought to do is say he's won, which he has, agree to compromise to make the thing sure, and wind the whole business up."

He had not taken into account Roosevelt's Dutch stubbornness. The president had a tantrum over the Court's liberal shift. He had been so sure the Wagner Act would be struck down—sealing the case for his bill—that he was unprepared. He believed the reversal was pure "playing politics" on the Court's part and was in no mood to make any deals.[7] A five-to-four majority was not dependable. He wanted his six new justices. If he settled for two, one would have to be Joe Robinson—who, although he was Roosevelt's loyal servant on Capitol Hill, might revert to his conservative Arkansas roots. The president would not yield and, in fact, was more resolved than ever to win.

On May 18, Justice Willis J. Van Devanter announced he would retire, and the Judiciary Committee voted ten to eight to report the Court bill unfavorably. Robinson's task now seemed impossible as it appeared Roosevelt was assured of a better than five-to-four majority. Tydings's opposition grew more determined, for some of Robinson's sure votes certainly would be vulnerable to overtures. There was great pressure on Roosevelt to compromise. Corcoran, Cohen, and Assistant Attorney General Jackson advised him against it, Jackson reasoning, "If you're going to pack a court at all you've got to really pack it." The president was undecided. He wanted to finesse the Robinson appointment until he was assured of more than one vacancy. After a long delay he summoned him to the White House on June 3 to talk.

Robinson, deeply wounded by Roosevelt's failure to appoint him to the Court immediately when Van Devanter retired, warned the president that his moderate votes had melted away; the cause would be lost without compromise. Roosevelt saw that Robinson was right and agreed to offer a somewhat softened measure in which retirement ages for judges would be raised from 70 to 75 and the president could appoint one new justice a year for those over 75 who failed to retire. He promised Robinson that, if he pressed on for the amended proposal, he would receive the promised appointment later. It was a bitter blow for Robinson to learn he would have to wait, but he accepted the setback and prepared to lead debate on the revised legislation.

During the late spring it was as if all of Washington was glued in place. Burke was heard to say, "While this bill is up I wouldn't leave sight of the Capitol Building for a round-trip to Heaven." Tydings refused the American Battle Monuments Commission's treasured invitation to tour the battlefields in France. The only Washington figure absent from the fray was Vice President Garner who, disgusted with virtually everything, packed his bags and departed for Uvalde, Texas, for the summer. Before he left he gave the opposition another shot in the arm when, speaking in a loud voice in the Democratic cloakroom, he called Tydings "a real patriot."[8]

Tydings's group determined to throw Roosevelt's slogan of "no compromise" right back in his face. At a secret meeting (where their first act had been to slam shut the transom so their discussion would not echo into the corridor), they decided to fight any compromise. Wheeler spoke for all when he said, "We are just taking the President at his word. He has said there ought to be no compromise." Tydings insisted everyone stay through the summer; squads of senators were primed to keep debate going, to talk the new plan to death.

Recruitment wars heated up all over again. What Washington *Evening Star* columnist Paul Mallon called the "cat-and-mouse game" became serious. Many whom the opposition had counted on were ready to jump ship. Mallon wrote, "You cannot poll the present convictions of senators and reach any worthwhile conclusions. Too many senators will not vote their convictions this time."

Wheeler and Tydings came to identical conclusions. Despite the blows the president had suffered—farm and labor indifference, Chief Justice Hughes's letter, the Court reversal, Van Devanter's resignation, the Judiciary Committee's negative vote and devastating report, and earlier the defection of many moderate Democrats—it looked now as if he would regain enough votes to win in a showdown. They had strong evidence for concern. Leslie Biffle, a Senate officer supposedly working for Robinson, kept Wheeler informed nightly by telephone as to who was weakening. Wheeler wrote in his autobiography, "I never knew for certain why he chose to tip us off. It could even have been done with the approval of Senator Joe Robinson."[9]

The steering committee carefully reviewed tabulations. Its membership redoubled efforts, buttonholing, threatening, pleading with those suspected of wavering. National sentiment was on their side: George Gallup's American Institute of Public Opinion showed 54 percent of the people surveyed opposed the Court plan; and *Fortune* magazine, too, found a preponderance against it. It was a coup for Tydings when his fellow Marylander, Senator George Radcliffe— one of the undecideds from the start—announced his opposition on July 1.[10]

During the arduous months of recruitment activity, some constituents and a decided minority of political analysts wrote that Tydings, fearful of losing his Senate seat in 1938, had avoided political damage by not taking a highly visible role in the battle. Tydings (whom Wheeler in speeches named as first leader of the fight) strategically had stayed mostly in the background, even after going on record against the bill. When the fight was over, he wrote to journalist Holmes Alexander, answering the criticism. "In order to hold my seat in the Senate, it is not necessary for me to go back on any of my convictions," he wrote, "but considering that Roosevelt is going to be President for three more years, my course should be to attack erroneous policies which I have consistently done, and in so doing, I may lose my seat, but I will certainly not lose my soul." His argument—not fully convincing—continued:

> To put it another way, about twenty years ago, I was in France as a soldier. When the Germans attacked heavily as they sometimes did, we took the best care of ourselves we could until the bombardment was over. . . . At no time did I consider going single handedly across "No Man's Land" because I believed my country was right. That would have been a beautiful gesture but what would it have accomplished? . . . [T]he net result of that maneuver would have been one less American soldier and no injury to the enemy.
>
> On the other hand, what I did was to use all the strategy at my command [so as to] shoot when it was the most effective. . . . Isn't that so now? . . . To get up and make a personal attack upon President Roosevelt would receive tremendous acclaim for a day, and then the very people who were pleased at my doing so would be the first to say, "That was a fine thing Tydings did, but it would have been better if he had held his fire to a more appropriate time."
>
> . . . [M]y guns speak out whenever I feel I can weaken the enemy and quite often they speak out under cover of darkness when the enemy cannot tell who is delivering the fire. In other words they are effective as the Supreme Court battle has just shown, for confidentially, again, I organized the Senators into the first group in opposition to the President's proposal and have been on the steering committee ever since. The President knows this but he has not been able to isolate me and destroy me.

Debate was scheduled to begin on July 6—Fourth of July fireworks followed by the greatest fireworks display of all: the Senate in full and magnificent voice. When Joe Robinson—Al Smith's running mate from the presidential race nine years earlier—stood to open the debate, the galleries were full with tourists, diplomats, jamboree-bound Boy Scouts, journalists, ex-senators, and senators' wives scrambling for seats. Representatives lined the Senate chamber's walls three-deep. Eleanor Tydings, the newspapers noted, came in from Oakington to "listen in." She and the wives of all steering committee leaders dashed out for lunch and then returned "to sit until the bitter end" each evening as the torrid debate—arguments, ridicule, and threats, the roar of insults hurled back and forth—filled the air with the sound and fury of the Senate at its turbulent best.

Robinson spoke with such passion that his face flushed red, and sweat rolled off his brow and down his cheeks. His appearance alarmed those around him; for all knew how hard he had worked, the disappointments he had been forced to swallow, and the precarious state of his health, given a touchy heart condition. Royal Copeland, who was a physician, grew so concerned he slid over to the seat beside him and whispered, "Joe, the cause you're fighting for isn't worth your life. For God's sake, slow down." But he would not or could not stop; and—hammering the air with a clenched right fist—he defended the president, reviled the Court, and threatened those who dared to consider filibuster. "Let them try," he bellowed. "It will not be tolerated!" For three days, all by himself, Robinson took on the opposition, fielding challenges thrown at him by Tydings and Burke and Wheeler and O'Mahoney and Clark.

By July 9, when Wheeler launched the opening salvo for his side, Joe Robinson was drained. His hands trembled. His complexion was purplish blue. He looked ill and exhausted and was worried because he could feel things were not going well. The opposition seemed to have the emotional and convictional edge—and a squad of devoted backers. Tydings sparred with those who tried to heckle Wheeler, mocking Roosevelt's comparison of the government to a three-horse team where one of the three refused to pull: What the president wanted, Tydings declared, was to hook up his team so that "the driver of the executive horse is also the driver of the other two." The American people must "drive all three." Roosevelt must not succeed, or future presidents might feel justified in packing the Court. Doris Fleeson wrote that "lanky, anti-Court Millard 'Glad' Tydings" threw his weight around so forcefully he surely would provide James Farley with a good target in the future.

Still, the power of the presidency and Robinson's ability to keep his troops in line were so strong that Wheeler and Tydings knew they did not have the votes. They knew many of Roosevelt's allies were uneasy with the prospect of his winning, but—when it came down to cold hard numbers—Robinson had 44 sure votes with seven grudging-to-unreliable ones. Tydings and Wheeler had 42. Wheeler reminded Tydings of the terms agreed to in February. Tydings was to meet with Corcoran and offer the president a two-justice compromise—with the vital caveat that the bill, which they would accept, must not apply to the present Court. An unhappy Tydings accepted the task.

"Millard didn't like it," his wife remembered, "but Wheeler said 'You said you would' "—and Tydings kept his word. He telephoned Corcoran, and on July 12 he informed Roosevelt's emissary that "we would accept the President's bill so long as it didn't apply to the sitting Supreme Court." He told him they would arrange for the resignation "of two of the elderly Justices so that Roosevelt would have two appointees on the Court." But he made sure that Corcoran knew it was the best they could get. In fact, Tydings added, he had been chosen spokesman because he was the only one who had a chance of persuading Carter Glass and Ed Burke to consent to the deal.

Corcoran replied that he would talk it over with "the Boss." Later that same afternoon he called Tydings. "The Boss won't accept it unless you give him the Chief Justice, too," he said rather flippantly, and gave Tydings the name of the person who could convince Hughes to retire. "Over my dead body," Tydings replied. "Nothing doing. This is show-down, Tommy, not poker!" The offer he had made that morning still stood. He told Corcoran he could be reached at Oakington over the weekend if Roosevelt changed his mind. He and Eleanor waited through what seemed an eternity. No call came from the White House. It appeared as though Tydings and Wheeler had lost.

On the morning of July 14, Joe Robinson was found dead of a heart attack in his broiling little Capitol Hill apartment. Sprawled on the floor in pajamas, he was found beside his bed with a copy of the preceding day's *Congressional Record* next to his right hand. The fight was over. Without Robinson there was no one who could hold the Democrats in line. Corcoran called Tydings to reopen negotiations. "Nothing doing," Tydings replied. On the funeral train carrying Robinson back to Arkansas for burial, Roosevelt's advisers still pushed to swing the Tydings compromise. No one would budge.

When the Senate reconvened, the vote to send the Court bill back to committee on July 21 passed by a lopsided 70 to 20. Hiram Johnson, venerable Republican senator from California, stood up and loudly asked, "The Supreme Court is out of the way?" Senator Marvel M. Logan of Kentucky replied, "The Supreme Court is out of the way." "Then glory be to God!" Johnson roared as the crowded Senate galleries burst into applause. Roosevelt had suffered the worst defeat of his presidency.

The opposition's unequivocal victory was prelude to a vigorous fight in the Senate for independence from executive domination. In the heat of battle, other New Deal legislation had languished through the 168 days. When the dust settled, the bulk of Roosevelt's 1937 agenda (wages and hours legislation, a farm bill, a little TVA bill, housing and slum clearance, and a plan to reorganize the executive branch) remained. It hung suspended in the highly charged atmosphere, dangling before conservatives and others who were mad at Roosevelt, like a convocation of red flags mocking a herd of angry bulls. The president would get almost nothing from Congress.

Resentment went well beyond the ill-advised Supreme Court fiasco. More Democrats now feared bankruptcy because of the failure to balance the budget, reduce the national debt, pare down relief expenditures. Progressives like Garner, Byrnes, and Harrison had joined Tydings and the conservatives in opposing Roosevelt's $1.5 billion relief request. Many resented his intrusion in selecting a new majority leader to replace Robinson. The contest pitted Pat Harrison against Alben Barkley; a Roosevelt letter to Barkley—the famous "Dear Alben" letter (clarifying Roosevelt's Court objectives and complaining that "advantage is being taken of what, in all decency, should be a period of mourning")—was correctly interpreted as an indication of his preference and was regarded as presidential meddling in a matter strictly up to the Senate.

In that hostile environment a heavily amended wages and hours bill barely cleared (before bogging down in the House until 1938); the farm tenancy bill eked its way through the legislative maze.

Robert Wagner's slum clearance and housing bill passed after it was watered down by two amendments: Byrd's slashed the cost per unit, and Tydings's limited the amount spent in a single state to 20 percent of the contemplated $700 million fund to keep it all from going to urban centers such as New York.

Even Roosevelt's nomination of Senator Hugo Black to the Supreme Court faced opposition. In an almost unheard-of reaction to a colleague's nomination, the Senate refused to waive hearings on his appointment. Tydings and others were distressed at his rumored membership in the Ku Klux Klan. Tydings suggested hearings be delayed until the charges could be investigated. A Southern liberal, Black was unpopular because of his caustic style of debate and aloof demeanor. Columnist Marquis Child believed he was inexperienced. The nomination cleared the Judiciary Committee and, after an acrimonious six-hour debate, passed 63 to 16.

Then, to Roosevelt's annoyance, while his programs were receiving rude treatment on the Hill, a Tydings measure he deplored cleared the hurdles. The Miller–Tydings National Fair Trade Enabling Act (cosponsored in the House by John E. Miller of Arkansas) would allow for regulating retail prices of standard manufactured articles by creating an exception to the Sherman Anti-trust Law. Tydings believed it unfair that big discounters and chain stores could reduce prices of popular trademarked products so drastically that they put small retail outlets out of business. "Small business is being crushed to the wall in a deliberate campaign," he argued. The world of Ma-and-Pa corner stores would be destroyed if huge chains continued to use "loss leaders" and unscrupulous juggling of prices to undercut competition and propel them into bankruptcy, causing unemployment for ordinary people.

A number of states (42 by August 1937) had enacted fair trade laws under which manufacturers could, by contract, establish a minimum price below which contract items could not lawfully be sold. The Supreme Court had upheld such legislation, with Justice Louis Brandeis writing in his opinion that loss leaders constituted fraudulent enticement of consumers to get them into the store where they might be induced to buy other items at higher prices. Under Tydings's Fair Trade Enabling Act, Congress would remove interference from the full and free operation of those state laws. His bill would legalize resale price agreements between manufacturers of trademarked merchandise and their dealers in states with fair trade laws.

The measure was attacked as a price-fixing device that would boost the cost of many articles. Roosevelt tried to sidetrack the bill by burying it in committee; the fight was into its second year. To ensure passage, Tydings finally attached it as a rider to the District of Columbia emergency tax measure. The Miller–Tydings Act landed on Roosevelt's desk for signature on August 6. The president detested the bill and Tydings, but he could not veto it without throwing the District of Columbia into financial disarray. When he finally signed it on August 17, pharmacy, book shop, liquor store, and small retail merchants and employees all over the country were jubilant because, for them, the Miller–Tydings Act meant survival of their neighborhood stores and a way of life.[11]

Tydings got his legislation. All Roosevelt managed to get was Black's confirmation and some watered-down gruel before Congress adjourned. Arthur Krock of the New York *Times* wrote that Congress was reestablishing its power. Oswald Garrison Villard had anticipated that Roosevelt might lose out to conservatives if he insisted on pushing the Court plan. "It would be sardonica, indeed," wrote Villard, "if the measure intended to speed up reform . . . should be the very weapon by means of which the conservatives could slow up all possible advances during the next three years."

It was those next three years that everyone had their minds fixed on, for the 1940 presidential election was at stake. A Senate realignment appeared in the making. If Democratic unity were destroyed, potential New Dealer successors to Roosevelt would face tough sledding. Some observers viewed the anti–expanded Supreme Court movement as an attempt by reactionaries to dominate the party at the end of Roosevelt's term. Columnists all over the nation—Villard, Mark Sullivan, Mark Foote of Detroit, the Baltimore *Sun*'s Henry M. Hyde, and Frank R. Kent—wrote that the party, so seemingly united in 1932 and 1936, now appeared split stem to stern. Roosevelt had lost control of his own party. More than one-third of the Senate's Democrats were in open revolt, including a few up for election in 1938 who had displayed extraordinary courage in expressing sentiments contradicting those of their party leader who remained popular with the public. Among those named, Tydings was prominent.

In August 1937, the bottom dropped out of the economy. The stock market plunged; businesses failed; industrial production dropped. By year's end, 2 million people had joined the unemployed. Because Roosevelt was given credit for the gains made since 1935, he also was blamed for the setback, which was labeled the "Roosevelt Depression." It seemed he had lost his touch. After a late-summer trip through the West to rally the people, a fresh but beleaguered president called Congress back into session in November.

He got precious little. His "seven little TVAs" went nowhere; his government reorganization bill never made it to the floor. (Too controversial, it was held over until 1938.) Democratic conservatives, quite aware of Roosevelt's diminished prestige, grew bold enough to contemplate a united and perhaps bipartisan bloc to oppose the New Deal. North Carolina's Bailey conceived the idea of drawing up a general policy statement—one conservative enough to satisfy progressive and conservative blocs in Congress, yet also basically acceptable to Roosevelt. If they could persuade the administration that their statement had widespread support, perhaps the president could be committed to a conservative platform. Historian James Patterson in his *Congressional Conservatism and the New Deal* has pointed out that Bailey's plan was more pie-in-the-sky than possible. "In retrospect," he wrote, "such an ambitious venture seems a little ludicrous, for the chasm between men like Bailey and the administration was already deep."

Bailey, however, quietly held a number of meetings, and Gerry hosted several dinners that Tydings joined. (The group initially included Bailey, Glass, Byrd, Burke, Copeland, and King, and later added Gerry, George, Smith, Van Nuys, and then Tydings.) Republicans Arthur Vandenberg and Warren Austin also attended the secret dinners, as Democrats wanted to broaden the coalition—a tricky business, given the difficulty inherent in allying with Republicans.

Although Tydings left no record of participating in writing the so-called manifesto, as a leading conservative Democrat he was credited with helping formulate plans to take control of the party so that at the 1940 convention no New Deal candidate—especially Roosevelt, who was suspected of coveting a third-term bid—could run away with the nomination. The manifesto was considered a part of the strategy to restore conservative control.

The group, needing as many signatures as they could get, circulated the statement in the cloakrooms in December. Although a number of colleagues were sympathetic with its goals—tax reduction, balanced budget, states' rights—they were hesitant to sign anything that might commit them publicly.[12] But before Bailey and Vandenberg could gather enough signatures, they were blown out of the water by a front-page article spilling the story. The bipartisan aspect made them seem to be plotting the New Deal's demise. At first they all ducked for cover. But as New Dealers crowed at their discomfort, Bailey took responsibility. The ill-fated effort showed, if nothing else, the depth of anti–New Deal feeling among a sizable number of Democratic senators.

Tydings long had surmised that the president was planning to run for a third term—as he had written Joe Davies during the Court fight—and was personally determined to do what he could to prevent it. Roosevelt, in turn, loathed Tydings. He had gotten away with more than Roosevelt could tolerate; his undisguised pleasure at needling the president (he had a gift for it, some said) gave Roosevelt indigestion. Tydings reveled in sweet little ironies, such as being asked to replace Roosevelt as commencement speaker at the University of Maryland in June 1937 when the president had to cancel at the last minute. Rather than hearing Roosevelt wax eloquent on the virtues of the New Deal, graduates, parents, faculty, and perhaps 5,000 spectators listened instead to Tydings warn against government experimentation and fundamental change without careful forethought: "May I charge you not to embrace new forms of government lightly and to abandon nothing so dearly won until you are certain the alternative is superior to that which you are relinquishing." Roosevelt's usually controlled propensity for vengeance was unleashed, and Tydings became number one on the 1938 hit list as Roosevelt began to consider retaliation.

Of Political Purges and Exculpations

Arthur Krock wrote of Roosevelt that he knew how to nurture a grudge and how to do something about it. Raymond Clapper also unhappily confessed that "back of that smile [Roosevelt] has a vindictive streak." Others came to see that he was more than "Dutch stubborn"; when his pride was injured, General Hugh Johnson said, he had a distinct wish to make adversaries "eat dirt." His tendency to coerce by threat of punishment—often through loss of patronage—evolved, after December 1937, into a policy of active retaliation.

On the last day of the Seventy-fifth Congress, Senator Joseph E. Guffey, rabid New Dealer from Pennsylvania, asked Roosevelt to use his influence to defeat those Democrats who had opposed him. Although Wheeler and others immediately poured what the Associated Press called a "vial of contempt and denunciation" on Guffey, the episode revealed the direction Roosevelt and his advisers were headed. Harold Ickes, Harry Hopkins, presidential secretary (and son) James Roosevelt, Joe Keenan, Ben Cohen, and especially Tommy ("the Cork") Corcoran became known as the "Elimination Committee" as the movement to purge some conservative Democrats evolved from what writer Alva Johnston called "high school girl revenge" to an openly declared political war.

Already committed to party realignment, New Dealers decided they could do it by purging the party of reactionaries—those Tory Democrats who refused to support the liberal and socially responsible direction that New Deal reforms symbolized. There should be one liberal party and one conservative party. If a person voted like a Republican, talked like a Republican, and thought like a Republican, then he damn well was a Republican and should be one in name as well as philosophy and stop wrecking New Deal programs. Realignment was the only way to ensure continuation of reforms.

But the idea of realignment was not intended merely to cleanse the party of reactionaries. Politically it was mandatory. If conservatives maintained their power after the 1938 elections, they would be in position to challenge the liberals in 1940. The real issue underlying the Sturm und Drang of purge talk was who would control the party in 1940—who would select its nominee for president. Ruby Black, Washington correspondent for the Madison (Wisconsin) *State Journal*, noted that conservatives were mounting a movement "to 'recapture' the democratic party," and some had overt presidential aspirations. Although Harry Byrd was "the senator most swollen by the stings of the presidential bee," she wrote, "others also hear its buzzing." Among them was Tydings, who, with his "beautiful young wife," routinely entertained "influential and conservative Democrats" at their Havre de Grace estate.

Prediction of a purge was nearly unanimous among political observers. Rodney Dutcher's column headlined "KNIFE IS OUT FOR DEMOCRATIC FOES OF PRESIDENT" described things as the "biggest party split since the Bull Moose bolt of 1912," and named the number-one target: the "wealthy and socially prominent" Tydings. Although conservative columnist Mark Sullivan hoped there would be no retribution (as it would further injure an already damaged party), and Frank Kent believed there would be no purge (because the Court plan had been a bad idea and the people knew it), most other commentators assessing the situation found it highly combustible. "Smoldering" was the word Jim Farley used to describe Roosevelt's anger.

There were ten conservative Democrats up for reelection in 1938: Tydings, George of Georgia, Cotton Ed Smith of South Carolina, Augustine Lonergan of Connecticut, Pat McCarran of Nevada, Adams of Colorado, George L. Berry of Tennessee, Clark of Missouri, Van Nuys of Indiana, and Gillette of Iowa. Roosevelt ultimately showed his resentment against Gillette, Van Nuys, McCarran, and Adams, and permitted his anger to boil over at George and Smith; but Tydings became primary beneficiary of his ardent hatred.[13]

By late January the president had dropped so many hints warning rival Democrats that Jim Farley, chairman of the Democratic National Committee—although unhappy—was not shocked when Roosevelt deleted crucial lines from a statement he had asked Farley to prepare and issue. Farley intended to reassure the flock that neither the DNC nor the administration would get involved in congressional primaries. But James Roosevelt telephoned Farley, "Father has struck the last two sentences out." Farley considered the offending phrases critical: "These nominations are entirely the affair of the States or the Congressional districts, and however these early battles result, the National Committee will be behind the candidate that the people themselves choose. This goes for every state and every Congressional district."

Perhaps Roosevelt believed the purges would be akin to a phoenix rising from the ashes of legislative defeat. But for Farley, who feared that the renewed Depression was strengthening the Republicans and believed his party needed unity, the purge was "an albatross, not of my own shooting, . . . hung from my neck." From then on, he wrote in his autobiography, his worst fears were realized as "conferences were latticed with a pattern of purge talk." On Capitol Hill he was inundated with complaints that "the vast power of the administration, in the manipulation of patronage and funds, was being mobilized to purge the party of all but 100% New Dealers." Vice President Garner was especially riled. He told Farley the idea was "unnecessary as hell," and was creating a solid block of senators who would vote Roosevelt down on anything he proposed.

Byrnes—never an avid fan of party ultraconservatives—nonetheless let Roosevelt know he would do everything in his power to save those "marked to fall under the ax." Tydings and Gillette were two he was able to assist with indirect financial aid. Connally and Wheeler also rallied to Tydings and spoke for him, aided him financially, and tried to convince the administration not to commit what they believed would be an act of transcendent stupidity.

But the president's wounds had festered. Although at times he would deny any intention of opposing fellow Democrats, he let his staff scheme away; from time to time he joined them. And Roosevelt had not waited until 1938 to take aim at Tydings. As early as August 1936, during his reelection campaign, he had begun a search for a candidate to unseat Tydings. A "mystery trip" into the Maryland countryside where he attended a "purely social" gathering at the Oxon Hill home of his good friend Undersecretary of State Sumner Welles brought him into contact with every Democratic bigwig in Maryland—except Tydings who was, not coincidentally, on vacation.

In January 1937, the Washington *Post*, reporting rumors "from an unusually authoritative source," remarked that "a great political chess game" was under way in the state. Referring to the past year's "hurriedly called conference of Maryland Democratic leaders . . . at the home of Sumner Welles," the dispatch reported that Roosevelt had taken steps that could result in "surprising moves to place in power . . . persons who will be more than lukewarm toward the Democratic regime." The next day the *Post* predicted that Tydings would be given an ambassadorship to remove him from the political scene, and further suggested that Welles might be persuaded to run: "It is said that Washington wants to see Maryland represented by two such friends of the President" as George Radcliffe and Welles, "and it is reported that President Roosevelt may even go so far as to offer Senator Tydings the ambassadorship to the Court of St. James." Welles made it clear, however, that he was not interested.

By November Roosevelt had fixed on Representative David J. Lewis as someone who could challenge Tydings. Lewis, from Western Maryland, was a dedicated New Dealer, a self-made man who had first gone to Congress in 1911. If he could be persuaded to run, Roosevelt's advisers agreed, he was one of the few who had a chance to depose Tydings. The local Democrats aligned with Roosevelt forces saw a chance to test Lewis's appeal at a November 18 dinner of the Young Democratic Clubs of Maryland in Baltimore. Everyone in the state hierarchy would be there: Tydings, Radcliffe, Democratic National Committeeman Howard Bruce, Mayor of Baltimore Howard Jackson, Maryland Attorney General Herbert O'Conor, and Sumner Welles. Also attending was big Jim Farley.

Tydings was ready. When shouts of "We Want Lewis!" arose from the audience, he mockingly said it sounded like "the love call of the hoot owls." He stole the show, according to the *Sun*, when he announced his intention to run and challenged those who wished him ill: Beat me on my not-a-rubber-stamp record. "Democrats would not be Democrats if there were not men who would assert their convictions," he averred. "I will be ready in the coming campaign to meet all comers on [my] record."

Tydings came out of the dinner under an anti–New Deal banner he unfurled himself, wrote the *Evening Sun*. H. L. Mencken wasted no time in endorsing him. Tydings, he noted, had supported the New Deal when it provided plausible programs, but when it "had only hooey to offer he voted against it, and not only voted against it, but also talked against it in a voice of brass. If that is a crime, then Tydings should be turned out of the Senate and an idiot put in. The job of a Senator is not simply to leap and prance as the White House whistles."

Lewis, under pressure to announce, hesitated. Then on December 9 he declared that he was running for reelection to the House.

His doctor had ordered him not to try for the Senate, he explained, for he was 69 and in less than perfect health. Roosevelt cast about for other candidates.

There was no lack of attractive figures who harbored no love for Tydings, given the struggles since Albert Ritchie's disastrous 1934 gubernatorial loss had thrown the Maryland party into disarray. Although Tydings had weathered the earlier storm generated by the Howard Jackson–Albert Ritchie rivalry, a number of peripheral players had bided their time, waiting to move up. Herbert O'Conor, William Curran, Lansdale Sasscer, and a newcomer, Baltimore City Councilman Thomas J. D'Alessandro, all nurtured ambition and believed their futures would be brighter if Tydings were eliminated from the scene. O'Conor coveted either the governor's mansion or a Senate seat and was weighing the odds as to which he might win.

And another figure emerged on the political scene: Harry Clifton "Curley" Byrd, president of the University of Maryland, gifted educator, administrator, and fund raiser, was also not lacking ambition, guile, or charm. He had, through persistence and deft application of political pressure, channeled $2 million in PWA and WPA funds to the university. The second million was approved right after Byrd paid a low-profile visit to the White House in early 1938. There were those who saw a connection between the quiet visit (Byrd had slipped out the White House back door) and subsequent grant. They suspected Roosevelt of greasing the skids in an effort to persuade Byrd to run for office. If Byrd were to seek the governorship, O'Conor, a young and popular fellow, could join Byrd's ticket as the senatorial candidate; or conversely, if O'Conor should run for governor, Byrd could try for the Senate on his ticket. Either way, Tydings would face a well-known and well-liked Marylander with an excellent shot at knocking him off.

Most would-be gubernatorial candidates had been struggling to line up supporters since 1936. There were two main contenders—Jackson and O'Conor—plus lesser rivals: Lansdale Sasscer, William Preston Lane, and Dr. Charles Conley (who had run in 1934). The situation created a dilemma for Tydings. If he supported Jackson for governor, O'Conor undoubtedly would train his guns on him, either by running for the Senate or by backing a viable challenger. If he aligned himself with O'Conor, Jackson's machine would turn against him. Because Tydings's support was based largely on a personal organization built up through distribution of patronage, he needed the active support of Jackson's forces. But given the clashes of 1934 (when Tydings had supported first Radcliffe and then, reluctantly, Ritchie for governor, forcing Jackson's withdrawal), a tension remained between them and their political camps, despite a popular perception that they enjoyed an alliance.

By mid-1936 enormous pressure was exerted on Tydings, viewed by many as titular leader of the party in Maryland, to intervene and settle who would run for governor. But, fearful of being bloodied, he preferred the sidelines. His wariness infuriated those who thought him cowardly, and his abstention from local politics frustrated others who could not win without his considerable weight. The situation grew increasingly messy. Jackson and his followers actively sought his endorsement. When Tydings allies Brooke Lee and William Walsh gave Jackson their support, newsreporters wrote incorrectly that Tydings had endorsed him. Tydings continued to walk a careful neutral line. By mid-1937 he was stalked by the press seeking a statement on Jackson. When reporters gathered at his office in reaction to Jackson's throwing his hat into the gubernatorial ring 15 months before the primaries, he let them fire away.

"Are you backing Mayor Jackson's candidacy?" he was asked.

"I have no comment to make, but I am reading the newspapers," he replied, wearing—the press noted—his best poker face.

When the reporters persisted—asking, "Are you responsible for the fact that the Mayor made this announcement so early?" and "What do you think of the views expressed yesterday . . . that a small group of men can dictate the nomination fifteen months in advance of the campaign"—he said, "The answer is the same." And news accounts noted, "There were signs of what might be described as a grin if it had appeared on the face of one less dignified than a United States Senator."

Would-be Baltimore boss William Curran was seen as gaining power at Jackson's expense and backing O'Conor. The spunky upstart Tommy D'Alessandro was challenging the Jackson forces. O'Conor was said to be trying to cut a deal with Sasscer; if he would bow out of the gubernatorial race, O'Conor would support him against Tydings. O'Conor also was seen as backing either David Lewis or General Milton A. Reckord, adjutant of the Maryland National Guard, as potential senatorial running mates. Lewis was considered his first choice despite the earlier refusal.

Meanwhile, some among the Washington New Deal's Elimination Committee were trying to get O'Conor to run for the Senate in their quest for Tydings's scalp. Curley Byrd was their preference to head the ticket for governor; but O'Conor by now was committed to run for governor and refused all entreaties to try for the Senate on a Byrd slate. Their gaze shifted to Congressman T. Alan Goldsborough, a committed New Dealer. He briefly had considered opposing Tydings, but was discouraged by advice from friends.

Drew Pearson, Tydings's antagonist since the Virgin Islands controversy, was obsessed with finding a worthy challenger. He floated the name of Dean Acheson, former undersecretary of the Treasury, as a possibility, but his first choice was Curley Byrd. He reported a "flirtation" between Byrd and "several gentlemen close to Mr. Roosevelt," in his column "The Maryland Merry-go-round." The flirtation, Pearson said, had as its goal not the governorship, but removing Tydings from office.

Friends of Byrd insisted that he might accept the governorship—if handed it on a silver platter with reassurances he could return to the university as president in four years—but that he had no interest in challenging Tydings, who was not only a friend but a fellow alumnus. Byrd's friends denied that his "success in forcing another $1,135,000 from the Federal Treasury via a WPA grant for his huge university construction fund" was significant.

Rumors continued. When Preston Lane withdrew from the race and threw his support behind Jackson, his links with Tydings made it seem a prelude to a Tydings endorsement. O'Conor angrily lashed out, saying, "One man or a few men [have no] right to speak for the entire party and its rank and file." He and Jackson insisted a primary was inevitable and essential.

Tydings carefully threaded his way through the mine field. He was seen as aloof, Machiavellian, and losing ground. "The senior senator might well do more visiting around to feel the pulse of the average man," noted the *Observer* in reporting complaints that he had grown "high hat." Certainly Tydings knew he could not avoid making enemies, but was trying to avoid making too many or too powerful ones. He wanted to keep his alliances sufficiently intact to fend off challengers; and he wanted to wield sufficient influence to protect himself, but not so much that he could be accused of running the state.

By late April 1938 Tydings's undeclared neutrality had driven everyone to distraction—particularly O'Conor. Without an official statement of neutrality, he could not control factions that would side with Tydings should he endorse Jackson. O'Conor decided to force Tydings's hand. He sent a messenger to tell Tydings that, unless he promised to remain "absolutely neutral," his camp would back someone against him. Tydings immediately telephoned Brooke Lee. Minutes later he slammed the receiver onto the cradle and stared out the window in silence. He risked alienating Jackson's machine, but it was obvious that Roosevelt's people would leap at the chance to join O'Conor against him. When he finally spoke he said, "I shall make it clear that I will remain neutral in the contest between Jackson and O'Conor."

On May 3, he stated his position. The forced impartiality cleared the air. O'Conor was delighted. Jackson's camp—although disappointed—was philosophical, saying, "Tydings made the Jackson alliance last year and has already delivered about all that he has to deliver." Columnists said O'Conor had made a good move. And so had Tydings. His neutrality did not prove fatal with Jackson's people. He now was linked to no group, had broken no ties, could nurture the fragile unity (despite an undignified performance).

Even more salutary, Tydings had scored an important victory. He had enlisted George Radcliffe, fellow Maryland senator and Roosevelt's friend, as his campaign manager. Appalled by Roosevelt's intrusion into congressional elections, Radcliffe did not hesitate to announce support for Tydings, but was not convinced so easily to manage his campaign. Nevertheless, Radcliffe's joining the staff was hailed as an ingenious maneuver and a major coup.[14]

It was far from over. The Elimination Committee remained determined to sidetrack Tydings. Columnists speculated that the president would not follow through with the vendetta because Radcliffe was heading Tydings's campaign and because Tydings's father-in-law was not only Roosevelt's ambassador to the Soviet

Union, but a heavy contributor to the New Deal. They reckoned wrong. On June 1, Davey Lewis, the "Little Giant of Western Maryland"—within an hour of a White House meeting—announced he would run. The press deduced the obvious: that Lewis was the president's handpicked candidate.

The contrasts between Lewis and Tydings were enormous. Born in Osceola, Pennsylvania, in 1869, Lewis was from an exceedingly humble background, son of a Welsh coalminer, and had entered the mines himself at the age of nine. He received no formal schooling, but in his early teens learned to read in Sunday School. He learned Latin, studied law at night, and settled in Cumberland, a Western Maryland mining town, where he practiced law before entering Congress to serve in the House of Representatives (from 1911 to 1917; he lost his 1916 bid for the Senate). He returned to Congress in 1931 after serving on the Tariff Commission during Wilson's presidency and practicing law. He was considered "father" of the Parcel Post; and Roosevelt, during the campaign, hailed him as the "father" of Social Security. He was erudite, bookish, intense, and—at five feet, with graying hair and thick wire-rimmed glasses— rather resembled a little gray owl. Still poor as a church mouse, he lived in an austerely furnished Washington boardinghouse. Lewis's campaign slogan, "The man from the mines vs. the man from the mansion," was calculated to emphasize the differences between the two men.[15]

Not long after Lewis's announcement, Roosevelt, in a fireside chat to the nation, called for a showdown between conservatives and liberals. Although he mentioned no names, he explained his belief that a party leader was entitled to support and oppose as he wished. "Do not misunderstand me," he said in self-defense, "I certainly would not indicate a preference in a state primary merely because a candidate, otherwise liberal in outlook, had conscientiously disagreed with me." But, he went on, "We all know that progress may be blocked by outspoken reactionaries." He was not speaking as president, he said, but as head of the Democratic party.

When Jim Farley heard the speech, he knew Roosevelt "had been won over to the purge wholeheartedly." As he readied himself for a trip to Alaska, the unhappy DNC chairman wondered if Alaska was far enough away.

Roosevelt's declared intention to rid the party of those he deemed Tories drew headlines. The campaign was viewed through the prism of the president's move—for, as hard as Lewis tried to run his own campaign, he inevitably was seen as Roosevelt's puppet. Lewis said he wanted a "hard-boiled, two-fisted fight by, with, and for Marylanders." But it was difficult for him to resist invoking the president's name, which hurt him by drawing attention to a question often posed: whether Roosevelt wanted a liberal party in progressive hands or a bevy of kowtowing stooges.

The Baltimore *Sun,* furious at the president's sponsorship of Lewis, ran an indignant editorial calling Lewis "the avenging angel of the Roosevelt administration." The paper thrashed the entire White House: "Mr. Lewis is the puppet of Mr. Roosevelt, of Mr. Farley, of Mr. Hopkins, of Mr. Ickes and of all the other masters of patronage and public purse." Tydings was "not alone and friendless," warned the *Sun;* the maneuver would backfire.

The appeal of a political slugfest proved irresistible. The donneybrook promised to be a lulu, pitting the droll and dapper Tydings against the bantering Roosevelt and little slugger Lewis— the "good gray gnome." It generated tremendous publicity for Tydings, attracting national attention. The New York *Times* predicted Roosevelt's retaliation would strengthen Tydings. The Springfield (Massachusetts) *Union* called Roosevelt's foray into the Maryland race "a crude, audacious attempt to penalize an able senator for the political crime of standing on the Democratic platform and refusing blindly to follow Mr. Roosevelt's weird experimental excursions." Administration denials that it was engaged in reprisals drew hoots of derision.

"Militant Millard," as Tydings was called by *Time* magazine, took heart when Guy Gillette of Iowa survived Harry Hopkins's attempt to purge him from the senatorial ranks. He suffered a few uneasy moments when Howard Jackson conferred with Farley, but Jackson honored his neutrality pledge. Tydings, of course, suffered the ubiquitous indignities served to candidates. A television skit aimed at humbling him proffered a wicked script:

Scene: Montgomery county [Maryland]. General Montgomery, for whom the county was named, sees an aloof, nose-in-air figure passing before him.

Montgomery: Who are you, sir?

The figure does not answer. The curtain goes down and rises, to denote the passage of three years—the passage of time to an election year. The same figure passes. General Montgomery hears him identify himself as Senator Tydings, and watches in amazement as he kisses babies, shakes hands and otherwise makes himself the friend of the people.

Initial Lewis–Tydings encounters were almost cordial. In early July they met and debated, often chatting amicably together before the debates got under way. But as outside elements joined Lewis, the campaign heated up when both labor and radical farm groups positioned themselves firmly with him. Tydings had not been particularly popular with farmers in 1938, but intrusion of the CIO into the election unexpectedly threw the agriculture vote into his lap. He appealed to farmers on the basis of independence. "Do you select a representative because you like the way he combs his hair? Or smiles? Or slaps you on the back?" he would ask rural constituents. "Or do you select a representative because he talks common sense? I have been known as a fellow who does not vote for everything that is proposed. If you send me back to Washington I am not going to change a bit."

Both William Green, president of the AFL, and John L. Lewis, president of the CIO, endorsed Lewis; but John L. Lewis and the CIO actually cost Davey Lewis support in some areas, especially the Eastern Shore, when John L. cast Tydings as a "renegade-to-be-beaten-at-any-cost." Natives of Maryland's Sho'—as inhabitants called it—virtually had thrown CIO organizers out of their region, and most of them declared they would vote for the devil before voting for someone endorsed by the CIO, Roosevelt or no Roosevelt.

Tydings made hay of John L.'s intrusion. At Crisfield, Maryland, he announced, "I'm no enemy of organized labor. I think labor ought to have the right to collective bargaining and to strike if working conditions do not suit it, and for that reason I like the American Federation of Labor, a level-headed and sane organization." Then he went for the kill. "I find this morning that Mr. John L. Lewis, head of the C.I.O., wants David J. Lewis in the United

States Senate. John L. Lewis doesn't live in Maryland and he wants David Lewis," he marveled before proclaiming, "If you want a C.I.O. Senator, don't vote for me. . . . Democrats, stand to arms! Do you want to turn this State over to a Senator run by John L. Lewis?" Quite naturally the crowd shouted back, "No!"

And the hapless Davey Lewis attracted another supporter whose influences Tydings questioned. Mauritz Hallgren, a former associate editor of the Baltimore *Sun* and the *Nation,* and chairman of the Maryland Civil Liberties Committee, had entered the race against Tydings but withdrew when Lewis filed. Stumping on Lewis's behalf, Hallgren labeled Tydings a "Tory Democrat," knowing the insulting phrase would irritate voters who saw themselves as inheritors of the true faith handed down by Jefferson. He warned he would "smash the Tydings–Radcliffe machine," thus threatening those appointed to office by either Tydings or Radcliffe. Many federal jobholders, political observers, and Tydings supporters interpreted Hallgren's words as extending the purge from Tydings alone to his followers.

Hallgren's actions on Lewis's behalf, which Tydings labeled "political terrorism," whetted his curiosity. He read books and articles Hallgren had written. What he read inspired one of the least noble aspects of the campaign: Tydings accused Hallgren of advocating communism. *Seeds of Revolt,* written in 1933, addressed national and international economic conditions, and seemed to credit communism with providing the answer to the world's financial crisis. In a radio speech in mid-July, Tydings read from it. "Here is what Mr. Hallgren wrote in that book, which I quote word for word," Tydings said. "He says, 'The only hope lies in the Communists. Their ideology prepared them, or should prepare them for insurrection and in this way they also have the rich experience of the Russian Bolshevik to draw upon.' That is what Mr. Hallgren said."

Lewis roared that Tydings was "red-baiting." Hallgren's response, "I am not now, never have been and in all probability never will become a member of the Communist Party, or a member of any organization affiliated with the Communist Party," was a harbinger of denials that years later reverberated through the Senate's marble caucus room as klieg lights and cameras captured the scene—

declarations rich with allusions that echoed across time when another election revealed the irony of such charges.

Hallgren also denied he ever wrote any such thing: "The quoted statement is a complete fabrication." That prompted a sarcastic and damaging rejoinder. Producing a photostatic copy of the page bearing the quotation, Tydings remarked, "What kind of memory can Mr. Hallgren have, I wonder, to have felt so intensely upon a subject only 5 years ago, for his book was published in 1933, and in this interval to have lost faith in his earlier convictions as to have forgotten even that he ever held them?" Elucidating further, he noted that Hallgren had just published an article in November 1937 in the magazine *Soviet Russia Today:* "Here are the exact words: 'One would have to be an arch-tory or a perfectionist, or perhaps a fair-weather liberal, not to be able to recognize the enormous, truly unprecedented contribution to social stability and social justice that has been made by the Soviet Union.' "

Tydings hastened to exclude Lewis from communist implications, saying, "I do not charge Mr. Lewis with being a Communist or with sharing Mr. Hallgren's view." But he strongly condemned Hallgren's promoting insurrection as the means of implementing the ends of communism. The *Sun* mulled it over and concluded that Lewis, by calling Tydings and his backers Tories, had initiated the problem. "People who start the calling of names ought not to whimper if they get a taste of their own medicine."

To regain the initiative, Lewis attacked Tydings's record, charging him with voting against every piece of legislation designed to help the poor. He berated the Miller–Tydings Act, which he called a price-fixing measure that hurt consumers and the poor. That was all the provocation Tydings needed to come roaring back. Lewis, he retorted, had not even bothered to show up to vote on Miller–Tydings. If the issue was so important to him now, perhaps he could explain his failure to register his opinion when it counted. Further, Tydings pointed out, Kent R. Mullikin, Lewis's campaign manager, happened to be one of those who took a leading role in guiding Maryland's fair trade law through the state legislature. Shouldn't Lewis reconsider his statement?

Missing the vote on Miller–Tydings was only a part of an overall pattern of absenteeism, Tydings told the voters. Lewis had missed 42 percent of all House votes during his terms in office. Tydings could hold his record up against anyone's—not just percentage of votes, but benefits derived to Marylanders.

He admitted opposing "wasteful," "unworkable" legislation such as the NRA, the AAA, the TVA, the National Labor Relations Board (NLRB); but to call him a "Tory Democrat," to say he had voted against all beneficial acts of the Roosevelt administration, was "silly propaganda." Roosevelt himself had said in 1936, "We all know now that the NRA went too far," Tydings told audiences. He had voted, he said, for the "bone and sinew" of the New Deal: the Reconstruction Finance Corporation (RFC), the Home Owners Loan Corporation Act (HOLC), the Civilian Conservation Corps (CCC), the Securities and Exchange Act (SEC), the Farm Credit Act, a wage and hours law. He could rattle off 22 of them, including one he had authored: the Philippine Independence Act.

And risking support from veterans, a group near and dear to his heart—and a politically well-organized faction—he had voted to sustain Roosevelt's unpopular veto of the costly war veterans bonus in 1936. In 1924 President Calvin Coolidge vetoed the World War Adjusted Compensation Act that promised to veterans bonus certificates due to mature in 1945. Tydings had voted for the bill; Congress overrode the veto. In 1932, in the depths of the Depression, 20,000 veterans marched on Washington demanding immediate payment. Roosevelt was forced to confront the problem. Lobbyists descended on Capitol Hill. By 1935 a number of bills finally had been drafted.

Tydings sponsored a plan based on self-liquidating loans. It offered a less generous bonus than two competing measures (one by Representative Frederick M. Vinson of Kentucky, and a second by Representative Wright Patman of Texas). In a speech Tydings spoke of his deep concern for veterans. "I am an ex-soldier myself," he said. "Many of the men at my command were killed in that terrific holocaust [and] I am not unmindful of their sacrifice." But, he pleaded, "we are still in the midst of a world-wide depression; . . . we should not lose sight of these conditions [and pay] the bonus 10 years before it is due." Congressional reluctance to cross powerful lobbies, and a clear sympathy for those who had risked their lives in war, led to passage of Patman's $2.5 billion plan, which Tydings derided as inflationary "printing press money." (Passed in January 1936 while Tydings was on his honeymoon, the Patman bill provided that bonuses be paid in "baby" bonds of $50 denomination paper notes, which the government would be obliged to cash on demand. No provision was made as to where the money would come from.)

Tydings, for all his concern over straining a stretched national economy, was reviled by bonus supporters as a Tory, a lackey of bankers, and a callous capitalist indifferent to starvation. Although newspapers praised his sense of responsibility and guts in refusing to pander to the "wildly inflationary" way out, when he later voted to sustain Roosevelt's veto he again was called every name in the book. The stand had not been easy to take; but concern for the economic crisis had surpassed emotional appeals, and Tydings voted what he believed best for the country. During the 1938 campaign he stood by his decision and claimed it as part of his "bone and sinew" New Deal support. He received endorsement by the Maryland American Legion.[16]

Tydings had wrapped his toga (now embroidered with New Deal emblems) around him and turned his opponent's charges against him. He was what a real senator should be, he told campaign audiences. He preferred to think issues through and vote accordingly, unlike certain puppets intent on getting patted on the head. He would make better use of his head than letting it become a resting place for Roosevelt's hand.

Running a traditional campaign against a tough opponent— and Lewis was formidable—was nothing compared to running against the full force of the president's power. Roosevelt himself had not as yet spoken out directly against Tydings, had not yet publicly named names of those he was out to get, but Tydings's troops feared the weapon of federal patronage cutbacks. When a Tydings appointee—Henry W. Webb, director of Maryland's Federal Housing Administration—was abruptly dismissed, Tydings saw it as a political attack on him. The reason given for Webb's firing—"longstanding inefficiency"—seemed specious; the timing—early July, as the Lewis–Tydings race was heating up—seemed suspicious. Tydings charged that Webb was "guillotined in the interest of political expediency." He further suspected that Kent Mullikin, Lewis's campaign manager, had been promised Webb's job.

Lewis supporter D'Alessandro explained that Tydings made appointments all the time for his own purposes. "The New Deal boys only did what Tydings has been doing and now he puts on a cry-baby act," he scoffed. But Tydings remained angry. Appointing people was a usual procedure; dismissing someone else's appointee was another use of patronage entirely.

Tydings's appointees were unnerved by Webb's dismissal. The *Evening Sun*'s Thomas O'Neill wrote that it was a warning: "Get behind our candidate in the Senate or you'll get off the pay roll." Krock's column in the New York *Times* stated that word had gone out that federal officeholders who failed to support Lewis would be dismissed. There was legitimate reason for concern. Presidential Secretary Stephen Early gave Roosevelt a secret strategy report prepared by Theodore Huntley of the Washington *Times–Herald*. Huntley wrote that the "practical thing to do is to take the organization away from Tydings through the judicious use of Federal patronage, thus bringing influential leaders into line and letting the lesser fry know . . . control of Federal patronage has passed from the hands of those who had controlled it into the hands of others who will work in harmony with the White House."

Webb was the only one fired. Oddly, Tydings did not demand investigation. A committee had been formed in early 1938 to study campaign irregularities—specifically regarding funding and patronage. The Special Committee to Investigate Senatorial Campaign Expenditures and Use of Governmental Funds in 1938 (the Sheppard Committee) studied hundreds of cases, including Webb; but that investigation was requested by Arthur E. Hungerford (a third Democrat running for the Senate) who did not believe charges that Webb was fired for failing to back Lewis. Ultimately the committee agreed with Hungerford, but the finding—made after the primary—received little attention. Likewise, when Mullikin *was* appointed to Webb's post in December, little interest was stirred because the election was over. But the timing of the dismissal had convinced Tydings and his supporters that the full range of weapons available to Roosevelt and his national machine would be unleashed against him.[17]

They did not have long to wait. Tydings's "bone and sinew" speech had given the Elimination Committee apoplexy. Ickes waded in. Two days after Tydings bragged about his "bone and sinew" votes, Ickes—substituting for Fulton Lewis, Jr., vacationing Mutual Radio commentator—delivered a searing rebuttal aired nationwide. A Maryland friend of his, Ickes said, had complained that "Tydings was doing a lot of beefing about a little bone and gristle." Well, Ickes growled, he should have "put a little heart into it" if he was truly dedicated. He was just trying to "muscle in" on the New Deal. Ickes gained the distinction of being the first member of the New Deal inner circle to attack Tydings by name in a public broadcast.[18] Unfortunately for Davey Lewis, Maryland stations did not air the broadcast.

Roosevelt, meanwhile, had set off on a cross-country tour in early July in his ten-car, air-conditioned train. From Kentucky to California he spoke in glowing terms of Democrats friendly to the New Deal and studiously ignored others, even if they stood squirming on platforms beside him. After sailing down the Pacific Coast, through the Panama Canal, and finally disembarking in Florida in early August, he reboarded the presidential train intent on opening fire on those he intended to destroy. Walter George of Georgia was first.

Senator George, Roosevelt told a crowd of 50,000 in Barnesville, Georgia, was "my personal friend," a "gentleman and a scholar," but he was not, in his judgment, a member of "the liberal school of thought." And, Roosevelt added, in case anyone missed the point, "if I were able to vote in the September primaries in this state, I would most assuredly cast my vote for Lawrence Camp"—a liberal he had encouraged to run against George. George calmly approached Roosevelt and shook his hand. "Mr. Roosevelt," he said, "I regret that you have taken this occasion to question my Democracy and to attack my record. I want you to know that I accept the challenge."

The president, traveling north toward Washington, next fired an indirect salvo aimed at Cotton Ed Smith of South Carolina. Without naming names he wound up his talk by saying, "I don't believe any family or man can live on fifty cents a day"—a swipe at Smith who was credited with insisting (during debates on the hours and wages bill) that in South Carolina such a thing was possible. Presidential Secretary Marvin McIntyre, realizing what Roosevelt was up to, quickly arranged for the train to leave.

Once back in the capital, Roosevelt put his own prestige on the line in Maryland as he pulled out heavy artillery aimed point-blank at Tydings. On August 16, one day after a coast-to-coast radio speech in which he singled out Lewis by placing him at the top of a list of social security "pioneers," he held a press conference. Handing out copies of an editorial from the New York *Post* entitled "Why the President Interferes," he instructed reporters to quote the words he read from the piece as his own. He was adopting, he said with an expansive smile, the *Post*'s editorial as his own statement.

Tydings, he said, "had betrayed the New Deal in the past and will again." He was trying "to run with the Roosevelt prestige and the money of his conservative Republican friends both on his side." If he were running as an outright anti–New Dealer, he said, there would be no reason for intervention; but by insisting that he supported the " 'bone and sinew' " of the New Deal, Tydings himself made it Roosevelt's "right and duty to tell the people what he thinks of Millard Tydings." He called for a Lewis victory.

Following the barrage, Tydings's Baltimore headquarters was unexpectedly serene. Supporters sensed that the president's labeling him a political Judas would help Tydings and hurt Lewis. Tydings blasted back the next day, asking sarcastically, "Do you want your Senator to be a Charlie McCarthy?"

His official response was an emotional masterpiece. A month before Roosevelt's attack, in a move that proved to be pure serendipity, Tydings had engaged every radio station in Maryland and one in Washington, D.C., for the evening of August 21. Luck and delicious irony provided that the time slot he reserved that sultry Sunday immediately preceded Edgar Bergen's *The Charlie McCarthy Show*, a coincidence noticed by everyone.

The issue of the "[sovereign] right of our people to pass judgment" on their representatives "without fear, intimidation or outside interference" had been raised and transcended all others, Tydings told his audience. "The word purge [begins] to creep into the Maryland newspapers, a word foreign to our ears in our dealings with each other," he warned. He narrated the story of Lewis's recruitment as an instrument of Roosevelt's will: Lewis had let himself be used by "persons who do not live in Maryland; who cannot vote in Maryland; who pay no taxes in Maryland; who have no homes in Maryland, but who are determined to dictate the policies of Maryland."

Tydings asked, "What is Mr. Lewis' position in the face of this invasion" by high government officials? "The same Mr. Lewis who denounced and denied that he would accept outside help last June now begs and pleads for outside help. I am running against the power of the Federal Government directed against me by the Chief Executive and his advisers," he said, enunciating each word. "What are you going to do about it, fellow Marylanders?" he cried. "This fight, this contest, is your fight and your contest. I am confident that on September 12 the people of Maryland will act, and act decisively to let the Federal Administration and all the people of the country know that the Maryland Free State shall remain free."

Tydings's appeal to state pride touched Marylanders' devotion to states' rights and home rule—values deep-rooted in 300 years of tradition. His shrewd exhortation also demolished the charge that he was a Tory Democrat or Republican sympathizer: He had not betrayed the New Deal or the party. A congressman's oath was to the Constitution, not to the chief executive. The New Deal had betrayed the Democrats by not adhering to the ideals Roosevelt himself had embraced in 1932.

Response to the speech was overwhelming—lavish and near unanimous with praise, locally and coast-to-coast. The New York *Times,* which printed a complete transcript, gave him front-page coverage and editorial support. The election assumed national importance because Roosevelt had pitted himself against a political opposite who epitomized independence, determination, and conviction. People would get to decide, wrote the St. Louis *Post Dispatch,* "whether they think the President is attempting to set up a one-man rule and carry the country down the 'perilous road to authoritarian government,' as Mark Sullivan terms it; or whether . . . he is simply attempting to bring a new degree of responsibility to party performance."

Raymond Clapper, who called Tydings a "suave reactionary," maintained that the purge was not a bad idea, but was being mangled by Roosevelt's "henchmen" who were acting like "prep-school boys." The White House image was tarnishing and needed big Jim Farley "back on the job." He called Tydings's "invasion" charge "hokum," although he admitted that it was the "natural political answer" to Roosevelt's actions.[19]

Clapper was almost alone in not chastising Roosevelt. The press wrote that he appeared to be swinging away from party government toward personal government. The same words were used over and over again to describe Roosevelt and his actions: meddling, devious, inconsistent, manipulative, unwise, perilously close to dictatorship, and New Deal juggernaut. Frederick William Wile in the Washington *Evening Star* warned that it—intellectual servitude—could happen here. He cautioned that it might be "Stalin-ism, Mussolini-ism, Hitler-ism rolled into one . . . with a Harvard accent and a billion dollar smile." Roosevelt's move smacked of Louis XIV's "*L'état c'est moi.*" A Washington *Post* editorial said, "In a dictatorship legislatures are chosen to cooperate with the executive. In a democracy they are chosen to represent their own constituents."

Liberal columnist Herbert Agar fumed at comments such as Wile's. Suggesting Roosevelt's actions resembled dictatorship "is the language of the psychopathic ward," he wrote. Roosevelt was just telling Marylanders that Millard Tydings was the enemy of the New Deal.

In the New York *Times* Krock suggested that Tydings had cleanly defined the issue: "If the Democratic voters want to turn over their Senatorship to Mr. Roosevelt as his personal property, guaranteeing an affirmative vote on whatever he may propose, they will do it with full knowledge of what they are doing." Krock believed the dictator charges were bunk, but saw how the dangers could be misconstrued. Roosevelt was trusted, but most people "do not admit, or even understand, the threat involved in the establishment of a one-man party in control of a government able to spend . . . billions of public monies to perpetuate itself and its disciples in office."

Billions of monies had been a hot subject in the spring of 1938. With the "Roosevelt Depression" deepening, the president's advisers pressured him to resume pump priming; and on April 14, Roosevelt presented Congress with his request for enormous sums for public works. Tydings and other conservatives were in a jam. It was an election year; voting against the bill would be tantamount to political suicide. As Wile remarked—quoting Al Smith's 1934 wisecrack that "nobody ever shoots Santa Claus"—running with extravagant New Deal spending was a lot easier than running against it. Tydings refused to vote for the $3.75 billion omnibus bill; but he could not vote against it. He finally ended up not voting at all.[20]

A comprehensive relief spending bill in an election year was but a part of the fiscal weapon wielded against conservatives. In Tydings's case, Ickes used federal spending specifically as reward or punishment—and Tydings had committed too many sins. Not only had he been one of that arrogant group of senators who, in occupying the first two rows of seats during the president's January state of the union address, showed contempt by refusing to applaud and by scowling peevishly throughout the address, but he had dared to join front-liners against Roosevelt's plan to reorganize the executive branch.

Roosevelt had submitted his plan in 1937 along with the Supreme Court reorganization bill, but the latter overshadowed the former. The slightly revised 1938 version met tremendous resistance in Congress. Consolidation of agencies, creation of new departments, and the addition of six presidential assistants—"men with 'a passion for anonymity' "—evoked fears of fascism. Hitler's Austrian *anschluss* was fresh in people's minds. Some feared the six new men would run a furtive government from the White House basement.

When Tydings opened debate on March 28, he argued against concentrating power in the hands of a few. "I am not attributing to the President . . . any motive to create a dictatorship in this country. That is not the point. The point is that the technique [has been used] in other countries." Krock wrote that the attitude of those who wanted "to send a message abroad that democracy is on the watch in this country . . . was completely expressed [by Tydings] when he said in effect that this is a good bill, but it is a bad time to give people anywhere even a mistaken reason to believe that the American democracy is surrendering any of its functions."

Tydings's and others' cautionary tales elicited 300,000 telegrams against the plan, but it squeaked through the Senate (perhaps because it was certain to meet defeat in the House, which it did). Roosevelt—in Warm Springs, Georgia, for a needed rest—clearly was unnerved by the charges and issued a statement. "I have no inclination to be a dictator. I have none of the qualifications which would make me a successful dictator," he said. "I have too much historical background and too much knowledge of existing dictatorships to make me desire any form of dictatorship for a democracy like the United States." Patterson in his book *Congressional Conservatism* noted, "This remarkable statement, so unnecessary and so plaintive, revealed that the charges of dictatorship had not fallen upon deaf ears."

Roosevelt's dreams of revenge and punishment remained undiminished. In Tydings's case, Davey Lewis and patronage threats were insufficient. Ickes knew Roosevelt need not restrict himself to the big stick of patronage; he held the bludgeon of New Deal billions. Maryland's hopes for WPA and PWA money to build bridges across the Chesapeake Bay, the Potomac at Morgantown, and the Susquehanna at Havre de Grace presented a perfect means for persuading voters to elect Lewis. Ickes also knew the depth of Roosevelt's hatred for Tydings. In the spring of 1937, before leaving for Raleigh to deliver his "Tidings of Victory" speech, Ickes was told by Roosevelt that he "hoped I would take Tydings' hide off and rub salt in it. I asked him if I was at liberty to go as far as I liked and he said that I was," Ickes noted in his diary.

For years Tydings had been pressing for bridges to span the bay and two rivers. As early as 1935 the *Sun* questioned the holdup: Someone was delaying funding to hurt Tydings. Tydings sometimes believed Ickes was "distinctly hostile" toward the Maryland projects; yet at other times he complained that local bankers and businessmen had been remiss in failing to underwrite the costs to be borne by private sources. By July 1937 Tydings had managed to push a bill through Congress providing for a Chesapeake Bay crossing. Roosevelt vetoed it. He said the War Department opposed any bay bridge south of Baltimore as in wartime it could adversely affect shipping.

The veto—ending 30 years of attempts to enact bay bridge legislation—came directly on the heels of the Court packing defeat and signing of the despised Miller–Tydings Act. It also killed the

Susquehanna span strongly endorsed by War Department engineers. Tydings and other state leaders could not avoid the suspicion that sour grapes and presidential wrath had played a part in thwarting those projects. Tydings met with War Department officials and engineers and in December announced he had won approval for a bridge south of Baltimore (where the Kent Narrows made construction feasible both in economic and engineering terms). Roosevelt killed the bill again on grounds of economics and national security. Republican Theodore McKeldin, rising political rival of Republican Governor Harry Nice, mentioned the connection between Roosevelt's veto and Tydings's voting record. In urging Marylanders to vote Republican, he paraphrased the president's attitude: "If you vote against my Court bill I'll vote against your bridge bill."

The bridges languished in limbo until 1938, when relief legislation and Roosevelt's rage at Tydings converged. Pump priming monies translated quite conveniently into poll priming monies. The Maryland bridges became bait in Roosevelt's obsession with driving Tydings from office. When Curley Byrd and Davey Lewis issued formal invitations for Roosevelt to visit Maryland, each specifically requested he inspect the bridge sites in question.

The foray against Senator George had been called the second march through Georgia. It was predicted that Roosevelt's first march through Maryland would end in a rout; treading on a border state's independence would be a colossal flop. In a nationwide poll of Democrats, 61 percent disapproved of the purge. Krock disdained Roosevelt's deviousness—how he had gone after Gillette in Iowa and Tydings, George, Smith, and Representative James J. O'Connor of New York. He inveighed against the way the president snapped the whip to teach heretics a lesson. Distinguishing between liberals and nonliberals was a far cry from going hammer and tongs and lucre against good men in his own party.

Dauntless, Roosevelt continued. In an August 23 press conference at Hyde Park, his estate in New York's Dutchess County, he told journalists he had heard credible reports that in Maryland "Republicans are being begged to enter the Democratic primary." The obvious implication—that Republicans were being asked to vote for Tydings—was more than misleading. It was wrong. The next day's newspapers set things straight: Maryland law prevented change of party affiliation within six months of an election, primary or general.

Also on August 23, the move that everyone in Maryland (and many elsewhere) had anticipated finally was made. Roosevelt accepted a formal invitation to speak in the state. Tydings, in his August 21 speech, had predicted that Roosevelt would "invade Maryland in person." Roosevelt eagerly agreed to visit the proposed Morgantown bridge site. The person who wired the invitation was none other than Curley Byrd, Tydings's friend and classmate. "Millard Tydings has been among my close personal friends for many years," Byrd said in the wire, "but I cannot go along with him" when he said Marylanders wanted the president to stay away. Byrd promised he personally would welcome Roosevelt. The president had needed Byrd's invitation over any other to refute Tydings's insinuation that he was a carpetbagger.

Byrd's action split the university. Prominent alumni sent telegrams endorsing Tydings to 100 alumni groups. They hated Byrd's dragging the school into national politics, even if it did mean more WPA funds. (Many people had noticed the link between the purge and the purse.) Byrd also was reviled for taking a shot at a major patron of the university—the man most responsible for its present status.

The *Evening Sun* was disdainful of Byrd's action. He was as ambitious as his university was needy, it scolded, and his "genius for grabbing every loose dime that happened to be lying around" merited a new descriptive category: "curlybyrd," as in "most of the curlybyrds managed to get worms." Historian George Callcott believed Byrd was maneuvered into extending the invitation as a part of a quid pro quo that the president extracted for the WPA largess. Callcott wrote in *A History of the University of Maryland,* "Speaking as if the words hurt him, Byrd invited Roosevelt to join him at Crisfield to launch a 'purge' of his old friend and classmate who had been one of the University's firmest supporters. . . . Two weeks later Roosevelt's yacht docked at Crisfield where Byrd welcomed him ashore as inconspicuously as possible."[21]

Lewis, D'Alessandro, Representative Alan Goldsborough, and others quickly followed up with invitations. Even Republican Governor Nice (running for a second term) saw a visit to the bridge locations as an excellent idea. To no one's surprise, Roosevelt's staff announced on August 29 that he would tour Maryland over Labor Day weekend. He would drive to Morgantown, inspect the bridge site, and then take an overnight cruise across the Chesapeake on the *Sequoia* to the Eastern Shore (with Lewis and Farley aboard as guests). By motor caravan, his entourage—which would include Lewis, Byrd, Goldsborough, Nice, Farley, and columnist Drew Pearson (in his own car)—would drive from Crisfield through a number of small towns (covering 300 miles and visiting seven Sho' towns) with a stop in Denton for a major address to be broadcast nationally.

Marylanders by the thousands sent letters and telegrams warning Roosevelt not to come. Even some Lewis and longtime New Deal supporters believed the move would boomerang. Krock warned of "dangers and embarrassments" to Farley as well as to Roosevelt and Lewis. If Tydings were renominated, how would Farley support Tydings and keep the Democratic party unified? Krock believed Roosevelt had "left the way clear to continued opposition if the Senator is renominated." In Krock's view, that gave the state primary "significance and portent beyond that of any other, quite out of proportion to the size of the State and the number of Democrats therein."

Roosevelt lent credence to the possibility that he would keep after Tydings even if nominated when he stated on September 2, "If there is a good liberal running on the Republican ticket, I will not have the slightest objection to his election. The good of the country rises above party." Krock noted the inconsistency of having declared that it would be "immoral" for Republicans to vote in a Democratic primary and then this. Tydings pounced on Roosevelt's remark yet refrained from attacking the president directly: "I personally am a Democrat. . . . I always supported the Democratic party and I'm willing to let the Republicans run their own affairs."

Tydings campaigned ferociously, losing ten pounds before the primary. When heckled, he was quick on the draw. Speaking to an initially hostile group of 3,000 shirt-sleeved, leather-faced farmers in Frederick, he was interrupted so many times he finally called out, "If there is a dairyman in the audience, there are a couple of cows here crying to be milked." Those who "came to jeer stayed to cheer," said the newspapers. Tydings shrewdly avoided attacking Roosevelt, but made reference to his own lack of subservience, saying the president obviously preferred a senator with a "detachable head which he must leave with his hat in the cloakroom before going on the floor of the Senate."

Lewis fought like a tiger, calling Tydings a Republican in Democratic garb. The Washington *Post* noted that the number of Lewis posters lining shop windows in Baltimore's working-class neighborhoods discouraged some of Tydings's friends. No one disliked Lewis. Many were embarrassed for him over his "out of character" escapade, as the *Post* labeled it. It was of no help when the Maryland Communist party endorsed him, an event described by one wag as "a bouquet of poison ivy if there ever was one." But Lewis's efforts drew far less attention than Roosevelt's most casual comment. Letters to the *Sun* scarcely mentioned him. The passionate ones were for Tydings and against Roosevelt. Roosevelt's men were likened to "circling hyenas." Roosevelt was a "political octopus," an "arrogant, self-willed, self-opinionated New York autocrat, who occupies the White House." "Does Roosevelt think Marylanders such morons that we need him to instruct and advise us?" one person asked.

Symbolic of Lewis being dwarfed was the seating arrangement in the president's limousine as it made its way through the Sho's small towns. Squeezed into the open back seat between Roosevelt and Governor Nice, men of generous proportion, Lewis had to sit on a pillow to be seen. Roosevelt had said, "Come on, Davey, you can use a few inches today."

Before Roosevelt's foray into Maryland, Tydings threw punches at the Elimination Committee, Drew Pearson, and "their New York cronies[—that little bunch of reformed Wall Street lawyers, conservatives until the depression, and now radicals," who campaigned against him. "Against whom am I running," he asked, "David J. Lewis or Drew Pearson, Tommy Corcoran, Ben Cohen and another group of New Yorkers?" He said Lewis had to duck into a phone booth to call Pearson to find out what to say in his next speech.

In turning Roosevelt's attack back onto the president—without mentioning his name—Tydings transformed White House opposition from a threat into an advantage. Charges of "outsider intervention" became a potent weapon, especially given the tangible evidence: Half of Roosevelt's Cabinet at one time or another participated in the war against Tydings. Roosevelt gave Tydings the classic advantageous role of underdog.

The president jeered that Tydings's reaction was "pathetic." He said he was "amused" and "saddened" by the "hysteria." But the high drama and political theater of his grand entry into Maryland, with bunting and banners, ruffles and flourishes, heightened the hysteria. If there was hysteria, Roosevelt himself created it.

Just before the president arrived, Tydings called his leaders together and forbade pro-Tydings demonstrations along Roosevelt's cavalcade route. His wife remembered him saying that anything of the kind would not show proper respect for the presidency. Still, supporters nailed Tydings campaign paraphernalia over Lewis posters, plastering telephone poles along the road. A typical poster read: "Preserve Your Civil and Religious Liberties Guaranteed to You Under Your Bill of Rights and State Constitution. Primary Day, September 12, Falls This Year on Historic Defenders' Day. Defend Your Rights on Defenders' Day and KEEP THE FREE STATE FREE!" Defenders' Day, as every Marylander knew, celebrated the battle in the War of 1812 when the guns at Fort McHenry saved Baltimore from the British, the battle that inspired the Star Spangled Banner, which had become the national anthem through Tydings's sponsorship.

The "invasion" began when Roosevelt disembarked from the *Sequoia* on a radiant September morning to begin the first leg of his journey. Sporting sunglasses, the president sat in the big back seat of his open limousine, with a rumpled Davey Lewis nearly lost between him and Governor Nice. He was met by a crowd estimated at 4,000, but, as papers reported, thousands stayed away from the caravan route. The flags and bunting everywhere were ample evidence that Sho' folk understood the reason for the trip. The day before, telephone poles and trees stood bare; but on that early Sabbath morning, Tydings banners and posters outnumbered Lewis's more than three to one, according to the New York *Times*. "Tydings placards stared at the President from trees and telegraph poles all the way down, and one man yelled 'Rah for Tydings' from the roadside. He smiled and the President smiled." There were no shouts of "Rah for Lewis," noted Thomas Stokes of the Washington *Daily News*. Banners strung across the highway read, "Don't Surrender Maryland to Outsiders—Vote for Tydings" and "Keep Democracy Democratic—Vote for Tydings."

Mere handfuls of people waited along the streets of small towns. The sun was hot but the atmosphere decidedly cold, given the thinness of crowds and the cheers that arose spontaneously for Tydings as Roosevelt's car motored by. Newark, New Jersey, newsman Henry Suydam, a writer who believed Tydings was of "somewhat limited capacities," found that the tour met with a mixed reaction. "[Roosevelt] was received with politeness, in some instances cold, in some cordial, in a few vociferous, but in no case with the numerical or emotional enthusiasm that his presence has been wont to elicit." Sensitive to the absence of cheers and piqued by the rudeness, Roosevelt remarked on one of the sullen onlookers: "I said 'Good Morning' to him and I got no response and somebody who evidently knew who he was told me about him. Apparently he is fond of sour pickles and believes what he reads in the *Sun* papers."

But at Salisbury (population 12,000) waited an enthusiastic crowd of about 15,000 on the high school lawn. Through traffic jams a steady stream of automobiles had poured into the town. Tydings supporters made sure that reporters noticed the preponderance of out-of-state license plates. Maryland Democrats, they implied, wanted nothing to do with Roosevelt's visit. As in Crisfield, where Democrats not firmly in either camp had a dilemma—whether to welcome the president or go to church or go fishing (Sho' fishermen spent the day on the bay, Tydings backers said)—Salisbury residents were torn over whether to stay home or see the president of the United States.

At Denton, Roosevelt was forced to endure the indignity of addressing the nation in front of a huge sign reading "WE WANT TYDINGS." Summoning all his charisma—the smile, the "fireside" voice, the eloquent words (which news reporters said were the only hopes for swinging Sho' votes)—Roosevelt never mentioned Tydings. He spoke of the Democratic party, saying that, as its leader, "I propose to try to keep it liberal." There always would be conservatives and liberals, he acknowledged, but "the nation cannot stand for the confusion of having [any man] pretend to be one and act like the other." He obliquely blasted Tydings's tactics, saying Maryland and the nation recently had been treated to a "deliberate attempt to create prejudice and class feeling which can be charitably explained only as political hysteria."

But his words cut no ice that hot afternoon. Maryland papers said that, if the trip was intended to damage Tydings, Roosevelt had failed dismally. Crowds were "disappointingly small," and his speech the mere "buzz of a stingerless bumble bee." The New York *Times* reviewed national editorial reaction under the revealing headline " 'INVASION' IS DEPLORED." From the calm, pro-Roosevelt Des Moines *Register* (Roosevelt's wish to realign the parties was sound, his method was not) to the colorful New York *Herald Tribune* ("the knife already between the Tydings ribs has been given an extra twist"), it was abundantly clear that Americans did not like the idea of being so frankly manipulated. The purge campaign swing was a colossal mistake.

The spectacle even made the London *Evening Standard,* which stated that the election had been the "chief subject of conversation these last 10 days in America." A West Virginia paper quoted Thomas Jefferson: "One thing I will say, that future interferences with elections, whether of the state or general government, by officers of the latter, should be deemed causes of removal, because the constitutional remedy by the elective principle becomes nothing, if it may be smothered by the patronage of the general government."

As Roosevelt prepared to retreat to Hyde Park on September 6, Tydings's Lord Baltimore Hotel headquarters reveled in the publicity generated by the spectacle. Work had come to a halt during the speech. Only one switchboard operator remained on duty as stenographers and campaign workers gathered to listen. The moment Roosevelt finished, the switchboard lit up with calls from all over the country. Tydings refused comment, but his staff and advisers were jubilant and told reporters he had smiled "like a cat that has just swallowed a mouse." The New York *Sun* printed the ultimate summary: "Undoubtedly the reception accorded to the President in Maryland was the coldest that he has ever received, particularly in a Democratic stronghold. From the moment he set foot on Maryland soil it was made apparent to him that his visit, because of its purpose, was an unwelcome one."

The Sho' response left Lewis glum. Curley Byrd, uncomfortable the entire day, stayed in the background. But D'Alessandro was ecstatic at having been part of Roosevelt's entourage. During a photo session he nearly was flattened by Secret Service agents when he rushed up to an astonished president and grabbed his hand to shake it for photographers. Jim Farley looked miserable. While still in Denton he told the press, "It's a bust."

Farley's role in the purge had been a matter of some dispute. In his autobiography he insisted he was against it and never took an active role in the races Roosevelt tried to influence. He argued that he only went to Maryland at the president's insistence. In an interview for the Columbia University Oral History Project, Farley declared, "I refused to go along with Mr. Roosevelt on the purge, and I issued a statement in which I said I wouldn't go along. He was trying to defeat Guy Gillette out in Iowa. I wouldn't go along. I wouldn't go along in his trying to defeat Tydings. I wouldn't go along in his trying to defeat Walter George. I took the position that it wasn't the duty of the Democratic National Committee or the Postmaster General to interfere in Congressional or Senatorial candidates."

When the interviewer noted that newspapers of the day and historians suggested otherwise, Farley insisted they were wrong. "The only time I got dragged in on it at all was in Maryland when I went with Mr. Roosevelt on his boat on Saturday, and we went down to the Eastern Shore of Maryland, where he made a speech for Dav(e)y Lewis who was running against Tydings. Now, I kept in the background pretty much that day, and I wouldn't get into the point where they could get my picture."

But hindsight and autobiography can be subject to memories disinclined to recall unpalatable episodes from the past. In 1938 columnists and political analysts credited Farley with staying out of Iowa, Georgia, and South Carolina; but he was widely seen as actively, if not happily, involved in Maryland. Krock acknowledged that Farley strongly disapproved of the overall strategy, but said that in Maryland he was "wholeheartedly with his chief."[22]

Among those present in Roosevelt's cavalcade was newsman Pearson, avid New Dealer and Tydings nemesis. He had been fanatically interested in finding a candidate to run against Tydings;

and once Lewis succumed, Pearson eagerly aided him. His columns described Tydings as a "bloated aristocrat." Maryland's Beau Brummel "was raised in ease in eastern Maryland, provided with a thorough schooling. Lewis went to work in the western mines. . . . Today Lewis is a great student, spends his leisure hours in the Library of Congress. Tydings, on the other hand, is to be seen at the horse races, Washington's swankiest dinners, or aboard his mother-in-law's yacht," one column stated. "Lewis lives at an obscure boarding house just around the corner from the Capitol, where board and room cost him and his wife $120 a month. Tydings keeps a house in Washington and a palatial estate on the upper Chesapeake."

Nowhere did Pearson mention that the Washington home belonged to Eleanor's mother—his actual mother-in-law—or that the yacht (on which Tydings was uncomfortable) belonged to his stepmother-in-law and at that time was berthed in the Baltic, far from Maryland. Pearson hammered away at Tydings through his famous shirttail relative. "Mrs. Davies, who is probably the richest woman in America, has long made no secret of her ambition to make her tall and handsome son-in-law president of the United States, and if money can do it, then Millard should be sitting in the White House soon."

And Peason did not limit his attacks to Tydings. His columns insulted Eleanor, wounding her deeply and driving Tydings to fits of fury. Describing her as "an ambitious lady when it comes to Washington society," he devoted gallons of ink to making her appear the epitome of social snobbery. When she broke an engagement with a Chicago congressman and his wife in favor of one at the Austrian embassy, Pearson transformed her decision into a headline: "MRS. TYDINGS MAKES SOCIAL ERROR." (Everything was fine until the rejected couple appeared as after-dinner guests at the Austrian legation: "Mrs. Tydings' face took on the color of a Chesapeake Bay sunset," Pearson wrote.) Another alleged gaffe—discontent over seating arrangements at a political banquet—merited another headline: "MRS. TYDINGS' SOCIAL DEMANDS MAY HURT SENATOR'S CHANCES FOR RE-ELECTION."

But Pearson's pièce de résistance was a pamphlet issued after Roosevelt's swing through the Eastern Shore. *The Life & Times of*

MiLord Tydings, a vicious satire comprising photographs and cartoons of Oakington Farms, further played up the senator's ties to Marjorie Davies. Published by "The Veterans League for Davey Lewis," the pictorial assault had the informal approval of Roosevelt and Farley, both of whom laughed heartily over it. About 100,000 copies were circulated through post office and rural letter boxes.[23]

Marylanders resented the pamphlet, and people in Harford County—who had known Tydings from way back—were angry at insinuations that he had used his position to increase the value of Oakington. The Pearson piece charged Tydings with having received an HOLC loan of $12,000 on his Havre de Grace house, $24,000 in WPA money to build a yacht basin in front of the home, and $7,200 for a private road built on his Oakington property—and with trying to finagle more WPA funds ($22,500) to dredge a deep sea channel near Oakington, allegedly so the *Sea Cloud* could anchor there.

The charges were disproved easily. HOLC loans were available to anyone—even senators. The yacht basin and channel dredging were first proposed in 1933, long before Tydings met the *Sea Cloud's* owner's future stepdaughter and purchased Oakington. The mayor of Havre de Grace, George T. Pennington, answered the charges himself, explaining that indeed the basin was near Tydings's old home, but that the site had been chosen because it was near the city park. The town gave $16,000 toward its construction after Havre de Gracians "voted in a special election in October 1935 on the question of a yacht basin. [Tydings] had nothing to do with putting it there," Pennington said. The road—an old public thoroughfare, maintained both by the county and area residents—was an extension of the Philadelphia Road that ran beside several properties to a public landing near Oakington. It had been rebuilt up to Tydings's property, but no improvements extended onto Tydings's estate.

All in all it was trivial stuff. Pearson (and Ickes, who gave Pearson much of the material used), in trying to inflate petty charges into full-blown political corruption—"trashy kitchen-stairs gossip," said the *Sun*—insulted the intelligence of Maryland citizens. The *Sun* noted that, if that was all they could come up with given Tydings's 20 years in public service, the man was as clean as they come.

Roosevelt's foray, the Pearson–Ickes attacks, the patronage

threats—the whole atmosphere provided an ideal climate for Tydings's final speech. In the words of the Washington *Herald,* he "trotted out his sharpest words, polished them bright with acid and arranged them in bristling order." On a statewide hookup, he demolished Lewis's chances by quoting four presidents on federal interference in local elections. George Washington insisted on 'scrupulous . . . caution . . . not to express a sentiment"; Thomas Jefferson said such "influence . . . should be deemed cause for removal"; John Tyler feared such behavior would "produce a spirit of crouching servilitude"; and last: Franklin Roosevelt. In attacking Herbert Hoover for meddling in New York, he had said, "We in this state, in every city, and on every farm, know the high impropriety of interference by the federal government in the purely local affairs of any state and we are fully conscious of the effective manner in which the people of this great state will at the polls show their resentment against such conduct." Tydings's speech blew Roosevelt and Lewis out of the running.

It rained on September 12, but lines at the polls were long, with record turnout. Tydings swept the election with 60 percent of the vote, winning, 189,719 to 124,439 as Lewis carried only four of Maryland's 23 counties. (Hungerford got 8,186 votes.) Across America his victory was hailed for serving Roosevelt right. Movietone newsreels headlined a smiling, victorious Tydings and Eleanor on their lawn at Oakington. The darling of the conservatives had put the grinning Roosevelt in his place.

The purge effort came a cropper. Gillette won, George won, as did Smith, Van Nuys, Lonergan, McCarran, Clark—every senator targeted. Tydings's win was the biggest as Roosevelt had put more into beating him than all the others combined. Louis Azrael, columnist for the Baltimore *News-Post,* wrote that Tydings should send Roosevelt a thank-you telegram.

Farley telephoned Roosevelt. "Boss," he said, "it's necessary for me to send a congratulatory wire to Tydings."

"I don't know why it should be," a peevish president retorted.

"I think I should at least express hearty congratulations," Farley said.

"Leave out the 'hearty' and all the other adjectives," Roosevelt snapped.[24]

Although furious at Roosevelt's attempt to control the Senate's political complexion, Tydings's first move after victory was to issue a healing statement: "This is no time for bias, malice or hatred." Congress would have its hands full "in charting the course properly" to avoid being drawn into the war in Europe, he said. Then he held a festive party at Oakington to celebrate both his victory and his father's seventy-ninth birthday.[25]

Roosevelt, on the other hand, was not ready to bind the wounds. Public humilation compelled him to have aides scurry into Maryland to look into the background and beliefs of Judge Oscar Leser, the Republican that Tydings would face in November. Pearson already was supporting him and wrote that Roosevelt's new motto was "Let's take the Leser of two evils." The president also foolishly reneged on the Morgantown and Havre de Grace bridges, immediately having Ickes announce that there was no PWA money available. His action transformed an already loaded subject (his promises of millions had been dubbed the "bridges bribe") into a sorry display of pettiness. Mencken split a gasket: Roosevelt's "lascivious flaunting of millions upon millions in bridge money, dole money," was "crude and trashy" and a "shameful" example of democracy in action. The Washington *News* printed an election box score: "Roosevelt and Ickes: no politics; Tydings: no purge; Maryland: no bridges."

Roosevelt blithely denied that the funding was related to the purge and criticized newspapers for linking them. When asked if he would back Tydings in the general election, he remarked that it was well known that he did not participate in local elections—and then "joined in the burst of laughter that followed," the press reported. But the "bridges bribe" and presidential reversal became a national news story. Published chronologies ran like this:

September 1. Ickes announced, "The question of approval [of the Morgantown bridge] will be decided on the project's merits."

September 4. Roosevelt, in Morgantown, gave the project his approval and called for immediate action.

September 10. Roosevelt directed Ickes to give the New York regional office instructions for a "right-of-way for two bridges: one at Morgantown and one at Havre de Grace. (A right-of-way mandated priority over other applications.)

September 12. In primary election, Lewis was defeated.

September 15. Ickes declared that the bridge projects were "just where they always were, [and that] we aren't ready to make a decision yet."

September 20. Roosevelt, at a press conference, suggested that the money set aside for the bridge projects be distributed to other Maryland works. Public outcry and editorial scorn apparently prompted White House reconsideration.

September 22. Ickes announced that one would be built (over the Susquehanna at Havre de Grace) to replace the antiquated double-decked span that had been a railroad trestle. Noting Tydings's hometown, Ickes smiled, "We are going to make it easy for the Senator to come and go as he pleases."

September 27. Lewis, responding to public outrage, personally appealed to Roosevelt regarding the bridge at Morgantown.

October 13. Roosevelt altered Maryland's PWA allotment, approving another $1,766,700 for the Morgantown bridge.

At that point the furor subsided. Tydings finally had won all the marbles, noted the Springfield (Massachusetts) *Republican*.

He was exhilarated over having thoroughly trounced Lewis and Roosevelt. His wife recalled hearing him roar with laughter one morning at campaign headquarters a few days after the primary and asking, "What is it?" "Oh," he said. "It was this man down in southern Maryland. I was talking to him and he was reporting there were 25 votes for Tydings in his precinct and one for Davey Lewis. He said, 'We got a posse out now lookin' for the son-of-a-bitch!' " When he stood up to speak before the Maryland Association of Commerce, she remembered, the audience "stood on their chairs and they cheered and they cheered and they went wild."

The general election was anticlimactic. Judge Oscar Leser, a tall man with a beautiful head of silver hair, defeated Galen L. Tait in the primary. Leser was considered "a cultured Maryland gentleman and expert in the field of taxation," who at 68 had no legislative training and no background in public service, according to the *Sun*. He had sat on the Supreme Bench of Baltimore for a year after having served as Maryland tax commissioner for 23. He was a conservative Republican ("There isn't anything much more conservative," the *Sun* remarked), and his ideas on government remained unknown. "He [says] he is an 'anti-Tydings Republican,' which may mean anything or nothing at all," a *Sun* editorial commented. He criticized Tydings's voting record, berated him for having spent too much money on the primary campaign,[26] and complained that the Senate was unbalanced with its huge Democratic majority. But he never uttered a word about what he would do or what he believed in.

Tydings's campaign focused exclusively on national and international issues. He barely mentioned Leser. Had he not often traveled in caravan with O'Conor (who defeated Jackson for the gubernatorial nomination), J. Millard Tawes (candidate for comptroller), and William Walsh (candidate for attorney general), Tydings's campaign could have been mistaken for a speaking tour exploring matters of national and international importance.[27]

He drew large crowds that listened intently as he explained how economic health rested on a tripod of agriculture, business, and labor. "The nation's prosperity will not stand on any two of its legs," he would say. "Any and all legislation must comprehend all three." And he addressed the precarious international situation. "Within the last month the world has been threatened by another great war," he said, referring to the famous "peace in our time" conference just ended at Munich. "I am not here to say that the manner in which the last crisis was averted was right or wrong." But nothing, he believed, had been settled. "There are in formation now other international crises that are going to threaten war. If you return me to the Senate, I am going to be for a big navy, second to none, . . . the surest guarantee for the country remaining out of war if it desires to do so."

He shunned isolationism. The United States should not adopt a "self-containment" policy, he argued, but must act on Cordell Hull's advice and develop foreign trade. Increased business relations and trade would pull America out of the Depression, and perhaps "rescue the [world from] armed conflict between nations." Democracy must be defended, he declared. "Our Democratic form of government is the culmination of 3,000 years of human struggle by man for the right to govern himself and become master instead of servants of the government. I beg of you not to squander this greatest of all inheritances."

Many political sophisticates read his campaign as positioning for a 1940 run for the presidency. He had staked out the issues and his solutions. Newswriters reported his appearances as "stirring, forceful, and fact-citing." People listened, they wrote, as he discussed the intricate problems facing the country and the world. He sometimes was introduced as the candidate for the Senate who should be made "the Democratic candidate for president in 1940."

His victory over the hapless Leser was overwhelming: a 204,000 vote majority (357,245 to 153,253)—the largest in Maryland history. Roosevelt's impressive win by 159,000 votes in 1936 had held the state record until then. Tydings felt thoroughly vindicated.[28]

The press endlessly analyzed the results of both the general election and the primary purges. Consensus held that Roosevelt had been rebuked. Tydings's victories showed that neither the president's influence nor his popularity translated to local contests. Questions were posed and answered in column after column: Had the president lost or had Tydings and the others won? Was Roosevelt impotent or were voters simply telling him to mind his own business? Predictably, conservatives declared that Tydings won and Roosevelt's policies had been rejected. Some liberals believed Tydings would have lost had Roosevelt stayed out. Most concluded that Roosevelt's method had been rebuffed but his policies and persona were still popular.

Nationwide the Democratic party incurred terrible losses: Republicans gained 81 House and 8 Senate seats. A number of astute political analysts suggested that Roosevelt's magic had vanished. He would face formidable opposition with conservative Democrats back in full force and with Republicans amassed in greater numbers. Such a coalition could wield tremendous power. Mark Sullivan called it "a sign of ascendancy for the orthodox wing of the party." Thomas Stokes predicted tough times for Roosevelt as Tydings, George, and the others would be immune to his efforts to control and intimidate them. The Republican resurgence also put Democrats on notice that party unity was essential to prevent defeat in 1940. The president's prestige had not just been eroded; it had been damaged badly. Raymond Clapper wrote that it appeared as if Roosevelt's career were over: The election results revealed "clearly, I think, that President Roosevelt could not run for a third term even if he so desired."

Roosevelt's New Deal supporters—those who had not authored the purge—were incredulous over the stupidity of the whole thing. "An amateur would know that no matter who you are, when you mix in those family fights, you're going to get the worst of it," one official said. Maurice Rosenblatt, ardent Roosevelt supporter, later was grateful that the purge and Court packing efforts failed. "History has borne out the fact that FDR was overreaching morally, legally and politically," he said in describing his sense that success would have inequitably shifted the federal balance of power. Clapper believed the election was wasted. It had presented an ideal opportunity for a clear-cut liberal versus conservative contest, a veritable philosophical showdown. "[But] both candidates and their supporting speakers [had] wandered off into a furious battle over trivialities, innuendo and ten-cent controversies. Both sides [had] sunk down into irrelevant details," he angrily wrote.

Clapper was not entirely correct. The issue of personality and "invasion" did capture a great deal of attention; but the matter of liberal versus conservative philosophy never was peripheral, despite the hullabaloo. Tydings focused on legitimate and key issues: conservative versus liberal; individual responsibility versus costly social programs; outside influence versus a state's own choice; states' rights versus federal power; and independent view versus rubber stamp— matters of principles and outlook. He and other conservatives were trying to check the course of what they saw as radicalism; Roosevelt was trying to cleanse the party of reactionary elements. There was nothing trivial about any of the battle lines in 1938. The election might have been a clearer debate on political philosophies had Roosevelt not intervened. His intrusions in South Carolina, Georgia, and Maryland muddied the issues. Secretary of Agriculture Henry Wallace was among those who believed Tydings would have been defeated had the president stayed home.

As a result of the purge's failure, Roosevelt was forced to

abandon the idea of permanent party realignment. Realignment may have been Roosevelt's ideological dream, but such a goal never was a viable possibility. From party disputes and polarities come changes and compensations that create the balances necessary to correct mistakes. Ideological differences may be infuriating, cumbersome, sometimes damaging, but they are central to the solution of long-standing problems.[29]

Roosevelt's failure portended a divided convention in 1940. The matter of which wing of the Democratic party would control the White House in 1940 had been, along with revenge, Roosevelt's prime motivation in undertaking the purge. He would be damned if he was going to let conservatives dictate the next Democratic nominee. If the housecleaning were successful, he could run without risking a full-blown split. Roosevelt, as was known, delighted in breaking precedents. He also was unhappy with potential successors to the White House. In conversations with Jim Farley he complained they all were "either too old or too young; too ambitious or too unknown; too conservative or too radical, or in too poor health or too lacking in personality."

Tydings, the president realized, was a very attractive political figure. In discussions with Farley over the pros and cons of Byrd and O'Conor as suitable rivals to Tydings, Roosevelt, who was keeping tabs on those he considered ambitious, described Tydings as a "hot presidential candidate." After the purge, Tydings was hotter than ever. Texas *Weekly* magazine wrote, "Tydings emerges as a national figure as a result of the President's effort to defeat him. He seems to be the one man who could work out a constructive anti–New Deal program between now and 1940 and who could rally the support of the conservatives of the country to such a program." Roosevelt was seen as fearing Tydings because he was aggressive, clever, articulate, and persuasive. Whether or not the Maryland senator would be a contender, he had stood up to Roosevelt's challenge and beaten him at his own game. Joseph Alsop wrote that Tydings was so sure of himself "that he already imagines himself the Democratic conservatives' ideal 1940 candidate."

Tydings was on every list of names for the nomination. The purge had given him more publicity than most politicians hope for in a lifetime. The Washington *Herald* noted that the size of his vote looked like a "blizzard of ballots" strong enough to fuel rumbles of "Tydings-for-President" throughout Maryland and the nation. An editor of the New York *Herald Tribune* approached Tydings for a job as his public relations man. He said to Tydings, "You're going to be president. You're the logical man to be president."[30]

Tydings-for-President clubs were organized in Baltimore. But not everyone thought a candidate from Maryland—a state with a meager eight electoral college votes—could make the grade. Charles P. Stewart, Central Press columnist, dismissed talk of Tydings for president as "hooey." "Tydings is smart, interesting and personally very likeable to folk he comes in close contact with—pretty 'tony' folk generally. He hasn't mass appeal, however," Stewart wrote. "Tydings, at least superficially, is a bit over-aristocratic. He looks it and he acts it. He'd rub any 'typical prairie state' the wrong way inevitably." Clapper believed if Tydings were nominated the country might as well go back to Hoover. But, as he pointed out once before regarding the depth of the party split, "news from Europe may change everything."

In November 1938 Tydings was on top of the world. He and Eleanor boarded the *Normandie* for Europe to rest. She remembered him being the happiest she had ever known him. When the ship's great whistle blew and their guests were ordered ashore by the captain, Tydings locked their stateroom door. They spent most of the voyage alone together. He wrote songs and verses that he sang and recited to her.

Eleanor's father had just left Moscow for Brussels, a major diplomatic listening post. They stayed with the Davieses at the Palais d'Asque, the U.S. embassy, where they were ensconced in a royal suite. On this, their second honeymoon, they hoped to fulfill their dream of adding a child to their family. It had been a deep disappointment, Eleanor wrote in her private memoirs, "that in the two and a half years of our marriage no baby had arrived." Marjorie escorted Eleanor into their room. "I think you may succeed in becoming pregnant here," she whispered. "This is the royal suite and the bed on which the King was born."

On an excursion to Paris, Eleanor and Marjorie bought fabulous hats at Suzy's, the famous Paris milliner. Tydings and Joe Davies spent the evening modeling them as the women howled with laughter. On another occasion they dragged their "indulgent husbands" through the shops and couturiers. The men amazed shop girls and convulsed their wives as they paraded about posing in hats and coats Eleanor and Marjorie were considering buying.[31]

They also talked politics. Davies ruminated on the European situation and asked about the purge.[32] After hearing the story, Davies remarked that he had heard Eleanor was becoming an "effective politician in her own right."

"You don't know the half of it, Joe," Tydings said proudly. "If she ever decides to run for the Senate, my goose is cooked!"

"Unless you have already been elected President," Davies chuckled.

"Not a chance," Tydings replied. "I wouldn't have that job if you gave it to me. It's a killer nowadays."

One of the main reasons Tydings had brought Eleanor to France was to show her the battlefields where he had fought during the war. He always felt he had left a part of himself in Alsace and the Meuse-Argonne. Together they drove through the Ardennes and revisited Verdun. On a cold, misty November day they walked Etraye's Ridge where he had set up the enfilading machine-gun barrage almost exactly 20 years before. They picked their way across hills and ravines where he had crawled from shell hole to shell hole trying to locate the front. As they moved through still-broken woods he found his way to the spot where the Germans had opened fire, killing the horses that drew food to the front. He knelt down and picked up a rusting soup kettle and tattered bits of bridle.

He showed her a dugout where someone he knew had carved his name. The name was visible still: R. H. Kelley, the commander of their battalions. As he pointed uneasily to the writing on the wall, she took his photograph. He took Eleanor to the cemetery there to see the graves of the men who were killed in France. He turned away as tears welled up in his eyes.

The couple returned from Europe for a Christmas family reunion at Oakington. Tydings's sisters Naomi and Kathryn, their husbands and children, and his father were there to open presents from

Paris, Brussels, and Verdun. Then they closed up the house for the winter and leased an apartment at the Wardman Park Hotel.

Tydings was rested and eager to go. The one shadow in his life at that time remained their disappointment that Eleanor and he never had a child of their own. In March, Eleanor wrote in anger and sorrow to her father: "More gossip: the Cassini column enclosed reporting my pregnancy is entirely erroneous. A catty Senate wife announced it at a Senate Ladies lunch when I wasn't present. The woman said I was annoyed [at being pregnant] as I couldn't be bothered! Dear Rose Gillette got up and said if it was true she knew I would be the happiest person in the world with the exception of Millard E. Tydings. Isn't it too bad it ain't so."

Roosevelt's prospects did not look encouraging in January 1939. Conservative Democrats—more powerful than ever—appeared to be closing in to dismember the New Deal. And the Republicans were waiting. During his state of the union address, the most noticeable feature of the evening was the lack of spontaneous applause. The relative silence was in contrast to the applause and demonstrations that had greeted the entrance of Tydings and George. Roosevelt was going to have his hands full dealing with a rebellious and angry Congress. He would need a miracle to keep control. But as Clapper had prophesied, "news from Europe might change everything."

Indeed, news from Europe pulled Roosevelt's chestnuts from the purge backfire. Realizing he would need all the support he could muster from Congress, he began reordering at home. He also realized the European crisis could deal him the cards he needed to beat the conservatives in 1940. He was quick to deflect attention from the election debacle by focusing on Hitler's designs for Europe. He was called lucky by those who were sorry to see the election's ugly aftermath blown right off the front pages.

Notes

1. The Supreme Court's membership in February 1937 included four men often reviled as Tories (James C. McReynolds, Pierce Butler, Willis J.

Van Devanter, and George Sutherland), three regarded as liberals (Louis D. Brandeis, Benjamin N. Cardozo, and Harlan Fiske Stone), and two moderates whose swing votes had generally determined controversial rulings (Owen J. Roberts and Chief Justice Charles Evans Hughes).

2. The dinner included Senators Peter Geolet Gerry of Rhode Island, Frederick C. Van Nuys of Indiana, Guy M. Gillette of Iowa, and Harry F. Byrd.

3. By February 9, Tydings had received 225 letters, three in favor; the next day, his 500 letters ran 50–1 against; by February 23, the tally was 4,000 letters, 125 in favor. Although the volume eased off by late March, the ratio remained about 30 to 1 despite an obviously orchestrated national campaign—mail favoring the plan exhibited identical texts, marking them as form letters.

4. Republicans, too, sensed that visible participation on their part might jeopardize the cause. Right after Roosevelt sprang the plan, three leading Republicans—William E. Borah of Idaho, Charles L. McNary of Oregon, and Arthur H. Vandenberg of Michigan—met secretly and agreed to a strategy of silence, to let Democrats fight it out. They kept Republican colleagues as quiet as they could. And Democrats had to silence the conservative Liberty League. Joseph Alsop called it a sensible "conspiracy of silence." It denied New Dealers the advantage of a noisy conservative leadership frightening away liberals.

5. Many of the Court-fight senators later were certain that their telephones had been tapped. Tydings heard that FBI agents were dispatched to Havre de Grace in a fruitless effort to dig up dirt on him and his family.

6. Steering committee members included Tydings, Wheeler, Gerry, Van Nuys, Burke, Byrd, George, Bailey, Clark, and Connally. Robinson's lieutenants were Alben W. Barkley of Kentucky, James F. Byrnes of South Carolina, Hugo L. Black of Alabama, Robert M. La Follette, Jr., of Wisconsin, Shermon Minton of Indiana, and Lewis B. Schwellenbach of Washington. None of the pro–Court plan senators was on the Judiciary Committee; but Van Nuys, Connally, and Burke were. Robinson received assistance from the administration. Corcoran, Cohen, Charles West, Joseph B. Keenan, and James Roosevelt were available to constantly remind the Senate that patronage originated in the White House.

7. Those who thought the moderate justices were intimidated by the plan and so reversed their positions were not exactly correct. The Washington minimum wage decision had been reached in January but was not announced until March. Undoubtedly the White House's deep displeasure over the reversal of New Deal legislation affected the justices, but the shift in the Court was ongoing before the plan was unveiled in February.

8. Garner was very fond of Tydings, who was a regular member of the vice-president's "Bureau of Education," which was what the feisty old Texan called his private office with its well-stocked liquor cabinet. There

Garner, Tydings, and their friends would toss down a few shots of bourbon. Garner called it "striking a blow for liberty."

9. James Farley also wondered if Robinson was behind the Wheeler–Tydings steering committee's excellent intelligence for he later informed Roosevelt that he had heard that "Wheeler was advised every night, with the knowledge of Robinson, what fellows were weakening on his side and what fellows were weakening on our side."

10. Tydings had handled Radcliffe—Roosevelt's good friend—with kid gloves for fear prodding would backfire. In an interview with the *Sun* in 1940, Tydings recalled, "I wondered what George would do. I didn't talk to him about it for some time. . . . We were riding back to Baltimore one night together and I ventured to raise the question. He told me at once 'I think your stand is the right stand. I'm going to take the same stand. I'm going to be against the President on this thing.' It was harder for Senator Radcliffe to do that than for any other member of Congress."

11. Roosevelt's umbrage over Tydings tacking on the legislation as an amendment to another bill was disingenuous. In 1935 he had tried to attach his controversial "soak the rich" tax proposal onto another bill and only reconsidered when congressional wrath over the issue and his means erupted.

12. Alva B. Adams of Colorado, Alvin V. Donahey of Ohio, Rush D. Holt of West Virginia, Francis T. Maloney of Connecticut, Arthur H. Moore of New Jersey, David I. Walsh of Massachusetts, and Champ Clark of Missouri were sympathetic but not ready to sign. Harrison and Byrnes, although disillusioned with Roosevelt, were even more hesitant.

13. The most publicly outspoken of the Court fight's commanders—Wheeler, Burke, and Connally—were not up for reelection until 1940; Glass and Bailey were safe until 1942. The Washington *Evening Star* in March 1937 dubbed the septet most at risk for retaliation—Adams, Clark, George, Gillette, Smith, Tydings, and Van Nuys—the "unterrified seven."

14. Radcliffe's memorandum on his political career states that, when Tydings asked for support in the primary, "without a moment's hesitation I said I would do so, without referring to the fact that such support would cost me a close friendship of many years of the most powerful man on earth. . . . Shortly thereafter . . . Senator Tydings asked me to be his campaign manager. I replied that to my way of thinking, it was rather unusual for one United States Senator to be campaign manager in the primary fight of his colleague. He insisted and I accepted and served in that capacity."

15. David John Lewis's name and background sometimes caused people to confuse him with John Llewellyn Lewis, also a Welsh coalminer's son linked in the public mind with liberal and New Deal issues. Although Tydings himself was careful not to capitalize on that confusion (John L.

Lewis was as unpopular a man as existed in Eastern Shore Maryland because of CIO efforts to unionize that conservative bastion), some supporters were not so scrupulous. For example, John L. Lewis owned an elegant and not inexpensive colonial home in Alexandria, Virginia; in answering the implications of "the man from the mines vs. the man from the mansion," Tydings supporters and news reporters often correctly stated that Davey Lewis had left the mines long before Tydings ever had a mansion, but also sometimes incorrectly added that Lewis had "a pretty fine home himself in Alexandria that many would call a mansion."

16. Because of his stand on the bonus issue, Tydings refused to apply for the bonus and declined disability compensation although entitled to both. In April 1937 he finally accepted his bonus and turned the entire $2,000 over to the Baltimore Memorial Post, Veterans of Foreign Wars, to fund education for veterans' children. He made his gift informally, hoping to avoid publicity; but grateful members leaked news of it. A 1936 *Saturday Evening Post* article exposing Washington nepotism and other misuse of official prerogatives noted a few public servants who were not selfishly out for themselves. Tydings, Tom Connally, and Edward Burke were the only three soldier-senators who voted no on the bonus and refused to apply for it.

By October 1983 World War I veterans had received $3.8 billion in bonuses, $14.3 billion in service-related compensation; and the government had spent another $19 billion in other costs, mostly medical. The original cost of the war had been $26 billion.

17. *Sun* reporter O'Neill's articles on patronage threats by another Lewis supporter, Eugene B. Casey, when studied by the Sheppard Committee were found to be fabrications. O'Neill quoted Casey as saying that, unless Maryland federal officials backed Lewis, "out they [would] go." He admitted inventing the quote to express his opinion; he was responsible for hyperbole nationwide over patronage threats. Krock's remarks were based on O'Neill's quotes.

18. Ickes's speech was also significant because it contained remarks widely construed as hinting at a third term for Roosevelt. "While he did not use the words 'third term,' there was little doubt as to what he intended to imply," the *Sun* wrote, citing from Ickes's broadcast: " 'If the reactionaries in the Democratic party want a real test of President Roosevelt's strength with the people, I suggest that they continue to work for a situation which will result in the people being given an opportunity to vote directly on the proposition of whether or not they are for President Roosevelt and his policies.' "

19. Clapper apparently forgot his 1935 advice that Roosevelt should

"allow some tolerance within the party [rather] than to risk having the whole New Deal overthrown because of too strict a purity test. . . . Petty vengeance is poor politics."

20. Only six Democrats voted against it (Burke, Byrd, Bailey, Copeland, Glass, and George L. Berry) and only one—Berry, appointed to finish out a term—was up for election.

21. Callcott also noted, "During the next few years Byrd continued to use Tydings' support, along with Roosevelt's friendship, to obtain a third $1,000,000 in PWA and WPA funds for campus construction."

22. It may be that Farley, whose strong dislike of Tydings dated back to the 1936 convention when Tydings only reluctantly made a terse seconding speech for Roosevelt, needed a push from White House staff to join the purge against Tydings. A sheaf of papers on 1938 campaign strategy among Roosevelt's papers at Hyde Park noted the need to draw Farley into open assistance: "At this time he may be more helpful than anyone in Washington outside of yourself [Roosevelt]. He has assured us that he will give us every cooperation and so far he has certainly done so. I know that he will probably not wish to accompany us on the trip but it is the opinion of the group that this would be the second most beneficial thing that can be done at this time because it would show clearly to the practical politicians that Senator Tydings, and Senator Radcliffe, are not going to receive much consideration in the matter of patronage no matter how the contest ends."

23. Roosevelt was aware of Pearson's activities. Campaign strategy files at the Roosevelt Library contain assessments of participants: "[Pearson] has been of invaluable service in this campaign. I cannot commend too highly his efforts which, in my opinion, have been wonderful. However, if he could be impressed with the idea that any publicity of certain movements of ours would be extremely disadvantageous to us at this time it would make the group feel very much more comfortable." Ickes's contributions were less valued: "It is the feeling of the group that absolute silence from this quarter is the best thing that can be done."

24. Farley noted in his autobiography that he and Roosevelt never were close again after the 1938 elections. He was disillusioned by the president's actions and hurt by his distant and cold attitude.

25. Senators George and Cotton Ed Smith also were conciliatory in public. But like Tydings, underneath they were angry. Smith said to George, "Roosevelt is his own worst enemy." George replied, "Not as long as I am alive."

26. Tydings spent $89,000 on the primary; his largest contributors were his wife and himself, who together gave $2,500. Lewis spent $54,000; his largest contributor was Drew Pearson, who, with his two sisters, gave

$17,000. Against Leser, Tydings spent $2,700. Leser's expenditures added up to exactly $436.20.

27. D'Alessandro, who defeated Representative Vincent Palmisano in the primary, seldom traveled with Tydings as he campaigned. Representative Alan Goldsborough, running for reelection, sometimes joined the caravan.

28. O'Conor defeated Harry Nice for the governorship. Tawes, Walsh, Goldsborough, and D'Alessandro all won.

29. Roosevelt never fully relinquished his goal, although he was not successful. In 1940 he had a personal emissary (Samuel Rosenman) approach Republican presidential candidate Wendell Wilkie to discuss working together for party realignment. Wilkie preferred to wait until after the election. With Wilkie's sudden and premature death, the idea also died. No head of party since Roosevelt has made a serious effort to effect such changes. The concept presents too many obstacles.

30. Tydings's wife said he turned the man down flat. "No. Nothing doing," she remembered him saying. When Joe Davies offered to pay the man himself, Tydings repeated his reply, adding that he did not want to be president. Eleanor Tydings Ditzen, in later years, strongly believed that Tydings had not wanted to run. But her husband may have been ambivalent; he did nothing to prevent his supporters from establishing Tydings-for-President clubs. In 1940 Tydings was nominated for president at the Democratic convention.

31. Eleanor Tydings Ditzen recalled the shopping expeditions as fascinating. "I have never seen anyone spend money with such joyous abandon as my stepmother!" she wrote. "Born heiress to a great fortune she considered it her duty to 'spread the wealth' and I thoroughly enjoyed helping her do it!"

32. Davies had offered to return home to help in the fight. He had said he would go "to bat for you with the Boss" to persuade him "to call off his dogs." But Tydings had declined the offer.

10

World War, Political Wars, Cold War

A s President Franklin D. Roosevelt, the Congress, and the nation focused on the great domestic problems created by the Depression (and on concomitant political struggles), the world outside the Western Hemisphere was battered by forces other than economic catastrophe. Beginning with Japan's invasion of Manchuria in 1932, no year went by without a major and violent change on the international scene: In 1933 Adolph Hitler assumed power in Germany; in 1934 Austrian Nazis assassinated Austrian Chancellor Engelbert Dollfuss; in 1935 Italy invaded Ethiopia and Hitler denounced the Versailles Treaty; in 1936 Hitler remilitarized the Rhineland, Benito Mussolini annexed Ethiopia, and civil war erupted in Spain; in 1937 Japan invaded China, and Italy withdrew from the League of Nations; in 1938 Hitler effected the Austrian *anschluss,* and Neville Chamberlain sought appeasement at Munich; in 1939 General Francisco Franco won in Spain, Czechoslovakia disappeared, and Germany invaded Poland, touching off World War II.

In late 1937 Roosevelt and Congress turned their attention to the ever-deteriorating overseas situation. With the recession and increased unemployment, Roosevelt's Court packing, government reorganization, and purge campaign setbacks, and dissatisfaction with the New Deal, the president's strength in Congress ebbed and his ability to lead appeared in jeopardy. Talk of a possible third term

369

was couched in pessimistic language. World turmoil ultimately thrust him back into the driver's seat and gave him unlikely allies—albeit cautious ones—such as Millard Tydings.

The war and postwar years were a time of evolution for Tydings. He began the decade in 1940 as an ardent fiscal conservative, but by 1950 had become a leading proponent of massive spending for foreign economic and military aid. In 1949 he gave up his seniority on the powerful Appropriations Committee to take a seat as a freshman on the Foreign Relations Committee to concentrate on foreign policy. So great was the transformation in his actions and attitudes that Thomas I. Emerson, an attorney for Roosevelt's NRA—in an interview as part of the Columbia University Oral History Project—characterized Tydings as having become one of the "liberals." Emerson overlooked the fact that Tydings had not changed when viewed through a domestic prism, but during the decade had turned his attention increasingly to issues of international concern.

During the late 1930s—until the United States entered World War II after the stunning attack at Pearl Harbor—Tydings played a significant role in the national debate over what course to follow in the face of threatened war and then actual war. He became one of Washington's leaders in the fight to assure American military preparedness in a world seemingly gone mad—and in a country where isolationism was gaining favor. Columnist Ray Tucker accurately wrote in 1939 that Roosevelt badly needed conservative Democrats if he were to overcome isolationist opposition to his foreign policy. Men who had been shut out of the White House—Senators Walter George, Carter Glass, and Tydings—suddenly found patronage available. The president especially needed every strong voice possible to revise neutrality legislation that no longer served a purpose and in fact aided aggressors.

In 1935 the emotional neutrality issue emerged due to a resurgence of isolationism in reaction to events abroad. Isolationist sentiment, which had fueled the Senate's 1920 rejection of President Woodrow Wilson's peace plan and membership in the League of Nations, had appeared dormant during the early years of the Depression, with Americans preoccupied by economic crisis. North Dakota Senator Gerald P. Nye's investigation of the munitions industry rekindled strong feelings. Initially intending to examine war profiteering in World War I, Nye shifted his 1934 study into an attack on how the United States entered that war. He blamed Wall Street bankers and munitions producers, anxious to protect foreign investments and reap huge profits, for duping Wilson and the nation into going to war. Nye's sensational charges reinvigorated the cause just as Mussolini launched his war against Ethiopia. Fears that the conflagration would spread to Europe—possibly draw the United States into another inferno—grew. For the next six years, debate raged over what role America should play as a tinderbox world relentlessly heated up.

Roosevelt, absorbed with domestic problems and anxious to stay out of the war, at first favored the idea of neutrality legislation—provided it gave him discretionary power to discriminate against aggressors. Tydings was uneasy with the concept of enacting legislation that seemed to have no practical value. And he disliked giving Roosevelt authority to decide foreign policy without Senate approval. When Nye and Secretary of State Cordell Hull each drafted neutrality bills in 1935 (Hull's measure was more flexible, allowing presidential discretion in applying an arms embargo), Tydings voted for Hull's but belittled it as well-meaning "New Year's resolutions, which will be broken as soon as war is declared."

He viewed neutrality legislation as a palliative, but voted with the administration for the Neutrality Act, and again in 1936 for its extension. In 1937 he drew the line, refusing to support a permanent law. He would do anything honorable to keep the country out of war, he said, but believed the best way to do that lay in readiness: production of planes and ships, training of air and naval personnel, and maintenance of the nucleus of a large army. "Wishing for peace is no substitute for being prepared," he said, explaining his vote. "We must blend idealism with what is real."

In spring 1939, after Germany swallowed Czechoslovakia, Roosevelt sought repeal of the Neutrality Act's arms embargo clause. Internationalists fought vigorously for supporters. The Senate balked until recess, infuriating the president. Tydings did not fall into line—was listed with the isolationist bloc by the Chicago *Tribune* and as "doubtful" by the Baltimore *Sun*. Hitler's September *blitzkrieg* reopened the issue. Roosevelt convened a special session of

Congress. Although most Democrats backed him right away, a noncommittal Tydings said, "I want to study the whole message very, very, carefully."

Bitterly criticized by administration internationalists, overwhelmed by a flood of 10,000 letters on the subject (largely against repeal of the arms embargo), and hounded by noisy delegations of Maryland isolationists, Tydings held public hearings. Almost 400 rambunctious Marylanders taunted him for even considering repeal. When several shouted, "We voted for you!" he snapped, "Now wouldn't I be pretty small potatoes if I were to vote on this question just because somebody voted for me." When they tried to corner him into making a decision on the spot, he refused, shouting, "I don't care for hell and a brown mule, I'm going to do what I think is right!"

By mid-October he was committed to arms embargo repeal and was named by the New York *Herald Tribune* as one of the outstanding orators on the bill, which passed on October 27. But because of his lukewarm votes for Roosevelt's compromise measures of 1935 and 1936, his outright refusal to vote for the permanent act, and because of animosity toward Roosevelt on domestic issues, impassioned interventionists saw Tydings as a friend of the isolationist bloc. On the other hand, because of his stand on military preparedness, he was seen as a staunch internationalist by others. His stance was easy to misconstrue. As a conservative, he was opposed to any law that delegated congressional power to the executive. He also opposed the legislation on principle: Neutrality might be a noble ideal; but given reality, it was worse than wishful thinking as it invited aggression.

Wayne Cole, scholar of prewar and wartime foreign policy attitudes in Congress and the nation, categorized American leadership into three groups: internationalists, traditionalists, and extreme isolationists. Tydings's stance put him somewhere between the first two—a cautious internationalist, but never an interventionist or isolationist. His wife Eleanor recalled that she would have been an interventionist, as was her father, had it not been for Tydings's words of caution. Graphically describing his own war experiences, he asserted that the United States was totally unprepared to fight the powerful German war machine. He had worked to strengthen the armed forces since he was elected, he told her, but Congress—hell-bent on funding the New Deal—would not spend the money. Eleanor wrote her father in March 1939 after Hitler's *Putsch*: "Millard and I talked for hours last night. . . . I am all for U.S. economic intervention immediately and declaration [of] our intent to apply sanctions against the Germans. But Millard says this country will never stand for that and we will probably pursue the same course we did in World War I."

Those who called his neutrality position anti-administration revealed ignorance of Tydings's overall record on international matters: support for the League of Nations and the World Court; his faith in conference diplomacy. In 1939 he played a major role in winning the largest peacetime naval appropriation ever: $733,049,151. He violently denounced the Ludlow Amendment (which, by constitutional amendment, would have required a majority public approval of a congressional declaration of war except in case of attack). He voted to fortify Guam (after Japan fortified the Caroline Islands). He called for bans on trade and credits to Japan and embargoes on Japanese goods. "Our economic weapon is our strongest one," he said. "Not to employ it is to invite ultimate danger." Tydings and Roosevelt were in closer agreement on foreign policy than the neutrality votes indicated. As Senator Robert Wagner pointedly told James Farley, Tydings was an administration stalwart in advocating vital defense programs, and Roosevelt should value him as such.[1]

In June 1940, Drew Pearson wrote, "Tydings has been vigorously behind Roosevelt's national defense program. In fact he has even gone so far in private conversations as to indicate he was reconciled to a third term for Roosevelt." Pearson was half right. Tydings was a leading proponent of Roosevelt's defense programs; but the two men—wary allies at best—remained rivals. So unreconciled to a third term was Tydings that he entered the 1940 race himself—a favorite son candidate from Maryland—in an election that for a time diverted attention from the international plight.

International events may have brought some conservatives into alliance with the White House on foreign policy, but little on the domestic scene had changed. Progressives and conservatives in great numbers and with great ferocity fought a third term. Speculation that Roosevelt might break with precedent had begun in November 1936. Other speculation centered on finding an "heir apparent." There was no end of strong candidates.

A spate of articles and polls appearing in papers nationwide unfailingly included Tydings along with two dozen other nationally known figures. Damon Runyon's "As I See It" column ranked his favorites: Tydings was eighth, behind such as Senators Bennett Clark of Missouri, Alben Barkley of Kentucky, Joe Robinson of Arkansas, and Secretary of Agriculture Henry A. Wallace; he was ahead of Representative Sam Rayburn of Texas, Governor Frank Murphy of Michigan, Senators Tom Connally of Texas, Walter George of Georgia, Harry Byrd of Virginia, and Secretary of Interior Harold Ickes.

George Gallup's top ten candidates between December 1936 and June 1940—assuming Roosevelt did not run—always included Farley, Cordell Hull, and Vice President John Nance Garner; Tydings was on Gallup's "long list" along with Alfred E. Smith, Relief Administrator Harry L. Hopkins, New York City Mayor Fiorello La Guardia, and Barkley, George, Connally, Byrd, Burton Wheeler, and the like. The *Christian Science Monitor* in August 1939, listing Republicans and Democrats, placed Tydings thirteenth among 22 contenders. (Roosevelt was third, after former Indiana Governor Paul V. McNutt and Garner; Republicans Arthur Vandenberg, Thomas E. Dewey, and Robert A. Taft were fourth, fifth, and sixth.)

Many articles, such as one in the Mason City (Iowa) *Globe Gazette,* featured Tydings, describing him as "very much the type of man" anti–New Deal Democrats were searching for. His reputation as a self-made man from small-town America had strong appeal. Articles mentioning Eleanor described her attentiveness to politics. "Perhaps she also heard those rumors that her husband was being groomed as the 1940 presidential candidate," noted a piece in the Washington *Daily News*. Tydings did not discourage the coverage.

In a searing column attacking him during the purge campaign, Joseph Alsop wrote that Tydings was "so sure of victory that he already imagines himself the Democratic conservatives' ideal 1940 candidate." And they were searching for a strong one. Vice President Garner's clique—the "Bureau of Education"—often met to discuss candidates. A long article in *Look* magazine by Pearson in January 1939 placed Tydings high on the list of challengers: "[Tydings] is another Garner favorite. . . . By marriage he has the Hutton–Davies–General Foods millions behind him. He would be acceptable to the old line South. However, the political insignificance of Maryland, plus the Senator's opportunistic law practice rule him out as a real contender."

Pearson was correct about Maryland's eight electoral votes being a drawback. Another was that Tydings's regional appeal did not translate well. Southern and Atlantic states might accept him, but he would not play well in Peoria. The insinuations that he had the General Foods fortune behind him were echoed elsewhere. A St. Louis *Post–Dispatch* feature article on Tydings said, "Mrs. Marjorie Post Close Hutton Davies has taken her stepson-in-law under her sponsorship. She is reported to have said: 'I have two ambitions in life, to make Joe Davies ambassador to the Court of St. James's and to make Millard Tydings President.' The backing of so determined and wealthy a woman is no small factor as Tydings himself must realize." The suggestions were nonsense. Marjorie's millions stayed put; and Davies, on return from Belgium in late 1939, announced his support for Roosevelt's third term.

The greatest disadvantage for Tydings, however, was Roosevelt—liberal, popular, and powerful Roosevelt. As long as he controlled the party, there was no chance that a conservative would get the nod; if there were to be an "heir apparent"—an uncertainty, given the way Roosevelt coyly evaded the question—he was determined not to let a conservative near the nomination. In talks with Farley in July 1939 at Hyde Park, Roosevelt voiced bitterness against Tydings and point-blank said he was unacceptable.

Rank-and-file Democrats and Davies, Ickes, Wallace, and Joseph P. Kennedy were keen for Roosevelt; but on Capitol Hill and elsewhere in Washington, there was strong sentiment against a third term. Hull, Farley, and Garner—the conservative, sharp-tongued "chairman" of his own so-called Bureau of Education—would have none of it. Garner openly worked to block such a move. He met with Farley in February 1940 along with a sizable number of Democratic senators willing to fight to the last ditch to stop Roosevelt: Tydings, Glass, Byrd, Clark, George, Ellison D. Smith of South Carolina, Frederick Van Nuys of Indiana, and Alva Adams of Colorado. United in the goal of saving the party from defeat—none of them believed Roosevelt could win—they would fight in different ways.

Tydings and Wheeler would come to Chicago as favorite sons; Byrd and Glass would pledge Virginia's slate to Hull; Farley and Garner eventually would declare as candidates and try to pick up delegates in the primaries. If they could command enough votes to stop a first-round Roosevelt draft, the party would have a chance. The Washington *Times–Herald* noted that the " 'Stop Roosevelt' Democrats planned to prevent a stampede to the President . . . by urging State delegations to cast more than the customary few complimentary votes for native-son or other favored candidates." In the effort to manipulate Roosevelt into not running, there even was talk of a third-party ticket. The press saw Garner, Tydings, Glass, and Byrd as the most viable leaders of such a movement.

Tydings had no desire to bolt for a third party. Although flattered to be considered, he knew the likelihood of winning the Democratic nomination was small. He would eagerly have accepted had lightning struck and the convention drafted him as a compromise candidate, but his run for the presidency in 1940 was less a genuine quest for the office than a crusade to stop Roosevelt.

The Tydings-for-President movement got off the ground in August 1939 when the Calvert Club of Baltimore endorsed him. Although he denied it constituted an official announcement on his part, he acknowledged that he approved of the action. His secretary told reporters, "Members of the [Calvert Club] called on the Senator last week and asked him if he had any objections if they gave him a boost for the presidency. Senator Tydings said he appreciated their interest in his behalf and that he had no objections." But, she emphasized, he wanted it understood that he was not initiating the move. "He certainly is not announcing his candidacy for the presidential nomination."

The political community read it as a deft anti-Roosevelt maneuver: He was asserting leadership to nail down Maryland's delegation as a contingent bound to a favorite son. Once in Chicago, Tydings could use his votes to bargain or trade with the other delegations and candidates lined up against Roosevelt. Maryland's official strategy would not be set until the Democratic state convention in May;

but, with his 1938 victory fresh in people's minds, Tydings was in a position to dominate the convention and control the delegation.

The 1940 political situation in Maryland involved more than presidential politics. Senator George Radcliffe, up for reelection, had been challenged by prominent banker Howard Bruce, DNC-man from Maryland since 1924. Bruce had the backing of Governor Herbert O'Conor, a potential rival for Tydings's seat in 1944. Tydings, mindful of Radcliffe's support in 1938, reciprocated. Radcliffe trounced Bruce. O'Conor's position in the state convention was weakened as Tydings's was strengthened.

The Baltimore *Sun*'s Thomas O'Neill (who declared Tydings the "author" of Radcliffe's "sweeping victory") said that Tydings and his allies—Baltimore Mayor Howard Jackson and Radcliffe—would control the convention. As no Democrat had entered the state primary (New York Governor Tom Dewey had entered the Republican primary), the Democratic state convention held the power to instruct delegates on how to cast Maryland's 16 votes.

It was not a given that Tydings could call the shots. He needed peace between the Radcliffe and Bruce factions; not all state Democrats were "Stop Roosevelt" Democrats. Brooke Lee, William Preston Lane, and O'Conor—knowing Roosevelt had at least 700 votes sewn up—threatened to split the convention, saying it was futile to bind themselves with "an iron-clad pledge" to vote for Tydings without provision for a third-term movement. James A. Newell of the Baltimore *News–Post* wrote, "Conviction is growing among some of the Maryland Democrats that Roosevelt will be drafted for a third term nomination, and they don't want to be in the position of trying to stem Niagara with a straw."

After protracted jockeying, the delegation adopted its resolution, authored in part by Tydings: Delegates were instructed to cast Maryland's 16 votes for Tydings except in the event that "the President should elect to accept the nomination to the third term," in which case they were free to vote "for whomever they choose." Tydings was named delegation chairman—showing unmistakably that he dominated the convention. The New York *Times* declared: "THIRD-TERM FOES CLINCH MARYLAND."

The special Tydings-for-President train, its rear observation platform festooned with star-studded bunting and pennants and posters, pulled out of Baltimore on July 13, 1940. But the Stop-Roosevelt movement was all but dead in its tracks because of two ineluctable factors: the growing "Draft Roosevelt" movement, and the worsening international crisis. The "phony war" in Europe had ended in May 1940 with Hitler's Panzer divisions' devastating rout of Belgium, Holland, Denmark, and France. Frightened Americans credited Roosevelt with keeping the United States out of the war, giving him a powerful boost.

Roosevelt, as evasive and cagey as the proverbial sly fox, never answered questions about whether he would run. From November 1936 until balloting began in Chicago in July 1940, he kept everyone guessing—including, some suspected, himself. Senator Wheeler told Eleanor Tydings in 1939 that he had "asked a man close to the president whether FDR would run again next year and the man said, 'Missy LeHand doesn't know, Mrs. Roosevelt doesn't know, and I don't know, but this I can tell you. Whenever we have discussed the half dozen leading candidates with FDR he has vetoed them all and he says, "of course, in the event of a war, all bets are off." ' "

Indeed, Roosevelt subtly or openly found fault with everyone, including his alleged favorites: Harry Hopkins, Solicitor General Robert Jackson, and Frank Murphy. He was deemed jealous of Farley's and Hull's popularity; and although publicly he encouraged Hull to run, eventually he responded blandly to mention of either in connection with the nomination. He favored no liberal and was death on Tydings, Garner, Wheeler, and other conservatives. Gradually it became clear there was to be no "heir apparent." He kept everyone in the dark until the convention was under way and he was "drafted" by his party.[2]

In Chicago, Wheeler withdrew, seeing that Roosevelt had it wrapped up; but Farley, Garner, and Tydings held firm. When Tydings was nominated, Farley later wrote, "there was a cheer, not a loud one, but Tydings had had the courage to voice his opposition." When it was over, Farley received 72½ votes, Garner 61, Tydings 9½, and Hull 5⅔—votes against the principle of a third term—while Roosevelt swept the first ballot with 946½ votes.[3]

Roosevelt's choice of Henry Wallace—an ex-Republican from Iowa—for vice-president was unpopular. Many agreed with Tydings that Jesse Jones or Sam Rayburn—"real Democrats"—would be better, and feared a party split resulting in defeat. Garner bolted for Texas to "just go fishing." Tydings, Glass, George, Smith, Clark, and Wheeler were seen as potential noncampaigners, if not bolters. A number of noncongressional Democrats came out for Republican Wendell Wilkie: former Director of the Budget Lewis Douglas, former Chairman of the Democratic National Committee Vance C. McCormack, former Senator James A. Reed of Missouri, and former Undersecretary of Treasury John W. Hanes.

Wayne Cole, in *Roosevelt and the Isolationists*, stated flatly, "Without Hitler there would have been no third term." Farley and George Gallup suggested as much at the time. Gallup in February 1940 wrote that the way to a third term was war. Farley's records of conversations frequently noted, that should an "unforeseen situation . . . develop abroad," Roosevelt would run—in spite of many private promises to the contrary.

Tydings was nauseated by the hyprocrisy and spectacle of the convention. During the "spontaneous" demonstration for Roosevelt, he had grimly clung to his Maryland banner—unlit cigar clenched in his teeth—as those surging about the floor indiscriminately grabbed banners and dragged unwilling delegates into the parade. Eleanor, enraged at an enormous red-headed man from Boston who kept trying to sweep her into the parade, hauled off and slugged him when he grabbed her by the waist to pull her down from the Maryland box. The famous "voice from the sewer" roared, "WE WANT ROOSEVELT"—over and over again.

Tydings's disgust over the sham draft was never voiced, even in private. His wife believed only his "iron self-control" prevented him from expressing his outrage. Publicly, before the convention crowd, he said, "Some of us in Maryland have stood out for a great principle of democracy. It was a fair fight and we lost. It is overwhelmingly evident that this convention wishes the renomination of President Roosevelt. We bow to your wishes and cast the 16 votes of Maryland for President Roosevelt."

But some observers noticed his anguish—saw him holding on for dear life lest his banner be carried off after half of his delegation (including Brooke Lee) deserted him. Louis Azrael wrote in the Baltimore *News-Post*, "And so, hurt but unable to fight, the dominant figure in Maryland politics stood before his friends and subordinates like a dismayed child, hurt, embarrassed, trying not to show it. . . . I could not help feeling sorry for him. And so, I suspect, did even those who stood and told him 'no.' "

Tydings returned to Maryland aboard his special train. "I'll have to go back and think things through quietly and seriously," he told reporters. His dilemma—whether or not to bolt, campaign for Radcliffe and "the Democratic ticket," or actively support Roosevelt—became a hot topic in local political circles. When there was talk that he would back Wilkie, he said, "Pure surmise." When news columns announced his emminent endorsement of Roosevelt, he dismissed them as "pure speculation. I said everything I had to say four or five days ago." His reference was to a cryptic, no-name statement of his position: "I am a Democrat, have always been a Democrat, have been greatly honored by the Democratic party, and I intend to remain a Democrat." He would have "nothing further to say on the subject," he added.

When he was thrown together with Roosevelt in an awkward tour of defense plants, the journalists reveled in reporting the story. He agreed to go because the trip was billed as a "non-political" tour of defense facilities. Roosevelt met Tydings's stiff greeting with a "Hello, Millard"; and for the greater part of the 117-mile journey (with a 30-car entourage), the two shared the backseat of an open limousine (Governor O'Conor sat between them) as Radcliffe faced the president. Roosevelt, reporters wrote, spoke to the group as a whole or just to Radcliffe after acknowledging Tydings's presence.

If Roosevelt hoped the meeting would lead to endorsement, he was wrong. Asked if the ride implied support for Roosevelt, Tydings replied, "I have made no statement in support of the third term. . . . My trip with the President was at his invitation, said to be on the Nation's business, and so far as I was concerned, that is all there was to the entire situation." For the rest of the campaign he supported Radcliffe, the Democratic party, "the ticket," but never mentioned Roosevelt's name. Eleanor came out for Wilkie. Other Democrats also suffered dislocations of loyalty. Garner remained in "virtual seclusion." Cotton Ed Smith was said to be "sulking on his plantation," and George was pictured as "not lifting a finger." Byrd and Glass did not "bolt," but passively supported "the nominee of the convention."

It was a romp for Democrats nationwide (Roosevelt, carrying 38 states, won 54 percent of the vote), and it was a romp in Maryland for the Democratic slate. Roosevelt had a 115,000 vote majority over Wilkie. But Radcliffe defeated former Governor Harry W. Nice by 185,000 votes, prompting the *Sun* to note that his victory surpassed all but one in the history of the state: 1938 when Tydings won by more than 200,000 votes.

New Dealers everywhere were angry with Tydings. But he believed he had followed the only course he could and still retain his integrity. Azrael, in remarking on the difficult choice he had faced wrote, "Millard Tydings tries hard to be intellectually honest and politically courageous. He succeeds much more than most politicians."

Columnist Ray Tucker had noted in 1939 that Roosevelt needed the support of conservatives if his foreign policy goals were to be met. But Tydings remained as independent as ever when it came to the president's "aid-short-of-war" policies. The struggle over neutrality intensified during the summer of 1940 as isolationists and noninterventionists came to view aid-short-of-war as deliberate steps toward war. From August 1940, when the "destroyers deal" upped the ante, until the devastating Japanese attack on Pearl Harbor, the debate raged. Isolationists would do anything to keep the United States out of a war they did not believe was America's fight. Interventionists, convinced the country must fight, worked incessantly to shape public opinion and propel the administration into action before Britain went down to defeat.

Tydings was in between. He held no brief for the isolationist view, but was unwilling to sanction steps he believed provocative until the military was better prepared. He sometimes was with the president, sometimes opposed—depending on the issue, its implications, and the method. He was especially wary of actions he thought would ignite the fuse, and the destroyers deal was just such an action. The idea of supplying destroyers to Britain originated with Winston Churchill, the empire's new prime minister. With German bombs raining fire on London, and with Britain's fleet of destroyers reduced by half from U-boat attacks, Britain needed U.S. help. Churchill pleaded with Roosevelt to part with 50 or more "overage" World

War I destroyers to keep the wolf packs at bay. If Britain could not control the seas to keep desperately needed military supplies steaming into port, all could be lost—and the United States might find itself directly at risk.

Roosevelt knew that giving Britain 50 destroyers (a proposal he had rejected once before) would arouse powerful opposition. The ships might prove vital to U.S. defense; if Britain went down, the Nazis might capture and use them. Leasing warships to a nation at war might violate international law. The move also would require congressional action. Roosevelt devised a deal to offer Churchill—destroyers for bases—bypassing Congress. Attorney General Robert Jackson obtained certification from the military that the ships were not essential to security (because bases were of greater value). Churchill promised that Britain's fleet never would be surrendered or scuttled—would be sent to Canada to fight on, if necessary. Roosevelt's September 3 announcement of the deal stirred the nation.

Supporters hailed the bargain as audacious statesmanship. Tydings and other critics considered the action reckless authoritarianism and exclaimed that he had defied the prerogatives of Congress, violated international law, and endangered the navy, thus imperiling security. The transfer of planes to Britain that had been approved by Congress in June (with Tydings's support) was inadequate precedent. It took only months to replace a plane but three or four years to build a destroyer, Tydings pointed out angrily; aid-short-of-war in general, and the destroyers deal in particular, were both dangerous. Taking belligerent action while one's army was in "a pathetic state" was like holding up someone "with an empty gun when the other person knows its empty," he warned. And he objected to Roosevelt's method—voicing the pretense of neutrality as he made an unneutral move. "I would rather be all the way in it than connive to be in it," he shouted in protest.

What worried Republicans and conservative Democrats was the age-old dilemma: executive versus congressional power. If Roosevelt could rationalize the destroyers deal, what was to stop him from making other arrangements—even declaring war—without consulting Congress? Tydings believed that Roosevelt had exceeded the limits of executive power. His method of sidestepping Congress was not well received by some who backed aid-short-of-war. Wilkie, a staunch interventionist, berated the president for committing "the most dictatorial and arbitrary act of any president in the history of the United States."

Tydings's opposition to the destroyers deal and the principle of aid-short-of-war was not motivated by animus toward the president. In almost all other foreign policy matters he backed the administration—voting for aid to Finland, to fortify Guam, to expand the Panama Canal, to increase appropriations for the army, and in support of a Selective Service bill. The New York *Times* credited him with the best argument for conscription: "I would rather have it and not need it, than need it and not have it." He was considered the leading proponent of a big navy. In the Naval Affairs Committee, where he ranked second, he overpowered its chairman, isolationist Senator David I. Walsh of Massachusetts. Tydings led the debate for a $3.5 billion expansion program that Chief of Naval Operations Admiral Harold R. Stark testified was vital. "Unless we go ahead," Tydings said, "we may get caught some day sitting in the Senate scared to death because a big naval battle is going on and we hadn't provided a Navy large enough." Two bills, passed four months apart in 1940, together increased the navy by 25 percent.

Although Tydings sympathized with Britain and voted for planes and war supplies to be sent there, he still believed the United States must not be drawn prematurely into the war. He opposed confirmation of Frank Knox as secretary of the navy and Henry Stimson as secretary of the army on grounds that their interventionist views might provoke war before the army, navy, and their air branches were ready. "Today the main thing for the country to do is to prepare, to prepare, to prepare, to prepare," he exclaimed. "I am going to be a realist so long as I'm walking around in a realistic world."

Throughout the spring he worked on an issue intimately linked with defense: paying for it. He argued for new taxes "all down the line" to meet the costs of pending armament programs. He called the federal deficit a "sixth column" menace. "It seems clear," he said, "that our front line of defense lies not upon the banks of the Rhine, nor the battlefields of Europe, nor upon the wide bosom of the Atlantic ocean, but within the marble walls of our National Treasury." Roosevelt was not thrilled with Tydings's promotion of a "pay-as-you-go" program. He emasculated Tydings's mandatory cuts amendment. The *Sun* was disgusted: "[Roosevelt] has no stomach for such unpleasant duties as cutting expenses." But the emergency tax bill, without Tydings's amendment, passed 75 to 5. Although Tydings called the final bill "inadequate," it was the largest peacetime tax increase in U.S. history, enacted to fund the largest peacetime defense buildup.

In 1941, when Roosevelt proposed the Lend Lease program, Tydings's first reaction was full support. But isolationists in and out of Congress labeled the measure the "War Dictatorship Bill." With the goal of winning over the Senate's most powerful noninterventionist voices, Wheeler, the leader of the opposition, exploited fears that Roosevelt would use Lend Lease as a means for accumulating power—power to do anything he wanted, including transferring warships to the British Navy. Wheeler's arguments made Tydings reassess. He was for the idea, he said, but not for a bill "that would permit the President to give away our Navy."

Tydings supported an amendment proposed by Walsh that forbade disposing of any unit of the navy unless it could be replaced within six months. No one knew the future, he warned. The French and English had made "solemn agreement that neither one of them—never, never, never, never, never—would make a separate peace with Germany. . . . Yet I lived to see the British Fleet fire on the French Fleet . . . and there on the northern coast of Africa, in the harbor of Oran, lies the flower, the finest ships, of the French Navy, sent to the bottom by British guns," he said. But after forcing his colleagues to consider what they were doing, Tydings voted with the administration on all amendments—save the one by Walsh—and for final passage of Lend Lease.

Tydings's stand against the destroyers deal, votes against Knox and Stimson, and caution on Lend Lease won him new enemies. *PM* magazine, which detested his labor record, wrote that in foreign policy he was "neither fish nor fowl. He co-operates privately with . . . isolationists but pays lip service publicly to the cause of aid to Britain." He was assailed from both sides—for supporting interventionist policies and for obstructing efforts to deal with a grave international crisis. His patriotism was questioned. Bewildered, he exclaimed in frustration that he was at a loss to know how so much misinformation could be spread and believed about him.

His major defection from administration policy came in opposition to revision of the Neutrality Act in November 1941. Roosevelt sought a bill authorizing merchant ships to arm and carry goods into combat zones and belligerent ports. An unarmed merchant ship, the *Robin Moor,* had been sunk in May (without loss of life— the U-boat commander ordered crew and passengers into lifeboats before firing). Later, when three U.S. destroyers were attacked by German submarines, Roosevelt used the incidents as justification for revision. On September 4, the *Greer* was fired on by two torpedoes (they missed); another submarine killed 11 men on the *Kearny* on October 17; the *Reuben James* was sunk by the Germans October 31, with great loss of life.

Roosevelt used the *Greer* assault to implement a "shoot-on-sight" policy in the Atlantic. In a speech to the American people on September 11, he claimed the U-boat fired without provocation. Interventionists leaped to take advantage of the three events, hoping they would incite the public into accepting the need to go to war. Shoot-on-sight was, in effect, a declaration of naval war on Germany. Revision of the Neutrality Act undoubtedly would provoke further incidents.

Tydings was undecided initially on revision. But through his position on the Naval Affairs Committee, he learned the circumstances surrounding the attacks. The *Greer* had been following the German submarine for hours in cooperation with a Royal Air Force bomber—radioing its location—and was fired on only after the British plane dropped depth charges. The *Kearny,* on active convoy patrol, dropped depth charges over a pack of U-boats attacking the convoy. The *Reuben James,* summoned from one convoy to another under attack by submarines, was aiding the convoy when fired on. Roosevelt's public claim that the destroyers had been fired on unprovoked was not true.

He waited until the last day of the tumultuous debate before unveiling his anger. In a dramatic speech on the floor, he accused Roosevelt of "lack of candor with the American people" for dealing in "deception, misinformation, and a withholding of the facts." The United States, he charged, "whether rightly or wrongly, was the aggressor in all three cases." The revision was a sham, "conceived in deceit, born in intrigue and reared in camouflage." A vote for revision, he claimed, was a vote for war. The president's protests that he was trying to stay out of war was "the epitome of disingenuousness." He had "snapped his fingers at this body" and ordered the navy to shoot on sight, Tydings shouted, and "now we have an Executive war, not a national war."

Tydings voted on November 7 to arm merchant vessels in light of what had happened to the *Robin Moor,* but he refused to vote to allow merchant ships in combat zones and belligerent ports. One month later (to the day), however, his concern over military preparedness and Roosevelt's propensity for the slick maneuver was rendered academic by the Japanese Empire's sneak attack at Pearl Harbor. On Sunday December 7, 1941, Tydings and Eleanor descended from the train at Aberdeen station near Oakington at midafternoon, returning from a luncheon at Tregaron, Joe Davies's Washington estate. Oakington's manager, Bob Livingstone, was waiting in an agitated state. He told them what had happened. Tydings could not believe it. Livingstone turned on the car radio.

On Monday morning the Naval Affairs Committee learned the extent of destruction.[4] Tydings's hard-fought struggle for a two-ocean navy seemed wasted—the heart of the Pacific fleet lay in twisted, smoking wreckage. There was but one comforting fact: The 15 cruisers he had fought for in 1929 came through mostly unscathed. They were an important part of the badly diminished forces standing between Japan and the California coast.

After the committee meeting, Tydings briefly spoke for the membership to reporters. "I am shocked and stunned and the situation is extremely grave," he said quietly. He and the others looked "long-faced and tight-lipped," the reporters wrote. In floor debate over initiating a probe of what went wrong, he made strong pleas for discretion and confidence in the president. There was "no doubt in my mind that the Japanese do not know definitely how much damage they have done," he said. It would be best to forget the recent political strife and gird for the war they now were committed to.

Roosevelt addressed Congress: "Yesterday, December 7, 1941—a date which will live in infamy—the United States of

America was suddenly and deliberately attacked by the naval and air forces of the Empire of Japan." He asked the assembly for a declaration of war. Reporters clamored for Tydings's reaction. "I have no word of criticism," he replied. The president had said precisely what needed to be said.

During World War II the role of Congress in foreign policy matters was largely attenuated. Roosevelt was commander in chief. The compelling demands of war required his attention, and the secrecy and urgency involved made consultation with a body as unwieldy as Congress untenable. Thus he operated primarily within the framework of the executive branch, establishing new departments and agencies as necessary. Until issues concerning postwar needs emerged, Congress dealt mainly with matters of budget, appropriation, labor strikes, industrial mobilization, conscription, and waste in government.

Concerned with accelerating the war effort, Tydings was one of a few senators who translated ideas into action. Harry S Truman of Missouri formed his famous "watchdog" committee to investigate defense industry profiteering, and Tydings established a committee in early 1942 to convert the government to wartime and streamline the federal bureaucracy. He intended to determine how employees in nonwar agencies could profitably be transferred to war agencies to prune the "Federal jungle."

"I am dissatisfied with the prosecution of this war . . . with the waste of public money on programs which have nothing to do with national defense. There is too much rhetoric and not enough action," he said in a radio speech. The Brookings Institution helped him develop a 26-page questionnaire designed to uncover duplication, waste, and inefficiency, and he sent copies to 2,500 department heads nationwide. What he found so incensed him that he sputtered, "I think we ought to make one great appropriation to import a lot of squirrels so that they can consume some of the nuts that are running around loose here in Washington." He went after the Office of Civil Defense for having Disney films and fan dancer Sally Rand as part of a physical fitness program—such "frills and furbelows" were sheer "boondoggling." The slogan coined: "Billions for defense, but not one buck for Donald Duck."

His efforts were praised and reviled. Arthur Krock credited him with playing a leading role in ensuring a sound economy in anticipation of the postwar period. Damon Runyon and the *Sun*'s Frank Kent supported his ideas. But the liberal *PM* regarded his "flyspeck" activities as a disguised attack on liberal agencies. And Drew Pearson could not resist crowing that Tydings was as guilty as his targets: One reply required 19 pounds of paper and cost $8,196, all to discover that there was waste in government. Pearson concluded, "Close intimates of Senator Tydings have made no secret of their idea that Millard's present move for economy was the right springboard for his sub rosa campaign for the presidency in 1944." The White House also took notice. Roosevelt's secretary, Marvin McIntyre, passed on a letter from Gardner Jackson of the Department of Agriculture, saying, "I don't know whether you want to take the trouble to read this or not." The last page said,

> When I tell you that Millard Tydings is planning a very subtle and major campaign against the Administration, using the military reverses and their impact on the public mind as his springboard you will not be surprised. From reliable sources I am told that Tydings told a group of his closest friends . . . that he has had confidential communication with McArthur [sic] through a newspaperman in Hawaii who is an intimate friend of both and that McArthur has told Tydings, "Keep it up." Tydings . . . told his associates that if McArthur is captured the effect on American public opinion will be so great that he (Tydings) and "the Army crowd" will be able to take over the running of the war and drive all of the Roosevelt people out of control. This sounds fantastic but I have made checks which confirm a portion of the pattern.

It was highly unlikely that MacArthur—confined to the rock of Corregidor in Manila Bay by the military might of Japan, desperate to save men besieged at Bataan—had time for political conspiracies with Tydings. There was no love lost between the general and the senator—ambitious men mistrustful of each other's role in the Philippines. Such White House paranoia no doubt abounded because Roosevelt detested Tydings as much as ever and because his committee was popular despite criticism. To preempt him, Roosevelt issued an order on federal manpower: The Civil Service Commission would transfer personnel by executive order. Tydings's bill authorizing mandatory shifts of personnel from peacetime to wartime agencies became superfluous.

Newspapers across the country and some indignant senators, including Tydings, noted that Congress itself was in danger of becoming superfluous. Chesley Manly of the Washington *Times–Herald* described defiance on the Hill: "Many members have charged that there is a concerted campaign to reduce Congress to the impotent status of Hitler's Reichstag." The Providence (Rhode Island) *Journal* expressed alarm over "the transfer of power to the President" and concluded, "The Tydings Committee report should be required reading." In fact, the first edition of the 58-page pamphlet became available on July 20, 1942, and was snapped up by nightfall.

Tydings's probe of the bureaucracy was widely viewed as the beginning of a congressional attempt to reassert independence. By congressional fiat it eliminated New Deal agencies, with Tydings arguing that their machinery could be put to more productive uses in war agencies and industries. But Roosevelt, through creation of new departments and bureaus, built up a bureaucracy that made the old New Deal "alphabetical monstrosities" pale in comparison: the Office of Production Management; Office of Economic Stabilization; of War Mobilization; of Petroleum Administration; of War Information; of Strategic Services; of Price Administration; of Science Research and Development; and the War Industries Board, War Production Board, War Maritime Commission, War Labor Board—it was enough to make any good conservative swoon.

Roosevelt's 1943 budget—a $109 billion "total war" budget—stunned everyone. Tydings demanded "close scrutiny" of each item. After the massive budget passed, he went on a pay-as-you-go tax rampage. Although Congress passed the Current Tax Payments Act in June, and the Tax Revenue Act of 1943 (overriding a Roosevelt veto), it made no other efforts to raise taxes for the duration of the war. Tydings judged the two measures inadequate. The cost of the war was being met by borrowing, and he feared that the postwar period would usher in another depression. As he continued the committee's work, he was regarded as a man looking ahead, thinking about the postwar federal power structure. Congress, he believed, must be prominent and must never—not in wartime or peacetime—surrender its duties, rights, or power.

Looking ahead to 1944, Tydings did not like what he saw as it gradually became evident that Roosevelt was planning to run again. Determined to stop him, he and a number of conservatives put their views on record: Roosevelt endangered the tripartite system of government as he steamrollered Congress, endlessly expanded the bureaucracy, and damaged future economic stability by running up a staggering deficit. And he was extending dangerously the power of centralized government in contravention of states' rights.

Although conservative Democrats (and Republicans) opposed a fourth term, it was clear that, as long as the country was at war, people would be unwilling "to change horses in mid-stream." And unlike the precedent-breaking third term, the idea of a fourth generated little controversy. The New York *Journal & American* noted in 1943 that there was "talk in Democratic Congressional cloak-rooms of booming Senator Byrd or Senator Tydings as 'stop Roosevelt' candidates, along with James A. Farley of New York." A hardcore group of conservatives did their best to drum up support for such a movement but made little headway. When a *Colliers* article mentioned Tydings among potential candidates and used the slogan "The Tide Runs for Tydings," he laughed, "But he [the writer] didn't say whether it was coming in or going out."

He did not try to control the Maryland delegation to the 1944 Democratic National Convention in Chicago or force it to oppose Roosevelt. Up for reelection himself, although not overly worried, he did not want to detract from his own campaign. Still, Marylanders like O'Conor and Jackson cared deeply about states' rights. Under their direction, the delegation declined to endorse a fourth term. But a week before the convention, when Roosevelt announced he would accept another term, O'Conor and Radcliffe said they would support it. Tydings was again in a tough spot. He opposed a fourth term; but since he had to run on the same ticket, he decided to remain mute.

In Chicago, while delegates cast their ballots (Farley got one vote, Byrd 89, Roosevelt 1,066), Tydings absented himself, saying he had a "previous engagement." So weak was enthusiasm among

Maryland delegates that only four of them joined the parade celebrating Roosevelt's renomination. The real fight was over the vice-
presidency. Henry Wallace was extremely unpopular. Maryland del-
egates decided to vote for O'Conor on the first ballot to see how
things shaped up. When the first round proved inconclusive—
Wallace led with Harry Truman, William Bankhead, and Alben
Barkley trailing—Tydings huddled with O'Conor, Radcliffe, and
Brooke Lee. They decided to back Truman. The announcement of
Maryland's 18 votes for Truman turned the tide as Southern and
"Bourbon" Democrats united behind him on the second ballot.

In Maryland, despite opposition from labor, leftists, and New
Dealers, Tydings had smooth sledding. In the primary he defeated
his ardent New Deal opponent, Willis R. Jones, four to one. In the
general election he faced a New Deal Republican named Blanchard
Randall, Jr.—considered the weakest candidate that party could have
fielded. With Republicans hopelessly split—they preferred Tydings
to the liberal Randall, and many courted him in hopes that he would
support Republicans Thomas E. Dewey and John W. Bricker—and
with New Deal Democrats dispirited by Tydings's obvious clout,
interest in the senatorial campaign dwindled.

The presidential race in Maryland, on the other hand, was
rough. Jackson refused to endorse Roosevelt, and sentiment among
states' righters was so strong that many prominent Baltimore County
Democrats bolted the party to form an organization called "Democrats for Dewey." Tydings sidestepped their efforts to woo him, and
by mid-October the Democrats for Dewey had pledged support to
the full Democratic slate. Yet Tydings declined to comment about
Roosevelt—a delicate and questionable endeavor. A *Sun* editorial
titled "Senator Tydings in Tortuous Channel" examined his predicament and concluded, "A man publicly engaged in such feats of
avoidance never looks very strong or very dignified." Still, as in
1940, he never uttered the president's name. He campaigned as a
Democrat, urged all Democrats to support the ticket, and ran on his
record of independence and on the need to "win the war, win the
peace, bring the soldiers home quickly."

Roosevelt's chances in Maryland were considered no better than
fifty-fifty. Tydings was seen as a sure bet. But the president squeaked
out a 316,000 to 293,000 victory in Maryland—a narrower margin

than in 1936 when he defeated Alf Landon by 95,000 votes. Nationally he received 53 percent of the vote, carrying all but 12 states. Tydings smashed Randall 344,000 to 213,000—but his tally, too, was slimmer than the 204,000 margin over Oscar Leser in 1938. Still, he won convincingly while Roosevelt barely eked by.

Tydings's theme—"win the war, win the peace, bring the soldiers home quickly"—contained a phrase that captured a sense of what was to come: "win the peace." The challenge (and later terror) implied ultimately concentrated the attention and energy of Congress, the president, and people and leaders everywhere. After the war, as world conditions grew increasingly unpredictable and posed greater difficulties, "winning" the peace took on both economic and military definitions. In the East and the West, Cold War tactics and weapons contradicted a vocabulary ostensibly dedicated to peace.

Earlier Tydings's main concerns had been budgetary, naval, and political—to contain spending, strengthen the navy, keep liberal Democrats in check. The war forced all Americans to think globally. Although Tydings played no role in establishing the United Nations, he backed the 1943 resolution that put the United States on record in support of an international peacekeeping authority.

Several specific events had irrevocable effects on his attitude toward the postwar world: a mission to the war-ravaged Philippines in May 1945; the singular experience of witnessing a terrifying new force in the universe at Bikini Atoll in June 1946; and stopovers in Okinawa, Tokyo, Athens, Rome, Berlin, and Potsdam as he returned from Philippine independence ceremonies in July. "Ruin! Everywhere!" he wrote in a journal he kept on the month-long journey in 1946. His determination to help resolve postwar dilemmas became a commitment of such magnitude that he gradually redefined his priorities and his Senate career shifted in a new direction.

Franklin Roosevelt died on April 12, 1945, a month after Tydings wrote him recommending a mission to the Philippines to spur rehabilitation. Tydings had learned that the Filipinos, enduring a catastrophic situation, needed American assistance desperately. Roosevelt agreed, but died before initiating action. When Truman took office, he made Tydings his special envoy to the Philippines, to assess the destruction and report on rehabilitation and independence.

What awaited him in Manila made a profound impact. The Philippines he remembered was gone. The devastation was beyond description.[5] Nothing he had witnessed in World War I prepared him for what he saw on every street in the old Intramuros section of Manila. The contrast between bustling wartime Washington and graceful Honolulu, where he stopped to study materials on the Philippines, was grotesque. Perhaps what lay ahead was foreshadowed by his visit to the royal mausoleum at Nuuanu where he placed a wreath of flowers on the tomb of Princess Kawananakoa. The last of the Hawaiian princesses had died on April 12—the same day as Roosevelt.

He stayed only a week in Manila, cutting short a planned month-long study as the conditions he found—the ruins, hunger, homelessness, the pockets of Japanese resistance throughout Luzon—demanded urgent action. He worked 16-hour days, conferring with MacArthur, Filipino President Manuel Osmeña, and trade experts, and then hastened home, flying 22 hours a day for three days, landing only for fuel, so he could report to Truman. They had only one year before the promised independence to develop revised long-range trade legislation and put in place programs to help the Filipinos rebuild.

Tydings gave Truman a verbal report and then, in a poignant speech to the Senate that won a rare standing ovation, described in harrowing detail the conditions in Manila. "Fighting took place from street to street, from house to house, from floor to floor, from room to room from one end of the city to the other." Bridges, docks, boats, buses, trains, trucks, homes, livestock, grain, food, currency, medicine, and communication, water, and electric systems—nothing in central Manila was left untouched. The extent of destruction was unimaginable, he said.

He described individual acts of courage and loyalty by the Filipinos that had saved thousands of Americans and shortened the war. "It is stated . . . without a single contradiction, that there is not a known case of an American refugee, an airman forced down on the islands, or a fleeing soldier whom the Filipinos did not hide, feed, and shelter, and on numerous occasions they planned and made successful his escape," he said. "Quite frequently Filipinos were tortured and sometimes shot, but not once did they give away any Americans." The emotion he felt was expressed in a compassionate appeal for a gift of $100 million to help rehabilitate and reconstruct the islands. "We would be a heartless and unappreciative nation if we did not recognize the dire straits of the Filipino people as a result of the fighting with the Japanese," he said. The United States had a moral obligation.

After unfortunate delays in a Congress overwhelmed by postwar problems, in spring 1946 the Bell Trade Act and the Tydings Rehabilitation Act were passed. Representative Jasper C. Bell's legislation provided for eight years of free trade and a gradual 20-year tariff increase; in 1974 the Philippines would reach 100-percent tariff. Tydings's plan provided $620 million in compensation: $100 million in surplus American property; $120 million to restore services and repair public property; and $400 million for distribution to enterprises and individuals who could prove they had suffered war damage.

It was threatening rain in Manila the morning of July 4, 1946, as Tydings, MacArthur, and Paul McNutt, U.S. high commissioner to the Philippines, arrived for the independence ceremony. The grim residue of war was visible everywhere. MacArthur's arrival stirred excitement in the vast crowd gathered, and Tydings was greeted with prolonged applause. He was the opening speaker as history recorded the first postwar transfer of power to a former possession. Many onlookers had tears in their eyes.

"It is a great day," Tydings said, for "freedom all over the earth." A new nation would take its place in the community of nations. But even as the political bonds were cut, he said, bonds of friendship would endure: "Though our governments may sever ties which for a half a century bound us together, our governments can never alter or repeal the history of Bataan and Corregidor, of Leyte, of Lingayen Gulf and Manila."

It began to rain after he finished; and by the time the American flag was lowered, the tropical downpour had drenched both it and the weeping crowd. As the red and blue flag of the Philippines— with its yellow sun on a field of white—was raised by the new Filipino president, Manuel Roxas, the sky cleared and the sun emerged. A blast of factory whistles and a twenty-one gun salute from the U.S. Seventh Fleet riding in Manila Bay broke the intensity of the moment. Roxas stepped up to the microphone and said, "The flag which was first raised in conquest here has been hauled down with even greater glory."

A few days earlier Tydings had witnessed another event that also symbolized a beginning, but of a very different nature. His flight to the Philippines set down on Kwajalein Island, a speck of land in the Pacific, 240 miles southeast of a tiny crescent-shaped atoll called Bikini. He witnessed the first public test of the atomic bomb—the fourth to be detonated. In a journal he brought along, he put his apprehension in writing: "Not only is the atomic bomb destined to change the entire concept of warfare but the long range bombers, guided missile, bacteriological warfare all threaten humanity with destruction. . . . We must find a substitute for war. In the meantime, of course, must keep prepared in case no substitute is found."

The sky above Kwajalein that evening was, he wrote, "indescribably lovely. Reds, greens, blues, aquamarines, pinks all splash the clouds and sky." While he and Stuart Symington (the assistant secretary of war for air, who had come to observe) watched the colors fade, someone pointed out a bomber—a B-29—under heavy guard just off the runway near the sea. It was already loaded with the bomb. "A beautiful sunset at one end of Kwajalein and a demonical contrivance at the other," Tydings wrote. "At the ends of the island God the creator at his best, and man the creator at his worst."

The next morning Tydings boarded a huge C-54 observer ship (nicknamed "Folklore One") and followed "Dave's Dream," the B-29 bearing "Gilda," to an eerie rendezvous with history. Over Bikini, high above its turquoise lagoon fringed with palms, 72 planes circled, stacked in soaring orbits ten miles wide, like enormous birds of prey. Below, 73 tethered ghost ships, prows to the wind, formed a spectral armada, with the battleship *Nevada*,—the principal target—painted bright red, guns painted white, so she would stand out at the bull's-eye. Anchored with her in that six-mile-wide display were the carriers *Saratoga* and *Independence*, the battleships *Arkansas, Pennsylvania, New York,* and three enemy ships—the German cruiser *Prinz Eugen,* the Japanese battleship *Nagato,* and the cruiser *Sakawa.* Some ships carried a bizarre cargo: 200 goats, some garbed in protective clothing, others partially shaved and smeared with ointment; 200 pigs; 3,000 caged rats and mice; thousands of fruit flies; and, on certain of the vessels, containers of flu virus and other lethal germs. High on steel towers on Bikini and the target ships, and aboard the circling B-29s, C-54s, Hellcat fighters, and B-17 drones, were 643 cameras set to shoot 50,000 still photographs and 1.5 million feet of film.

Tydings put on his Mae West, goggles, and parachute harness, and sat down on a little life raft attached to the harnesses. "Bomb away, bomb away, bomb away!" shouted the bombardier over the radio monitor, and then came the flash—a brilliant orb of fire. A tumbling tower of smoke rose instantly, high above the *Nevada,* reaching up seven or eight miles, its top a mushroom billowing "scores of circular folds like a Corinthian column," he scrawled in his journal in shaky handwritten pencil. He watched, transfixed, as the great cloud faded to nothing in perhaps 20 minutes.

The *Nevada* remained afloat, as did all but two unarmored transports. The *Independence,* closest to impact, sustained very heavy damage and a number of ships were on fire. A few goats were still alive. Bikini's palm trees fluttered unharmed. Later a destroyer and two transports sank. Red drone planes, sent through the radioactive cloud to measure its intensity, returned to their bases. The test tower on Bikini literally had evaporated.

Tydings flew to Manila while Symington stayed on. What they had witnessed horrified them. When Symington caught up with Tydings they had time to talk as they flew from Japan (where they visited Hiroshima and Nagasaki) to China, French Indochina, Thailand, India, Trans-Jordan, Egypt, and, finally, Europe. Symington saw that the explosion and its lethal message had made a "stunning impression" on Tydings, and came to understand the link between Tydings's military experience and his determination to work for a world without weapons or war. "Tydings was a combat man, a fighter, with many decorations for courage," Symington explained years later. "I have found in my lifetime perhaps the people most against war, except professional peaceniks, are military men who have actually seen the blood."

Tydings had seen the blood. Now he had seen Bikini—battleships rolled over like toys. When he returned home, moody and preoccupied, Eleanor was distressed at his visceral upset. "He was in such a state," she would recall later, "that I said, 'Look, I have to know what this is all about.'" He brought her literature unavailable to most people and what she read frightened her so that she confessed she was never entirely free of the fear.

Long before Bikini, Tydings had been concerned with disarmament, pleading for a world conference on disarmament throughout the 1930s. Then in October 1945 he was appointed to sit on the Senate Special Committee on Atomic Energy, chaired by Brien McMahon of Connecticut—a committee Truman had urged to shape legislation formulating national policy for development and control of such energy. Tydings and his fellow members took a course in nuclear physics at the National Bureau of Standards (to grasp the technical language and nature of atomic research and the problems peculiar to nuclear energy) and attended hearings where atomic scientists, military officials, and Cabinet members testified on the range of problems to be solved. The formidable quandary over international control of atomic weapons would be dealt with mainly elsewhere, but complex domestic aspects had to be defined and effected: the composition and duties of an atomic energy commission; policies for research (private and government); control of fissionable materials; security; issues of production, licensing and patents; and what role, if any, the military should play in administering a national atomic energy program.

Edward U. Condon of the Bureau of Standards became scientific adviser to the committee; the senators became his pupils. It was essential they realize that atomic energy was more than the bomb, that they not be so overwhelmed by fear of the weapon that they were unable to focus on other social, industrial, and scientific uses— applications of benefit to civilian welfare and quality of life, if properly developed and harnessed. Yet the implications of the atom as weapon were impossible to ignore. Tydings came home from the first hearings in November 1945 with a chilling description. The atmosphere inside the committee room, he told Eleanor, had been as gloomy and unnerving as the rain and the armed guards waiting outside. As one of the august scientists was leaving, a senator asked, "Tell me, Doctor, is it possible to blow up the earth?" The man paused at the door. "Why no, Senator." He hesitated only a moment before adding, "As of today."

McMahon's bill, S. 1717, was approved unanimously in committee and accepted by the Senate (and by the House after two months of intense political negotiation). The final legislation, the Atomic Energy Act of 1946, created the Atomic Energy Commission (AEC) to administer domestic controls and carry out research, development, and production programs. It established civilian control over the AEC but provided for a Military Liaison Committee to report Defense Department atomic activity to the AEC, receive information on AEC activitives in the military field, and make recommendations regarding military application of atomic research. It also created the Joint Committee on Atomic Energy, to comprise nine members each from the House and Senate.

Most sections of the Atomic Energy Act focused on private and federal research and development, dissemination of information, and control of fissionable materials. But it also addressed matters of international control: There must be no development of weapons in contravention of international agreements; and construction and stockpiling of weapons, and production of fissionable materials, would be firmly regulated by the AEC until worldwide objectives could be defined and effected. That would preclude the military from engaging in weapons programs that could endanger international negotiations.

Tydings became increasingly anxious over the threat of atomic weapons. Instead of concentrating on the details of domestic policy at hearings, he focused on arms control—specifically, the dilemma over controlling the atomic bomb while conventional weapons proliferated. He asked Dr. Harrison Davies, representative of the Federation of Atomic Scientists, how nations could agree on control of the bomb "without a corresponding diminution in the other arms of all other countries." If arms control applied to atomic weapons only, would not the world remain hostage to war? Davies conceded his point—that any agreement, to provide a lasting solution, must in some way be contingent on corresponding reductions across the board.

The problems were easier to define than to solve. Tydings agonized over many facets of the issue: the linkage of atomic and conventional weapons; the need for inspection and the difficulty of assuring its effectiveness; the setting and process that might ensure successful resolution of the problems. Should it be done through the United Nations? By separate conference? How could new weaponry developed during the war—atomic and conventional—be prevented from becoming malignant threats to survival?

In January 1946 he spent days and nights writing and rewriting a speech on world disarmament. His wife had never seen him so agitated. Night after sleepless night he paced the floor, obsessed by the possibility of total annihilation. In his endless nocturnal reflections he finally came to the conclusion that "control" of atomic weapons, without fundamental changes in the approach and mechanisms of control, would prove futile.

On January 28, interrupting a filibuster on the fair employment bill, he launched a plea for peace that was widely regarded as a major contribution to the effort to deal with the postwar nightmare. "It begins to appear as if the nations of the earth are headed directly into World War III," he lamented. Mankind had learned nothing in the past three decades. But now, through representatives to the new United Nations Organization, the government was "asking the other great powers to join with us in the control of the atomic bomb. Mark you," he stressed, "it is not proposed that it be prohibited by all nations. The great powers are engaged only in the control of the atomic bomb. There are few words in the English language more elusive than the word 'control.' " What was needed was total disarmament worldwide—with atomic and conventional weapons and standing armies, navies, and air forces to be dismantled and eliminated by January 1, 1950. It was time for a "showdown" on the good faith and conscience of the world.

The proper venue for negotiations on such a radical step was not the United Nations, "a very fragile and insufficient reed" already overwhelmed with "a tremendous multitude of problems," he suggested, but a special world conference of nations. He offered a resolution calling on Truman to convene a conference devoted to the single goal of seeking total world disarmament—a plan with inspection safeguards and provision for each country to maintain a small army for keeping civil order within its borders.

His call for a world conference received strong bipartisan commendation. Brien McMahon, Robert Taft, and William Fulbright, among many others, called his speech and resolution constructive and bold. Editorial reaction—from the New York *Times* to small publications of fraternal, civil, and church groups—was largely positive. Liberal columnist Oswald Garrison Villard quoted widely from Tydings's speech in an article for the *Peace News and the Citizens on World Disarmament*. The entire text of the two-hour speech was reprinted in the prestigious magazine *Vital Speeches of the Day*.

Truman was distinctly unenthusiastic. He had instructed Bernard Baruch to work through the United Nations to negotiate control of atomic weapons and was annoyed at the suggestion to bypass his own representative. Tydings was also condemned for expressing fears about the United Nations—his concern that emerging contradictions in its purpose and principle might render it "a snare and a delusion" doomed by "the same hypocrisy which bedeviled the League of Nations." Cartoons depicted him in baseball garb shouting to take the pitcher out of the game before a batter stepped up to the plate.

Undeterred, he kept on talking. What he had seen—worldwide devastation, political chaos, desperate poverty, and the power of the bomb—confirmed his belief that global disarmament was imperative for human survival. "I am not afraid to be a radical on this subject," he said in a radio broadcast. "We still have time to act to preserve the peace of the world. We cannot act after World War III starts." On radio, before civic groups, in the Senate, he prodded people to consider what civilization was facing. "At Bikini," he told listeners, "we saw more than two score of war planes, some of them giant four-engine planes, take off from the ground, fly in and near the great atomic bomb smoke plume. . . . These planes," he said, "had not a human being in them. They took off from the ground, were guided by radio and came back and alighted on the ground without a human hand touching them. . . . These events should stir the dullest intellect into rapid thought. . . . Either we find means of preventing another war," he said, "or we will likely wreck civilization all over the earth. No other problem approaches this one."

When in March 1947 he reintroduced his resolution asking Truman to convene disarmament talks, the president, through the Department of State, quickly threw cold water on the idea. An official rejection of his proposal was sent to Senator Vandenberg: The matter would be approached through the United Nations; American atomic policy was resolved to achieve agreement on control of atomic energy before tackling other issues. Tydings got the message. He refrained from publicly calling for an international disarmament conference again until February 1950, after Truman gave the go-ahead on the hydrogen bomb in reaction to the Soviet Union's possession of the bomb.

In mid-1946, when the first Joint Committee on Atomic Energy was created, Tydings decided not to retain a seat on it. The committee's role was too passive—a "watchdog" capacity—and he believed his efforts could be used more productively elsewhere. The Naval Affairs and Military Affairs Committees were being merged into one Armed Services Committee as part of a postwar governmental restructuring, also intent on unifying the Navy and War Departments into one National Military Establishment. Those complex endeavors, along with U.S. foreign policy—the Marshall Plan, establishment of a North Atlantic alliance, and military assistance to Europe—required Tydings's attention.

The reorganization of Congress and the executive branch was designed to streamline government. The number of committees was reduced from 33 to 15—some, including Territories and Insular Possessions, being abolished. Senators were limited to serving on two committees. Tydings supported restructuring for its cost-effectiveness and efficiency. When the bill effecting changes (Legislative Reorganization Act of 1946) was signed, Tydings became ranking Democrat on the new Armed Services Committee and moved up in seniority on the Appropriations Committee.

Unification of the armed services was far harder to accomplish than was congressional reorganization. Both navy and army were loath to relinquish power. The navy in particular argued vociferously against the proposal that a single Department of Defense, under civilian leadership, provide integrated strategic planning and preside over a unified military program and budget. Before the Naval Affairs Committee, Navy Department witnesses fought for their independence. Interservice bickering and rivalry were bitter.[6]

Tydings—despite sentimental attachment to the navy—understood the need for a central authority, yet knew that compromise was essential if legislation were to succeed. He agreed with Truman that there should be a single department to administer the coordinated services—army, navy and newly created air force—each on a parity, each headed by a civilian secretary charged with internal management, and each retaining autonomy subject to the authority of the secretary of defense. Although pressured by the navy and ranking officials at the Naval Academy in Annapolis, he refused to show partiality. Symington, who worked with Tydings for unification, respected his grasp of the strategic value. "I think he felt the battleship was dying . . . and was keen for air power, including naval air," Symington recalled later. He also admired the way Tydings handled pressure from the navy's top brass.

The National Security Act of 1947 created the National Military Establishment. Former Secretary of the Navy James Forrestal became its first secretary. The act also created a National Security Council and Central Intelligence Agency. It incorporated the Joint Chiefs of Staff system originated during the war, but with no single military chief of staff. The act's significance went beyond national security; it validated the realization that the military had a pivotal role to play in shaping policy in peacetime as well as war.

The act did not achieve an actual merger, although the old Navy and War Departments were abolished; for the three military branches remained separate departments headed by their own secretaries. The act's vague language—the secretary of defense shall "establish *general* policies and programs for the National Military Establishment" and shall "exercise *general* direction, authority and control over such departments and agencies" (italics added)—created problems. Forrestal was unable to keep his subordinate secretaries from quarreling, especially over funding. Each had the authority to go directly to the president and used that authority. The Joint Chiefs of Staff, playing an impossible dual role as senior officers of their service branches and as advisers to Forrestal, gave him conflicting advice on critical issues. The chain of command was flawed grievously. Forrestal grew distressed over the lack of harmony.

In 1949, when Tydings became chairman of the Armed Services Committee, he drafted new legislation designed to solve the problem created by the lack of central authority. His measure—the Tydings Bill—strengthened and clarified the powers of the secretary of defense with "direction, authority, and control over the Department of Defense." There would be an undersecretary and three assistant secretaries of defense—responsible to the secretary and unable to appeal over his head. The secretaries of the navy, army, and air force would be departmental officials, rather than officials of the executive branch. Control and accountability clearly was centered in the secretary of defense. And the Joint Chiefs of Staff would have a chairman as presiding officer.

Forrestal, who initially had reservations about unification, became convinced that a strong secretary was crucial. Exhausted and depressed by his failure to make an untenable system work, he resigned, but appeared before the Armed Services Committee as lead witness in favor of reorganization. The navy again opposed strengthening the secretary of defense, however, and argued that Tydings's bill—by concentrating military power in the hands of one person—would create a dictatorship. A new member of the Senate, Joseph R. McCarthy of Wisconsin (elected in 1946), entered the fray. Fearing unification might injure the prestige and power of his beloved marine corps (a department of the navy), he offered several amendments intended to cripple Tydings's bill.

With the backing of virtually the entire Senate and House, Tydings overcame efforts to obstruct passage and easily outmaneuvered the Wisconsin freshman. After two months of hearings, in which Tydings reconciled differing views as fairly as he could, he shepherded the bill through the Senate where it passed without major debate. The National Military Establishment became the Department of Defense. Washington analysts considered the Tydings Bill to be the most important piece of domestic legislation to come before Congress in several years. A greatly relieved Truman signed Tydings's milestone legislation into law on August 10, 1949.[7]

In 1947, as the first unification measure was being debated, events overseas redefined with a vengeance the role America would play in the world. The Soviet Union's refusal to withdraw troops from the Iranian province of Azerbaijan, its political and military domination in Eastern Europe, and growing communist threats in Greece and Turkey compelled the U.S. government to rethink its foreign policy—from economic and military perspectives. Winston Churchill's March 1946 speech at Fulton, Missouri—where he declared, "From Stettin in the Baltic to Trieste in the Adriatic, an iron curtain has descended across the Continent"—vividly captured the sense of dread. The need to formulate a coherent foreign policy strategy (one that took into account the military's role—and one that would require huge sums of money) intensified.

Conditions in Europe were desperate. Freak storms had destroyed the wheat crop, bringing starvation. More than just human well-being and the economy appeared in extremis; the very survival of democracy in Europe seemed at risk. If conditions did not improve, communist agitators might make headway in France, Italy, Greece, and Turkey. Truman believed he must help rebuild the Continent and deter further communist aggression. To assure success, he needed support on Capitol Hill. Because Republicans had gained control of both houses of Congress in the 1946 midterm elections, he particularly needed Democrats such as Tydings—conservatives strong on defense, knowledgeable in foreign affairs, and articulate in debate.

For Tydings the postwar years were a time of great change. Long outside the inner circle of power as he battled Roosevelt for 12 exhausting years, he now was positioned to join the Democratic clique that dominated party politics and shaped policy. Observers in Washington remarked that, for a man weary of constantly fighting the leader of his party, the opportunity to be on the inside must have appeared irresistible. And Tydings and Truman were friends from the Senate. They disagreed on issues relating to labor, housing, and agriculture, but shared a rural background, were sympathetic to small business, believed in less government rather than more, and shared the bond of having served in World War I. Tydings enjoyed a very different relationship with Truman from the one he had endured with Roosevelt.

The issues facing the country were different, too. Although domestic matters demanded resolution, foreign issues came to command greater attention. Following the war, Tydings evolved from being known as guardian of domestic solvency to being recognized as a firm supporter of foreign aid, willing to argue for vast sums of money in the effort to provide a democratic, stable future for Europe—for world conditions demanded changes.

When in 1947 Republicans introduced a tax-reduction bill, Tydings opposed it. When the tax cut passed anyway, and Truman vetoed it, Tydings voted to sustain the veto because of the European situation. When Truman requested emergency aid for Europe, Tydings worked to convince conservative Democrats not to vote to slash the program as Republicans were trying to do. He agreed with Vandenberg's assessment that there was no advantage in throwing a 15-foot rope to a man drowning 20 feet from shore.

Truman needed Senate leaders to speak in favor of his expensive foreign policies, and Tydings became one of Truman's most reliable advocates. On March 12, 1947, when Truman asked Congress for $400 million in military and economic aid to Greece and Turkey to prevent communist penetration in the Eastern Mediterranean, Tydings supported him. In June 1947, when Secretary of State George C. Marshall spoke at Harvard University on helping Europe rebuild, Tydings said that such a course was urgent, that delay would be costly, financially and politically. "It will cost us far, far less money in the long run," he told constituents, "than a policy of unpreparedness." He realized that the Truman Doctrine and the Marshall Plan represented a departure in foreign policy and told radio audiences that the alternative to "embarking on a new course"—Soviet domination in Europe, in the Mediterranean, and perhaps elsewhere—would be worse.

Although Truman disagreed with Tydings on certain domestic issues, the president had high regard for Tydings's grasp of military matters. In mid-September he sent him on a fact-finding mission to Europe to study economic and military conditions. Tydings went in a dual role: as a member of the Appropriations and Armed Forces Committees; and, as he said, because he needed to be in "a better position" to help shape policy. "New legislation affecting [the] general unsettled European conditions is sure to come before the next Congress," he said to the assembled press corps on departure. He would meet with civilian and military representatives in Germany, Austria, Italy, Greece, Switzerland, France, the Low Countries, and Britain, to observe conditions, assess the advisability (and cost) of the proposed European Recovery Program, and analyze its effect on both the national and international economy.

Returning on October 17, he declined to make any public conclusion regarding what course the United States should follow. He had collected data from government and military leaders everywhere he went, he said, but wanted to study it before issuing formal statements. Publicly noncommittal, privately he was convinced that the European situation was desperate and warranted action. In early November, in a series of four articles published nationwide through the American Newspaper Alliance distribution service, he finally answered questions asked repeatedly on his return.

He described in grim detail the horror of entire cities destroyed, the rampant disease, widespread starvation, and terrible—nearly debilitating—uncertainty over the future. Remembering Berlin in 1923 where, he wrote, he experienced the deadly inflation, he recalled paying 1 million marks for a single cigarette—a prewar value of $250,000—and was especially concerned about Germany. Germans were anxious and insecure, worried over how they would be treated. "If no help comes to Germany, and if all the armies were now to withdraw, there is a golden made-to-order opportunity for a new 'man on horseback.'" Anything that could help avoid such an outcome must be sought and supported, he wrote.

Italy and Greece also endured severe economic and political distress. Their ports were badly damaged and fishing fleets sunk. They lacked fuel and natural resources and suffered serious food shortages. Their currencies were weak, and Italy's government finance was "far from orthodox." The Greeks were engaged in a bitter civil war, and the Italians—"making a commendable bid for a better and a democratic way of life"—were working hard digging themselves out of their predicament. Aid to the two nations was "indispensable."

As bad as things were in Austria, France, the Low Countries, and Britain, they were better off than the rest of Europe. Conditions were austere, but most areas of society and industry were functional.

With assistance, they would rapidly regain their former standard of living.

Aid to Europe, Tydings concluded, would mean security and might prevent another war. It would strengthen "the security of the world, and our own security along with it. . . . [O]ur own interests are served by aiding the rehabilitation of Europe. Indeed, we cannot afford not to do so." World War II had cost the United States $400 billion.

After that trip he became one of the strongest voices in Congress for the European Recovery Program (the Marshall Plan). Later, Tydings would battle for entering into the North Atlantic Treaty pact, for offering a costly military assistance program (MAP), and for continued and increased financial aid to help Europe help itself. In late 1947 he spoke throughout the Eastern states in support of Truman's call for economic aid to Europe.

Tydings's national visibility—due to his high profile in the Senate during Roosevelt's tenure and his prominent roles in military unification and European aid—brought him mention for the vice-presidency in 1948. Because Truman had succeeded to office on Roosevelt's death, there was no sitting vice-president. Gossip speculated that Tydings was willing and available, and political analysts in countless articles contended that he was highly qualified. He did nothing to check such talk and admitted to close friends and associates that he would accept the nomination if it were offered.[8]

Stewart and Joseph Alsop in August 1947 suggested that Truman's men were shopping for a good running mate, "poking and sniffing at the selection of available candidates like a set of careful housewives looking for a good brisket of beef on a badly-stocked butcher's counter." Mentioning Secretary of Agriculture Clinton Anderson and Tydings as prime choices (although, they hedged, Anderson was too unknown in the East and Tydings too conservative), the Alsop brothers wailed that, besides them and the "I'm-a-Fugitive-from-the-Supreme-Court" candidates (Fred M. Vinson and William O. Douglas), all that was left were dark horses: Alben W. Barkley, James V. Forrestal, W. Averell Harriman, and Representative A. S. Mike Monroney of Oklahoma. And they were saddled with even greater drawbacks: Barkley too old, Forrestal and Harriman too rich, and Monroney—well, Monroney was Catholic.

The *U.S. News and World Report*'s "Washington Whispers" column put Tydings in the top tier of candidates, as did the *Christian Science Monitor*'s Roscoe Drummond. *Time* magazine included him in the "swarm of prospects," all of whom had flaws—Tydings "stood too far to the political right." A December 1947 poll of Senate Democrats gave Senator Scott Lucas of Illinois eight votes, Tydings seven, and others—including Forrestal, Jim Farley, and George Marshall—one or two.

Conservative columnist Gould Lincoln wrote that, if one set Tydings's labor record aside, he was "a strong and aggressive campaigner [and] geographically 'right' to run with a Missourian." Veteran correspondent Bascom N. Timmons labeled him the "hottest tip" in private chambers where the nomination was hashed over. But, he wrote, "Should Tydings eventually round out the 1948 Democratic ticket it would be in defiance of the old tradition that a President and Vice President must not have a surname beginning with the same letter. No winning national ticket ever was so made up."[9]

Political writer Harry Haller tried to boost Tydings's chances in articles aimed at overcoming wounds inflicted in the 1946 primary in Maryland. Senator Radcliffe had lost to Herbert O'Conor as Tydings took refuge on the sidelines—much to Radcliffe's disgust. Tydings reasoned that he had campaigned hard for Radcliffe in 1940, paying off the 1938 IOU that Radcliffe had acquired for helping Tydings during the purge campaign. But Radcliffe remained furious. And Tydings had opposed Preston Lane for the governorship in 1946, backing instead the popular comptroller of the treasury, J. Millard Tawes.[10] Observers had been incredulous at Tydings's dabbling in a gubernatorial race, as—no matter who won—he stood to lose political leverage by alienating one faction or the other. Haller wrote in January 1948 that "if [Tydings] is nominated, he will add materially to the strength of the ticket because he does enjoy national confidence. . . . In spite of his admitted mistake in opposing Lane in 1946, he will get united Democratic support in Maryland."

Tydings helped himself at the White House by being among

the first of the Democratic leaders to call for Truman's reelection. By early 1947 the feisty Missouri progressive was unpopular with many in the Democratic hierarchy—especially Southerners—and it appeared his renomination would be challenged because of fears that he could not be elected. At a New Haven, Connecticut, Jefferson Day speech in April, Tydings declared that the cry for 1948 must be "We want more of Truman and Truman's high, constructive, courageous and sound leadership." Washington's press corps believed his early and unequivocal endorsement raised Tydings's stock at 1600 Pennsylvania Avenue.

Another factor in Tydings's favor was the support he had given Truman's nominee for assistant secretary of the navy, Edwin Pauley, in 1946. Roosevelt had intended to appoint Pauley, and Forrestal favored him. But Secretary of Interior Harold Ickes violently opposed him. Pauley was an oil man, and Ickes said the appointment reeked of conflict of interest because of the navy's huge oil reserves. At hearings before the Naval Affairs Committee, Ickes pronounced him unfit for office, charging that Pauley had made the "rawest proposition" he had ever heard (allegedly promising enormous contributions to the Democratic party if the navy would refrain from suing to recover certain offshore oil reserves). Tydings, who nurtured no affection for Ickes and saw a chance to help Truman, lit into Ickes. Columnist Louis Azrael noted that the case "gave [Tydings] a good chance to establish himself as a White House favorite" after years of being "odd-man out in Washington."

Ickes resigned, as he had resigned many times before to get his way with Roosevelt. Truman, unlike Roosevelt, accepted his letter. Pauley, mauled by the hearings, withdrew from contention. Truman was furious at Ickes. Tydings's loyalty did not go unnoticed.

In February 1948 Tydings was hospitalized at Bethesda Naval Hospital with a serious case of pneumonia. On release he reentered the political scramble—resulting in a relapse that saw him back in bed, then back in the hospital, gravely ill, for more than a month. When allowed to go home the second time, his doctors took no chances, enforcing a regimen that kept him out of the political game. He knew his chances for the nomination had been affected and told news reporters in mid-April that he was not seeking office—for the time being.

By the time the state Democratic convention met in Baltimore on June 1 to select delegates to the national convention at Philadelphia (convening on July 12), Tydings was back in the thick of it. Having edged out Governor Lane as the dominant figure at the convention, he found himself endorsed by O'Conor and Baltimore Mayor Thomas D'Alessandro (elected in 1947) as favorite son for the vice-presidency. Over his protests, Maryland's Democratic leaders—including Lane, Tawes, Radcliffe, and Brooke Lee—voted unanimously to commit the delegation to what D'Alessandro had dubbed a "T-formation": "Truman and Tydings—T'n'T—you can't beat that. It's dynamite."

Although Tydings made it clear he would accept the nomination if it were offered, he denied in public statements that he had campaigned for it. "I am not a candidate, and that's the truth," he told reporters. His insistence was made, perhaps, to avoid disappointment if he were passed over (which appeared likely as Truman's platform was being shaped in a liberal mold, with a strong civil rights statement). It was most probable, however, that he believed accepting the favorite son role would keep his delegation in line behind Truman. Since taking office, Truman had pushed the issue of civil rights and had alienated large blocs of powerful political leaders from the South, including Maryland's Eastern Shore.

It was Southern disaffection that again centered attention on Tydings just before convention time. Bradford Jacobs, correspondent for the Baltimore *Sun*, wrote that Truman needed someone Southern and conservative to conciliate that wing of the party and unify the Democrats to beat the Republican ticket—New York's Tom Dewey and California's Governor Earl Warren. Maryland's location and Tydings's conservatism as well as national and senatorial stature (fourth in seniority)[11] placed him back among the top contenders, Jacobs said. Democratic National Chairman J. Howard McGrath admitted the race was "wide open": Barkley looked good but was 71; O'Mahoney was another possibility but was Catholic; Tydings, McGrath said as reporters peppered him with questions, "is generally regarded as one of the most potent political campaigners in his party . . . at 58, is a veteran of Senate and party councils. He enjoys the confidence of many Southern Democrats who have been bitter about Mr. Truman's civil-rights programs." Columnist Doris Fleeson found "tepid" reaction to all prospective candidates. Tydings's only real drawback, she wrote, was his vote for the Taft–Hartley labor law and then voting to override Truman's veto.

The South was fully on the warpath over Truman's civil rights program. Determined to stop him, Southern leaders had Senator Richard B. Russell of Georgia contact Tydings the day before the convention opened in Philadelphia to see if he would run for president against Truman. Russell controlled more than 200 delegates, but Tydings could muster broader support nationally. Tydings turned Russell down flat. Russell replied, "If you won't take it, Millard, I'm going to take it myself. But I am under instructions to get a definite 'no' from you first." A definite no was what he got.

In later explaining why he declined, Tydings said he "didn't see eye-to-eye" with the Southern rebels. He liked Truman and wholeheartedly supported his nomination. He believed in equality as expressed in the Constitution and its amendments. But he also did not like a platform that threatened states' rights and forced a civil rights program on those not yet willing even to consider change, and was uncomfortable with the concept of total integration. Tydings described himself as caught in the middle.

When Tydings arrived in Philadelphia, he and Eleanor headed for the Bellevue Stratford Hotel, site of the convention. On the hotel's porte cochère, the Democrats had erected an enormous electrified donkey that nodded its head, switched its tail, and wiggled its five-foot ears as sparks shot from its eyes and smoke belched out of its nose. Something went wrong with the mechanism; and for a short time, smoke poured out of the wrong end of the donkey, making them and the crowds roar with laughter.

Tydings had tentatively made up his mind to decline a nomination for vice-president before his arrival in Philadelphia; when he got there and saw "certain aspects" of the platform—the strong civil rights provisions—he declared himself out of the race and threw his support to Barkley, releasing his delegates on Monday July 12. They ultimately agreed unanimously to line up behind Barkley.

The convention was a humdrum affair—"dull," "apathetic," "lackluster," were adjectives used by reporters—until the Dixiecrats set off fireworks when 35 rebels from Alabama and Mississippi stormed out waving a huge Confederate flag after Truman's aggressive plank on civil rights was approved. But Truman was nominated, with Barkley for vice-president. Later that week in Montgomery, Alabama, Senator Strom Thurmond of South Carolina accepted the nomination for president on the States Rights Democratic party (or Dixiecrat party) ticket, with Governor Fielding L. Wright of Mississippi as his running mate.

Truman was given little chance of winning. The Truman–Barkley ticket met with ambivalence in Maryland. Newspapers accused Tydings of having forced Truman on Maryland delegates in his usual high-handed manner. And competition for votes was not limited to Strom Thurmond and the Dixiecrats. Henry Wallace was running for president on the Progressive party ticket (with Senator Glen H. Taylor of Idaho); and Norman Thomas, campaigning on the Socialist party ticket, appealed for votes.

The 1948 election was vitally important to the Democrats. If Truman lost, he probably would take the party down with him. If that happened, they would fail to regain control of Congress— which meant control of committee chairmanships. Tydings campaigned strenuously, stressing the issue of war and peace. The Republican stance, he said—opposition to the European Recovery Plan and a general intransigence on foreign policy—weakened the United States and increased the danger of war.

For the first time in 60 years, Marylanders failed to vote for the winner of a presidential election. Dewey took Maryland by 8,000 votes—a margin so slim that, if some Wallace (10,000), Thurmond (2,500), and Thomas (3,000) votes had shifted to Truman, he would have carried the state. But he eked out a national victory, winning 50 percent of the vote and 303 electoral votes.[12] His upset kept the White House in Democratic hands, and the party recaptured Congress.

On October 28, 1948, before the election, Tydings wrote Alben Barkley requesting a position on the Foreign Relations Committee. Senator Carl Hatch was retiring, the letter said, and he wanted to get off Appropriations and take Hatch's place on Foreign Relations. His move was a big surprise to his colleagues. It was unusual for a ranking member of a powerful committee to leave it in order to become a freshman on another, no matter how important the other committee was. Before Congress convened in 1949, Tydings also had sought and gained a seat on the Joint Committee on Atomic Energy. That made him the only member of Congress to sit on three vitally important committees: Armed Services, Foreign Relations, and Atomic Energy.

He also had challenged Kenneth McKellar of Tennessee for the prestigious position of president pro tempore of the Senate. McKellar had held the honorary title before 1946 and wanted it back. Secretary of the Senate Leslie Biffle managed Tydings's campaign. But Biffle's maneuvering and the "high-pressure campaign" alienated some of Tydings's colleagues. Newspaper reports described Biffle's get-togethers as "curious conspirings [in his] famous 'diner' in the northwest corner of the Capitol [where] Senators were invited in for lunch to partake of Biffle's soft drawl, Tydings' gleaming smile, and good food and drink." Tydings lost the vote at the Democratic caucus, 27 to 25. He graciously accepted defeat, saying he was "greatly complimented" to have lost by such a small margin. Given that McKellar had held the office for so long, columnists interpreted the vote as a show of Tydings's strength.

He had demonstrated his clout and was poised to become a legislative force in military and foreign relations. With access to information on national defense, diplomatic efforts, and in the atomic energy field, Tydings would have his finger on the pulse of the areas of government that determined what role the United States played in the world. He would use his influence to support American adherence to the proposed North Atlantic Treaty pact (which would take skillful selling as it represented a departure from U.S. policy of avoiding "entangling alliances"). He would press for aid to Europe through the Marshall Plan and the new military assistance plan (which would require deft management to get approval in Congress). He would propose again a world disarmament conference to end the arms race before increasingly powerful thermonuclear weapons made Armageddon more than a word from Revelation 16:16.

Tydings already was regarded as a global statesman. As he sought to increase his visibility and power in 1949, many political observers and colleagues thought he was positioning himself for a run at the highest office in 1952. Richmond *Times–Dispatch* correspondent Jack Bell opened an article headlined "TYDINGS EYED

AS PRESIDENTIAL TIMBER IN 1952" thusly: "Democrats who have been looking over the field for possible 1952 presidential nominees think they see a gleam in the eye of Senator Millard E. Tydings." Tydings's wife had written to her father Joe Davies, describing the 1948 Philadelphia convention: "So many delegates and people want to back Millard for President or Vice President. I can't tell you how popular he is. It's too bad, but maybe we'll have some fun in 1952."

Drew Pearson, who had written Tydings off as "an ardent has-been" when he lost to McKellar (whom he also dismissed as "an ardent has-been"), devoted a number of paragraphs to Tydings's future. "A strange Romeo has showed up under the White House balcony singing love songs," he began. "He is dapper Senator Millard Tydings of Maryland who used to make sarcastic slurs against the Administration but now devotes his tongue to the Truman cause." Tydings was playing a "cagey political game," Pearson said, hoping to get his foot in the White House door. "The shrewd Maryland senator let the cat out of the bag the other day by disclosing his ambition to close political friends. He admitted going along with the Administration in part so he can move into Truman's shoes in case Truman doesn't run again."

Tydings let them write what they wanted, shrugging off their remarks. He was a towering figure in Washington, and there were no storm clouds on his horizon. Considered a shoo-in for 1950—Democratic National Chairman J. Howard McGrath had publicly scoffed in June 1949 at the suggestion that anyone could take his seat away from him—Tydings didn't care for hell and a brown mule what people speculated. He was strategically positioned to make things happen in the three areas he considered crucial to the future of the country and the world. He was riding high and rolled up his sleeves to go to work.

Notes

1. Tydings also had urged increased defense for the Hawaiian Islands and the Philippines. In 1934 he had inspected the U.S. naval station at Cavite and made a secret trip to Bataan Peninsula and Corregidor, the great

fortress rock guarding the entry to Manila Bay. General Douglas A. Mac-Arthur called Corregidor "the strongest single fortified point in the world," believing it impregnable. Tydings became convinced it was vulnerable. Accompanied by Major General Frank Parker, he studied the terrain and remarked, "Magnificent fortress this is; no Navy in the world could ever take this rock." But when Parker said, "Yes, they can, Senator, from upstairs," he realized Corregidor's uncamouflaged guns were exposed. "How much money would it cost to protect you from the air?" he asked. When the colonel replied, "$500,000,000," Tydings had said, "You'll never get it from Congress. They won't give it to you."

2. Jim Farley unequivocally believed Roosevelt "engineered his own nomination." In his autobiography Farley wrote, "What I did not like was the hypocrisy: the effort put forth to make it appear that the President was being drafted, when everyone knew it was a forced draft fired from the White House itself."

3. Alabama delegate William Lovard Lee broke with his state's third-termers during the Alabama caucus. "I'm going to vote for this fellow Tydings," he announced. "He is aggressive. He is a fighter. He is nobody's deputy. That's the kind of man I like. Mark me down for Tydings." Thus Tydings received 8½ votes from the Maryland delegates and one from Alabama.

4. The battleships USS *Arizona, California, Nevada, Oklahoma,* and *West Virginia* were sunk; three others were badly damaged, as were three cruisers and three destroyers. The public was told only that the *Oklahoma* had capsized and the *Arizona* was sunk.

5. Frederica M. Bunge in *Philippines: A Country Study* wrote that, during the war, "An estimated 1 million Filipinos had been killed, a large portion during the last months. The final fighting for Manila left the city one of the most extensively damaged of any major city in the world." American war dead, in both Atlantic and Pacific theaters, numbered just over 400,000.

6. Truman's special counsel, Clark Clifford, paraphrased the president's irritation over rivalry: "He said, being faintly humorous, that from time to time if the Army and Navy had shown the same zeal in fighting the enemy as they had shown in fighting each other, the war wouldn't have lasted so long."

7. Although Tydings was proud of his role as arbiter in bringing a modicum of harmony to the rival services, the signing ceremony at the White House had an underlying somberness. Forrestal, severely depressed, had plunged to his death from the sixteenth floor of the Bethesda Naval Hospital in May—an apparent suicide. Tydings wept openly at his funeral.

At the White House on August 10, Forrestal's absence was felt acutely by Tydings.

8. Although Tydings's family consistently maintains that the senator had no ambition to be president—that his 1940 run was aimed solely at stopping a Roosevelt third term (a statement borne out by the evidence)—his son Joseph did concede that in 1948 there was "maybe a little bit" of ambition for attaining the office of vice-president.

9. Timmons noted that talk of Sam Rayburn of Texas joining Roosevelt on the 1944 ticket moved a friend of Roosevelt's to bawl, "Why, the Republicans would have a slogan of 'Roosevelt, Rayburn and Ruin' before nightfall." (He also cited Alf Landon's refusal to accept Senator Styles Bridges of New Hampshire as his running mate for fear the Democrats would pounce on the catchy refrain "Landon Bridges Falling Down.")

10. In 1946, O'Conor narrowly won over Republican D. John Markey (who would run unsuccessfully against John Marshall Butler in the Republican senatorial primary in 1950). Lane defeated Republican Theodore R. McKeldin by a small margin; McKeldin would run again in 1950 and trounce Lane, who headed the Democratic ticket and whom many blamed for taking Tydings down to defeat with him.

11. He was tied for fourth in seniority with Alben W. Barkley of Kentucky, Carl T. Hayden of Arizona, Elmer Thomas of Oklahoma, and Robert F. Wagner of New York.

12. Dewey–Warren got 46 percent and 189 electoral votes, while Thurmond–Wright carried several Southern states for 38 electoral votes; Wallace–Taylor took a million votes away from Truman but failed to win any electoral votes.

11

The Final Battles

The contributions Tydings contemplated making in the realms of foreign affairs and disarmament remained incomplete. For in 1950, at the zenith of power, considered by many as the logical successor to Harry Truman, he was appointed by Foreign Relations Committee Chairman Tom Connally of Texas to chair a subcommittee charged with investigating Senator Joseph R. McCarthy's shocking accusations that large numbers of disloyal Americans—card-carrying Communists—were employed by the Department of State.

Before the smoke had cleared after the 1950 election, Tydings had taken the loss philosophically. After having paid a call at the White House in late November, he said to reporters—who anticipated that Truman would give Tydings a juicy appointment—"Well, the President offered to resign and give me his job but I wouldn't take it." When the lame duck congressional session resumed on November 27, he ambled up to Democratic Majority Leader Scott Lucas, who had been defeated in Illinois, and said with a broad grin, "I feel five years younger, don't you?"

The night of the election, after the results indicated conclusively that John Marshall Butler had defeated him, he delivered a gracious farewell speech over the radio, thanking the citizens of Maryland for their support over the years. On the way home he and Eleanor, driving with friends, heard Butler's victory speech in which he continued to insult Tydings. Tydings listened and then, chuckling, turned around to Eleanor and the others in the backseat and said, "Say, we better stop the car." They said rather anxiously, "Why?" "Didn't you hear that awful thud?" he asked. "No," they chorused in alarm. "Oh, that was just 25 years in the Senate falling off my shoulders," he said. Even at home alone in the evenings as Eleanor wept with rage, he comforted her saying, "Now, now, it's not the end of the world."

In an interview with the *U.S. News and World Report*, he blamed his defeat on the primary for the governorship: "[It] was so bitter that it demoralized the Democratic Party and brought on a situation that has no parallel in Maryland politics, where the party was split completely down the middle." He noted that even in losing he ran 50,000 votes ahead of badly defeated Governor William Preston Lane (who won a bitter primary fight with George Mahoney). When asked to what extent the result was influenced by McCarthy's actions he replied, "I don't think that McCarthy as a person did any damage, but I think the issue raised and the propaganda about it had some effect, but it would be secondary to what I have already told you."

But after the smoke cleared, as he worked amid the wreckage of his career packing 400 filing cases of letters and documents from 28 years in Congress, as he began to hear reports of behind-the-scenes skulduggery waged against his campaign, he launched a private, quiet investigation of the rumors. As the facts emerged, the anguish and anger he felt became visible.

After careful thought, he and Eleanor canceled their daughter's coming-out party. Young Eleanor's Christmas-time debut was to have been the most lavish of the season. The Mayflower Hotel's grand ballroom had been reserved two years in advance, the orchestra hired, invitations sent, gowns fitted. But reverses in the Korean War cast a pall on Washington—the vice president canceled a dinner for Truman—and Tydings's loss cast its unhappy shadow on the family. They decided a festive celebration would be inappropriate. Tydings issued a statement saying that he and Mrs. Tydings found it advisable to cancel the ball "in keeping with the austerity of the times." A "small and simple" dance would be held at the Chevy Chase Club instead.[1]

After Christmas, Marjorie Davies insisted that Eleanor persuade

Tydings to accept as a gift a holiday voyage to the warm Caribbean on a cruise liner. Concerned about his fatigue, Eleanor did coax him into going. Onboard ship she realized how bitterly he suffered from the defeat. "He withdrew completely inside himself behind a wall which I could not breach," she wrote in her private memoirs. "He never admitted his hurt. I wept on his shoulder but he would not weep on mine." The other passengers stared, and they experienced the pain of being the target of constant gossip.

Tydings's personal investigation of possible election abuses provided sufficient evidence for him to take action. In mid-December, armed with examples of illegal activities, he complained orally and in writing to the Subcommittee on Privileges and Elections of the Senate Committee on Rules and Administration. On February 3, 1951, the subcommittee agreed unanimously to hold public hearings on the Maryland senatorial election of 1950. The investigation was conducted by a special subcommittee composed of Democratic Senators A. S. Mike Monroney of Oklahoma (chairman), Thomas C. Hennings, Jr., of Missouri, and Republicans Robert C. Hendrickson of New Jersey and Margaret Chase Smith of Maine. Tydings did not challenge the election results or contest the seating of Butler, but he wanted investigation into the possible illegal use of funds, fraudulent and malicious campaign literature and advertising, and illegal outside interference. He hoped the proceedings would result in laws drawn to prevent the kind of abuses that led him to file his complaint.

Tydings was the first witness as hearings opened on February 21, 1951. He launched a scathing attack on "scandalous, scurrilous, libelous, and unlawful" campaign practices. Four times he used the phrase "moral squalor" to characterize deliberate falsification of facts in campaign advertisements; fraudulent literature; illegal funding and money unaccounted for; indirect campaign contributions by Mutual Broadcasting Corporation commentator Fulton Lewis, Jr., Chicago *Tribune* owner Robert McCormick, Washington *Times–Herald* editor Ruth "Bazy" McCormick Miller; and illegal outside influence by Colonel Roscoe C. Simmons (McCormick family retainer) and Chicago public relations man Jon Jonkel who, as a non–Maryland resident, was by law ineligible to serve as Butler's campaign manager.

In particular, Tydings targeted the tabloid "From the Record" with its infamous composite photograph (purporting to show him in intimate conversation with Earl Browder, former head of the American Communist party) and articles devoted to skewering Tydings that bore the designation: "Authorized by the Young Democrats for Butler." Tydings had learned that the group's membership included at most six people, only one of whom had any knowledge of the tabloid before its circulation and none of whom had helped with or paid for it. Only John B. Purnell was willing to say he authorized it.

Tydings spoke angrily about the fraudulent attribution and what he considered its fraudulent contents; many of the articles were demonstrably untrue. He decried the composite photograph and the tabloid's last-minute appearance. "It was conceived, printed, and circulated in moral squalor by the dishonorable conspirators and perpetrators, who knew in advance it was a tissue of lies from beginning to end," he declared. Its timing was calculated to capitalize on the disastrous reverses in Korea. The perpetrators knew, he said, "that there was a high degree of receptivity for its message at the time it was circulated. It was designed to make votes dishonorably and to fraudulently capitalize on the anxieties and fears" of Americans. The timing gave him "little or no opportunity to expose its many calculated and deliberately false and malicious lies," he pointed out.

Butler's responsibility was important and relevant. His headquarters had denied authorizing the tabloid, but the checks paying for "From the Record" came directly from his headquarters. "The Butler campaign committee paid for it. The Butler campaign committee circularized it. The Butler campaign committee took all the advantages which flowed from these malicious falsehoods," Tydings raged. Yet, "when it was called to Mr. Butler's attention, neither he nor those associated with him had the fundamental manhood or decency to denounce it for what it was."

The essentially chimerical Young Democrats for Butler also allegedly had sponsored a full-page advertisement in the Baltimore *American*. But it, too, represented evidence of fraudulent attribution (written by a housewife named Margaret T. Berndt, it was paid for by the Butler headquarters), and its contents also were false. In large boldface type it charged that during the State Department loyalty hearings the "Republican counsel was never allowed to question a witness," and that the "Republican counsel was never admitted to closed executive sessions." Tydings exploded, for Robert Morris, Republican counsel, had questioned numerous witnesses and had attended ten executive sessions. The advertisement, Tydings said, was "a total and complete lie," and Butler knew it at the time. "Yet he willfully, deliberately, and calculatingly published this lie," Tydings averred. "Mr. Butler knows he has no defense for this highly dishonorable action."

Tydings described the outside interference by the two McCormicks and their newspapers, by Simmons and Jonkel, indirect campaign contributions by Lewis and the McCormicks, illegal use of funds by Jonkel, how McCormick (owner of the *Times–Herald* as well as a large percentage of Mutual Broadcasting Corporation) had connived with his niece Bazy to bring Simmons to Maryland for six weeks to speak against Tydings in Baltimore's black communities; how Lewis used his Mutual broadcasts in a political manner; how Bazy McCormick used the *Times–Herald* staff to subsidize and print "From the Record" and devise the composite photograph; how Simmons used the names of three black ministers as sponsors for a campaign pamphlet, "Back to Good Old Dixie," which in reality was paid for by Butler headquarters; and how Jonkel used campaign contributions without accounting as required by Maryland and federal law. And Tydings introduced information about an episode of Byzantine intrigue that had come to his attention during his own private investigation—a bizarre tale of intimidation by way of a midnight ride, "Chicago gangland style," suffered by a diminutive Baltimore printer, William H. Fedder.

Fedder was the second witness. In a trembling voice, Fedder recounted his adventure. He had been hired to do a number of printing and distributing jobs for the Butler campaign; but when a lot of invoices remained unpaid, he telephoned Butler at home one night in very early November to complain. He told Butler that, if he failed to receive reimbursement, he would not release a substantial amount of campaign material he had orders to distribute. He referred to himself on the telephone as a man who could not guarantee that Butler would win the election, but was probably the only man in Maryland who could guarantee that Butler could lose.

Fedder immediately received a letter from Butler personally guaranteeing payment—a violation of state laws because the amount (approximately $12,000) exceeded the maximum ($2,500) a candidate could himself contribute to pay debts incurred in a campaign. The next day Butler was distressed to find out that what he had done was not legal. When McCarthy's office learned of the letter, it assured Butler that "McCarthy's boys" would get it back. Donald A. Surine, a surly, physically menacing administrative assistant to McCarthy, and two other good-size men arrived in Baltimore late at night, ostensibly to discuss with Fedder a postcard job they previously had hired him to handle. (The job involved finding a pool of women to hand-address and stamp postcards on which they were to write messages asking addressees to vote for Butler. Jean Kerr, a clerk on McCarthy's staff—and later his wife—had suggested to a fellow staff clerk that Fedder could handle it. Fedder was told to drive to Washington to pick up the 50,000 postcards and stamps.)

Using the postcard project as the pretext for their visit—there were problems with Fedder's management of it and probably legitimate concern regarding his designs on the 50,000 one-cent stamps—the two other men arrived early and grilled Fedder about how many cards were done. When Fedder said only 5,000 or 6,000, they became so angry that, in hopes of appeasing them, Fedder claimed he had mailed a large quantity already. That made them more furious because he had been ordered not to mail any—so he could not pocket the stamps. Fedder told the subcommittee that when Surine arrived at the Baltimore post office at 1:00 A.M. and heard the story—plus an agitated confession that no cards had been mailed—Surine became abusive.

"His eyes looked like they were going to pop out of his head," Fedder said. When he began to walk toward the door, "Surine reached out and jerked me back by the coat. He said, 'Listen, I want that letter back.' I said, 'What letter?' He said, 'The guaranty letter you got from Butler.' I told him that he wasn't going to get the letter. He told me that if I didn't give him the letter they would fix me up and put me through a McCarthy investigation." Fedder went on, "He bragged about being good at that sort of thing. . . . I asked him to please let me finish [the job] and go home. He said that where they came from 'my kind' would be lucky to get home at all."

Surine and the others drove Fedder around until 6:00 A.M. in an apparent attempt to retrieve the damaging letter—which Fedder wisely had given to his attorney for safekeeping. During the five-hour ordeal, Fedder testified, he was questioned and threatened while driving to various houses to pick up finished cards. After a 4:00 A.M. stop at Fedder's house to get the $500 check Fedder had been paid for the postcard work (Surine demanded its return), the four drove to an all-night restaurant where Surine wrote and forced Fedder to sign a statement absolving the Butler campaign of all further payment and admitting that much of the work contracted to him was not properly done. Desperate to get away, Fedder signed it and left for home.

The Fedder story was but one sordid aspect of what the subcommittee and the public learned was done in Butler's name. As the testimony unfolded over a three-month period, 48 witnesses spoke some 750,000 words about what went on in Maryland. Little by little, Tydings and the subcommittee learned that the Mc-Cormicks also had connived to hire Jonkel, made loans to people associated with Butler's campaign, and raised big money from outside the state. And they learned that McCarthy originated the idea and provided the material for "From the Record." Clearly, McCarthy had done more than make three speeches in Maryland; he and his staff devoted thousands of hours to the Butler campaign. His entire crew was placed at Jonkel's disposal, with Jean Kerr assigned full time to the campaign. McCarthy raised money (including huge donations from wealthy Texas and Oklahoma oil men), designed literature, and planned the postcard campaign. He brought Robert E. Lee (of the Lee list from the State Department loyalty hearings) and his wife Rex into the campaign; met frequently with Jonkel, Bazy Miller, and Robert Morris, the loyalty hearing's minority counsel; and shared a speech writer, Ed Nellor, with Fulton Lewis. The evidence was inescapable that McCarthy had run the show from behind the scenes. "Never before," wrote historian Thomas C. Reeves in his book *The Life and Times of Joe McCarthy,* "had this sort of vindictiveness been displayed by a United States senator against a colleague."

Don Surine and his henchmen denied Fedder's story and accused Tydings of subornation of perjury. Ewell G. Moore, one of

Surine's men, prefaced his every refutation with the phrase "contrary to Mr. Fedder's statement, which is a lie," and concluded, "As we all know so well, ex-Senator Tydings has been turned out to pasture by the voters of Maryland. His cries of anguish indicate that the wound to his ego would be somewhat eased if he could convince the public that those who accomplished his defeat did so by lies, with the aid of kidnappers and extortionists. I respectfully request this committee to turn over the record of these proceedings to the Department of Justice, with a recommendation that Mr. Fedder be prosecuted for his perjury, and that . . . ex-Senator Tydings be investigated for subornation."

Tydings was recalled to testify on April 10. He denied he had suborned perjury and expressed deeper concern over the election abuses because the evidence had exposed the full extent of Mc-Carthy's involvement. When asked by Senator Margaret Chase Smith, "Is it your contention that the tabloid From the Record caused your defeat and the election of Senator Butler?" he responded, "At the time the election took place, if you had asked me that question, I probably would have said I doubt it. I think it was a contributing factor. Since the election, I have come in contact with a great many people, some of them have been good enough, Senator Smith, to write me letters and tell me that they voted against me and are very sorry they did, that they had been taken for a ride. [That From the Record had a terrific influence there is no doubt in my mind."

When pressed about his postelection statement attributing his defeat to the split in the Democratic party and dismissing the importance of McCarthy, Tydings said that initially he had no "comprehension of the widespread skulduggery and deceit and fraud which has since been laid bare before this committee." And the danger from such practices was very real: "There are many people who will resist money corruption, but even the honest Sunday-school teacher . . . can be ensnared and seduced to cast a false ballot [because of] malicious and falsely conceived statements." His vehemence betrayed the passion he felt, and he apologized, saying, "Excuse me for getting a little heated, gentlemen, but I am a little long suffering over this."

Tydings returned to the subject of perjury. Since he was questioned about subornation of perjury, he said, he would like the committee to recall Don Surine for questioning. Specifically he suggested that Surine had lied in testifying that he had resigned from the Federal Bureau of Investigation. Tydings said, "Let me say I have something in my possession that the committee doesn't have." It was proof that the FBI had fired Surine for unacceptable behavior. Surine's insistence that he left voluntarily was perjured testimony and must cast doubt on the rest of Surine's statement, Tydings believed.[2]

The committee apparently agreed. After calling Surine back to testify again, its members wrote in an unanimous report issued in August 1951, "The testimony of Surine before this subcommittee contains an apparent willful and knowing misstatement of a material fact relating to the circumstances of the termination of his services with the Federal Bureau of Investigation." Surine's possible perjury "should be transmitted to the Department of Justice for such action as it deems appropriate." In regard to Fedder's story of the midnight ride, the report stated, "The explanation given by Surine, [George] Nilles, and [Ewell] Moore for their activities on this occasion is not convincing; and it is the opinion of this subcommittee that the 'picking up and mailing of addressed post cards' was not the only purpose of their mission."

The report confirmed the validity of Tydings's charges. In every case involving campaign literature and illegal use of funds, the subcommittee found fault with Butler's campaign. Campaign manager Jonkel's misuse of funds was referred to the Justice Department for follow-up, and he was subsequently fined $5,000 for his failure to report contributions and expenditures worth over $27,000. There unquestionably was "outside influence": "Almost all the charges against the conduct of Senator John Marshall Butler's campaign can be attributed directly or indirectly" to those influences. Jonkel, McCarthy, members of his staff, the *Times–Herald,* its publisher, chief editorial writer, assistant managing editor, and other personnel—all projected their influence on the campaign, to Tydings's detriment. But there was no violation of election laws save for Jonkel's belated listing of campaign funds and ineligibility to be Butler's campaign manager, the report asserted.

"From the Record" contained "misleading half truths, misrepresentations, and false innuendos that maliciously and without foundation attacked the loyalty and patriotism [of Tydings] disregarding simple decency and common honesty." If such a publication constituted " 'fair comment' within the intent and meaning of the law [covering libelous defamation], then surely the law must be changed," the members agreed. The composite picture "was a shocking abuse of the spirit and intent of the first amendment to the Constitution." Further, the misrepresentation of the tabloid's sponsorship was judged "a violation of the Federal and State laws" requiring publishing organizations and their officers to be listed. The same was true for the pamphlet "Back to Good Old Dixie."

Condemnation of Butler's campaign was unequivocal. But the subcommittee distinguished between Butler's conduct and that of his "outsider" supporters. Butler, who was only mildly chastised for not keeping rein on certain elements of his campaign, waged a "front street" campaign. The subcommittee would not recommend that he be unseated. It noted that, although Butler could escape "legal responsibility" for acts of his agents, he had "a moral responsibility" to keep the campaign "above the low level of 'exploiting the doubt' as to the loyalty and patriotism of former Senator Tydings." The report's concluding sentence pointedly remarked, "To this date Senator Butler has not disclaimed responsibility for the tabloid, the faked photograph, or any other aspect of his campaign under investigation."

The report's harshest language scored the "despicable 'back street' campaign conducted by non-Maryland outsiders." The practices employed in the Maryland race were "unreservedly" denounced as "destructive of fundamental American principles." The "poison of unfounded charges and doubts as to alleged subversive leanings . . . eats away like acid at the very fabric of American life," the report asserted. "The right of disagreement is an inherent American right and privilege. But to recklessly imply to those with whom you disagree the taint of subversive leanings will rob democracy of its priceless heritage of the right to make up its mind as it sees fit."

McCarthy himself was indirectly but sternly rebuked. The report directly referred to his having avoided appearing before the subcommittee. Invited three times to attend and make "any statement or explanation" he felt appropriate, he artfully replied that he was not "seeking an 'opportunity' to appear." The subcommittee, possibly reluctant to tangle with the contentious McCarthy, did not demand his presence. But its report stated that, while he was not duty bound to testify, "the prominence of his personnel in the anti-Tydings campaign and the activity attributed to the Senator himself by certain witnesses might properly have been explained by him." Given the testimony, "it appears Senator McCarthy was a leading and potent force in the campaign against Senator Tydings." And in an obvious reference to McCarthy, the report concluded, "The question of unseating a Senator for acts committed in a senatorial election should not be limited to the candidates in such elections. Any sitting Senator, regardless of whether he is a candidate in the election himself, should be subject to expulsion by action of the Senate, if it finds such Senator engaged in practices and behavior that make him, in the opinion of the Senate, unfit to hold the position of United States Senator."

To no one's surprise, McCarthy attacked the report as "an attempt to whitewash Tydings," and he called the subcommittee members "puny politicians." The report was accepted, nonetheless, by the parent Committee on Rules and Administration (of which McCarthy was a member) by a 9–3 vote—a victory for the subcommittee and a setback for the adversarial senator from Wisconsin. (McCarthy, Kenneth S. Wherry of Nebraska, and William E. Jenner of Indiana were the three Republicans who voted against it.)

Although offering no specific recommendations for election procedures legislation or for the establishment of Senate rules for declaring a Senate seat vacant, the report inspired strong favorable reaction in the press.[3] *Commonweal,* the prestigious Catholic magazine, said in an editorial on a West Point scandal as well as the Senate subcommittee report: "If the West Point cadets are to be tried for cheating, why not McCarthy? Has he done less than these cadets to debase the integrity and honesty of our national life?" The Baltimore *Sun* wrote that the subcommittee unanimity and Rules Committee vote meant that "Republicans as well as Democrats were ashamed of the tactics which were employed in the campaign. Marylanders, above all others, should share this shame." Columnist Marquis Childs wrote that the ghosts of John C. Calhoun, Daniel Webster, Henry Clay, and a few senators less ancient but no less known for rectitude—Carter Glass, William E. Borah, and Robert M. La

Follette, Sr.—would be sickened. "Their contemporaries often thought them wrongheaded, stubborn, cantankerous. But they stood for beliefs, for a way of life, with certitude, with passion, with heart and soul and mind."

The report and general reaction was a salve for Tydings's wounded ego. Although he was unsatisfied by the lack of recommendations for legislative changes, and although McCarthy's continued misuse of the communist issue—and increased power—galled him, life had to go on. He joined Joseph Davies's law firm, which became Davies, Richberg, Tydings, Beebe & Landa. He pursued hobbies he could not make time for when he was in the Senate. After he and Eleanor attended the New York boat show in 1951, he purchased a powerboat and named it the *Elona*—*lona* is Spanish for "wild duck"; the "El" was for Eleanor. He took her on a cruise up the Atlantic coast to New York and up the Hudson River, through the 13 locks between the Hudson and Lake Champlain to Marjorie Davies's beautiful retreat on Lake Champlain in Upstate New York. And Tydings at last found time for his beloved farm at Oakington.

Throughout the 1940s whenever Congress was not in session he had thoroughly enjoyed running the farm. His first venture had been raising white Leghorn hens for eggs. He had fancy boxes constructed, and Oakington eggs arrived daily at Washington embassies and the Senate restaurant. When the hens—apparently unimpressed by the exalted status of their customers—went on a sit-down strike, Tydings had music piped into their commodious quarters. When they became cannibalistic and actually ate their own young, Eleanor told him they had to go. So he went into the hog business.

He spent time and money developing the finest herd of purebred, pedigreed white-belted Hampshire hogs in Maryland. At auction he bid on the boar Glory Bound, Wisconsin grand champion and reserve champion of all American Hampshire hogs. The new sire to his herd increased the size and quality of his stock, bringing state and national awards. He designed a "lying-in" hospital and nursery houses for the sows and piglets and also what he called "Hog Honeymoon House"—an odd wooden contraption painted a delicate rose with a broad platform that provided sufficient support for Glory Bound's tremendous weight (so he could not injure female swine brought to him for fertilization). When Emlen Knight Davies visited her daughter at Oakington, one of her friends asked the senator about the unusual barnyard furniture: "What is that for?" "Why that is the marriage bed," Tydings had explained. "You see, Glory Bound weighs a great deal more than the female hogs." "Well, isn't that just too cute!" the woman exclaimed. "I suppose you turn the little girl pigs over on their backs." Eleanor recalled that he turned purple from trying not to laugh.

Hogs proved as unprofitable as eggs so he tried his hand at cattle. When one of his prize young white-faced Hereford bulls lost the tuft of his tail to a barbed wire fence, it upset him to no end. He raised wheat, barley, corn, hay, and alfalfa, rotating the crops on his 550 acres. Talking about the farm could reduce him to boyish excitement. He loved the house with a passion and refused to sell the property even when offered $750,000.

And he wrote plays. One of them, *Barren Victory*—written in his last year in the Senate—was the story of the captain of a machine-gun battalion during World War I who served on the front lines in Alsace. He submitted it to a New York publisher and asked for an honest evaluation. He got it. "Rudimentary job on all counts—writing, characterization and construction": stilted dialogue, superficially drawn characters. Stay in the Senate, the publisher wrote, "and, unless you enjoy using the typewriter, stop playwriting." Tydings thanked him for his candid reaction. "Politics is so often so filled with baloney that it is refreshing when one enters a different field of endeavor to find an honesty and frankness which I wish were more entwined in the side of life which has occupied most of my energies."

None of what Tydings turned to filled the void. He enjoyed his law practice, was earning a great deal of money for the first time in his life, but the reality of having lost his power base in a city based on power was devastating. The loneliness was painful. No one was interested in the opinion of an ex-senator. He felt adrift, invisible. The shock of defeat under such publicly humiliating circumstances compelled him to return to the scene of what he considered McCarthy's crime. He found himself driven to fight McCarthy—both to stop him and to clear his own name—and offered his help to the few who were grouping to take on the senator from Wisconsin.

Democrat William Benton of Connecticut, a newcomer to the Senate, was shocked by McCarthy's behavior and was aghast at the Senate's apparent refusal to do anything about it, such as holding him accountable for abuse of office and lying. When the Rules Committee issued the Maryland Report on August 3, 1951, Benton read it and was spurred to action. Consulting only Secretary of the Senate Leslie Biffle and Senator Lister Hill of Alabama, on August 6 he introduced on the Senate floor an unexpected and unprecedented resolution requesting that the Rules Committee make an investigation to ascertain whether or not it should take "action with a view toward the expulsion from the United States Senate" of Joseph McCarthy. Benton did not actually believe that the necessary two-thirds of the Senate would vote for expulsion, but he intended to bring the kind of attention to McCarthy that might "encourage the voters of Wisconsin to expel him in 1952."

An enormously successful man, Benton was a mover and shaker in the world of business who had cofounded the New York advertising agency of Benton and Bowles in 1929, served as vice-president of the University of Chicago, then chairman of the board of Encyclopaedia Britannica. In 1949 he was appointed to fill the unexpired term of Connecticut Senator Raymond Baldwin, who had resigned. Benton was outgoing and friendly, but was a political neophyte lacking clout on Capitol Hill (his Washington experience was limited to two years as assistant secretary of state under Truman). Impulsive and a born maverick, he refused to let himself be intimidated by the precedents, customs, and aura of mystery that enveloped Senate proceedings. His defense of the State Department during the Tydings loyalty hearings brought him more notoriety than credit—except among a few defiant liberals, none of whom were part of the Senate's powerful inner circle.

It did not take Benton long to realize he needed advice from someone who knew how to work the Senate establishment, so he wrote to Tydings on August 9. "I know that you will have a particular interest in my Resolution," he began, "and I may say that I have had very little support for it and need a great deal of help and guidance." Tydings was more than willing.

They conferred by telephone and met at Tydings's office where he advised Benton to specify charges against McCarthy and that the best chance lay in nailing him for perjury because of testimony during the loyalty hearings. McCarthy had sworn that he had not said in his Wheeling speech that he had in his hand "a list of 205 [persons] that were made known to the Secretary of State as being members of the Communist Party." But employees of WWVA radio of Wheeling had signed affidavits stating McCarthy did make the statement, and a news reporter for the Wheeling *Intelligencer* had used the precise phrase in his story for the next day's edition.

In a September letter to Benton—written before a date had been set for Benton's testimony before the Rules Committee—Tydings wrote, "If these radio people committed perjury before the United States Senate, they should be called to account for it. If you have a perjurer sitting in your midst, then he should be kicked out of the United States Senate." Tydings also warned Benton of his own mistakes and advised him to give McCarthy no chance to turn the proceedings into a forum. "I want to warn you of a technique which McCarthy employs, which I didn't detect at first in my own case and which he is now beginning to use on you," Tydings wrote—referring to McCarthy statements implying that Benton was after his scalp because of his efforts to expose communists. He outlined "a counter-technique" to prevent McCarthy from "practicing his old game." If Benton were to state that it was a crime for a member of the Communist party to work for or receive a salary from the U.S. government, and then note that—because McCarthy had said he had the names of "205" in the State Department—McCarthy was in a position to take his case to a grand jury, then he would have given McCarthy the stage. "The way McCarthy would answer this would be to attack General Marshall or Dean Acheson, and say he would be glad to go before a jury (not a Grand Jury) at any time and prove his case against Acheson, if Acheson would meet him there," Tydings cautioned. "In other words, he has changed the subject, issued a new challenge which is impossible of fulfillment, in order to evade yours."

Tydings advised Benton to preface his question with a precise statement, then phrase the question so it could be answered only yes or no—explain that it is a crime for Communist party members to work for the government, note McCarthy's statement regarding 205 card-carrying Communists, and say, "Now, what I want to know is: will the Senator go before the Grand Jury and have these alleged traitors to our Government indicted, brought to trial, convicted and punished? The answer to this is a simple Yes or No. If it is No, then [McCarthy] puts himself in the position of having knowledge of these Communist law breakers [whom he could get out] tomorrow morning by the simple medium of appearing before the Grand Jury." If McCarthy tried to shift attention, Benton must cut in: "Now don't let's change the subject. Don't let's attack Acheson, whom the Senator has not so far accused of being a card-carrying Communist, or General Marshall, whom likewise he has not accused. . . . Will the Senator accept my challenge or will he just go off on another tirade and evade the issue?"

Benton must anticipate McCarthy, counter his accusations, stick to the subject. "Bill, you have simply got to hold him to the one issue. My mistake was in allowing him to wander all over the map, out of Senatorial courtesy, instead of holding his feet to the fire, which in my judgment would have brought about a different result. I hope you won't repeat my error. You have a great issue for showing this faker up and a technique that is unanswerable."

Benton asked him what witnesses to call. Tydings wrote, "Summon . . . the two radio men from Wheeling. . . . Then summon Edward Morgan [majority counsel from the loyalty hearings], Brien MacMahon [sic] and Millard Tydings, who will all testify that McCarthy said he never made any such statement. If having a charge of perjury hanging over a U.S. Senator is not enough reason for a Senate investigation, I would advise the Senate to march down to the Treasury en masse with trucks and shovels, and proceed to load them up with currency of the realm—for they will not be bothered."

A week before Benton was scheduled to testify, Tydings reiterated that Benton should make perjury the outstanding charge and "Lustron" the second most important charge. (The Lustron Corporation, which made prefabricated housing, had paid McCarthy $10,000 for an article he had written on housing while he was engaged in amending the Taft–Ellender–Wagner Housing Act to provide RFC loans of $7 million to Lustron.) Tydings advised that Benton should show "a general pattern of fraud, deceit and misrepresentation—in short, just plain lying—to show the character of the man who is occupying a Senate seat. . . . [D]on't let McCarthy choose the battleground. . . . And by all means get whatever you say to the press . . . for its influence on the Senate."

Benton followed Tydings's advice. Tydings firmly believed McCarthy would be unable to wiggle out this time. He said to Benton and friends, "If this matter is handled with a reasonable degree of competence . . . I cannot for the life of me see how the Senate investigating committee can fail to take up a charge of perjury." Not many people familiar with the Senate agreed. Except for a few tenacious liberals, the Senate by and large saw Benton's move as poorly conceived and impulsive. Some thought that Tydings was urging him on because he had an axe to grind with McCarthy.

But Tydings's involvement with Benton sprang from both personal hurt and a sense of altruism, those close to him believed. Ed Morgan described Tydings's efforts as a fight against the "evil" that McCarthy represented, and said, "He had enough grit in his system and enough guts . . . to feel that somewhere along the line this man, McCarthy, had to be brought to toe whether he was in the Senate or not." And he remained available to help others accomplish that. Senator William Fulbright, too, thought that Tydings's primary concern was to destroy the "evil influence" of McCarthyism.

When Benton testified before the Subcommittee on Privileges and Elections on September 28 in support of his resolution, he made ten specific charges, six relating to the loyalty hearings and two pertaining to the Maryland election:

1. McCarthy had committed perjury in regard to statements he made on the radio at Wheeling.
2. He engaged in unethical behavior by accepting a $10,000 fee from Lustron Corporation for an article written on housing.
3. He had charged George Marshall with being part of a "conspiracy to aid Russia."
4. He had made deceitful statements when he said he was forced to publicly name possible Communists at the State Department.
5. He had engaged in deceit and fraud in the Maryland election.

6. He falsely said he would not claim senatorial immunity.
7. His reference to a fraudulent FBI chart on the Senate floor during the loyalty hearings was a deliberate attempt to mislead the Senate.
8. His claim of knowing the names of "81" Communists was fraudulent, and he had falsified the source of the names.
9. His accusations relating to the Malmedy massacre of American soldiers by the German SS in 1944 were false.
10. He kept on his payroll a man charged with perjury.

McCarthy, Benton declared, had besmirched the integrity of the Senate, had lied repeatedly on and off the floor, had abused his colleagues. He detailed McCarthy actions that had contributed to Tydings's defeat. "From the earliest time," Benton remarked, "Senate rules have strictly forbade one Senator from impugning the character or the integrity of another Senator. As the case now stands, Senator McCarthy is the only individual in Senate history who has been granted immunity from this rule." If his resolution was not adopted, the record would show that the Senate "accorded to the Wisconsin member the rare privilege of falsifying the facts about another member because the Senate was afraid to enforce its own rules."

Benton's resolution was far from popular. Guy Gillette, chairman of the Subcommittee of Elections and Privileges—not eager to stir up McCarthy or the anti-communist hornets' nest on the eve of an election year (with a third of the Senate up for reelection)—had not planned to hold hearings on the resolution, hoping it would die by pigeonhole. What undoubtedly saved it from dropping out of sight was McCarthy's arrogance. His August 20 assault on those who wrote the Maryland election report—particularly Republicans Robert Hendrickson and Margaret Chase Smith (whom he denigrated as unqualified to judge him)—and his September 18 attack on Democrat Tom Hennings (whom he impugned because his law partner served as counsel to John Gates, editor of the *Daily Worker*) ultimately guaranteed Benton his hearing.

Even after Benton's September 28 session, the resolution again seemed doomed when no follow-up action was taken. McCarthy berated the subcommittee in November for its "dishonest" attempt to sabotage his reelection. In December he wrote Gillette two letters, released to the press, charging that the subcommittee was "guilty of stealing" from the taxpayers in its efforts to "aid Benton in his smear attack." He challenged their jurisdiction and demanded that Gillette provide him with information on its staff salaries and backgrounds. He persuaded Henry Cabot Lodge to help him get Hendrickson and Smith bumped from the subcommittee in favor of two pro-McCarthy Republicans. Smith bowed to Lodge's pressure. An angry Hendrickson would not. But it seemed McCarthy's intimidation had derailed the investigation.

Mike Monroney, who characterized the loss of Smith as "catastrophic," made an astute move that gave Benton's fight new life. He suggested that the subcommittee ask the full Senate for a vote of confidence. Since McCarthy had challenged the honesty and authority of the subcommittee, he should be asked to propose that the Rules Committee be discharged from considering Benton's resolution. The maneuver pitted McCarthy against the Senate's loyalty to its own institutions. If compelled to choose between McCarthy and one of its committees, Monroney was certain McCarthy would lose. When McCarthy refused to make the necessary motion, Rules Committee Chairman Carl Hayden of Arizona introduced it himself, and debate began on April 10.

True to his style, McCarthy counterattacked—to divert attention from Hayden's resolution and to throw Benton on the defensive. He introduced a resolution charging Benton with protecting Communists when he was assistant secretary of state and demanding investigation of Benton's public and private conduct. But he could not forestall a vote. The Senate voted 60 to 0 against discharging the Rules Committee; the subcommittee voted to open hearings on the Lustron charge. (The other charges they either conceded—e.g., the two stemming from his role in the Maryland election—or found "so controversial in nature that it would not be feasible for this Subcommittee, or perhaps any other agency, regardless of its resources, to resolve.")

Tydings's advice on how to handle McCarthy was never put to the test, for McCarthy refused to appear before the subcommittee. Six times between October 1951 and July 1952, McCarthy sidestepped invitations to appear. Although he testified in July to present what he called a "bill of particulars" on Benton (handing out 62 exhibits that "proved" Benton was a "clever propagandist" whose actions paralleled the Communist party line "down to the last period, the last comma"), he again avoided urgent requests in November that he give them the benefit of his testimony before drafting the final report. By then, he had been reelected (by 39,042 votes) and haughtily wrote to Tom Hennings (the subcommittee's new chairman), "I thought perhaps the election might have taught you that your boss and mine—the American people—do not approve of treason and incompetence and feel that it must be exposed."

Benton was defeated by Connecticut Republican Prescott S. Bush. Tydings's often repeated remark, "I cannot for the life of me see how the Senate investigating committee can fail to take up a charge of perjury," had failed to consider the unpopularity of Benton's resolution—and the Senate's fear of McCarthy. For many, including Tydings, believed it was fear, rather than senatorial courtesy, that deterred the subcommittee from subpoenaing McCarthy. The wish to avoid tangling with him clearly was stronger than the interest in Benton's resolution—a fact reflected in the final report.[4]

Tydings was determined to fight on and pushed Benton to continue too, telling him, "Under no circumstances should the matter be allowed to drop." Benton needed no persuading. Both were committed to stopping McCarthy by keeping his misdeeds in the public eye.

Tydings initiated his own campaign against McCarthy in November 1951 when he wrote Republican Senator William E. Jenner of Indiana, McCarthy stalwart, a caustic letter. Jenner had issued his own "minority report" on the Maryland election; in it, he dwelled almost entirely on the loyalty hearings, rehashing the charges of whitewash. "Here is an opportunity for you or McCarthy to make $5000 with great ease," Tydings wrote, challenging both Jenner and McCarthy to "show what a red-blooded American" could do when opportunity knocked. Since McCarthy knew the names of 205 (or 57) "card-carrying Communists" in the State Department, it should be simple for either of them to "go before the Grand Jury in the District of Columbia . . . and expose these rascals." He gave them until the second anniversary of McCarthy's Wheeling speech to collect the reward. "Don't put this off, Bill," he admonished, "because I am awfully anxious to pay you or McCarthy the money."

Mentioning Jenner's upcoming race for governor, Tydings suggested that, if he did expose Communists, "even the intelligent people in Indiana might vote for you"—but then noted that Jenner's voting record on the Marshall Plan, NATO, and arms aid to Korea mirrored the *Daily Worker* and American Communist party's positions. "Look out that you are not charged with 'guilt by association,' or with 'having an affinity for Communist causes,' " Tydings wrote scornfully. He gave the letter to the press and, in a postscript, asked Jenner to do him "the favor" of putting it in the *Congressional Record*.

Very early in 1952, Tydings upped the amount to $10,000 (a figure that matched the Lustron fee, he said) and widely advertised his offer. If McCarthy would bring even a single Communist employee of the State Department before a grand jury and the appearance led to indictment and conviction, McCarthy could claim the money. Tydings had fed Milwaukee *Journal* reporter Robert Fleming information on McCarthy, and in autumn 1952 he sent a photograph of the frozen corpses of unarmed American soldiers gunned down by the German SS at Malmedy to the Madison *Capital Times* and hundreds of other Wisconsin newspapers. "I am certain they will want the 'facts' about a man up for reelection, who has performed such patriotic services in defending the murderers of surrendered American soldiers," he said in his accompanying press release.

In October 1952, shortly before the election, in response to a challenge by McCarthy—he had invited Tydings to show up in Wisconsin—Tydings shot off a telegram accepting, on condition that McCarthy meet him in debate. Tydings elucidated exactly what he intended to say regarding the loyalty hearings. "When he got my telegram, he ducked and disdained to debate it with me," Tydings recalled in a December 1954 letter to a colleague.

He and Benton stayed in touch and exchanged information about Tydings's $10,000 advertisement and Benton's "I Believe" campaign. The I Believe crusade began as a result of McCarthy's $2 million libel suit filed against Benton, which accused the latter of using congressional immunity as a refuge so he could "smear" McCarthy. Benton waived his right to immunity for anything he said on or off the Senate floor. The moment McCarthy had Benton's word in writing, he filed suit. In 1954, as the suit was nearing trial, McCarthy suddenly dropped it, saying he could not find anyone who believed Benton's charges. Benton launched his I Believe campaign, asking people who believed his ten charges against McCarthy to write. In April Benton told Tydings, "It is amazing the response I am getting here. I now have over 2000 names of people who want to volunteer to testify that they believe my charges."

He also told Tydings that a respected New York ad writer thought the ten charges should be "renewed and revived and dramatized, in line with McCarthy's withdrawal of his suit against me. . . . Millard, if you are in a mood to give some time to this case again, you might be surprised to review once more the charges I made against McCarthy." Tydings replied, "I have noted that many people are willing to accord [McCarthy] a degree of elasticity concerning statements, both under and not under oath, which seems not to be accorded to anybody else where lying or perjury is concerned."

It was a depressing time for those invested in stopping McCarthy. Tydings wrote in reply to a lawyer friend in Dubuque, Iowa, "The truth of the matter is that my old colleagues do not care to get involved in a hydrated contest. . . . It is a sad commentary, however, that with all the investigations of fraud and crime which the Senate has conducted, it seems unwilling to ferret out matters in its own body where it would appear much more than a prima facie case of venality exists."

But there were individuals willing to battle McCarthy. When they formed a group dedicated to that purpose, Tydings aided them. A lobbying organization devoted to furthering the election of "men of caliber whose general outlook is liberal"—the National Committee for an Effective Congress (NCEC), headed by a young and dynamic Washington lobbyist, Maurice Rosenblatt—took McCarthy and McCarthyism very seriously. Rosenblatt realized that a campaign against McCarthy would require more than courage, it would need organization, media and congressional connections, and advice. He and a few others created the group in early 1953. Men such as Tydings provided advice. The Clearing House, as they called it, became the center of the stop-McCarthy movement. Tydings's role, Rosenblatt later recalled, was symbolic as well as advisory. "I think he was a moral support. It was important to have a guy like that with you."

Tydings and the Clearing House liberals made strange allies. Rosenblatt for years had opposed Tydings, whom he considered a rigid conservative and a *"Monsieur"*—a man so far above the crowd, so detached from his roots and grass roots, that he "was blinded— he was disarmed—by his own security, by his own position, by the fact that he was a *Monsieur*. . . . And he was a little obtuse, politically." But when Tydings and Rosenblatt initially met, "the man I met," he said, "was not the Grand Señor of Havre de Grace. The man I met was a smart, sharp politician whose ox had been gored and who was fighting for a principle." The trauma of the loyalty hearings and the election debacle had forced a turning point in his life, Rosenblatt believed—had brought out different facets of his character.

One element of his value to the Clearing House was that "Millard saw what [McCarthy] was," Rosenblatt said. He knew what they were up against from firsthand experience. "He had been bloodied and he was with us in every way." His very presence was a potent reminder that McCarthy was to be taken seriously. And his activism might embolden others.

As much as the Clearing House needed his support and input, Tydings's role in converting his former Senate colleagues to its cause was attenuated by reality. Overt activity by him would risk further politicizing the situation on Capitol Hill to McCarthy's benefit. "He did not go up to the Hill on our behalf . . . because I think he very directly felt that, as a defeated ex-Senator on this issue, he was bad news rather than good news because he reminded these fellows that they'd misinterpreted the McCarthy power." Rosenblatt was certain that he was privately in contact with those who had brushed up against McCarthy, but—as Rosenblatt put it—Tydings realized that "you never mention rope in a house where there's been a hanging."

Tydings understood the Senate's procedural and traditional institutions, and he understood the McCarthy modus operandi. To fight McCarthy, one had to do it dispassionately. "He wasn't going to get down there and compete with McCarthy to see who could roll in the mud better," Rosenblatt said. What he did was warn those who contemplated challenging McCarthy to avoid the face-to-face brawls that invited his famous attacks. Becoming another McCarthy victim would not help—and it was easy to be victimized by McCarthy because he played by no rules that would be considered fair. Stick to the facts, Tydings told anyone who would listen, and publicize everything in the press.

When Senator Stuart Symington publicly crossed swords with McCarthy as the preliminaries to the Army–McCarthy hearings were heating up in early 1954, Tydings appeared at his office with advice. McCarthy had charged the Army Department with "coddling Communists" and had accused Robert T. Stevens, secretary of the army, of abetting efforts to promote and protect Communists. When the army fought back and charged McCarthy (and his chief counsel on the subcommittee, Roy Cohn) of having demanded special treatment for Private G. David Schine, McCarthy made countercharges of "blackmail." The Army–McCarthy hearings commenced when the Permanent Subcommittee on Investigations—as no other committee would conduct the inquiry—voted to explore the accusations made by and against its chairman (and chief counsel).

Subcommittee Democrats, led by John L. McClellan, insisted that all other hearings be put off so they could focus exclusively on the matter. Republicans joined them when McCarthy tried to side-step the restriction. The Democrats demanded that the hearings be public. In the struggle over procedure, McCarthy won the right to cross-examine, but lost his seat on the subcommittee. He could not be prosecutor, witness, and judge on his own case, as he had attempted to be. Democrats searched carefully for an unbiased attorney to replace Roy Cohn as counsel (as he obviously could not serve on matters involving himself), and accepted Illinois Senator Everett Dirksen's recommendation of Ray H. Jenkins, a trial lawyer from Tennessee with no ties to McCarthy. (The army's counsel was Joseph L. Welch, a temperate, judicious, and consummately skilled attorney from Boston; McCarthy and Cohn were represented by up-and-coming Washington attorney Edward Bennett Williams.) Hearings began on April 22, 1954.

McClellan and Senator Henry Jackson of Washington approached McCarthy cautiously, but Stuart Symington was spoiling for a fight. At one point in committee, before the hearings had begun, Symington later remembered saying, "I can't go along with this, Joe, I am going to have to take you on." McCarthy had replied, "Don't do it, Stu. I'm fond of you, and if you do, I'll destroy you." Symington remembered it was "just as simple as that."

Tydings, watching from the sidelines, became concerned and decided to intervene. Arriving unexpectedly at Symington's door in February, he warned him that his telephones probably would be tapped, that he must be careful not only about what he said but also about what he wrote—even "casual writing"—because there were pro-McCarthy people on various Senate and subcommittee staffs, at the Pentagon, and among their friends. Symington was certain Tydings also spoke to McClellan and Jackson to warn them about how they handled McCarthy, to stay away from him. "What Millard was saying to me was 'be careful.' . . . He wanted to advise me about what he had learned."

But Symington did not heed the warning. "I did this [take McCarthy on during the Army–McCarthy hearings] against Tydings's advice." When Tydings could see that Symington was going to do it anyway, he counseled, "avoid personal confrontation; stick to objective facts. . . . What Millard was saying was, 'This fellow is dangerous because he doesn't play the rules you and I think are important; so watch it.' " Symington recalled with a rueful smile that he should have taken Tydings's warnings more seriously. "Ironically, I gave his advice to Bob Stevens, secretary of the army, but he didn't listen, got really embroiled with him," he added. "We found out later some of our phones were tapped; very sad."[5]

Perhaps the only time Tydings appeared on Capitol Hill in open support of the Clearing House was during the Army–McCarthy hearings. Republicans had begun trying to end them prematurely in May. The television cameras that carried the hearings into millions of homes were not kind to McCarthy. His antics—bullying and interrupting incessantly with what became a parodied refrain, "Point of order, Mr. Chairman"—had done little for the Republican party's image. But the Democrats were determined not to let the hearings end until the Eisenhower administration was forced to deal with McCarthy.

Tydings feared that a "temporary" recess the Republicans had managed to win was actually a ploy intended to terminate the hearings. He met with Rosenblatt and Dean Francis P. Sayre of the

Washington Cathedral, another Clearing House activist, to discuss the situation; then, accompanied by Rosenblatt, Tydings went to see McClellan to alert him to the dangers of falling for such a ruse. With McCarthy looking vulnerable, they must not let the moment go by. Sayre met with Symington. On the heels of those meetings, McClellan and Symington released separate, blunt statements declaring that the subcommittee would not be sidetracked and that the hearings would continue—which they did until June 17, a week after the famous dramatic clash between McCarthy and the army's attorney, Joseph Welch.

McCarthy's attack on Frederick G. Fisher, a young associate of Welch's Boston law firm, Hale and Dorr, evoked the impassioned reaction from Welch: "Until this moment, Senator, I think I never really gauged your cruelty or your recklessness. . . . If it were in my power to forgive you for your reckless cruelty, I [would] do so. I like to think I am a gentleman, but your forgiveness will have to come from someone other than me. . . . Have you no sense of decency, sir, at long last? Have you left no sense of decency?"

The Army–McCarthy hearings of springtime 1954 proved to be the beginning of McCarthy's undoing. But the instrument that delivered the coup de grâce was handed to the Senate by an elderly and dignified gentleman, Ralph Flanders of Vermont—a principled and conservative Republican senator (conservative in the philosophical sense, for politically he called himself a liberal) who had finally had enough. On June 11, 1954, Flanders publicly took the singularly courageous step of offering a resolution that would strip McCarthy of his Senate chairmanships if he did not answer the six questions asked in the 1952 report on William Benton's charges.

Flanders's resolution was resisted stoutly on both sides of the aisle, fearing a precedent would be set that could threaten their system (and could alienate one bloc or another among their constituents). But on August 2, the Senate voted 75 to 12 to go ahead. The Clearing House, convinced Flanders was motivated by principle and would not back down, offered him support. He accepted, and they set out to rally public opinion by keeping the press briefed and by getting influential citizens and the leadership of labor, civic, and religious groups to pressure their senators to support the Flanders measure. But the Senate as a whole was unwilling to take a stand on McCarthy.

Sensing that the situation could be salvaged, Flanders announced on July 16 that he was substituting another resolution for the one depriving McCarthy of his chairmanships. Senate Resolution 301 called instead for the censure of McCarthy, charging him with conduct "unbecoming a member of the United States Senate"— "contrary to Senatorial traditions"—that would "bring the Senate into disrepute." Flanders's resolution was the weapon that humbled McCarthy and vindicated Tydings, Benton, and the other men and women who had tried for four frustrating years to make the country see him for what he was.

On August 2, a committee of six was appointed to hear charges against McCarthy. Republican Arthur V. Watkins of Utah, gaunt, tall, and a Mormon of scrupulous conscience (of whom Richard Rovere wrote, "He could play variations on the crack of doom with a chairman's gavel"), was appointed chairman. The other members were Democrats Edwin C. Johnson of Colorado, John C. Stennis of Mississippi, and Samuel J. Ervin, Jr., of South Carolina, and Republicans Frank Carlson of Kansas and Francis H. Case of South Dakota. The choices were widely acclaimed—although columnist Stewart Alsop remarked that a "man-eating tiger" was going up against an "elderly mouse."

The Watkins Committee went about its business without concession to several McCarthy demands. "We are not unmindful of *his* genius for disruption," Watkins noted. When the committee finished, it had conducted a fair and somber investigation that exposed in deliberate recital every instance of abuse, defiance, and impudence committed by McCarthy and found him culpable on two counts: his contemptuous treatment of the Subcommittee on Privileges and Elections in 1951 and 1952, and his abuse of General Ralph W. Zwicker in 1954. McCarthy's behavior was labeled "contemptuous, contumacious, and denunciatory, without reason or justification."

By the time the Senate reconvened in November (Democrats regained control of both houses in the midterm elections), McCarthy had defiantly scored the committee in the interim. He accused the Watkins Committee of having become the "unwitting handmaiden . . . involuntary agent . . . and attorneys in fact" of the

Communist party, prompting Sam Ervin to call for McCarthy's expulsion. Minority Leader Lyndon B. Johnson of Texas declared that the kind of language McCarthy used about his colleagues could be "fittingly inscribed on the wall of a men's room."

McCarthy's defiance hammered the last nails into the coffin of his career. Debate on Flanders's resolution began on November 29. On December 2 the Senate dropped the Zwicker charge but voted to censure McCarthy on two counts: for contempt and abuse of the Subcommittee on Privileges and Elections in 1951 and 1952, and for contempt and abuse of the Senate itself and its Select Committee in 1954.

The vote was a resounding repudiation of McCarthy. Forty-four of the Democrats, one Independent (Wayne Morse), and half of the Republicans voted to condemn. Just three senators—McCarthy himself; Wisconsin's other senator, Republican Alexander Wiley; and Democrat John F. Kennedy of Massachusetts—were unrecorded. After it was over, McCarthy told reporters, "Well, it wasn't exactly a vote of confidence, but I don't feel I've been lynched. I'm happy to have this circus ended so I can get back to the real work of digging out Communism, crime, and corruption."

McCarthy had not been lynched. He retained his seat. The man who once told a young woman he was courting—the daughter of a senator who repeated his confidence to Tydings's wife Eleanor—that he would end up either in the White House or in jail, ended up in neither. But his career was as dead as if it had been hanged from the Capitol dome.

The Clearing House, many members of Congress, and especially William Benton and Millard Tydings were elated at the outcome. Tydings and Benton felt personally vindicated and felt that their efforts to stop McCarthy in 1951 and afterward finally were justified. Despite the apparent failure of Benton's resolution to expel McCarthy or censure him in 1951 or 1952, in the long run it proved anything but a failure. That resolution, the ensuing exchanges between McCarthy and the members of the Subcommittee on Privileges and Elections, and its final report (the Hennings Report) played a central role in the final censure of Joe McCarthy.

The censure of Joseph McCarthy provided Tydings with needed vindication. But the Senate's action, although it spoke volumes about McCarthy's rectitude, did not repair the damage to Tydings's reputation. The perception lingered that he had engaged in some kind of whitewash of the State Department. He wanted to clear his name once and for all. Only then would he feel both vindicated and exonerated.

To that end, Tydings answered those who still questioned his handling of McCarthy's charges in late 1954. A Baltimorean who suggested he had used a "spraying machine" in whitewashing Owen Lattimore was reminded that evidence proving Lattimore was either a Communist or disloyal to the government was never presented. "Now the thing that irks me is this," he said. "Many of the same employees that I was called upon to investigate are still working in the State Department. If I 'whitewashed' them, why haven't they been reinvestigated during the last two years when the Wisconsin Senator has been in charge of that matter? No one gives me an answer to this," he lamented.

As accusations continued to surface, Tydings realized that, unless he could produce a statement from officials in President Dwight D. Eisenhower's administration that not one State Department employee had been proven to be either a Communist or disloyal to the government, the shadow of McCarthy's charges would darken his name forever. He asked Senator Olin D. Johnston of South Carolina, ranking Democrat on the Post Office and Civil Service Committee, to request in writing the status of all persons investigated by Tydings's committee and the ultimate disposition of their cases.

Accordingly Johnston wrote Secretary of State John Foster Dulles on November 24, 1954, and posed questions designed to clear up any remaining doubts over Tydings's investigation. Specifically, Johnston asked, who among the ten individuals named by McCarthy in public testimony had been proven to be disloyal or Communist, and who among the group of 80 whose names were not made public (the Lee list names) had proven to be disloyal or Communist? How many of those named still were working at the State Department? And he asked that the department advise him whether any employees or former employees of the State Department had been indicted and found guilty—and, if so, who?

The State Department's January 10, 1955, reply, made by Assistant Secretary of State Thruston B. Morton, stated in writing that

11	of those in question never were employed by the State Department	3	were removed under Public Law 733 (security)
10	still were employed by the State Department	2	resigned during Executive Order 9835 proceedings (old loyalty program)
11	transferred to other agencies	1	was removed under Executive Order 9835 proceedings
6	were terminated by reason of completed assignments	1	resigned during Executive Order 10450 proceedings (new loyalty program)
8	separated by reduction-in-force	2	were removed for suitability reasons
1	retired	32	resigned for other reasons (and 1 was mislisted)
1	died		

Morton noted that neither Executive Orders 9835 and 10450 nor Public Law 733 "requires that it be proved that a person is a Communist before he may be discharged, and no findings to this effect were made" in cases where individuals were dismissed in connection with those regulations. And he noted that "no present or former employee has been indicted and found guilty under the provisions of Public Law 759," which made it a felony for a "member of an organization that advocates the overthrow of the government of the United States by force and violence" to accept federal employment.

Johnston issued a press release on January 16, 1955, declaring that the State Department had informed him that not one of the persons investigated by Tydings's committee had been found to be a Communist or disloyal to the government, and concluded, "Realizing that [Tydings's] 1950 investigation . . . and the publicity following that investigation has left a great deal of doubt and confusion in the public mind as to the true facts in the case, the letter to me from the State Department . . . should clear up this matter for all time." He was gratified, he said, that "charges of widespread Communism" under a Democratic administration had "been contradicted by the letter to me from the present Republican Administration."

Johnston's statement received wide coverage in the national press. McCarthy immediately accused Johnston of "torturing the truth" in an attempt to "bring [Tydings] back to life" before the 1956 Senate elections. McCarthy insisted Morton's letter substantiated his claims that subversives had infiltrated the State Department. His challenge again confused the issue because Morton's language was vague. Dulles refused to clarify the matter.

Tydings refused to be denied his public exoneration. He and Ed Morgan studied the wording of Morton's letter. After much thought, Tydings decided that the best way to prove there had been no whitewash was to acquire an official confirmation—Republican confirmation—that most of the cases McCarthy gave the Tydings Committee to investigate had been investigated previously by two House committees in 1947 and 1948—under a Republican-controlled Congress—and that a substantial number of them still worked at the State Department. Johnston wrote Morton asking him to state how many of the 80 cases came from the list of 108 names reviewed in 1947 and 1948. Morton's reply: 69.

Johnston's subsequent press release made clear that most of McCarthy's cases had undergone multiple investigation under the Republicans, none were dismissed from service, and many of those that McCarthy had Tydings investigate remained on the government payroll the entire time McCarthy was chairman of the Committee on Investigations—with ten still at the State Department. "The above facts," Johnston said on July 31, 1955, "should completely exonerate the Tydings Committee from any charge of 'whitewashing' for we now learn from high officials in the Eisenhower Administration the true facts."

Simultaneous with McCarthy's censure and Johnston's initial letter to John Foster Dulles, Tydings had begun to emerge from his political cocoon. In November 1954 he launched a "decency" drive, challenging John Marshall Butler and McCarthy to "come out of their holes and fight like men." He dared Butler to meet him in debate. Butler refused. Tydings's move was interpreted by political analysts as the opening gambit of a return to public life. When questioned about it, he told reporters, "I haven't crossed that bridge yet."

His reply exemplified an uncertainty he felt. When asked by constituents eager to see him reenter politics whether he was testing the water, he stated, "As far as my own personal wishes and that of my family are concerned, I have no desire whatever to stand again for elective public office. I know that my recent excursions in the press have been interpreted as a bid on my part to go back to the Senate. Having served in the Senate longer than any other Marylander in the history of the United States, my appetite for public office has been pretty well satisfied." But ambivalence surfaced in the next breath: "I do feel that the campaign of 1950, with its composite picture and totally now proved false propaganda, left a scar on what I had hoped to be an honorable record. I do not feel I can go to my ultimate grave without putting the record straight."

Tydings's son Joseph, a recent law school graduate intensely interested in local politics—he had just won election to the Maryland House of Delegates and was working hard to establish Young Democrats Clubs throughout the state—feared his father's health would suffer if he reentered public life. Joe tried to dissuade him, but knew the issue transcended politics, knew it involved emotional and logical considerations that were at odds. Reflecting on the ambivalence years later, Joe Tydings said, "I don't think he ever recovered from losing the election [in 1950]. On the other hand he enjoyed the sudden affluence [and success] his law practice brought. . . . But it wasn't compensation enough. He never showed it, but he was very thoroughly wounded."

Tydings's law practice may have been financially remunerative, but it was not emotionally satisfying; it was small compensation for the loss of position, power, and prestige—much less the purity of name and reputation. The humiliation rankled; the injuries were slow to heal. As another political figure, reflecting on his own defeat, said, "I have friends who lost a campaign 20 years ago and if you get two drinks in them it comes back."

The big money, the knowledge that he had served long and well, and the possibility that his health was ill suited to the rigors of a campaign competed with siren songs of exoneration and restoration of power. Ed Morgan summed up what he thought finally made Tydings run in 1956: "Once a man has [reached] that pinnacle of power . . . there's a certain bug [that] never gets out of his system. I think that might have been it more than anything else. And the idea of vindication."

When Tydings was wooed in late 1954 and afterward—by Maurice Rosenblatt, Ernest Gruening of Alaska, Ed Morgan, Baltimore Mayor Thomas D'Alessandro, E. Brooke Lee, and countless others, including many liberals—it was hard for him not to channel residual anger into action, hard not to dispel the periodic bouts of self-pity by reentering politics.

In summer 1955 the *Sun* reported that Tydings said he would be "tempted" to run in 1956 if "that arch-demagogue, Senator Joseph R. McCarthy, could be persuaded to come to Maryland and meet me face-to-face." "Among other epithets," the paper noted, Tydings called McCarthy a "consummate liar," a "coward," and a "hypocrite of the first water." News articles commented that Tydings had passed up the chance to run in 1952 when Herbert O'Conor retired, and speculated that he was waiting for a rematch with Butler. And so Tydings's November 1954 "decency" drive ultimately became his reelection drive, even though his ambivalence demonstrated itself up to the filing deadline.

The idea of a Tydings–Butler rematch intrigued the entire Democratic community. He was deluged with telegrams, calls, and letters; editorials begged him to run; and Oakington was invaded by visiting party leaders urging him to enter the race. He remained uncertain, saying, "I haven't any definite timetable. It depends on events"—by which he meant a genuine draft. Eleanor wrote her father that "all Hell had broken loose" at home from the pressure. "Joe says I should try to dissuade him, that his health couldn't stand the kind of strenuous campaigning he would have to do. He is sixty-five. I am afraid to do so. He might regret it all his life if he doesn't run and I would be to blame! I am torn about what to do. He is happy with his law practice and I am happy too. It must be his decision."

Joe listed the pros and cons. Tydings agreed that Joe was right; it would mean an exhausting fight. He decided not to run. But in February 1956, two weeks before deadline, under pressure from

D'Alessandro and leaders from all over the state—many pledged to announced candidate George P. Mahoney—Tydings agreed to file. Maryland Democrats had dual motives. They feared that Mahoney, who had wrecked four elections since 1948, would win the nomination and again bring the party defeat. If they could persuade Tydings to run, they assured themselves of a candidate with the stature to beat Butler—and rid themselves of a four-time loser and spoiler.

But Tydings wavered anew, changing his mind just at deadline. When D'Alessandro, who had wrung from him the promise to run, learned of the reversal, he tracked him down in New York City (where Tydings had gone on business) and called four times, saying, "You're making a hell of a mistake. You've got us all out on a limb. This isn't the thing to do. What the hell is the matter with you, you crazy?" D'Alessandro arranged for others to call Tydings, and together they finally convinced him to run for the sake of the party. "Joe remonstrated and so did I," Eleanor wrote her father, "but he had made his own decision. He could beat Mahoney and he would beat Butler. He would erase the 1950 campaign smear against him."

He campaigned as if he were an unknown. He sought the advice of people he had never listened to before—notably his son and D'Alessandro, who became unofficial campaign advisers. Joe educated him on issues pertaining to civil rights and labor. Tydings had never taken Joe's advice seriously before; but "this time he accepted it," Joe Tydings remembered with pride. "He changed his position on civil rights because of me. He had always taken the position, 'separate but equal' educational facilities. I explained to him [what] the Supreme Court had ruled in *Brown vs. Board of Education* and [that was] the law of the land. And he sat down, listened, and agreed." On labor, Tydings "had always been bitterly opposed to organized labor. . . . I got him to moderate his position with respect to labor issues. . . . He listened. That was the first time he listened to me," he said. Joe campaigned hard for his father in Annapolis, at the University of Maryland—he had been student body president—and through the Young Democrats Clubs he had founded (and of which he was then state president).

D'Alessandro served as a sort of father-confessor who gave him undiluted feedback—sans sugar coating. After his first speech he came to D'Alessandro for an opinion. "He came in and I said, 'You stunk.' Oh, he went wild. I said, 'There's no use fighting with me, I'm here to help you. Who in the hell wants to hear about potatoes and cabbage . . . in East Baltimore?' " He told Tydings: "Nobody knows who in the hell you are. You ought to have a name plate in front of your place because your face has changed. . . . I gave him hell. So he got mad and I said let him get mad. . . . He got mad every time he didn't have his way—like a kid. You'd tell him not to do this, and he breaks all the dishes in the house. Then you'd tell him not to do it [again] and he'd break some more dishes."

But Tydings heard him. The next time he spoke he asked the Baltimore mayor to listen. "That's fine," D'Alessandro said. "That's a good speech. Now put a little force in it and put a name plate there and smile at the end."

Tydings campaigned with a new humility and ran the legs off Mahoney. He traveled at times with others running for office— newcomers like Louis Goldstein, a young man just entering public life. He outwalked, outtalked, and outlasted them. He astonished his driver with his knowledge of remote areas. When they were trying to find a place in the mountains of Western Maryland, the driver interrupted him from reading papers in the backseat as they came to the end of the paved road, asking, "Where to now, Senator?" Tydings glanced up, indicated a dirt road and continued reading. When the road appeared to have ended and the driver said, "Now, where to, Senator?" Tydings looked up. "Take that way to the left." Just as the driver was convinced they were hopelessly lost, he saw a mountain cabin where an old man sat on the front porch chewing tobacco. The old fellow stood up and beamed, "Lawd God, Millard boy, I ain't seen you in thirty years! Come in and have a drink." He was the Democratic leader of that part of the mountain country.

The man who filed the day before deadline beat Mahoney, who had started with the machine in his pocket (if not the wholehearted support of his colleagues). It was a narrow victory; the unit vote was tied at 76 to 76, but Tydings won the popular vote 142,238 to 134,246. "I'm a tired boy," he told reporters after his May 7 victory.

He was more than tired. In the last week of the campaign, his driver had sought out Eleanor and told her, "The Senator is very ill, Mrs. Tydings, and I have put him to bed in a room. Nobody knows this. You had best go to him quickly." She found him burning with fever. Their physician prescribed antibiotics and he appeared to recover. But he stayed tired. Even after a week's rest at Hot Springs, Virginia—where he slept most of the time—he told her he had no intention of campaigning strenuously in the general election.

Back at Oakington he continued his "rest cure." One morning Eleanor went into Aberdeen, leaving him in bed. He told her he was going to drive to Baltimore to meet with Democratic leaders and have lunch with Mahoney. She had read in the newspaper that Mahoney had gone to Florida, but thought little of it. When she returned in perhaps an hour, she found him still in bed. She said, "I thought you were going to Baltimore." "I did go," he said. "But Millard," she said, "you couldn't have had lunch. It's only noon now." "Well, I did," he insisted.

Distressed, she went downstairs where Robert Livingstone had been polishing floors and asked him if Tydings had gone out. "No, ma'am, he hasn't left his room." That night Tydings complained of a terrible pain in his head, all around his left eye. By 11:00 P.M. he was in such agony that she called the doctor and her husband was rushed by ambulance to Johns Hopkins Hospital. He was there for 46 days. That was the first inkling Eleanor had of the nature of the devastating illness—initially thought to be shingles, then encephalitis, but never diagnosed conclusively—from which Tydings never recovered.

At first the family put up what Eleanor called "a happy nonchalant front" and acted as though his illness were merely fatigue. But the hospitalization became a nightmare when the press descended in a mob, demanding information and demanding to see him.

The doctors were baffled. Top men on the staff examined him and thought he might have a brain tumor. A Boston specialist was brought to do tests (a brain X ray and spinal tap) that ruled out a tumor. In conference with ten physicians, Eleanor was told that her husband was suffering from encephalitis. They said he could not head the state delegation to the Democratic National Convention in Chicago as planned, and they insisted he must not continue his campaign. A stunned Eleanor argued, realizing what a blow withdrawal from the race would be to him; but they were adamant. When they explained to her what encephalitis was—a viral infection of the lining of the brain—it was with a real sense of dread that she accepted their counsel. She asked his private physician about eventual recovery. "The doctor tried to let me down easily," she wrote in her memoirs, "but finally told me gently: 'The best you can hope for is that the Senator will get worse slowly.' "

After Tydings returned to Oakington in late July, where Eleanor arranged round-the-clock nursing, his convalescence went well. Not fully aware of the gravity of his condition, he nevertheless knew he would not be able to go on with the campaign. Eleanor summoned his closest advisers to tell them. After talking with Tydings and Eleanor, they conferred among themselves before D'Alessandro and Brooke Lee urged Eleanor to take his place as candidate. When she protested that she could not with her husband so ill, they requested she keep his condition—and withdrawal—a secret until after the convention. Otherwise, they said, the party would be reduced to chaos and Mahoney would capture the nomination. She reluctantly agreed, but found the duplicity painful as swarms of reporters pounded on the gates of her home.

In early August, Tydings suffered a serious relapse and went into virtual seclusion. Three days after the Democratic convention, on August 19, his withdrawal from the race was announced. His statement said that his health made it impossible for him to conduct a vigorous campaign: "This has been the most painful decision of my life and has been reached upon the unanimous advice of the finest doctors, and after the entreaties of my family."

Immediately D'Alessandro, Lee, and others went to work on Eleanor to persuade her to accept the nomination. Joe was too young, Mahoney undesirable, she had to do it for the party because only the Tydings name could beat Butler, they said. She again refused. But articles about an Eleanor Tydings candidacy appeared, and she received calls from other leaders asking her to consider it seriously. The Democratic National Committee member for Maryland persuaded her to meet with him, Lee, D'Alessandro, and others before a speech she was scheduled to deliver to the United Democratic Women's Club (UDWC) in Ocean City on August 26.

The first thing she saw as she neared the boardwalk were crowds of women waving banners and signs reading "WE WANT ELEANOR" and "ELEANOR FOR THE SENATE." Her first thought was, "What is Eleanor Roosevelt running for here in Maryland?" Under pressure from D'Alessandro and Lee, flattered by their confidence, and perhaps overwhelmed by it all—especially by the strain she was under—she found herself saying she would accept the nomination if the state convention drafted her, and she telephoned her husband for advice. "It was one of his better days," she recalled. He laughed and told her to "ask Brooke Lee if it really was 'in the bag' " for her to win. Lee replied that "nothing was ever a sure thing in politics but that this was the closest thing to a 'draft' " he had ever seen.

"What about it?" the men asked impatiently when she returned from talking to Tydings. "All right, I'll do it," she said. When Joe caught up with her as she entered the UDWC hall, he said, "My God, Mother, what have you done?" At Baltimore's grand Belvedere Hotel in dozens of smoke-filled rooms, frantic infighting ensued on August 27 among rival groups caucusing furiously for votes. Eleanor was escorted to a suite of rooms and left there while the men joined what was a confusing melee over procedure. D'Alessandro's Baltimore district fell apart. His son went up to the room where Eleanor waited and drew his thumb across his throat. "We wuz robbed, Mrs. T," he growled. "The bastards bought the bastards." Eleanor lost in the unit vote 97 to 55 on August 27, and George Mahoney faced Butler in November.[6]

Eleanor knew it was just as well she had not won. Her heart had never been in it, and her husband's illness worsened, as predicted. At times he appeared to have recovered. He returned to the practice of law in 1957, was mentioned for the Senate in 1958 (he said only that those who wanted him were "very kind" but that "my future plans are indefinite"). Periods of recovery were sporadic. One day he would be in great form, advising his law partners, consulting with his son, conversing animatedly at dinner, admiring his grandchildren. Then the next day he could become fearful, angry, ill, and forgetful. The man who made extemporaneous speeches detailing flaws in the national budget, who cited facts and figures without using notes, would forget the point of an anecdote in the middle of telling it, or would repeat the story a few minutes later as if he hadn't told it.

Sometimes Tydings would sit alone for hours in the darkened library at Oakington, or would go into the solarium where young Eleanor's baby, Suzy, lay in her bassinet, and he would spend long periods of time watching her face as she slept, perhaps mourning the children he and Eleanor never had. Other times he would sink into illness, drift away to a place where the physical and emotional pain meant nothing, slip back in time to the battlefields of France where he had endured and survived the greatest challenge of his life. "We had a tough time in the battle of Verdun drive," he called out to visitors at his bedside. It was unbearable for Eleanor to watch illness lift him out of the realm of reality, cast him into an abyss of madness induced by pain.

For almost five years Millard Tydings ranged between sickness and health until at last his spirit gave up the struggle. On February 9, 1961, he died of pneumonia in his sleep. The obituaries eulogized him as "one of America's political greats," and noted in their praise how "few men in public life have the distinction of having been pilloried by partisans of both sides." Many in Maryland, the Baltimore papers remarked, suffered guilt over their treatment of him. He was a man who never ran from a fight, said the Washington *Post,* who "never hesitated to disagree with powerful political figures." The New York *Times,* in an editorial piece called "A Fighting Senator," said that his "two sensational battles"—against Franklin D. Roosevelt and Joe McCarthy—earned him a place in history. He was "a distant and rather an austere man," the *Times* acknowledged, but he possessed "the personal courage and the deep conviction" required of men who would stand up to those they opposed. He was, said the *Times,* a man who "impressed even those who disagreed with him."

The family was grateful he could not know he was pilloried anew after his death by McCarthy partisans. They wrote letters denouncing his "perfidious" handling of the loyalty hearings, letters complaining that McCarthy had been "defamed" by those "eulogizing" Tydings's alleged courage. But the convocation of honorary pallbearers would have pleased him. Vice President Lyndon B. Johnson headed the group that included Speaker of the House Sam Rayburn; Supreme Court Justice Tom Clark; Senators Stuart Symington, William Fulbright, Lister Hill, Estes Kefauver, Richard

Russell, Carl Hayden, and Henry Jackson; General Carlos Romulo of the Philippines; and every major figure in Maryland: Governor J. Millard Tawes, Comptroller Louis Goldstein, Thomas D'Alessandro, George Radcliffe, and all his longtime friends from the war, E. Brooke Lee, William Preston Lane, William C. Walsh, and General Milton Reckord, the man who had helped him form the unit of national guardsmen sent by Woodrow Wilson to Eagle Pass, Texas, in 1916—a lifetime earlier.

The night before Tydings's funeral it snowed, the heaviest snow in many years. Oakington's mile-long private lane was blocked with six-foot drifts. There was no public road service to clear the way to the church and cemetery. The city fathers of Havre de Grace manned the city's plows themselves to open the roads.

American Legionnaires and veterans came by the hundreds to Oakington to pay tribute and last farewell to their comrade. President John F. Kennedy sent a wreath of red roses. Tydings lay in his casket in the great bay window of the solarium at Oakington, the window that looked out over the snow-covered Chesapeake Bay. A young Maryland opera star traveled down from New York City to sing the Lord's Prayer at an overflowing St. John's Church, a church that Tydings's great-great-grandfather had helped to build.

Millard Tydings was buried beside an evergreen tree on a snow-mantled slope at Angel Hill Cemetery in Havre de Grace. The tall, lanky, lantern-jawed senator famous for his acid tongue and rapier wit and hard-fought political wars was at peace.

Notes

1. The debut was not called off in a fit of pique as insinuated by some in the press, but the defeat surely played a part. The family had considered cancellation as early as October, as Eleanor Tydings wrote to her stepmother Marjorie Davies that month; but General Lawton Collins of the Joint Chiefs of Staff, just back from Korea, had told Tydings not to cancel because the situation would not worsen. In November and December, however, military reverses seriously damaged the United Nations' position after the Chinese entered the war. The family concluded that the extravagance would be unfitting.

2. Surine was fired because he misused his position in a white slavery

case in Baltimore. Surine made use of a prostitute's services in a manner more befitting a customer than an agent of the FBI.

3. No Senate or election reforms resulted from the Maryland senatorial election of 1950 investigation, primarily because of First Amendment concerns.

4. The Subcommittee on Privileges and Elections' final—and unanimous—report of January 2, 1953, avoided the issue of communists in government or "McCarthyism." That would have forced them to act on what a sitting senator said from the Senate floor—a task all were unwilling to tackle. Instead the report indirectly confronted McCarthy by repeating six questions Hennings had asked him in a November 1951 letter: Was it ethical for McCarthy to receive $10,000 from Lustron? Were contributions made to his anti-communist campaign diverted to personal use? Did he use family and friends to mask income, stock speculation, receipts, and the like? Had he used his influence on behalf of special interest groups? Did his financial dealings violate federal and state banking and tax laws? Did he violate federal and/or state corrupt practices acts in his 1944 and 1946 Senate campaigns? Clearly the suggested answer in each case was yes. The appendix of exhibits reinforced that implication. A 15-page history of the investigation—including McCarthy's refusals to appear and his arrogant responses—laid the foundation for its "inescapable conclusion that Senator McCarthy deliberately set out to thwart any investigation of him by obscuring the real issue and the responsibility of the Subcommittee by charges of lack of jurisdiction, smear, and communist-inspired persecution." His behavior demonstrated "disdain and contempt for the rules and wishes of the entire Senate body, as well as the membership of the Subcommittee on Privileges and Elections." But the report made no recommendations. The Senate's failure to confront McCarthy was denounced by the liberal press.

5. What Symington had said to Stevens was, "If you are going to play with McCarthy, you have got to forget about any of those Marquis of Queensbury rules." Army transcripts of that conversation were made part of the record, and McCarthy unsuccessfully tried to use them to disqualify Symington.

6. Mahoney lost the general election by 52,951 votes. (Butler undoubtedly was helped by Dwight D. Eisenhower's crushing victory over Democrat Adlai E. Stevenson.) Mahoney continued to be a disruptive force in the Maryland Democratic party. In 1966 he won the nomination for governor and ran against Republican Spiro Agnew. Agnew won and went on to join Richard M. Nixon as his running mate in the 1968 campaign for the presidency. Agnew became the first vice-president forced to leave office for unethical behavior.

Afterword

While the most dramatic episode in Millard Tydings's life was his fateful collision with Joseph McCarthy, that experience was unrelated to any central political theme embodied in his career. In exploring his public life, I had not expected to discover one dominant theme representing a significant thread running through American political history. Indeed, I did not want to view Tydings's life or career solely through the prism of a political ideology and thus narrowly define him. But as I wrote and reflected on my finished manuscript, it became clear that his real importance in American history lay not in his combat with McCarthy and Franklin Roosevelt, but in his role as one of the leading and most articulate spokesmen for the traditional conservative Democratic point of view.

The conservative point of view fell on hard times during and after the New Deal years of the Depression. Fiscally orthodox Jeffersonian Democrats like Tydings who believed in balanced budgets, states' rights, and who waged war against the growth of the federal government as a result of New Deal programs and policies, were reviled as "Tory Democrats." They were seen as prisoners of fixed ideas and not as men fighting to achieve economic stability, to maintain the institutional balance of power, and to preserve existing power relationships. By the 1960s, conservative Democrats were held in such low esteem in their own party that they became conspicuous by their absence in the ruling political hierarchy, leading many to become Republicans. Now the traditional conservative view, and the values it represents, appears to be making a comeback in an era of trillion-dollar debts.

Tydings called himself a "moderate progressive"—not a conservative—in the early 1930s. He had entered politics in 1915 during the Progressive Era, attracted to the ideals and principles of Woodrow Wilson. But like the Progressive Era—which was rife with contradictions—the early Tydings record was more than inconsistent when measured in progressive terms. Although he detested the cronyism and corruption of machine bosses, as did progressive leaders, and was unequivocal in his disdain for the injustices of colonialism and the Ku Klux Klan, he had little use for the central progressive belief that government should function as the agent of reform, that it should intrude in social and economic relations in order to protect and advance the common good. He held to the Jeffersonian credo that the government that governs least governs best. And although he initially supported such policies as a state-level workmen's compensation law, relief for farmers, and laws settling claims for those displaced by the Aberdeen Proving Grounds, and in the U.S. Senate authored legislation giving independence to the Philippines (satisfying the progressive commitment to abjure colonialism), he also firmly opposed women's suffrage, federal ownership of public utilities, federal child-labor laws, and the concept of collective bargaining for labor unions—the heart of the progressive program.

If Tydings ever was a moderate progressive, it was a short-lived affiliation. His entry into politics in 1915 was followed by four years of military service—far removed from the niceties of debate over political philosophy and the merits of progressive values. His reentry into politics in 1919 coincided with the demise of the Progressive Era as Wilson's New Freedom moved away from regulatory activity and a retrenchment of sorts set in. Any inclination he may have had to promote progressive policies (as distinct from ideals) apparently never was reinforced. At Annapolis he compiled a strong record for economy, writing legislation to abolish useless state offices—diminishing the size of government rather than increasing it. Thus his orthodox fiscal conservatism was highly visible from the beginning. In other words, Tydings represented the ambiguities of the reform effort, rather than evidencing real commitment to it.

But he became an unambiguous adherent of conservative Jeffersonian democracy and was a disciple of the so-called Bourbon Democrats. He was a product of a rural mainstream America rooted in a Southern border state—where traditional individualism and self-sufficiency were admired; where Thomas Jefferson's ideals were revered; and where being a protector of business, big or small, was not an ignoble calling nor business a dirty word. He came to conservatism naturally.

When Franklin Delano Roosevelt's New Deal moved from recovery to reform, and proliferation of new and huge federal bureaucratic domains threatened to alter the balance within government—increasing the power and size of the executive branch at the expense of the legislative and judicial branches—Tydings's conservatism solidified. It was then that he matured into an outspoken and passionate advocate for the virtues of the conservative point of view. He believed he was defending a way of life that was threatened, for he saw the New Deal reforms as politically destabilizing—radical departures from the status quo. As the executive branch and president steadily accumulated power, Tydings delivered impassioned warnings that the balance of the three branches of government must not be altered because it was crucial to democracy; existing power relationships must be preserved. He saw the cost of the New Deal, and its deficit financing, as economically destabilizing and cautioned against burdening future generations with enormous public debt. He fought against the surrender of congressional authority. His greatest success came when he helped preserve the institutions of government by working to defeat Roosevelt's assault on the Supreme Court, for especially then did the personal nature of Roosevelt's presidency threaten to change the concept of government by laws, not men.

Another institution of American government (traditional rather than constitutional) that Tydings regarded as fundamental to democracy was the two-party system. His role as conservative advocate stirred ongoing tensions between the extreme wings of the Democratic party and revealed the uneasiness of alignments, the flirtations with party realignment. Because the existence of a robust and representative Democratic party was important to Tydings, he opposed realignment. He believed that the party must not be limited to one voice but must be a choir of voices. When the Liberty League, a group of powerful Democrats enraged at the direction Roosevelt was taking the country, sought to woo Tydings (and other conservative Democrats) to join them outside the party—which would have had the effect of realignment—he rejected their advances. When New Dealers—disgusted with the intransigence of the outspoken Tydings and his fellow "irreconcilables," and sick of fighting them—sought to stifle all who publicly dissented, he and the others refused to bolt. Tydings stood his ground so he could continue to give voice and muscle to the doctrines he believed were essential to draw the country back from the brink of bankruptcy and autarchy. Instead of bolting, he sought to counter the New Deal's leftward pull, tried to move the party toward the center and draw it back to its ancestral roots.

The purge election of 1938 was an overt (and extraordinary) attempt to rid the party of dissent and achieve a homogenous—and therefore more effective and efficient—unity. That blatant assault on political diversity made Tydings more determined to speak out, for silencing dissident opinion was inimical to democracy. The full range of ideas that comprised the political spectrum deserved representation if the party were to reflect its constituency accurately and lead successfully—not to mention win elections and preserve the traditional political system. Roosevelt's realignment and purge attempts failed to dispose of the party's conservative wing. Nevertheless, his reforms became an integral part of the American system—so woven into the political texture that today few would try to unravel them. Roosevelt's legacy saw liberalism become the new Democratic orthodoxy; his heirs dominated the party. With consolidation of New Deal policies, the ultimate dominance of liberals in the party eventually forced the minority conservative wing (those who did not switch parties) into abeyance.

The idea of party realignment is a recurring theme in American history. Polarization due to disagreement is inevitable, given the inexorability of political swings, and has led in the past to third-party movements and even to the dissolution of major parties. But Tydings did not believe that realignment of the Democratic party into an entity where only liberals and progressives need apply was a workable or desirable end. He knew that disagreement and diversity are the magic ingredients—the yeast—of democracy, to be safe-guarded and treasured. He believed a party was weakened intellec-tually when differing viewpoints were smothered. When one wing was excluded, the whole party was diminished. And the very act of exclusion was inconsistent with the democratic concept. Realign-ment was counterproductive; the trick was to remain open to all points of view.

Reconciliation of differing views apparently was left for others to contemplate and attempt, for Tydings played no role as concilia-tor of voices raised in disagreement. He fought so all voices could be heard. Thus the phrase used to describe a Democratic move toward the center in the late 1980s—"politics of inclusion"—un-doubtedly would have appealed to Tydings; the nomination of conservative Senator Lloyd M. Bentsen of Texas for vice-president on the Democratic ticket in 1988 suggested that the party might voluntarily nudge itself back toward the center by making room for the "Tory Democrats." Perhaps the ideological move to the right since the 1960s will force Democrats to reconsider and broaden the party, to acknowledge that—for balance and victory—the reality of internal dissent must be accepted. And dissenters must be tolerated, respected, and included.

Tydings throughout his career stood for political balance in and victory of the Democratic party. He fought for balance among the government's institutions of power—traditional and constitutional. And he defended eloquently and with passion the conservative point of view, thus filling a role that is essential to the health and vitality of a political democracy.

Discussion of Sources

Because Tydings destroyed much of the material from his years of service in Congress, I relied very heavily on contemporary accounts from newspapers and magazines. I was fortunate to enjoy access to letters, unpublished manuscripts, and memorabilia still in possession of the Tydings family.

I also made extensive use of published government documents and material relating to his contemporaries—archival and manuscript collections; interviews (author's interviews and those of Columbia University's Oral History Project and the U.S. Senate Oral History Collection); diaries, memoirs, and autobiographies; published biographies; unpublished manuscripts; material from the National Archives Record Groups 46, 128, and 319; the Enoch Pratt Free Library, Baltimore; the Military History Institute, Carlisle, Pennsylvania; and Movietone, Fox, and Paramount newsreels. See the General Bibliography that follows this chapter of citations.

Prologue

Author's interviews with Eleanor Tydings Ditzen, Joseph D. Tydings, William Fulbright, Maurice Rosenblatt, and Edward P. Morgan provided insight into Tydings's personality and position in the Senate, augmented by author's interviews with Stuart Symington, Claude Pepper, Clark Clifford, Thomas D'Alessandro, Louis

Goldstein, Morris Rosenberg, and Carlos Romulo. Newsman's query on 1948 campaign: 1945 King Features Syndicate article. Anecdote relating to vanity: David Oshinsky, *A Conspiracy So Immense.* Comments on committee behavior: interview, Ditzen; *Philippine Mail,* Salinas, California, Nov. 1940. Harold Ickes's remark: Scrapbooks, Box 39, Tydings Papers.

1   Neither Witch Hunt nor Whitewash

Literature on McCarthy and McCarthyism is voluminous, but the Army–McCarthy hearings of 1954 generally are covered in greater depth than the 1950 State Department loyalty hearings. I found Tydings's papers (Series V) much more intact than those for his earlier career. Of especial value is the comprehensive scrapbook collection. Augmenting its use, I relied on the Washington *Post,* the Washington *Evening Star,* the Baltimore *Sun* papers, and the New York *Times* as well as contemporary national news magazines (which together provided coverage ranging widely across the political spectrum). Interviews with Edward Morgan, extensive use of the published two-volume hearings transcripts (*Tydings Committee Hearings*—hereafter *TCH*), the *Tydings Report, Congressional Record* (cited as *CR*), and the Truman Papers were supplemented by use of William Evjue, William Benton, and Robert Fleming's papers at the Wisconsin Historical Society; Record Group 46, National Archives; interviews with Eleanor Tydings Ditzen and Maurice Rosenblatt; and several biographies of great value: Richard M. Fried's *Men against McCarthy;* Robert Griffith's superb *The Politics of Fear: Joseph R. McCarthy and the Senate;* David M. Oshinsky's *A Conspiracy So Immense;* Thomas C. Reeves's comprehensive *The Life and Times of Joe McCarthy: A Biography;* and Richard Rovere's brilliant portrait, *Senator Joe McCarthy.*

Let the Games Begin

McCarthy use of the **numbers:** Box 2, Folder 1, Fleming Papers; Rovere, *Senator Joe McCarthy.* Foreign Relations Committee **dis-**

putes: Executive Sessions of the Senate Foreign Relations Committee (Historical Series), 81st Cong., 1st and 2nd sess., 1950, pp. 208–40. **Hearings opening** exchanges: pp. 1–32, *TCH;* press commentary: Washington *Daily News,* 2/27/50; Washington *Post,* 3/9/50. **108 names** (Robert E. Lee lists): interview, Edward Morgan; Records of the Foreign Relations Committee, Senate Subcommittee, Boxes 7, 8, RG 46, NA; Series V, Box 8, and Scrapbooks, Box 49, Tydings Papers. **Panuch case:** Washington *Post,* 3/10/50; Oshinsky, pp. 119–20. **Hearings second day:** pp. 33–84, *TCH.* **March 9** executive session: Washington *Post,* 3/10/50. **Third day:** pp. 87–107, *TCH.* **Kenyon** testimony, **Hickenlooper** remark: pp. 186–210 and pp. 207–08, *TCH;* **Jessup** statement: pp. 217–48, *TCH.* Tydings–McCarthy arguments over **names** and entering speech as **sworn testimony:** pp. 171–75, ibid.; McCarthy **boast:** *CR,* Feb. 20, 1950. Tydings press conference disparaging **evidence:** Baltimore *Sun,* 3/21/50. **81 names:** interview, Morgan. **Kent:** *Sun,* 4/1/50; **Rayburn, Benton, Biddle:** Washington *Evening Star,* 3/26/50. Tydings–McCarthy exchanges on **Jessup:** pp. 215–17, *TCH;* Hickenlooper, p. 225, ibid. **"Top Russian** espionage agent" remark: Washington *Daily News,* 3/21/50. **Stimson, Dulles, Vandenberg** letters: Baltimore *Sun,* 4/2/50. **McGrath:** examination of **Lattimore file,** Lodge response: Baltimore *Sun,* 3/26/50; New York *Times,* 4/8/50, 4/11/50. Tydings–Truman correspondence on release of **loyalty files:** Series V, Box 5, State Department Folder, Tydings Papers; OF419-K, PSF, Truman Papers; Records of Foreign Relations Committee, Senate Subcommittee, Box 13, RG 46, NA. **Justice** memo on **loyalty files:** OF419-K, Truman Papers. Truman to **Early:** ibid. **McCarthy speech:** *CR,* Mar. 30, 1950. *Amerasia* case background: see Griffith, pp. 93–100, *Politics of Fear;* Records of Foreign Relations Committee, Senate Subcommittee, Boxes 7, 11, RG 46, NA; Series V, Boxes 1, 2, 3, 5, Tydings Papers. **Lattimore** statement: Washington *Post,* 4/2/50. For Lattimore's side of the story, see autobiography, *Ordeal by Slander;* his testimony appears at pp. 418–84, *TCH.* **Tydings's exoneration of Lattimore:** *TCH,* p. 454, Washington *Post,* 4/7/50 and 4/12/50.

The Beginning of the End

Taft: *Labor,* 4/1/50; *Sun,* 4/6/50; interviews, Ditzen, Morgan; interview, Benjamin H. Reese, Columbia University Oral History Project. **Hickenlooper–McGrath–Lodge** breaks: Baltimore *American* and *Labor*, 4/8/50; Washington *Post*, 4/8/50, 4/12/50. **FBI** investigation of **Lattimore** and Tydings's response to Hickenlooper: Washington *Post*, 4/9/50. Pro-McCarthy **letters:** *Newsweek*, 6/5/50; Washington *Evening Star*, 3/25/50; Washington *Post*, 3/27/50, 3/28/50; Series V, Box 2, Correspondence Folder, Tydings Papers. *Sun*, 3/28/ 50. Tydings–McCarthy **three-letter exchange:** Series V, Box 4, Joseph R. McCarthy 1950–1952 Folder, Tydings Papers. **Note** on evidence: *Reporter*, Aug. 19, 1952. Tydings's reply to **Taft:** Baltimore *News–Post*, 4/20/50. **Executive sessions** warning to McCarthy on files' integrity: Series V, Box 2, Correspondence Folders, Tydings Papers; interview, Morgan. **Set record straight:** ibid.; *Reporter*, Aug. 19, 1952. **Censure memo,** April 12 memo to Truman: Series V, Box 2, Correspondence Folder, Tydings Papers. Support on **Capitol Hill:** interview, Morgan. **"New avenues":** Washington *Post*, 4/17/50. **Budenz** testimony: pp. 487–528, Budenz questioning: pp. 533–67, 571–89 and 590–630, *TCH*; Baltimore *News–Post*, 4/20/ 50; **William White,** New York *Times*, 4/28/50; **Krock,** ibid., 4/23/ 50. **Jenner** assault: *CR*, Apr. 25, 1950; *Sun*, 4/26/50; Washington *Times–Herald*, 4/26/50. **Dodd** testimony: pp. 631–43, *TCH*. **Browder** testimony: pp. 669–733, ibid. **Field** testimony: pp. 709–35, ibid. **Jenner** remark: Fried, p. 74. **Utley** testimony: pp. 737–98, ibid. **Lattimore** reappearance: pp. 799–871, ibid. Tydings giving material to **FBI:** Washington *Post*, 4/24/50. Morgan interview on **81 cases:** Series V, Box 8, Tydings Papers. **Democratic offensive:** *CR*, May 3, 1950; *Sun* and Washington *Post*, 5/4/50. Origin of **205 and 57:** *CR*, July 26, 1946; Fleeson, Washington *Evening Star*, 5/3/50; Griffith, pp. 50–51. **"A Bomb":** *CR*, May 9, 1950; Washington *Evening Star*, 5/4/50. Truman **release of files:** Washington *Post*, *Sun*, 5/5/50; Tydings press release: Series V, Box 5, State Department Folder and Box 2, FBI 1950 Folder, Tydings Papers. **Tydings's disarray:** Benton memorandum, Feb. 21, 1955, Box 4, Benton Papers; interview, autobiography, Ditzen. **Benton, Chavez** speeches: *CR*, May 9, 1950. **Bipartisan commission:** Washington *Post*, 4/4/50; *Sun*, 4/6/50; *Labor*, 4/8/50; Washington *Evening Star*, 5/28/50; Griffith, p. 112. **Blair House** meeting: Series V, Box 4, Loyalty and Security Folders 1945–1950 Folder, Tydings Papers; Spingarn June 23 and June 26 memos, OF, Truman Papers; **Pearson,**

"Washington Merry-go-round" syndicated column, 7/9/50. Examination **loyalty files:** *Evening Sun*, 5/10/50. McCarthy to Morgan claiming **file-rape:** Series V, Box 2, FBI 1950 Folder, Tydings Papers. *Amerasia* examination: interview, Morgan; Records of Foreign Relations Committee, Senate Subcommittee, Boxes 7, 11, RG 46, NA; *Wall Street Journal*, 6/1/50; *Sun*, 5/21/50; Series V, Boxes 1, 2, 3, 5, Tydings Papers. *Amerasia* testimony: pp. 923–1471, *TCH*; **Van Beuren** telegram: Box 2, Folder 2, Fleming Papers; interview, Morgan; **Krock** comment, New York *Times*, 5/5/50. Tydings **"reward"** article: Washington *Times–Herald*, 5/11/50. **Legislation** sidetracked: *Evening Sun*, 5/18/50. Tydings **draft** bill: *CR*, June 1950. **Hearings termination** decision: *Sun*, 6/29/50. FBI study of loyalty files, Tydings–McGrath–McCarthy correspondence: Papers of J. Howard McGrath, Truman Library. **Tydings's report** and aftermath: interview, Morgan; *Tydings Report*; Executive Session of the Senate Foreign Relations Committee, 81st Cong., 1st and 2nd sess., 1950, pp. 551–99; **Connally** press conference: Records of Foreign Relations Committee, Executive Session Transcripts and Minutes, Box 10, RG 46, NA; *Christian Science Monitor*, 7/18/50; *Sun*, 7/18/50; New York *Times*, 7/25/50; Washington *Post*, 7/21/50; **Tydings July 20 speech:** *CR*, July 20, 1950; interview, Morgan; Washington *Evening Star*, Washington *Post*, New York *Times*, 7/21/50. Margaret Chase **Smith,** *Declaration of Conscience*. For additional discussions of hearings significance, see Griffith, pp. 101–14; Reeves, pp. 245–46; Fried, 89–94.

2   A Despicable "Back Street" Campaign

Again, Tydings's papers are more intact in this area (Series III). In addition, I used the William Benton, Robert Fleming, and William Evjue Papers at the Wisconsin Historical Society; Record Group 46, National Archives; contemporary newspaper and magazines; authors and other interviews; Eleanor Tydings Ditzen unpublished autobiography; Louis Bean pamphlet, *Influences in the 1954 Mid-term Election;* Griffith, Fried, Reeves, and Rovere biographies; Stanley Kelley, Jr.'s valuable *Professional Public Relations and Political Power;* John H. Fenton's *Politics in the Border State*.

"X": Washington *Post*, 7/25/50. **McCarthy tax** issue: Box 2, Folder 1, Fleming Papers. **"Unjudicious"** clearance of Lattimore: *Sun*, 4/7/50. **O'Conor** on Lattimore: *Sun*, 4/18/50. Tydings's **political troubles:** interviews, Thomas D'Alessandro, Stuart Symington, William Fulbright, Joseph D. Tydings; Series III, Subseries II, Box 8, Tydings Papers; Fried, *Men against McCarthy*, pp. 124–25; *CR*, June 22, 1946. Tydings's **primary opposition:** *Sun* and *Evening Sun* papers, Aug. 17, 19, 31, Sept. 1, 16, 17, 1950; Records of the Subcommittee on Privileges and Elections, SEN 82–F16, Box 8, RG 46, NA; Griffith, *Politics of Fear*, pp. 126–29; Fried, pp. 125–27; U.S. Senate, *Maryland Senatorial Election of 1950. Hearings before the Subcommittee on Privileges and Elections of the Committee on Rules and Administration, Pursuant to S. Res. 250*, 82nd Cong., 1st sess., 1951 (hereafter *Maryland Hearings*); U.S. Senate Committee on Rules and Administration, *Maryland Senatorial Election of 1950*, 82nd Cong., 1st sess., 1951 (hereafter *Maryland Report*). **Tydings's record:** Series III, Subseries II, Box 10, Tydings Papers; interview, Symington. Questionnaires, Series III, Subseries 2, Box 5, Tydings Papers. Remark to **O'Conor**, Harry W. Kirwin, *Inevitable Success: Herbert R. O'Conor*, p. 509. **Personal material:** interview, autobiography, Ditzen. **Schapiro** letter: Series V, Box 4, Tydings Papers. **Primary** results and aftermath: *Maryland Manual*; Series III, Subseries 2, Box 8, Tydings Papers; Fried, pp. 129–30; *Evening Sun*, Sept. 19, 25, 30, Oct. 2, 3, 4, 16, 27, 1950; *Maryland Hearings*; Stanley Kelley, Jr., *Professional Public Relations*, ch. 4. Tydings **campaign:** Series III, Subseries II, Boxes 5, 9, Tydings Papers. Material on McCarthy-inspired **pamphlets, brochures,** Butler–McCarthy campaign workers and participants **Jonkel, Miller, Simmons, McCormick, Fulton Lewis,** et al.: Series III, Subseries II, Tydings Papers; Records of the Subcommittee on Privileges and Elections, SEN 82–F16, RG 46, NA; *Maryland Hearings*; *Maryland Report*; Kelley, ch. 4; Griffith, pp. 126–31, 153–57; Fried, pp. 127–37. Tydings **strategy memo, supporters,** and **campaign material:** Series III, Subseries II, Box 9, Tydings Papers. **Fulton Lewis** broadcast: *Maryland Hearings*, pp. 579–93, *Maryland Report*, pp. 21–36. Angry constituent **letters:** Series V, Box 2, Tydings Papers. Tydings final **statement** and **speech:** Series III, Subseries 2, Box 9, ibid.

Election results and aftermath: *Maryland Manual*; *Evening Sun*, 11/
8/50; New York *Times*, 11/12/50; interviews, Maurice Rosenblatt,
William Fulbright; Kelley, ch. 4; Bean, pp. 25–32. **Note** on Mc-
Carthy's anger, Jack Anderson and Ronald May, *McCarthy: The Man,
the Senator, the Ism*, p. 290. McCarthy **war record:** Box 3, Folder 4,
Box 4, Folder 10, Fleming Papers; Box 81, Evjue Papers; *Time*
magazine, 10/22/51. McCarthy **legal problems:** Box 2, Folder 10,
Fleming Papers. *Time* and *Newsweek*, Scrapbooks, Box 49, Tydings
Papers.

3   Chesapeake Childhood

Background information on **Havre de Grace history:** Elias
Kidwiler, *History of Havre de Grace, "The Town We Live In"*; C.
Milton Wright, *Our Harford Heritage*; J. Thomas Scharf, *History of
Maryland: From the Earliest Periods to the Present Day*; Peter A. Jay,
Havre de Grace: An Informal History, supplemented by material from
town newspapers the *Record* (formerly the Havre de Grace *Republi-
can*) and the Havre de Grace *Democratic Ledger*. Background infor-
mation on Tydings and O'Neill **family histories** and Tydings's
childhood: interviews, Eleanor Tydings Ditzen, Joseph D. Tydings,
and O'Neill descendant Jane Kirkendahl; autobiography, Ditzen;
Tydings's personal papers, Series I, III, and VI, Tydings Papers.
WRC radio interview, "Coffee with Congress," April 12, 1947;
Tydings Vertical Files, Enoch Pratt Free Library, Baltimore; Holmes
Alexander, "Millard E. Tydings: The Man from Maryland," in
American Politician, J. T. Salter, ed.; Myron I. Scholnick, "The
President and the Senator: Franklin Roosevelt's Attempted 'Purge'
of Maryland's Millard Tydings in 1938," unpublished. Material on
John **O'Neill defense** of Havre de Grace: Series I, Box 1, Tydings
Papers; Claude Swanson, *Perilous Fight*; Kidwiler; Jay; Wright; inter-
view, autobiography, Ditzen; **Alsop** column: Washington *Star*, 9/
12/38. Background on Tydings's **entry into politics** and early
career: Series I, Box 1 and Series VII, Subseries 1, Box 1, Tydings
Papers; Tydings Vertical Files, Enoch Pratt Free Library; interviews,
Ditzen, Joseph Tydings; Alexander, "Man from Maryland."

4   This Is the End, God Take Care of Me

Material on Tydings's wartime experiences was taken primarily from the lengthy manuscript he wrote after the war, some parts of it still in possession of the Tydings family and some housed in Series VI, Box 1, Tydings Papers. Use of Tydings's written recollections were supplemented by interviews with Eleanor Tydings Ditzen and Joseph D. Tydings; conversations with personnel at the Carlisle Military History Institute Library, Carlisle Barracks, Carlisle, Pennsylvania; and use of the following monographs: U.S. Government, *Order of Battle of the United States Land Forces in the World War: American Expeditionary Forces*; John Cutchins and George Scott Stewart, Jr., *History of the Twenty-ninth Division "Blue and Gray," 1917–1919*; George C. Marshall (director), *Infantry in Battle*; and Tydings's *The Machine Gunners of the Blue and Gray Division (Twenty-ninth)*.

Information relating to Milton **Reckord,** Eagle Pass, Texas, and **Anniston,** Alabama: interviews, Tydings, Ditzen; autobiography, Ditzen; Baltimore *Sun* papers, Jan. 1918; *Order of Battle*, pp. 151–55; *History of the Twenty-ninth*, pp. 1–62. Tydings's **overseas service:** material drawn largely from his handwritten manuscripts, augmented by his book, *Machine Gunners; Order of Battle*, pp. 156–59; *History of the Twenty-ninth*, pp. 72–204; interviews, Ditzen, Tydings; contemporary news accounts; other materials in Series VI, Boxes 1–6, Tydings Papers. Post-**armistice** and **postwar** information: interviews, Ditzen, Tydings, Thomas D'Alessandro, Edward Morgan; *Machine Gunners; Infantry in Battle*, pp. 77–82, 108, 306; Series VI, Tydings Papers; autobiography, Ditzen; newsclips, Scrapbooks, Box 4, Tydings Papers.

5   The Accidental Senator

Tydings's papers relating to his early career are sketchy at best so I relied heavily on the *Congressional Record*, contemporary news accounts, and the Vertical Files at Baltimore's Enoch Pratt Free Library to track his political positions and evolution. Dorothy

Brown's chapter, "Maryland between the Wars," in *Maryland: A History—1632 to 1974*, Richard Walsh and William Fox, eds., provided invaluable background on the time period, as did George Callcott's excellent study, *A History of the University of Maryland*. Interviews with Joseph D. Tydings and Eleanor Tydings Ditzen and the papers of Mary E. W. Risteau at the Maryland Historical Society filled in important gaps.

Return from France: interview, Ditzen; Series I, Box 1, Tydings Papers. **Reentry into politics:** interview, Tydings; Scrapbooks, Boxes 1, 4, Tydings Papers; *Maryland Manual*; Holmes Alexander, "Millard E. Tydings: The Man from Maryland"; Tydings to Alexander, Series I, Box 1, Tydings Papers. **University of Maryland:** interviews, Ditzen, Tydings; Callcott, *A History of the University of Maryland*, pp. 276–80; *Journal of the House of Delegates of Maryland, 1920*; Brown, "Maryland between the Wars," pp. 728–30. **House race:** Vertical Files, Tydings, John J. "Sonny" Mahon, Frank S. Kelly, Albert C. Ritchie, Enoch Pratt Free Library; Westminster (Md.) *Democratic Advocate*, 6/6/22; Tydings interview, *Sun*, 10/29/50; Brown, pp. 774–75; Havre de Grace *Democratic Ledger*, 5/17/22; Boxes 11, 13, Risteau Papers; Scrapbooks, Box 4, Tydings Papers; *Maryland Manual*; **Drinking escapade:** Scrapbooks, Box 4, Tydings Papers; Box 13, Risteau Papers; *Sun*, 9/7/22; Baltimore *American*, 9/7/22; *Evening Sun*, 3/21/24. **In Congress:** Montgomery (County) *Press*, 12/25/25; **Anti-Klan letter:** *Sun*, Oct. 1924, Scrapbooks, Box 4, Tydings Papers; **Coolidge anecdote:** Tydings interview, *Sun*, 10/29/50; **Prohibition debates:** *CR*, Mar. 9, 1926; *Sun*, 3/10/26; Philadelphia *Public Ledger*, 3/11/26. **Senate race:** Vertical Files, Tydings, Ritchie, Mahon, Kelly, Ovington Weller, Enoch Pratt Free Library; Tydings to Alexander, Series I, Box 1, Tydings Papers; Alexander, "Man from Maryland"; James B. Levin, "Albert C. Ritchie: A Political Biography," unpublished, pp. 253 passim; interview, Tydings; New York *Times*, 2/5/26; *Sun*, 3/27/26, 6/8/26; Westminster (Md.) *Democratic Advocate*, 6/19/26; Oswald Garrison Villard, *Forum*, Dec. 1936; Brown, "Maryland between the Wars," p. 688; *Evening Sun*, 9/24/26; Scrapbooks, Box 4, Tydings Papers. **Victory:** *Maryland Manual*; Alexander, "Man from Maryland"; Havre de Grace *Democratic Ledger*, Washington *Daily Mirror*, Nov.

26; Scrapbooks, Box 4, Tydings Papers. **Publicity:** *Sun*, 12/11/27; New York *Times*, 3/9/28. **Muscle Shoals:** *CR*, May 24, 25, 1928; *Evening Sun*, 5/26/28; New York *Times*, 5/26/28; *Sun*, 5/30/28. **Rise in Senate: Kent** column, *Sun*, 8/25/28; Scrapbooks, Box 4, Tydings Papers. **1928 campaign:** Brown, "Maryland between the Wars," pp. 692–94; **religious and racial bigotry,** ibid.; *Sun*, 4/23/28; New York *Times*, 9/3/28; *Observer*, 9/15/28, 11/3/28; New York *Times*, 4/8/28; Utica (N.Y.) *Daily Press*, 9/27/28; **media:** Scrapbooks, Box 4, Tydings Papers; **Tydings's power:** New York *Herald Tribune*, 6/17/29. **Prohibition:** *CR*, Apr. 24, 1928, June 19, 1929, Jan. 1930, Apr. 1, May 13, 14, 1930, Feb. 16, 1931, Jan. 9, 16, 1932; Tydings, *Before and After Prohibition*; Scrapbooks, Box 5, Tydings Papers. **Defense and debts:** *CR*, May 4, 1928, Jan. 4, 17, 26, 29, 1929, Mar. 3, 1930, Jan. 27, 1931; New York *Times*, 1/18/29; *Wall Street Journal* article and reply: 1/21/29 and 1/30/29; Scrapbooks, Box 5, Tydings Papers; reply to **criticism:** Baltimore *Post*, 1/4/32. **Art** bill: *CR*, Dec. 9, 1931; Scrapbooks, Box 5, Tydings Papers. **Personal:** *Sun*, 10/19/30; St. Louis *Dispatch*, 4/21/30; Montgomery (County) *Press*, 5/2/30. **Depression and tariff:** *Sun*, 10/31/29; *CR*, Oct. 27, 1929, Nov. 1, 12, 1929, Jan. 1930, Mar. 25, Oct. 3, 1930; **Kent** column: *Sun*, 3/18/30; **Mencken** comments: Mar. 1930; Scrapbooks, Box 5, Tydings Papers; **Smoot–Hawley** comment: Oct. 17, 1930 speech. **Counter-Attack:** Washington *Post*, 6/11/33; Washington *Evening Star*, 6/18/33; Scrapbooks, Box 6, Tydings Papers. **RFC:** *CR*, Jan. 9, 18, Feb. 2, 11, 15, 16, Apr. 26, May 17, 20, June 13, 20, 21, 22, 1932; **Copeland:** *CR*, Feb. 11, 1932; **Black:** *CR*, Feb. 16, 1931; **Huey Long:** *CR*, May 27, 1932; **Sun** editorial, 5/24/32; **Mencken** column: 6/6/32; **Tydings's power: Wile** Oct. 1930 comment, *Sun*, Scrapbooks, Box 5, Tydings Papers; Baltimore *Post*, 11/24/32; Alexander, "Man from Maryland"; Kirwin, *Inevitable Success*, pp. 401–02; Baltimore *Post*, 1/4/32 and 6/8/32; *Sun*, 11/1/32.

6   The Squire of Havre de Grace Takes Aim
at the Squire of Hyde Park

Tydings's papers relating to President Franklin D. Roosevelt's first term are thin. Besides contemporary news accounts and the

Congressional Record, I used the Roosevelt Papers at Hyde Park, New York; the George L. Radcliffe Papers at the Maryland Historical Society, Baltimore; Harold Ickes's comprehensive and colorful diaries; Enoch Pratt Free Library Vertical Files; author's interviews with Eleanor Tydings Ditzen, Joseph D. Tydings, and Morris Rosenberg, Tydings's law partner. I am indebted to William E. Leuchtenberg for his seminal study, *Franklin D. Roosevelt and the New Deal, 1932–1940* and to James T. Patterson for his invaluable *Congressional Conservatism and the New Deal*. Samuel Lubell's *The Future of American Politics*, Samuel I. Rosenman's *The Public Papers and Addresses of Franklin D. Roosevelt*, vol. 1, and Holmes Alexander's "Millard E. Tydings: The Man from Maryland" also provided valuable material.

Lippman remark: Leuchtenberg, *New Deal*, p. 10. **FDR platform:** ibid., p. 9; **FDR speech** of 10/19/32, Rosenman, *Public Papers and Addresses*. Tydings **campaign remarks:** Scrapbooks, Box 5, Tydings Papers; **election results:** ibid., Box 6, *Maryland Manual*. **Prohibition** material: Scrapbooks, Boxes 5, 6, Tydings Papers. **FDR policies:** Lubell, *American Politics*, pp. 21 passim; Leuchtenberg, *New Deal*, pp. 11–12, 37. **Tydings's AAA** position: Washington *Evening Star*, 4/26/33; *CR*, Apr. 1933; Scrapbooks, Box 6, Tydings Papers; **Tydings's attitude** toward New Deal: *Sun*, 5/18/34; interviews, Tydings, Ditzen; Patterson, *Congressional Conservatism*, p. 25. **Acheson** nomination: Scrapbooks, Box 6, Tydings Papers. **Patronage:** ibid.; *Sun* editorial, 1/7/33; *Sun* 6/7/33; *Evening Sun*, 10/12/33; Alexander, "Man from Maryland." **Maryland Politics:** Vertical Files, Tydings, Howard W. Jackson, Albert C. Ritchie, George L. Radcliffe, Enoch Pratt Free Library; *Sun*, 5/23/33; Scrapbooks, Aug. 1933, Box 6, Tydings Papers. **1934 campaign:** Scrapbooks, Boxes 7, 8, ibid; Washington *Post*, 5/17/34; *Sun*, 11/2/34 and 10/2/34; **1934 results:** Leuchtenberg, p. 116; **Hopkins remark:** ibid., p. 117. **FERA fight:** *CR*, Feb. 15, Mar. 13, 18, 19, Apr. 2, 1935; Washington *Post*, 3/14/35; *Sun*, 3/5/35; *Evening Sun*, 3/19/35, New York *Times*, 4/3/35. **Watchdog label:** *Evening Sun*, 4/12/34; **Washington *Evening Star* editorial:** 4/6/35. **Biltmore speech:** New York *Times*, 5/8/35. **FDR reaction:** Scrapbooks, Box 8, Tydings Papers; OF419, Box 73, Roosevelt Library. **Virgin Islands:** history and background: OF6Q, Box 17, ibid.; material on **Eli Baer:** interview, Morris Rosenberg; on **Paul Pearson,** OF6Q, Box 17, Roosevelt Library. **Yates's letter:** ibid.; **Ickes's role:** interviews, Ditzen, Tydings; Ickes, *The Secret Diaries of Harold L. Ickes,* vol. 1, pp. 402, 393, 388 passim; **Ickes–Tydings letters:** New York *Herald Tribune,* 7/11/35; **Hearings action:** Series III, Subseries 1, Box 4, Tydings Papers; Ickes, *Secret Diaries,* 1, pp. 390–97; Washington *Evening Star,* 7/2/35; New York *Times,* 7/11/35; *Sun,* 7/16/35; Scrapbooks, Boxes 7, 8, Tydings Papers. **Pearson** transfer: OF6Q, Box 17, Roosevelt Library; Ickes, *Secret Diaries,* 1, pp. 405–08; **Cramer, Wilson,** ibid.; Scrapbooks, Boxes 7, 8, Tydings Papers. **Organic Act:** interview, Tydings; OF6Q, Box 17, Roosevelt Library; **Drew Pearson** material: interviews, Ditzen, Rosenberg. **Second New Deal:** Patterson, *Congressional Conservatism,* pp. 17–31; Leuchtenberg, *New Deal,* pp. 150–63. **Wagner bill:** *CR,* May 16, 1935; *Sun,* 5/17/35. **Public Utility bill:** Patterson, pp. 38–41; Leuchtenberg, pp. 154–57; Scrapbooks, Boxes 7, 8, Tydings Papers; **tax the wealth:** *CR,* June 28, 1935; Patterson, pp. 58–69; Leuchtenberg, pp. 152–53; Scrapbooks, Boxes 7, 8, Tydings Papers. **Rivers and harbors bill:** *CR,* Aug. 24, 25, 1935; New York *Times,* 8/26/35; *Sun,* 8/26/35. **Anti-FDR movement: Pearson** remark, Washington *Post,* 8/24/35; **Colby,** Patterson, pp. 252–53; Washington *Post,* 6/1/35; **Tucker** column: Scrapbooks, Box 8, Tydings Papers; **Liberty League:** Patterson, pp. 251–57; Washington *News,* 8/24/34; **Ickes** remark, Washington *Evening Star,* 8/24/34; **Tydings statement:** Scrapbooks, Box 7, Tydings Papers. **Tucker** column: Flint (Mich.) *Journal,* 8/5/35. **Tydings's challenge:** Wheeling *Intelligencer,* 8/10/35; New York *Times,* 12/11/35; Washington *Herald,* 4/9/35; Baltimore *News–Post,* 7/7/35; Washington *Herald,* 12/12/35; Jan. 1936, Scrapbooks, Box 11, Tydings Papers. **Al Smith** statement: New York *Herald Tribune,* Feb. 1936; ibid. **FDR retaliation:** Washington *Post,* 11/4/35; Nov. 1935, Scrapbooks, Box 7, Tydings Papers; **Clapper** editorial: Washington *Post,* 11/4/35. **Tydings conciliation:** Feb. 18, 1936, Scrapbooks, Box 11, Tydings Papers; Baltimore *News–Post,* 2/21/36; **Kent:** *Sun,* 2/28/36; Tydings **speech:** Washington *Post,* 3/6/36; **Waltman** comment: *Post,* 3/7/36; **Mencken:** Mar. 1936, Scrapbooks, Box 11, Tydings Papers. **1936 convention:** June 1936, Scrapbooks, ibid.; *Sun,* 6/24/36; Washington *Evening Star,* 6/24/36;

Farley: *Sun*, 6/27/36; Tydings **speech:** *Sun*, 6/27/36; **Waltman:** Washington *Post*, 6/27/36; Bel Air (Md.) *Times*: 7/3/36. **1936 campaign: Tweedle Dee** remark, Tydings to Alexander, Series I, Box 1, Tydings Papers; **with Farley,** *Sun*, 8/19/36; **Oakington rally,** interview, Ditzen; *Sun*, 9/6/36. **Victory:** Farley quip, Leuchtenberg, p. 196; Washington *Post*, 11/4/36; New York *Times*, 10/1/36; *Sun*, Scrapbooks, Box 11, Tydings Papers.

7   A New and Independent Nation

The Tydings Papers contain legislative materials relating to the Philippine Islands but beyond that, and with the exception of the Scrapbooks, are not strong on issues relating to Philippine independence. The *Congressional Record*, contemporary news accounts, and Philippine newspapers from the Tydings Scrapbooks and the Library of Congress, all provided material of great value. Several general histories aided me in exploring the history of the islands, Filipino–American relations, and the struggle for independence: David Joel Steinberg's *The Philippines: A Singular and Plural Place*; David Bernstein's *The Philippine Story*; Frederica M. Bunge, *Philippines: A Country Study*; and Garel A. Grunder and William E. Livezy, *The Philippines and the United States*. Additionally, I used the Franklin D. Roosevelt Library, Hyde Park, New York, and the Key Pittman Papers at the Library of Congress, and consulted the Stanley Hornbake Papers at the Hoover Institution Archives, Stanford University, and the Frank Murphy Papers at the Bentley Historical Library, University of Michigan. Interviews with Carlos Romulo and Eleanor Tydings Ditzen as well as Manuel Quezon's autobiography, *The Good Fight*, also contributed material of use. But of extraordinary value was Theodore Friend's magnificent *Between Two Empires: The Ordeal of the Philippines, 1929–1946*, which guided me through the complicated political maneuverings of the Filipino leaders. Because Tydings's role in independence was attenuated before 1934, I relied on Friend's interpretations of the interactions among Quezon, Osmeña, and Roxas, and I equally trusted his accuracy regarding the many opposing American interests.

Tydings's interest in Philippines: interview, Ditzen. **History** and background of islands: Report No. 494, Philippine Independence, Committee on Territories and Insular Affairs, Mar. 15, 1934, 73rd Cong., 2nd sess.; *CR*, Mar. 18, 1932; Bunge, pp. 3–36; Steinberg; Bernstein; Grunder and Livezy; Friend, pp. 1–11. **Military–Pacific** aspects of independence: *CR*, Feb. 20, 1929. **1932 debate:** for pro- and anti-independence arguments in Senate, *CR*, Apr., July, Dec. 1932; for Filipino pro- and anti-independence stances, see Friend, part 3. **Quezon** on T. Roosevelt: Friend, p. 58; **Hawes** to Roxas, Osmeña: ibid., p. 71. **Quezon–Osmeña rivalry:** ibid., pp. 95–108; Steinberg, pp. 52–53. **Vandenberg–**Tydings debate: *CR*, Dec. 12, 1932. **Long–Broussard–**Tydings exchange: ibid., Dec. 14, 1932. **H–H–C bill** provisions: Series IV, Box 1, Tydings Papers. **Stimson quote** on Quezon: Friend, p. 109. **Quezon–Osmeña** maneuvering: ibid., pp. 109–35. **Aquino** role: Scrapbooks, Box 7, Tydings Papers; **Robinson** remark: Philippines *Free Press*, 6/10/33. **Quezon** role, *Good Fight*. **Romulo** switch: Friend, p. 115n. **Roxas** on Quezon, ibid., p. 136. **Pittman** remark, ibid., p. 137. **Tydings** on H–H–C: Scrapbooks, Dec. 1932, Box 5, Tydings Papers; *pronunciamento*: *CR*, Jan. 24, 1934; Baltimore *Evening Sun*, 1/24/34; Philippines *Free Press*, 3/31/34. **Quezon** to Stimson, Friend, p. 139. **Tydings–Quezon** maneuvering: ibid., pp. 139–48; OF400, Boxes 15, 16, Roosevelt Library; Scrapbooks, Jan. to Mar. 1934, Box 7, Tydings Papers; Quezon, *Good Fight*; interviews, Ditzen, Romulo. **Roosevelt** assessment: *Sun*, 2/17/34. **Tydings letter, memo** to Roosevelt, OF400, Box 15, Roosevelt Library. **Tydings bill debate:** *CR*, Mar. 14, 21, 22, 23, 1934; Baltimore *Sun*, 3/2/24. **Quirino** and **Hawes** anecdotes: Friend, p. 145. **Quezon letter** to *Sun*: 3/29/ 34. **Philippines *Free Press:*** 3/31/34. **Tariff fights:** *CR*, Apr. 10, 11, 1934. **Trade privileges** fears: Washington *Herald*, 10/11/34; OF400, Box 16, Roosevelt Library; Scrapbooks, Boxes 7, 10, Tydings Papers. **Mission to Manila:** Philippine newsclips, Dec. 1934, Box 10, ibid.; Frank Murphy Papers, University of Michigan; Grunder and Livezy, pp. 225–27; **Aguinaldo–Tydings** quotes: Scrapbooks, Philippine newsclips, Box 10, Tydings Papers; *delicadeza:* Friend, p. 30; **Tydings speech:** Series II, Box 3, Tydings Papers; Scrapbooks, Philippine newsclips, Box 10, ibid.; **Reaction of Quezon, Osmeña, Roxas, Paredes, Quirino:** ibid.; **of Romulo:**

author's interview. Manila *Advertiser*, 12/27/34; Manila *Daily Bulletin*, 12/24/34; Philippines *Herald* editorial and column: 12/29/34 and 2/1/35. **Aguinaldo response:** Scrapbooks, Philippines newsclips, Box 10, Tydings Papers. **Malacañan meeting:** Philippines *Herald*, 12/26/34; *Tribune*, 12/27/34. **Tydings interview:** Philippine *Free Press*, 4/6/35. **Tydings departure** quotes: *Tribune*, 12/18/34; Scrapbooks, Box 7, Tydings Papers. **Quezon–Quirino** pro Tydings–McDuffie remarks: Manila *Daily Bulletin*, 2/9/35. **Quezon 1935** delegation: New York *Herald Tribune*, 3/14/35; Baltimore *News–Post*, 3/23/35; Quezon, *Good Fight*. **Tydings speech:** Series II, Box 3, Tydings Papers. **Quezon election,** Philippine Constitution: Friend, pp. 151–58. **Tydings speech:** *CR*, May 15, 1935. **Joint Committee:** Quezon, *Good Fight*; Grunder and Livezy, pp. 230–31; Friend, pp. 157–59; Scrapbooks, Boxes 11, 14, Tydings Papers; **Osmeña letter** to Quezon: Friend, p. 158. **Villard:** *Forum*, Dec. 1936.

8   At Home in Maryland

For material on Tydings's political role in Maryland, I found the Tydings Scrapbooks and the Vertical Files at Baltimore's Enoch Pratt Free Library to be of great value, as were George Radcliffe's papers at the Maryland Historical Society. Dorothy Brown's "Maryland between the Wars," Holmes Alexander's "Millard E. Tydings: The Man from Maryland," Jo Ann Argersinger's article, "Toward a Roosevelt Coalition: The Democratic Party and the New Deal in Baltimore," and several unpublished dissertations also were quite useful. Tydings's poetry collection is housed with his papers at the University of Maryland. Material relating to his personal life and marriage comes largely from interviews with Eleanor Tydings Ditzen and Morris Rosenberg, from Mrs. Ditzen's unpublished autobiography, and news accounts.

Tobacco, crabbing industries: Scrapbooks, Oct.–Nov. 1935 and Crisfield (Md.) *Times*, 6/7/35 and 6/14/35, Box 7, Tydings Papers. **Saint Lawrence Seaway:** ibid.; *CR*, Jan. 17, Feb. 1, 1934. **PWA** projects: *Sun*, 1/29/35, 3/1/35; Scrapbooks, Sept. 1935, Box 7,

Tydings Papers. **Patronage:** Bel Air (Md.) *Times*, 8/21/36. **King-maker:** Alexander, "Man from Maryland"; Tydings to Alexander, Series I, Box 1, Tydings Papers; *Evening Sun*, 4/11/34. Material on **Ritchie–Jackson** power struggle and nomination melee: Vertical Files, Albert Ritchie, Howard Jackson, E. Brooke Lee, William Curran, Herbert O'Conor, George Radcliffe, Tydings, Enoch Pratt Free Library; Scrapbooks, Jan.–Sept. 1934, Box 7, Tydings Papers and specifically *Sun*, 1/31/34, 2/5/34; Baltimore *Post*, 4/11/34; Tydings to Alexander, Series I, Box 1, Tydings Papers; **Tydings offer to resign:** *Sun*, 6/25/34; **Radcliffe** role: Radcliffe Memorandum, Box 45, Radcliffe Papers. **Ritchie** anger at Tydings: Baltimore *News–Post*, 4/24/34 and **Tydings reply:** *Sun*, 4/26/34; **Tydings peace statement:** Scrapbooks, Apr. 1934, Box 7, Tydings Papers; **Curran:** Brown, "Maryland between the Wars," p. 760; *Sun*, 5/2/34; see also Rothman's unpublished dissertation, "Factional Machine Politics— William Curran and the Baltimore City Democratic Party Organization, 1929–1946"; **Radcliffe:** see Memo, Box 45, Radcliffe Papers; **O'Conor:** Scrapbooks, June–July, 1934, Box 7, Tydings Papers; Kirwin, *The Inevitable Success: Herbert R. O'Conor*, pp. 153–59; **Conley:** Brown, "Maryland between the Wars," pp. 762–63; **Tydings criticized:** Scrapbooks, Aug.–Sept. 1934, Box 7, Tydings Papers; Newell column, *News–Post*, 12/12/34. **Ritchie defeat:** New York *Times*, 11/9/34; *Sun*, 11/10/34; Kirwin, pp. 160–61; Tydings to Alexander, Series I, Box 1, Tydings Papers. **Navy/War "Disaffection Bill":** *Sun*, 7/17/35 and 8/17/35; **Mencken:** *Evening Sun*, 7/29/35; *Sun*, 2/12/36; *Evening Sun*, 2/12/36; Tydings to Alexander, Series I, Box 1, Tydings Papers; **Villard:** *Forum*, Dec. 1936. **Personal:** Jennings, *Herald*, 4/16/34; Scrapbooks, 1934, Box 7, Tydings Papers; Washington *Herald*, 3/7/35; **cocktail party:** ibid., 8/24/35 and Washington *Evening Star*, 8/23/35; **Warfield Simpson** anecdote: interview, autobiography, Ditzen; **poetry:** Series II, Subseries 2, Box 10, Tydings Papers; **marriage:** material relating to Eleanor Davies drawn largely from author's interviews and Ditzen autobiography; **Oakington:** *Sun*, 12/6/35 and 4/18/37; interviews, Morris Rosenberg, Joseph D. Tydings, Ditzen; autobiography, Ditzen; **gossip columns:** Scrapbooks, Sept. 24–25, 1935, Dec. 5–6, 1935, Apr. 2, 27, 1936, Box 7, Tydings Papers; *Sun*, 10/25/35 and 12/6/35; **Drew Pearson:** Washington *Herald*, 11/27/35; **Martinsburg**

(W. Va.) *Journal:* 12/10/35; **wedding:** interview, autobiography, Ditzen; Washington *Herald* and Washington *Post*, 12/28/35; **Davies's dinner:** Washington *Post*, 1/24/37.

9   The Squire of Oakington at War with the Squire of Hyde Park

In addition to using the Tydings Papers, the Roosevelt Library, and the Harold Ickes and George Radcliffe Papers, a number of autobiographies, interviews, and histories proved invaluable to my examination of the Supreme Court packing fight and purge election of 1938. Autobiographies include Tom Connally and Alfred Steinberg, *My Name Is Tom Connally*; Henry Ashurst, *A Many Colored Toga: The Diary of Henry Fontain Ashurst*; James Byrnes, *All in One Lifetime*; Harold Ickes, *The Secret Diaries of Harold L. Ickes*, vol. 2, *The Inside Struggle*; Burton Wheeler, *Yankee from the West*; Eleanor Tydings Ditzen's unpublished autobiography; and Jim Farley's *Jim Farley's Story*. Biographies and monographs of substance include William Leuchtenberg, *Franklin D. Roosevelt and the New Deal*; James Patterson, *Congressional Conservatism and the New Deal*; James MacGregor Burns, *Roosevelt: The Lion and the Fox*; Joseph Alsop and Turner Catledge, *The 168 Days*; Samuel Rosenman, *The Public Papers and Addresses of Franklin D. Roosevelt*; Bascon Timmons, *Garner of Texas*; Holmes Alexander, "Millard E. Tydings: The Man from Maryland"; Myron Scholnick, unpublished thesis. Additionally I used the Enoch Pratt Free Library Vertical Files, the *Congressional Record*, and contemporary news and magazine accounts.

Of Justices and Justice

Budget resolution: *CR*, Jan. 12, 1937; *Wall Street Journal*, 1/14/37. **Court** plan: for discussion of FDR's aims and tactics, see Patterson, pp. 85–124; Leuchtenberg, pp. 232–39; Alsop and Catledge, pp. 55 passim; Byrnes, pp. 65, 97–104; PSF Box 186, Supreme Court Folder, Roosevelt Library; **Kent:** Sun, 3/28/37. **White House** meeting: Alsop and Catledge, pp. 65–67. **Reaction to plan:** interview, autobiography, Ditzen; Alsop and Catledge, pp. 68–71, 74. **Tyd-**

ings dinner: ibid., pp. 103–04; interview, autobiography, Ditzen; Wheeler, pp. 322–23. **Corcoran:** ibid. **National reaction:** Alsop and Catledge, pp. 72–73; Leuchtenberg, p. 235; Scrapbooks, Feb. 1937, Box 13, Tydings Papers. **White House strategy:** Alsop and Catledge, pp. 80–89; **Norris:** ibid., p. 95. For discussions of Tydings's and **opposition's strategy:** Connally, pp. 184–92; Wheeler, pp. 319–40; and see Patterson, pp. 99–127; Leuchtenberg, pp. 231–38; Alsop and Catledge. **Tydings to Davies:** in possession of Tydings family. **Vote count:** Alsop and Catledge, pp. 93–94. **Tydings on record:** *Sun* and Washington *Post*, 2/24/37. **Agriculture and labor:** Scrapbooks, Box 13, Tydings Papers; Alsop and Catledge, pp. 115–19, 163–76. **Roosevelt speech:** Wheeler, pp. 325–26; **Alsop** column, Scrapbooks, Mar. 1937, Box 14, Tydings Papers; **Glass:** ibid.; **Tydings:** *CR*, Mar. 2, 1937. **Raleigh dinner:** Tydings speech, Series II, Subseries 1, Box 1, Tydings Papers; **Mallon:** Washington *Evening Star*, 3/5/37; **Ehringhaus,** Alexander, "Man from Maryland"; **OSWALD:** *Evening Sun*, 3/5/37; **Tydings retort:** Scrapbooks, Mar. 1937, Box 14, Tydings Papers; **Ickes:** vol. 2, pp. 91, 95–96; Washington *Post*, 3/11/37. **Hearings:** Wheeler, pp. 327–33; Connally, pp. 189–91; Alsop and Catledge, pp. 119–28, 177–78; **Ashurst,** ibid., p. 193; **Dieterich:** Alsop and Catledge, pp. 90–91; **Wheeler–Brandeis–Hughes:** ibid., pp. 126–27; Wheeler, pp. 327–33. **Garner–Byrnes–Harrison:** *Sun*, 4/7/37, 4/8/37; Alsop and Catledge, pp. 131–32. **Court switch:** ibid., pp. 140–41; Leuchtenberg, pp. 236–37. **Promise to Robinson:** Alsop and Catledge, pp. 156–57, 207. **Van Devanter:** ibid., pp. 206–09. **Garner:** interview, autobiography, Ditzen. **No compromise:** Scrapbooks, Apr. 1937, Box 14, Tydings Papers. **Biffle:** Wheeler, p. 323; Connally, p. 189; Farley, p. 124. **Public opinion:** Washington *Post*, 5/24/37. **Radcliffe stance:** Memorandum, Box 45, Radcliffe Papers; *Sun*, 3/7/40; Tydings to Alexander, Series I, Box 1, Tydings Papers. **Senate debates:** *Sun* and Washington *Post*, 7/7/37; *CR*, July 6, 7, 8, 9, 1937; Alsop and Catledge, pp. 254–65; **Copeland:** Wheeler, p. 337. **Corcoran meeting:** interview, autobiography, Ditzen; New York *Herald Tribune*, 9/2/38; Alsop and Catledge, p. 275. **Robinson's death:** ibid., p. 268. **Hiram Johnson:** *CR*, July 22, 1937. **Dear Alben letter:** PSF, Box 188, U.S. Senate Folder, Roosevelt Library. **Relief bills and Black nomination:** *CR*, Apr. 5, 7, Aug. 2,

4, 5, 6, Nov. 26, Dec. 15, 1937; Leuchtenberg, pp. 238–51; Byrnes, pp. 104–05; *Sun*, 4/8/37, 5/12/37, 11/27/37; Patterson, pp. 134–39, 152–55. **Miller–Tydings Act:** author's interviews, Joseph D. Tydings, Morris Rosenberg, and Columbia University Oral History interview, Robert Jackson; Morgenthau Diaries, 4/6/37, 6:175, Roosevelt Library; *N.A.R.D. Journal,* Aug. 26, 1937; Rosenman, 7, pp. 333–35. **Manifesto:** Patterson, pp. 190–210; *Sun*, 12/18/37. **University of Maryland speech:** Series II, Subseries 1, Box 4, Tydings Papers; *Sun*, 6/6/37.

Of Political Purges and Exculpations

Grudges and **Elimination Committee:** New York *Times*, 6/9/38; Farley, pp. 120, 127; Patterson, p. 262; Leuchtenberg, p. 266. **Realignment:** ibid., pp. 268–69; Patterson, pp. 251, 262–63, 271–72, 277–80, 284–87; Clinton Rossiter, *Parties and Politics in America;* **Ruby Black:** Madison *State Journal*, 7/15/37; **Dutcher, Sullivan, Kent:** Scrapbooks, May 1937, Box 15, Tydings Papers; Washington *Evening Star*, 3/26/37; **Farley:** p. 95, 120–21, 128–33; **Byrnes:** p. 101. **Mystery trip:** Vertical Files, Sumner Welles, Enoch Pratt Free Library; Philadelphia *Evening Bulletin*, 6/3/38; Washington *Post*, 1/17/37, 1/18/37. **David Lewis:** Vertical Files, Enoch Pratt Free Library; *Sun*, 11/19/37, 6/2/38, 6/3/38; Ickes, vol. 2, p. 282; Farley, p. 134; **Mencken:** *Evening Sun*, 11/29/37. **Maryland politics:** see Franklin L. Burdette, "Modern Maryland Politics and Social Change," in *Maryland: A History—1632 to 1974*, Richard Walsh and William Fox, eds., pp. 773–81; Callcott on **Curley Byrd:** pp. 325–26; Kirwin, pp. 193–95, 206–11 and New York *Times*, 4/26/38 and Cumberland (Md.) *Times*, 8/24/38; Vertical Files, Tydings, Howard Jackson, Herbert O'Conor, Curley Byrd, William Curran, Thomas D'Alessandro, Enoch Pratt Free Library; *Evening Sun*, 7/9/37; **O'Conor:** *Sun*, 7/10/37; Kirwin, p. 209; Farley, 122–23. **Drew Pearson:** "The Maryland Merry-go-round," Scrapbooks, 1938, Tydings Papers; **Jackson:** *Evening Sun*, 4/28/38; **Radcliffe:** Memorandum, Box 45, Radcliffe Papers; *Sun*, 4/21/38. **FDR speech:** Rosenman, 7, p. 381; Farley, pp. 140–41; New York *Times*, 4/26/38; Springfield *Union*, 6/3/38; **Sun editorial:** 4/27/38. **Time** magazine: Sept. 12, 1938. **Skit:** Scrapbooks, Box 15, Tydings Papers. **AFL**

and CIO speeches: Washington *Post*, 7/17/38; *Sun*, 7/23/38. **Hall-gren:** *Sun*, July 15, 16, 17, 19, 1938; Washington *Evening Star*, 7/15/38, Washington *Post*, 7/15/38, 7/17/38; Vertical Files, Hallgren, Mulliken, Enoch Pratt Free Library; see also Scholnick, pp. 44–47. **Bone and sinew:** *Sun*, 7/24/38. **Veterans bonus:** *CR*, June 2, 1933, Mar. 18, 1935; *Sun*, 3/6/65, 3/19/35; Washington *Evening Star*, 3/25/35, 3/26/35; **turns over bonus:** *Sun*, 4/27/37; *Saturday Evening Post*, 6/13/36; **Webb:** D'Alessandro, Krock, Scrapbooks, July, Aug. 1938, Box 14, Tydings Papers; **O'Neill,** *Evening Sun*, 9/11/38; Scholnick, pp. 66–80; **Early** report: PSF, Box 189, U.S. Senate 1938–1939 Folder, Roosevelt Library; U.S. Congress, Senate, *Report of the Special Committee to Investigate Senatorial Campaign Expenditures and Use of Government Funds in 1938*, Senate Report No. 1, 76th Cong., 1st sess., 1939, pp. 128–37. **Ickes** reply to **bone and sinew:** *Sun*, 7/26/38 and Ickes, vol. 2, pp. 429–30. **FDR attacks George and Smith:** Leuchtenberg, p. 267; Burns, pp. 362–64. **FDR attacks Tydings:** Washington *Herald*, 8/16/38; Rosenman, 7, p. 381; New York *Post*, 8/16/38; Rosenman, 7, pp. 488–89; **Tydings's reply:** *Sun*, 8/17/38 and 8/22/38; New York *Times*, 8/22/38; *St. Louis Dispatch,* **Clapper, Wile,** and **Agar,** Scrapbooks, Aug. 1938, Box 14, Tydings Papers; **Krock,** New York *Times*, 8/23/38. **Pump priming:** *Sun*, 4/12/38, 4/15/38; Patterson, pp. 240–41. **Executive reorganization:** Ickes, vol. 2, pp. 287–88; Patterson, 216–33; Leuchtenberg, 277–80; *CR*, Mar. 28, 1938; **Krock,** New York *Times*, 4/8/38. **Bridges: Ickes,** vol. 2, p. 95. **Tydings's efforts:** in mid-1930s countless articles appeared in the *Sun* and regional papers discussing Tydings's efforts to get Maryland bridges funded; see Scrapbooks, Tydings Papers. **FDR's "invasion"** of Maryland: **Krock's** columns, **FDR's** press conferences and speeches, **Tydings's** replies and speeches, **Byrd's** role, **Lewis's** efforts, public opinion, color and action leading up to FDR's Labor Day entry into Maryland from Scrapbooks, Sept. 1937, Box 14, Tydings Papers; **Byrd:** Callcott, pp. 325–27; interview, Ditzen; Farley, p. 144; **Farley:** pp. 137, 145–47; Farley interview, Columbia University Oral History Project, vol. 1, p. 20, vol. 2, pp. 254–55; PSF, Box 189, U.S. Senate 1938–1939 Folder, Roosevelt Library. **Pearson:** Baltimore *American*, 3/22/38; Philadelphia *Record*, 4/3/38; **MiLord** satire; PSF, Box 189, U.S. Senate 1938–1939 Folder, Roosevelt Library. **Tydings's**

final speech: Washington *Herald*, 9/9/38. **Election:** Maryland Secretary of State, *Maryland Manual;* Fox-Movietone News; National Archives, Sound and Video Branch; **Azrael:** Baltimore *News–Post*, 9/13/38; Farley, p. 145; **Senator George:** Byrnes, p. 103. **Bridges: Mencken,** *Evening Sun*, 9/18/38; Washington *News*, 9/21/38. **Post-primary:** interview, Ditzen; portrait of **Leser,** Tydings's **speeches** and **campaign efforts:** Scrapbooks, Sept.–Oct. 1938, Box 14, Tydings Papers. **Election results:** *Maryland Manual; Sun*, 11/5/38. **Analysis:** editorials and columns, Scrapbooks, Sept.–Dec., 1938, Box 14, Tydings Papers; **analysis** also drawn from Leuchtenberg, pp. 269–72, Patterson, pp. 284–87; Burns, pp. 363–66; Farley, pp. 146–50; Columbia University Oral History Project interviews with Samuel Bledsoe (p. 207), Marvin Jones, Claude Wickard. **Wilkie:** Scholnick, p. 110. **Europe:** interview, autobiography, Ditzen. **Clapper:** Washington *Post*, 9/15/38.

10   World War, Political Wars, Cold War

Tydings's papers contained useful information for the war and postwar periods. Also helpful were the Roosevelt Library, Truman Library, Douglas MacArthur and George Radcliffe Papers, National Archives Record Group 128 (Nuclear Energy Records) and 319 (Modern Military Records), the *Congressional Record* and contemporary news accounts. Author's interviews with Eleanor Tydings Ditzen, Joseph D. Tydings, Stuart Symington, Clark Clifford, and Columbia University Oral History Project interviews with James Farley, Thomas Emerson, and others also were of varying value. Jim Farley's autobiography was of interest, and again, Theodore Friend's *Between Two Empires: The Ordeal of the Philippines, 1926–1946*, James Patterson's *Congressional Conservatism and the New Deal*, William Leuchtenberg's *Franklin Roosevelt and the New Deal*, James MacGregor Burns's two biographies, *Roosevelt: The Lion and the Fox* and *Roosevelt: The Soldier of Freedom* were of great use. Of exceptional value were Steven L. Rearden's *History of the Office of the Secretary of Defense: The Formative Years, 1947–1950* and Wayne S. Cole's perceptive and definitive work, *Roosevelt and the Isolationists, 1932–1945*.

Tydings's transformation: interview, Thomas Emerson, Columbia University Oral History Project; **Tucker:** Scrapbooks, Box 22, Tydings Papers. **Isolationism:** for analysis of the isolationist–Roosevelt struggle over control of foreign policy, see Cole. **Neutrality legislation:** *CR*, Aug. 20, 1935, Apr. 29, 1937; *Chicago Tribune, Sun*: Scrapbooks, July 1939, Box 24, Tydings Papers; **September 1939:** *Sun*, 9/22/39; **constituent hearings:** *Sun*, 10/13/39; **Cole:** p. 163; autobiography, Ditzen; **Japan:** Scrapbooks, Jan. 1938, Box 22; **Wagner:** Farley, p. 204; note on **Philippines:** interview, Ditzen; Series II, Box 6, Tydings Papers; **Pearson:** "Washington Merry-go-round," 6/23/40. **Third Term: Runyon,** Washington *Times–Herald*, 1/20/37; **Gallup:** see George H. Gallup, *The Gallup Poll, 1935–1971; Christian Science Monitor* and Mason City (Iowa) *Globe Gazette*, Scrapbooks, Aug. 1939, Box 24, Tydings Papers; **Eleanor:** Washington *Daily News*, 6/21/37; **Alsop:** Washington *Evening Star*, 9/12/38; **Pearson:** *Look*, 1/31/39; St. Louis *Post–Dispatch*, Scrapbooks, Aug. 1939, Box 24, Tydings Papers; **Farley:** Farley, pp. 182, 184; on **Garner,** see Bascom Timmons, *Garner of Texas: A Personal History*, pp. 261–76; Scrapbooks, Feb. 1940, Box 27, Tydings Papers. **Tydings-for-President:** Washington *Post*, Washington *Times–Herald*, 8/5/39. **Maryland politics: O'Neill:** *Sun*, 7/21/39, 5/8/40, *Evening Sun*, 5/22/40; **Tydings maneuvering:** Baltimore *News–Post*, 5/22/40, *Sun*, 5/23/40, New York *Times*, 5/8/40; **Newell:** Baltimore *News–Post*, 5/20/40. **Roosevelt candidacy: Wheeler:** autobiography, Ditzen; **Roosevelt attitude** toward other candidates: see Timmons, pp. 266–74; Ickes, *Secret Diaries*, vol. 3, pp. 65–67, 154, 184, 201, 232; Wheeler, *Yankee from the West*, 353–58; Robert Sherwood, *Roosevelt and Hopkins: An Intimate History*, pp. 94–98; Burns, *Lion and Fox*, pp. 411–15, 424–26; Farley, pp. 184–85, 224–33, 250–56. **Convention:** Farley, pp. 271–306; Wheeler, pp. 358–66; Burns, pp. 426–30; **Alabama** note: Scrapbooks, July 1940, Box 28, Tydings Papers; **Cole:** p. 383; **Gallup:** Washington *Post*, 2/3/40; autobiography, interview, Ditzen; **Tydings's quote:** *Evening Sun*, 8/2/40; **Azrael:** Baltimore *News–Post*, 7/19/40. **Campaign:** Tydings return and **attitude:** ibid., 9/25/40; *Evening Sun*, 8/30/40; Scrapbooks, Aug.–Sept. 1940, Boxes 23, 28, Tydings Papers; **Roosevelt–Tydings tour:** *Sun*, 10/1/40, 10/2/40; **Smith, George, Byrd, Glass:** Washington *Post*, 10/24/40; **Azrael:** Baltimore *News–Post*, 9/25/40. **Destroyers deal:** Cole, pp. 370–74; Burns, *Lion and Fox*, pp. 437–52; *CR*, Aug. 15, 1940; **Wilkie:** Burns, *Lion and Fox*, p. 441. **Tydings support** for administration: **New York Times,** 8/29/40; *CR*, Aug. 28, 1940. **Stimson/Knox:** ibid., July 9, 1940. **Pay-as-you-go:** ibid., May 13, 28, June 14, 18, 19, Aug. 21, 22, 1940. **Lend Lease:** *Sun*, 6/20/40, 2/28/41, Washington *Daily News*, 3/8/43, *CR*, Feb. 11, 18, 27, 28, Mar. 5, 8, 1941; **PM:** Scrapbooks, Box 29, Tydings Papers. **Neutrality 1941:** Cole, pp. 446–54; *CR*, Nov. 7, 1941; *Sun*, 11/8/41; **Pearl Harbor:** autobiography, interview, Ditzen; interview Joseph Tydings; *Sun*, 12/9/41. **War years: Tydings Committee:** speech, Series II, Subseries 1, Box 4, Tydings Papers; **Questionnaires:** *Sun*, 2/18/42, Washington *Post*, 3/1/42; various quotes from *CR*, Feb. 13, 23, 1943, and Scrapbooks, Box 31, Tydings Papers; **Pearson** quote: "Maryland Merry-go-round," 6/12/42; **McIntyre:** DNC, Box 1174, Roosevelt Library; **committee report** material: PSF, Box 189, U.S. Senate 1941–1944 Folder, ibid.; *Sun*, 5/31/42; **Manly:** Washington *Times–Herald*, 5/29/42; *Sun*, 7/21/42. **1943 budget:** *Sun*, 1/12/43; *CR*, Mar. 21, June 9, 30, 1943. **1944 election:** for general discussion of election, see Burns, *Soldier of Freedom*, pp. 497–513; **New York Journal American:** 3/21/43; **Colliers:** see *Sun*, 7/6/43; **Maryland delegates** in Chicago: *Sun*, June 1, 27, July 13, 19, 21, 22, 1944; Kirwin, pp. 366 passim; interview, autobiography, Ditzen; **Tydings campaign:** *Sun*, 4/21/44, 5/5/44, Baltimore *News–Post*, 5/8/44, and Scrapbooks, Box 35, Tydings Papers; **Republicans for Tydings:** see Series III, Subseries 1, Box 1, ibid.; **Roosevelt race** in Maryland and Tydings's role: ibid.; *Sun*, Sept. 15, 16, 17, Oct. 17, 1944; **Tydings's theme:** Series II, Subseries 1, Box 6 Tydings Papers. **Results:** *Maryland Manual*. **Philippines:** for Tydings–MacArthur correspondence, see RG 5, Tydings Folder, MacArthur Memorial; for Tydings–Truman correspondence, see OF400 and 521, PPF105 and 445, Truman Library; newspapers from Scrapbooks, Box 37, Tydings Papers; **Tydings speeches:** Series II, Subseries 1, Boxes 3, 6, ibid., and *CR*, May 23, June 7, 1945; *Bataan Magazine*, June, July 1945; *Sun*, 6/6/45; **Tydings Rehabilitation Act,** Series IV, Boxes 1, 2, Tydings Papers; *CR*, Nov. 27, Dec. 5, 1945; **Independence:** Series II, Subseries 1, Box 7, and Scrapbooks, July 1946, Box 37, Tydings Papers; Friend, pp. 262–63. **Bikini:** descriptions are from

Tydings's personal journal, in possession of Tydings family; *Newsweek*, July 8, 1946; Washington *Times–Herald*, 6/1/46; interview, Symington; interview, Ditzen. **Disarmament** and the **Joint Committee:** Series II, Box 1, Atomic Energy Folder, Tydings Papers; *Sun*, 10/31/45, 11/2/45; interview, autobiography, Ditzen; Harold Green and Alan Rosenthal, *The Joint Committee on Atomic Energy: A Study in Fusion of Governmental Power*; Richard Hewlett and Oscar Anderson, Jr., *A History of the United States Atomic Energy Commission: The New World, 1939/1946*, vol. 1, and *Atomic Shield, 1947/ 1952*, vol. 2; see also Hearings Transcripts: *Atomic Energy Act of 1946: Hearings before the Special Committee on Atomic Energy*, U.S. Senate, 79th Cong., 2nd sess.; also Records of Joint Committee on Atomic Energy, General Correspondence, Speeches Files, Boxes 8, 9; History AEC, Boxes 29–31; General Advisory Committee, Box 34; Broadcasts, MET, Box 107; Hearings Transcripts, Boxes 365– 67; Legislation, Legislative History, Box 398, RG 128, National Archives. **Tydings's January 1946 speech:** interview, Ditzen; *CR*, Jan. 28, 1946; New York *Times*, 1/29/46; *Vital Speeches of the Day*, Mar. 1, 1946. **Radio broadcasts:** Series II, Subseries 1, Box 7, Tydings Papers; **Truman:** PSF, "T" folder, Truman Library; interview, Thomas Emerson, Columbia University Oral History Project, p. 1725 passim. **Unification of military:** rivalry/background: interviews, Clark Clifford, Stuart Symington; on unification, see Rearden, *History of the Office of the Secretary of Defense: The Formative Years, 1947–1950*, pp. 11–56 and 63–107; *Hearings before the Committee on Armed Services, National Defense Establishment*, U.S. Senate, 80th Cong., 1st sess., and *Hearings before the Committee on Armed Services, National Security Act Amendment of 1949*, U.S. Senate, 81st Cong. 1st sess.; *CR*, May 12, 23, 26, 1949; **McCarthy:** autobiography, Ditzen; **Forrestal** note: Washington *Post*, 5/25/49. **Cold War** policies: Tydings speeches on Marshall Plan, Series II, Subseries 1, Box 7, Tydings Papers; **Mission** to Europe: *Sun*, 9/18/ 47, 10/18/47; **Articles:** New York *Times*, Nov. 5, 6, 7, 8, 1947. **1948 Election:** See Series III, Subseries 1, Box 2, Tydings Papers; autobiography, interview Ditzen; *U.S. News & World Report*, 10/31/ 47, 11/7/47; **Alsop:** Scrapbooks, Aug. 1947, Box 43, Tydings Papers; **Drummond, Senate poll:** ibid.; *Time* magazine: 5/5/47 and 1/17/47; **Lincoln:** Washington *Evening Star*, 7/12/47; **Tim-**

mons: *Sun*, 4/16/47; **Haller:** Series III, Subseries 2, Box 6, Tydings Papers; **Radcliffe:** Memo, Box 45, Radcliffe Papers. **Pauley** nomination: *Oilman's Newspaper*, 3/21/46; *Evening Sun*, 4/16/47; **Azrael:** Baltimore *News–Post*, 3/11/46. **Philadelphia: T'n'T:** *Evening Sun*, 6/2/47, *Sun*, 7/1/48; interview, D'Alessandro; **Jacobs:** Sun, 7/7/48; **Dixiecrats: Russell:** *Sun*, 11/5/48; **Bellevue Stratford Hotel:** interview, autobiography, Ditzen; **Convention:** Scrapbooks, July 1948, Box 45, Tydings Papers; **Election:** Franklin Burdette, "Modern Maryland: Politics and Social Change," pp. 796–97. **Tydings post-election** career: Tydings to **Barkley:** General File, Box 17 (1948–1949), Alben Barkley Papers, University of Kentucky Libraries; **McKeldin challenge:** Scrapbooks, Dec. 1948, Box 45, Tydings Papers. **On 1952: Bell:** Richmond *Times–Dispatch*, 1/28/49; **Eleanor** Tydings to Davies, autobiography, Ditzen; **Pearson:** "Washington Merry-go-round," Box 48, Tydings Papers.

11 The Final Battles

As for earlier chapters dealing with Tydings–McCarthy issues, the material available is substantial. Tydings's papers were helpful as were the William Benton, Robert Fleming, and William Evjue papers at the Wisconsin Historical Society; the Truman Library contained some information as well. Author's interviews with Eleanor Tydings Ditzen, Joseph D. Tydings, Stuart Symington, Edward Morgan, Maurice Rosenblatt, Thomas D'Alessandro, Louis Goldstein, and William Fulbright, and the Ditzen autobiography offered interesting insights and details. In addition, contemporary news accounts, transcripts of the *1950 Maryland Senatorial Election Investigation* (cited as *Maryland Hearings*) and the *Maryland Senatorial Report* (cited as *Maryland Report*), and Record Group 46 of the National Archives provided material of great use. Again I am indebted to Richard Fried, Robert Griffith, David Oshinsky, Thomas Reeves, and Richard Rovere for their biographies of McCarthy.

Tydings initial remarks: *Sun*, 11/26/50, 11/28/50; **driving home:** interview, Ditzen; *U.S. News & World Report*, 11/17/50. **Debut:** interview, autobiography, Ditzen; Washington *Times–Herald*, 12/

15/50, Washington *Post*, 12/28/50. **Investigation:** *Evening Sun*, 11/ 29/50; *Sun*, 12/17/50; **Tydings to Gillette:** Records of the Subcommittee on Privileges and Elections, *1950 Maryland Senatorial Election Investigation*, Box 6, RG 46, NA; **Tydings statement** before subcommittee: pp. 7 passim, *Maryland Hearings*; **Fedder** testimony: pp. 32 passim, ibid.; Reeves, p. 337. **Ewell Moore:** pp. 597–98, 622, *Maryland Hearings*; **Tydings reappearance:** pp. 1057–102, ibid.; **Surine:** see ibid., pp. 692–93, 703, 706, and Box 4, Folder 7, Fleming Papers and *Maryland Report*, pp. 33–34; **subcommittee judgments:** Fedder story: p. 33, ibid.; **"outside influence":** p. 5, ibid.; **"From the Record":** pp. 4, 6–8, ibid.; **Butler:** pp. 2–3, 5– 6, 37–39, ibid.; **"despicable 'back street'"** practices: pp. 6–7, ibid.; **McCarthy:** pp. 23, 34–35, 8–9, ibid.; **McCarthy response:** see "Individual Views of Mr. McCarthy," pp. 41–74, ibid., and Milwaukee *Journal*, 8/3/51. **Note on election reform:** author's telephone conversation and correspondence with Bruce C. Frame, press secretary of Maryland Senator Paul Sarbanes, 3/2/85 and 6/28/ 85. **Press reaction** to report: *Commonweal, Sun*, and Marquis Childs from Scrapbooks, Box 3, Tydings Papers. **Tydings private life:** interview, autobiography Ditzen; interview, Tydings; interview, Symington. **Playscript:** Series II, Subseries 2, Box 10, Tydings Papers. **Benton:** for Tydings–Benton correspondence and material relating to Benton's role in challenging McCarthy, see Boxes 4 and 5, Benton Papers; Series III, Subseries 2, Boxes 13, 14, and Series V, Boxes 1, 2, 5, 7, and 8, Tydings Papers; Box 81, Folder 4, Box 128, Folder 3, Evjue Papers. **Benton** profile: Griffith, pp. 157–59, and interview, Rosenblatt; **Benton resolution:** *CR*, Aug. 6, Sept. 28, 1951; **McCarthy retaliation:** *Sun*, 8/21/51, 11/30/51; **McCarthy letters:** *Sun*, 12/7/51, 12/8/51; for discussion of **McCarthy's maneuvering,** see Griffith, pp. 164–73. **Subcommittee report:** *Investigation of Senators Joseph R. McCarthy and William Benton Pursuant to Senate Resolution 187 and Senate Resolution 304*, Report of the Subcommittee on Privileges and Elections of the Committee on Rules and Administration, 82nd Cong., 2nd sess., 1952, pp. 12– 15, 42–45 and 52. Tydings to **Jenner:** PSF445, Truman Library. Tydings to **Fleming:** Box 4, Folder 9, Fleming Papers. **Tydings– Benton** correspondence, Boxes 4, 5, Benton Papers; Series V, Box 1, Tydings Papers. **NCEC:** interview, Rosenblatt; interview, Symington; Box 3, Folder 3, Box 4, Folder 9, Fleming Papers; see Griffith, pp. 224–42; **Welch clash:** *Sun*, 6/10/54. **Flanders challenge:** see Griffith, pp. 270–91, 294–315; **Watkins:** Rovere, p. 223; **Alsop:** Reeve, p. 647; Griffith, p. 296 and pp. 294–315; interview, autobiography, Ditzen. **Tydings vindication:** constituent correspondence, Series III, Subseries 2, Box 14; **Olin Johnston:** all material relating to Tydings's correspondence with Johnston from Series V, Box 8, Tydings Papers; **Johnston press release:** *Sun*, 1/17/55; **McCarthy response:** Washington *Post*, 1/18/55; **Morgan:** correspondence from Series V, Box 8, Tydings Papers; interview, Morgan; press release, Series V, Box 8, Tydings Papers; *Sun*, 8/1/55. **Reentry into politics:** Washington *Post*, 11/24/54; **correspondence on subject:** Series III, Subseries 2, Box 15, Tydings Papers; interview, Tydings; **loss of power:** quote from Walter Mondale sometime after his defeat by Ronald Reagan, Washington *Post*, c. 1987; interview, Morgan; being **wooed:** letters in Series III, Subseries 2, Box 15, Tydings Papers, and Tydings Correspondence Folder, Susquehanna Museum of Havre de Grace Archives; interview, Rosenblatt; *Sun*, 2/12/55 and 2/13/55; Ditzen, Tydings interviews. **Campaign:** interviews, D'Alessandro, Goldstein; **Primary results:** *Sun*, 5/8/56. **Illness:** interview, autobiography, Ditzen; Tydings letter, Tydings Correspondence Folder, Susquehanna Museum of Havre de Grace Archives; **withdrawal** from race: New York *Times*, 8/20/56; **Eleanor campaign:** interview, autobiography, Ditzen; interview, D'Alessandro; Washington *Post*, 8/28/56. **Obituaries and tributes:** *Sun*, 2/10/61, 2/11/61; New York *Times*, 2/10/61; *CR*, Feb. 13, 1961.

Afterword

I am deeply indebted to Dr. George Callcott of the University of Maryland for discussing with me the issues central to Tydings's political philosophy. I also owe a debt of gratitude to the following authors whose works examine conservatism, progressivism, and/or liberalism—the mainstream political traditions that together make up American political history: Richard Hofstadter, *The American Political Tradition: And the Men Who Made It*, and *The Age of Reform*; Gabriel Kolko, *The Triumph of Conservatism: A Reinterpretation of*

American History, 1900–1916; Samuel Lubell, *The Future of American Politics*; Mary Beth Norton, *A People and a Nation: A History of the United States*; James T. Patterson, *Congressional Conservatism and the New Deal: The Growth of the Conservative Coalition in Congress*; Stephan Therstrom, *A History of the American People*; and Robert H. Wiebe, *The Search for Order, 1877–1920*. I also drew on interviews with Joseph D. Tydings, Maurice Rosenblatt, and William Fulbright in shaping the material in this essay.

General Bibliography

Manuscript Collections

Archives, Libraries, and Manuscript Collections Used

Theodore McKeldin Library, University of Maryland, College Park, Maryland
  Papers of Senator Millard E. Tydings

Enoch Pratt Free Library, Maryland Room, Baltimore, Maryland
  Vertical Files:
    Howard Bruce
    Harry Clifton Byrd
    William Curran
    Mayor Thomas J. D'Alessandro
    Frank A. Furst
    Phillip Lee Goldsborough
    Maurice Hallgren
    Mayor Howard W. Jackson
    John Frank Kelly
    Senator William Cabell Bruce
    William Preston Lane
    John "Sonny" Mahon
    Kent R. Mulliken
    Governor Harry W. Nice
    Senator Herbert R. O'Conor
    Senator George L. Radcliffe

Governor Albert C. Ritchie
Senator Millard E. Tydings
Governor William C. Walsh
Senator Ovington Weller
Sumner Welles

Maryland Historical Society, Baltimore, Maryland
Papers of Senator George L. Radcliffe
Papers of Maryland Delegate Mary E. W. Risteau

Susquehanna Museum of Havre de Grace, Havre de Grace, Maryland
Papers of Senator Millard E. Tydings

Franklin D. Roosevelt Library, Hyde Park, New York
Franklin D. Roosevelt:
    President's Secretary's File
    President's Official File
    President's Personal File
Papers of Samuel I. Rosenman
Papers of Henry Morgenthau
Democratic National Committee Papers

Harry S Truman Library, Independence, Missouri
Papers of Harry S Truman:
    Confidential Files
    Official File
    President's Secretary's Files
    President's Personal File
Papers of Dean Acheson
Papers of Oscar L. Chapman
Papers of Tom C. Clark
Papers of J. Howard McGrath

Wisconsin State Historical Society, Madison, Wisconsin
Papers of William E. Benton
Papers of William T. Evjue
Papers of Robert Fleming

National Archives and Records Center, Washington, D.C.
Record Group 46 (Congressional Records)
Record Group 128 (Nuclear Energy Records)
Record Group 319 (Modern Military Records)

Manuscript Division, Library of Congress, Washington, D.C.
Papers of Joseph and Stewart Alsop
Papers of Senator Tom Connally

Papers of Joseph E. Davies
Papers of James A. Farley
Papers of Senator Theodore F. Green
Papers of Harold L. Ickes
Papers of Senator Key Pittman
Papers of Dean Francis Sayer

MacArthur Memorial Archives, Norfolk, Virginia
Papers of General Douglas MacArthur

Military History Institute, Carlisle Barracks, Carlisle, Pennsylvania

Other Archives, Libraries, and Collections Consulted

Hoover Institution Archives, Stanford, California
Papers of Stanley Hornbeck

Bentley Historical Library, University of Michigan, Ann Arbor, Michigan
Papers of Frank Murphy

Seeley G. Mudd Manuscript Library, Princeton University, Princeton, New Jersey
Papers of Bernard M. Baruch
Papers of John Foster Dulles
Papers of Ferdinand Eberstadt
Papers of Adlai E. Stevenson

University of Kentucky Libraries, Lexington, Kentucky
Papers of Senator Alben W. Barkley

Government Documents and Publications

Cole, Alice C., and Alfred Goldberg, et Al. (Editors). *The Department of Defense: Documents on Establishment and Organization, 1944–1978.* Washington, D.C.: Historical Office, Office of the Secretary of Defense, 1978.

Maryland Secretary of State. *Maryland Manual.* Annapolis: State Printer, 1919–1957.

Rearden, Steven L. *History of the Office of the Secretary of Defense: The Formative Years, 1947–1950.* Volume 1. Washington, D.C.: Historical Office, Office of the Secretary of Defense, 1984.

U.S. Government. *Order of Battle of the United States Land Forces in the World War: American Expeditionary Forces*. Washington, D.C.: Government Printing Office, 1931.

U.S. Government, U.S. Congress. *Congressional Record*. 1922–1951.

————. Senate Committee Hearings Transcripts
  I used virtually all hearings transcripts published relating to important committees on which Tydings served:
  Committee on Naval Affairs
  Committee on Territories and Insular Possessions
  Committee on Appropriations
  Committee on Armed Services
  Committee on Foreign Relations
  Joint Committee on Atomic Energy

Work Projects Administration, Writers Program. *Maryland: A Guide to the Old Line State*. New York: Oxford University Press, 1941.

Newspapers

Besides using the excellent scrapbooks in Tydings's collection at the McKeldin Library Archives, University of Maryland, which contained newspaper clippings from all regions of the state of Maryland and the United States, I relied heavily on:

The Baltimore *Sun* papers
The Washington *Post*
The Washington *Star*
The New York *Times*

And also used:

Christian Science Monitor
CIO News
Des Moines *Register*
Labor
Madison *Capital Times*
The *Wall Street Journal*
Washington *Times–Herald*
Various Philippine Newspapers at the Library of Congress

Magazines

American Mercury
Atlantic Monthly
Business Week
Colliers
Congressional Digest
Forum
Harper's
Life
Nation
Nation's Business
New Republic
Newsweek
New York *Times Magazine*
Progressive
The Reporter
Saturday Evening Post
Time
U.S. News & World Report
Vital Speeches of the Day

Interviews

Interviews Conducted by Author

Clark M. Clifford

Thomas J. D'Alessandro, Mayor of Baltimore and U.S. Representative

Mrs. Eleanor Davies Tydings Ditzen, Tydings's Wife

Senator William Fulbright

Louis Goldstein, Comptroller, State of Maryland

Jane Kirkendahl, Tydings's Cousin on O'Neill Side, Havre de Grace, Maryland

Edward P. Morgan

Senator Claude Pepper

Carlos Romulo

Morris Rosenberg, Law Partner of Millard E. Tydings

Maurice Rosenblatt, National Committee for an Effective Congress

Senator Stuart Symington

Senator Joseph D. Tydings, Tydings's Son

Columbia University Oral History Project Interviews

Senator Raymond E. Baldwin of Connecticut

Samuel B. Bledsoe

Thomas I. Emerson

James A. Farley

Senator Ralph E. Flanders of Vermont

Bernard L. Gladieux

Senator Thomas C. Hart of Connecticut

Phillip C. Jessup

Marvin Jones

Arthur Krock

Robert E. Lee

Senator Herbert H. Lehman of New York

Eugene Meyer

Benjamin H. Reese

Senator Leverett Saltonstall of Massachusetts

Claude Wickard

Henry A. Wallace

U.S. Senate, Historians Office, Oral History Collection Interviews

Darrell St. Claire, Chief Clerk, Rules Committee

Visual Materials

Fox–Movietone News Newsreels. 450 West 54th Street, New York, New York.

Joseph R. McCarthy: Thunder on the Right. Video Cassette. Hornbake Library, University of Maryland, College Park.

National Archives. Motion Picture, Sound and Video Branch. Washington, D.C.

Sherman Grinberg Film Libraries (Paramount 1927–1957; ABC News). 630 Ninth Avenue, New York, New York.

Unpublished Manuscripts

Benton, William E. (?) "America's Shame." Unpublished Manuscript on McCarthyism. Tydings Papers, University of Maryland.

Ditzen, Eleanor Davies Tydings. Unpublished Autobiography, C. 1973.

Levin, James B. "Albert C. Ritchie, A Political Biography." Ph.D. dissertation, City College of New York, 1970.

MacLean, K. Elizabeth. "Joseph E. Davies." Ph.D. Dissertation, University of Maryland, 1986.

Ross, Hugh. "The Third Term Campaign in 1940." Ph.D. Dissertation, Stanford University, 1960.

Rothman, Edwin. "Factional Machine Politics: William Curran and the Baltimore City Democratic Party Organization, 1929–1946." Ph.D. Dissertation, Johns Hopkins University, 1949.

Scholnick, Myron I. "The President and the Senator: Franklin Roosevelt's Attempted 'Purge' of Maryland's Millard Tydings in 1938." Master's Thesis, University of Maryland, 1962.

Tydings, Joseph Davies. Unfinished Manuscript. Opening Chapter of Biography of Millard E. Tydings.

Tydings, Millard E. Manuscript on World War I Experiences, N.D. but C. Mid to Late 1920s.

———. *Barren Victory.* Unpublished Playscript, 1949.

————. *Her Excellency's Day*. Unpublished Playscript, C. 1939.

————. "Thoughts of a Madman." Unpublished Poetry Manuscript, C. 1920–1930s.

Published Memoirs, Autobiographies, Diaries

Acheson, Dean. *Present at the Creation: My Years in the State Department*. New York: New American Library, 1970.

Anderson, Clinton P. *Outsider in the Senate*. New York: World Publishing, 1970.

Ashurst, Henry F. *A Many Colored Toga: The Diary of Henry Fontain Ashurst*. Tucson: University of Arizona Press, 1962.

Barkley, Alben W. *That Reminds Me*. Garden City, N.Y.: Doubleday, 1954.

Bohlen, Charles E. *Witness to History, 1929–1969*. New York: W. W. Norton, 1973.

Budenz, Louis. *This Is My Story*. New York: McGraw-Hill, 1947.

Byrnes, James F. *All in One Lifetime*. New York: Harper & Brothers Publishers, 1958.

Connally, Tom, and Alfred Steinberg. *My Name Is Tom Connally*. New York: Thomas Y. Crowell, 1954.

Evjue, William T. *A Fighting Editor*. Madison, Wis.: Wells Printing Company, 1968.

Farley, James A. *Jim Farley's Story: The Roosevelt Years*. New York: McGraw-Hill, 1948.

Flanders, Ralph F. *Senator from Vermont*. Boston: Little, Brown, 1954.

Forrestal, James, and Walter Millis (Editors). *The Forrestal Diaries*. New York: Viking Press, 1951.

Hoover, Herbert. *The Memoirs of Herbert Hoover: The Cabinet and the Presidency 1920–1933*. Volume 2. New York: Macmillan, 1952.

Hull, Cordell. *The Memoirs of Cordell Hull*. 2 Volumes. New York: Macmillan, 1948.

Ickes, Harold L. *The Secret Diaries of Harold L. Ickes.* 3 Volumes. New York: Simon and Schuster, 1954, 1955.

Lattimore, Owen. *Ordeal by Slander.* Boston: Little, Brown, 1950.

Lilienthal, David E. *The Journals of David E. Lilienthal: The Atomic Energy Years, 1945–1950.* New York: Harper & Row, 1964.

Lodge, Henry Cabot. *The Storm Has Many Eyes.* New York: W. W. Norton, 1973.

MacArthur, Douglas. *Duty, Honor, Country.* New York: Rolton House Publishers, 1962.

————. *Reminiscences.* New York: McGraw-Hill, 1964.

McCarthy, Joseph R. *McCarthyism: The Fight for America.* New York: Devin-Adair, 1952.

Moley, Raymond. *After Seven Years.* New York: Harper & Brothers, 1939.

Morris, Robert. *No Wonder We Are Losing.* New York: Bookmailer, 1958.

Quezon, Manuel Luis. *The Good Fight.* New York: D. Appleton–Century, 1946.

Reilly, Michael F. *Reilly of the White House.* (As Told to William J. Slocum.) New York: Simon and Schuster, 1947.

Romulo, Carlos P. *Crusade in Asia: Philippine Victory.* New York: John Day, 1955.

Roosevelt, Eleanor. *This I Remember.* New York: Harper & Brothers, 1949.

Roosevelt, Elliott (Editor). *F.D.R.: His Personal Letters, 1928–1945.* 2 Volumes. New York: Duell, Sloan, and Pearce, 1950.

Sayre, Francis B. *Glad Adventure.* New York: Macmillan, 1957.

Truman, Harry S. *Memoirs: Years of Decision.* Volume 1. Garden City, N.Y.: Doubleday, 1955.

————. *Memoirs: Years of Trial and Hope.* Volume 2. Garden City, N.Y.: Doubleday, 1956.

Watkins, Arthur V. *Enough Rope.* Englewood Cliffs, N.J.: Prentice-Hall, 1969.

Wheeler, Burton K., with Paul F. Fealy. *Yankee from the West.* Garden City, N.Y.: Doubleday, 1962.

Biographies

Abell, Tyler (Editor). *Drew Pearson Diaries 1949-1959*. New York: Holt, Rhinehart & Winston, 1974.

Adams, John G. *Without Precedent: The Story of the Death of McCarthyism*. New York: W. W. Norton, 1983.

Alexander, Holmes. "Millard E. Tydings: The Man from Maryland." In *The American Politician*, Edited by J. T. Salter, Chapel Hill: University of North Carolina Press, 1938.

Anderson, Jack, and Ronald W. May. *McCarthy: The Man, the Senator, the Ism*. Boston: Beacon Press, 1952.

Belfrage, Cedric. *The American Inquisition, 1945-1960*. Indianapolis: Bobbs-Merrill, 1973.

Buckley, William F., and L. Brent Bozell. *McCarthy and His Enemies*. Chicago: Henry Regnery, 1954.

Burns, James MacGregor. *Roosevelt: The Lion and the Fox*. New York: Harcourt, Brace & World, 1956.

———. *Roosevelt: The Soldier of Freedom, 1940-1945*. New York: Harcourt Brace Jovanovich, 1970.

Cantril, Hadley (Editor). *Public Opinion 1935-1946*. Princeton, N.J.: Princeton University Press, 1951.

Coffin, Tristram. *Senator Fulbright: Portrait of a Public Philosopher*. New York: Dutton, 1966.

Cohn, Roy M. *McCarthy*. New York: New American Library, 1968.

Cole, Wayne S. *Roosevelt and the Isolationists, 1932-1945*. Lincoln: University of Nebraska Press, 1983.

Cook, Fred J. *The Nightmare Decade: The Life and Times of Senator Joseph R. McCarthy and the Catholic Church, 1950-1957*. Chapel Hill: University of North Carolina Press, 1978.

Demaris, Ovid. *The Director: An Oral Biography of J. Edgar Hoover*. New York: W. W. Norton, 1982.

Donovan, Robert J. *Tumultuous Years: The Presidency of Harry S Truman, 1949-1953*. New York: W. W. Norton, 1982.

Ewald, William Bragg, Jr. *Who Killed Joe McCarthy?* New York: Simon & Schuster, 1984.

Ferrell, Robert H. *Off the Record: The Private Papers of Harry S Truman.* New York: Harper & Row, 1980.

Flynn, John T. *The Lattimore Story.* New York: Devin-Adair, 1953.

Freidel, Frank. *Franklin D. Roosevelt.* 3 Volumes. Boston: Little, Brown, 1952–1956.

Fried, Richard M. *Men against McCarthy.* New York: Columbia University Press, 1967.

Goldston, Robert C. *The American Nightmare: Senator Joseph R. McCarthy and the Politics of Hate.* Indianapolis: Bobbs-Merrill, 1973.

Gosnell, Harold F. *Champion Campaigner Franklin D. Roosevelt.* New York: Macmillan, 1952.

Greer, Thomas H. *What Roosevelt Thought: The Social and Political Ideas of Franklin D. Roosevelt.* East Lansing: Michigan State University Press, 1958.

Griffith, Robert. *The Politics of Fear: Joseph R. McCarthy and the Senate.* Lexington: University Press of Kentucky, 1970.

Gunther, John. *Roosevelt in Retrospect: A Profile in History.* New York: Harper & Brothers, 1950.

Herndon, Booton. *Praised and Damned: The Story of Fulton Lewis, Jr.* New York: Duell, Sloan, and Pearce, 1954.

Hoffman, Nicholas von. *The Life and Times of Roy Cohn: Citizen Cohn.* New York: Doubleday, 1988.

Huthmacher, J. Joseph. *Senator Robert F. Wagner and Urban Liberalism.* New York: Atheneum, 1968.

Hyman, Sydney. *The Lives of William Benton.* Chicago: University of Chicago Press, 1969.

Johnson, Gerald W. *Roosevelt: Dictator or Democrat?* New York: Harper & Brothers, 1941.

Johnson, Haynes B., and Bernard M. Swertzman. *Fulbright the Dissenter.* New York: Doubleday, 1968.

Joslin, Theodore. *Herbert Hoover Off the Record*. Garden City, N.Y.: Doubleday, 1934.

Kirwin, Harry W. *The Inevitable Success: Herbert R. O'Conor*. Westminster, Md.: Newman Press, 1962.

Leuchtenberg, William E. *Franklin D. Roosevelt and the New Deal, 1932–1940*. New York: Harper & Row, 1963.

Levine, Erwin L. *Theodore Francis Green*. Providence, R.I.: Brown University Press, 1963.

Lowitt, Richard. *George W. Norris: Triumph of a Progressive, 1933–1944*. Champaign: University of Illinois Press, 1978.

Manchester, William. *American Caesar*. New York: Dell Publishing, 1978.

Matusow, Allen J. (Editor). *Joseph R. McCarthy*. Englewood Cliffs, N.J.: Prentice-Hall, 1970.

Matusow, Harvey. *False Witness*. New York: Cameron & Kahn, 1955.

Miller, William J. *Henry Cabot Lodge: A Biography*. New York: Heineman, 1967.

Oshinsky, David M. *A Conspiracy So Immense: The World of Joe McCarthy*. New York: Free Press, 1983.

Patterson, James T. *Mr. Republican: A Biography of Robert A. Taft*. Boston: Houghton Mifflin, 1972.

Perkins, Dexter. *The New Age of Franklin Roosevelt 1932–1945*. Chicago: University of Chicago Press, 1959.

Pilat, Oliver. *Drew Pearson: An Unauthorized Biography*. New York: Harpers Magazine Press, 1973.

Potter, Charles E. *Days of Shame: Army McCarthy*. New York: Coward, McCann & Geoghegan, 1965.

Reeves, Thomas C. *The Life and Times of Joe McCarthy: A Biography*. New York: Stein and Day Publishers, 1982.

Rogin, Michael Paul. *The Intellectuals and McCarthy: The Radical Specter*. Cambridge, Mass.: MIT Press, 1967.

Rorty, James, and Moshe Decter. *McCarthy and the Communists*. Boston: Beacon Press, 1954.

Rosenman, Samuel I. (Editor). *The Public Papers and Addresses of Franklin D. Roosevelt.* 13 Volumes. New York: Harper & Brothers, 1938–1950.

———. *Working with Roosevelt.* New York: Harper & Brothers, 1952.

Rovere, Richard. *Senator Joe McCarthy.* Cleveland: World Publishing, 1962.

Schlesinger, Arthur M., Jr. *The Age of Roosevelt.* 3 Volumes. Boston: Houghton Mifflin Company, 1957–1960.

Sherwood, Robert E. *Roosevelt and Hopkins: An Intimate History.* New York: Harper & Brothers, 1948.

Smith, Rixley, and N. Beasley. *Carter Glass: A Biography.* FDR and the Era of the New Deal Series. New York: Da Capo Press, 1972.

Steele, Robert V. P. *When Even Angels Wept: The Senator Joseph McCarthy Affair—A Story without a Hero.* New York: Morrow, 1973.

Stromer, Marvin E. *The Making of a Political Leader: Kenneth S. Wherry and the United States Senate.* Lincoln: University of Nebraska Press, 1969.

Swain, Martha H. *Pat Harrison: The New Deal Years.* Jackson: University Press of Mississippi, 1978.

Theoharis, Athan G. *Seeds of Repression: Harry S Truman and the Origins of McCarthyism.* Chicago: Quandrangle Books, 1971.

Timmons, Bascom N. *Garner of Texas: A Personal History.* New York: Harper, 1948.

Tugwell, Rexford G. *The Democratic Roosevelt: A Biography of Franklin D. Roosevelt.* Garden City, N.Y.: Doubleday, 1957.

Weinstein, Allen. *Perjury: The Hiss–Chambers Case.* New York: Knopf, 1978.

White, William S. *The Taft Story.* New York: Harper, 1954.

Zion, Sidney. *The Autobiography of Roy Cohn.* Secaucus, N.J.: Lyle Stuart, 1988.

Monographs

Abaya, Hernando J. *Betrayal in the Philippines.* New York: A. A. Wyn, 1946.

Alsop, Joseph, and Turner Catledge. *The 168 Days.* New York: Da Capo Press, 1973.

Bean, Louis. *Influences in the 1954 Mid-term Election*. Washington, D.C.: Public Affairs Institute, 1954.

Bernstein, Barton J. (Editor). *Politics and Policies of the Truman Administration*. Chicago: Quandrangle Books, 1972.

Bernstein, David. *The Philippine Story*. New York: Farrar, Straus, 1947.

Block, Herbert. *The Herblock Book*. Boston: Beacon Press, 1952.

Brown, Dorothy M. "Maryland between the Wars." In *Maryland: A History—1632 to 1974*, Edited by Richard Walsh and William Lloyd Fox. Annapolis, Md.: Hall of Records Commission, Department of General Services, 1983.

Bunge, Federica M. (Editor). *Philippines: A Country Study*. Washington, D.C.: American University, 1983.

Burdette, Franklin L. "Modern Maryland Politics and Social Change." In *Maryland: A History—1632 to 1974*, Edited by Richard Walsh and William Lloyd Fox. Annapolis, Md.: Hall of Records Commission, Department of General Services, 1983.

Callcott, George H. *A History of the University of Maryland*. Baltimore: Maryland Historical Society, 1966.

———. *Maryland and America 1940–1980*. Baltimore: Johns Hopkins University Press, 1985.

Cutchins, John A., and George Scott Stewart, Jr. *History of the Twenty-ninth Division "Blue and Gray," 1917–1919*. Philadelphia: Division Historical Committee, 1921.

Divine, Robert A. *Second Chance: The Triumph of Internationalism in America during World War II*. New York: Atheneum, 1971.

Fenton, John H. *Politics in the Border States*. New Orleans: Hauser Press, 1957.

Friend, Theodore. *Between Two Empires: The Ordeal of the Philippines, 1929–1946*. New Haven: Yale University Press, 1965.

Gaddis, John Lewis. *The United States and the Origins of the Cold War*. New York: Columbia University Press, 1972.

Gallup, George H. *The Gallup Poll, 1935–1971*. 3 Volumes. New York: Random House, 1972.

Goldman, Eric F. *The Crucial Decade—And After, 1945-1960.* New York: Vintage Books, 1960.

Green, Harold P., and Alan Rosenthal. *The Joint Committee on Atomic Energy: A Study in Fusion of Governmental Power.* Washington, D.C.: George Washington University, 1961.

Griffith, Robert, and Athan Theoharis (Editors). *The Specter, Original Essays on the Cold War and the Origins of McCarthyism.* New York: New Viewpoints, 1974.

Grunder, Garel A., and William E. Livezy. *The Philippines and the United States.* Westport, Conn.: Greenwood Press, 1973.

Hamby, Alonzo L. (Editor). *Beyond the New Deal: Harry S Truman and American Liberalism.* New York: Columbia University Press, 1973.

———. *New Deal Analysis and Interpretation.* New York: Weybright and Talley, 1969.

Heinemann, Ronald L. *Depression and New Deal in Virginia: The Enduring Dominion.* Charlottesville: University Press of Virginia, 1983.

Hewlett, Richard G., and Oscar E. Anderson, Jr. *A History of the United States Atomic Energy Commission: The New World, 1939/1946.* Volume 1. University Park: Pennsylvania State University Press, 1962.

Hewlett, Richard G., Oscar E. Anderson, Jr., and Francis Duncan. *A History of the United States Atomic Energy Commission: Atomic Shield, 1947/1952.* Volume 2. University Park: Pennsylvania State University Press, 1969.

Hofstadter, Richard. *The Age of Reform: From Bryan to F.D.R.* New York: Vintage Books, 1955.

———. *The American Political Tradition: And the Men Who Made It.* New York: Alfred A. Knopf, 1951.

Hyman, Sidney. *The American President.* New York: Harper & Brothers, 1954.

Jay, Peter A. (Editor). *Havre de Grace: An Informal History.* Havre de Grace, Md.: Susquehanna Publishing, 1986.

Kelley, Stanley, Jr. *Professional Public Relations and Political Power.* Baltimore: J. H. Press, 1956.

Kidwiler, Elias W. *History of Havre de Grace: "The Town We Live In."* Havre de Grace, Md.: Havre de Grace Record, 1947.

Kirk, Grayson. *Philippine Independence: Motives, Problems, and Prospects.* New York: Farrar and Rinehart, 1936.

Kolko, Gabriel. *The Triumph of Conservatism: A Reinterpretation of American History, 1900–1916.* Chicago: Quandrangle Books, 1963.

Lubell, Samuel. *The Future of American Politics.* New York: Harper & Row, 1965.

Marshall, George C. (Director). *Infantry in Battle.* Washington, D.C.: Infantry Journal, 1934.

Matthews, Donald R. *U.S. Senators and Their World.* Chapel Hill: University of North Carolina Press, 1960.

Meyer, Milton Walter. *A Diplomatic History of the Philippine Republic.* Honolulu: University of Hawaii Press, 1965.

Norton, Mary Beth. *People and a Nation: A History of the United States.* 2nd Edition. Boston: Houghton Mifflin, 1986.

Pacis, Vincente Albana. *National Defense: A Basic Philippine Problem.* Manila, 1937.

Patterson, James T. *Congressional Conservatism and the New Deal: The Growth of the Conservative Coalition in Congress, 1933–1939.* Lexington: University of Kentucky Press, 1967.

———. *The New Deal and the States: Federalism in Transition.* Princeton, N.J.: Princeton University Press, 1969.

Pearson, Drew, and Robert S. Allen. *The Nine Old Men.* Garden City, N.Y.: Doubleday, Doran & Company, 1936.

Porter, David L. *Congress and the Waning of the New Deal.* Port Washington, N.Y.: Kennikat Press, 1980.

Roseboom, Eugene H. *A History of Presidential Elections.* New York: Macmillan, 1957.

Rossiter, Clinton. *Parties and Politics in America.* Ithaca, N.Y.: Cornell University Press, 1960.

Saint-Etienne, Christian. *The Great Depression 1929–1938: Lessons for the 1980s.* Stanford, Calif.: Hoover Institution Press, 1984.

Scharf, J. Thomas. *History of Maryland: From the Earliest Periods to the Present Day.* Baltimore: J. B. Piet, 1879.

Smith, Margaret Chase. *Declaration of Conscience*. Garden City, N.Y.: Doubleday, 1972.

Smith, Robert Aura. *Philippine Freedom, 1946–1958*. New York: Columbia University Press, 1958.

Steinberg, David. *The Philippines: A Singular and Plural Place*. Boulder, Colo.: Westview Press, 1982.

Swanson, Neil H. *The Perilous Fight*. New York: Farrar and Rinehart, 1945.

Therstrom, Stephen. *A History of the American People*. Volume 2. San Diego: Harcourt Brace Jovanovich, 1984.

Tydings, Millard E. *Before and After Prohibition*. New York: Macmillan, 1930.

———. *Counter-Attack: A Battle Plan to Defeat the Depression*. Indianapolis: Bobbs-Merrill, 1933.

———. *The Machine Gunners of the Blue and Gray Division (Twenty-ninth)*. Aberdeen, Md.: Harford Printing and Publishing, 1920.

Wentworth, Evelyn L. *Election Statistics in Maryland, 1934–1958*. College Park: Bureau of Governmental Research, University of Maryland, 1959.

White, William S. *Citadel: The Story of the United States Senate*. New York: Harper, 1956.

Wiebe, Robert H. *The Search for Order, 1877–1920*. New York: Hill and Wang, 1967.

Wright, C. Milton. *Our Harford Heritage: A History of Harford County, Maryland*. Baltimore: French-Bray Printing, 1967.

Articles

Argersinger, Jo Ann E. "Toward a Roosevelt Coalition: The Democratic Party and the New Deal in Baltimore." *Maryland Historical Magazine* 82 (Winter 1987).

Benton, William. "The Big Dilemma." New York *Times Magazine*, April 26, 1959.

Bernstein, Barton J. "The Quest for the Super Bomb." *Stanford Magazine* (Winter 1984).

———. "Roosevelt, Truman, and the Atomic Bomb." *Political Science Quarterly* 90 (Spring 1975).

Bernstein, Joseph M. "The Philippines and the Netherlands East Indies." *Amerasia* (October 25, 1943).

Clapper, Raymond. "Roosevelt Tries the Primaries." *Current History* (October 1938).

Committee on the Philippines. "Recommendations as to the Future of the Philippines." *Foreign Policy Committee Reports,* Number 2, January 1934.

Heald, Robert L., and Lyon L. Tyler, Jr. "The Legal Principle behind the *Amerasia* Case." *Georgetown Law Journal* 39, 2 (January 1951).

High, Stanley. "Party Purge." *Saturday Evening Post* (August 21, 1937).

Maskell, Jack. "Campaign Activities by Congressional Employees." American Law Division of the Congressional Research Service, October 1, 1982.

Patterson, James T. "The Failure of Party Realignment in the South 1937–1939." *Journal of Politics* 27 (August 1965).

———. "The New Deal and the States." *American Historical Review* 73 (October 1967).

Porter, Catherine. "The Future of Philippine–American Relations." *Public Affairs* (September 1943).

Ross, Hugh. "Roosevelt's Third Term Nomination." *Mid-America* 44 (April 1962).

Shannon, J. B. "Presidential Politics in the South: 1938." *Journal of Politics* (August 1939).

Tydings, Millard E. "An Inadequate Navy Is Worse Than None." *Forum* (December 1938).

———. "McCarthyism: How It All Began." *Reporter* (August 19, 1952).

———. "World Disarmament: UNO Not Equipped for Task." *Vital Speeches of the Day* (March 1, 1946).

———. "World Disarmament: A Verdict Built on Acts and Facts beyond Reasonable Dispute." *Vital Speeches of the Day* (March 1, 1950).

———. "The World's One Great Hope." *Progressive* (May 1950).

Villard, Oswald Garrison. "Pillars of Government: Millard E. Tydings." *Forum* (December 1936).

Index